INTERNATIONAL ECONOMIC LAW
AFTER THE GLOBAL CRISIS

This collection explores the theme of fragmentation within international economic law as the world emerged from the 2008 global financial crisis, the subsequent recession and the European sovereign debt crisis which began in early 2010. The post-crisis 'moment' itself forms a contemporary backdrop to the book's focus on fragmentation as it traces the evolution of the international economic system from the original Bretton Woods design in the aftermath of the Second World War to the present time. The volume covers issues concerning monetary cooperation, trade and finance, trade and its linkages, international investment law, intellectual property protection and climate change. By connecting a broad, cross-disciplinary survey of international economic law with contemporary debate over international norm and authority fragmentation, the book demonstrates that ours has been essentially a fragmented and multi-focal system of international economic regulation.

c. l. lim is an international lawyer and former trade negotiator. He is currently Professor of Law at the University of Hong Kong and chairs the East Asian International Economic Law and Policy Programme. He is also Visiting Professor at King's College London and a barrister.

bryan mercurio is Professor and Vice Chancellor's Outstanding Fellow of the Faculty of Law at the Chinese University of Hong Kong. He has also worked in government and private practice and has advised law firms, international organisations, NGOs and several governments on a wide range of international trade and investment matters.

INTERNATIONAL ECONOMIC LAW AFTER THE GLOBAL CRISIS

A Tale of Fragmented Disciplines

C. L. LIM
University of Hong Kong

BRYAN MERCURIO
Chinese University of Hong Kong

CAMBRIDGE
UNIVERSITY PRESS

CAMBRIDGE
UNIVERSITY PRESS

University Printing House, Cambridge CB2 8BS, United Kingdom

Cambridge University Press is part of the University of Cambridge.

It furthers the University's mission by disseminating knowledge in the pursuit of education, learning and research at the highest international levels of excellence.

www.cambridge.org
Information on this title: www.cambridge.org/9781107075696

First published 2015

A catalogue record for this publication is available from the British Library

Library of Congress Cataloguing in Publication data
International economic law after the global crisis : a tale of fragmented disciplines / edited by C. L. Lim, University of Hong Kong;
Bryan Mercurio, Chinese University of Hong Kong
pages   cm
"The collection began life partly as a collection of papers delivered during the second conference of the Asian International Economic Law Network (AIELN) . . . held at the University of Hong Kong during the summer of 2011"
ISBN 978-1-107-07569-6 (Hardback)
1. International finance–Law and legislation.   2. Foreign trade regulation.
3. Investments, Foreign–Law and legislation.   4. International economic relations.
I. Lim, C. L., 1947– editor.   II. Mercurio, Bryan, editor.
K4430.I58 2015
343'.03–dc23
2014030592

ISBN 978-1-107-07569-6 Hardback

CONTENTS

v

TABLES

CONTRIBUTORS

DOUGLAS W. ARNER is a professor at the Faculty of Law of the University of Hong Kong.

EMILIOS AVGOULEAS is the inaugural holder of the International Banking Law and Finance Chair at the University of Edinburgh, the Head of the Commercial Law (subject area) Group in the Law School, and the Director of the Edinburgh LLM in International Banking Law and Finance.

LORAND BARTELS is a senior lecturer in law in the Faculty of Law and a fellow of Trinity Hall at the University of Cambridge.

TOMER BROUDE is the Sylvan M. Cohen Chair in Law and Vice Dean, Hebrew University of Jerusalem Faculty of Law and Department of International Relations.

ROSS P. BUCKLEY is the CIFR King & Wood Mallesons Chair of International Finance Law, and a Scientia professor, at UNSW Australia.

ELISABETTA CERVONE is Consulting Counsel at The World Bank, Finance and Markets Global Practice.

JULIEN CHAISSE is an associate professor at the Chinese University of Hong Kong, Faculty of Law.

ANDREW FILIS was a research fellow at Queen Mary University of London (Centre for Commercial Law Studies) (2012–14). Previously, as a policy official at the UK's Ministry of Justice (2004–11), he had been involved in a variety of civil and family justice policy related work.

AN HERTOGEN is a lecturer at the University of Auckland, Faculty of Law.

HOLGER HESTERMEYER is a référendaire at the Court of Justice of the European Union.

ANITA K. KRUG is an assistant professor at the University of Washington, School of Law.

RAFAEL LEAL-ARCAS is a reader in law at Queen Mary, University of London.

C. L. LIM is an international lawyer and former trade negotiator. He is currently Professor of Law at the University of Hong Kong and chairs the East Asian International Economic Law and Policy Programme. He is also Visiting Professor at King's College London and a barrister.

ANTOINE MARTIN is a recent Ph.D. graduate consultant specializing in international relations and policy affairs.

BRYAN MERCURIO is Professor and Vice Chancellor's Outstanding Fellow of the Faculty of Law at the Chinese University of Hong Kong.

ANDREW MITCHELL is Professor of Law at Melbourne Law School and Future Fellow of the Australian Research Council.

JAMES MUNRO is a doctoral (PhD) candidate at the University of Melbourne.

JUNJI NAKAGAWA is a professor of international economic law at the Institute of Social Science, University of Tokyo.

MARTINS PAPARINSKIS is a lecturer at University College London, Faculty of Laws.

SHIN-YI PENG is a professor of law at National Tsing Hua University currently serving as Commissioner of the National Communications Commission, the Executive Yuan, Taiwan.

JUAN IGNACIO STAMPALIJA is an assistant professor of law at the Universidad Austral School of Law in Buenos Aires, Argentina.

TANIA VOON is Professor of Law at Melbourne Law School and former legal officer in the Appellate Body Secretariat of the World Trade Organization.

ROLF H. WEBER is Professor of civil, commercial and European law at the University of Zurich, Switzerland, and a visiting professor at the University of Hong Kong.

PREFACE

In this collection, we set out to provide a reliable guide and analyses of key, contemporary issues in international economic law. The period following the global financial crisis, and thereafter the global economic crisis marked by the great recession and the European debt crisis, seemed an especially good time to revisit the broader manner in which the post-Second World War Bretton Woods system has evolved, and to ask whether current institutions and arrangements are adequate to the task of handling the kinds of issues which we have included in this survey. Our aim has therefore been to provide a snapshot of the field during the years following the global financial crisis of 2008.

Although we believe this single volume will be a useful complement in the university classroom, our aim is to appeal not only to academics, scholars and university students but also to lawyers, diplomats and policy-makers.

The book began life partly as a collection of papers delivered during the second conference of the Asian International Economic Law Network (AIELN). AIELN, which is spearheaded by Junji Nakagawa of the University of Tokyo, is a regional sub-group of the Society of International Economic Law (SIEL), and is therefore open to those who are members of SIEL. The conference – dubbed 'AIELN II' – was hosted by Doug Arner and C. L. Lim of the University of Hong Kong, and Bryan Mercurio of the Chinese University of Hong Kong and held at the University of Hong Kong during the summer of 2011 following a world-wide call for papers. Colleagues came from afar – London, Oxford, Washington, DC and Zurich, among other places, in addition to AIELN's lively membership of Asian, Australian and New Zealand scholars. The 2011 conference focused on the emerging issues that the international economic system confronts today, ranging from the adequacy of financial regulation systems to the regulation of credit rating agencies, cross-border cooperation in securities regulation, investment in agricultural land abroad and the expropriation of intellectual property rights.

This collection is not, however, a mere reproduction of the proceedings of that conference. Following a post-conference assessment, we selected a core of papers while identifying what we thought of as gaps and other new issues which were quickly emerging, but which had not been discussed during those proceedings: for example, the Chinese currency policies which continued to be an issue throughout 2011, and the European Emissions Trading Scheme, which was extended in January 2012 to airlines worldwide, having an impact on air traffic (or transport) rights within the EU. The European Debt Crisis unfolded with the focus on Greece and the capabilities of the EU in taking collective action. In light of these developments, we sent out further invitations to other international experts in an effort to provide as richly textured a snapshot of current issues scattered across the whole landscape of international economic regulation as possible.

When we turned our focus to how common issues were conceived, conceptualized and regulated we found a variety of ways by which this was done by what remains, essentially, a fragmented and multi-focal system of international economic regulation. At the same time, the world trading system continues to fragment and regionalize, in turn causing ever newer forms of regulatory systemic friction particularly at a time when regional trade agreements continue to venture far beyond regulatory concerns in Geneva. And so this volume is intended as a survey of a broad range of legal and regulatory instruments, indeed a range of legal regimes, by organizing our inquiry around some of the most salient and pressing economic, legal and regulatory issues of the day, issues which acknowledge the existence of a globalized economy against the backdrop of imperfect global economic design.

So this is not a study of the various crises as such, but does involve some questions of what they might mean for the international economic order. By and large, we have focused upon two important aspects of what theses crises do not mean – they do not or do not yet mean any great structural change in the way the global economy continues to be designed and regulated, and they do not mean that other real challenges will not continue to emerge from all sides, often unrelated to the crises but in a way which seems very much related to economic globalization.

By way of a caveat, comprehensiveness is impossible. Choices had to be and were made. In general, however, we have tended to venture into areas which are important but have to date been under-explored in the literature, particularly in light of our principal focus on the still fragmented – and fragmenting – nature of global economic regulation.

Towards the end of the volume, we felt we knew more about what this means, and we have tried to spell out some of that understanding in our conclusion.

Our greatest debt is to our contributors who were sheer joy to work with, and to Finola O'Sullivan and Kim Hughes at Cambridge University Press who have been such magnificent and rigorous supporters of the project. We thank the University of Hong Kong, not least for providing generous financial support through its Strategic Research Themes funding programme and a venue for the AIELN II Conference, AIELN's Steering Committee of committed scholars, the Chinese University of Hong Kong, and our fellow co-organizer at HKU, Professor Douglas Arner to whom we attribute much of the success of that conference. Similarly, we are indebted to Ms Flora Leung at HKU for her consummate skills as conference administrator. Mr Kalana Senaratne, currently a doctoral student at the University of Hong Kong, and Ms Jackie Cheng, a JD student at the Chinese University of Hong Kong, provided invaluable editing assistance. Finally, C. L. Lim would like to record his appreciation to the HKU–KCL Fellowship and HKU Sabbatical Leave Schemes for funding support, to HKU law school for six months' leave, and to King's College London and the World Trade Organization's Visiting Scholar-in-Residence Programme for offering such conducive working environments during the preparation of this volume.

C. L. Lim and Bryan Mercurio

University of Hong Kong and the Chinese University of Hong Kong

Hong Kong SAR

The fragmented disciplines of international economic law after the global financial and economic crisis: an introduction

C. L. LIM AND BRYAN MERCURIO

I. Introduction

This book explores the theme of fragmentation within the discipline of international economic law. More specifically, it focuses on the fragmented nature of international economic law at a period of time of particular interest; that is, as the world emerged more fully from the 2008 global financial crisis, the subsequent great recession and the European sovereign debt crisis which began in early 2010.

The book acknowledges the contemporary theoretical debate today in the field of international economic law which is concerned with how different norms (e.g. deriving separately from trade law and environmental law, or trade law and investment rules or the rules of monetary cooperation) relate to each other within the larger discipline of international economic regulation. Perhaps deriving from earlier concern among public international lawyers about the multiplication of international tribunals, this practical problem which the theoretical debate seeks to address is often characterized in terms of '*norm fragmentation*', however elastic that characterization has proved to be. There is a corresponding concern in this debate with how different norms are addressed within different institutional arrangements or sites of authority – the so-called problem of '*authority fragmentation*'.[1] Viewed from the

---

[1] See e.g. 'Conclusions of the Work of the Study Group on the Fragmentation of International Law: Difficulties Arising from the Diversification and Expansion of International Law 2006', adopted by the ILC at Its Fifty-eighth session, A/61/10 (2006), para. 51; *Yearbook of the International Law Commission* (2006), vol. II, pt 2; T. Broude, 'Fragmentation(s) of International Law: On Normative Integration as Authority Allocation', in T. Broude and Y. Shany (eds.), *The Shifting Allocation of Authority in International Law* (Oxford: Hart, 2008), 99.

perspective of trade lawyers, there is also an overlapping concern with how individual disciplines such as trade law should take on board environmental and other rules, and often this has been referred to as the 'trade and ...' debate or, simply, the trade 'linkages problem'.[2] Finally, there are some very interesting proposals today about how the difficulties caused by diffuse institutions within international economic law may be handled or addressed.[3]

While such 'fragmentation' is the focus of the present volume, its theme or the tale we wish to tell in this book is more reserved, and more discrete than the theoretical debate(s) described above would suggest. The key aim of the present volume is to study actual fragmentation at this particular moment without having too many preconceptions about what we are likely to find. We have chosen this path not only because it is useful to take stock of the underlying factual realities of the theoretical debate but also because we do not believe a mature intellectual consensus has yet emerged from such theoretical debate. In short, this collection seeks to present a wide-ranging and complex picture of the fragmentation of the discipline (and its sub-disciplines) during an important period of economic uncertainty.

---

[2] See e.g. T. Broude, 'Principles of Normative Integration and the Allocation of International Authority: The WTO, the Vienna Convention on the Law of Treaties, and the Rio Declaration', *Loyola Univ. Chicago Int'l L. Rev.* 12(5) (2009), available at http://ssrn.com/abstract=1249432

[3] Examples of suggestions in this regard include the proposal to seek greater convergence in the substantive norms to be applied in different fora or within different international economic institutions. These may occur either within the same field or sub-discipline, or across different fields or the different sub-disciplines of international economic law. For an example of the former, see Broude, 'Fragmentation(s)', 105; C. L. Lim and H. Gao, 'Competing WTO and RTA Jurisdictional Claims', in T. Broude, A. Porges and M. Bush (eds.), *The Politics of International Economic Law* (Cambridge University Press, 2010), 282. For an example of the latter, see the debate on the application (or misapplication, that being part of the debate) of trade law conceptions of non-discrimination by investment treaty tribunals – i.e. in search of a 'cohesive international economic law': R. P. Alford, 'The Convergence of International Trade and Investment Arbitration', *Santa Clara JIL* 12(35) (2013), 44; R. Howse and E. Chalamish, 'The Use and Abuse of WTO Law in Investor-State Arbitration: A Reply to Jürgen Kurtz', 20 (2009) EJIL, 1087, 1094; J. Kurtz, 'The Use and Abuse of WTO Law in Investor-State Arbitration: Competition and Its Discontents: A Rejoinder to Robert Howse and Efraim Chalamish', 20 (2009), EJIL, 1095; and Jürgen Kurtz's seminal article 'The Use and Abuse of WTO Law in Investor-State Arbitration: Competition and its Discontents', 20 (2009), EJIL 749. The political science literature on complex regimes is relevant to this latter debate. See e.g. the discussion of complex regimes, and of overlapping and nested regimes, in Karen J. Alter and Sophie Meunier, 'The Politics of International Regime Complexity' 7 (2009) *Perspectives on Politics* 13, 15.

The next two sections explain these twin themes of the collection – 'fragmentation' and 'uncertainty' – and how we view their correlation in marking out the bounds of our current enterprise.

II. 'Fragmentation' as the principal focus: revisiting the Bretton Woods system

At its core, this collection is an international economic law book focusing on *norm* fragmentation in a *historical* sense. We hope, though, that this is not to say that those who are merely interested in a snapshot of some very interesting issues and debates in the field during the current post-crisis phase will find the volume to be any less valuable. Discrete issues raised by the crisis – e.g. financial regulation,[4] and the regulation of credit rating agencies[5] – are dealt with in the present volume. So too are related or knock-on developments outside the fields of financial regulation. For example, increased trade competition post-crisis has led to disputes such as the dispute over China's currency policies and is therefore addressed in the present collection of chapters.[6] Nonetheless, the post-crisis 'moment' itself forms only the context and backdrop to our focus on fragmentation as we trace the evolution of the international economic system from its original Bretton Woods design in the aftermath of the Second World War to the present day.

In this volume we therefore refer to fragmentation in a more traditional way in which international economic lawyers have routinely viewed the issue – in a more historically sensitive manner than the theoretical debate (mentioned earlier) would suggest. We are interested in fragmentation in the specific context of the historical development of international economic law and regulation.

Our historical approach towards fragmentation in the international economic law field focuses not only on the conceptual, conflictual and institutional design puzzles with which the theoretical debate is most concerned. Instead, our approach revisits the way in which international economic regulation was designed to work in the aftermath of the Second World War. Going back to the early days of Bretton Woods,[7] the global

---

[4] See Chapter 4 in this volume.   [5] See Chapter 3 in this volume.
[6] See Chapter 6 in this volume.
[7] See F. D. Santos, *Humans on Earth: From Origins to Possible Futures* (Heidelberg: Springer, 2012), 209; A. F. Lowenfeld, *International Economic Law* (2nd edn, Oxford University Press, 2008), 600.

system originally envisaged was preoccupied with reinvigorating trade flows. Great Britain, for example, needed an increase of 50 to 100 per cent in its exports to balance its post-war international accounts.[8] In the monetary field the concomitant concern was to have something as consistent as a pre-war gold standard in order to facilitate trade,[9] while at the same time maintaining closed capital accounts. Readers today are sometimes surprised to be reminded that this was the original role of the International Monetary Fund (IMF).

John Maynard Keynes originally proposed an international currency pegged against gold, and a clearing union or global central bank.[10] It was Harry Dexter White's efforts to achieve the control of the United States which saw the role of the US dollar replacing the gold standard instead.[11] Nonetheless, the dollar itself was pegged to gold, and but for a few currencies such as the Swiss franc which remained pegged to gold other currencies were to be pegged to the US dollar under the original (version of) Article IV of the IMF Articles of Agreement.[12] This became the so-called 'par value system' which lasted more or less as conceived from 1945 until 1971, and for a brief period there was an attempt to repair the fixed exchange rate system. But by 1973 major currencies were floating – a system which has lasted until now with the major currencies now in one form of 'dirty float' or another.[13] As we shall see in this volume, the system which resulted and its relation to trade has since come under public scrutiny in the aftermath of the 2008 crisis; in the form of allegations that China has been maintaining its currency at a substantively undervalued rate in order to improve its terms of trade.[14]

Bretton Woods was, in short, about *rebuilding trade, stabilizing currencies and post-war reconstruction* and within that compass a

---

[8] D. E. Moggridge, *Maynard Keynes: An Economist's Biography* (London: Routledge, 1992), 671.
[9] For the history of the gold standard from the 1870s, see P. Issard, *Globalisation and the International Financial System: What's Wrong and What Can Be Done?* (New York: Cambridge University Press, 2005), 14–27.
[10] Moggridge, *Maynard Keynes*, 672–3.
[11] Together with US control over the IMF and World Bank secured through the system of weighted voting ultimately adopted in respect of the governance of these key institutions of the Bretton Woods system. See Santos, *Humans on Earth*, 210. See further R. B. Craig, *The Harry Dexter White Spy Case* (Lawrence, KS: University Press of Kansas, 2004), 135, 149; R. Skidelsky, *John Maynard Keynes, Volume III: Fighting for Britain 1937-1946* (London: Macmillan, 2000), 233ff.
[12] Lowenfeld, *International Economic Law*, 598–9, 622–3.
[13] *Ibid.*, 624–7.   [14] See Chapter 6 in this volume.

more-or-less coherent system developed which parceled out these functions among the separate Bretton Woods institutions, the essential architecture of which remains with us, roughly speaking, in the form today of the World Bank Group and the regional development banks, the IMF and regional international financial institutions, and the World Trade Organization (WTO). To us, that architecture remains at the *core* of global economic regulation notwithstanding the increased shift in elite decision-making before the crisis towards the various 'Gs' and, after the 2008 crisis, towards the central role of the G20 as the premiere forum for global economic governance.[15]

As international economic lawyers know, this Bretton Woods 'system' evolved over several decades during the second half of the twentieth century, and in many ways is unrecognizable today from what had been envisaged during the post-war years. *These changes, and others, have given rise to what we see now as a fragmented discipline of international economic law* – a system whereby trade, investment, monetary and exchange rate cooperation, financial regulation, intellectual property (IP) protection, the regulation of trade in goods and the trade in services, and international development law have evolved away from an initially coherent Bretton Woods design. This, in turn, *produced a multiplicity of norms which are not always easy bedfellows, a plurality of international institutions*, and in some cases global norms of a different kind altogether – namely, certain norms which are characterized by the total absence of formal institutional anchorage. It is in this way that normative and institutional differences have come to matter and that is the way we have *situated* the theoretical debate about norm and authority fragmentation – i.e. by situating the theoretical debate as only a discrete sub-issue within our broader and more historically inclined field of investigation.

For our part, it is the growth of this vast discipline and its systematization which has become our principal concern.

III.   The post-crisis theme

Four aspects of the post-crisis theme of this collection deserve further explanation.

---

[15] Giovanni Grevi, 'The G20: Panacea or Window Dressing?', FRIDE Policy Brief, 2 September 2010. For background, see further J. F. Linn and C. I. Bradford Jr., 'Summit Reform: Towards an L-20', in J. F. Linn and C. I. Bradford Jr. (eds.), *Global Governance Reform: Breaking the Stalemate* (Washington, DC: Brookings, 2007), 77.

One of the popular questions which arose after the crisis was: *first*, whether there would be a grand redesigning of the system itself, and to this extent the 'post-crisis' theme in this volume is of direct relevance and salience to an investigation of disciplinary fragmentation from a historical, evolutionary perspective. That connection has shaped our study of the aftermath of the crisis; in light of expectations in certain quarters that 2008 could have led to calls for the redesigning of the international financial system and even global economic regulation more broadly.[16]

So to this extent *the post-crisis theme* is relevant to the investigation of the fragmentation of the discipline from a historical, evolutionary perspective. We cannot of course ignore the larger aspects of the crisis, which at the time of writing continues to capture public attention. The global financial crisis could become one of the defining moments of the discipline. It is already one of the defining moments of the twenty-first century, together with the September 11 terrorist attacks in the United States. But while we had embarked upon this project with an acute awareness of that fact, we *cannot* make the claim that 2008 and its aftermath was necessarily a pivotal moment *for the discipline of international economic law*. This is our *second point*. Instead, for us, capturing the state of international economic law at this time became an essential part of discovering the answer to that question. There is every suggestion that short of discrete and specific reforms affecting the international financial and banking sector – especially in achieving financial stability in light of the consistent limitations of financial regulation[17] – and the emergence of the G20 as, in the words of Ross Buckley (Chapter 5 in this volume), the 'high table of economic governance' globally, there has been little structural or substantive change in the methods of international economic regulation.

Much of the rest of the field of international economic law did not undergo any significant change, structural or otherwise. Aside from an impetus towards reform in the regulation of global finance and some evidence of increased trade friction owing to pressures caused by the Great Recession, *it is fragmentation which remains a persistent feature of international economic law*.

---

[16] See e.g. D. W. Arner and R. P. Buckley, 'Redesigning the Architecture of the Global Financial System', *Melbourne JIL*, 11 (2010), 185.

[17] J. Dalhuisen, *Dalhuisen on Transnational Comparative, Commercial, Financial and Trade Law* (4th edn, 3 vols., Oxford: Hart, 2010), vol. III, 448ff.

We therefore make no deeper claim about the moment itself, nor do we claim that this is a moment in which a fragmented discipline becomes coherent. The present collection of chapters suggests that the opposite is just as likely to be true. Thus, state-to-state cooperation, particularly to achieve coherence and convergence in norms, has received a significant amount of attention in this volume.[18]

Putting aside the question of a grand redesigning of the global economic system, a *third* issue emerging from the 2008 global financial crisis and 2010 European debt crisis is *geopolitical* in nature. Many now believe that 2008 accelerated the so-called BRIC nations' (Brazil, Russia, India and China) – and particularly China's – reach in international economic affairs.[19] There is a sense that in light of the origins of the crisis in the United States and the subsequent European debt crisis, greater attention should now be paid to the role of Asia – and not least, East Asia – in the global economy. To be sure, the 'Rise of the Rest' as Fareed Zakaria who coined the phrase calls it, has been a pre-crisis phenomenon but there is also a sense that the United States' economic troubles have accentuated a global economic shift.[20] A question then arises about the likely repercussions, if any, on international economic regulation.[21] Underlying such questions is a longer-standing question about the extent to which China has been integrated into the global economy through its 2001 accession to the World Trade Organization.[22]

---

[18] See Chapters 7 and 12 in this volume.

[19] Subsequently this appellation was taken to include South Africa – e.g. 'BRICS'. See further, 'The BRICS at the WTO Doha Development Round', Working Papers, North–South Institute, available at: www.nsi-ins.ca/equitable-growth/the-brics-at-the-wto-doha-development

[20] A recent collection of essays exploring this theme highlights the connection between concerns about the crisis and perceptions of a geopolitical shift: 'In fact, even as the carnage from the financial meltdown recedes, a chronic deficit problem remains ... Not since Tsarist Russia has a great empire relied on so much borrowing abroad' (S. Clark and S. Hoque, 'Introduction', in S. Clark and S. Hoque (eds.), *Debating a Post-American World: What Lies Ahead* (Abingdon, Oxon.: Routledge, 2012), 4). Zakaria himself comments on the scenario after the 2008 crash, see 'Preface to the Paperback Edition', in Fareed Zakaria, *The Post-American World and the Rise of the Rest* (London: Penguin, 2009).

[21] On the shift of power at the WTO, see C. L. Lim, 'On Free Trade and the Post-American World', in Clark and Hoque, 230.

[22] See, e.g., D. M. Blumenthal, 'Applying GATT to Marketising Economies: The Dilemma of WTO Accession and Reform of China's State-Owned Enterprises (SOEs)', *Journal of International Economic Law* (1999), 113; J. Y. Qin, 'WTO Regulation of Subsidies to State-Owned Enterprises – A Critical Appraisal of the China Accession Protocol', *Journal of International Economic Law*, 7 (2004), 863; J. Chen, 'China, India and Developing Countries in the WTO: Towards a Proactive Strategy', in M. Sornarajah and J. Wang

Thus, a number of the chapters in this volume reflect an interest in China's recent policies, disputes, and treaty and other conduct.[23] Again, these chapters are not intended to make a deeper claim about the post-crisis state of international economic law but merely reflect the times we live in, witnessing an enlarged curiosity about how China – and indeed the other nations just mentioned – will 'behave' in the international economic system as rule-subjects and rule-makers.

Fourth, other new issues remain salient to an understanding of the development of international economic law. Unlike the Chinese currency or Greek bond issues which are related to the 2008 and 2010 crises,[24] climate change has been an independent issue standing at the forefront of public attention.[25] Likewise, the recent bilateral investment treaty (BIT) disputes over cigarette-packaging laws have prompted investigation of the intersection of the (fragmented) regimes of IP and investor/investment protection.[26] BITs continue to engage attention because of their impact on health and social policies. Other similar issues which stand more or less apart from the 2008/2010 crises include recent food price crises, beginning in 2008,[27] and one chapter in this volume deals with the intersection between agricultural shortage, the food price crisis and investment. Its subject is the relatively new phenomenon of foreign investment in agricultural land.[28]

Hence our focus on the persistence of fragmentation. To appreciate this persistence fully, it is necessary to consider the history of international economic law from the mid-twentieth century to the present time. The next section therefore takes this up.

IV.   The evolution of the Bretton Woods system and the fragmentation of the discipline

At the risk of repeating what may be well known, it may be useful to recall some of the key features of the evolution of the Bretton Woods system, starting from the 1940s to the present time. Our aim in this

---

(eds.), *China, India and the International Economic Order* (Cambridge University Press, 2010), 53; H. Gao, 'Taming the Dragon: China's Experience in the WTO Dispute Settlement System', *Legal Issues of Economic Integration*, 34 (2007), 369; C. L. Lim and J. Wang, 'China and the Doha Development Agenda', *Journal of World Trade*, 44 (2010), 1309.

[23] See Chapters 5, 6, 8, 9 and 14 in this volume.

[24] See Chapters 6 and 13 in this volume.

[25] See Chapters 18 and 19 in this volume.   [26] See Chapter 16 in this volume.

[27] V. Walt, 'The world's growing food-price crisis', *Time*, 27 February 2008; J. Blas, J. Farchy and C. Belton, 'Wheat soars on Russia ban', *Financial Times*, 6 August 2010.

[28] See Chapter 15 in this volume.

condensed account is to show how Bretton Woods had originally been viewed as an *integrated* or *cohesive* system of global economic regulation coming out of the ruins of the Second World War. In our view, a historical perspective provides a more acute appreciation of the struggle which is now required to make sense of the contemporary issues which the several authors in this volume have sought to address.

The following account describes exchange rate cooperation, sovereign lending and current account convertibility as key ideas which were originally meant to foster the re-liberalization of post-war trade. We then describe how the idea of closed capital accounts came to an end with the re-globalization of finance, paving the way for international banking and financial regulation. Having established this distinction between how global trade and finance were viewed originally, and how global finance re-emerged and was regulated because it then needed to be, we turn to trade – including trade in services – and then to investment, the growing sophistication of IP protection and the contemporary challenge of climate change. In between, we mention the tale of developmental concerns, and the concerns of developing nations within the confines of the disparate regimes for the regulation and protection of trade, investment and IP, and for building a climate change regime as an independent endeavour. Ours is a story about how global economic regulation emerged piecemeal, resulting in fragmented regimes which persist to the present day as new issues continue to emerge.

1. Exchange rate cooperation: from par value to dirty float

In relation to exchange rates, after the Second World War, the Bretton Woods design had resulted in a treaty-based institution which sought to police exchange rates and foster exchange rate cooperation between sovereign nations. The aim was to have orderly exchange rates for the trade-facilitative effect that would then ensue.[29] That aim is well captured still in Article I of the IMF Articles of Agreement. The aim, to be sure, was to give confidence to countries in order that they not devalue or adjust currencies in seeking to address maladjustments in their balance of payments. It has been observed that such practices were a contributory cause of the Second World War. Thus, the IMF was designed to provide two ways to deal with maladjustments – institutional, intergovernmental

---

[29] For the historical backdrop, see Lowenfeld, *International Economic Law*, 599–600.

assistance (1) in readjusting exchange rates, and (2) to address the causes/conditions of maladjustment. To that extent, the scheme of the IMF Articles (I and IV(4)(a) in particular) remain unchanged today.

Originally Article IV of the IMF Articles stated that each nation's currency shall be expressed in gold or in US dollars. This was the so-called 'par value' system. However, that system – originally contained in Article IV(3) – was changed entirely following the effort to amend the Articles, which culminated in the Jamaica amendments in 1976. The changes which have so altered the IMF's Articles occurred during the 1970s. The background to that, in very brief terms, was that the Vietnam war had proved costly for the United States, not least in light of that country's period of unprecedented fiscal expansion (improving social security, retirement plans, etc.). The end result was that the US government was spending more, it was importing more, and this in turn led to exchange instability. Some readers may recall the famous quote of Treasury Secretary John Connally, in 1971, that the US dollar is 'our currency, but your problem'. At that point, the decision had been taken to devalue the US dollar against gold, which had triggered a fundamental discussion. The USA ended its treaty obligation unilaterally in August 1971.[30] The United States could say the US dollar was still expressed in US dollars, and thus there was no legal violation of its obligation. However, other nations were faced with the problem that the reserve currency country, the United States, which had been the fundamental link in international monetary arrangements had ended its support of the global system. So other nations were faced with a difficulty, as a result of which the Group of Seven (G7) through the Smithsonian Agreement in December 1971 attempted to come up with a new level for US dollar to gold. This, had it succeeded, would have preserved the fixed exchange rate system but that last attempt was given up in June 1972. The 1976 Amendments to the IMF Articles of Agreement were the result.[31] This upheaval eventually led from a system of managed exchange rates and exchange rate adjustments to one of floating exchange rates. To that extent the original Bretton Woods design no longer reflects the contemporary system for monetary and exchange rate cooperation. Furthermore, the trade-facilitative function which the par value system had played was undermined by these changes. The manner in which the world trading regime (discussed further, below) and the IMF regime interact is complex. Put simply, the system was

[30] *Ibid.*, 624–5.   [31] *Ibid.*, 625–33.

designed to allow exchange-related action to involve, account for, and perhaps defer to the IMF's purview in exchange-related matters, but significant questions remain about the precise interaction of the fragmented regimes of exchange rate and trade regulation.[32]

2. The function of sovereign lending

As for the function of sovereign lending, its aim had been to bolster the confidence of sovereign nations by making the IMF's resources available, thus ensuring that nations facing balance-of-payment difficulties do not engage in measures destructive of international prosperity. This underlies the IMF's loan-making function and the concomitant imposition of IMF conditionalities.[33] That function came into focus with the 1982 debt crisis, during which Mexico and Brazil could no longer service their loans, and in successive crises, not least during the 1990s.[34] Today, the IMF is viewed mainly as a lending institution and the line between what it does and what the World Bank does has become blurred. In this regard, the IMF functions as a credit union in addition to its function of facilitating international monetary cooperation and regulation, and in maintaining exchange rate stability. This system of a US dollar-based credit union emerged at Bretton Woods, as opposed to John Maynard Keynes' idea of an international central bank with a global currency.

Likewise, the International Bank for Reconstruction and Development, originally established to address the economic distress in Europe, had over time become a development aid organization once the Truman administration took over the function of rebuilding Europe through the Marshall Plan.[35] Professor John Head has also observed that while the IMF shifted its focus to debt issues as a result of the collapse of the par

---

[32] See Chapter 6 in this volume.

[33] Although this function had grown up without express authorization under the IMF Articles of Agreement, it was subsequently defined and regulated under the amended Articles of Agreement (for which, see arts. XXX(b) for the definition of a stand-by arrangement, and V(3)(b), V(3)(c) and V(4) in particular for conditions and conditionalities. See further, Lowenfeld, *International Economic Law*, 613ff. and 644ff.

[34] D. W. Arner, *Financial Stability, Economic Growth, and the Role of Law* (Cambridge University Press, 2007), 23ff.

[35] J. W. Head, *Losing the Global Development War: A Contemporary Critique of the World Bank, the IMF and the WTO* (Leiden: Nijhoff, 2008), 101.

value system, the World Bank realized that the model of reconstruction on which it had been built was inadequate to 'build new economies from whole cloth' and thus turned towards prescribing economic and financial policies for national governments.[36]

3. Current account convertibility and the elimination of foreign exchange restrictions versus restrictions on capital account convertibility

The idea of current account convertibility was also to fall within the purview of the IMF; namely, to assist in the establishment of a multilateral system of payments for current transactions and the elimination of foreign exchange restrictions.[37]

However, from the beginning of the preparations for a post-war global economic system, the free movement of capital was not envisaged. Keynes had written thus:[38]

> Nothing is more certain than that movement of capital funds must be regulated; – which in itself will involve far-reaching departures from laissez-faire arrangements.

Thus, in contrast, in relation to capital account transactions by which we largely mean to refer to investment funds, flows of money for investments or payments for investments, nowhere in the IMF Articles would we find provision for *capital account convertibility*.[39] Indeed, Article VI(3) states that: 'Members may exercise such controls as are necessary to regulate international capital movements'. This was due in part to British fear of capital outflows from the United Kingdom at the close of the Second World War.[40] The imposition of capital controls would, however, be subject to the non-restriction of payments for current transactions. This

---

[36] *Ibid.*, 102. For a useful critique, see N. Woods, *The Globalizers: The IMF, the World Bank and their Borrowers* (New York: Cornell University Press, 2006).

[37] Art. VIII, IMF Articles of Agreement.

[38] Moggridge, *Maynard Keynes*, 673.

[39] 'Free movement of capital was never itself considered part of the new order after World War II. The Bretton Woods Agreement of 1944, including the IMF...Treaty and the creation of the..."World Bank"...did not mean to liberalise capital movements and accepted that each country could insulate its own capital market' (Dalhuisen, *Transnational Comparative*, 597–8).

[40] Lowenfeld, *International Economic Law*, 608.

caveat is especially important where the distinction between capital and current account transactions may not always be easy to discern.[41]

Nonetheless, international capital found a way to flow again across borders. Part of that story has to do with the emergence of the European dollar market following the Second World War, the other part having to do with the subsequent emergence of 'petrodollars'. The market for the US dollar had meant the emergence of a 'Eurobond' market in Europe which developed and grew together with euro deposits.[42] That period witnessed loans and trade finance in US dollars and here began an offshore, international market denominated in US dollars. During the late 1960s and early 1970s, the role of the oil-producing countries also meant that should countries like Saudi Arabia sell oil in US dollars, they could repatriate those oil profits only if there existed effectively functioning financial markets at home. Thus, the choice was made instead to deposit such dollar profits in European banks. Those banks in turn loaned the money to oil-consuming countries which needed funds to buy oil for production.[43]

That process continued gradually until the 1990s and witnessed the re-globalization of finance, paving the way ultimately for the formal liberalization of financial services under the General Agreement on Trade in Services (the GATS), discussed further below.[44]

4. Financial regulation and central bank cooperation

This brings us to the subject of financial regulation as a sub-discipline of international economic law. In contrast to the 'hard law' model of trade regulation and the institutionalized modes employed by the IMF and World Bank and other regional, international financial institutions, a distinctively soft law model of regulation emerged to cope with international financial regulation.[45]

In respect of central bank cooperation, for example, this is more a model of global economic 'coordination' rather than 'regulation' per se. While the Bank of International Settlements (BIS) did not have a role in

---

[41] *Ibid.*
[42] Dalhuisen, *Transnational Comparative*, 590, 593.
[43] See Issard, *Globalization and the International Financial System*, 57–8.
[44] Dalhuisen, *Transnational Comparative*, 592. See further, L. E. Panourgias, *Banking Regulation and World Trade Law: GATS, EU and Prudential Institution Building* (Oxford: Hart, 2006), 23–103 for the interaction of trade and banking regulation.
[45] This is discussed, for example, in Chapter 2 in this volume.

the Bretton Woods plan at all, one important evolution is that it has come to play an important role in the aftermath of the 2008 crisis in raising bank liquidity requirements via 'Basel III', which at the time of writing is being implemented by national central banks worldwide.

Originally, the BIS's role had been to effect reparations following the First World War, and to engage in reconstruction between the wars. As we have seen, following the establishment of the Bretton Woods system, finance began to move again across international borders in a process described as the 'spontaneous globalisation' of the financial markets.[46] It was, as we have said, related to the emergence of a European dollar market and the creation of 'petrodollars'.

The most prominent committee housed in the BIS was the Basel Committee which in part had itself come about following the failure of the Herstatt Bank on 26 June 1974, causing the cross-border failure of US counterparty banks. The US and German financial systems, by the early 1970s, were no longer isolated. The eleven countries of the G10 eventually formed the Committee on Banking Regulations and Supervisory Practices (the 'Basel Committee') leading to the Basel Concordat.[47] Some readers may also recall the failure in 1982 of the Banco Ambrosiano, leading to a revision of the Concordat. During the 1980s, discussions in Basel became more frequent. The failure of BCCI in 1991 led to further refinements of banking supervision; in the allocation of supervisory jurisdiction between host state and home state.[48]

Aside from the Basel Concordat and its amendments in respect of international banking supervision, the Basel Committee is well known today for its work in ensuring capital adequacy and risk management through the Basel Accords (Basel I, Basel II, etc.).[49] This, of course, goes to the heart of some of the principal concerns concerning financial stability and systemic risk arising out the 2008 crisis.

Perhaps the most important point, for our purposes, is that financial regulation is not addressed within a single cohesive regime. Instead, the GATS – operating under the WTO regime, further discussed below – addresses the separate but related issue of financial services liberalization,

---

[46] Dahuisen, *Transnational Comparative*, 589.
[47] Lowenfeld, *International Economic Law*, 812–13. That is, viewed historically. For the argument that the importance of banks require special regulation, see L. E. Panourgias, *Banking Regulation and World Trade Law: GATS, EU and Prudential Institution Building* (Oxford: Hart, 2006), 18–21.
[48] Lowenfeld, *International Economic Law*, 815ff.   [49] *Ibid.*, 820–45.

albeit treating regulation as the subject of prudential carve-outs or exceptions to trade liberalization commitments. Thus GATS merely acknowledges the need for financial services regulation but does not provide for it.[50] Financial services regulation is fragmented.

5.   From GATT to the WTO

But it is the facilitation of global trade which lies at the heart of the original Bretton Woods design.

Throughout the late nineteenth century and until the First World War, early globalization stirred by industrial inventions and reduced barriers expanded trading relationships beyond what was imaginable just decades earlier. The advent of the First World War halted trade flows, and while there was talk of liberalizing and regulating trade through the League of Nations, this did not come to pass.[51] Instead, the intervening years between the two World Wars came to be characterized by protectionism and a corresponding sharp decline in the importation and exportation of goods. We have seen that in the aftermath of the Second World War, trade – along with monetary stability and reconstruction – became one of the three pillars to rebuild and safeguard the global economy. While not directly discussed at Bretton Woods, in 1945 the USA had circulated a document entitled 'Proposals for Expansion of World Trade and Employment', which proposed the creation of the International Trade Organization (ITO).

The proposal was well received, as governments shared the objective of reversing the mistakes of economic isolationism which had characterized the pre-war years and believed that freer international trade would be mutually advantageous for both economic and security reasons. Working through the United Nations Economic and Social Council and the United Nations Conference on Trade and Employment, fifty-seven nations finalized a proposal on 21 November 1947, which became the

---

[50] See further the GATS and more specifically, the WTO Annex on Financial Services.
[51] The 1919 treaties had contained references to the MFN principle, and we find a trace of the rule in the Covenant of the League of Nations. The final draft of the League was adopted in 1919, which contains a reference to 'equitable treatment for the commerce of all members of the League', in art. 23(e). Wilson's own '14 Points' speech of 8 January 1918 prescribed 'the establishment of an equality of trade conditions among all the nations consenting to the peace' which was explained to mean 'whatever tariff any nation might deem necessary for its own economic service, be that tariff high or low, it should apply equally to all foreign nations'.

Havana Charter.[52] At the same time, several nations had entered into negotiations to conclude a multilateral agreement to reduce tariffs, eventually becoming known as the General Agreement on Tariffs and Trade (GATT). While the two negotiations were technically separate, the negotiators were the same individuals and the negotiations intertwined. The negotiators had a dual purpose: they were to draft an ITO Charter while at the same time negotiate for the reduction and binding of thousands of individual tariff commitments.

While awaiting US approval of the ITO, eight of the twenty-three signatories to the GATT agreed to apply it provisionally as of 1 January 1948, with the others joining shortly thereafter. Designed only to be temporary pending the creation of the ITO, provisional application of the GATT lasted longer than expected due to the refusal of the US Congress to approve the ITO. Thus the GATT, without a constitutional or institutional foundation, was left to serve as the sole world forum for international trade matters. This created a number of institutional difficulties, but through discovery and legal creativity the GATT functioned well during its forty-seven years as the sole multilateral forum for international trade.[53]

Following the previous seven rounds of negotiations – the Annecy, Torquay, Geneva, Dillon, Kennedy and Tokyo Rounds, respectively – the eighth negotiating round of the GATT, called the Uruguay Round, was by far the most ambitious and far-reaching. The Uruguay Round continued the liberalization of trade through tariff reductions and the elimination of non-tariff barriers to trade, but it also did much more. Importantly, and controversially, it expanded the multilateral trading system beyond goods to include trade in services (through the GATS) and IP (via the TRIPs Agreement). The incorporation of these two topics was (and continues to be) controversial for a number of reasons, not least because they are perceived to be trade issues which favour the developed countries. Additionally, services trade and IP protection are both topics of interest in bilateral and regional trade treaty negotiations.

The Uruguay Round also strengthened the dispute settlement mechanism, improving the procedural, substantive and enforcement elements

---

[52] The records of these meetings run to over 100 volumes and contain over 27,000 pages. See J. H. Jackson, *The World Trading System, Law and Policy of International Economic Relations* (2nd edn, Cambridge, MA: MIT Press, 1997), 37.

[53] See generally S. Lester, B. Mercurio and A. Davies, *World Trade Law* (Oxford: Hart Publishing, 2012), 55–60.

of the system. Systemically, the Round changed the entire governance structure of the GATT, not only abandoning most plurilateral agreements in favour of a multilateral approach to almost every topical issue but also creating the WTO (and with it obligations on all members), a formal organization that would unify all of the various agreements within one institutional framework.

Since the conclusion of the Uruguay Round, the WTO has functioned well but had few major successes and has faced substantial criticism. Perhaps the biggest successes have been the admission of China (2001) and Russia (2011) into the multilateral system. The biggest disappointment is no doubt the failure to conclude the Doha Round, the current WTO negotiating round launched in 2001. There were serious concerns that the round would fail, and in December 2011 an official 'impasse' was declared. It is widely believed that members, and in particular the US, EU, Brazil, China and India, must offer more market access and other trade concessions in order to restart the negotiations and successfully conclude the round. Looking beyond the Doha Round, internal governance, energy, climate change and export restrictions are but a few unaddressed issues which require attention. As time passes, other urgent issues will emerge and the Doha Development Agenda will take on the appearance of a creature of a different age. In addition, it should be noted that three of the four so-called 'Singapore issues' (i.e. competition, procurement and investment) were dropped from the Doha negotiations in 2004 for lack of consensus, with the exception of trade facilitation. As this chapter goes to press, the fresh success of a breakthrough in respect of the fourth issue, trade facilitation, in the 2013 Bali Ministerial Conference brings only some small measure of comfort to some.

What is noteworthy is that investment is only thinly regulated under the WTO regime; more specifically under the Agreement on Trade Related Investment Measures (TRIMS) concluded as part of the Uruguay Round negotiations. Thus global regulatory fragmentation extends to the fragmentation of trade and investment regulation.

6.   The protection of investments and international investment law

As early as the eighteenth century, there was an implicit assumption that states would protect the property of citizens of other countries. The assumption was that such protection would form part of domestic law. The protection of foreign property from state intervention also clearly became customary international law, a notion which was not seriously challenged until the Bolshevik Revolution in Russia in 1917. This despite the fact that in 1868, the Argentine jurist Carlos Calvo had rebelled against the 'gunboat diplomacy' of the day by calling for a major reinterpretation which would entail a reduction in the property rights of foreign property holders. Calvo believed that foreign property holders should have recourse only to national courts, not to international tribunals or diplomatic channels. The debate focused on the protection of the rights of foreign property rights holders according to a 'domestic' or 'national' standard, and such protection according to a (higher) 'minimum international standard'.

The uncompensated expropriations in Russia in 1917 resulted in the Lena Goldfields Arbitration in 1930 which sided with the investor (based upon a theory of unjust enrichment) and reopened the debate. Shortly following the arbitration, Mexico adopted the Calvo Doctrine and expropriated several US agricultural and oil industries. Unsurprisingly the USA disagreed, with Secretary of State Cordell Hull informing Mexico that while international law allowed for expropriations, this was premised upon the payment of 'prompt, adequate and effective compensation'.[54] International law substantiated the US position, as the emergence of the 'international minimum standard of international law' protected aliens from 'unacceptable measures of the host state', independent of the laws of the host state.[55]

While this principle was challenged, if not eroded with the emergence of several independent developing countries in the decades following the Second World War, customary international law (and Hull's position) arguably became crystallized with the emergence of BITs and other similar international investment agreements. Beginning in 1959 with a treaty between Germany and Pakistan, BITs provided investor protection through obligations on the host state, most of which are enforceable through investor-state dispute settlement. By the early 1990s, even the most ardent supporter of the Calvo Doctrine had to admit that almost every developing country had begun concluding BITs which were contrary to the Doctrine. Even BITs concluded between developing countries included substantial investor protection at odds with the Calvo Doctrine.[56]

---

[54] R. Dolzer and C. Schreuer, *Principles of International Investment Law* (Oxford University Press, 2012), 2.

[55] *Ibid.*, 3.

[56] There is however vigorous debate over the extent to which such BITs affected the content of customary international law. See F. A. Mann, 'British Treaties for the Promotion and Protection of Investments', BYIL, 52 (1981), 241.

Currently there are over 2,750 BITs in force with an additional 150 free trade agreements (FTAs) containing comprehensive investment chapters.

Unlike finance and trade, there is no overarching multilateral framework regulating international investment. Instead, each BIT or other investment agreement is a stand-alone system. As the legal language differs between differing agreements, so too do the obligations and interpretation. Here is fragmentation at a sub-disciplinary level – i.e. within investment law itself notwithstanding the existence of common concepts and principles. However, this cannot be overemphasized as no one questions the unity of public international law, despite the existence of consensual treaty rules applying solely between the parties to those treaties. Furthermore, there is a high degree of convergence between the various treaties and one speaks only of the 'US model', 'UK model', 'French model', and so on.

For many years, most investors were either unaware or were ignorant of the protections afforded by BITs and other agreements and there were only a few investment arbitrations. This changed in the early 1990s with the conclusion of the North American Free Trade Agreement (NAFTA) between Canada, Mexico and the USA. Investors in these nations began regularly using the NAFTA to challenge measures in the other partner countries, and in time investors around the globe likewise began utilizing agreements to bring claims and extract monetary awards from host states. International investment arbitration has now emerged as an important sub-discipline of international economic law. The financial crisis, and the number of pending and potential disputes arising out of the crisis also attest to this fact.

Two of the chapters in this volume highlight the issues, respectively, of convergence, and the specific nature of a newly emergent 'Chinese model' – or more precisely, 'models' – of investment treaty.[57] Others look at the manner in which investment disciplines interact with other areas – from the restructuring of sovereign debts to IP.[58]

7. *Global intellectual property protection – from the 1880s to the present*

While many believe that the 'internationalization' of IP protection, and the link between IP and trade, began with the WTO TRIPs Agreement in

---

[57] See Chapter 12 and Chapter 14 in this volume.
[58] See Chapter 16 and Chapter 13 in this volume.

1995, this is incorrect. The internationalization of IP law, regulation and policy began much earlier. Elements of IP had appeared in eighteenth- and nineteenth-century Friendship, Commerce and Navigation (FCN) treaties.[59] These bilateral treaties were then multilateralized in the latter part of the nineteenth century in two important treaties – the Paris Convention for the Protection of Industrial Property (1883) and the Berne Convention for the Protection of Literary and Artistic Works (1886). Importantly, both treaties multilateralized key obligations and introduced certain minimum standards and other regulations. Both treaties, however, leave large and important gaps, merely serving as a rough framework for developing IP policy. Signatories retained a wide discretion to draft and implement their own laws, and while recourse to the International Court of Justice (ICJ) in the event of a dispute was envisaged, both treaties lacked a true dispute settlement and enforcement mechanism. For these reasons, intellectual property rights (IPRs) and protection continued to vary widely from country to country throughout most of the twentieth century.

Moreover, these treaties, and thus the entire framework for the international IP system, were essentially negotiated and concluded by developed countries. Developing countries joined, particularly in the wake of decolonization, but played little part in rule formation. This began to change in the 1960s, when developing countries called for transfers of technology and the liberal use of compulsory licences in order to promote local production of goods. Implementation of such strategies largely failed to lower prices or lead to economic development. Indeed, such policies left many developing countries with more expensive, inferior products, and a large number of inefficient industries operating without the threat of competition. The newfound spirit of independence did, however, influence the future direction of international IP. For instance, the Stockholm Protocol of 1967 (revising the Berne Convention) contained special rights for developing countries, including special reservations regarding translations, reproduction, broadcasting and educational use of copyrighted works.[60] Developing countries also pressed for the revision of the Paris Convention, but their

---

[59] A 1778 FCN between France and the USA is reputed to be the first such treaty. M. Sornarajah, *The International Law on Foreign Investment* (Cambridge University Press, 2004), 209.

[60] See generally S. Ricketson, *The Berne Convention for the Protection of Literary and Artistic Works: 1886–1986* (London: Sweet & Maxwell, 1987).

efforts were less successful as developed countries rebuffed the demands.[61]

This push from developing countries, in combination with the realization among the industrialized world that their economic future was not in manufacturing but in advancement through information, knowledge and intellectual creation, led to a radical shift in strategy which would change the direction of international IP protection. With the emergence of the knowledge economy on the horizon, developed countries recognized that in order to fully exploit innovative advantages, stronger laws were needed to avoid misappropriation through counterfeiting and piracy.

The US first sought to change direction through the unilateral enforcement of IP rights by virtue of the authority of the United States Trade Representative (USTR) under Section 301 of the US Trade Act of 1974. In essence, the USA initiated litigation against other countries in the US Court of International Trade (USCIT) under its domestic unfair trade practices laws, even though the respondent countries had not violated any international agreement. The USA filed cases against several developing countries, most notably Brazil, Argentina, India, China and Taiwan, and extracted concessions from the respondents in a number of cases.[62] Subsequently, the EU adopted and utilized a similar law.[63] In doing so, the USA and EU also effectively promoted the direct linkage of IP and international trade.

At the same time, developed countries began to seek an alternative forum to address IP policies. Basing their arguments for the direct linkage on the fact that a country with weak or otherwise insufficient IP protection engages in unfair competition as it can benefit through the cheap production and sale of fake and counterfeited goods, the developed

---

[61] See P. S. Haar, 'Revision of the Paris Convention: A Realignment of Private and Public Interests in the International Patent System', *Brooklyn Journal of International Law*, 8 (1982), 77; R. A. Loughran, 'United States Position on Revising the Paris Convention: Quid Pro Quo or Denunciation?', *Fordham International Law Journal*, 5 (1981–2), 411; S. K. Sell, 'Intellectual Property as a Trade Issue: From the Paris Convention to GATT', *Legal Studies Forum* 13 (1989), 407.

[62] A. O. Sykes, 'Constructive Unilateral Threats in International Commercial Relations: The Limited Case for Section 301', *Law & Policy in International Business*, 23 (1992), 263–330.

[63] See W. W. Leirer, 'Retaliatory Action in United States and European Union Trade Law: A Comparison of Section 301 of the Trade Act of 1974 and Council Regulation 2641/84', *North Carolina Journal of International Law & Commercial Regulation*, 20 (1994–5), 41–96. The EC repealed the regulation upon the creation of the WTO.

countries (led by the USA, EU, Switzerland and Japan) argued that such unfair competition could drive costlier original goods out of the market. These same countries also attempted to convince the developing world that effective IP protection and enforcement would lead to substantial gains through increased investment, which would provide jobs, technology and increased exports.

The trade-off was therefore acceptance of IP as a negotiating topic in exchange for an end to unilateral action. Rejecting such a deal would have meant the continuation of unilateralism and perhaps other sanctions, such as a reduction of trade and aid flowing from developed countries to the developing world.[64] After initial opposition, developing country objections waned and attention turned to negotiating the agreement.[65] In the process, developing countries secured several important TRIPs-related concessions, most notably deferred implementation of substantial portions of the agreement and promises of technology transfer and assistance.[66] They also received concessions in other trade areas, notably increased access to developed country agriculture and textiles markets.[67]

The resulting compromise, the TRIPs Agreement, expands IP coverage beyond that of pre-existing international agreements. It explicitly includes seven sectors of IPRs (i.e. copyright and related rights; trademarks; geographical indications; industrial designs; patents; layout-designs of integrated circuits; and the protection of undisclosed information).[68] Like other covered agreements, the basis of TRIPs is most-favoured nation

---

[64] See M. Blakeley, *Trade-Related Aspects of Intellectual Property Rights: A Concise Guide to the TRIPs Agreement* (London: Sweet & Maxwell, 1996), 6; D. Matthews, *Globalising Intellectual Property Rights: The TRIPs Agreement* (London: Routledge, 2002), 33.

[65] For a succinct history of the origins of the TRIPs Agreement and its negotiating process, see Matthews, *Globalising Intellectual Property Rights*, ch. 1 (origins) and ch. 2 (negotiations). For more detailed background on the TRIPs Agreement, see S. K. Sell, *Power and Ideas: North–South Politics of Intellectual Property and Antitrust* (New York: State University of New York Press, 1998).

[66] See e.g. D. Matthews and V. Munoz-Tellez, 'Bilateral Technical Assistance and TRIPS: the United States, Japan and the European Communities in Comparative Perspective', *Journal of World Intellectual Property*, 9 (2006), 629; T. P. Trainer, 'Intellectual Property Enforcement: A Reality Gap (Insufficient Assistance, Ineffective Implementation)?', *John Marshall Review of Intellectual Property Law*, 8 (2008), 47.

[67] The benefits of the concessions are debated. See e.g. E. Durán and C. Michalopoulos, 'Intellectual Property Rights and Developing Countries in the WTO "Millennium" Round', *Journal of World Intellectual Property*, 2 (1999), 853.

[68] TRIPs also requires members to provide for the protection of plant varieties, either by patent or an effective *sui generis* system such as plant breeders' rights established in the International Union for the Protection of New Varieties of Plants Convention.

(MFN) treatment and national treatment (NT). The TRIPs also establishes minimum levels of protection and enforcement provisions. In formulating minimum standards, TRIPs incorporates the substantive obligations of the Paris and Berne Conventions and certain provisions of the Treaty on Intellectual Property in Respect of Integrated Circuits and the Rome Convention. In addition, TRIPs also sets standards in areas which were either not addressed or, according to members, not sufficiently covered in the WIPO Agreements.

Much has occurred since that time, such as developing countries mounting a pushback against IP enforcement, particularly in relation to essential pharmaceuticals. This resulted in the first significant 'win' for developing countries at the WTO: the Doha Declaration on TRIPs and Public Health (2001), a document which reiterates that the TRIPs Agreement should not restrict members from taking measures for the protection of human health, as well as the follow up Implementation Agreement (2003) which provides a waiver for countries with no or insufficient manufacturing capabilities to import pharmaceuticals under a compulsory licence. Pending ratification from a number of members, this waiver will be turned into the first ever amendment of the TRIPs Agreement.

At the same time, developed countries began raising the minimum standards and adding to the substantive and procedural aspects of the TRIPs Agreement through bilateral or regional FTAs and even stand-alone agreements (most notably through negotiating an Anti-Counterfeiting Trade Agreement). TRIPs-Plus provisions now appear in almost every comprehensive FTA involving a developed country party, and extend rights and protections in all areas of IP.[69] In most cases, these provisions not only increase levels of protection but also restrict or eliminate flexibilities existing in the TRIPs Agreement.

Finally, as we have already seen, IP overlaps with other areas such as investment, demonstrating the effects of fragmentation on the global IP regime.

8.   Climate change and international economic law

In the last two decades, climate change has moved from being a peripheral topic of marginal importance to a mainstream topic of concern.

---

[69] See M. Handler and B. Mercurio, 'Intellectual Property', in S. Lester and B. Mercurio (eds.), *Bilateral and Regional Trade Agreements: Commentary and Analysis* (Cambridge University Press, 2009).

Efforts to combat climate change have taken many forms, and there is an abundance of literature debating, discussing and relating to the science behind climate change.

International efforts to combat climate change gained notoriety in 1997 with the adoption of the Kyoto Protocol to the United Nations Framework Convention on Climate Change (UNFCCC). Designed to produce binding reductions and limitations on greenhouse gases on developed countries, the Kyoto Protocol did not place any binding targets on developing countries. Likewise, developed country parties to the agreement have failed to meet targets. Thus, while the Kyoto Protocol was successful in getting the world interested in the issue, it has largely failed to curb greenhouse gas emissions.

More recently, delegates at the fifteenth session of the Conference of Parties to UNFCCC drafted and agreed to 'take note of' the Copenhagen Accord, a document which endorses the continuation of the Kyoto Protocol and otherwise addresses global emissions.[70] While environmentalists and others would have hoped for more progress than has been achieved, the issue is firmly on the international agenda and will remain so for the foreseeable future. In the absence of a meaningful global agreement, however, the movement is shifting its attention to the domestic level and to other international forums. At the domestic level, an increasing number of nations, and states or territories of nations are considering implementing laws and regulations pressing for lower greenhouse gas emissions. These laws will affect the trade in a number of products, including oil and gas, and must be drafted in a manner which is consistent with WTO commitments. Internationally, the WTO itself is now discussing climate change and the wider environment as a matter which directly pertains to trade.

V.   Outline of the Chapters in this book

Part I Monetary cooperation, trade and finance

In setting out to investigate the importance of the post-crisis moment to the larger, historical evolution of the Bretton Woods system, particularly

---

[70] For information and analysis on the Copenhagen Conference and its perceived failure to deliver meaningful results, see M. Levi, 'Beyond Copenhagen: why less may be more in global climate talks', *Foreign Affairs* (22 February 2010), online: www.foreignaffairs.com; D. Bodansky, 'The Copenhagen Climate Change Conference: A Postmortem', AJIL, 104 (2010), 230.

in its immediate aftermath, this collection has necessarily looked towards those aspects of the international system which the financial and economic crises have drawn attention to. None of these aspects detract much from the overall design for a stable system of international trade which Harry Dexter White, who together with John Maynard Keynes had been a principal architect of the Bretton Woods system, had envisaged; principally because global financial regulation was never envisaged when closed capital accounts were originally intended after the Second World War.

Chapter 2 by Rolf H. Weber deals with perceived weaknesses in the making, force and application of global financial law by virtue of its 'soft law' nature; while in Chapter 3 Elisabetta Cervone explores the regulation of credit rating agencies whose activities – and perceived shortcomings in their regulation – have been alleged to have contributed to the crisis. Emilios Avgouleas and Douglas W. Arner analyse the more recent European debt crisis in Chapter 4.

Buckley, in Chapter 5, sets his sights on the widely acknowledged importance of East Asia and discusses what he sees as an 'imbalance' in East Asian participation in global financial regulation. He explores how this could matter to the long-term development of global financial and economic regulation; particularly China's role and the so-called 'Beijing' consensus.

Chapter 6 by C. L. Lim explores an event occurring in the aftermath of the 2008 crisis, in which China acted to devalue its currency. This caused critics to accuse China of currency manipulation, and to allege that such manipulation should attract trade remedy action against Chinese goods. However, as Lim discusses in his chapter, it is not entirely clear how the global system for exchange rate cooperation and the world trading regime interact and apply in dealing with this issue. His chapter explores increased trade friction with China regulated under the world trading regime spilling over into the 'fragmented' regime for exchange rate cooperation between sovereign nations. The chapter serves to bridge Part I and Part II.

Part II Trade and some of its linkages

Part II goes on to focus on trade and related issues. While the WTO provides the overarching framework for trading relations, the proliferation of FTAs together with a host of 'trade and…' issues mean that the regulation of 'trade-related' issues can be highly fragmented.

In Chapter 7 An Hertogen argues that structural imbalances in the exercise of sovereignty – by which she means the disparity between areas of sovereign discretion coupled with issues in respect of which there is little sovereign control – block the development of cooperative responses to problems of increasing economic and financial interdependence. Her chapter attempts to balance state sovereignty and cooperation by suggesting a reinterpretation of the tools available to states to protect their domestic affairs. The chapter focuses on the substantive concepts that can drive reinterpretation, taking the current interpretation of the central provisions of the GATS as a prime example.

Junji Nakagawa explores a different kind of fragmentation in Chapter 8 – that between trade regulation and development law – by looking at China's development through its industrial policy. The chapter evaluates the policy space afforded to developing trading nations by using China as a case study. Nakagawa discusses some of China's domestic polices pre- and post-accession to the WTO. Based upon the evidence presented, he argues that a 'retrenched policy space' argument is unsound – at least in this case – but that further empirical research is still needed to establish an optimal set of industrial policies for developing countries under WTO law.

In Chapter 9 Tomer Broude and Holger Hestermeyer turn to the potential opportunities that fragmentation of international law offers. Taking Google's experience in China as an example, some have suggested that international trade law can be used to promote the freedom of speech and access to information in China and elsewhere – i.e. by targeting internet censorship as a trade barrier. Thus, international trade law – in this case, principally but not limited to the law concerning the liberalization in online information services under the GATS – might protect a human right in the face of adverse political restrictions. Doing so could serve as a powerful vindication of economic liberalization where such liberalization is otherwise more often than not considered to contradict or to at least compromise human rights concerns. Broude and Hestermeyer are more sceptical. They argue that the WTO's jurisprudence indicates indifference towards the freedom of expression and ultimately promotes economic interests with little, if any, impact on restricted speech. Thus, any positive effects of trade law are incidental. Nonetheless, lawyers cannot ignore the fragmented nature of international law; including the possible benefits of other regimes.

Shin-yi Peng in Chapter 10 continues the treatment of services trade. Illustrating what might still be described as a particular type of norm fragmentation at the sub-disciplinary level, Peng first describes the stalled negotiations on emergency safeguard measures for services before asking if there is an emerging common approach utilized in recent regional trade agreements (RTAs) which could be used as a raw model in the GATS negotiations. She concludes, however, that no common approach has emerged in the context of RTAs negotiations. Moreover, the chapter argues that the current GATS jurisprudence provides only limited guidance to negotiators addressing the issues of emergency measures, leaving key questions unanswered and open for future discussion. She takes the China–Taiwan Economic Cooperation Framework Agreement as an illustration.

Part II concludes with Chapter 11 by Martins Paparinskis, which also serves as a prelude to the chapters on investment in Part III. His chapter engages the issue of fragmentation directly. Taking the example of the ASEAN Comprehensive Investment Agreement, Paparinskis asks whether an ASEAN member can exercise the ASEAN-authorized suspension of concessions in breach of WTO obligations.

Part III Investment law and intellectual property protection

The issues of investment and IP law dealt with are topical given the ongoing global economic malaise. Each chapter illustrates the fragmented nature of the various regimes and treaties regulating investment and IP law.

Chapter 12 by Anita K. Krug addresses an important gap in the literature by extending transnational convergence analysis to the investment company context. Focusing on the divergent approaches of the USA and EU, the chapter finds this heterogeneity may be attributable to entrenched interests and practices. The chapter then considers whether transnational convergence of investment company laws and norms is normatively desirable for global economies before evaluating and suggesting models of investment company regulation.

Chapter13 by Julien Chaisse seeks to answer two fundamental questions in the context of international investment agreements (IIAs) and the European sovereign debt crisis: (1) whether public debt obligations are covered by IIAs; and (2) whether private bondholders can file arbitral claims under IIAs. The questions are asked in the context of the introduction of collective action clauses by Greek legislation. To answer these questions, Chaisse's chapter reviews the forty BITs entered into by Greece and the key provisions which would enable a lawsuit against banks and the Greek state on behalf of holders of Greek bonds who had no other choice but to take part in the biggest sovereign restructuring in history. His chapter illustrates how the absence of an international regime for debt restructuring interacts with the international protection of foreign investments and investors given by a patchwork of BITs.

Chapter 14 by Juan Ignacio Stampalija, continues the examination of investment law through a survey of China's BITs, particularly China's approach to negotiating BITs. Stampalija's chapter gives a nod to China's importance in the global economy today and, against the background of fragmented investment treaty obligations, explores the application to China of those investment treaty rules China has consented to. While China has negotiated well over a hundred BITs, foreign investors have only exceptionally relied on these treaties in order to settle their investment disputes. Stampalija discusses the principal features of Chinese investment agreements and gauges the level of protection afforded to foreign investors in light of the decisions of tribunals in investment disputes, and also the changing nature of China's treaties where this last should also be understood against the background of increasing Chinese investment activity abroad. As we have seen, post-war investment has been regulated by a large number of BITs and there is divergence – another form of 'intra-disciplinary fragmentation' – where general or customary international law has long been confronted by highly specific treaty rules of a non-general nature; often of a bilateral nature. Stampalija teases out some of the more uncharacteristic features specifically in respect of the Chinese treaties.

Chapter 15 by Antoine Martin explores a further form of fragmented norm interaction between the emerging norms concerning food security, water and biodiversity resources, and traditional investment law. This is one of the first scholarly works which analyses the trend of both private and sovereign international investors in acquiring land in foreign jurisdictions for the purpose of producing and exporting food back to the home country. Much maligned, these so-called 'land grabs' are often large-scale investments in arable land with controversial impacts in terms of water and biodiversity resources, food production, and also job creation and population displacement/resettlement. Given the recent increase in such activities, foreign direct investment in agriculture constitutes a key aspect of contemporary international economic law characterizing the period following the global financial crisis. This chapter engages with questions as to the future of global economic relations – especially in relation to poverty, hunger and climate change issues– which have been framed, thus far, by imperfect global economic regulation. Implicitly, it understands fragmentation to mean under-regulation. Martin focuses on the reasons why host states offer their land to foreign investors and identifies some negative impacts that such investments will have on populations unless more regulation is put in place. It draws its conclusions from a cross-analysis of various reports to provide an overview of the trend and identify who invests and where.

Chapter16, deals with the issue of IP rights as an investment. Using Australia's plain packaging of tobacco products as a case study, Tania Voon, Andrew Mitchell and James Munro map out the broad level of IP protection afforded by international investment agreements, their exceptions and areas of controversy. The chapter highlights the complex interrelationship between international investment law, international trade law and IP protection.

Finally, in Chapter 17 Bryan Mercurio completes Part III by analysing the current trend in international IP law. Mercurio argues that instead of meeting its goal of increasing and harmonizing enforcement of IP rights, the Anti-Counterfeiting Trade Agreement (ACTA) further fragments international IP law by essentially allowing parties to maintain the status quo. The author questions how an agreement can curb counterfeiting and piracy when it does not require parties to amend their existing law. The chapter then seeks to uncover the ACTA's long-term effects and its intersection with existing international IP regimes, both as an alternative forum for IP rule-making and on the 'governance' of international IP more generally at the bilateral, regional and multilateral levels.

Part IV Aspects of climate change regulation

Part IV of the book turns to the issue of climate change, and its relationship with international economic law. Without a global treaty, countries are left to tackle the issue of climate change at the domestic level. This creates a host of issues, including the free-rider problem. In Chapter 18 Lorand Bartels looks at one particular scheme in which the EU seeks to export its emission-trading system. Bartels evaluates the WTO consistency of the EU scheme which now requires airlines to acquire and 'surrender' allowances for the carbon emissions produced by their flights. Due to its impact on trade in goods and services, the scheme has implications for the EU's obligations under WTO law; specifically, under the GATT and the GATS. Some of these issues are specific to this scheme, but in other respects they are connected with the current debate on the WTO legality of border carbon adjustments.

Chapter 19 by Rafael Leal-Arcas and Andrew Filis examines the degree to which the existing WTO normative framework grants members the policy space to take measures aimed at the promotion of renewable energy. Following a detailed review of the existing jurisprudence, the chapter finds that environmentally focused measures that, incidentally, distort or otherwise restrict cross-border trade will likely be deemed to be consistent with WTO obligations system so long as they are bona fide, applied evenhandedly and not unduly restrictive. That said, the authors express a certain degree of caution as the current interpretation of the WTO rules and obligations may change in the future. The current issues discussed in Part IV are non-crisis related but continue to spark controversy and lead to contemporary questions about the future directions of international economic law.

Part V Concluding observations

Chapter 20 contains the editors' concluding observations on the current state of international economic law, in light of its fragmented nature, and the possibilities for convergence and harmonization in the future.

PART I

Monetary cooperation, trade and finance

2

Does financial law suffer from a systemic failure?
A study of the fragmentation of legal sources

ROLF H. WEBER[*]

I. Introduction

International financial law is based on legal instruments enacted by public bodies (such as parliaments, executive authorities, international organizations) as well as by self-regulatory agencies acting on their own or by directive of public bodies. In fact, reality shows that international financial law is often implemented through inter-agency institutions with ambiguous legal status,[1] such as the Bank for International Settlement (BIS), the International Organization of Securities Commissions (IOSCO), the International Association of Insurance Supervisors (IAIS) or the Financial Stability Board (FSB). The Basel III framework, for instance, which consists of a comprehensive set of reform measures to strengthen the regulation, supervision and risk management of the banking sector, illustrates how an inter-agency institution approaches the need for international financial regulation.[2]

From a substantive point of view, the key elements of the respective regulations consist in the referral to best practices that promote sound regulatory supervision through rules of thumb,[3] comprising core principles released by the respective organizations. Best practices come into existence by application of two steps: first, agencies develop the best practices informally, by copying one another; in a second step, the best practices are acknowledged more formally. Hence, the process is not driven by a centralized legislator but represents rather a harmonization

---

[*] This contribution reflects the research state of the existing publications at the end of 2011.
[1] See R. H. Weber and D. Arner, 'Towards a New Design for International Financial Regulation', *University of Pennsylvania Journal of International Law* 29 (2007), 393–401; C. Brummer, 'Why Soft Law Dominates International Finance – And Not Trade,' *Journal of International Economic Law* 13 (2010), 623, 627.
[2] Basel Committee on Banking Supervision, www.bis.org
[3] D. Zaring, 'Best Practices,' *New York University Law Review* 81(2006), 294.

of agreed principles.[4] Furthermore, regulatory reports and observations generating normative undercurrents help define the appropriateness of national regulatory approaches;[5] in addition, the cooperation between the supervisory authorities must be improved, for example by providing for information sharing in case of cross-border activities of financial institutions or by outlining procedures for joint enforcement mechanisms; such kind of rules can improve the procedural level of the regulations.[6]

Many legal sources are of an informal quality helping to spur agreement between regulators, thereby limiting the risks of often uncertain costs and benefits accompanying the adoption of standards.[7] This informal quality has partly been an 'escape' since the globalization of the financial markets might have undermined the authority and control of 'national' authorities.[8] Nevertheless, 'escape' does not need to have a negative connotation since informal legal instruments are usually well accepted by the market participants and are mostly designed in a flexible way for future adjustments.

However, the question can be raised whether such kinds of intermingled regulation actually meet the need for a clear legal framework for financial markets. A legal framework of whatever nature must fulfill certain basic requirements such as regulatory stability, legal certainty and foreseeability of consequences of certain behaviors. In light of these elements, the following thoughts of this contribution assess the present international financial law framework in view of its systemic viability.

II. From systemic risks to systemic failure

A widely accepted definition of systemic risk does not yet exist; indeed, systemic risk is not easy to define and quantify. For some authors the problem of systemic risks is rooted in individual large and complex financial institutions with global reach; therefore, a need for a refocus on international regulatory initiatives seems to be unavoidable.[9]

---

[4] *Ibid.*, 309, 318.
[5] R. H. Weber, 'Overcoming the Hard Law/Soft Law Dichotomy in Time of (Financial) Crises,' *Journal of Governance and Regulation* 1 (2012), 8.
[6] Brummer, 'Why Soft Law Dominates International Finance,' 628–630.
[7] C. Brummer, 'How International Financial Law Works (and How It Doesn't),' *Georgetown Law Journal* 99 (2011), 257, 261.
[8] Weber, 'Overcoming the Hard Law/Soft Law Dichotomy,' 9.
[9] E. H. G. Hüpkes, '"Too big to save" – towards a functional approach to resolving crises in global financial institutions,' paper for the Chicago Federal Reserve Bank Conference on Systemic Financial Crises: Resolving Large Bank Insolvencies, 2004, 11.

Irrespective of this argumentation, looking at the consequences of systemic risks, it can be said that this phenomenon can cause severe disruption in the functioning of the financial system and consequently also adversely affect the real economy.[10] Generally speaking, systemic risk additionally relates to financial stability.[11] According to the International Monetary Fund (IMF), the Bank for International Settlements (BIS) and the Financial Stability Board (FSB), systemic risk can be defined as 'disruption' to the flow of financial services that is (1) caused by an impairment of all or parts of the financial system; and (2) has the potential to have serious negative consequences for the real economy.[12]

Based on this definition, a systemic risk leads to the temporary unavailability or the substantial impairment of the provision of financial services and the fact that such impairment has significant spillovers to the real economy. Consequently, the ESRB Regulation of the EU (Art. 2(c)) defines systemic risk as the "risk of disruption in the financial system with the potential to have serious negative consequences for the internal market and the real economy."[13]

Systemic risk mainly occurs in connection with large banks due to the sheer size of the banks' balance sheet, the complexity of their structures and their interconnectedness with other financial markets and institutions.[14] All three situations make it difficult for authorities to assess the impact and scope of a financial crisis situation, leading to panic or delays in the real solution of such crisis. The interconnectedness of a bank in particular tends to cause the risk of spillover effects.[15] Systemic risk also occurs where the performance of certain functions by a financial

---

[10] A. J. Levitin, 'In Defense of Bailouts,' *Georgetown Law Journal* 99 (2011), 443–446.

[11] International Monetary Fund, 'Chapter 2, Systemic Risk and the Redesign of Financial Regulation,' in *Meeting New Challenges to Stability and Building a Safer System, Global Financial Stability Report*, April 2010, 10.

[12] International Monetary Fund/Bank for International Settlement/Financial Stability Board, 'Guidance to assess the systemic importance of financial institutions, markets and instruments: initial considerations,' background paper, October 2009, 5–6.

[13] Regulation (EU) No. 1092/2010 of November 24, 2010, OJ 2010 L 331/1 of December 15, 2010.

[14] H. Brouwer, G. Hebbink, and S. Wesseling, 'A European Approach to Banking Crises,' in Mayes and Liuksila (eds.), *Who Pays for Banking Insolvency?* (Basingstoke: Palgrave Macmillan, 2004), 209, 214–215.

[15] R. H. Weber and V. Menoud, 'Systemic Risks as a Topic of Financial Conglomerates' Prudential Supervision,' *Banking and Financial Law Review*, 22 (2007), 382–384.

institution is indispensable for the real economy and cannot be substituted
by another provider within a reasonable time and at reasonable cost.[16]

Systemic failures can have many causes; in general, the following
aspects might play a major role:[17]

- A misalignment of the incentives of different national regulators precludes
  global solutions, i.e. leads to an undesirable regulatory heterogeneity.
- Informational asymmetries and regulatory competition hinder information sharing among authorities, which are imperative in a world of
  globally acting financial conglomerates.
- Legal uncertainty arising from different legal regimes makes it difficult
  to plan a stable regulatory framework which is the basis for the execution of business activities.

Systemic failure of the legal system means that the existing regulations do
not fulfill the functions as provided by the overarching legal concept. For
example, legal uncertainty can lead to non-compliance with regulatory
provisions or to reluctance in enforcing norms. If the legal system is too
complex, its coherence might suffer and the concerned persons and
organizations no longer clearly acknowledge the key features of the legal
framework.[18] Regulations relating to financial markets which are not
stable can also cause uncertainties in other fields of society. Consequently, the legal framework must avoid systemic failures.

III.   Does talking about the hard law v. soft law controversy help?

1.   Setting the stage

As mentioned, new rules regulating the financial markets have emerged in
recent years, mainly on a 'half-governmental' level; this source of legal
instruments has been chosen since national regulators and international
organizations were not in a position to react as quickly as necessary with
appropriate regulations protecting financial markets from problematic developments. Since this kind of international financial law through inter-agency
institutions not having a very clear legal status has become more important,
the stability and predictability of the legal framework seems to be increasingly
uncertain and its foundation might be built on relative shaky grounds.[19]

---

[16] IMF/BIS/FSB, 'Guidance to assess the systemic importance,' 9, 16.
[17] Hüpkes, 'Too big to save,' 2 (but in another context)
[18] For a general overview, see E. Posner, *Law and Social Norms* (Cambridge, MA: Harvard
University Press, 2000).
[19] Weber, 'Overcoming the Hard Law/Soft Law Dichotomy,' 10.

Not surprisingly, in view of this 'half-governmental' rule-making approach the relatively old discussion in international economic law about the merits of 'hard law' and 'soft law' has revitalized. In particular the question is asked, to what extent 'soft law' could replace 'hard law' under certain circumstances?[20]

2.   Is hard law really robust?

In contrast to international financial regulation, trade matters as well as monetary matters are governed by international treaties. Here lies an important difference between the 'trade and monetary law model' of international economic regulation, and global financial regulation. Trade rules are stated in the WTO Agreements (GATT, GATS), while monetary rules can be found in the Articles of Association of the IMF and World Bank. Compared to the global regulation of finance, there is a 'fragmentation' of legal sources.

In the context of trade and monetary cooperation, these multilateral treaties are designed to align incentives with the public interest and to prevent regulatory capture.[21] Furthermore, multilateral treaties usually encompass a dispute settlement mechanism ensuring accountability and enforceability of the rules; as a consequence, non-compliance with the treaties can lead to sanctions. Therefore, the legal framework of the WTO and the IMF/World Bank is acknowledged as member-driven, rule unitary, comprehensive, and nearly universal.[22] As a consequence, such system is often viewed to be more 'robust.'

The following elements and characteristics are typical of such a 'robust' regulatory system:

- The legal framework is rule-oriented, focusing on the predictability and stability of the legal provisions for all participants in the concerned arrangement.[23]

---

[20] The term 'soft law' was introduced by R. J. Dupuy, 'Declaratory Law and Programmatory Law: From Revolutionary Custom to "Soft Law,"' in Akkerman, Krieken, and Pannenborg (eds.), *Declarations on Principles* (Leyden: Sijthoff, 1977), 252; see also D. Thürer, 'Soft Law,' in Wolfrum *et al.* (eds.), *The Max Planck Encyclopedia of Public International Law* (2008) online available at www.mpepil.com; E. Ferran and K. Alexander, 'Can Soft Law Bodies Be Effective? Soft System Risk Oversight Bodies and the Special Case of the European System Risk Board,' *Legal Studies Resource Paper Series* 36 (2011), 1.
[21] Weber, 'Overcoming the Hard Law/Soft Law Dichotomy,' 10.
[22] R. M. Gadbaw, 'Systemic Regulation of Global Trade and Finance: A Tale of Two Systems,' *Journal of International Economic Law* 13 (2010), 551.
[23] See J. H. Jackson, *The World Trading System: Law and Policy of International Economic Relations* (Cambridge University Press, 1997), 85–88.

- The universal scope of application can avoid national regulatory capture of the legislator by protectionist groups.[24]
- The legal framework, if aligned with the public interest, can be designed in a way that the behavior of the 'ruled' entities takes the public interest appropriately into account.[25]
- A dispute settlement mechanism is established and implemented as central pillar of the system in order to make the rules enforceable and to hold the concerned institutions/persons accountable for their behavior.[26]
- Transparency should be foreseen as prerequisite for good governance, i.e. transparency is the "best of all disinfectants."[27]
- Adequate governance principles help to develop a decision-making model based on consensus.[28]

While such a robust system seems to be stable, some weaknesses cannot be overlooked: on the one hand, no progress is achievable if the member states of the international agreement are not prepared to apply negotiation flexibility in order to adjust the rules to the new (market or technology) needs. This problem is obvious within the WTO: the Doha Round has almost come to a standstill for many years. On the other hand, a long-standing arrangement such as the IMF Agreement might have to be adjusted if the market circumstances substantially change, as the collapse of the fixed-rate Bretton Woods regime (1973) and the liquidity needs during the recent financial crisis have shown.[29]

3. Can soft law have a replacing function?

As has previously been mentioned, soft law consists of rules issued by public or private bodies which do not observe specific procedural

---

[24] H. Siebert, *Rules for Global Economy* (Princeton, NJ: Princeton University Press, 2009), 76; Gadbaw, 'Systemic Regulation of Global Trade and Finance,' 570.

[25] K. W. Dam, *The GATT: Law and International Organization* (Chicago, IL: University of Chicago Press, 1970), 6; Gadbaw, 'Systemic Regulation of Global Trade and Finance', 568.

[26] L. D. Brandeis, 'What Publicity Can Do', in *Other People's Money and How the Bankers Use It* (New York: Seven Treasures, 1914), 92; see also C. Kaufmann and R. H. Weber, 'The Role of Transparency in Financial Regulation,' *Journal of International Economic Law* 13 (2010), 797ff.

[27] Gadbaw, 'Systemic Regulation of Global Trade and Finance', 572.

[28] See R. H. Weber, 'Multilayered Governance in International Financial Regulation and Supervision,' *Journal of International Economic Law* 13 (2010), 683, 703.

[29] Weber, 'Overcoming the Hard Law/Soft Law Dichotomy,' 11.

formalities as provided by state law.[30] At the same time, legal doctrine seems to have accepted that soft law does not necessarily have a lower quality than hard law;[31] the notion that legalization entails a specific form of discourse, requiring justification and persuasion in terms of applicable rules and pertinent facts is not only an element of hard law, but also of soft law.[32]

As a consequence, soft law can entail several functions previously tied to hard law, for example the notion of a coordination device and the objective of loss avoidance as efficient means.[33] However, soft law is only an adequate legal instrument if it does not enable market participants to disregard public interest by assuming inadequate systemic risks.[34]

This appreciation is not a new result derived from 'legislative' reactions to the financial crises, but corresponds to manifold theories developed during the last few years. The key term used is 'informal lawmaking' which can be based on a number of different concepts:[35]

- Anne-Mary Slaughter has developed principles for government networks, being set out as relatively loose, cooperative arrangements across borders between and among like agencies that seek to respond to global issues and managing to close gaps through coordination, thereby creating a new sort of power, authority, and legitimacy;[36] Slaughter advocates the establishment of such government networks since they permit the realization of coordination at a global level and create a new authority responsible and accountable for the development of rules.[37]

---

[30] See A. T. Guzman and T. L. Meyer, 'International Soft Law,' *Journal of Legal Analysis* 2 (2010), 171, 179–183; for a general overview, see C. Brummer, *Soft Law and the Global Financial System: Rule Making in the 21st Century* (Cambridge University Press, 2012), 210ff.

[31] Weber, 'Overcoming the Hard Law/Soft Law Dichotomy,' 11.

[32] K. W. Abott and D. Snidal, 'Hard and Soft Law in International Governance,' *International Organization* 54 (2000), 429.

[33] Guzman and Meyer, 'International Soft Law,' 188ff.

[34] For a general framework that can help to explain why market participants tend to make risk-taking choices without adequate regard to the overall financial system, see I. Anabtawi and S. L. Schwarcz, 'Regulating Systemic Risk: Towards an Analytical Framework', *Notre Dame Law Review* 86 (2011), 1349–1412, 1362ff.

[35] For further theoretical approaches (for example H. L. A. Hart, M. Foucault, G. Teubner), see Weber, 'Overcoming the Hard Law/Soft Law Dichotomy,' 11, with further references.

[36] A.-M. Slaughter, *A New World Order* (Princeton, NJ and Oxford: Hart, 2004), 14.

[37] *Ibid.*, 12–13 and 262–263; see also A.-M. Slaughter and D. Zaring, 'Networking Goes International: An Update', *Annual Review of Law and Social Science* (2006), 215.

- Similarly, David Zaring enumerates six principles in order to explain how global financial regulation works and in order to make understandable how legal obligations function when there is no court that could enforce them. The developed principles encompass: first, a national treatment principle; second, a most-favored nation principle; third, a preference for rule-making over adjudication; fourth, a subsidiarity principle of enforcement; fifth, a peer review model of enforcement; and sixth a network model of institutionalization. Zaring claims that global financial regulation now functions similar to a legal system, despite the fact that its initiators do not act with the force of law.[38] By analyzing these set of principles, he suggests that it would be possible to characterize and describe the structure and implementation of global financial policy-making choices. The principles proposed by Zaring exemplify how financial policy-making is currently realized, and illustrate that they are not unlike hard law and institutional principles.[39]

- Joost Pauwelyn distinguishes between (1) process informality leading to norms developed not in treaty-based forms, but in networks, fora or G-groups often without international legal personality; (2) actor informality encompassing private actors, industry associations, civil society, and other organizations or networks; and (3) output informality leading to norms that are not formal hard law sources, but standards, non-binding guidelines or indicators most of which are outside of the remit of the traditional legal order.[40]

- Warren Chik analyzes the disjuncture between the law and practices in cyberspace caused by the developments of information technologies, including the socio-economic problems and proposed the framework of 'Internet-ional' legal principles based in the history of customs as source of law.[41] Irrespective of the fact that Chik looks at Internet law, not at financial market law, it should be appreciated that from a regulatory perspective the differences are not so substantial and that

---

[38] D. Zaring, 'Finding Legal Principle in Global Financial Regulation,' *Virginia Journal of International Law* 52 (2012), 683–722, 685.

[39] *Ibid.*, 687.

[40] J. Pauwelyn, 'The Rise and Challenges of "Informal" International Law-Making,' in Muller, Zouridis, Frishman, and Kristemaker (eds.), *The Law of the Future and the Future of Law* (Oslo: Torkel Opsahl Academic, 2011), 125, 126.

[41] W. B. Chik, '"Customary International Law": Creating a Body for Customary Law for Cyberspace,' *Computer Law & Security Review* 26 (2010), 3ff.

the suitability of customary international rules as a template for for-mulating regulations also applies in financial markets.[42]

- A related approach can be seen in the theory of Cally Jordan, who develops the thought that hard law emanates from 'customary law upon which it draws' or the disputed *lex mercatoria* as a powerful undercurrent in finance, rather than from the state and its courts.[43] This theory provokes the question whether the global financial crisis was caused by a breakdown of a *lex mercatoria* of finance.[44] Jordan classifies the *lex mercatoria* neither as soft law nor as hard law; she states with a view to international commercial practice that the *lex mercatoria* would constitute an independent powerful source of norm-making in international financial markets.

The challenge of informal lawmaking consists in maintaining the laws' neutrality and protective force and in balancing informality which may be needed to enable effective cooperation or to avoid traditional stric-tures; such an approach will require a shift in international law from being a value-free instrument enabling state-to-state cooperation to a genuine regulatory order as well as a process balancing effectiveness with democratic accountability.[45] The advantage of this approach con-sists in the fact that it reduces formal requirements and increases dynamic adaptation potential.[46] Thereby, informal (lawmaking) is suit-able to implement an adequate degree of organization of the market participants as well as appropriate decision-making structures. But informal lawmaking should be 'supervised' by a legislative regime in order to make this model more accountable which is a centerpiece of any stable order.

Being a regulatory model which develops and establishes rules inde-pendently of the principle of territoriality and which is responsive to changes in the concerned environment, informal lawmaking follows the principle of subsidiarity, meaning that governments only intervene if the participants of the concerned community are not able to find suitable solutions themselves.[47]

---

[42] *Ibid.*, 185ff.
[43] C. Jordan, 'Transnational Law: Practice Inspiring Theory,' *Melbourne Legal Studies Research*, Paper No. 578 (2011), 1–22.
[44] *Ibid.*, 5.   [45] Pauwelyn, 'The Rise and Challenges,' 137–139.
[46] On the benefits and risks of informal lawmaking in general, see Weber, 'Overcoming the Hard Law/Soft Law Dichotomy,' 12–13.
[47] *Ibid.*, 12; Brummer, 'How International Financial Law Works,' 284.

Furthermore, it is fair to say that informal lawmaking leads to more extensive capacity building: its enabling functionality in financial markets serves the facilitation of the coordination process while at the same time providing directionality to the provision of cross-border standards; an informal lawmaking quality allows the regulators to enter into agreements by varying scope and specificity, and then to clarify (or change) the expectations of the concerned parties.[48]

IV.   Overcoming the hard law–soft law dichotomy

Referring to rules considered by the 'governed' persons to be adequate guidelines, an actually different legal quality of provisions based on statutes (hard law) and provisions based on private regulations (soft law) is difficult to identify. The legitimacy of soft law is also based on the fact that private incentives lead to a need-driven rule-setting process.[49] Informal lawmaking is justified if it is at least as efficient as traditional hard law and if compliance with its rules is equally likely.[50]

Nearly half a century ago, Louis Henkin phrased the often cited view that "almost all nations observe almost all principles of international law and almost all of their obligations almost all of the time."[51] This assertion is no longer convincing. The increasingly dense framework of rules with different legal qualities does not seem to improve the compliance with hard law (in particular international treaties).

Other models rely on specific compliance aspects: for example it is argued that states obey international rules not because they are threatened, but because they are persuaded by the dynamic created by the treaty regimes to which they belong.[52] Others rely less on managerial processes than on the fairness of international rules themselves.[53] Both

---

[48] Weber, 'Overcoming the Hard Law/Soft Law Dichotomy,' 12.
[49] On the notion of self-regulation, see A. Campbell, 'Self-Regulation and Media,' *Federal Communications Law Journal*, 51 (1999), 758ff.; J. Black, 'Constitutionalizing Self-Regulation,' *Modern Law Review*, 59 (1996), 32ff.
[50] L. J. Gibbons, 'No Regulation, Government Regulation, or Self-Regulation: Social Enforcement of Social Contracting for Governance in Cyberspace,' *Cornell Journal of Law and Public Policy*, 6 (1997), 509.
[51] L. Henkin, *How Nations Behave* (2nd edn, New York: Columbia University Press, 1979), 47.
[52] See A. Chayes and A. Handler Chayes, *The New Sovereignty: Compliance with International Agreements* (Cambridge, MA: Harvard University Press, 1995).
[53] T. M. Franck, *Fairness in International Law and Institutions* (Oxford University Press, 1995).

approaches, however, underestimate procedural elements, i.e. the complex processes of internalization of global norms.[54] Furthermore, it cannot be overlooked that the concept of Thomas Hobbes, outlined in his famous *Leviathan*,[55] that law is to be defined in political terms, which means in terms of power, no longer fits the highly complex structures of international financial markets.

Therefore, overcoming the dichotomy of hard law and soft law should be an important objective in international financial regulation.[56] In fact, already some time ago, theoretical analyses came to the conclusion that collective awareness and attention can be mutually beneficial in rule-making processes: cooperative arrangements are in a position to create a reasonable international framework.[57]

V.   Multilayered governance in financial law

Regulations are usually not 'invented' by coincidence. Moreover, a process-oriented approach developing mechanisms of evolution for future legal norms makes sense.[58] An evolutionary approach can encompass substantive and procedural elements; in the light of the rapidly changing technologies and financial markets, any approach relying on substantive elements risks becoming quickly outdated. Therefore, procedural elements seem to be better suited to comply with changing 'needs', since processes are more likely adaptable to new needs of society.

In view of the continuing integration and globalization of financial markets, the regulatory landscape has become increasingly multifaceted, encompassing manifold entities operating in various business sectors and on different geographic scales. The rapid increase in cross-border financial activity calls for a reassessment of the nationally based regulatory and supervisory system, which has developed on the given historical and

---

[54] H. H. Koh, 'Why Do Nations Obey International Law?,' *Yale Law Journal*, 106 (1996/97), 2599, 2602, 2645–2646, 2655–2656; G. Shaffer, 'Transnational Legal Process and State Change: Opportunities and Constraints,' University of Minnesota Law School, Research Paper No. 10-28 (2010).

[55] T. Hobbes, *Leviathan or the Matter, Forme & Power of a Common-Wealth Ecclesiastical and Civil* (London, 1651).

[56] This is discussed in more detail by Weber, 'Overcoming the Hard Law/Soft Law Dichotomy,' 14.

[57] J. G. Ruggie, 'International Responses to Technology: Concepts and Trends,' *International Organization* 29 (1975), 557, 562, 570.

[58] See M. Amstutz, 'Mechanisms of Evolution for a Law of the Future,' in Muller *et al.*, *Law of the Future*, 395ff.

political backgrounds and which fails in many ways to respond to the regional and international dimensions of today's financial reality.[59]

The acknowledgement that financial markets are to be regulated and supervised at different levels of global governance inevitably requires the development of a concept of multilayered governance. By means of standard-setting, the different layers of governance must be dynamically interlinked to enable them to address developments in the ever-evolving financial markets.[60]

Different layers with manifold interlinkages of manifold governing bodies tend to lead to too much complexity which could cause a system failure.[61] If governance is constructed in a non-transparent way, financial institutions will not be able to fully comply with the regulations. A too complex financial system will prove to be less reliable. In addition, a system that is too interlinked and too complex could also run the risk that the individuals lose orientation in decision-making processes. Looking at the complex financial products and markets Anabtawi and Schwarcz refer to a system that is "just too complex to understand" and leads to information uncertainty. Overcoming this information asymmetry will be costly but necessary to prevent the functioning of the financial system from impairment; standardization could provide one feasible response.[62]

Possible approaches for a harmonization of rule-making processes should consider that states might have an interest in participating in hybrid forms of regimes; this could possibly be done for example through delegated experts. A further task of states would be the transposition of transnational rules into their legal framework.[63] From a substantive point of view, the minimum level of a combined hard law–soft law approach should be set in view of the generally accepted industry standards and the given international customary law. In concretizing vague terms, the behavior of the 'reasonable man,' understood as an expression of common sense, could be applied as possible guideline.[64]

---

[59] Weber, 'Multilayered Governance,' 703.   [60] *Ibid.*, 704.

[61] See regarding complexity in a similar context, Anabtawi and Schwarcz, 'Regulating Systemic Risk,' 1368ff.

[62] *Ibid.*, 1389ff.

[63] M. Koskenniemi, 'Fragmentation of International Law: Difficulties Arising from the Diversification and Expansion of International Law,' in *Report of the Study Group of the International Law Commission* (Geneva: ILC, 2006), 65–67 and 99–101.

[64] A. D. Miller, 'The "Reasonable Man" and Other Legal Standards,' California Institute of Technology, Social Science Working Paper No. 1277, September 2007.

Stabilization of the financial market should figure among the key targets in any design of a regulatory system that aims to prevent further financial crises. What is crucial is that the behavior of individual financial institutions is also taken into account. Hence the existing financial legal system needs to be constructed with a wider scope of application.[65] In all regulatory segments, the relevant actors of the rule-making processes need to be identified; (institutional) actors structure incentives in human exchange whether political, social, or economic.[66] Actors also institute processes by producing and disseminating rules that determine the behavioral patterns of the 'participants.'[67] Such regulation encompassing hard law and soft law moves the decision-making processes to the most concerned actors of a specific market segment.[68]

In a multilayered governance concept the scope of financial activities, the importance of regulatory objectives, and the levels of supervisory activities could serve as criteria for assessing how financial regulation should be allocated to the different regulatory bodies in financial markets. On such a basis, standards could be a key to establishing multilayered governance as they allow for flexible adaptation of internationally agreed rules to national or regional particularities.[69]

If the partly existing dichotomy between hard law and soft law can be overcome along the lines set out herein and if the concept of multilayered governance can be realized an adequate legal framework for international financial markets can be achieved. Therefore, the efforts of the 'legislators' (in a wide sense) should go into the direction of aligning the present (international and national) statutory legal sources with the growing body of informal lawmaking. The more such alignment can be effected, the less financial law will suffer from a systemic failure.

---

[65] Anabtawi and Schwarcz, 'Regulating Systemic Risk,' 1401.

[66] R. H. Weber, 'New Rule-Making Elements for Financial Architecture's Reform,' *Journal of International Banking Law and Regulation* 25 (2010), 512, 516.

[67] See also Weber, 'Multilayered Governance,' 698–699.

[68] Weber, 'Overcoming the Hard Law/Soft Law Dichotomy,' 14.

[69] Weber, 'Multilayered Governance,' 683.

3

Credit rating agencies:
the development of global standards

ELISABETTA CERVONE

I. Introduction

The global financial crisis exposed some of the regulatory and market failures of a more and more globalized financial system and led to far-reaching discussions about a broad range of academic and policy issues on the regulation of financial services. While the causes of the financial crisis remain controversial, one factor clearly deserves our attention: the lack of substantive principles and 'hard law' in the international financial architecture and its accompanying regulatory apparatus, particularly regarding cross-border financial institutions, such as credit rating agencies (hereafter 'CRAs').

CRAs are major players in today's financial markets, with ratings having a direct impact on the actions of investors, borrowers, issuers, and governments. The 'Big Three' global CRAs – the US-based Standard & Poor's and Moody's, and the dual-headquartered (in New York and London) Fitch Ratings – have been under intense scrutiny. They were initially criticized for their favorable pre-crisis ratings of insolvent financial institutions like Lehman Brothers, as well as risky mortgage-related securities that contributed to the collapse of the US housing market. Since the spring of 2010, CRAs have focused on US and European sovereign debt. That resulted in Standard & Poor's unprecedented downgrade of the US' long-held triple-A rating in August 2010. Greece, Portugal, and Ireland have all been downgraded to 'junk' status. As the current Eurozone crisis highlights, a sovereign downgrading can have vast implications not only in the financial markets, but also for the respective state itself.

However, financial multi-polarity and re-regulation make global regulatory consolidation and full harmonization from a *top-down* approach in the CRAs industry an even more distant prospect than was the case before the crisis. It would be easier to harmonize when one country or one bloc dominates than when many diverging voices need to concur for a decision to be made; the latter being a condition more conducive to global regulatory fragmentation than the achievement of global standards. The declining relative importance of US capital markets in recent years and the lessons learned from the inward-looking Sarbanes–Oxley Act; emerging markets that have developed sophisticated and highly liquid financial centers that attract foreign investors, including US investors; fierce competition among both established and up-and-coming global financial centers in Asia and the Middle East. All have created an entirely new atmosphere. It would be also easier to harmonize rules in an era of deregulation, by reaching agreement on a low common denominator. Expectations as to what the rules should achieve, levels of financial development, governments' interest in financial regulation (and technical capacity to discuss it), may vary hugely from one jurisdiction to another.

Against this backdrop, the purpose of this chapter is to explore the prospects of harmonization and the development of global standards in light of a current fragmentation of regimes as well as the actors involved in rule-making. It does so by proposing the idea of imposing higher regulatory standards via extraterritoriality and private sector governance in the CRAs industry.

In particular, this chapter investigates the role of the European Union (EU) 'territorial' authority, providing a view on the role of the EU regulator as source of international financial law in the wake of the recent global financial turmoil. Although scholars have long recognized the extraterritorial effects of various financial rules, extraterritoriality is generally examined in the context of the conflicts-of-law literature. This chapter intends, instead, to explore the possibilities of extraterritoriality as a regulatory strategy, specifically looking at equivalence clauses used to export the EU regulatory model. This under-explored issue is contextualized in the credit rating industry by investigating how EU law interacts with global law and standards in the industry. To carry out this analysis, we scrutinize the 'equivalency' device, the legal means by which the EU regulator unilaterally exerts its influence in the CRA industry. First mover dynamics, linked to equivalence mechanisms, are evident in the EU CRAs Regulation (hereafter the 'EU Regulation').[1] The *equivalence* device serves to 'export' the EU regulatory model. If a non-EU regulator

---

[1] Regulation No. 1060/2009 of the European Parliament and of the Council of 16 September 2009 on credit rating agencies, OJ L 302, 17.11.2009.

wishes to allow CRAs domiciled within its jurisdiction the right to issue ratings for use in the EU, but does not already have a regulatory regime at least as stringent as the EU's one, it may have to comply with the EU Regulation, including entering into cooperation agreements with EU regulators. There are some early indications that the equivalence regime has been used by the EU to press for changes to the US, Japanese, and Canadian rating regime. This may make the EU forging ahead of global standard-setters.

The credit rating industry is an excellent area in which to show readers how this concept might work. CRAs and the markets they serve have global nature. This sector is characterized by the mobility of the rating service, which may be easily provided from varying locations (e.g. a German analyst operating in a London office of an American CRA producing a rating on an Italian company) and by the cross-border impact of ratings on users located beyond the geographical limits of a jurisdiction (e.g. ratings issued by a Japanese CRA may be used for calculating risk capital by banks in various EU member states).

Beside territoriality, we examine the capacities of private governance in the industry. We find that there is a role also for the CRA industry private sector governance – via their self-regulatory code – in informing the strength of international financial standards in the industry.

In such a heterarchic system of governance, efficiency does not seem to result from a clear hierarchy of norms, but draws from open competition and cooperation among various types of regulators.

II.   Credit rating agencies regulation after the crisis

CRAs play a powerful and highly contentious role in the global financial system. The regulatory system relies on their assessments, transferring a 'quasi-regulatory,' and thus public authority, to the agencies. This reliance is observed in bank regulation, which in some circumstances sets banks' capital requirements in relation to asset risks as assessed by the rating agencies. Similar regulations exist for insurance and other financial market participants.[2]

---

[2] The regulatory incorporation of CRAs has been more developed in the USA. In 1975, the SEC adopted the term 'nationally recognized statistical rating organization' (NRSRO) to determine appropriate capital charges for broker-dealers under the SEC's net capital rule according to an objective benchmark. In 1981, the SEC changed its historic practice of precluding the disclosure of ratings in securities offerings and encouraged such

Basel II contributed to the increasing use of credit ratings for regulatory purposes on a global scale.[3] Meanwhile, credit ratings continued to play a major role in global banking-sector regulations under Basel III, which mandates banks to justify their tier-one assets as part of liquidity requirements with reference to CRAs.

The incorporation of ratings in standards and regulations contributes significantly to market reliance on ratings, thus dramatically reducing banks', institutional investors', and other market participants' own capacity for credit risk assessment. This in turn was a cause of the 'cliff effects' of the sort experienced during the recent crisis, through which rating downgrades can amplify procyclicality and cause systemic disruptions.

The inherent conflict between their *status* as private, profit-seeking entities and the status of a quasi-public regulator is even more remarkable because they not only have continued to operate with little government regulation, but have also been largely exempted from established legal standards applying to traditional forms of investment advice in the USA and the EU. Even worse, market discipline such as reputation – which has traditionally been the preferred course of action – did not provide sufficient restraint during the crisis. There appeared to be an 'accountability gap.'

The extensive reforms that have been introduced internationally in the CRAs industry as a result of the crisis have brought to a halt the reliance on self-regulation and market discipline as primary regulatory mechanism. A strong consensus emerged that international self-regulatory efforts should have been supplemented with regulation of CRAs by national competent authorities. This consensus was encapsulated by the G20 in 2009,[4] which stated that all CRAs whose ratings are used for regulatory purposes should be subject to a regulatory oversight regime that includes registration and is consistent with the IOSCO Code on

disclosure. See Disclosure of Ratings in Registration Statements, Securities Act Release No. 6,336, 46 Fed. Reg. 42,024 (Aug. 6, 1981); Adoption of Integrated Disclosure System, Securities Act Release No. 6,383, 47 Fed. Reg. 11,380 (March 3, 1982). Marketplace and regulatory reliance on credit ratings then gradually increased, and the concept of 'investment grade' securities, as approved by an NRSRO, became embedded in a wide range of US regulation of financial institutions, as well as laws relating to credit worthiness.

[3] Banks were permitted to use ratings from certain accredited CRAs (ECAIs, External Credit Assessment Institutions) to determine minimum credit risk capital requirements under Pillar I of the Basel Capital Accord (Basel II).

[4] G20, *Declaration on Strengthening the Financial System.*

CRAs.[5] Overall, reviews by regulators in the EU, USA, and other jurisdictions (including Japan, Australia, Mexico, and Hong Kong), led to
greater regulation and supervision in the industry, in order to ensure
good governance, manage conflicts of interest, and improve transparency
and quality of ratings.

In the USA, initiatives to establish government regulation of CRAs
began before the emergence of the crisis. They culminated with the
enactment of the Credit Rating Agency Reform Act in 2006,[6] which
established a system of registration and regulation of NRSROs and
instructed the SEC to formulate implementing rules. The Commission
adopted rules in 2007[7] and 2009[8] implementing the requirements of the
Act and reflecting concerns about the performance of the CRAs in the
lead up to the financial crisis.

Several important reforms affecting CRAs were then included in the
omnibus financial services reform legislation, the Dodd–Frank Wall
Street Reform and Consumer Protection Act[9] (hereafter, Dodd–Frank
Act). The Dodd–Frank Act provides for more intensive and effective
regulation of NRSROs, overseen by the Office of Credit Ratings at the
SEC. The Act requires the SEC to adopt rules that will significantly
increase the regulation of CRAs under the securities laws. The statute
and its implementing regulations affect everything from rating methodologies to the corporate governance of the organizations themselves. At
the same time, they will make the ratings of NRSROs much more
transparent and easier for third parties to evaluate. The sanctions for
failure to adhere to the statute and regulations are severe and may lead to
the revocation of the registration of an agency with the SEC.

One key change redefined CRAs as 'experts' and exposed CRAs to
'expert' liability.[10] This would allow investors to bring private rights of

---

[5] *Code of Conduct Fundamentals for Credit Rating Agencies*, Report of the Technical
Committee of IOSCO. The IOSCO Code, published in December 2004 and updated in
May 2008, is "a set of robust, practical measures that serve as a guide to and a framework
for implementing" (IOSCO, *Statement of Principles Regarding the Activities of Credit
Rating Agencies* ('IOSCO Principles') of 2003).
[6] Credit Rating Agency Reform Act of 2006, Pub. L. No. 109-291 (2006).
[7] SEC Release No. 34-55857 (June 18, 2007).
[8] SEC Release No. 34-59342 (February 2, 2009).
[9] Pub. L. No. 111-203, 124 Stat. 1376 (2010).
[10] Issuers in the USA at times have included the rating for a security in the related public
offering registration statement. Under the SEC's Rule 436(g), issuers have been able to
include those ratings without obtaining consent from the NRSRO issuing the rating. The

action against the agencies if their ratings are found to be inadequate.[11] Other provisions of the legislation that have received public attention and concern are the repeal of the NRSRO exemption to Regulation Fair Disclosure (Reg. FD)[12] and a change in the pleading standard for federal securities fraud claims against CRAs.[13] The Act also removes statutory references to credit ratings in several areas of federal law and calls for federal agencies to review their use of credit ratings in rules and regulations.

III.   The EU regulation and its extraterritorial effects

Prior to the financial crisis, there was no comprehensive regulation of CRAs in the EU.[14] Their regulation consisted primarily of self-regulatory guidelines established pursuant to the IOSCO Code. This self-regulatory approach (with minimal statutory obligations) has been viewed to be sufficient.

The crisis caused a sharp reversal of regulators' opinions. Rapid action was taken to significantly reinforce and expand the IOSCO Code through the enactment of the first comprehensive regulation on CRAs in the EU,[15] requiring their registration and oversight.[16] It requires that all CRAs established in the EU seek authorization from the relevant national authorities and, among other things, provides that only credit ratings issued by CRAs subject to the new Regulation can be used by entities based in the EU for regulatory purposes. The EU Regulation was amended in May 2011[17] to entrust the European Securities and

---

legislation repeals 436(g), potentially exposing NRSROs to 'expert' liability if they provide consent for ratings to be included in registration statements.

[11] However, all the major CRAs have indicated they will not consent to their ratings being used in registration statements and prospectuses.

[12] The NRSRO exemption from the SEC's Reg. FD has permitted issuers to share material non-public information with NRSROs without triggering broader disclosure requirements. The legislation eliminates this exemption.

[13] The legislation changes the pleading standards for CRAs. This could potentially lead to more suits as the change may permit claims of federal securities fraud to be brought against a CRA that allegedly "knowingly or recklessly failed to conduct ... a reasonable investigation ... or to obtain reasonable verification" of the data it relies on to determine credit ratings.

[14] The Market Abuse Directive regulated only limited aspects of CRAs' activities.

[15] See n. 1.

[16] CRAs were required to apply the majority of the regulation by December 7, 2010, while the provisions relating to endorsement by June 7, 2011 (art. 41).

[17] Regulation (EU) No. 513/2011 of the European Parliament and of the Council of 11 May 2011 amending Regulation (EC) No. 1060/2009 on credit rating agencies, OJ L 145, 31.5.2011.

Markets Authority (ESMA) with exclusive supervisory powers over CRAs registered in the EU in order to centralize and simplify their supervision at European level.

The EU Regulation imposes a comprehensive set of binding rules, taking a much more prescriptive approach to regulation than both the IOSCO Code and the Dodd–Frank Act. It addresses substantive operational and organizational issues and involves detailed requirements pertaining to registration, corporate governance, rating methodologies, and ongoing supervision.

The scope of the EU Regulation extends to CRAs located outside of the EU, allowing the use of a credit rating issued by a third-country CRA only when the rating activities are either endorsed by a CRA located in the Community[18] or comply with certification based on equivalence.[19]

The endorsement regime allows CRAs registered in the EU to endorse credit ratings issued in third countries if the conduct of credit rating activities by the third-country CRA complies with requirements (relating to conflicts of interest, rating analysts, methodologies, outsourcing, disclosure, and transparency) that are at least *as stringent as* the EU requirements, achieving the same objective and effects in practice.[20] In order to respond to concerns that lack of establishment in the Community may be a serious impediment to effective supervision, third-country CRAs are required to set up subsidiaries in the EU.[21]

The other option for the use of credit ratings issued in third countries is certification based on *equivalence*. One of the certification conditions for a foreign CRA is that the Commission has adopted an equivalence decision recognizing the legal and supervisory framework of the third country as equivalent to the requirements of the Regulation.[22] The equivalence mechanism does not grant automatic access to the EU, but offers the possibility for qualifying third-country CRAs to be assessed on a case-by-case basis and be granted an exemption from some of the organizational requirements for CRAs active in the EU, including the requirement of physical presence in the EU. For example, the requirement of physical presence in the EU has been adjusted in certain cases, notably as regards smaller CRAs from third countries with no presence or affiliation in the EU.[23]

The endorsement regime was designated primarily for the initial stage of the application of a new regulatory regime for credit ratings in the EU,

---

[18] EU Regulation, art. 4.   [19] *Ibid.*, art. 5.   [20] *Ibid.*, art. 4(3)(b).
[21] *Ibid.*, art. 4(3)(a).   [22] *Ibid.*, art. 5(1)(b).   [23] *Ibid.*, art. 5(1).

until decisions on *equivalence* are made in respect of major jurisdictions. Equivalence decisions should later enable relatively more flexibility for credit ratings issued by CRAs established in countries deemed to have an equivalent regulatory regime as those to be used for regulatory purposes in the EU. Secondarily though, as was discussed during the negotiation, was that CRAs whose credit ratings may have significant impact on the European financial markets should always have physical establishment in the EU in order to be supervised directly by the competent authorities from the EU and eventually to be held responsible for complaints of users of their credit ratings. This means that any third-country CRA which is considered *systemically important*[24] must establish a subsidiary within the EU.

It was questioned whether the EU Regulation establishes two different tests for third-country CRAs depending on which mechanism is used: 'at least as stringent as' versus 'equivalent to.' According to ESMA,[25] there are no objective reasons to set different requirements: where the European Commission has recognized that the regulatory regime of a third country is equivalent to the CRA Regulation, it is possible to refer to this decision in respect to the 'as stringent as' test for endorsement.

Both the certification and endorsement provisions could have considerable extraterritorial implications.

The EU Regulation is imposed on CRAs regardless of where they are domiciled. The three largest CRAs – Standard & Poor's, Moody's, and Fitch – are based in the USA, but have a significant cross-border presence in all financial markets, including the UK and, more generally, Europe.[26] They are now subject to conflicting regulations in the USA and the EU[27] and may also feel compelled to comply with the revised IOSCO Code.[28] Because other jurisdictions (including Japan, Australia, and Mexico)

---

[24] *Ibid.*, art. 5(1)(d). *Systemic importance* is not defined in the regulation, but presumably implies the largest CRAs based in the USA, Canada, and Japan. CESR considered the matter of determining systemic importance an issue for competent authorities of all member states.

[25] ESMA, *Final Report, Guidelines on the application of the endorsement regime under Article 4(3) of the Credit Rating Agencies Regulation No. 1060/2009*, ESMA/2011/139.

[26] Although the head offices, main management teams, and main administrative hubs are in the USA, they operate in the EU through subsidiaries established in a number of European countries. However, Fitch is dual headquartered in the USA and the UK.

[27] Anr Sy, 'The Systemic Regulation of Credit Rating Agencies and Rated Markets,' 24–26, IMF Working Paper No. WP/09/129, 2009.

[28] See n. 5. The EU regulation states that CRAs should apply the IOSCO Code of Conduct on a voluntary basis.

enacted regulations on CRAs and several others are in the process of developing regulations for CRAs, CRAs headquartered outside of the EU are now tasked with implementing the complex rules and procedures promulgated in the various territories which may not conform to the detailed standards promulgated by the European Commission. In particular, they are required to implement the stricter of any conflicting rules if they wish to issue ratings for use in the host country. This is a significant undertaking, as the regulations permeate all aspects of the CRAs' daily operations.

In the event that no CRA were exempted and no regulatory regimes were deemed *equivalent to* or *at least as stringent as* the EU Regulation, only those ratings developed entirely within the EU would have been eligible for regulatory purposes.[29]

An inability to assess third-country CRA regimes as *equivalent* would make lending to or investment in non-EU sovereigns, financial institutions, and corporates prohibitively expensive for EU banks and securities firms owing to the material increase in regulatory capital requirements associated with not being able to recognize the relevant ratings. This scenario may be complicated further by the instance, particularly in the Asia-Pacific region, of CRA arrangements whereby lead analysts are located in regional hubs and rate firms and debt issues across several economies. If the EU-based CRAs choose not to, or are unable to, rate securities outside of the EU, the EU financial institutions would not be able to invest in non-EU debt securities. Even if the smaller EU CRAs did rate debt outside of the EU, their ratings may not be viewed as being of sufficient quality and their regulatory use by EU financial firms may raise concerns among other market participants. This could hinder the flow of capital between Europe and non-EU jurisdictions, thus lessening European investment opportunities.[30] It could also impact the ability of foreign governments or companies to raise capital in the EU. This in turn may lead to unintended consequences for the management of liquidity in Europe, increased credit concentration risks across the market, and the non-viability of some business models.

The EU Regulation's certification requirement could also have anti-competitive effects, serving as a barrier to entry into the EU market.

---

[29] EU Regulation, art. 5.

[30] Letter from Yasuhiro Harada, Chairman and Co-Chief Executive Officer, Rating and Investment Information, Inc., to Jörgen Holmquist, Dir. Gen., Internal Market and Services, European Commission 4 (Sept. 5, 2008).

The requirement of having a subsidiary or branch in the Community could prevent some third-country CRAs from operating in the Community completely. While many of the US-based CRAs have subsidiaries in the EU, two of the largest CRAs in Asia, Rating and Investment Information, Inc. and Japan Credit Rating Agency, Ltd., do not currently have subsidiaries in the EU.[31] Rating and Investment Information, Inc. primarily assigns ratings on bonds issued in Japan, but it also assigns ratings to bonds issued in the EU markets.[32] Similarly, Japan Credit Rating Agency, Ltd. primarily rates corporations and financial institutions in Japan, but those ratings can be utilized by banking institutions in the EU for risk weight assessment. They are both large CRAs likely to be deemed 'systemically important' and thus would not be able to use the certification procedure. Instead, these CRAs would have the burden of establishing EU-based subsidiaries to issue these ratings. Such an action may be deemed too costly in relation to the amount of revenue such rating activities would generate, causing CRAs like Japan Credit Rating Agency, Ltd. or Rating and Investment Information, Inc. to withdraw from the Community altogether.

Even for entities not found to be systemically important, many jurisdictions' regulations likely will not be deemed equivalent and ratings issued by these unqualified CRAs would be disbarred, thereby limiting competition within the EU.[33]

The introduction of an elaborate and prescriptive regime for third-country CRAs to be used in the EU for regulatory purposes may lead to a sort of protectionism, making the EU at risk of falling behind the USA in international awareness.[34] This may to a significant level eliminate the benefits of equivalence as a form of mutual recognition of regulatory standards among countries and, generally, recognition of compliance with global standards.

---

[31] *Ibid.*, 3.   [32] *Ibid.*

[33] E. Parker and M. Bake, 'Regulation of Credit Rating Agencies in Europe,' *Butterworths Journal of International Banking and Financial Law* 24 (2009), 401, 402.

[34] The USA has appeared more mindful of international constraints in recent times. The Dodd–Frank Act gives rise to fewer problems of extraterritorial application than the Sarbanes–Oxley Act had. Much of the controversy surrounding the extraterritorial effect of Sarbanes–Oxley was related to the new rules of corporate governance and accountability. See P. Lanois, 'Between a Rock and a Hard Place: The Sarbanes–Oxley Act and Its global Impact,' *Journal of International Law and Policy* 5(4) (2007), 1–19.

IV.   The 'equivalence' regime as a coordinating mechanism

The following discussion on the EU Regulation and its extraterritorial effects is part of an intense political debate – created by the increased rate and significance of cross-border financial flows across the Atlantic and exacerbated after the financial crisis – over regulatory jurisdiction and extraterritoriality, which focuses on equivalence and mutual recognition.[35]

An inescapable implication of the extraterritorial effects of the EU Regulation is that it could lead to overlapping jurisdictions, conflicting legal regimes and, possibly, over-regulation.

Divergent developments in the industry concern, for example, the 'issuer website' rules. In US, the Securities Act Rules 17g-2 and 17g-5 have been amended to require NRSROs to disclose more credit rating history information and disclose information relating to an initial rating provided by an issuer to certain non-hired NRSROs. The amended rules also require issuers to provide information to both hired and non-hired NRSROs. Non-US CRAs or branches of US CRAs that are not registered with the SEC as NRSROs are not subject to the regulations. In addition, even in the case of NRSROs regulated by Rule 17g-5, ABS issued by non-US issuers to non-US persons are exempt from the application of the rule until 2 December 2011. In the EU, Article 8 of the amendment to the CRA Regulation EC 1060/2009 proposed that issuers of structured finance instruments (or related third parties) must give non-hired EU CRAs access to the same information they give to the EU CRA they hire to rate the instrument. This was similar to Rule 17g-5 in the US, but was voted down, apparently heavily influenced by the observation that, in the US, the rule did not have the intended effect of generating competitive unsolicited ratings, but had only added to the administrative cost and burden of effecting a securitization. Given these divergent developments on the parallel Rule 17g-5 and Article 8 reforms, it will be interesting to see what coordination action is taken (if any) as between the SEC and ESMA when the exemption for non-US ABS comes to an end in December 2011.

---

[35] The EU has been instrumental in moving the US SEC from a policy of national treatment of non-US issuers to a policy of mutual recognition of financial disclosure regulation based on convergence between US GAAP and international accounting standards (IFRS). See R. S. Karmel, 'The EU Challenge to the SEC,' 31 (2008), *Fordham International Law Journal* 1711.

The EU and the USA differ also in disciplining CRAs liability. While US CRAs are now subjected to 'expert liability,' currently the EU CRA Regulation does not establish a specific civil liability regime itself.[36] Investors' claims against CRAs are legally difficult to treat under the predominant issuer-pays model, where investors do not have a contractual relationship with the CRA. Consequently, an investor suffering a loss due to a flawed rating, in breach of the CRA Regulation, cannot base claims for compensation directly on contract law. Whether and under what conditions an investor can claim compensation based on the law of tort varies largely according to the legal orders of member states.[37] Often, liability of CRAs vis-à-vis investors outside contractual relationships is subject to restrictive conditions, so that in practice investors do not seem to have an effective right of redress. This is confirmed by the very limited case law in EU member states on CRAs' civil liability toward investors. Also, the fact that the conditions under which investors can claim damage against CRAs are often either not very clear or left to courts' discretion may in practice prevent investors from claiming damage even in cases of clear infringements and gross negligence.

In general, there are fundamental differences in terms of the philosophy that the USA has in relation to their regulation and supervision of CRAs.[38] The US approach relies very heavily on upfront and detailed disclosure being made during the application process. Once the information is in the public domain, the US system relies on the SEC and on the ability of the market to exercise its own judgment regarding the credibility of the NRSRO itself, the robustness of the rating processes and procedures and the reliability of the ratings it produces. The SEC has chosen then to make relatively modest changes to the ways in which CRAs operate, favoring the introduction of greater competition for ratings and a scaling back of the use of ratings as a means of regulatory compliance.

However, the two systems are comparable. The goals are the same and, at the end, there appears to be consensus on the broad parameters of

---

[36] Nevertheless, Recital 69 of the CRA Regulation states that any claim against a CRA in relation to any infringement of the provisions of the Regulation should be made in accordance with the applicable national law on civil liability.

[37] Differences between member states' civil liabilities regimes applicable to CRAs lead to different levels of protection for investors and could even incentivize forum shopping, with CRAs choosing jurisdictions where civil liability for infringements of the CRA Regulation would be less likely.

[38] CESR, *Technical Advice*, May 21, 2010, Ref.: CESR/10-332.

CRA regulation: registration of CRAs with regulatory bodies, disclosure of key rating processes and methodologies, rules governing conflicts of interest.

Furthermore, recent proposals to amend the EU Regulation are more focused on market mechanisms.

Not only an obligation of due care of CRAs toward investors is specified in many requirements of the EU Regulation,[39] but a proposal for a regulation amending the EU Regulation foresees that CRAs should disclose information on their rating methodologies and underlining assumptions, on any proposed changes to their methodologies or on specific information on certain types of credit ratings, such as sovereign ratings.

Small and medium-sized CRAs would be encouraged to exchange information which could facilitate new market entrants entering the rating industry and offer a wide range of services. In addition, comparison of ratings from distinct CRAs could be facilitated by promoting common standards for rating scales and a European Rating Index (EURIX). Furthermore, improved transparency on pricing policies and fees would not only facilitate competition in the rating market, but would also enable ESMA to effectively monitor potential conflicts of interest resulting from the 'issuer pays' model. Finally, mandatory rotation of CRAs would not only substantially reduce the familiarity threat to CRA independence resulting from a long business relationship between a CRA and an issuer, but would also have a significant positive effect on improving choice in the rating industry by providing more business opportunities for smaller CRAs.

In both jurisdictions, the level of access enjoyed by investors to information about, from or concerning the CRA and its activities is increasing. With access of the investors to such information, control will be enhanced. The principle of 'stating the reasons' for making a regulatory decision applies now also in the CRAs industry. Stating the reasons will allow shedding light on the deliberative dynamics, and on the arguments at play, and will make the control of CRAs all the more objective.

---

[39] The obligation of a CRA to take all necessary measures to ensure that the information it uses in assigning a credit rating is of sufficient quality (art. 8(2) CRA Regulation) or the obligation to monitor and regularly update its credit ratings (art. 8(5) CRA Regulation) are obviously in the interest of investors. Breaching these obligations may lead to faulty ratings and could cause damage to investors who have based investment decisions on these ratings.

Because of conflicting regulatory philosophies of national authorities, differing costs of adjusting to foreign regulatory standards and competition among financial centers, traditional unilateral extraterritoriality, whether accidental or intentional, is in the process of changing into a mixture of standardization, exemptions, and agreed unilateral or multinational recognition.[40] The approach taken by the EU, during the past decade, in respect to financial information on securities issuers and accounting standards,[41] in which equivalency focused more on whether the regulatory regime broadly achieved equivalent outcomes, may be used as a template. A flexible approach to equivalency provides foreign market actors de facto preferential access to local investors over market actors in non-participating jurisdictions if they comply with foreign regulations that are *comparable* to the local market. If the US system would be deemed equivalent under the EU Regulation on CRAs, such recognition could significantly reduce barriers to capital between the two markets.

As economic theory suggests, where regulators of two large markets negotiate market access, the positive public goods benefits will be equally distributed. Even though the regulator of a small market must adopt standards that are not preferred, and even though adjustment costs are high, access to the EU markets can provide incentives to compromise and adjust. From this perspective, a series of strategic bilateral coordination arrangements by one actor could potentially lead to a global standard, or at least something close to it that is widely adopted by many jurisdictions. By picking off smaller countries and having them converge at its standard, a regulator of a large capital market, such as the EU market, could create network-size advantages that overwhelm the adjustment costs of other regulators. Standards can thus converge with those of the larger regulator.

---

[40] As far as US securities law is concerned, the US Supreme Court has recently put limits on its extraterritorial reach: *Morrison* v. *National Australia Bank*, June 24, 2010, www.supremecourt.gov/opinions/09pdf/08-1191.pdf. See generally E. Reuveni, 'Extraterritoriality as Standing: A Standing Theory of the Extraterritorial Application of the Securities Laws,' 43 *UC Davis L. Rev.* 1071 (2010); Xla Licht and Ji Siegel, 'What Makes the Bonding Stick?: A Natural Experiment Involving the Supreme Court and Cross-Listed Firms,' Harvard Business School Working Paper 11-072, 2011.

[41] In 2008 the EU deemed the GAAP of the US, Canada, and Japan equivalent to its IFRS, despite some major differences. Council Directive 2008/961, Commission Decision of 12 December 2008 on the Use by Third Countries' Issuers of Securities of Certain Third Country's National Accounting Standards and International Financial Reporting Standards to Prepare Their Consolidated Financial Statements, 2008 OJ (L 340) 112 (EC).

Equivalence is, at least potentially, a highly coercive instrument. However, it could significantly – perhaps even radically – liberalize markets, depending on the standards required of foreign regulators to be deemed *comparable*. Comparability is a process that could involve considerable domestic regulatory reform and presupposes a sufficient degree of confidence in the effectiveness of each other's supervisory systems. It implies a thorough analysis of each other regulatory framework and the common assessment of a sufficient if not high degree of equivalence. Where comparability can be demonstrated, mutual recognition and equivalence offer the benefit of operating not as an exclusionary tool, but as a coordinating mechanism by synchronizing the existing national and regional regulations and developing common approaches.

V.   The EU regulatory export and the 'hardening' of global standards

The EU Regulation does not seem to have deterred market entry. So far, twenty-three CRAs have submitted an application for a license with ESMA. In October 2011 all European entities of Fitch, Moody's, and Standard & Poor's, were registered under the endorsement regime. That means that the 'Big Three' (that already had subsidiaries in the EU) demonstrated to the EU regulator that the ratings they issue in third countries fulfill requirements that are at least *as stringent as* the requirements set out in the Regulation.

In implementing the EU Regulation, any potential extraterritorial and anti-competitive effects of the Regulation seems to be substantially reduced: the EU has already adopted – or it is in the process of adopting – equivalency decisions without forcing countries to implement the Regulation in full.

In 2009 CESR (as ESMA's predecessor) has been mandated by the European Commission to review the equivalence of various countries, including Australia, Canada, Japan, and the USA, and it has been carrying out some initial work on a further number of jurisdictions such as Hong Kong and Singapore.

By November 2011, the EU Commission only adopted an equivalence decision concerning the Japanese framework for CRAs. It did not adopt any decision with respect to the US framework. However, several other third countries were in advanced state of aligning their regulatory framework to the requirements of the CRA Regulation. A transitional period was granted, then, until April 30, 2012. This transitional period allowed market participants to continue using credit ratings issued in third countries, while the convergence assessment with the CRA Regulation requirements continued.

According to its advice on the equivalence between the US and EU regulatory regimes,[42] CESR identified certain weaknesses in the US regulatory regime, mainly relating to the methodologies used, the quality of ratings, and disclosure requirements. However, despite the significance EU regulators place on these provisions and the fact that the USA prohibits regulators from interfering with the substance of ratings, CESR's analysis is that the two regimes are broadly equivalent in achieving the overall objective of ensuring "that users of ratings in the EU would benefit from equivalent protections in terms of the CRA's integrity, transparency, good governance and reliability of the credit rating activities."[43] Because the US regulations are essentially designed to achieve the same ultimate goals as the EU Regulation, CESR deem them equivalent to the EU Regulation despite differences in the means used to achieve those goals, as was the case when the EU made prior equivalency determinations regarding financial reporting standards.[44] While no formal equivalence decision has yet been taken, ESMA is monitoring the improvements to the legislation anticipated by the Dodd–Frank Act and will continue its assessment as the draft secondary legislation is disclosed by the SEC.

In Japan, the Revised Financial Instruments and Exchange Act of 2010 introduced a registration system for CRAs and the Revised Cabinet Office Ordinance of 2009 prescribes obligations regarding quality control in the rating process. CESR pointed out that it considers the Japanese legal and supervisory framework for CRAs very comprehensive and in many respects similar to that of the EU Regulation. There are no areas where the Japanese requirements did not meet the objectives of the EU requirements and as such CESR had no recommendations to make in respect of the regime as a whole for the purposes of an equivalence determination. The European Commission has identified Japan's regulatory regime as equivalent through a formal decision in September 2010.

---

[42] CESR Technical Advice to European Commission on the equivalence between US regulatory and supervisory framework and EU regulatory regime for credit rating agencies (April 21, 2010).

[43] CESR Technical Advice to European Commission on the equivalence between US regulatory and supervisory framework and EU regulatory regime for credit rating agencies (April 21, 2010), 4.

[44] Council Directive 2008/961, Commission Decision of 12 December 2008.

Work is continuing on the regimes of Canada, Australia, Hong Kong, and Singapore.

In an effort to appease European regulators, the Canadian Securities Administrators (CSA) are planning to regulate CRAs rigorously. The latest version of its rules, published for comment on March 2011, introduces a new oversight regime for CRAs. In the original version regulators were taking a 'comply or explain' approach, requiring agencies to comply with a code of conduct, or explain why they are deviating from that code. Now, the CSA is dropping the 'explain' option; instead, firms must simply comply. The CSA indicated that it is requiring compliance because the CESR had determined that the proposed Canadian approach would not be considered equivalent to the EU Regulation. The failure to obtain an equivalency determination from the European Commission, and the consequent inability of a CRA that issues ratings out of Canada to rely on the endorsement or certification models, would have a negative impact on such CRA. The issuers that such agencies rate might also be negatively impacted to the extent those ratings are used for regulatory purposes in the EU. Consequently, the CSA is proposing to require compliance with a code of conduct that incorporates a list of provisions set out in the rule (which are based substantially on the IOSCO code and have been augmented to meet developing international standards).

Since June 2011 the Hong Kong Securities and Futures Commission (SFC) licenses and regulates CRAs pursuant to amendments to the Securities and Futures Ordinance. The Commission has also adopted a Code of Conduct for persons providing credit ratings. Among other things, the Code provides that a CRA should implement and enforce procedures to document reporting lines and allocate functions and responsibilities and ensure that the credit ratings it prepares are based on a thorough analysis of all relevant information known to the agency. In addition, rating methodologies should be rigorous, systematic and, where possible, result in ratings that can be subjected to objective validation based on historical experience, including back-testing. The regulation of CRAs will bring Hong Kong's regulatory regime in line with international developments in this area. Hong Kong is the base from which major multinational CRAs conduct business in the Asia Pacific region. Some smaller CRAs also have offices in Hong Kong.

ESMA has adopted a flexible approach to assessing equivalence of any third-country regulatory regime, at least in the early stages of the new regime. Instead of a 'plain' equivalence assessment, specific case-by-case review of compliance with EU standards has been required. This would have the benefit of ensuring that major jurisdictions could be considered equivalent from the beginning, while recognizing, though, that further work will need to be undertaken. This approach would avoid potential market disruption or distortions arising from the authorities' inability to complete the work necessary by the deadline due to insufficient resource available.

There are some early indications that the equivalence regime has been used by the EU to press for changes to countries that host strong financial centers with a heavy international aspect (like the US, Japanese, and Canadian rating regimes) in a *race to the top*.

We doubt, at least in the case of CRAs, that the inevitable competition in a world of several financial centers creates a regulatory race to the bottom and to the under-enforcement of established regulations.[45] To the extent to which it has authority, the EU can be an important and indeed decisive player in the international regulatory arena, enhancing international convergence in the CRAs industry and promoting mutual recognition of substantively similar regimes. The EU Regulation can be characterized as part of more ambitious plan by the EU to "lead by example"[46] in an attempt to position itself at the vanguard of "an emerging, rules-based, global order"[47] of which it is the author.

VI.   A multimode governance structure

We explored the possibilities of extraterritoriality as a regulatory strategy in the credit rating industry, specifically looking at equivalence clauses used to export the EU regulatory model. Is there a role also for the CRA industry private sector governance in building and 'hardening' global standards in the industry?

Financial governance, in Europe and beyond, is increasingly influenced by multilevel decision-making in private and public, national and international governance institutions. Regulating the activity of CRAs "very much highlights the multi-level governance of financial services and the 'uploading,' 'downloading' and 'cross-loading' of rules across jurisdictions and levels of governance."[48]

---

[45] R. S. Karmel and C. R. Kelly, 'The Hardening of Soft Law in Securities Regulation,' *Brooklyn Journal of International Law* 34(3) (2008–9), 883.

[46] J. Barroso, 'Leading by example: The EU and global governance,' speech by President of the EC, May 12, 2009, Brussels.

[47] *Ibid.*

[48] L. Quaglia, 'The Politics of Regulating Credit Rating Agencies in the European Union,' Centre for Global Political Economy WP 5/2009.

The public–private dynamics, increased by the interplay between various levels of governance, are complex.

At the international level, the CRAs' activity has been regulated by the IOSCO Code, the rules of which have been incorporated, to a large extent, into the EU legislation and, partly, into the Dodd–Frank Act. Mostly important, the guidelines adopted by the heads of governments representing the G20 group of systemically important economies have been implemented by worldwide, regional, national, and non-governmental organizations cooperating in the contest of international organizations.

At regional level, extraterritorial effects are evident not only in the EU Regulation (as discussed in the article), but also in the Dodd–Frank Act. For example, Section 929P of the Act gives federal district courts jurisdiction over enforcement actions by the SEC alleging violations on the part of CRAs, even if the conduct occurs outside the USA and involves foreign investors, as long as the former includes "significant steps" within the US, or has a "foreseeable substantial effect" within the USA.[49] In a report released in August 2010, the SEC stated that CRAs should expect that the former would pursue enforcement action against extraterritorial misconduct.[50] This in turn raises issues about the extraterritorial effects of US rules for CRAs operating in Europe and the prospect of an indirect downloading (or cross-loading) of such rules in the EU. These extraterritorial effects of both the EU and US regulation on CRAs raise the prospect of an indirect "uploading" or "cross-loading" of the new EU and US rules in, respectively, non-EU jurisdictions and non-US jurisdictions.[51]

Market initiatives such as the CRAs own Code of Conduct – which can supplement and complement incomplete, intergovernmental regulations – may add complexity to the regulatory framework.

---

[49] Dodd–Frank Wall Street Reform and Consumer Protection (Dodd–Frank) Act, Pub. L. No. 111-203, § 929P(b)(1) (2) (2010).

[50] SEC, Report of Investigation Pursuant to Section 21(a) of the Securities Exchange Act of 1934: Moody's Investors Service, Inc., Exchange Act Release No. 62802 (2010).

[51] Quaglia, 'Politics of Regulating Credit Rating Agencies.' "Uploading" is defined as the incorporation of EU rules (or part of them) into international financial regulation (L. Quaglia, 'The European Union in Regulating Global Finance,' Working Paper EUSA conference, Boston, 2011, 4). "Cross-loading" is defined as the incorporation of rules agreed in one jurisdiction into another, without the adoption of these rules by international regulatory for a (*ibid.*).

CRAs produced regulations of global relevance and application. These are an important source of discipline. The IOSCO Code has served as an industry code and promoted the establishment of internal CRA policies and procedures to give effect to the IOSCO Principles. The mechanisms for implementing the IOSCO Code took the form of any combination of, among other things, government regulation, industry codes, and internal CRA policies and procedures. The new government regulation in place can provide a mechanism for implementing the principles in combination with the IOSCO Code. A number of CRAs (including the three largest ones) were found to have substantially implemented the IOSCO Code. A somewhat larger group of CRAs had partially implemented the IOSCO Code.[52] In addition, recent voluntary initiatives have been undertaken by the major CRAs to enhance rating quality.[53]

Also, the IOSCO evaluation of CRA regulatory programs across different jurisdictions (Australia, EU, Japan, Mexico, USA) reveals that while the structure and specific provisions of those programs may differ, the objectives of the four IOSCO Principles[54] – quality and integrity of the ratings process, management of conflicts, transparency, and treatment of confidential information – are embedded into each of the programs, albeit in varying degrees of implementation.[55] Despite the differences among the jurisdictions, in each jurisdiction reviewed the Principles appear to be the building blocks upon which CRA regulatory programs have been constructed.

Both the Dodd–Frank Act and the EU Regulation encompass – broadly speaking – comparable measures to address three similar objectives. *First*, a lack of competition among CRAs shall be cured by installing a registration system with lowered premises to become a recorded organization. *Second*, formerly missing transparency shall be established by extensive disclosure obligations. *Third*, investor protection shall be strengthened through maintenance of objectivity of CRAs by avoiding conflicts of interest. Measures taken to achieve these objectives are essentially well known from the IOSCO Code. The Dodd–Frank Act as well as the EU Regulation only transfer already voluntarily applied

---

[52] www.iosco.org/library/pubdocs/pdf/IOSCOPD233.pdf
[53] Commission Staff Working Paper, Impact Assessment, at http://ec.europa.eu/internal_market/securities/docs/agencies/SEC_2011_1354_en.pdf
[54] IOSCO Principles.
[55] Regulatory Implementation of the Statement of Principles Regarding the Activities of Credit Rating Agencies, February 2011.

provisions into binding regulations which reasonable-acting CRAs have already followed voluntarily.

Regrettably, with the move to more intensive regulation, market discipline has been largely avoided in the EU Regulation.

Minimum harmonization and optionality appear to be in permanent retreat in the new regime. For example, the EU Regulation does not envisage admissibility of a dual system of compliance with its requirements, whereby local/regulatory duties in a third country would be 'topped up' by policies and procedures voluntarily followed by the third-country CRA or the EU-registered, endorsing CRA. In fact, the requirements *as stringent as* those set out in Articles 6 to 12 may only be established in law or regulation of that third country in order to satisfy the condition laid down in Article 4(3)(b). The EU Regulation does not provide any exceptions for such a situation. The reasoning is that "if the requirements for endorsement could be established on a voluntary basis, the risk of non-compliance by the third-country CRA would be significantly higher."[56]

It seems unfair to bar the use of credit ratings in the EU if they are issued by non-EU CRAs who are otherwise in compliance with all provisions in the EU Regulation. It would have been wise to consider the possibility for the endorsing CRA to confirm to EU authorities that the non-EU CRA has met the requirements on a self-imposed basis if there were no equivalent local regulatory regime. This is what the EU Regulation provided just for the eighteen-month transition period until June 7, 2011.[57] After that date, the CRAs without an exemption and whose home regulatory regimes are not deemed *equivalent to* or *as stringent as* the EU Regulation have to establish and register a subsidiary within the EU and conduct all rating activities for use in the EU through that entity.[58]

While this move in 'regulatory paradigm' in the EU Regulation is an understandable reaction to the financial crisis, it must not be forgotten that the regulatory process more and more infiltrates in the private law domain and enhances the role of private actors in the process of financial markets regulation. The strengths of a market-based approach, which is sufficiently flexible to accommodate changing market circumstances, are particularly important in a sector which is renowned for innovation.[59]

---

[56] CESR, Consultation Paper, paras. 94–95.
[57] EU Regulation, art. 41.   [58] *Ibid.*, art. 5.
[59] Karmel and Kelly, 'Hardening of Soft Law in Securities Regulation,' 885 (noting that soft law is relied upon "because of the need for speed, flexibility and expertise in dealing with fast-breaking developments in capital markets").

The problem was not self-regulation per se, but the failure to integrate structures of private governance of CRAs effectively within a larger institutional setting. While monitoring by reputation can be less effective in an uncompetitive dimension,[60] the reputational incentive *does* exist. Rather, it is sacrificed as a tradeoff with regulation-induced incentives.

A successful reform of the credit rating industry must be accompanied by the withdrawal of rating-based regulations. When the CRAs will abandon their quasi-governmental function, contenting themselves with their position as private-sector entities, market forces are expected to play their disciplining role and CRAs' revenues will directly relate to the substantive value of their credit ratings and not to any 'regulatory privilege.' Investors would then be required to make credit judgments of their own. The interplay of market forces by way of more informed investor decision-making may sanction inappropriate or suboptimal behavior by CRAs and incentivize them to alter their conduct. The CRAs are not the only source of creditworthiness information. Above all, the bond market is largely an institutional market, where bond managers at financial institutions – not retail investors – make the buy-and-sell decisions. Improved disclosure by issuers to investors will facilitate the build-up of capabilities at banks, investment managers, and institutional investors to conduct their own assessment of the creditworthiness of the financial products they invest in and thus enhance their ability to avoid mechanistic reliance on CRA ratings. While it may take a number of years for market participants to develop enhanced risk management capability so as to enable reduced reliance on CRAs, authorities should take actions to incentivize the necessary enhancements to be made.

Following failures of ratings in the US subprime mortgage-based securities market, work has been undertaken to reduce regulatory reliance on credit ratings. At the global level, the Financial Stability Board (FSB) reviewed this issue and drew up principles to reduce reliance on credit ratings in standards, laws, and regulations.[61] The FSB principles aim to catalyze a significant change in existing practices, to end

---

[60] For an extremely chastising view, see F. Partnoy, 'The Paradox of Credit Ratings,' University of San Diego School Law and Economics, Research Paper No. 20, 2021 (2001), 658, according to which "the reputational capital view of CRAs is not supported by history or economic analysis."

[61] Financial Stability Board, Principles for Reducing Reliance on CRA Ratings. The principles were endorsed by the G20 Seoul Summit in November 2010.

mechanistic reliance by market participants and establish stronger internal credit risk assessment practices instead.

Some jurisdictions have already implemented or are considering actions to remove or replace references to CRA ratings in their laws and regulations. The US Dodd–Frank Act marks a turning point by requiring the complete removal of regulatory references to credit ratings.[62] In the EU, the proposals for a new Capital Requirement Directive[63] and other proposals,[64] reduce the number of references to external ratings and require financial institutions to do their own due diligence.

However, reducing regulatory reliance is proving difficult at times, not least because it complicates the adoption of global supervisory standards such as Basel III that do refer to ratings. It may take a number of years for market participants to develop enhanced risk management capability to enable reduced reliance on CRAs. In the short term, we need institutional safeguards for holding CRAs legally and democratically accountable.

In light of the cross-border activities of certain CRAs and the global nature of ratings generally, the most effective way to minimize potential regulatory gaps and address the regulatory frictions resulting from different regulatory regimes and levels of governance in the CRAs industry is through international coordination and bilateral dialogues.[65] It is important that the USA and EU continue to work together to ensure that equivalence determinations for CRAs follow an outcomes-based assessment rather than requiring an exact duplication of rules.

This dialogue should be soon guided to ensure CRAs regulation is globally consistent. The reforms of the US regulatory system, which still represents the largest and most liquid market in the world, on one hand, and of the EU regulatory system, on the other hand, are a critical

---

[62] US Dodd–Frank Act of 2010, Sec. 939–939A.

[63] COM (2011) 453 final (July 2011), which replaces the current Capital Requirements Directives (2006/48 and 2006/49).

[64] Commission proposal of 15 November 2011 for a Directive of the European Parliament and of the Council amending Directive 2009/65/EC on the coordination of laws, regulations and administrative provisions relating to undertakings of collective investment in transferable securities (UCITS) and Directive 2011/61/EU on Alternative Investment Funds Managers in respect of the excessive reliance on credit ratings, COM(2011) xxx final; Commission Proposal of 15 November 2011 for a Regulation amending Regulation (EC) No. 1060/2009 on credit rating agencies.

[65] K. L. Casey, Commissioner US SEC, testimony concerning international cooperation to modernize financial regulation, before the US Banking Subcommittee on Securities and International Trade and Finance (September 30, 2009).

component of a more effective global system, but in and of themselves they will not be sufficient to create such a system. Increased participation of China, India, and the emerging Middle Eastern financial centers in the debate is critical for success in achieving an international regulatory system that supports the goals of market integrity and investor protection.

The interplay between domestic and global level is a core element to develop and 'harden' global standards and to monitor compliance with the G20 agenda. The IOSCO provides a forum for CRA regulators and supervisors, aiming to help them in enhancing international regulatory and supervisory cooperation in the implementation of their respective jurisdictions' programs, as well as in addressing potential conflicts that may arise from the different regulatory requirements imposed by different jurisdictions upon globally operating CRAs.

These informal, ad hoc activities stretch the boundaries of permissible sovereign activity in reciprocal ways. If all regulators share information with each other, then each regulator simultaneously cedes sovereignty in a manner that is evenhanded.

What informal arrangements fail to address is the enforcement issue. The potential for multiple layers of enforcement exists, with fifty states in the USA and twenty-eight member states in the EU. In the building of a cross-border regulatory system on CRAs, equivalence assessments should consider the differences in enforcement, which vary widely across markets. The multiplicity of supervisors involved gives rise to an unworkable patchwork of legal risks, complexities, and compliance costs for CRAs that could threaten their viability.[66] Due to the specific nature of the rating activity, in which the division lines between geographical competences of supervisors are not set too firmly, the risk of conflicts over competences may lead to ineffective and/or inefficient supervision, regulatory arbitrage, or unlevel playing field.

Can regional supervisors cope with the global dimension of CRAs? Competent authorities may perceive the dimension of CRA supervision mainly from a regional perspective missing the full picture of the global nature and impact of a CRA's activity. Especially in situations where the main impact of a CRA lies outside the jurisdiction where it is registered, there is the risk that the regional competent authority does not allocate

---

[66] Despite the Reform Act's framework for exclusive federal regulation of NRSROs, the New York and Connecticut attorneys general have sought to impose far-reaching reforms on the three largest CRAs using actual or threatened litigation under state law.

sufficient resources for the supervision of this CRA. The competent supervisor, which is used to being responsible for its regional financial market and accountable to its national political institutions, has to take the main responsibility for CRA activities with global reach affecting primarily financial markets outside its home jurisdiction.

To promote transatlantic coordination, consistent enforcement of the regulatory standards within a jurisdiction and accord with the broad nature and impact of CRAs activities, responsibility for enforcing regulatory laws and rules applicable to CRAs should be vested exclusively at the highest governmental level within a jurisdiction. Perhaps most notably for the EU financial market is the centralization of licensing, supervisory, and enforcement powers over CRAs in a central EU authority, the European Securities and Markets Authority (ESMA). The traditional distinction between the home competent authority and the other competent authorities and the use of supervisory coordination by colleges is no longer necessary. The possibility of sanctioning CRAs is not a substitute for an efficient right of redress for investors (sanctions imposed in the public interest do not compensate investors for their losses). However, the ESMA 'rule-making' and supervisory powers over CRAs and local supervisory authorities are of potentially dramatic significance to the EU financial market regulation.

Within the proposed 'constitutional framework,' based on reducing regulatory reliance on CRAs, enhanced CRAs' accountability and cooperation among regulatory entities, constitutional pluralism does not represent an academic utopia.

VII.   Conclusions

In analyzing the EU Regulation on CRAs and its extraterritorial effects, this chapter addresses conceptual challenges for contemporary financial regulation and supervision based on the idea of imposing higher regulatory standards via extraterritoriality.

The financial crisis has dealt a serious blow to the previously existing international dialogue and the fear exists that the main regulators would retreat. However, we found that the equivalence regime introduced by the EU Regulation on CRAs enhances the benefits of equivalence as a form of mutual recognition of regulatory standards among countries and, generally, recognition of compliance with global standards. The extraterritorial effects of the EU Regulation – which is accompanied by robust additional requirements for certification of third-country credit ratings to be used in the EU – may then lead to stronger global standards in the industry.

The European Commission, in assessing equivalence of third-country regulatory regimes, adopts a flexible approach, taking account of the inevitable differences in regulatory philosophy and approach, and that an exact replication of all the EU requirements will not be necessary. The process is not limited to a passive finding of equivalence in regulation, but consists of an active search for common or at least compatible solutions. As a result, there are early indications that regulations on CRAs in some major jurisdictions, such as the USA, Japan, Canada, Hong Kong, and Australia are converging toward the EU regulatory framework.

In this approach to regulation, we tend to be critical of authoritarian *top-down* conceptions of intergovernmental economic regulation and promote, instead, competing liberalization at multiple levels and in multiple modes. Disciplining mechanisms such as territoriality and private-sector governance may render global financial standards more coercive than traditional theories of international law predict. The literature that dismisses international financial rules on the basis of their legal informality should not overlook the context in which the rules operate.

Postscript

Since the writing of this chapter, the European Commission has published an equivalence decision on Argentina, Brazil, Mexico, Hong Kong, and Singapore, concluding that their legal and supervisory framework for CRAs are equivalent to the EU regulatory regime for CRAs. In addition, amendments were made in the EU to the CRAs Regulation, which entered into force in 2013. Among other things, the new rules will make CRAs more accountable for their actions, ensuring that a CRA can be held liable where it infringes intentionally or with gross negligence the CRAs Regulation, thereby causing damage to an investor or an issuer. Following these amendments, the EU and the USA will not differ substantially in disciplining CRAs' liability.

These new events indicate that regulations on CRAs in some major jurisdictions are converging toward the EU regulatory framework. This is consistent with, and even supports, the approach toward the regulation of CRAs adopted in this chapter, the purpose of which has been to explore the prospects for the harmonization and development of global standards in the CRAs industry via extraterritoriality.

4

The broken glass of European integration: origins and remedies of the Eurozone crisis and implications for global markets

EMILIOS AVGOULEAS AND DOUGLAS W. ARNER

I. Introduction

Following decades of effort to build a single financial market, the European Union (EU), as a supranational organization and almost all of its member countries lacked proper resolution mechanisms in the event of a financial crisis.[1] Thus, with the advent of the global financial crisis (GFC) the single market faced the prospect of widespread bank failures and near collapse of national financial systems. Today, in the context of the Eurozone financial crisis, the EU is at a critical crossroads. It has to decide whether the road to recovery runs through closer integration of financial policies and of bank supervision and resolution, or whether to take the path of fragmentation with a gradual return to controlled forms of protectionism in the pursuit of narrow national interest, although the latter is bound to endanger the single market. The policy dilemmas facing the EU and contemporary institution building within the Eurozone offer us a looking glass into the future of both global and regional financial integration.

The complexity of the financial integration process and its significance means that it is impossible to understand contemporary developments within the Eurozone without a discussion of the different forms of integration and of the history of financial integration in Europe. It is important to draw a distinction between economic, monetary and political forms of integration, before looking at the specific properties of EU

---

[1] See E. Avgouleas, *Governance of Global Financial Markets: The Law, the Economics, the Politics* (Cambridge University Press, 2012), ch. 6. See also F. Recine and P. G. Teixeira, 'The New Financial Stability Architecture in the EU', Paolo Baffi Centre Research Paper No. 2009-62 (November 2009). Available at SSRN: http://ssrn.com/abstract=1509304 or http://dx.doi.org/10.2139/ssrn.1509304

financial integration. Economic integration normally refers to integration of national commercial and economic policies and elimination of trade barriers and of obstacles to foreign direct investment (FDI).[2] Monetary integration[3] refers to formal currency alignments and interest rate cooperation between states. On the other hand, financial sector integration refers to the elimination of restrictions to cross-border capital flows that may involve transactions concerning loans, debt and equity securities, and of barriers to cross-border market access by financial intermediaries, as well as to rights of foreign firm establishment. The market for a given set of financial instruments and/or services is fully integrated if all potential market participants with the same relevant characteristics deal with a single set of rules, when they decide to transact in financial instruments and/or provide financial services, and firms and consumers have non-discriminatory access to such financial instruments and/or services. It must also provide non-discriminatory regulatory oversight arrangements.[4] Finally, political integration is equally important. It involves the voluntary sharing/pooling of sovereignty, whether in commercial and financial affairs, trade–policy cooperation/coordination, or in relation to justice and national security.[5] Thus, lack of political integration can hinder the flow of benefits emanating from monetary and financial integration.

The design of institutions underpinning financial integration has to be a step-by-step process, as in the EU over several decades, starting with the European Coal and Steel Community and the European Economic Community (EEC) and from there to the EU and ultimately to the European Economic and Monetary Union (EMU) and the introduction of the single currency.[6] Yet problems inevitably arise when a

---

[2] For Ropke, the free and reciprocal flow of trade between the various national economies is what defines economic integration. See, Ropke, W. (1950).

[3] Monetary arrangements that supplement trade relationships have existed for centuries. See E. E. Meade, 'Monetary Integration', *Rethinking Finance: Harvard International Review*, March 21, 2009, at: http://hir.harvard.edu/rethinking-finance/monetary-integration

[4] See L. Baele, A. Ferrando, P. Hördahl, E. Krylova and C. Monnet, 'Measuring Financial Integration in the Euro Area', Occasional Paper Series No. 14, European Central Bank, April 2004, 7.

[5] On the main tenets of political integration in an intergovernmentalist rational bargaining framework, see A. Moravcsik, 'Preferences and Power in the European Community: A Liberal Intergovernmentalist Approach', *Journal of Common Market Studies*, 34 (1993), 473–524.

[6] The Maastricht Treaty established the European Union (EU) in 1993. The same treaty introduced the charter of the European Monetary Union. The EU Treaty has undergone a

supranational market exhibits a high degree of integration but the development of cross-border regulatory mechanisms lags significantly behind. This shortcoming has become acutely evident in the course of the current Eurozone crisis.

This chapter is in six sections. Following the present introduction, section II provides an analytical overview of economic and institutional developments relating to the EU single market for financial services in the pre-crisis period. Section III discusses the evolution of the EU single financial market and the causes of the Eurozone crisis. Section IV discusses the initial post-crises responses. Section V reviews the main tenets of the European banking union and considers how this new set of EU institutions will affect EU economic and political integration. Section VI concludes with discussion of potential implications of EU experiences for the future of financial integration. This chapter reflects developments as of the end of 2103, with the policy concerns addressed largely unchanged as of the end of 2014.

II.   Development of the EU single financial market

1.   Challenges of European financial integration

The European experience constitutes the most advanced global laboratory for regional economic, legal and political integration.[7] Thus, it is worth examining the process of regional financial integration, as it developed in Europe, in order to discern inherent and artificial obstacles to efficient financial governance regimes for an integrated market. The establishment of pan-European banks has, of course, been the most potent integrative factor, in an environment marked, at least in the earlier stages, by absence of regulatory cohesion. At the same time, it was inevitable that the concurrent presence of pan-European banks and of incoherent regulatory structures would lead to financial instability across the single market and especially across the single currency area, in the event of serious market turbulence.

The establishment of a single currency area (the Eurozone) and the pan-European presence of a number of large banks with large cross-border

series of amendments as its ambit and reach, both in terms of new members and powers, has expanded. The latest amendment of the EU treaty was the Treaty of Lisbon (2009).

[7] J. Wouters and T. Ramopoulos, 'The G20 and Global Economic Governance: Lessons from Multilevel European Governance?', *Journal of International Economic Law*, 15(5) (2012), 15(3): 751–75.

operations lent urgency to questions about long-term protection of EU-wide financial stability in the absence of appropriate institutional arrangements.[8] The so-called financial stability trilemma,[9] which states that the (three) objectives of financial stability, financial integration and national financial policies cannot be combined at the same time, has precisely described this acute policy trade-off which holds that one of these objectives has to give in to safeguard the other two.[10] In spite of assertions to the contrary,[11] the recent crisis has proved beyond doubt that a common currency area is not viable without building, at the same time, transnational supervisory structures in the field of fiscal monitoring and responsibility and bank supervision.

Arguably, an essential prerequisite of financial market integration is importation of a harmonized set of core rules, which border on uniformity[12] and are binding in all jurisdictions comprising the single market. Absence of such uniformity can, in theory, seriously hinder market integration as it can give rise to regulatory arbitrage and hidden protectionism and harm efficient group approaches to capital allocation and risk management within cross-border banks.[13] There is no area where divergence of national rules and regulations is more important than cross-border bank failures. Thus, protection of financial stability in an integrated financial market characterized by cross-border financial institutions becomes a very challenging task, especially when there are incongruent policy measures between national preferences and regional integration requirements. While, at the later stages of single market development the EU has moved very

---

[8] See D. Schoenmaker and S. Oosterloow, 'Financial Supervision in an Integrating Europe: Measuring Cross-Border Externalities', *International Finance*, 8 (2005), 1–27.

[9] See D. Schoenmaker, 'The Financial Trilemma', Duisenberg School of Finance, Amsterdam/Finance Department VU University Amsterdam; Tinbergen Institute Discussion Paper (February 2011); N. Thygesen, 'Comments on the Political Economy of Financial Harmonisation in Europe', in J. Kremer, D. Schoenmaker and P. Wierts (eds.), *Financial Supervision in Europe* (Cheltenham: Edward Elgar, 2003).

[10] See R. M Lastra and J.-V. Louis who (describe the same trade-off as an 'inconsistent quartet' of policy objectives: free trade, full capital mobility, pegged (or fixed) exchange rates and independent national monetary policies ('European Economic and Monetary Union: History, Trends, and Prospects', *Yearbook of European Law*, 2013).

[11] See T. Padoa-Schioppa, *The Road to Monetary Union in Europe: The Emperor, the Kings and the Genies* (Oxford University Press, 2000).

[12] Uniformity in this context only means the need to have coherence and compatible rules and regulations across jurisdictions.

[13] J. D. Larosière, 'Report of the High Level Group on Financial Supervision in the EU', Brussels: European Union (February 2009).

close to maximum harmonization in the field of financial market regulation, the overall European regulatory edifice lacked strong uniformity/consistency both in terms of rule construction and rule enforcement in this area. In addition, there has been a marked absence of institutions that could provide binding guidance, in the event of difference of opinion between national regulators, as regards the application and enforcement of financial regulation, or could resolve eventual conflicts of national regulatory actions.

2. Early stages of European financial integration

Financial integration in Europe is a phenomenon that pre-dates the twentieth century, at least for the leading European markets. There is convincing evidence, which shows that by the mid-eighteenth century European equity markets were well integrated.[14] This was, in general, a period characterized by a transition from autarky to integrated world capital markets, and, thus, it is widely seen as the era of the first globalization. The term 'financial integration' however, was not used in this sense before the mid 1950s.

When the six-state EEC was established, in 1957 (by the Treaty of Rome), furthering member states' growth was the apparent but not sole objective of the founders. Political integration was a stronger long-term objective. Namely, building a single market was seen as an essential prerequisite to political integration and not a self-standing goal. The fact that political integration in the EU is still nowhere close to what was envisaged by the founding fathers can easily explain the lack of adequate institutions supervising the single financial market and securing financial stability. For example, one of the EU fundamental freedoms, the free movement of capital, became effective only after the signing of the Maastricht Treaty in 1992, a full thirty-five years after the Treaty of Rome, as it was essential in building a European monetary union and national restrictions in the free flow of capital could no longer be retained.

---

[14] L. Neal, 'Integration of International Capital Markets: Quantitative Evidence from the Eighteenth to Twentieth Centuries', *Journal of Economic History*, 45(1985), 219–26; *The Rise of Financial Capitalism: International Capital Markets in the Age of Reason* (New York: Cambridge University Press, 1990); 'The Disintegration and Re-integration of International Capital Markets in the 19th Century', *Business and Economic History*, 2 (1992), 84–96.

3.   The role of the EU treaties: an ever closer union?

The European economic integration process and the establishment of the euro as the common currency of (as of today) seventeen EU member states has been incremental with periods of strong progress and of painfully slow growth. In general, it has been the product of political expediencies as much as of economic efficiency rationales and it has witnessed major crises and setbacks.[15]

Western European economies have shown in the post-war era a marked preference for exchange rate stability. When the first set of European arrangements aiming at exchange rate stability failed, following the collapse of the requisite Bretton Woods arrangements, and the post-war world entered the era of floating exchange rates, EEC members created the European Monetary System (EMS) in 1979,[16] in order to manage and control currency fluctuations among EMS members. EMS was viewed as the first step towards permanent exchange rate alignment and paved the way for the establishment of EMU. Eventually, EMU member states irrevocably pegged the exchange rates of member country currencies, which were replaced by the single European currency.

At this point it should be noted that the establishment of the single currency was itself a matter of politics as much as of economic necessity. Of course, through a currency union, EU members could answer the classic monetary trilemma, which is built on the Mundell–Fleming model of an open economy under capital mobility.[17] The monetary trilemma famously states that a fixed exchange rate, capital mobility and national

---

[15] See P. Pierson, 'The Path to European Integration: A Historical Institutionalist Analysis', *Comparative Political Studies*, 29 (1996), 123–63; J. Story and I. Walter, *Political Economy of Financial Integration in Europe: The Battle of the Systems* (Manchester University Press, 1997).

[16] See Resolution of the European Council of 5 December 1978 on the establishment of the European Monetary System (EMS) and related matters (1978) Bulletin of the European Communities. December, No. 12, 9–13. Regulations Nos. 380 and 381/78, 18 December 1978, OJEC, No. L379, 30 December 1978 (and their modifications); Agreement of 13 March 1979 between the central banks of the Member States of the European Economic Community laid down the operating procedures for the European Monetary System. Available at http://ec.europa.eu/economy_finance/emu_history/documentation/compendia/a791231en1771979compendiumcm_a.pdf. See for analysis, F. Giavazzi and A. Giovannini (1989).

[17] See R. A. Mundell, 'Capital Mobility and Stabilization Policy under Fixed and Flexible Exchange Rates', *Canadian Journal of Economics*, 29 (1963), 475–85 available at http://jrxy.zjgsu.edu.cn/jrxy/jssc/2904.pdf

monetary policy cannot be achieved at the same time; one policy objective has to give. Therefore, under capital mobility and national monetary
policy, fixed exchange rates will invariably break down.[18] However, as the
EU has been very far from being an optimal currency area under the
Mundell model,[19] and there was no fiscal integration or debt mutualization it was only a matter of time before the first strains would appear. It
is, thus, arguable that the founders of the EMU just hoped that a single
currency would pave the way for a fiscal and political union, something
that has not yet happened. Moreover the desire for a political union
might not have been the whole story.

From a political economy viewpoint European financial and monetary
integration was not just an intergovernmental goal, or merely dictated by
the conditions of increasing market integration and capital mobility in
the EU. The interests of professional intermediaries may have also been a
strong force behind the push for further integration. In fact, the early
Eurobond market might have played the role of an imperfect substitute
to financial integration, given that capital mobility was only a secondary
EU goal until the 1990s.[20] Conversely, the 1966 Segré report was both
very cognizant of the growth potential attached to financial integration
and of the potential for this objective to be confounded by commercial
interests.[21]

(i)   EMU membership criteria and realities

The path to monetary integration that was adopted by the Maastricht
Treaty was based on a three-stage process and the fulfilment of convergence criteria. Only countries, which met the appropriate criteria, could
gain Eurozone membership. The transitional framework under the treaty
provided some flexibility in terms of the time required for the weaker
candidate economies to converge with the strongest, especially as regards

---

[18] See M. Obstfeld, J. C. Shambaugh and A. M. Taylor, 'The Trilemma in History: Tradeoffs
among Exchange Rates, Monetary Policies, and Capital Mobility', *Review of Economics
and Statistics*, 87(2005), 423–38.

[19] R. A. Mundell, 'A Theory of Optimum Currency Areas', *American Economic Review* 51
(1961), 657–65.

[20] R. Genillard, 'The Eurobond Market', *Financial Analysts Journal*, 23 (1967), 144;
K. Richebacher, 'The Problems and Prospects of Integrating European Capital Markets',
Journal of Money, Credit & Banking, 1 (1969), 337.

[21] See C. Segré *et al.*, *The Development of a European Capital Market: Report of a Group of
Experts appointed by the EEC Commission* (Brussels: European Economic Community,
1966).

their macroeconomic outlooks and policies. However, such convergence proved in many cases no more than drawing-board plans.

The Maastricht Treaty's convergence criteria included two basic conditions for euro membership: first, a 3 per cent limit on general government annual deficit and a 60 per cent limit on general government gross debt limit.[22] It also included three other important criteria, which were inflation, long-term interest rates and exchange rate fluctuations. Inflation was to be kept within 1.5 per cent margin over that of any of the three EU countries having the lowest inflation rate. Long-term interest rates were to stay within a 2 per cent margin over that of the three states with the lowest borrowing rates in the EU. As regards exchange-rate fluctuations, there was a requirement of participation for two years in the Exchange Rate Mechanism II (ERM II), which provided for a narrow band of exchange-rate fluctuations.

Reality was, however, in glaring contrast with the spirit of the Treaty, due to political pressures and the actual condition of the European economies, which even in the 1990s were mildly to grossly indebted states with considerable budget deficits. The Treaty itself had exceptions to provide political leverage in extending membership to certain countries while restricting it to others.[23] In practice, these differences meant a much lesser degree of economic integration than had been envisaged in the Werner (1970)[24] and Delors reports (1989).[25] Moreover, the difference in the macroeconomic 'initial conditions' of the founding member states made it politically difficult to enforce the strict fiscal criteria laid down for EMU membership.

---

[22] Art. 104c of the Maastricht Treaty on European Union and the Treaties Establishing the European Communities Protocols (7 February 1992), at: www.eurotreaties.com/maastrichtprotocols.pdf

[23] Art. 104c of the Maastricht Treaty stated that countries could exceed the 3 per cent deficit target if 'the ratio has declined substantially and continuously and reached a level that comes close to the reference value' or 'excess over the reference value is only exceptional and temporary and the ratio remains close to the reference value'. Euro area countries could similarly exceed the 60 per cent gross debt target provided that 'the ratio is sufficiently diminishing and approaching the reference value at a satisfactory pace' (*ibid.*)

[24] Werner Committee, 'Report to the Council and the Commission on the Realisation by Stages of Economic and Monetary Union', Luxembourg, 8 October 1970, at http://ec.europa.eu/economy_finance/emu_history/documentation/chapter5/19701008en72realisationbystage.pdf

[25] Jacques Delors Committee for the Study of Economic and Monetary Union 'Report on Economic and Monetary Union in the European Community', presented to the Council on 17 April 1989, at: http://aei.pitt.edu/1007/1/monetary_delors.pdf

4. EU Harmonization legislation 1985–2009: market impact, gaps and loopholes

Consistency of the legal and regulatory framework has always been regarded as an essential prerequisite of EU financial integration. The first step towards this direction was to develop a harmonized set of minimum regulatory standards based on consensus.[26] This seemed more aligned with the overall objective of achieving a single market without having to endure excessive concessions on idiosyncratic national policy designs and preferences, which might make the harmonization process politically untenable.

(i) Harmonization principles

The Delors Commission's 1985 White Paper[27] preceded the enactment of the first amendment to the Treaty of Rome in thirty years, the so-called Single European Act.[28] The White Paper outlined the reforms required in the pre-existing EEC legal framework in order to build a truly single market in the EEC (as it then was) and pave the way for monetary integration.[29] The White Paper noted at the same time that: 'the legislation adopted by the Council and the European Parliament is either too detailed, or insufficiently adapted to local conditions and experience; often in stark contrast to the original proposals'.[30] However, maximum harmonization proved impossible for many areas of activity in the single market and the European Commission adopted instead the principles of mutual recognition, minimum harmonization and home country control. These three principles were subsequently enshrined in harmonization legislation in a number of areas, including financial services. The internal market was to be based on minimum harmonization of national regulatory systems and mutual recognition[31] through which member states would recognize each other's laws, regulations and

---

[26] This has been defined as the first EU financial services consensus. See E. Avgouleas, 'The New EC Financial Markets Legislation and the Emerging Regime for Capital Markets', *Yearbook of European Law*, 23 (2004), 321–61.

[27] European Commission, *Completing the Internal Market: White Paper from the European Commission to the European Council* (1985) Com.(85), 310 final.

[28] Single European Act [1987] OJ L 169/1.

[29] The Delors report provided for the establishment of a new monetary institution that would be called a European System of Central Banks (ESCB) responsible for carrying out monetary policy and the Community's exchange rate policy vis-à-vis third currencies.

[30] *Ibid.*   [31] *Ibid.*

authorities.[32] The use of minimum regional requirements was intended to limit competitive deregulation by state actors and regulatory arbitrage by commercial parties.[33] It was also a reflection of how political collaboration can encourage adoption of sound market principles and practices.[34]

The EU framework for financial services provided minimum standards for the establishment and operation of banks and other financial inter-mediaries, conduct of public offers on a national and pan-European basis, and extended to accounting, company law and regulation of insti-tutional investors, in the form of collective investments schemes. It also provided access to the single market unfettered by national borders or restrictions on activity, the so-called single passport facility.[35] Essentially, the purpose of the passport facility was to allow intermediaries to deliver products or services into any part of the internal market and promote cross-border competition.[36] As a result, the 'passport directives' in finan-cial services defined the kind of financial intermediary to which they applied, its activities and the market segment, the conditions for initial and continuing authorizations, the division of regulatory responsibility between the home (domicile) state and the host state, and aspects of the regulatory treatment of non-EU member states.[37]

The Maastricht Treaty, which established the EU as a successor to the EEC, provided an impetus for states to implement prior financial services directives. One important influence in the success of the harmonization mechanisms adopted at this stage of EU integration process was the role played by the rulings of the European Court of Justice (ECJ). Being part of the EU obligated its member states to adopt and implement EU legislation, as national governments could be held liable in damages for failing to comply with EU-level decisions.[38]

---

[32] B. Steil, *The European Equity Markets: The State of the Union and an Agenda for the Millennium* (Washington, DC: Brookings Institution Press, 1996).

[33] D. W Arner and M. W. Taylor, 'The Global Credit Crisis and the Financial Stability Board: Hardening the Soft Law of International Financial Regulation?', *University of New South Wales Law Journal*, 32 (2010), 488–513.

[34] D. W. Arner, P. Lejot and W. Wang, 'Assessing East Asian Financial Cooperation and Integration', *Singapore Yearbook of International Law*, 12 (2009), 1–42.

[35] See R. Cranston (ed.), *The Single Market and the Law of Banking* (2nd edn, London: Lloyds of London Press, 1995); G. Ferrarini, *European Securities Markets: The Investment Services Directive and Beyond* (The Hague: Kluwer Law, 1998).

[36] *Ibid.*   [37] *Ibid.*

[38] Judgment of the Court of 19 November 1991, *Andrea Francovich and Danila Bonifaci and others* v. *Italian Republic*, References for a preliminary ruling: Pretura di Vicenza and

B.   The gradual shift to maximum harmonization

The 'passport directives' have clearly enhanced financial integration in the EU, although areas of marked divergence, such as retail financial services, remained.[39] But, minimum harmonization left the EU with an incomplete regulatory framework, since, in many cases, it merely augmented rather than replaced pre-existing national laws.[40] Thus, the drive towards harmonization intensified in the early 2000s, following the introduction of the euro and the publication of the Commission's Financial Services Action Plan (FSAP) in 1999.[41] Arguably, the most important integrative instrument of that era (which can be viewed as the second EU financial services consensus)[42] was the Directive on Markets in Financial Instruments (MiFID),[43] which established a detailed pan-European regime with respect to conditions of establishment and operation of financial markets and investment intermediaries and the conduct of cross-border financial activities.

To answer a number of challenges pertaining mostly to enactment and consistent implementation of financial services legislation, the EU adopted the so-called Lamfalussy process in 2001. It consisted of four levels that started with the adoption of the framework legislation (Level 1) and more detailed implementing measures (Level 2). For the technical

---

Pretura di Bassano del Grappa, Italy, failure to implement a directive, liability of the member state, Joined cases C-6/90 and C-9/90 (European Court reports 1991 Page I-05357), at http://eur-lex.europa.eu/LexUriServ/LexUriServ.do?uri=CELEX:61990J0006: EN:HTML

[39] E. Grossman and P. Leblond, 'European Financial Integration: Finally the Great Leap Forward?', *Journal of Common Market Studies*, 49 (2011), 413–35.

[40] See for a discussion of this issue and the gaps left behind by minimum harmonization, E. Avgouleas, 'The Harmonisation of Rules of Conduct in EU Financial Markets: Economic Analysis, Subsidiarity and Investor Protection'. *European Law Journal*, 6 (2000), 72–92.

[41] Commission Communication, Financial Services: Implementing the Framework for Financial Markets: Action Plan, Com.(1999), 232. On the important changes FSAP implemented in the field of EU regulation of financial services and its impact on the single market, see E. Ferran, *Building an EU Securities Market* (Cambridge University Press, 2005).

[42] On this and for a critical discussion of FSAP legislation, see E. Avgouleas, 'Evaluation of the New EC Financial Market Regulation: Peaks and Troughs in the Road Ahead', *Transnational Lawyer*, 18 (2005), 179–228.

[43] EC, Directive 2004/39/EC 2004 of the European Parliament and of the Council of 21 April 2004 on markets in financial instruments amending Council Directives 85/611/EEC and 93/6/EEC and Directive 2000/12/EC of the European Parliament and of the Council and repealing Council Directive 93/22/EEC, [2007] OJ L 145/1. For a discussion of the contours of MiFID, see E. Avgouleas (ed.), *The Regulation of Investment Services in Europe under MiFiD: Implementation and Practice* (West Sussex: Tottel, 2008).

preparation of the implementing measures, the Commission was to be advised by the committees made up of representatives of national supervisory bodies from three sectors: banking, insurance and occupational pensions, and the securities markets. These committees were CEBS,[44] CEIOPS[45] and CESR.[46] The Level 3 committees would then contribute to the consistent implementation of Community directives in the member states, ensuring effective cooperation between the supervisory authorities and convergence of their practices (Level 3) and finally, the Commission was to enforce timely and correct transposition of EU legislation into national laws (Level 4).[47] These arrangements underwent a major overhaul in the aftermath of the GFC.[48]

III.   The global financial crisis and the Eurozone debt crisis

As mentioned earlier, it was not until the 2008 crisis and in earnest after the outbreak of the Eurozone debt crisis in 2010 that the vexed issue of preservation of financial stability in an integrated market came to the

---

[44] Decision 2004/5/EC (the Commission's decision dated November 2003 is available at http://europa.eu/legislation_summaries/internal_market/single_market_services/financial_services_banking/l22025_en.htm). On 1 January 2011, this committee was replaced by the European Banking Authority (EBA), which took over all existing and ongoing tasks and responsibilities of the Committee of European Banking Supervisors (CEBS).

[45] CEIOPS (2003–10) was established under the European Commission's Decision 2004/6/EC of 5 November 2003. In January 2011 CEIOPS was replaced by EIOPA under the Decision 2009/79/EC in accordance with the new European financial supervision framework.

[46] The Committee of European Securities Regulators (CESR) was an independent committee of European securities regulators established by the European Commission on 6 June 2001. On 1 January 2011, CESR was replaced by the European Securities and Markets Authority (ESMA) in accordance with the new European financial supervision framework. See more at www.esma.europa.eu/index.php?page=cesrinshort&mac=0&id=

[47] See A. Lamfalussy, *Final Report of the Committee of Wise Men on the Regulation of European Securities Markets Brussels*, 15 February 2001, at http://ec.europa.eu/internal_market/securities/docs/lamfalussy/wisemen/final-report-wise-men_en.pdf. For a review on the process recommendations, see E. Ferran, 'Understanding the New Institutional Architecture of EU Financial Market Supervision', in G. Ferrarini, K. J. Hopt and E. Wymeersch (eds.), *Rethinking Financial Regulation and Supervision in Times of Crisis* (Oxford: Oxford University Press, 2012), ch. 5, where Ferran examines the recent EU institutional reforms on financial market supervision to assess their significance; A. Schaub, 'The Lamfalussy Process Four Years On', *Journal of Financial Regulation and Compliance*, 13 (2004), 110–20.

[48] See 'Report of the High Level Group on Financial Supervision in the EU', February 2009 (the de Larosière report), at http://ec.europa.eu/internal_market/finances/docs/de_larosiere_report_en.pdf

forefront of EU policy-makers' attention. Both crises have emphasized the need to revisit existing models of financial market integration with a view to enriching them with institutions and structures that underpin financial stability as well as economic growth. It should be noted here that the Maastricht Treaty (1992) did not include 'financial stability' as a key objective of the ECB, although, Article 127(5) of TFEU underscores 'financial stability' as a classic central banking good. Thus, financial stability has not been designed as one of the four basic tasks to be carried through the ESCB (Article 127(2) of TFEU) and has rather been clustered with prudential supervision under the 'non-binding tasks' of the ECB.

1. Background

The EU legislative framework based on harmonized standards for financial markets sought equivalence among disparate regulatory and legal systems, so that regional initiatives could recognize national legal and regulatory regimes.[49] But a multilevel governance system involves far more complexities than a regime based on minimum harmonization can foresee. These mainly arise out of the conflicting and sometimes misunderstood national priorities and transnational requirements.

Political considerations also undermined the credibility of rule-based frameworks for coordination of national fiscal policies in the euro area.[50] For example, the Stability and Growth Pact (SGP) was originally designed to safeguard sound public finances and to thwart individual Eurozone members from adopting fiscal policies leading to unsustainable debt levels by enforcing budgetary discipline. Arguably, the Maastricht Treaty itself allowed sufficient flexibility to the interpretation of SGP and its enforcement as to allow it to become part of the political bargaining process in the EU at the expense of objective economic criteria.[51] As a result, during the period that the debt crisis was building up, the Eurozone was deeply marked by economic and financial imbalances and the

---

[49] See B. Steil, *The European Equity Markets: The State of the Union and an Agenda for the Millennium* (Washington, DC: Brookings Institution Press, 1996), 113.

[50] See C. F. Bergsten and J. F. Kirkegaard, 'The Coming Resolution of the European Crisis', electronic resource, Peterson Institute for International Economics, Washington, DC (2012), at: www.ciaonet.org/pbei/iie/0024277/f_0024277_19801.pdf

[51] European Council Presidency Conclusions, Council of the European Union. (22–23 March 2005), Brussels, at: www.consilium.europa.eu/uedocs/cms_data/docs/pressdata/en/ec/84335.pdf

Union itself lacked a central fiscal authority, which would have afforded it a credible mechanism to enforce budget discipline. In addition, trade imbalances due to accelerating competitiveness imbalances and lack of exchange rate flexibility meant that there were no realistic prospects for fiscal convergence.[52] Yet, preserving, in the long term, any currency union, including EMU, requires a sufficient level of economic convergence, together with a properly functioning internal market, and an effective system for economic and budgetary policy surveillance and coordination.

Accordingly, when the Eurozone debt crisis erupted with force, European financial stability was hampered by a number of pre-existing problems which had simply been ignored for far too long. These included colossal pre-crisis public and private debt piles, a flawed macroeconomic framework and absence of institutions capable of handling effectively a cross-border banking crisis. The incomplete institutional design was the true mark of an 'imbalanced' and disjointed monetary union, also characterized by the absence of effective fiscal convergence mechanisms. In part, the reason for these imbalances was the fact that during the first decade of its life, EMU was premised on a weak institutional framework that was more suitable to a 'fair weather currency',[53] rather than a monetary union with asymmetrical member economies, which were about to experience massive macroeconomic shocks. It is clear that EMU founders assumed that any macroeconomic or banking system stability shocks could be dealt with at the national level without requiring any transfers from the strongest to the weakest members of the Eurozone, due to the no bailout clause in the EMU Treaty.[54]

While the 2008 crisis intensified reform efforts to a great extent, the true big bang for the mooted pan-European supervisory and bank resolution structures has been the ensuing Eurozone debt crisis, which has shaken to its foundations the banking system of the Eurozone. The EU had to devise mechanisms, in the midst of crisis, first, to prevent an immediate meltdown of its banking sector and ensuing chain of sovereign bankruptcies and, second, to reform its flawed institutions, in order to prevent the Eurozone architecture from collapsing. Namely, Eurozone

---

[52] See P. de Grawe, *Economics of Monetary Union* (9th edn, Oxford: Oxford University Press, 2012), pt 2.
[53] Bergsten and Kirkegaard, *Coming Resolution of the European Crisis.*
[54] See art. 101 TEU (now enshrined in art. 125 Treaty on the Functioning of the European Union).

members had to build both a crisis-fighting capacity and support bailout funding mechanisms. This led to the establishment of the European Financial Stability Facility (EFSF), which was superseded by the European Stability Mechanism (ESM), discussed in section V. At the same time, serious steps have been taken to build a European banking union based on structures safeguarding centralization of bank supervision and uniform deposit insurance arrangements, as well as centralization of crisis resolution.

2. Problems of integration – cross-border banking

The premise of home country control and the principle of minimum harmonization were bound to undermine at some point the stability of the EU banking system. The integration process continued in an increasingly deregulated market following the intensification of liberalization efforts in the last quarter of the twentieth century, but the regulatory standards and supervisory principles were not adjusted to new realities. The Eurozone crisis has brought home with devastating force the potential risks of financial market integration, which inevitably leads financial institutions operating in the single market to develop very tight links of interconnectedness, allowing thus shocks appearing in one part of the market to be widely and quickly transmitted across all other parts. Examples of such rapid transmission of shocks include the failure of Icelandic banks, the botched rescue of Fortis bank, the threat of collapse of the financial systems of Ireland and Spain, and the possibility of a sovereign default (e.g., Greece), or of a chain of sovereign defaults. Each of those crises brought serious tremors to European markets and exposed their fragility and the dearth of policy options available to Eurozone decision-makers. Naturally, the rapid amplification of those crises and their grave consequences has raised serious questions regarding the survival of the Eurozone.

In the USA the response to the crisis was rapid and came in the form of state purchase of distressed bank assets (the so-called Troubled Asset Relief Programme (TARP)), innovative intervention schemes by the Federal Reserve and (complex) re-regulation of the financial sector. In the EU, however, the diversity of member state economies and issues arising out of inherent contradictions between national policy priorities meant a much lower degree of responsiveness to the crisis. This became evident as soon as some of the EMU states, which experienced a more severe crisis than other members, had to adopt policies based on their own national needs and interests – which may not necessarily have been in conformity with single market policies. For example, lack of common deposit insurance in a well-integrated banking market at a time of cross-border crisis led to several conflicting policy choices and responses in an effort by the states to protect their own citizens.

(i)   The Icelandic banking crisis

The collapse of the Icelandic banks – Glitnir, Kaupthing and Land-sbanki[55] – which operated branches in EU member states on the basis of the single passport presents a classic case of home country control failure and of the disastrous consequences of lack of centralized supervision and resolution mechanisms in the EU. The single passport, which was also used by firms from European Economic Area countries such as Iceland, a non-EU member, gave Icelandic banks the ability to expand their asset and deposit base in the EU through branches and through internet-based operations offering cross-border banking services. As European depositors were lured by the high interest rates offered by Icelandic banks, gradually Icelandic banks built a large depositor base in certain European countries.

However, by 2008 both the country's economy and even more its banks were in serious trouble. While trouble was brewing over several months Icelandic bank operations within the EU were supervised by the home country authorities, which were unwilling to take any radical restructuring or rescue measures, thus, nothing was done to prevent the ensuing panic. So when Icelandic banks faced difficulties in refinancing their short-term debt, a run on the Icelandic banks' deposits in the Netherlands and the UK became inevitable, as domestic depositors were not covered by the deposit protection scheme of their home countries. While both the Netherlands and the UK, were, in the beginning unwilling to extend protection to Icelandic bank depositors, at the same time, Iceland could provide no comfort to foreign depositors, because it was already in the middle of a deep financial crisis, and its government did not want to pay for the mistakes made by private banks, assisted by politicians and 'home' supervisory authorities. Harsh responses followed from both UK and Netherlands authorities,[56] which, though entirely

---

[55] The collapse followed from difficulties in refinancing their short-term debt and a run on deposits in the Netherlands and the UK.

[56] The UK used provisions in sections 4 and 14 and Schedule 3 of the Anti-terrorism, Crime and Security Act 2001 to issues a freezing order over Landsbanki assets. Under the order

necessary, annulled the single passport principle. In order to prevent the crisis spreading to the UK banking system the UK Prime Minister, Gordon Brown extended protection to UK depositors, which essentially meant that the UK deposit protection scheme would cover the loss. Thus, the UK Treasury proceeded with the unprecedented step of issuing a compulsory freezing order on Icelandic bank assets and deposits under the Anti-terrorism, Crime and Security Act 2001, which, of course, antagonized relationships with Iceland. In addition, the UK government announced that it would launch legal action against Iceland over any losses connected to the compensation of an estimated 300,000 UK savers.[57] Icelandic authorities later reached an agreement separately with both the UK and Netherlands governments. Thus, Iceland will be paying the UK and Netherlands a percentage of GDP from 2019 to 2023 to compensate for the deposit protection made available by these two countries to their own consumers holding deposits in Icelandic banks.

The collapse of Icelandic banks led to economic crisis and the mishandling of the crisis brought down the political machinery of the government. The Icelandic banking crisis and the more recent Cyprus banking crisis hold serious lessons as they underscore the risks arising from the 'nurturing' of over-grown financial sectors which much outstrip a country's GDP, although this places smaller country industries into a disadvantageous competitive position.[58]

(ii)   The botched rescue of Fortis Bank

When the collapse of Lehman Brothers hit global markets, Fortis – a big European bank with strong cross-border presence in France, the Netherlands, Belgium and Luxembourg – came very close to collapse.[59] In Belgium, Fortis was the country's biggest private sector employer and

the UK Treasury froze the assets of Landsbanki within the UK, to prevent the sale or movement of Landsbanki assets within the UK, even if held by the Central Bank of Iceland or the government of Iceland, at: http://en.wikipedia.org/wiki/2008%E2%80% 932012_Icelandic_financial_crisis – cite_note-55; 2001 Act, at: www.legislation.gov.uk/ ukpga/2001/24/contents
[57] C. Marshall and I. Martin, 'UK government launching legal action against Iceland' (8 October 2008), at: www.citywire.co.uk/money/update-uk-govt-launching-legal-action-against-iceland/a316803 (retrieved 24 November 2011).
[58] Another lesson that the Icelandic banks crisis might hold is that *default* in the face of mounting and unreasonable debt might not be such a bad thing.
[59] Basel Committee on Banking Supervision (BCBS), 'Report and Recommendations of the Cross-border Bank Resolution Group', Basel, September 2009, 10.

more than 1.5 million households – about half the country – banked with the group. In 2007, Fortis had acquired parts of ABN AMRO through a consortium with Royal Bank of Scotland and Santander. In 2008, Fortis had difficulties realizing its plans to strengthen its financial position. Over the summer of 2008, its share price deteriorated and liquidity became a serious concern. Insolvency fears saw Fortis's shares fall to their lowest level in more than a decade and its shares gradually lost more than three-quarters of their value.

Fortis was deemed to be systemically relevant in the three countries. Thus, the ECB and ministers from the Netherlands, Belgium and Luxembourg agreed to put €11.2bn. ($16.1bn.; £8.9bn.) into Fortis to save the bank. As part of the weekend deal to rescue Fortis, the bank would have to sell its stake in the Dutch bank ABN AMRO, which it had partially taken over the previous year. The Fortis deal would have seen Belgium contribute €4.7bn., the Netherlands €4bn. and Luxembourg €2.5bn. However, European bank shares fell sharply, from worrying that other banks could have problems, and from concerns over the $700bn. bailout plan in the United States (TARP). One of the biggest casualties was Fortis's rival Dexia, which French and Belgian governments also promised to step in to support. Eventually the joint rescue of Fortis broke down along national lines and each of the three countries (Belgium, the Netherlands, Luxembourg) concentrated only on the part of the group that was most important for their market,[60] in defiance of single market principles/ideals.

---

[60] The Dutch government purchased Fortis Bank Netherlands, Fortis Insurance Netherlands, Fortis Corporate Insurance and the Fortis share in ABN AMRO. 'The Belgian government raised its holding in Fortis Bank Belgium to 99 per cent. The Belgian government also agreed to sell a 75 per cent interest to BNP Paribas (BNP) in return for new BNP shares, keeping a blocking minority of 25 per cent of the capital of Fortis Bank Belgium. BNP also bought the Belgian insurance activities of Fortis and took a majority stake in Fortis Bank Luxembourg. A portfolio of structured products was transferred to a financial structure owned by the Belgian State, BNP and Fortis Group' (BCBS, Report and Recommendations, 10 (12 December 2008)). The Court of Appeal of Brussels suspended the sale to BNP, which was not yet finalized, and decided that the finalized sales to the Dutch state and the Belgian state as well as the subsequent sale to BNP had to be submitted for approval by the shareholders of Fortis Holding in order for these three sales to be valid under Belgian law. After initial rejection by the shareholders, certain transactions were renegotiated and financing of the portfolio of structured products was modified. The renegotiated transaction with the Belgian state and BNP was approved at the second general meeting of shareholders and the latter transaction was finalized on 12 May 2009 (ibid.).

3.   The Eurozone debt crisis

The Eurozone crisis should be seen as a sequence of four interlocking crises resulting from imbalanced monetary integration. This resulted in a competitiveness crisis that transformed into a marked loss of fiscal revenues and widening fiscal deficits which led to debt accumulations (particularly in Greece, Italy, Portugal, and Spain) that were financed by the surpluses of the northern countries, leading, in turn, to massive payment imbalances within the Eurozone (in particular, Germany, the Netherlands and Finland vis-à-vis the European South). As these surpluses had to be reinvested, they found their way to investments in the bonds of deficit countries (Greece, Italy) or to the banking systems of the Eurozone periphery (Ireland, Spain) and financed gigantic real estate bubbles in Ireland and Spain. Thus, they led to accumulation of unsustainable levels of public or private debt or both.[61] The fact that many EU banks had invested in EU members' bonds and are also adversely affected by the continuous recession ravaging the periphery of the Eurozone only made things worse.

The Eurozone crisis has signalled a fundamental shift in the political dynamics underpinning the EU. While the exact remedies of the crisis, austerity, more integration, mutualization of Eurozone members' debt and other measures remain topics of heated discussion, one remedy is viewed as uncontroversial: breaking up the link between bank debt and sovereign indebtedness. This will in turn break the vicious circle of ever more bank bailouts and ever higher levels of national debt. Yet implementation of such a mechanism, which would inevitably work as a form of mutualization of Eurozone bank debt, required centralized bank supervision and resolution mechanisms that the EU did not possess. Since its establishment the EMU lacked these crucial supporting institutions that could have helped it to restore financial stability during times of acute uncertainty and market volatility.[62]

In order to break the vicious circle between bank bailouts and levels of sovereign indebtedness, the Eurozone members have established a

---

[61] E. Avgouleas, 'Eurozone crisis and sovereign debt restructuring: intellectual fallacies and new lines of research'. Paper presented at the Society of International Economic Law (SIEL), 3rd Biennial Global Conference, Centre for International Law (CIL) and Faculty of Law, at National University of Singapore (July 2012).

[62] C. F. Bergsten and J. F. Kirkegaard, 'The coming resolution of the European crisis', electronic resource, Peterson Institute for International Economics, Washington, DC (2012), at: www.ciaonet.org/pbei/iie/0024277/f_0024277_19801.pdf

funding facility, the European Stability Mechanism (ESM), which, subject to a strict conditionality, will be employed to directly recapitalize Eurozone banks.[63] The use of ESM funds for such recapitalizations would put a stop to further increases of the indebtedness of the sovereign concerned due to bank bailouts. The inevitable transfer of payments from the richer to the weaker Eurozone members through ESM, which enjoys the guarantee of all Eurozone members, and the need to tighten the framework for bank regulation, supervision and resolution have meant that the countries in the core of the Eurozone have promoted the centralization of bank supervision and resolution functions in EMU. These demands have given birth to a new set of bank authorization, supervision and resolution arrangements: the European banking union. However, the European banking union, plausible and necessary as it may be, has also reinforced rather than calmed the centrifugal forces within the EU and has the potential to lead to a serious split of the internal market.[64] Important members of the EU, chiefly the UK, have resolutely remained outside important European banking union arrangements. It is, thus, reasonable to infer that political expediency, and not economic necessities, will in the end seal the fate of the single currency.

IV.   EU financial regulation infrastructure in the post-2009 period

1.   Phase I: from the Lamfalussy process to the ESFS

In November 2008 the Commission appointed a High Level Group (chaired by Jacques de Larosière) to study the Lamfalussy framework in light of the GFC and the threats to cross-border banking and the internal market that the GFC uncovered, and to make recommendations for a new EU regulatory set-up.[65] The proposals advanced by the de Larosière report were instrumental to subsequent developments. In order to implement the recommendations of the de Larosière committee the EU established (through a series of regulations, normally referred to as the ESAs founding regulations) an integrated European System of Financial

---

[63] The ESM is discussed in section V. For a detailed description of ESM's functions, see www.esm.europa.eu/about/index.htm

[64] R. Lastra, 'Banking Union and Single Market: Conflict or Companionship?', *Fordham International Law Journal*, 36 (2013), 1190.

[65] J. D. Larosière, *Report of the High Level Group on Financial Supervision in the EU.* Brussels: European Union (February 2009).

Supervision (ESFS), which came into effect in December 2010.[66] It consists of the European Systemic Risk Board[67] and a decentralized network made up of existing national supervisors (who will continue to carry out day-to-day supervision) and three new European Supervisory Authorities (ESAs): the European Banking Authority (EBA),[68] the European Insurance and Occupational Pension Authority (EIOPA), and the European Securities Markets Authority (ESMA), which respectively replaced the corresponding Lamfalussy Level 3 Committees (CEBS, CEIOPS, CESR). Furthermore, colleges of supervisors[69] are to be put in place for all major cross-border institutions because supervision of strategic decisions at the consolidated level requires a college of supervisors to understand the global effects and externalities of those decisions.[70] Last but not least, a Joint Committee[71] was formed by the ESAs to coordinate their actions on cross-sectoral rule-making and supervisory matters which naturally extend to supervision of financial conglomerates.

---

[66] Art. 2 ESA Founding Regulations, see Regulation (EU) No. 1095/2010 of the European Parliament and of the Council of 24 November 2010 establishing a European Supervisory Authority (European Securities and Markets Authority), amending Decision No. 716/2009/EC and repealing Commission Decision 2009/77/EC (2010), 84–119: OJ, at www.esma.europa.eu/system/filesReg_716_2010_ESMA.pdf

[67] ESRB was established under EU Regulation No. 1092/2010 of the European Parliament and of the Council of 24/11/2010 on European Union macro-prudential oversight of the financial system and establishing a European Systemic Risk Board (the 'ESRB Regulation'), at: www.esrb.europa.eu/shared/pdf/ESRB-en.pdf?efba86ec695eea33d6b673acc62578d9

[68] The European Banking Authority was established by Regulation (EC) No. 1093/2010 of the European Parliament and of the Council of 24 November 2010, at: www.esrb.europa.eu/shared/pdf/EBA-en.pdf?79016e649558f0a9a741da6c169b806b

[69] The colleges are a mechanism for the exchange of information between home and host authorities, for the planning and performance of key supervisory tasks in a coordinated manner or jointly, including all aspects of ongoing supervision, and also for the preparation for and the handling of emergency situations. These are permanent, although flexible, structures for cooperation and coordination among the EU authorities responsible for and involved in the supervision of the different components of cross-border groups, specifically large groups. See further at: www.eba.europa.eu/Supervisory-Colleges/Introduction.aspx; Colleges of Supervisors – 10 Common Principles. (27 January 2009) (Vol. CEIOPS-SEC-54/08, CEBS 2008 124, IWCFC 08 32), at: http://eba.europa.eu/getdoc/aeecaf1a-81b5-476a-95dd-599c5e967697/Clean-V3-formatted-CEBS-2008-124-CEIOPS-SEC-08-54-.aspx

[70] In a sense this followed similar propositions on how regulation of cross-border banking in the EU had to be structured. See C. Lamanda, 'Cross-Border Banking in Europe: What Regulation and Supervision? Unicredit Group Forum on Financial Cross-border Groups', Discussion Paper No. 01 (March 2009), at: www.unicreditgroup.eu/content/dam/unicreditgroup/documents/inc/press-and-media/cross_border_banking_discussion_paper.pdf

[71] Art. 54 ESA Founding Regulations.

Apart from issuing guidance and recommendations to national supervisors,[72] ESAs also seek to formulate a single EU rulebook and harmonize technical standards on the basis of powers conferred by the EU Commission,[73] which will be subsequently adopted by the European Commission to become formal/binding EU law.[74] To safeguard consistent application of harmonized legislation, if the ESAs find a national supervisory authority failing to apply EU law, they have the power to investigate infractions.[75] The ESAs will conduct regular peer reviews of national supervisory authorities across the EU.[76] They will be able to collect information from national supervisors to allow them to fulfil their role.[77] This information will be used for analysing market developments, coordinating EU-wide stress tests and macro-prudential analysis undertaken by the ESRB.[78] Therefore, ESAs work with the ESRB to ensure financial stability. They also have a remit to consider consumer protection issues.[79]

The ESFS did not remedy the 'mismatch' between the geographic scope of European bank activities and the regulatory remit of the authorities supervising them. On the contrary, the ESFS might be accused of just providing yet another layer of complexity in the EU structures.[80] Therefore, even after the implementation of the de Larosière reforms, cross-border supervision and bank resolution at the EU level remained decentralized and in want of further clarifications as to how ESAs would be able to control and manage their complicated tasks when parties involved would include non-EU countries.

Moreover, the structures developed under the ESFS for cross-border bank supervision remained complex and involved too many levels of overlapping competences that could lead to critical delays during a crisis.

---

[72] *Ibid.*, art. 8, defining tasks and powers of the Authority; see also arts. 10–17 (*ibid.*).

[73] *Ibid.*, art. 11, exercise of delegation.   [74] *Ibid.*, art. 10, regulatory technical standards.

[75] *Ibid.*, art. 18, action in emergency situations.

[76] *Ibid.*, art. 30, peer reviews of competent authorities.

[77] *Ibid.*, art. 36, relationship with the ESRB.

[78] *Ibid.*; art. 23, identification and measurement of systemic risk; see also the ESRB Regulation.

[79] *Ibid.*, art. 9, tasks related to consumer protection and financial activities; art. 26, European system of national Investor Compensation Schemes (*ibid.*).

[80] Part of the ESFS will of course become redundant once the EBU enters into force. As a result of this reality but, in part, as an implicit expression of the Commission's dissatisfaction with the ESFS, the Commission started a wide-ranging review of the ESFA in April 2013. See EU Commission, 'Public consultation ESFS review Background Document' (26 April 2013), at: http://ec.europa.eu/internal_market/consultations/2013/esfs/docs/background-document_en.pdf

Then if any major European bank or a financial institution fails, it would certainly have repercussions outside EU,[81] though no provision is made for formalized cooperation structures with third-country regulators beyond those provided in the (informal) context of the G20 and the FSB. The most important international cooperation issue is of course the need to draw up clear fiscal burden-sharing arrangements.[82]

Finally, under the EFSF extensive reliance was placed on the judgments and decisions of the home supervisor. A binding mediation mechanism is required to deal with such cross-border supervisory problems. Without such an effective and binding mechanism, member states could attempt to limit the branching activities of any firm regulated only by a home supervisor, who is judged to have failed to meet the required standards of supervisory practice. Such fragmentation would represent a major step backwards for the single market.[83]

2.   Phase II: from the ESFS to the European banking union

(i)   A new approach to integration

The nature of the regulatory architecture itself may not be an important cause of a financial crisis. Yet the 'institutional design' can be very important for the prevention and resolution of a major financial crisis. Prevention is dealt with through a framework of systemic risk control and robust prudential regulations. Crisis management and resolution, on the other hand, require established supervisory and resolution structures, which in an integrated market, must have a cross-border remit, in order

---

[81] See T. Beck, *The Future of Banking*, a VoxEU.org eBook (25 October 2011), at: www.voxeu.org/sites/default/files/file/the_future_of_banking.pdf

[82] C. A. E. Goodhart and D. Schoenmaker have proposed binding burden-sharing arrangement among national governments. If a cross-border bank faces difficulties, the governments would share the costs according to some predetermined criteria – for example, according to the distribution of the troubled bank's assets over the respective countries. Under such a burden-sharing approach, a common solution can be found upfront. By pre-committing to burden sharing, governments would give up some of their sovereignty, but, in return, the single market in banking serving Europe's businesses and consumers would be saved ('Burden Sharing in a Banking Crisis in Europe', *Sveriges Riksbank Economic Review*, 2 (2006), 34–57). This proposal was refined and suggested to become an integral part of group-level recovery and resolution plans for cross-border banks in E. Avgouleas, C. Goodhart and D. Schoenmaker, 'Bank Resolution Plans as a Catalyst for Global Financial Reform', *Journal of Financial Stability*, 9 (2013), in press.

[83] Country-specific recommendations on economic and fiscal policies: European semester (22 June 2012). Luxembourg: Council of the European Union, at www.consilium.europa.eu/uedocscms_Data/docs/pressdata/en/ecofin/131135.pdf

to override or subsume the principle of home country control.[84] For a very long time and until the different pillars of the European banking union come into place, the regulatory structures of the EU have been characterized by three principles: decentralization, lack of coordination and segmentation. A careful look at the developmental phase of European institution-building reveals this has been a process of experimentation rather than design.[85] The preceding analysis of the crisis and of the responses to it has shown that the inadequacies of the EU financial and institutional framework have played an important role in undermining the stability of the Eurozone financial sector during the crisis.

The EU treaties did not establish clear institutional borders as a prerequisite for the efficient functioning of 'multilevel European governance'. This flaw was most evident in the Eurozone sovereign debt crisis. European responses to this crisis highlighted the current role of and power balance among EU institutions and member states where the Union continues only to react to, and very rarely foresees, urgent needs and international developments which call for prompt reaction.

To remedy several of the aforementioned shortcomings the EU, as a whole, has embarked on a number of initiatives to build an integrated surveillance framework with respect to: (1) the implementation of fiscal policies under the Stability and Growth Pact to strengthen economic governance and to ensure budgetary discipline; and (2) the implementation of structural reforms. As a first step, Eurozone heads of state adopted the intergovernmental Euro Plus Pact, to strengthen the economic pillar of EMU and achieve a new quality of economic policy coordination, with the objective of improving competitiveness and thereby leading to a higher degree of convergence. As this remains outside the existing institutional framework a constitutional amendment to the EMU will be required to implement it.[86] In addition, the European Parliament and

---

[84] L Garicano and R. M. Lastra, 'Towards a New Architecture for Financial Stability: Seven Principles', *Journal of International Economic Law*, 13 (2010), 597–621; see also on the new supervisory framework in the EU, H. T. Arroyo, 'The EU's Fiscal Crisis and Policy Response: Reforming Economic Governance in the EU Directorate General for Economic and Financial Affairs' (2011), European Commission, at: www.oecd.org/gov/budgetingandpublicexpenditures/48871475.pdf

[85] D. Schoenmaker, 'The Financial Crisis: Financial Trilemma in Europe Vox: Research-Based Policy Analysis and Commentary from Leading Economists' (19 December 2009), at: www.voxeu.org/article/financial-crisis-and-europe-s-financial-trilemma

[86] Conclusions of the European Council, 24–25 March 2011, EUCO 10/1/10 Rev. 1, and subsequently revised conclusions, EU (25 January 2012). Conclusions of the European Council (9 December 2011) (Vol. EUCO 139/1/11 Rev. 1).

the Council adopted a 'six pack' set of new legislative acts, aimed at strengthening the Eurozone's economic governance by reduction of deficits through tighter control of national finances.[87] The reforms represent the most comprehensive reinforcement of economic governance in the EU and the euro area since the launch of EMU almost twenty years ago. This legislative package aims at concrete and decisive steps towards ensuring fiscal discipline to stabilize the EU economy and to avert future crises.

(ii)   EMU bank debt mutualization and centralization of bank supervision and resolution

Moreover, EMU is currently in the process of adopting a number of radical institutional reforms with a view to addressing the existential challenges it faces. Radical measures have been adopted, which aim at stabilizing market conditions and containing the impact of the Eurozone debt crisis on the banking system and vice versa, containing negative feedback loops between banks and sovereigns.[88] Conditional on measures

---

[87] The legislative 'sixpack' set of European economic governance architecture reforms comprised five regulations and one directive, proposed by the European Commission to come into force on 13 December 2011. See Regulation (EU) No. 1173/2011 of the European Parliament and of the Council of 16 November 2011 on the effective enforcement of budgetary surveillance in the euro area, OJ 2011, L 306/1; Regulation (EU) No. 1174/2011 of the European Parliament and of the Council of 16 November 2011 on enforcement measures to correct excessive macroeconomic imbalances in the euro area, OJ 2011, L 306/8; Regulation (EU) No. 1175/ 2011 of the European Parliament and of the Council of 16 November 2011 amending Council Regulation (EC) No. 1466/97 on the strengthening of the surveillance of budgetary positions and the surveillance and coordination of economic policies, OJ 2011 L 306/12; Regulation (EU) No. 1176/2011 of the European Parliament and of the Council of 16 November 2011 on the prevention and correction of macroeconomic imbalances, OJ 2011 L 306/25; Council Regulation (EU) No. 1177/2011 of 8 November 2011 amending Regulation (EC) No. 1467/97 on speeding up and clarifying the implementation of the excessive deficit procedure, OJ 2011 L 306/ 25; Council Directive 2011/85/EU of 8 November 2011 on requirements for budgetary frameworks of the member states, OJ 2011 L 306/41, at: http://ec.europa.eu/economy_ finance/economic_governance/index_en.htm. See also Regulation (EU) No. 1175/2011 of the European Parliament and of the Council of 4 October 2011 amending Regulation (EC) No. 1466/97 on the strengthening of the surveillance of budgetary positions and the surveillance and coordination of economic policies, OJ 2011 L 306/12, 15–16.

[88] See also E. Ferran, 'Understanding the New Institutional Architecture of EU Financial Market Supervision', in G. Ferrarini, K. J. Hopt and E. Wymeersch (eds.), *Rethinking Financial Regulation and Supervision in Times of Crisis* (Oxford University Press, 2012).

implemented at the national level, these policy initiatives will also support fiscal consolidation and private sector deleveraging.[89]

EU members need to complete the adjustment of internal and external imbalances, to repair financial sectors and to achieve sustainable public finances.[90] Responding to the ever growing pressure for more bank and sovereign bailouts the European Commission initiated the establishment of institutions that would support the use of funds from the European Stability Mechanism (ESM)[91] for bank bailouts, leading to the establishment of a more integrated banking union in the EMU.[92] Other important measures that could lead to the resolution of the Eurozone's banking and sovereign debt crisis are the ECB's decision to signal its readiness to undertake Outright Monetary Transactions (OMTs) in secondary markets for the bonds of Eurozone countries and the Liikanen report,[93] which has proposed solutions to separate deposit-taking banking from riskier banking activities. However, a comprehensive EU mandate on structural reform of the EU banking sector may take some time, as the EU faces so many existential problems on numerous fronts.

V. The European banking union

1. The role of the European Stability Mechanism

The Eurozone members have established a funding facility, the ESM, which is both essentially a fund that will employ, under strict conditionality, member state funds and funds it will obtain in the money and capital markets in order to operate as a liquidity provision and bank

---

[89] EU (autumn 2012). European Economic Forecast (Vol. European Economy: 7/2012). European Commission: Directorate-General for Economic and Financial Affairs, at: http://ec.europa.eu/economy_finance/publications/european_economy/2012/pdf/ee-2012-1_en.pdf

[90] EU (spring 2012). European Economic Forecast (Vol. European Economy: 1/2012). European Commission: Directorate-General for Economic and Financial Affairs, at: http://ec.europa.eu/economy_finance/publications/european_economy/2012/pdf/ee-2012-1_en.pdf

[91] See art. 81 of Regulation (EU) No. 1093/2010; Regulation No. 1094/2010; Regulation (EU) No. 1095/2010

[92] See speech of the President of the EU Commission Manuel Barroso, at: http://ec.europa.eu/commission_2010-2014/president/news/archives/2012/06/20120626_speeches_2_en.htm

[93] E. Liikanen, High-level Expert Group on reforming the structure of the EU banking sector. Brussels (2 October 2012), at: http://ec.europa.eu/internal_market/bank/docs/high-level_expert_group/report_en.pdf

recapitalization mechanism.[94] The use of ESM funds for bank recapitalizations is supposed to stem further increases in the indebtedness of the sovereign concerned due to bank bailouts.

Specifically, the Eurogroup of 20 June 2013 approving the establishment of the ESM as a direct recapitalization instrument for Eurozone banks imposed four conditions for ESM funds:[95]

(1) Risk of sovereign over-indebtedness or adverse impact of a member state's access to debt markets.
(2) Risk to financial of the Eurozone or of the member states.
(3) Risk of bank insolvency/failure and lack of alternative sources of funding.
(4) Systemic risk: the institution has a systemic relevance or poses a serious threat to the financial stability of the euro area as a whole or the ESM member making a request.

In part in order to counter moral hazard and in part because ESM funds are limited (around €700bn., with expected lending capacity of up to €500bn., member states having so far contributed only €80bn., and €620bn. remaining in callable pledges), there is a strict limit to ESM lending of €60bn. per member state seeking recapitalization assistance. Therefore, private capital resources will be sought as a first solution, including contributions from existing shareholders and creditors of the beneficiary institution. If shareholders' equity is, as expected, insufficient, then an appropriate level of write-down or conversion of debt will have to take place, following a burden-sharing arrangement between ESM, bank creditors and the member state.[96]

2. The Single Supervisory Mechanism

As mentioned earlier, the EU's reliance on national supervisory structures for the single market proved to be flawed. The failure of the rudimentary crisis management coordination mechanisms that were in place, through the Lamfalussy level 3 committees, lacked both the

---

[94] ESM's mandate is quite broad. See www.esm.europa.eu/about/index.htmat www.esm. europa.eu/index.htm#
[95] See Eurogroup, 'ESM Direct Bank Recapitalisation Instrument – Main Features of the Operational Framework and Way Forward', Luxemburg, 20 June 2013, at: www.eurozone.europa.eu/media/436873/20130621-ESM-direct-recaps-main-features.pdf
[96] *Ibid.*

competence and the resources to cope with a cross-border banking crisis that endangered taxpayers' money. Lack of appropriate coordination structures was nowhere more evident than bank recovery and resolution. Similarly the complete absence of a centralized EU structure dealing with systemic risk monitoring was incomprehensible. The most important of those gaps in the Eurozone institutional edifice is about to be remedied through the establishment of the first and most significant pillar of the proposed European Banking Union: the Single Supervisory Mechanism (SSM).

On 12 September 2012 the Commission proposed the SSM for Eurozone banks, which will be run by the ECB, in order to strengthen EMU. The SSM is the first step towards an integrated 'banking union' which includes further components such as a single rulebook, common deposit protection and single bank resolution mechanisms. The Commission called on the Council and the European Parliament to adopt proposed regulations by the end of 2012, together with the other three components of an integrated 'banking union' – the single rulebook in the form of capital requirements (IP/11/915), harmonized deposit protection schemes (IP/10/918) and a single European recovery and resolution framework (IP/12/570).

The desirable ambit of the ECB's supervisory powers has been the subject of considerable debate. Several member states have wanted the SSM to be restricted to 'systemically important' banks. For example, there is controversy as to whether German savings and cooperative banks should come under the remit of the SSM, as these banks consider themselves as local regional banks with passive assets and low-risk exposures, hence subject to different policy regimes from commercial banks. However, small or medium-size banks can also endanger the stability of EU financial system, e.g., the failures of banks like Northern Rock or the Spanish Caixas. Thus, the SSM is probably a more effective option. Furthermore, the existence of two supervisory mechanisms for banks, operating in the same market, would inevitably create conflicts of jurisdiction and competence ('turf wars') undermining the banking union. Early indications say that the ECB will be empowered to take over the supervision of any bank in the Eurozone if it so decides, in particular if the bank is receiving public support. That is, the ECB will set the rules and be able to assume directly all relevant supervisory tasks, if it considers it appropriate, over the 6,000 Eurozone banks. However, in principle, the ECB will focus its direct supervision only on those banks that can generate significant prudential risks through their size or risk profile.

Thus, within the unified supervisory system, the ECB will have direct responsibility for around 150 banks with assets of more than €30bn., or those with assets representing more than 20 per cent of a member state's GDP. National supervisors within the same unified supervisory system will primarily supervise the remaining banks. Finally, while the ECB will have the power to assume direct supervision at any moment, if need be, national supervisors will remain in charge of tasks like consumer protection, money laundering and branches of third-country banks. ECB supervision will be phased in automatically in late 2014.

The legislative proposals[97] published by the Commission establishing the SSM have still to work out appropriate solutions for some outstanding issues. First, the geographical reach of membership, i.e., which EU member states to include or not in the EBU. While the need for a banking union is stronger within a currency union, as the close link between monetary and financial stability is stronger and the link between government and banking fragility is exacerbated,[98] some non-euro area member states, including countries in Central Europe and Scandinavia, may want to join. And they have a veto over decisions under Article 127(6). The UK has categorically stated that it will not join the SSM.

Second, there is a legitimate concern that adding supervision – a politically charged task – to the ECB's responsibilities may compromise its impartiality and independence. Therefore, the supervisory function needs to be kept discrete and independent from the rest of the ECB structures to preserve its institutional autonomy. This is a very important distinction since banking and monetary policy, though interlinked, are not identical. However, there are contrasting views as regards the extent and form of separation between the two functions.[99]

---

[97] Issued on 12 September 2012; see 'Commission proposes new ECB powers for banking supervision as part of a banking union', press release. Brussels/Strasbourg: European Commission; also, 'Communication from the Commission to the European Parliament and the Council: A Roadmap towards a Banking Union' (Vol. Com.(2012) 510 final), at: http://ec.europa.eu/internal_market/finances/docs/committees/reform/20120912-com-2012-510

[98] T. Beck, 'Banking Union as a Crisis Management Tool, in Banking Union for Europe Risks and Challenges', electronic resource, Centre for Economic Policy Research (2012), at: www.dsf.nl/assets/cms/File/Events/Thorsten%20Beck_Banking_Union.pdf

[99] For example, there is overlap of representatives between the Supervisory Board and the Governing Council. Therefore, as T. Beck and D. Gros conclude, raising Chinese walls between the two highly overlapping bodies would make no sense ('Monetary Policy and Banking Supervision: Coordination instead of Separation', European Banking Centre Discussion Paper No. 2013-003; published as CEPS Policy Brief (March 2013)).

Finally, the issue of the lender of last resort remains unresolved. The ECB together with the Central Banks of the EU member states (NCBs) comprises the European System of Central Banks (ESCB). This configuration produces in itself structural complexity,[100] which has its roots in the dual role performed by the NCBs. The NCBs are national agencies while performing non-ESCB functions, but, at the same time, NCBs constitute an important part of the ESCB and play a role in the conduct of EMU monetary policy. This functional complexity has deeper roots that relate to their constitutive laws. Whereas the ECB operates solely under EC law, NCBs are governed by both EC law and national legislation.

NCBs remain the effective lenders of last resort within the Eurozone, an arrangement that made sense when supervision was not centralized and most NCBs also had a regulatory function. However, following the advent of the EBU, this arrangement is bound to create overlapping competences and confusion.

3.   The new EU Resolution Framework and the EBU Single Resolution Mechanism

(i)   Single Resolution Mechanism

To provide for common mechanisms to resolve banks and guarantee customer deposits, the Commission has proposed instituting a Single Resolution Mechanism (SRM), which would govern the resolution of banks and coordinate in particular the application of 'resolution tools' to banks within the EU. The SRM is envisaged as an indispensable supplement to the SSM and one of the cornerstones of the Banking union. The SRM would ensure that – not withstanding stronger supervision – if a bank that was subject to the SSM faced serious difficulties, its resolution could be managed efficiently with minimal costs to taxpayers.[101] This mechanism would be more efficient than a network of national resolution authorities particularly in the case of cross-border failures, given

---

[100] Lastra and Louis, 'European Economic and Monetary Union'.

[101] EU Commission press release, 'Commission proposes Single Resolution Mechanism for the Banking Union', IP/13/674, 10/07/2013, at: http://europa.eu/rapid/press-release_IP-13-674_en.htm?locale=en. At the 27–28 June European Council, EU leaders set themselves the target of reaching agreement on the mechanism by the end of 2013, so that it could be adopted before the end of the European Parliament term in 2014. This would enable it to apply from January 2015, together with the Bank Recovery and Resolution Directive (ibid.)

the need for speed and credibility in addressing the issues in the midst of a crisis.[102]

In addition to the prescribed resolution architecture, a Single Bank Resolution Fund would be set up under the control of the Single Resolution Board to ensure the availability of medium-term funding support while the bank was restructured. It would be funded by contributions from the banking sector, replacing the national resolution funds of the euro area member states and of member states participating in the banking union.[103]

The SRM aims at safeguarding the continuity of essential banking operations, to protect depositors, client assets and public funds, and to minimize risks to financial stability. Resolution decisions will be taken in line with the principles of resolution as set out in the single rulebook consistent with international best practices and in full compliance with Union state-aid rules, in particular, that shareholders and creditors should bear the cost of resolution before any external funding is granted.[104]

The Commission has also proposed the harmonization and simplification of protected deposit regimes, faster pay-outs and improved financing of schemes, notably through ex-ante funding of deposit guarantee schemes and a mandatory mutual borrowing facility between the national schemes. Therefore, if a national deposit guarantee scheme finds itself depleted, it can borrow from another national fund. The mutual borrowing facility would be the first step towards a pan-EU deposit guarantee scheme, and would be a natural complement to the establishment of a single supervisory mechanism. The single rulebook could include rules on the structure of the banking sector.

4. Evaluation of EU regulatory reforms

Weaknesses in the institutional framework have affected EU financial integration in two ways. First, the incomplete or partial harmonization of the pre-crisis supervisory and regulatory framework prevented the

---

[102] See Beck, 'Banking Union as a Crisis Management Tool'; G. Schinasi (5 November 2012) also distinguishes between immediate crisis resolution and intermediate to long-term measures.

[103] *Ibid.*

[104] Communication from the Commission to the European Parliament and the Council: A Roadmap towards a Banking Union (Vol. COM (2012) 510 final), EC (9 September 2012).

benefits of full integration from being reaped and allowed fragilities in the financial sector to build up. Second, the occurrence of the GFC and more critically that of the Eurozone debt crisis exposed the vulnerabilities and gaps in the national and EU-wide crisis management frameworks in such a menacing way as to lead to partial disintegration of the internal market, which, in certain areas, has split along national market lines.[105] Thus, for the EU, progression to a framework of tighter financial integration and risk controls for the banking system – together with improved governance standards in the monetary and fiscal spheres and centralization of responsibility for financial stability – has become a one-way road.

Current EU reforms promise to create a stronger financial and institutional framework in order to strengthen the resilience of the single market and mitigate the risk of vicious circles of market instability and fragmentation observed during the GFC and the ongoing Eurozone debt crisis.[106] Nonetheless, current integration efforts are high risk, as their core only extends to the seventeen EMU members and, thus, it might create irreparable fractures for the internal market, which remains incomplete at this stage.[107] Moreover, the new arrangements under the SSM need to become a 'first-best'[108] framework in order to stabilize the euro-area sovereign debt crisis and financial instability. Effective supervision, however, will challenge the fiscal sovereignty of Eurozone members.[109] This initiative, which essentially centralizes control over Eurozone finances by reducing the power of national governments, has attracted criticism from different quarters with respect to the role of the ECB, which will end up mustering an enormous amount of power without having a democratic mandate. At the same time, the legal basis for the new arrangements must be robust and include a mechanism for judicial review.

The establishment of the SSM is only a significant first step on a much longer path towards building crisis management and resolution institutions for the EU banking union. There remain several essential components such as a European banking charter, a fully-fledged single

---

[105] ECB (April 2012). Financial Integration in Europe: European Central Bank, 87.
[106] *Ibid.*, 12.   [107] Lastra, 'Banking Union and Single Market'.
[108] Schinasi elaborates on 'first-best' mechanism in the EU context comprising single supervisor, uniform deposit insurance and European resolution mechanism.
[109] G. Schinasi, 'European Banking Union: Pros and Cons – A View from Across the Atlantic' (5 November 2012). Presentation, at: www.dsf.nl/assets/cms/File/Events/Garry%20Schinasi_European%20Banking%20Union%20.pdf

rulebook, a single resolution authority and a common deposit insurance scheme whose detailed arrangements are still to be worked out. Finally, there remains unanswered for now the sensitive question of whether the doors of a new integrated financial supervisory mechanism are to be closed on non-EU countries.

VI. Conclusion: the importance of EBU for global financial integration

The reform of the EU integration mechanisms in the aftermath of the GFC and in the context of the Eurozone debt crisis marks an important milestone in international economic integration processes, especially because it has exposed the failure of various institutional mechanisms supposed to ensure financial market stability. Moreover, the EU crisis response bears significant implications in the development and functioning of single market operations and has emphasized the need to improve international and regional coordination on fiscal, monetary and financial policies affecting other states.

Over a period of several decades, the progressive development of an integrated single financial market in the EU combined with a single currency among seventeen of its members led to the imbalances that became visible when the GFC erupted in 2008.[110] Unfortunately, despite the vast amount of effort expended in developing both the EU single financial market and EMU, important design features necessary to support financial stability had not been put in place or were not sufficiently robust, particularly in relation to burden sharing, resolution of cross-border financial institutions, deposit guarantee arrangements, regulation and supervision, and fiscal arrangements and affairs.

It is not controversial, even though it does challenge orthodox thinking, to argue that financial integration is not always beneficial. Risks flowing from cross-border financial crises tend to intensify within integrated markets. The Eurozone crisis is a powerful reassertion of the same reality that reflects on the vulnerability of economically integrated markets in times of crisis when national responses prove insufficient to deal with the common issues in an economically integrated area. The

---

[110] J. Stark, 'Crisis and Recovery in Emerging Europe: The Policy Response in Retrospect and Challenges Ahead', in T. Bracke and R. Martin (eds.), *From Crisis to Recovery: Old and New Challenges in Emerging Europe*, electronic resource (Basingstoke: Palgrave Macmillan, 2012).

more integrated a regional market is, the higher the propensity for cross-border contagion. The cascading effects of the ongoing Eurozone crisis are a vivid reminder of the contagion risk in a highly integrated system.

The Eurozone debt crisis has clearly exposed the weaknesses of regulatory structures divided along national lines when these have to deal with integrated cross-border financial markets. As a result, the EU faces a number of hard choices extending to the intractable trade-off between national sovereignty and collective financial stability. The plans to establish a European banking union within the boundaries of the Eurozone, which will include a single supervisor and, in the future, a single resolution authority and a pan-European deposit guarantee scheme, have clearly tilted the balance towards further centralization and pooling of sovereignty. While the EBU and the treaty for a fiscal union do constitute decisive steps towards political integration, they may not be seen as entirely irreversible developments. A very important test about the cohesion of the EBU will come the next time that the EU decides to follow, through the ESM, the route to bank rescues applied in Cyprus, where it apportioned the costs to private stakeholders, such as shareholders, bondholders and large depositors, treating the latter essentially as investors.[111] Moreover, taxpayers and governments from both the core and the periphery of the Eurozone may, in the end, decide that the wider and abstract good of further European integration and of the stability of the single market is not worth the loss of sovereignty, and perennial austerity and sacrifice of national interest that they seem to entail.

On the other hand, the EU experience is invaluable in supplying policymakers with irrefutable evidence about the axiom that, although financial markets may be established anywhere, provided that certain property rights are recognized by local law, in the absence of restrictions on cross-border flows, their stability may only be guaranteed through appropriate institutions and not by reliance on the rationality and coordination of market forces. Therefore, arrangements to safeguard the stability of global markets ought to be intensified as, financial market integration, in many areas, including shadow banking operations, transcends regional borders and may only be dealt with at the global level.

The complexities involved in harmonizing common practices, standards and specifically the legal rules for diverse economies mean that EBU-type institutions may not be feasible at the global level in the

---

[111] For a complete analysis of the Cyprus bailout plan and of its implications, see *Financial Times*, 'Cyprus bailout', at: www.ft.com/in-depth/cyprus-bailout

foreseeable future. Yet in an increasingly globalized world, formal international cooperation in the field of financial stability and cross-border bank supervision and resolution, might in the long run come to be seen as a necessary ingredient of national prosperity in an environment where national financial markets are closely integrated.[112] This would become especially the case if ongoing national and regional reforms prove to be less successful than expected.[113]

Naturally, building multilevel or centralized financial governance structures in a region as economically and politically integrated as the EU is infinitely less complicated than a similar attempt at the global scale. But, these may, in the end, prove more challenges to be overcome rather than insurmountable stumbling blocks. Either way policy-makers should not assume that they have time to deliberate before another major crisis occurs. They should urgently start with the business of augmenting the global and regional financial stability mechanisms in order to safeguard the future economic prosperity; the lessons drawn from the Eurozone crisis may prove very useful in this process.

---

[112] For an example of such a model for the governance of global financial markets, see Avgouleas, *Governance of Global Financial Markets*.

[113] e.g. James Barth contends that not everyone is convinced of the new regulations in place (in case of the USA, the Dodd–Frank Act) has solved the too-big-to-fail problem, yet, the biggest banks have not been downsized, despite the presence of a general consensus from various stakeholders. He quotes from Sheila Bair (former FDIC chair, *Fortune*, 6 February 2012), Richard Fischer and Harvey Rosenblum (FRB of Dallas, *Wall Street Journal*, 4 April 2012) and Simon Johnson (professor at MIT, Bloomberg, 10 October 2011). See J. R. Barth and A. P. Prabha, *Breaking (Banks) up Is Hard to Do: New Perspectives on Too Big to Fail*. Financial Institutions Centre (3 December 2012), at: http://fic.wharton.upenn.edu/fic/papers/12/12-16.pdf

5

From regional fragmentation to coherence: a way forward for East Asia

ROSS P. BUCKLEY

I. Introduction: fragmentation and regionalism

Disciplinary fragmentation in international economic law occurs between its sub-disciplines of trade, monetary cooperation, global financial regulation, investment, and so on. However, within each sub-discipline, further fragmentation occurs in a variety of ways owing to a variety of factors. One of these is said to be regionalism. Some view regionalism as a building block of wider multilateral convergence, while others view regionalism as a threat to multilateralism such as the threat that regional trade agreements appear to pose to the global multilateral trading system. The Trans-Pacific Partnership (TPP) negotiations, the initiative for a Regional Comprehensive Economic Partnership (RCEP), and the proposal for a Free Trade Agreement between China, Japan and Korea are examples of attempts at regional trade integration in East Asia and the Asia-Pacific, that mirror earlier developments in Europe and North America.

Others see regions not in terms of disciplinary fragmentation but as a source of ideas about global economic governance, for example, the emergence of a 'Beijing' or 'East Asian' or 'Seoul Development' consensus.

This chapter explores the prospects for East Asian regionalism. It does so by placing East Asian monetary and financial cooperation – characterized by a predictably 'soft law' framework – against the backdrop of the collective underrepresentation of the region at the global level. It then goes on to show how history and contemporary events and circumstances prevent cooperation in East Asia, let alone the emergence of a coherent regional economic framework. Because of the centrality of East Asia to the global economy in the foreseeable future, this lack of coherence will impact how international economic law and regulation develops. In many ways, the situation in East Asia emphasizes the truth in the observation that the greatest source of fragmentation in the international economic order remains the fact that large domains of law and policy remain within the jealously guarded, sovereign purview of sovereign nations. What is worse than regionalism is sovereignty. In East Asia what lies behind the retreat to sovereignty, and the prevention of cooperation, and at what cost, is the subject of this chapter. And so the chapter concludes by looking at Japan's historical baggage and, more extensively, China's own role today in stifling an 'East Asian voice' in the regulation of international economic affairs. Put simply, ironic as it is, the primary obstacle to the emergence of a unifying Beijing Consensus for international economic governance is Beijing.

East Asia is naturally a fragmented, not a cohesive, region. Its nations are divided by religions, political systems, degrees of development and historical distrust. Some of the region's nations reject religion all together while others embrace Buddhism, Christianity and Islam. Some nations are communist directed but promote free markets such as China, others are democracies with a high degree of government influence over industry such as Japan, Korea and Singapore, and others are laissez-faire free market democracies such as Hong Kong. Some nations are highly developed such as Japan and Singapore, others are desperately under-developed such as Myanmar and Laos, and others, such as China, have pockets of both stages of development within them.

The road to the degree of unity seen today in Europe has been long and tortuous, yet Europe shares a common religion, political system and degree of development. The principal divisive factor in Europe has been historical distrust. East Asia has a much steeper road to climb on the path to unity with deep divisions in religion, political systems and levels of development and with at least as much historical distrust due to past wars and conflicts as has Europe.

This high degree of regional fragmentation has greatly limited the impact the region has been able to have in global economic governance. The usual pattern in the G20 and other fora has been for Japan and/or South Korea to argue against proposals put forward by China and for China to do likewise when a proposal originates from their neighbours to the east. The net result is that the voices of the region's major nations tend to cancel each other out, and the very large areas of agreement on economic and development policy within the region are not effectively promoted or argued for in the bodies of global economic governance.

This is a great loss because East Asia matters and its views on how to encourage and support economic growth deserve a global audience. East

Asia has mattered for a long time. The region's high growth rates have supported global growth. The region's, and especially China's, capacity to produce manufactured goods, clothing and other items ever more efficiently and cheaply has kept a lid on inflationary pressures in virtually all developed economies. For Australia, Brazil and other commodities exporters China's growth has provided a massive market for minerals and other commodities. Indeed, the rise of East Asia generally has underpinned global prosperity for the past twenty-five years.

Since the global financial crisis of 2008 the region has mattered even more. As economic growth has slowed dramatically or even stalled in the EU and the USA, the world has come to rely upon East Asia (bolstered by Brazil, India and Australia) to provide markets for exports and maintain economic activity.

So what we have today is a situation in which the region that is underpinning global economic activity has relatively little input into global economic governance and the rules of the global economic game are being set by the two regions that are faltering economically: the EU and USA.

This doesn't have to be so. This chapter explores what will be required for East Asia to begin to speak with a more unified voice in the councils of economic governance. It lays out a road map for the region to follow if it wishes to transcend its natural fragmentation and begin to exercise the influence and power that its economic success has earned it.

II. History and background: the Washington Consensus, the Beijing Consensus and the Seoul Consensus

Historically, East Asia enjoyed only a minor role in global economic and financial governance. Sixty years ago, in terms of its economic significance and influence, this made sense. Today it does not. For decades, East Asian nations have charted their own economic course, and enjoyed extraordinary growth. For over twenty years China has grown at an average rate above 9 per cent[1] that has recently decreased to about 7.5 per cent,[2] Malaysia has grown at an average rate of above 6 per cent,

---

[1] W. M. Morrison, 'China's Economic Conditions', Congressional Research Service, Report for Congress, 26 (2012), 4–5.

[2] I. Johnson, 'China's growth rate slowed in the 2nd quarter', *New York Times* (12 July 2012), at: www.nytimes.com/2012/07/13/business/global/chinas-growth-rate-slowed-in-the-2nd-quarter-down-sharply-from-a-year-ago.html. For a highly insightful analysis of

Singapore at above 7 per cent, and South Korea, Taiwan and Thailand at well over 5 per cent.[3] When Japan was outperforming the world, from 1950 to 1965, its economy expanded on average at over 10 per cent per annum.[4]

China is today the second largest economy in the world in purchasing power parity (PPP) terms, the terms that economists generally accept as best for comparative purposes, and, even more impressively, the second largest economy in unadjusted US dollar terms.[5]

Of worldwide official foreign currency reserves China holds about 30 per cent, Japan about 15 per cent and South Korea about 3 per cent.[6] China and Japan have long been the principal buyers of US Treasury bonds. The Chinese and Japanese have saved and lent, so Americans can borrow and spend. China has been assisted in amassing these reserves, in my view, by keeping its currency, until recently,[7] significantly

how China is now pursuing more equitable and sustainable development in a quest for social peace and stability, see C. L. Lim, 'China's State-Centric Model of Steered Economic Liberalization', Conference on European and Global Economic Governance, Brussels, 2011.

[3] Data spanning 1987–2011, World Bank, 'GDP growth (annual%)' (accessed 1 August 2012), at: http://data.worldbank.org/indicator/NY.GDP.MKTP.KD.ZG; International Monetary Fund, 'World Economic Outlook Database' (accessed 1 August), at: www.imf.org/external/pubs/ft/weo/2012/01/weodata/index.aspx

[4] K. Beida, The Structure and Operation of the Japanese Economy (New York: Wiley, 1970), 12.

[5] International Monetary Fund, 'World Economic Outlook Database' (accessed 1 August), at: www.imf.org/external/pubs/ft/weo/2012/01/weodata/index.aspx

[6] See International Monetary Fund, 'Currency Composition of Official Foreign Exchange Reserves' (29 June 2012), at: www.imf.org/external/np/sta/cofer/eng/cofer.pdf; S. White, 'Japan gives China's yuan $10 billion stamp of approval', Reuters (13 March 2012), at: www.reuters.com/article/2012/03/13/us-japan-china-investment-idUS-BRE82C0BL20120313; J. Lee, 'South Korea's foreign-exchange reserves rise to $316.84 billion', Bloomberg (3 May 2012), at: www.bloomberg.com/news/2012-05-02/south-korea-s-foreign-exchange-reserves-rise-to-316-84-billion.html

[7] In mid 2010 China ended the freeze of the yuan against the US dollar and began to allow a gradual change in the value of the yuan. In April 2012 the government accelerated this process (see E. Fung and S. Hong, 'China widens yuan trading band vs. dollar', Wall Street Journal (14 April 2012)), at: http://online.wsj.com/article/SB10001424052702304444604577342580742454656.html). The IMF has of late revised its position on the renminbi, calling the currency 'moderately undervalued' – a shift from its earlier consistent position that the renminbi was 'substantially undervalued'. The IMF said China's shrinking trade surplus and the renminbi's appreciation in recent years meant that it was now closer to fair value (IMF, 'People's Republic of China', IMF Country Report No. 12/195, 2012 Art. IV Consultation, July 2012).

undervalued.[8] However, while China may well have been manipulating the value of its currency, it did so without breaching its obligations under the Articles of Agreement of the IMF or the various WTO treaties.[9]

The path to development promoted by the International Monetary Fund, World Bank and US Treasury is a bundle of policies generally known as the Washington Consensus.[10] The focus of these policies has been to grow the debtor's economy, to alleviate poverty within the country so as to generate sufficient foreign exchange resources to stay current on its debts.[11] It has been taken as axiomatic that higher growth rates lead to less poverty and that the road to higher growth involves devaluing exchange rates, reducing budget deficits, charging more for state-produced goods and services such as electricity and water; privatizing state-owned companies, and deregulating the labour market. In summary, the Washington Consensus calls for a much-reduced role for government and a much-increased role for markets.[12]

Diverse policies have been pursued by different East Asian nations, so the region's economic success does not present a simple story. However, the three leading countries' economies have much in common. Their public finances are healthy, their banking systems and corporate balance sheets are less stressed than most Western countries, and their massive foreign exchange reserves serve as potent insurance against external shocks.[13] China, Japan and Korea share a common perspective that government should have a major role in directing economic activity:

---

[8] There is a vigorous debate on whether China has manipulated the value of the yuan (which it steadfastly denies) and on whether the yuan has long been undervalued. See for example: R. Wolverson and C. Alessi, 'Confronting US–China Economic Imbalances' *Council on Foreign Relations* (2 November 2011), at: CFR: www.cfr.org/china/confronting-us-china-economic-imbalances/p20758#p3

[9] B. Mercurio and C. Sze Ning Leung, 'Is China a "Currency Manipulator"?: The Legitimacy of China's Exchange Regime under the Current International Legal Framework' (2009) 14 *International Lawyer* 1257.

[10] The term 'Washington Consensus' was coined in 1989 by John Williamson, a British economist: 'A Conversation with John Williamson, Economist', *Washington Post* (12 April 2009), online: www.washingtonpost.com/wp-dyn/content/article/2009/04/09/AR2009040903241.html

[11] A. Saad-Filho, 'Life Beyond the Washington Consensus: An Introduction to Pro-poor Macroeconomic Policies', *Review of Political Economy* 19 (2007), 521; H. Askari, *Third World Debt and Financial Innovation: The Experiences of Chile and Mexico* (Paris: OECD Development Centre, 1991), 22.

[12] R. P. Buckley, 'The Economic Policies of China, India and the Washington Consensus: An Enlightening Comparison' *Wisconsin International Law Journal* 27 (2010), 707.

[13] I. Husain, 'Asia and global governance', *International Policy Digest*, 15 October 2011.

not for them is the Washington Consensus approach of leaving strategy
to the market.[14] Their domestic economic policy settings are strongly
pro-business with relatively meagre social welfare safety nets and their
policies generally prefer domestic businesses over consumers through a
mix of low interest rates on savings and high tariffs on imports. All have
pursued export-led models of growth.

In summary, the three leading East Asian nations manage their economies in broadly similar ways when it comes to the relative size and role
of government in an economy, the preferred size of foreign exchange
reserves, and a pro-business bias in policy setting. In particular, China,
Japan and Korea all favour far larger roles for government than the
Washington Consensus would permit.

The policies that have served the region so well often contradict those
of the Washington Consensus. This is self-evidently true in China,[15] but
even Japan has consistently preferred regulatory approaches 'that rein in
rather than let loose market forces'.[16] Indeed, the only East Asian economy to consistently follow Washington Consensus policies has been
Hong Kong (treating it as a separate economy for these purposes).

The term 'Beijing Consensus' was coined in 2004 by economist and
journalist Joshua Cooper Ramo.[17] According to Ramo the Beijing Consensus comprises three theorems 'about how to organize the place of a
developing country in the world'.[18] The first emphasizes the value and
necessity of innovation, the second emphasizes sustainability and equality as first-order considerations, and the third the importance of self-
determination.[19] Ramo also stresses that, unlike the 'prescriptive' Washington Consensus, the Beijing consensus 'does not believe in uniform
solutions for every situation'.[20]

Williamson (who coined the term 'Washington Consensus' in 1989)
argues that Ramo's concept is so ill-defined, that it must be imputed to

---

[14] China has the largest foreign exchange reserves, Japan the second largest, Korea the
eighth largest, see: 'Top 10 forex reserves by country', *Forexspace* (April 25, 2012), online:
www.forexspace.com/forex-insights/309/top-10-forex-reserves-by-country

[15] As recently as 2004, state-owned enterprises accounted for over 50 per cent of China's
GDP and over 40 per cent of its exports: Jayati GHOSH, 'China and India: The Big
Differences' *International Development Economics Associates* (25 August 2005), online:
IDEAs: www.networkideas.org/news/aug2005/news25_China_India.htm

[16] P. Lipsey, 'Japan's Asian Monetary Fund Proposal', *Stanford Journal of East Asian Affairs*
3 (2003), 100.

[17] J. C. Ramo, *The Beijing Consensus* (London: Foreign Policy Centre, 2004), http://fpc.org.
uk/publications/TheBeijingConsensus

[18] *Ibid.*, 11.   [19] *Ibid.*, 12.   [20] *Ibid.*, 4.

describe the actual development policies pursued by China.[21] Accordingly, Williamson argues that the Beijing Consensus in fact comprises five central pillars: incremental reform; innovation and experimentation; export-led growth; state capitalism; and authoritarianism.[22] If we are seeking an East Asian Consensus we need only tinker a little with Williamson's conception of the Beijing Consensus to come up with: incremental reform; innovation and experimentation; export-led growth; state capitalism and a major directive role for government.

I agree with Williamson that Ramo provided a neat term bereft of real content. The G20 went on to provide a 'Seoul consensus' bereft of any substantive connection to East Asia.

The G20 endorsed its first development agenda[23] in November 2010 in the form of the 'Seoul Development Consensus for Shared Growth'. This Consensus contends that the G20 must 'enhance the role of developing countries' because for 'prosperity to be sustained it must be shared'; because global interconnectedness disproportionately affects the poorest countries; because as the 'premier forum' for international economic cooperation the G20 has a role to play in helping developing countries; and because the global economy needs less industrialized economies to fuel global demand.[24] The document notes that 'there is no "one-size-fits-all" formula for development success', but then goes on to establish six broadly applicable 'G20 Development Principles' and nine 'key pillars' where the application of these principles are most critical. None of the principles or pillars relate particularly to policies pursued in East Asia. The Seoul Development Consensus is a G20 policy, not an East Asian consensus.

Other nations should be grateful that China and the other nations of East Asia have consistently ignored IMF advice and Washington Consensus policies, and taken their own paths, because for decades the stellar economic growth of East Asia has lifted that of the world, while Washington Consensus policies have never worked this well in the countries in which they have been applied.[25]

---

[21] J. Williamson, 'Is the 'Beijing Consensus; Now Dominant?' *Asia Policy* (2012) 13, 1–16, 6.

[22] *Ibid.*

[23] AusAID, 'The G20 Seoul Development Consensus for Shared Growth', 7 April 2012, available from: http://ausaid.gov.au/HotTopics/Pages/Display.aspx?QID=230

[24] 'G20 Development Summit 2010, Annex 1: Seoul Development Consensus for Shared Growth', www.g20.org/Annex/20101112/780968426.html

[25] D. Rodrik, 'Goodbye Washington Consensus, Hello Washington Confusion?' *Journal of Economic Literature*, 44 (2006), 974.

In finance China has marched to the beat of its own drummer. For twenty years the EU and USA have been pushing for China to open up, allow in foreign capital, and allow the renminbi to float on international markets. China has resisted most of these demands. Foreign banks have been allowed in when, and on the terms, that suited China, and only in limited ways. Foreign capital has been allowed in only in tightly controlled ways so that longer-term investments in businesses are welcomed but short-term hot money flows are denied access.[26]

So China has consistently called the shots in terms of its interaction with the global financial system. Yet, to date, China, and East Asia more broadly, have punched well below their weight in shaping international financial and economic governance. China has been happy to interact on its terms with global capital, without taking the next step of becoming heavily engaged in how the global financial system is structured and regulated.

III. Global economic governance

Until 2009 global economic governance was principally exercised by the G7 grouping of nations, in which Japan was the only Asian member. With the advent of the global financial crisis in 2008 it quickly became apparent that the G7 nations did not have the moral authority, or the right nations at the table, to craft a credible response to the crisis. So the G7 resolved to pass its role on to the G20, a pre-existing meeting of finance ministers that was promptly upgraded to a heads-of-government meeting.[27] The G20 grouping includes all members of the G7 plus China, Indonesia and Korea as well as other developing nations including Brazil, India and South Africa.

So for the first time, of late, East Asia has had four representatives seated at the high table of economic governance: Japan, China, Indonesia and Korea; five, given that ASEAN is usually extended an invitation to participate; and seven if one includes Australia and India as Asian nations. While India is indubitably Asian, and Australia in an economic

---

[26] R. P. Buckley and W. Zhou, 'Negotiating the International Economic Legal Order: Who Has Done Best, China or the West?', in C. Picker, L. Toohey and J. Greenacre (eds.), *China and the International Legal Order* (Cambridge University Press, 2013).

[27] D. Arner and R. Buckley, 'Redesigning the Architecture of the Global Financial System', *Melbourne Journal of International Law* 11 (2010), 207–8.

sense strongly arguably so, this chapter focuses upon East Asia rather than the region more broadly conceived.

While global economic governance is in the politician's hands in the G20, global financial governance is managed by the technocrats of the International Monetary Fund, Bank for International Settlements and Financial Stability Board. Yet in none of these bodies does East Asia have adequate representation.

Even after the reallocation of voting rights in the IMF in 2010–11, the ten ASEAN nations plus China, Japan and Korea have only 15.20 per cent of the total votes available to be cast,[28] whereas these thirteen nations generate 25.52 per cent of global GDP.[29]

There are sixty member central banks of the Bank for International Settlements, yet only nine are from East Asia (China, Hong Kong SAR, Indonesia, Japan, Korea, Malaysia, the Philippines, Singapore, Thailand)[30] and while there are nineteen members of the Board of the BIS, only two are from East Asia, both from Japan.[31]

The Financial Stability Board (FSB) has 52 seats on it for nations and 18 for organizations making 70 seats in total.[32] Yet China has 3 seats, Hong Kong has 1; Indonesia 1; Japan 3; Korea 2; and Singapore 1 – giving East

---

[28] International Monetary Fund, 'IMF Executive Directors and Voting Power' (14 August 2012), online: IMF: www.imf.org/external/np/sec/memdir/eds.aspx (Japan has 6.23 per cent and China 3.81 per cent of the votes).

[29] The GDP of the ASEAN+3 nations is US$16,120.4 billion compared to gross world product of US$63,170 billion (Central Intelligence Agency, 'Field Listing – GDP (Official Exchange Rates)', *The World Factbook*) (accessed 16 March 2012), www.cia.gov/library/publications/the-world-factbook/fields/2195.html

[30] Bank for International Settlements, 'Organisation and Governance', Bank for International Settlements (last updated 19 December 2011), www.bis.org/about/orggov.htm. In relation to voting shares, the BIS website states that 'The BIS currently has 60 member central banks, all of which are entitled to be represented and vote in the General Meetings. Voting power is proportionate to the number of BIS shares issued in the country of each member represented at the meeting.'

[31] The Board at the time of writing comprised: Christian Noyer, Paris (Chairman); Masaaki Shirakawa, Tokyo (Vice-Chairman); Ben S Bernanke, Washington, DC; Mark Carney, Ottawa; Agustín Carstens, Mexico City; Luc Coene, Brussels; Andreas Dombret, Frankfurt am Main; Mario Draghi, Frankfurt am Main; William C Dudley, New York; Stefan Ingves, Stockholm; Thomas Jordan, Zurich; Mervyn King, London; Klaas Knot, Amsterdam; Anne Le Lorier, Paris; Baron Guy Quaden, Brussels; Fabrizio Saccomanni, Rome; Ignazio Visco, Rome; Jens Weidmann, Frankfurt am Main; Zhou Xiaochuan, Beijing: see Bank for International Settlements, 'Board of Directors' (last updated 10 August 2012), BIS: www.bis.org/about/board.htm

[32] Financial Stability Board, 'Members of the Financial Stability Board' (7 August 2012), www.financialstabilityboard.org/about/plenary.pdf

Asia as a region only 11 seats.[33] Article 10(1) of the FSB Charter provides that the number of the seats in the Plenary (i.e. the decision-making body of the FSB) 'reflects the size of the national economy, financial market activity and national financial stability arrangements of the corresponding Member jurisdiction' – yet somehow it fails to come close to this for East Asia, at least in terms of the sizes of the national economies.

Therefore it is only in the G20 that East Asia's representation equals its economic heft – the region has 20 per cent of the seats (i.e. four seats out of 20) and 25.52 per cent of global GDP. Furthermore, the pattern has become to invite the chairperson of ASEAN to G20 summits to represent ASEAN's position on issues. The ASEAN chair was first invited to the summit in London in 2009,[34] and has been invited to all subsequent summits.[35] ASEAN is pushing for a formal seat at the G20, rather than relying on ad hoc invitations from the nation hosting the relevant G20 summit, but a permanent seat for ASEAN has not yet been institutional-ized. If it is, or for so long as the tradition of ad hoc invitations is continued, East Asia will have 24 per cent of the representatives at G20 meetings, which means the region's representation very nearly equals its contribution to global GDP.

The G20 is the primary body directing global economic and financial regulation – a role it has been given by the G7. The G20 often directs the activities of the more technical bodies like the IMF or the FSB. In this sense, if East Asia had been able to choose just one organ of global governance on which to have fair representation it could not have done better than choose the G20. The G20 is certainly the region's best chance to play a major role in global economic governance. What stands

---

[33] Financial Stability Board, 'Members of the Financial Stability Board' (7 August 2012), www.financialstabilityboard.org/about/plenary.pdf

[34] G. Capannelli, 'Asian Regionalism: How Does It Compare to Europe's?' *East Asia Forum* (21 April 2009), East Asia Forum: www.eastasiaforum.org/2009/04/21/asian-regionalism-how-does-it-compare-to-europes

[35] For attendance at both 2009 summits, see: 'How can Asia strengthen its voice at the G20?' *East Asia Forum* (29 June 2010), www.eastasiaforum.org/2010/06/29/how-can-asia-strengthen-its-voice-at-the-g20/; for attendance at both 2010 summits, see: 'Chair of ASEAN, President SBY of Indonesia Invites Members of G20 to Join ASEAN in Search of Lasting Solutions to Global Challenges', *ASEAN* (4 November 2011), www.aseansec. org/26712.htm; for 2011 attendance, see: R. C. Severino, 'Cambodia Hosts First East Asian Summit for 2012', *East Asia Forum* (27 April 2012), www.eastasiaforum.org/2012/04/27/cambodia-hosts-the-first-asean-summit-for-2012/; for 2012 attendance, see: 'Cambodian PM heads for Mexico to attend G20 Summit', *Global Times* (16 June 2012), www.globaltimes.cn/content/715285.shtml

between the region and its playing that sort of role is the subject of enquiry of this chapter.

IV. Why East Asia has had little input into global governance

There are four principal reasons why the region's input into global governance has not matched its economic performance:

(1) The economic rise of East Asia has been a relatively recent phenomenon and there is considerable inertia in international governance arrangements.
(2) The region has not been able to agree within itself – its voice at meetings of the G20, the BIS, the FSB and other bodies is fragmented.
(3) The United States has actively worked to discourage regional cooperation.
(4) The region does not possess confidence in international institutions and their policies.

1. Inertia in global governance arrangements

The first reason needs little explanation – power in international affairs is attractive, nations do not like ceding it once they have it, and power sharing is a zero-sum game, i.e. more influence and power for East Asian nations means less for other nations. The region that is overrepresented in membership entitlements at the IMF, the G20 and the various international financial regulatory bodies is generally Europe, so any push for greater representation for East Asia (and developing nations more generally) almost inevitably requires Europe to give up some of its power. For instance, on the FSB on which East Asia has eleven seats, European nations hold eighteen seats, and the European Central Bank and European Commission each hold an organization's seat while there are no distinctively Asian organizations on the Board.[36] So Europe enjoys almost double the representation of East Asia on the FSB while producing roughly the same proportion of global GDP.[37]

---

[36] Financial Stability Board, 'Members of the Financial Stability Board' (7 August 2012), www.financialstabilityboard.org/about/plenary.pdf
[37] East Asia's GDP from the IMF database is US$16.4 trillion (www.imf.org/external/pubs/ft/weo/2012/01/weodata/index.aspx), while from the same database, the European Union's GDP is approximately US$17.6 trillion.

2. The absence of unity among East Asian nations

As was explored in the introduction to this chapter, East Asia is a region fragmented by religion, political systems, degrees of development and history. Furthermore, the idea of Asia or East Asia is yet to gain as much traction as the idea of Europe had acquired by the 1970s.[38] Asia is not a term one hears used regularly in the region. Speakers are far more likely to speak of other nations specifically than of the region as a grouping. Asia and East Asia are terms used more often by outsiders to define and limit the region than by those living within it to engender feelings of camaraderie and a shared future.

The hand of history weighs heavily on aspirations for regional unity.[39] The general perception in the region is that Japan has never properly apologized or taken responsibility for the atrocities it committed in its imperial period from 1895 to 1945.[40] This view is most strongly held in China, which through atrocities such as the Rape of Nanking suffered grievously at Japanese hands.[41] Reconciliation between China and Japan is essential for the development of a regional architecture, as Simon Tay has pointed out,[42] yet China and Japan are in no sense natural allies. Nonetheless reconciliation is needed, and for it to occur, 'Japan must come to terms with its history'.[43] This is a difficult challenge for Japan, given its domestic politics. Extreme right-wing elements within its body politic who wish to argue that the rape of Nanking never happened will always receive disproportionate media coverage in places like China, as will Japanese school texts that choose to portray Japan as a victim in the Second World War rather than an aggressor.[44] This is a difficult

---

[38] For a comparison of the development of the idea of European regionalism as compared to Asian regionalism, see Capannelli, 'Asian Regionalism'.

[39] R. Foot, 'Asian's Cooperation and Governance: The Role of East Asian Regional Organizations in Regional Governance: Constraints and Contributions', *Japanese Journal of Political Science*, 13 (2012), 139.

[40] D. Nagashima, 'Japan's Militarist Past: Reconciliation in East Asia?', *Yale Journal of International Affairs* (2006), 117; S. Narine, 'The Idea of an "Asian Monetary Fund": The Problems of Financial Institutionalism in the Asia-Pacific' *Asian Perspective*, 27 (2003), 84–5.

[41] Narine, 'The Idea of an "Asian Monetary Fund"', 84–5.

[42] S. C. T. Tay, 'Attempts at a Regional Architecture', in Simon C. T. TAY (ed.), *Pacific Asia 2022: Sketching Futures of a Region* (Japan: Japan Center for International Exchange, 2005), 200.

[43] *Ibid.*

[44] J. H Miller, 'The Outlier: Japan Between Asia and the West', Asia-Pacific Centre for Security Studies, Occasional Paper, March 2004, at 10.

challenge for Japan but is one to which it simply must rise – for its own sake and for the region's. Korea has its own similar sources of historical distrust with Japan, most prominently the way in which Japan forced Korean women to serve as comfort women (prostitutes) for Japanese soldiers in the Second World War and its continuing refusal to compensate the women.[45] Again, Japan needs to come to terms with its history.

The cause of East Asian unity is further held back by the absence of a clear regional leader. Until perhaps fifteen years ago, the obvious economic leader of the region was Japan,[46] but the distrust mentioned above limited its capacity to play this role, and in any event Japan tended to keep its distance in regional councils playing the role of a somewhat aloof developed nation in a developing region. Today the economic leader of the region is China, but Japan remains unwilling to concede this role and instead the two nations continue to jostle each other for leadership of the region.

3. The USA works actively to discourage regional cooperation

The USA has not historically seen a unified East Asia as being in its national interest. It has therefore worked in more and less subtle ways against regional unity and cooperation. When Japan proposed, and was willing to fund, an Asian Monetary Fund in the aftermath of the 1997 crisis, the USA was strongly opposed to the idea – principally because this Fund could have led to far greater regional cooperation and diminished US influence.[47]

More recently, however, as the region has progressed along a road towards regional community building, the USA has come to realize it best get on the bus, or risk being left behind. America's attitude towards

---

[45] Y. P. Hsu, '"Comfort Women" from Korea: Japan's World War II Sex Slaves and the Legitimacy of Their Claims for Reparations', *Pacific Rim Law and Policy Journal*, 2 (1993), 97.

[46] So in 1996 Björn Hettne was able to write, 'Asia-Pacific is becoming the new centre of global capitalism. It can also be seen as an emerging trade bloc under the leadership of Japan' and later describe Japan as 'a hegemonic contender' ('Globalization, the new regionalism and East Asia', Global Seminar Shonan Session, United Nations University, 2–6 September 1996).

[47] Z. Pan, 'Dilemmas of Regionalism in East Asia', *Korea Review of International Studies*, 10 (2007), 23.

East Asian regionalism is far less antagonistic than it was one or two decades ago, but it still doesn't actively support the process.[48]

4. East Asia's historical distrust of international institutions

The principal contemporary reason for the region's general scepticism about global economic governance is the region's deep disillusionment with the intervention of the IMF in the Asian crisis in 1997 and 1998.[49] The IMF's high-handedness in imposing stringent conditions on Indonesia, Korea and Thailand was perceived as a humiliating affront to sovereignty and still looms large in the region's collective memory. This is particularly so because the IMF's initial diagnosis of Asia's troubles in 1997 was quite wrong, as even the Fund itself was forced to admit in under two years.[50] The strongly interventionist and directive style of the IMF in that crisis was in direct contrast to the region's strong preference for consensus-led cooperation, and so the region remains deeply distrustful of global economic institutions.[51] Be that as it may, the region is losing the opportunity to shape the global debate and the resulting regulatory measures due to this historical distrust, and it is surely time for the region to rise above its history and to start to play the role which its economic success has earned it and which will serve it best. After all, it is not as if China is content with the international financial system as it is. The Governor of China's central bank has been calling since 2009 for a new reserve currency regime;[52] and China is hard at work bringing this to pass. It has entered into currency swap agreements with Australia,

---

[48] Januzzi, at 129–130; I. Go, 'Regionalism in the Asia-Pacific and US interests' *Nanzan Review of American Studies*, 30 (2008), 167.

[49] C. R. Henning and M. S. Khan, 'Asia and Global Financial Governance', Peterson Institute for International Economics, Working Paper, October 2011, at 10; 'Bitter IMF pills difficult for Asia to swallow', *China Daily*, 3 December 2008, www.chinadaily.com. cn/world/2008-12/03/content_7264255.htm

[50] R. Buckley and S. Fitzgerald, 'An Assessment of Malaysia's Response to the IMF during the Asian Economic Crisis', *Singapore Journal of Legal Studies* (2004), 96.

[51] For a nuanced analysis of other reasons for this distrust, see I. Sohn, 'East Asia's Counterweight Strategy: Asian Financial Cooperation and Evolving Monetary Order', UNCTAD G-24, Discussion Paper No. 44, March 2007, 2–3.

[52] Z. Xiaochaun, 'Reform the IMF', *China Org* (26 March 2009), www.china.org.cn/international/2009-03/26/content_17504019.htm (accessed 11 October 2011); F. Bergsten, 'We should listen to Beijing's currency idea', *Financial Times* (8 April 2009), www.ft. com/cms/s/0/7372bbd0-2470-11de-9a01-00144feabdc0,s01=1.html#axzz1aWgJGjgs; 'Beyond Bretton Woods 2: is there a better way to organise the world's currencies?', *The Economist* (4 November 2010), www.economist.com/node/17414511; J. Anderlini, 'China

Brazil, Hong Kong, Indonesia, Malaysia, New Zealand, Singapore and South Korea to facilitate trade with those countries being denominated in their local currencies or renminbi, rather than US dollars.[53] As a result of these agreements and their projected expansion in the future, HSBC predicts that by 2015 the renminbi will be one of the three leading currencies for the conduct of international trade.[54] China remains of the view that there are better alternatives for a global reserve currency than the US dollar, with which I agree,[55] and if it could bring all of East Asia with it in that view, it would have a far better prospect of one day seeing it realized.

V. Regional integration

Integration within East Asia is an odd phenomenon. The region is highly integrated in terms of production – China is increasingly the manufacturing hub to which industries in other regional nations contribute inputs in their niches of comparative advantage. It is also well integrated in formal trade terms with a veritable noodle bowl of bilateral and regional free trade agreements in place or under negotiation.[56] However, the region is poorly integrated in financial and political terms.[57] The financial systems of most East Asian nations are far more

---

calls for new reserve currency', *Financial Times* (24 March 2009), online: FT: www.ft. com/intl/cms/s/0/7851925a-17a2-11de-8c9d-0000779fd2ac.html#axzz24FUqz5a5

[53] M. Dwyer and J. Murphy, 'Historic $A pact seals China ties', *Australian Financial Review* (23 March 2012), http://afr.com/p/national/historic_pact_seals_china_ties_3EnHQZ Q0Awvcj176ecKMjM

[54] *Ibid.* See also J. Wheatley, 'Brazil and China in plan to axe dollar', *Financial Times* (18 May 2011), www.ft.com/cms/s/0/996b1af8-43ce-11de-a9be-00144feabdc0.html#axzz1a WgJGjgs

[55] R. P. Buckley, 'Resilience and global financial governance', in S. Cork (ed.), *Resilience and Transformation: Preparing Australia for Uncertain Futures* (Melbourne: CSIRO, 2009), 70.

[56] There are currently seventeen implemented free trade agreements among East Asian nations, one free trade agreement under negotiation (Japan–Korea) and a further five under proposal (Y. Zhang and M. Shen, 'The Status of East Asian Free Trade Agreements', ADBI Working Paper Series No. 282, May 2011, 32–3). In addition, in May 2012, China, Japan and Korea agreed to begin negotiations on a free trade agreement ('China plans talks with Japan, Korea on free-trade area', *Bloomberg* (14 May 2012), www. bloomberg.com/news/2012-05-12/china-japan-korea-to; 'Regional Economic Outlook: Asia and Pacific', International Monetary Fund, World Economic and Financial Surveys, October 2011.

[57] D. Cowen and R. Salgado, 'Globalization of Production and Financial Integration in Asia', in D. Cowen, R. Salgado, H. Shah, L. Teo and A. Zanella (eds.), 'Financial

closely integrated with financial systems in North America or Europe than with those of other East Asian nations. This is perplexing given the high savings rates and foreign exchange reserves that characterize regional nations. East Asia's massive savings as a region give it enviable options in dealing with global capital, and provide the opportunity to interact with global capital more on its own terms.

Immediately after the East Asian crisis in 1997 Japan offered to fund the establishment of an Asian Monetary Fund, with a view to enhancing regional financial integration, but the idea met stern opposition from the United States and the IMF, and a lack of support from China, and was dropped.[58] In its place, the much less ambitious Chiang Mai Initiative (CMI) was pursued, a series of bilateral commitments by which regional nations committed to make bilateral swap arrangements and security repurchase agreements available to each other in times of need.

The CMI was not called upon during the 2008 global crisis with regional nations preferring to arrange extended credit lines from the US Federal Reserve. In the face of this failure, the swap agreements were multilateralized in early 2009 and increased by US$40bn. to US$120bn. in an agreement known as the Chiang Mai Initiative Multilateralized (CMIM).[59] And in May 2012, the swap lines were doubled to US$240bn.[60] China, Japan and Korea provide 80 per cent of these commitments, with the balance from ASEAN nations.

Originally only 20 per cent of the amounts available under the CMIM were available if a nation did not have an IMF programme in place. As IMF negotiations are typically slow, 80 per cent of the funds would not be available promptly – when they are needed in a crisis. The reason given for conditioning CMIM credit upon an IMF programme is that the CMI lacked a surveillance capacity. This has now been remedied with a surveillance authority established, in Singapore, in 2012.[61] However,

Integration in Asia: Recent Developments and Next Steps', IMF Working Paper No. 06/196, 2006 at 4.

[58] Lipsey, 'Japan's Asian Monetary Fund Proposal', 100.

[59] J. Rathus, 'The Chiang Mai Initiative's multilateralisation: A good start', *East Asia Forum*, 23 March 2010.

[60] Ministry of Strategy and Finance, Korea, 'ASEAN+3 Finance Ministers and Central Bank Governors' meeting successfully concludes', press release, 3 May 2012, http://english.mosf.go.kr/upload/mini/2012/05/FILE_A66G81_20120503182819_1.pdf

[61] The ASEAN+3 Macroeconomic Research Office (AMRO) was officially opened on 31 January 2012. It is responsible for monitoring the macroeconomic and financial situation of, and identifying vulnerabilities within, the ASEAN+3 region (Ministry of Finance, Singapore, 'Opening ceremony of ASEAN+3 Macroeconomic Research Office',

the immediately available amount was only increased to 30 per cent of available funds, with a view to a further increase to 40 per cent in 2014.[62]

Jayant Menon has noted that 'Asia's recent doubling of its financial safety net looks impressive. But it's more icing than cake.'[63] Menon is right. The amount of funds available under the CMIM need at least to be doubled and preferably tripled,[64] and the limits on the availability of the funds radically altered, before the CMIM will be a real substitute for credit lines from the US Federal Reserve or the IMF in any future crisis. However, while ASEAN and the region moves slowly, it is persistent, so achieving a CMIM of this size and ability to react swiftly is by no means unforeseeable.

A series of substantial credit lines coupled to a serious surveillance (and thus advice-giving) capacity is very close to a monetary fund, in this case, an Asian Monetary Fund. If the CMIM's credit lines are tripled, and the conditions upon which they be made available be determined entirely by the CMIM's surveillance authority in Singapore, not the IMF, then the CMIM could begin to function like an Asian Monetary Fund and thereby greatly enhance the region's control of its economy and allow the region to insulate itself, to some extent, from the vagaries and volatility of global capital.

VI.   The need for a unified regional voice in global governance

If East Asia is going to be able to exercise the influence it should have, given its foreign exchange reserves and its contribution to global GDP growth, China, Japan and Korea are going to need to cooperate. Yet, rather than cooperating, the three countries repeatedly clash at G20 summits. For instance at the G20 Finance Ministers meeting in Paris in February 2011, Korea and China were in conflict over the internationalization of the renminbi; at the G20 seminar in Nanjing in late March 2011, Japan openly supported the current role of the US dollar as the global reserve currency in opposition to the wishes of China.[65]

press release, 31 January 2012), www.amro-asia.org/wp-content/uploads/2012/01/01-Press-Release_AMRO-Opening-Ceremony.pdf

[62]   Ministry of Strategy and Finance, Korea, 'ASEAN+3 Finance Ministers'.

[63]   J. Menon, 'Asia's financial safety net a dead loss', *Bangkok Post* (15 June 2012), www.bangkokpost.com/news/local/298107/asia-financial-safety-net-a-dead-loss

[64]   And then of course regularly increased to keep pace with inflation.

[65]   Y. Tiberghien, 'Big Picture: The Context of the Seoul G20 Summit and the Northeast Asian Paradox', East Asia Institute Issue Briefing No. MASI 2011-04, 26 August 2011, at 6.

The region's economic strength and stability, and its role as a driver of growth globally, should give rise to considerable economic clout for the region in G20 deliberations but for this to happen the region needs to speak with one voice. The two principal reasons it doesn't are (1) the lingering, potent historical animosities between China and Japan and Korea and Japan, and (2) Japan's and Korea's concern about China's military rise and its increasing bellicosity.

So the way forward is going to require action from Japan and China. What is needed from Japan has already been explored,[66] so the focus now turns to China.

VII.   China's change of course

For twenty years China's foreign relations policies were, in the main, a model of the subtle but effective pursuit of national self-interest. In the past few years, all this has changed.

For years in classes about the region, I would contrast the use by Japan and China of aid funds to secure influence. Every year Japan would heavily outspend China on regional aid, and achieve far less bang for their yen. Japan funded worthy projects that gave its neighbours what Japan believed they needed, and what they often did need. China on the other hand gave what recipient governments wanted.[67] It was as if Japan were the parent who knew best, and China the grandparent who bought soft toys and ice cream.

As the developed nation in East Asia, Japan acted as if it had earned the right to solve other nations' problems. China behaved like a good friend who listened first, and then helped. In the words of Mauzy and Job, 'China's attempts to woo Southeast Asia consist of a package of well crafted policies featuring economic incentives and goodwill measures along with a strong diplomatic effort.'[68]

Unsurprisingly, China won friends and influenced nations, whereas Japan spent a lot of money and did a lot of good, but not much for itself.

---

[66] See text accompanying n. 35 and following.

[67] J. Weston, C. Campbell and K. Koleski, 'China's Foreign Assistance in Review: Implications for the United States', US–China Economic and Security Review Commission Backgrounder, 1 September 2011, at 2; H Tanaka and A. P. Liff, 'Japan's Foreign Policy and East Asian Regionalism', Council on Foreign Relations, December 2009, at 3–4.

[68] D. K. Mauzy and B. L. Job, 'US Policy in Southeast Asia: Limited re-engagement after years of benign neglect', *Asian Survey* 47 (2007), 632.

There were tensions in these years which diminished other nation's trust in China such as China's 'integration' of Tibet, China's desire to reunify Taiwan as part of China, and an unsettled land boundary with India.[69] However, it is fair to say that China's star was on the ascendant as a potential regional leader. All this started to change in the past few years with the rise of Chinese bellicosity.

China is pushing its claims to islands in the South China and East China Seas, and few in the West draw distinctions between these claims. They tend to be seen as undifferentiated acts of Chinese aggression. China's perspective is utterly different.

China is pushing its claim to the Spratly Islands in the South China Sea vigorously against the Philippines, Vietnam, Malaysia, Taiwan, Brunei – all of whom maintain claims to at least some of the islands. A quick look at a map shows the validity of the Philippines', and perhaps Vietnam's, claims to the Spratlys and the vast oil and gas reserves beneath them. Any map also shows the fatuousness of China's claims to the Spratlys, which are a long way away from China. This doesn't deter China as it bases its claims on history – for reasons related to the idea of China that I will explore later. In July 2012, to reinforce its claims, China resolved to garrison troops on one of the islands, and appointed forty-five legislators to govern them.[70]

Likewise, in mid 2012, China established a military garrison on the Paracel Islands in the South China Sea, which are claimed by Vietnam. This was described by one of Australia's most perspicacious commentators as 'an extraordinary act of provocation'.[71]

Formerly China would have sought oil and gas exploration rights over the Spratlys and the Paracels by offering the Philippines and Vietnam production-sharing agreements, plus large amounts of aid and large, cheap loans. Today China bases its claims not on persuasion and largesse, but on military might. China will prevail by relying on its military strength but at what cost to its longer-term ambitions to be a genuine

---

[69] S. M. Ali, 'Asia's Century one of Turbulent Transition and Volatility' *East Asia Forum* (24 April 2012), online: East Asia Forum: www.eastasiaforum.org/2012/04/24/asias-century-one-of-turbulent-transition-and-volatility/

[70] J. Perlez, 'Tensions rise as China sends troops to disputed islands', *Sydney Morning Herald* (25 July 2012), www.smh.com.au/world/tensions-rise-as-china-sends-troops-to-disputed-islands-20120724-22n76.html

[71] P. Hartcher, 'Any China conversation better than none at all', *Sydney Morning Herald* (14 August 2012), 11.

regional and global leader, and to start to shape the global system so that
it serves China's, and East Asia's, ends?

In the East China Sea there is a territorial dispute over the Diaoyu
Islands (which are known as the Senkakus in Japan) and over fishing
rights in nearby waters. In the words of an article on Xinhuanet

> There is ample historical evidence to show that the Diaoyu Islands have
> been Chinese territory since the Ming Dynasty (1368–1644). The fact is
> recorded in many historical documents. Even a map published by Japan
> between 1783 and 1785 ... labelled the Diaoyu Islands as Chinese
> territory.
>
> The islands were unfortunately seized by Japan during the 1894–1895
> Sino-Japanese war and had since been under its occupation until its defeat
> at the end of World War II. However, they were not returned to China, its
> rightful owner, and were wrongly assigned to the then U.S.-controlled ...
> Japan ... under an illegal treaty signed between Tokyo and Washington
> in 1951.[72]

Japan has rather different views, stating that the islands have been under
Japanese control since 1895, and dismissing all the grounds that China
relies upon as baseless.[73] This dispute is about five uninhabited islands
comprising a total area of about 7 kilometres, and three barren rocks,
which just happen to be near important shipping routes and which
probably sit above substantial oil reserves. At the time of writing it
continues to generate considerable heat with allegations that China has
locked missile guidance systems on to Japanese vessels in the area and the
like.[74] This dispute poses a genuine threat to regional stability.

There have been extensive protests within China about Japan's occupation of these islands.[75] Most Chinese scholars to whom I have spoken

[72] J. Hanlu, 'Japanese rightists' landing at Diaoyu Islands infringes Chinese sovereignty',
Xinhua (19 August 2012), http://news.xinhuanet.com/english/indepth/2012-08/19/
c_131794676.htm

[73] Ministry of Foreign Affairs of Japan, 'The basic view on the sovereignty over the Senkaku
Islands' (August 2012), www.mofa.go.jp/region/asia-paci/senkaku/senkaku.html

[74] See A. P.Q. Wittmeyere, 'Why Japan and China Could Accidentally End up at War'
(22 March 2013) *China–US Focus*, www.chinausfocus.com/peace-security/why-japan-
and-china-could-accidentally-end-up-at-war (accessed 4 April 2013); and 'Locked on',
The Economist (9 February 2013), www.economist.com/news/asia/21571466-danger-
ous-dance-around-disputed-islets-becoming-ever-more-worrying-locked (accessed 4
April 2013).

[75] 'Japanese firms close offices in China as islands row escalates', *Guardian* (17 September
2012), www.guardian.co.uk/world/2012/sep/17/japanese-firms-close-offices-china; 'China–
Japan protests resume amid islands row', *BBC News* (18 September 2012), www.bbc.co.uk/

are of the view that the government could do much to reduce these tensions and defuse the situation.[76] Yet, as the words of Xinhuanet quoted above suggest, the Chinese government for its own reasons is not seeking to do so.

The George W. Bush administration fixated on the Middle East and ignored East Asia. Upon coming to power in 2009 the Obama administration sought to rectify this oversight. But the conventional wisdom was that America was by then so resented in the region that reclaiming its former influence would be likely impossible.[77]

Yet, of late, China's aggressive postures have so scared regional nations that they have been lining up to ask America to re-engage. So we see the Philippines asking America to reopen Clark Air Base and Subic Bay, military bases the Filipinos ordered closed over 20 years ago.[78] We see the USA announcing it will move the bulk of its navy to the Pacific, so that 60 percent of its fleet, including six aircraft carrier groups, will be based in the Pacific by 2020.[79] And we see Indonesia taking the unprecedented step of sending its newest Sukhoi fighter aircraft offshore for the first time ever – to Australia for joint training exercises in July 2012.[80]

So China in the past four years has given to the USA the extraordinary gift of allowing it to re-establish its regional credibility and influence; which raises the question of why would China do such a thing?

The answer to this question lies not in what China expects the results of its actions to be, but in what is motivating its actions. In the decades when China's foreign relations policies were a model of the subtle but

news/world-asia-china-19632042; 'More protests in China over Japan and Islands', *New York Times* (18 September 2012), www.nytimes.com/2012/09/19/world/asia/china-warns-japan-over-island-dispute.html

[76] See also S. Raine and C. Le Mière, 'Chapter Two: Beijing's Multifaceted Approaches', *Adelphi Series*, 53 (2013), 55; I. Storey, 'Slipping Away? A South China Sea Code of Conduct Eludes Diplomatic Efforts', *East and South China Seas Bulletin*, No. 11, Center for a New American Security (20 March 2013).

[77] R. C. De Castro, 'The Obama Administration's (Neoliberal) Reengagement Policy in East Asia: Implications for US–China Relations in the Twenty-first Century', *Issues and Studies* 47(2011), 1.

[78] R. Johnson, 'The US will open massive Philippine bases not occupied since the Cold War', *Business Insider* (8 June 2012), www.businessinsider.com/the-us-is-reopening-massive-philippine-military-bases-not-used-since-the-cold-war-2012-6

[79] L. Panetta, 'US to deploy 60% of navy fleet to Pacific', *BBC News* (2 June 2012), www.bbc.co.uk/news/world-us-canada-18305750

[80] L. Murdoch and M. Bachelard, 'Indonesian jets in Australian war games', *Sydney Morning Herald* (18 July 2012), www.smh.com.au/world/indonesian-jets-in-australian-war-games-20120717-228f3.html

effective pursuit of national self-interest, China was seeking regional influence and supporters in global fora. It was not, however, dealing with issues of territoriality. When China's foreign relations policies have tended to be self-defeating, they have dealt with claims to territory seen by China as traditionally belonging to China. And here the idea of China becomes very important. Just as I wrote earlier that the idea of Asia is not particularly strong, the idea of China is both powerful and resonant for Chinese people.

So when territory that historically was part of the idea of China, or that today is seen as having formed part of that idea whether at the time it really did so or not, is not accepted by other nations for reasons of geography as being part of China, China becomes aggressive and assertive in ways that do not serve it in the bigger picture. Yet we must bear in mind that these actions of the Chinese government which I have characterized as aggressive are criticized internally within China as being too weak. For what is at stake for China is not just some small collection of islands, even with potential oil and gas reserves, what is at stake is part of the historical idea of China. It is the idea of China as the central kingdom, China as mother of the world's most populous people, China as the 'moral guardian' of her people in Confucian terms.[81] This is part of the reason that China treats as its nationals people who were born there but have since renounced their Chinese citizenship and assumed that of other nations.[82] It is part of the reason why when China first opened to foreign investment under Deng Xiaoping the investment that was most welcomed by provincial and national governments, and was most likely to succeed, was investment by overseas Chinese.[83]

---

[81] In Confucianism the state is the 'moral guardian' of the people, the relationship between the individual and the state is understood in consensual rather than adversarial terms, and neo-Confucian ideals held it was the responsibility of the educated individual to serve the state. See R. Martin (ed.), 'Central Themes for a Unit on China', *Asia for Educators* (2009), http://afe.easia.columbia.edu/main_pop/kpct/ct_china.htm. Confucianism prescribes a lofty ideal to the state with the governor as 'father' to his people who should look after their basic needs (J. Wang, G. G. Wang, W. E. A. Ruona and J. W. Rojewski, 'Confucian Values and the Implications for International HRD', *Human Resource Development International*, 8 (2005), 315).

[82] J. Garnaut, 'China fetes Abbott like "PM-in-waiting"', *The Age* (23 July 2012), www.theage.com.au/opinion/political-news/china-fetes-abbott-like-pminwaiting-20120723-22k9e.html; D. Rothwell, 'Chinese law is Australia's business', *Drum* (29 November 2010), www.abc.net.au/unleashed/41544.html

[83] K. C. Fung, H. Iizaka and S. Tong, 'Foreign Direct Investment in China: Policy, Trend and Impact', paper prepared for conference 'China's Economy in the 21st Century', 24–25 June 2002, Hong Kong, at 6–7; C. S. Fan, 'Overseas Chinese and Foreign

Important insights into this idea can be gleaned from a speech delivered by Professor Wei-Wei Zhang in the Netherlands in 2011. He writes:

> China is a civilisational state and the world's only civilisational state. China is the only country in the world with a history of unified state for over 2000 years. It is the only country with a continuous civilisation lasting over 5000 years. The Chinese are the indigenous people to their own land. . . . China is the only country which is . . . an amalgamation of an ancient civilisation and a huge model state.[84]

Professor Zhang sees China as somewhat like what the Roman Empire might have been if it endured to this day as a massive unified state in which all inhabitants spoke Latin. He sees China as an amalgamation of four factors: a super-large population, a super-sized territory,[85] a super-long history and a super-rich culture.

As Amartya Sen has observed:

> high technology in the world of 1000 A D included paper and printing, the crossbow and gunpowder, the clock, the iron chain suspension bridge, the kite, the magnetic compass, the wheelbarrow and the rotary fan. Each one of these examples of high technology . . . a millennium ago was well-established and extensively used in China and . . . practically unknown elsewhere.[86]

Most people in the West are unaware that China gave these inventions to the world 1,000 years ago and led the world in technology, but this is common knowledge in China. Indeed, in discussions in China, it seems the statistic that as recently as 1820 China produced 33 per cent of global GDP is forefront in the mind of most educated Chinese.[87] In 1820

Investment in China: An Application of the Transaction Cost Approach', Centre for Asian Pacific Studies Working Paper Series, Paper No. 39, 1997, 8–10.

[84] Wei-Wei Zhang, 'The Allure of the Chinese Model', conference 'Power Shifts in a Changing World Order: The Role of the European Union and the Position of the Netherlands', Senate of the Netherlands, 4 February 2011, at 11.

[85] Professor Zhang seems unaware that the contiguous continental United States, Australia and Brazil are all within 5 percent of the land mass of China.

[86] A. Sen, 'Global doubts as global solutions' (Alfred Deakin Lecture, Melbourne, 15 May 2001), www.abc.net.au/rn/deakin/stories/s296978.htm

[87] See for example: 'Hello America: China's economy overtakes Japan's in real terms', *The Economist* (16 August 2010), www.economist.com/node/16834943; Derek Thompson, 'The economic history of the last 2,000 years in 1 little graph', *Atlantic* (19 June 2012), www.theatlantic.com/business/archive/2012/06/the-economic-history-of-the-last-2-000-years-in-1-little-graph/258676/; D. Thompson, 'The economic history of the last 2000 years: Part III', *Atlantic* (22 June 2012), www.theatlantic.com/business/archive/2012/06/

China's GDP was 42 per cent higher than Western Europe's and over 18 times that of the US; and East and South Asia's GDP combined was 2.5 times that of Western Europe.[88] China has been a superpower before and the Chinese know this. They believe 'the rise of China is granted by nature' and China's decline 'is a historical mistake which they should correct'.[89]

For most Chinese people, the period from 1820 to 1970 was a historical anomaly – a period in which Asia was not the most productive part of the planet.[90] For these people, the economic rise of China and India is merely the world returning to its natural state.

In short, China is an idea at once larger, more influential and more powerful than the ideas that underpin almost any other nation. Ironically, probably the only other nation in the world that is as defined and influenced by its own idea of itself – in this case the ideas surrounding its founding – is the United States.

The power and resonance of this idea of China is why the nation is behaving so counter-productively over the territorial disputes in the South China and East China seas. And any resolution of these conflicts is going to have to accommodate the present day reality and influence of this idea. China is going to need to be assisted to see its interests through a lens that is larger than one merely of sovereignty. It would be well served by assistance in seeing its pivotal role in a world of two superpowers, a role that is so much bigger, and with more far-reaching consequences for China and others, than historical ideas of the geographical ambit and limits of China.

China is the regional superpower in East Asia. It now has real muscles to flex. Perhaps doing so provides some sort of steroidal satisfaction – we are doing this because we can. But there is a clear pattern here – when

the-economic-history-of-the-last-2000-years-part-iii/258877/; 'China's historical GDP share in the world', *China Whisper* (29 August 2012), www.chinawhisper.com/chinas-historical-gdp-share-in-the-world; Z. Jelveh, 'Merely following a megatrend', *New York Times* (15 October 2005), www.nytimes.com/2005/10/15/technology/15interview.html?_r=1 and ex=1287028800 and en=6e9fe66df56bd0aa and ei=5090 and partner=rssuserland and emc=rss

[88] A. Maddison, 'China in the World Economy', *International Journal of Business* 11(2006), 242 (table 1).

[89] Y. Xuetong, 'The Rise of China in Chinese Eyes', *Journal of Contemporary China* 10 (2001), 33.

[90] Certainly for China this period was utterly anomalous as its GDP measured in constant dollars increased only 5 per cent in total over the 130 years: Maddison, 'China in the World Economy', 242.

China is seeking to gain access to resources or influence with other nations it behaves adroitly and subtly but when the issue at stake touches on China's territorial sovereignty the subtlety gives way entirely to bellicosity. This regional aggression is distinctly at the expense of China's national interests. China's former course of building its soft power and trustworthiness was far better calculated to advance its own interests. Its current behavior has seen American influence rise in the region far more than anyone believed possible three or four years ago.[91]

China's new aggressive posture on security issues also effectively derails any possibility of a unified voice on economic governance issues. By driving Japan and Korea ever more strongly under the American military umbrella, China inevitably gives the USA the power to shape the Japanese and Korean positions on economic issues to an extent that would not otherwise be possible.

This is to the detriment of all. The G20 would be a more effective institution of global economic governance with a strong and unified policy input from East Asia. The region with the highest growth rates in the world must have useful things to say in global economic deliberations and deserves to be listened to carefully. The capacity to bring this about lies in China's hands, but it is going to require many years of careful, considerate regional behavior as China convinces the region it has the region's best interests at heart and can be trusted to deliver to it prosperity and security.

The first step in this journey towards reclaiming its natural regional leadership may lie in the negotiations towards a free trade agreement among China, Japan and Korea which commenced in March, 2013.[92] Some commentators believe these negotiations may provide a forum and way in which to deal with the territorial issues.[93] This free trade

---

[91] J. Bajoria, 'How the US should stay relevant in Asia', *Council on Foreign Relations* (18 November 2011), www.cfr.org/asia/us-should-stay-relevant-asia/p26546; I. Johnson and J. Calmes, 'As US looks to Asia, it sees China everywhere', *New York Times* (15 November 2011), www.nytimes.com/2011/11/16/world/asia/united-states-sees-china-everywhere - as-it-shifts-attention-to-asia.html?pagewanted=1 and _r=2 and ref=world

[92] Ministry of Economy, Trade and Industry (Japan), 'First Round of Negotiations on a Free Trade Agreement (FTA) Among Japan, China and the ROK' (28 March 2013), www.meti.go.jp/english/press/2013/0328_01.html (accessed 4 April 2013); Xinhua, 'China, Japan, S. Korea end 1st FTA talks with progress', *China Org* (28 March 2013), www.china.org.cn/business/2013-03/28/content_28386884.htm (accessed 4 April 2013); and Ministry of Foreign Affairs (Republic of Korea).

[93] 'China Japan and South Korea eye free trade agreement', *BBC News: Business* (26 March 2013), www.bbc.co.uk/news/business-21934726 (accessed 4 April 2013).

agreement could therefore be doubly important – for the potential it offers to achieve a degree of regional unity on trade issues and as a forum and means to resolve other issues that are presently utterly undermining regional unity.

VIII. Conclusion

East Asia has been important to the global economy for decades, and of central importance since 2008. However, the region's natural fragmentation, and the forces of history, have greatly limited its ability to contribute to global economic governance and therefore to the development of a less fragmented and more coherent discipline of international economic law. While the substance of the Washington Consensus is widely understood, that of the Beijing Consensus is less well defined. I have defined here an East Asian Consensus as comprising incremental reform; innovation and experimentation; export-led growth; state capitalism and a major directive role for government. But the fact that an East Asian Consensus is not a settled and influential term speaks to the region's inability to (i) articulate why it has led the world in economic growth for two decades and (ii) grasp the thought leadership role that such economic success should confer. It should have long been obvious to China that the region was unlikely to collectively support a Beijing Consensus. The failure to promote an East Asian Consensus is a lost thought leadership opportunity and one that has done nothing to lessen the fragmentation in the discipline of international economic law.

The region's economic strength should also have given rise to considerable economic clout in G20 deliberations but for this to happen the incoherence in the region's voice needs to stop. The two principal reasons it doesn't are (i) the lingering, potent historical animosities between China and Japan and Korea and Japan, and (ii) Japan's and Korea's concern about China's military rise and its increasing bellicosity.

So the way forward is going to require action from Japan and China.

As previously considered, the only answer to the potent historical distrust is for Japan to take responsibility for its history, give unconditional apologies for past abuses, and ensure its school texts and other histories don't whitewash Japan's role as the aggressor in WWII and the abuses committed by its troops.

Equally there is only one answer to the rising concerns about China's current aggression. China needs to stop resorting to threats and military intimidation or security tensions will continue to irreparably undermine any convergence of the region's voice. China is paying a huge price in lost international influence for taking its utterly uncompromising stance on territorial issues. This is a real loss for the region which is destabilized and spends much more than it would otherwise need to do on military expenditures. It is tragedy for China, Japan and Korea who spend their energy squabbling among themselves rather than shaping the international regulatory and other agendas in ways that would serve them and the region.

Since opening up to foreign investment under the leadership of Deng Xiaoping, China's strategies have been characterized by subtle, astute, long-term thinking – three elements missing from its current approach. A return by China to its former policies of seeking regional leadership and influence through soft power and the strategic use of aid funds and largesse may require China to share the oil and gas resources in the South China Sea but the cost to China of sharing these resources would be far less than the cost to China of the loss of the opportunity to shape the global economic and regulatory agenda.

China is now a major global player. It is playing for stakes far higher than fidelity to the historical idea of China or access to some oil and gas or fishing rights. China, Japan and East Asia would all be far better off if each could realize that the bigger game they are playing in is the opportunity to shape the global economic and financial architecture and to bring coherence, and a distinctly Asian sensibility, to the rules by which the global economy is governed – those of the discipline of international economic law.

6

'The law works itself pure': the fragmented disciplines of global trade and monetary cooperation, and the Chinese currency problem

C. L. LIM

I. Introduction

This chapter considers the long-standing controversy over the Chinese yuan – the primary unit of account of the renminbi, or RMB, the official currency of the People's Republic of China.[1] The currency valuation interventions of the People's Bank of China (PBC) have been the subject of international disagreement, not least between the USA and China. Criticism of China in the USA became especially heated during the 2009 to 2012 period, occurring in the aftermath of the global financial and economic crisis and coinciding with the period of the great recession. Other countries, such as Brazil, also drew critical attention to the issue inside the World Trade Organization (WTO) during this period.[2] But

With the usual caveat, I am indebted to Joel Trachtman and Patrick Low for so generously sharing their thoughts with me. My former student, Kelsey Ng, assisted me with her research on US Congressional Bills.

[1] See M. Benitah, 'China's Fixed Exchange Rate for the Yuan: Could the United States Challenge It in the WTO as a Subsidy?', *ASIL Insights*, October 2003.

[2] M. Dalton, 'WTO to examine complaint on yuan', *Wall Street Journal*, 16 November 2011; J. Leahy, 'US seeks pact with Brazil over renminbi', *Financial Times*, 8 February 2011. To be sure, this controversy is not confined to China's currency policies, and China is here chosen only because of the ample record derived from the longer disagreement with its currency policies in light of China's successful export-based economy. As this chapter goes to press, the focus of congressional dissatisfaction with 'currency manipulation' has now also shifted to South Korea, and particularly Japan. Dissatisfaction with Japan's currency policies is also noteworthy following the latest appeal to the US Trade Representative by 43 Democrat and 17 Republican Senators for the issue to be addressed in the ongoing Trans-Pacific Partnership (TPP) Negotiations to which both the USA and Japan are party. This would at least suggest that a regional treaty solution (i.e. further fragmentation of international economic regulation along global–regional lines) could gain interest in the future. See J. Politi and S. Donnan, 'Currency manipulation should be part of trade talks, senators say', *Financial Times*, 24 September 2013. For the TPP, generally, see C. L. Lim,

while the problem has arisen in the context of trade competition and was often framed as a trade dispute – in terms of 'cheap goods' or unlawful subsidization[3] – a larger question concerns the extent to which the matter is adequately governed by existing rules under the post-Second World War Bretton Woods framework for the regulation of global trade and monetary cooperation.

The debate is ostensibly legal, or at the very least takes place under the colour of law. However, there is scant trade regulation under existing trade rules. This does not mean the answer automatically lies with a different set of international rules, given the fragmented disciplines of international economic law. There is even less that the International Monetary Fund (IMF) can do in terms of the actual enforcement of legal discipline. Here, disciplinary fragmentation means that the issue is likely to fall between the cracks; unlike the more familiar problem in international economic law of overlapping, or competing authority – i.e. of having too much incoherent regulation, as opposed to too little regulation.[4] This is the familiar problem of gaps – lacunae – in international law, leading to a professional lawyers' phenomenon which I call 'rule tolerance'.

Making the currency issue actionable under the WTO Subsidies and Countervailing Measures (SCM) Agreement is often discussed but difficult because that shoe does not fit; resulting only in some highly strained interpretations of trade law. Equally, the mandatory rules under the IMF Articles of Agreement are few, as befits a tradition of soft monetary rules. One exception is a core 'anti-manipulation' rule which we will return to. Yet framing dissatisfaction over China's currency interventions as a 'manipulation' (i.e. monetary cooperation) problem recalls a man equipped with a hammer, for whom all things resemble a nail. The legal meaning of 'currency manipulation' is unclear. Furthermore, it is

---

D. Elms and P. Low (eds.), *The Trans-Pacific Partnership: A Quest for a 21st Century Trade Agreement* (Cambridge University Press, 2012).

[3] Leahy, 'US Seeks Pact'; K. Bradsher, 'Washington asks WTO to examine Chinese aid', *International Herald Tribune*, 8–9 October 2011.

[4] See e.g. 'Conclusions of the Work of the Study Group on the Fragmentation of International Law: Difficulties Arising from the Diversification and Expansion of International Law 2006', adopted by the ILC at its Fifty-eighth session, A/61/10 (2006), para. 51; *Yearbook of the International Law Commission* (2006), vol. II, pt 2; T. Broude, 'Fragmentation(s) of International Law', in T. Broude and Y. Shany (eds.), *The Shifting Allocation of Authority in International Law* (Oxford: Hart, 2008), 99; C. L. Lim and H. Gao, 'The Politics of Competing Jurisdictional Claims in WTO and RTA Disputes', in T. Broude, M. L. Busch and A. Porges (eds.), *The Politics of International Economic Law* (Cambridge University Press, 2011), 282.

not an anti-manipulation rule per se, but rather a rule against manipulation *with* the deliberate intent of affecting a nation's terms of trade (i.e. by increasing net exports).[5] At the same time, economists have faced an equally difficult time marking out the correlation between currency volatility and the sorts of assumed trade effects which China's critics say its currency policies entail.[6] Another difficulty is the lack of a proper adjudicatory mechanism in relation to controversies over international monetary policy.

This chapter surveys and compares the rules and regimes for trade and monetary cooperation against the backdrop of persistent calls for unilateral action against Chinese goods, especially following the 2009 to 2010 period when China had intervened to maintain an undervalued yuan. Eventually, it also became a prominent electoral issue during the 2012 presidential elections in the United States. The central arguments in this chapter are that (1) the rules governing trade and monetary cooperation 'tolerate' a wide scope of discretion in currency policies; (2) under trade law, China's trading partners are constrained by trade rules in the national responses they may wish to adopt, and that (3) the sort of national action in response to China's currency policies which ought to be permitted is one which is justified by the kinds of rule arrangements we have. Without either counselling action against or attempting to defend China, this chapter argues that (4) of all the trade law arguments which are available against the backdrop of a fragmented international economic system, anti-dumping action is what global rules are most likely to permit. Framing the issue as a dumping issue, coupled with the prospect of WTO litigation, could also point a way forward for the future refinement of global rules. Particularly when we consider the legal methods lawyers use to work out such issues, fragmentation and the absence of adequate global rules do not mean a regulatory free-for-all, either for China, the USA, or anyone else.

---

[5] See further, the 2007 decision on bilateral surveillance of IMF's executive board, 15 June 2007.

[6] See 'The Relationship between Exchange Rates and International Trade: A Review of Economic Literature'. Note by the Secretariat, WT/WGTDF/W/57, 27 September 2011; 'The Relationship between Exchange Rates and International Trade: A Short Update of Recent Economic Literature'. Note by the Secretariat, WT/WGTDF/W/65, 18 July 2012. See further, the discussion by A. Hertogen, 'The Forgotten GATT Articles on Exchange Rates', PEPA/SIEL conference, January 2012, on file.

II.   Calls for unilateral action against unfair trade

Difficulties with global rules, coupled with domestic protectionist pressures in the post-crisis global economic climate, have led to calls throughout the past decade for unilateral action by the United States – principally, unilateral rules to block Chinese goods in circumstances where China is not perceived to be 'playing fair'.[7] The argument for such unilateral action takes place against the backdrop of ineffective – or what is perceived to be ineffective – global regulation. There are 'gaps in the rules'. Thus, according to such reasoning, even a nation like the United States which believes in international rules may need to resort to self-help. More so, if all that is truly involved is 'self-defence'.[8]

International economic lawyers have however tended to focus their writings on what the rules say. To the extent that they find the rules uncertain, these writings underscore the apparent permissibility of the PBC's policies and also the fact that unilateral action by China's trading partners may be permissible where such action doesn't contravene the rules. International lawyers routinely 'tolerate' unilateral, sovereign action in such a manner where, as here, our fragmented legal regimes – the WTO and the IMF – are incapable of providing practical guidance. 'Tolerance' may not be the exact word. I use it here only to denote professional acceptance of the limits of legal rules, and – as I shall argue further, below – acceptance that there are 'gaps' in the law where specific issues fall through the cracks between the fragmented, yet sometimes overlapping, regimes which characterize the discipline of international economic law. A further reason which makes such tolerance bearable to the lawyer's professional sensibilities may be that if unilateral action incentivizes or even compels international consultation and negotiation, and prompts authoritative rule interpretation or legislation (i.e. the creation of new treaty rules in the longer run), legal practitioners in the field might yet ask if that would be such a bad thing from the viewpoint of the international legal order.

In a sense, the debate is as old as that between the natural lawyers who would not *confine* all that we would call 'law' to that which may be traced

---

[7] Bradsher, 'Washington Asks WTO', 8–9.

[8] For raising the argument of 'self-defence', in these contexts, see R. Hudec, 'Thinking about the New Section 301: Beyond Good and Evil', in J. Bhagwati and H. T. Patrick (eds.), *Aggressive Unilateralism: America's 301 Trade Policy and the World Trading System* (Ann Arbor, MI: University of Michigan Press, 1990).

to the voluntary consent of sovereigns to international rules,[9] and so-called legal positivists who would.[10] It requires us to come up with further justifications for unilateral action when the rules have run out. In any event, thinking about whether unilateral action may ever be *normatively justified* is familiar to international economic lawyers. A clear example can be found in the writings of the late Robert Hudec. His writings sought out the strength of moral–political justification for a range of unilateral trade devices which were the subject of heated public debate. These ranged from anti-dumping to anti-subsidy action against foreign goods, to the search for a normative justification for 'Section 301' in the United States.[11] Hudec's underlying concern in all these instances was seemingly constant – when, if ever, would it be *justified* to act unilaterally? Today, the issues raised by the currency issue are similar to those confronted in Hudec's search for a justification – if any – for anti-dumping action, anti-subsidy action and Section 301 action.

In short, there is a currently a close search in international economic law writing for a way forward where existing international rules do not seem adequate, and the prospect of unilateral sovereign action has again raised its head.[12] Yet there is no suggestion of a

---

[9] See e.g. F. de Victoria, in E. Nys (ed.), *De Indis et de Iure Belli Relectiones* (Washington, DC: Carnegie, 1917); John Pawley Bate (trans.), 'First Reflectio of the Reverend Father, Brother Franciscus de Victoria, On the Indians Lately Discovered' (hereafter, 'First Reflectio'), 115: 'the law of nations (*jus gentium*), which either is natural law or is derived from natural law ... What Natural reason has established among all nations is called the *jus gentium*' (151). Hence custom is evidence, but not a source, of law ('And, indeed, there are many things in this connection which issue from the law of nations, which, because it has a sufficient derivation from natural law, is clearly capable of conferring rights and creating obligations' (153)); positive law being subordinate to natural law ('And if there were any human law which without any cause took away rights conferred by natural and divine law, it would be inhumane and unreasonable and consequently would not have the force of law' (152)).

[10] See A. Gentili, *De Jure Belli Libri Tres*, John C. Rolfe (trans.), with intro. by Coleman Phillipson (Oxford: Clarendon, 1933), vol. II, bk 1, ch. 1, 8: 'The law of nations which is that which is in use among all nations of men, which native reason has established among all human beings, and which is equally observed by all mankind. Such a law is natural law. *The agreement of all nations about a matter must be regarded as a law of nature*' (my emphasis).

[11] R. Hudec, 'Mirror, Mirror on the Wall: The Concept of Fairness in US Foreign Trade Policy', in R. E. Hudec, *Essays on the Nature of International Trade Law* (London: Cameron May, 1999), 227; Hudec, 'Thinking about the New Section 301'.

[12] See e.g. J. Trachtman, 'Yuan to Fight about It: The WTO Legality of China's Exchange Rate Regime', in Simon Evenett (ed.), VOXEU e-book, 10 April 2010; R. W. Staiger and A. O. Sykes, '"Currency Manipulation" and World Trade', *World Trade Review* 9 (2010),

regulatory free-for-all, implying that all manner of unilateral, sovereign responses may be permissible. This raises the question of when, and *what sorts of, national responses to China's currency policies would be permissible under international law.* That is the only question addressed in this chapter, as opposed to whether action should be taken against China at all or, if so, what strategies would be legally most advantageous.

III.   The Chinese currency issue

Since 2005, the Chinese RMB has been pegged to a basket of currencies comprising the US dollar, the Japanese yen and the euro.[13] The PBC has the power to intervene in the currency markets. It does so by buying and selling, principally the US dollar, in the international currency market. The PBC's stated purpose is to maintain the RMB's exchange rate, a legitimate aim, but the claim that the PBC's exchange rate policies are maintained strictly in accordance with purely domestic imperatives has nonetheless drawn a critical response.[14] Its critics claim that the PBC is, in reality, taking exchange action against the US dollar with the intent of keeping the RMB at an artificially low rate – i.e. to promote China's exports and/or restrict imports – while, at the same time, building up China's foreign reserves.[15] It is alleged that China intervened to prevent its currency from appreciating between 2009 and the first half of 2010, causing its reserves to swell by US$540 billion over an eighteen-month period.[16]

The controversy involves a difficulty in distinguishing between the pursuit of a legitimate domestic policy, and allegations of currency

583; B. Mercurio and C. S. N. Leung, 'Is China a "Currency Manipulator"?: The Legitimacy of China's Exchange Regime under the current International Legal Framework', *International Lawyer*, 43 (2009), 1257; Hertogen, 'The Forgotten GATT Articles'. For a slightly earlier but near contemporaneous piece, see R. Bhala, 'Virtues, the Chinese Yuan and American Trade Empire', *Hong Kong LJ* 38 (2008), 183.

[13] Prior to 2005 it was pegged to the US dollar, but under pressure from the Bush administration in 2005, it was allowed to float within a narrow band enabling it to rise by 21 per cent ('Renminbi (Yuan)', *New York Times*, *Global Edition*, Times Topics, 18 October 2012), http://topics.nytimes.com/top/reference/timestopics/subjects/c/currency/yuan/index.html

[14] This is also the 'standard defence', typically accepted by the IMF without question (see J. E. Sanford, 'Currency Manipulation: The IMF and WTO', CRS Report for Congress, 28 January 2011).

[15] Trachtman, 'Yuan to Fight about It'.   [16] 'Renminbi (yuan)', *New York Times*.

manipulation with the aim of boosting China's export performance and terms of trade. Two distinct sets of rules – embodied in China's IMF obligations (particularly under Article IV of the IMF Articles of Association) and its WTO obligations – both appear to apply. The next section offers a brief summary of the two bodies of rules, and discusses their differences. The section following that discusses how unilateral action (e.g. by the USA) may be viewed under these separate legal regimes.

IV. The 'trade' and 'monetary cooperation' methods of legal analysis compared

1. Monetary cooperation: the International Monetary Fund

Under Article I of the IMF Articles of Agreement, the purposes of the IMF include the following:

> (ii) To facilitate the expansion and *balanced growth of international trade,* and to contribute thereby to the promotion and maintenance of high levels of employment and real income and to the development of the productive resources of all members as primary objectives of economic policy.
>
> (iii) To promote *exchange stability,* to maintain orderly exchange arrangements among members, and *to avoid competitive exchange depreciation.*
>
> (iv) To assist in the establishment of a *multilateral system of payments* in respect of current transactions between members and in the *elimination of foreign exchange restrictions* which hamper the growth of world trade.
>
> (v) To give confidence to members by *making the general resources of the Fund temporarily available to them* under adequate safeguards, thus providing them with *opportunity to correct maladjustments in their balance of payments without resorting to measures destructive of national or international prosperity.*

Article I(ii) reflects a belief on the part of the framers of the Bretton Woods system in the importance to 'employment, income and development' of international trade. Equally important is a global system for trade payments.[17] Here, the IMF had originally been intended to administer a system of freely convertible currencies,[18] using fixed exchange

---

[17] As we shall see below, hence art. I(iv)'s reference to the establishment of a 'multilateral system of payments'.

[18] Hence art. I(iv)'s reference to 'the elimination of foreign exchange restrictions'.

rates.[19] The thinking was that the enhanced ability of traders to predict both the convertibility of a currency and its value would facilitate trade payments which would, in turn, facilitate trade.[20] For this system to work, Article I(v) also provides for a system of 'temporary' IMF loans for members facing balance-of-payment difficulties.[21]

For our purposes, it is Article I(iii)'s reference to the need to 'avoid competitive exchange depreciation' which goes directly to the heart of the Chinese currency issue. It reflects the experience of the inter-war period, during which competitive depreciations in order to boost a nation's trade terms reflected a policy best summed up idiomatically: beggar thy neighbour and the Devil take the hindmost.

The key provision which had maintained the fixed currency value (so-called 'par value') system for the currencies of its members was Article IV. As it originally stood, it was based on a variation of the gold standard. Broadly speaking, the US dollar was pegged to gold and other currencies were pegged to the US dollar. Members were generally prohibited from revaluing their currencies by more than one per cent without IMF authorization. Article IV(3) as it stood imposed a duty on members to collaborate with the Fund to 'avoid exchange alteration'. Under the amended Article IV today, however, IMF members are now free to choose their own currency arrangements. The history to this is that, during the 1970s, exchange rate policies reverted to a high level of discretion in sovereign decision-making by IMF members in events taking place after the United States unilaterally announced on 15 August 1971 that the dollar would no longer be pegged to gold. Article IV was, in due course of time, amended.[22]

According to the Smithsonian Agreement in the autumn of 1971, a system of 'central rates' had originally been envisaged instead, together with a devaluation of the US 'dollar to gold' rate while other major currencies were to appreciate against the dollar. Fixed exchange rates would be preserved, but with wider margins for deviation. Following Britain's departure from the Smithsonian Agreement, by 1973 all the major currencies were in a float. The par value system had been relegated to history.[23] The so-called 'Second Amendment' to

---

[19] Hence, art. I(iii)'s reference to 'exchange stability'.
[20] J. W. Head, *Losing the Global Development War* (Leiden: Nijhoff, 2008), 105–6.
[21] *Ibid.*, 106.   [22] *Ibid.*
[23] A. Lowenfeld, *International Economic Law* (2nd edn, New York: Oxford University Press, 2008), 625–27.

the IMF Articles in 1978 now contains the version of Article IV which we have today.[24]

It is worth noting that the Committee of Twenty had originally proposed a further alternative – a system of 'symmetry'. This envisaged a system where excessive surpluses and deficits were *equally* to be avoided. This would have obligated 'surplus countries' to import more, stimulate domestic demand, revalue their currencies.[25] That such a system was not adopted shows that what we have today under Article IV was the result of deliberate policy choice. The obligations of a surplus country under the 'symmetry' proposal would have reflected precisely the measures which China has now been subjected to by way of moral pressure to adopt in light of its massive trade surplus. The point, as Professor Andreas Lowenfeld had so carefully described it, is that the IMF members chose otherwise, in favour of sovereign freedom. Some pegged their currencies against special drawing rights, some against the dollar, and some against each other while floating together.[26] Nations such as the United States, Japan, Canada and the United Kingdom have since moved to a system of 'managed' or 'dirty floats' (i.e. as opposed to having freely floating currency regimes),[27] as has China since 2005 under pressure from the Bush administration.

Legally speaking, there is nothing wrong with the PBC intervening to manage the value of the Chinese currency. The argument that the PBC is engaging in internationally wrongful behaviour has to proceed a little further; by drawing our attention to the language of Article IV(1)(iii)'s current 'anti-manipulation' rule. It states that IMF members '*shall avoid* manipulating exchange rates or the international monetary system in order to prevent effective balance of payments adjustment *or to gain an unfair competitive advantage over other members*' (emphasis added). The allegation against China is that the PBC is manipulating exchange rates '*to gain an unfair competitive advantage* over other members'. Thus, a judgement about that correlation needs to be made in applying that rule, and as we shall see below Professors Staiger and Sykes have questioned that correlation. 'Unfairness' is another difficult criterion which involves the making of a moral value judgement.[28]

---

[24] *Ibid.*, 633; see, more generally, 629–37 for an excellent account of the events leading to (and the effects of) the Second Amendment.

[25] *Ibid.*, 629–30.   [26] *Ibid.*, 634.   [27] *Ibid.*

[28] See further, for the nature, interpretation and application of such rules generally, W. J. Waluchow, *Inclusive Legal Positivism* (Oxford: Clarendon, 1994).

A trade lawyer if called upon to interpret this rule against the backdrop of the professional trade lawyer's sensibilities may be tempted to distinguish between 'manipulation' which may not be per se wrongful, and manipulation judged against what trade lawyers call an 'aims and effects' test.[29] One reason 'manipulation' per se may not be wrongful lies in the risk of overbreadth for treating it otherwise. IMF member states do routinely intervene in the currency markets. Talking about the possible need to look at 'aims and effects' would not be just a fanciful way of discussing the meaning of the rule in Article IV(1)(iii). Clearly the history of Article IV has led to a preference by IMF members to leave themselves a large degree of discretion in managing exchange rates. To the extent that many of them tend to intervene in the currency markets, such intervention may be said to amount to 'manipulation'. To be clear, it is not much of an answer for China to say that 'Everybody does it', even if China may be fully justified in saying so. One way around the problem is to note that, so far as the framers of the Articles were concerned, there must be something more than 'manipulation defined as simple intervention'. Accordingly, should the United States choose to design a national response to currency manipulation by, for example, imposing countervailing duties on Chinese goods, such currency interventions by China must still be shown to have been intended to have and/or produce the effect of having an unfair advantage in international trade.[30] This was the approach taken in the Currency Manipulation Prevention Act, which was proposed

---

[29] See J. Trachtman and A. Porges, 'Robert Hudec and Domestic Regulation: The Resurrection of "Aims and Effects"', *Journal of World Trade* 37(2003), 783.

[30] Other aspects of the language of art. IV(1) (my emphases in the extracts below) support a reading of an anti-manipulation 'rule' (i.e. 'shall...avoid') does not exist in a vacuum:

> Recognizing that the essential purpose of the international monetary system is to provide a framework that facilitates the exchange of goods, services, and capital among countries, and that sustains sound economic growth, and that a principal objective is the continuing *development of the orderly underlying conditions that are necessary for financial and economic stability*, each member undertakes to collaborate with the Fund and other members to assure orderly exchange arrangements and *to promote a stable system of exchange rates*. In particular, each member shall:
>
> (i) endeavor to direct its economic and financial policies toward the objective of fostering *orderly economic growth with reasonable price stability, with due regard to its circumstances*;
> (ii) seek to promote stability *by fostering* orderly underlying economic and financial conditions and *a monetary system that does not tend to produce erratic disruptions*;

in the US House of Representatives in 2003.[31] Section 6(1) defined currency manipulation as the manipulation of exchange rates by a country *in order to gain an unfair competitive advantage as stated in Article IV of the Articles of Agreement of the International Monetary Fund.*

The principal difficulty with the 'soft law regime' of international monetary cooperation, however, is that the IMF Articles do not provide for binding dispute resolution. Article IV(3) only states that the IMF can oversee compliance. Thus unilateral action, ostensibly taken to implement IMF obligations, would appear to be subject to even greater 'tolerance' under IMF rules than would necessarily be the case under global trade rules.

2.   Global trade rules: the World Trade Organization

In principle, tolerance would have no place under world trade rules (i.e. under the GATT 1994) wherever there is a clearly applicable rule (i.e. in both content and scope) prohibiting particular trade conduct. The task is to identify a clear, prohibitive rule. The usual complaint that the Chinese currency is undervalued involves saying that, as a result, Chinese goods become artificially cheap in exchange rate terms. In other words, an undervalued currency is an 'exchange subsidy' which distorts the price of Chinese exports.

(i)   'Currency dumping'

Brazil appears to have proposed a novel form of 'exchange rate antidumping measure' by referring to 'currency dumping',[32] but this is not

> (iii) avoid manipulating exchange rates or the international monetary system in order to prevent effective balance of payments adjustment or to gain an unfair competitive advantage over other members; and
>
> (iv) *follow exchange policies compatible with the undertakings under this Section.*

[31] H. R. 3269 8/10/2003.

[32] J. Leahy, 'Brazil to seek new arms for currency battle', *Financial Times*, 19 September 2011; D. Kinch, 'Brazil files currency dumping complaint in WTO, *Dow Jones Newswire*, 15 November 2011. This is based on a proposal of 20 September 2011 (WT/WFTDF/W/ 56), submitted to the WTO's Working Group on Trade, Debt and Finance; see 'Brazil Pushes Forward with Currency Discussion at the WTO', *Bridges Weekly Trade News Digest* 15(32) (28 September 2011). This was a follow-up to an earlier Brazilian proposal in May 2011, proposing that the WTO should examine the impact of fluctuating rates on international trade (*ibid.*). See further: 'The Relationship between Exchange Rates and International Trade: A Review of Economic Literature'. Note by the Secretariat, WT/ WGTDF/W/57, 27 September 2011; 'The Relationship between Exchange Rates and

currently a known legal concept. It is however more than mere shorthand for saying that China's currency interventions would provide *moral* justification for national trade remedy action (since dumping is not illegal under WTO rules). It could be, and probably is, taken to mean that currency manipulation should *lawfully* be taken account of in calculating dumping margins (i.e. in identifying sales at less than normal value).[33]

According to this argument, the PBC's policies should be taken into account in national anti-dumping investigations. To the extent this may be permissible under GATT–WTO rules (i.e. the rules of the Anti-Dumping Agreement), it would not amount to unilateral but permissive action. Article 2.4 of the Anti-Dumping Agreement merely requires, indeed it demands, a 'fair comparison'. And goes on, with my emphasis, to add that:

> Due allowance shall be made in each case, on its merits, for differences which affect price comparability, *including* differences in conditions and terms of sale, taxation, levels of trade, quantities, physical characteristics, and *any other differences which are also demonstrated to affect price comparability.*

This is perhaps the strongest case for saying that the PBC's policies violate national trade laws – i.e. for saying that it justifies internationally lawful national trade remedy action.[34] There are two aspects to be aware of. The first is Article 2.4.1 of the Anti-Dumping Agreement which states in part that: 'Fluctuations in exchange rates shall be ignored *and in an investigation the authorities shall allow exporters at least 60 days to have adjusted their export prices to reflect sustained movements in exchange rates during the period of investigation*' (my emphasis). However, the italicized portion suggests that the requirement that fluctuations should be ignored does not preclude taking currency misalignment or manipulation into account, but is instead intended to facilitate commercial certainty and trade. The opening words of that provision appear to support this interpretation: 'When the comparison under paragraph 4 requires a conversion of currencies,

---

International Trade: A Short Update of Recent Economic Literature'. Note by the Secretariat, WT/WGTDF/W/65, 18 July 2012.

[33] Another way of reading press reports of Brazilian statements may be to say that what Brazil really means is unlawful subsidization, not dumping. If so, the discussion below on anti-subsidy law will apply instead.

[34] Bhala, 'Virtues', 248.

such conversion should be made using the rate of exchange on the date of sale.' Second, Article 2.4.1 as a whole speaks of fairness, and the question that arises is whether it could mean the same thing as the reference to an 'unfair' trade advantage in Article IV(1)(iii) of the IMF Articles.

We will come back to the relationship between the GATT and IMF Articles. Suffice to note for now that 'fairness' is the ghost in the machine – be it in interpreting the IMF's anti-manipulation rule for its effects on trade or in determining the correct dumping margin calculation in light of the PBC's policies.

The anti-dumping route was the approach taken in the proposed Currency Exchange Rate Oversight Reform Act of 2007 (s. 1607).[35] Curiously, this approach has not been subjected to much scrutiny in the current debate; probably because it does call for unilateral action in the first instance whereas the weight of professional opinion appears to weigh in favour of 'tolerance' – i.e. against an overtly unilateral response. At the very least, it calls for a 'unilateral redefining of the rules'.[36] It remains, as at the end of 2011, a component of the proposed Currency Exchange Rate Oversight Reform Act 2011 (s. 1619).[37]

(ii)   Anti-subsidy law

The main way in which the Chinese currency issue seems to have been characterized however is by thinking about it as a kind of unlawful

---

[35] *Ibid.*, 247. See also the proposed Currency Exchange Rate Oversight Reform Act 2010, 'Bipartisan Group of Senators unveils new legislation to crack down on unfair currency manipulation by countries Like China', press release, Office of Senator Jim Webb, 16 March 2010; and in 2011, the proposed Currency Exchange Rate Oversight Reform Act 2011 (S. 1619), 'Currency Exchange Rate Oversight Reform Act 2011 (S. 1619) Legislative Bulletin', DPCC press release, 3 October 2011. At the time of writing, this latest proposal continues to languish in the House of Representatives; see e.g. 'Brown leads 21 senators in calling on speaker Boehner not to adjourn until the House passes Bipartisan China Currency Bill', Office of Senator Sherrod Brown, press release, 20 September 2012. For the 'bevy of Bills' since 2000, see Bhala, 'Virtue', 232.

[36] Bhala, 'Virtue', 232. Under Title VII of the Tariff Act 1930 in the USA, 'export price' and 'constructed export price', in the determination of sales lower than fair value are governed under USC §1677a, while 'normal value' is governed under USC §1677b. USC §1677(35) defines 'dumping margin'. The focus of any amendment should be on the definition of export price/constructed export price – i.e. an amendment of USC §1677a. See further, Bhala, 'Virtue', 247–8.

[37] 'Currency Exchange Rate Oversight Reform Act 2010 (S. 1619) Legislative Bulletin'.

subsidization.[38] Anti-subsidy law, contained principally in the WTO SCM Agreement would look to two categories of subsidization: (1) unlawful (Art. 3) and (2) actionable (Art. 5) subsidies. The SCM Agreement requires subsidization to be unlawful or actionable as a precondition to the imposition of countervailing duties. However, there is genuine doubt whether China's currency policies can be framed – from a legal viewpoint – as a subsidy in the first place notwithstanding that this is how it is primarily viewed.[39]

For it to amount to subsidization in the first place, that policy will have to be framed as a *financial contribution* pursuant to Article I.1(a)(1). But where there is (1) no real or potential direct transfer of funds involved (through some sort of grant, loan or equity infusion),[40] (2) government revenue is not foregone which otherwise would be due,[41] (3) the government (i.e. the PBC) is not providing goods or services other than the general available infrastructure within which Chinese economic activity takes place,[42] and (4) the Chinese government is not making payments to a funding mechanism, or is otherwise entrusting or directing a private entity to carry out any of the functions referred to in (1)–(3),[43] the requirements of Article I.1 of the SCM Agreement would not be met.

The argument here is that the Chinese government is providing renminbi at an artificially low cost to exporters – i.e. it is providing a

---

[38] Currency Exchange Rate Oversight Reform Act 2010; R. E. Lighthizer, 'Evaluating China's role in the World Trade Organization over the past decade', testimony before the US–China Economic and Security Review Commission, 9 June 2010 (calling China's policy 'currency manipulation' and stating that such manipulation is 'a prohibited export subsidy').

[39] Lighthizer, 'Evaluating China's role in the World Trade Organization'.

[40] See *Canada – Export Credits and Loan Guarantees for Regional Aircraft*, Panel Report, WT/DS222/R, 19 February 2002.

[41] See *US – Tax Treatment of 'Foreign Sales Corporations'*, Appellate Body Report, WT/DS108/AB/R, 24 February 2000 (hereafter, *US – FSC*)

[42] See *US – Final CVD Determination with Respect to Certain Softwood Lumber from Canada*, Panel Report, WT/DS257/R, 29 August 2003.

[43] This is the so-called 'anti-circumvention' device where governments might otherwise do that which they are prohibited to do (i.e. through the private sector), see the 'Hynix case', involving Korea's challenge to US countervailing duties imposed as a result of an alleged Korean bailout of Hynix semiconductors by entrusting or directing the bailout to private actors – *US – CVD Duties Investigation on Dynamic Random Access Memory Semiconductors from Korea*, Appellate Body Report, WT/DS296/AB/R, 20 July 2005. See further, J. F. Francois and D. Palmeter, 'US – CVD Investigation of DRAMS', *World Trade Review*, 7(2008), 219.

service, specifically an exchange service.[44] Unless this argument can be cast in terms of Article I.1(a)(1), there would be no 'subsidy' at the outset.

It might also be asked whether, *where there clearly is a benefit* (under Article I.1(b) of the SCM Agreement) conferred by a trade distorting measure,[45] a 'financial contribution' would need to be shown. The jurisprudence of the GATT–WTO has nonetheless been against such a broad reading. The point was tested in *US – Export Restraints* where the USA argued that by virtue of the distortive effect of Canadian export restraints, the USA was justified in imposing countervailing duties.[46] In that case, export restraints conferred a benefit on Canadian producers (i.e. it had a production relocation effect), but the difficulty lay in showing that there was a financial contribution. The United States defended itself in that case and lost the argument that in construing the requirement that a benefit should have been conferred, it would be justified in looking at the *effects* of the restrictions.[47] This litigation loss now haunts a further attempt to impose a broad reading of the SCM Agreement.

According to the panel, export restrictions could not be seen as a subsidy according to Article I.1. Doing so would deviate too much from the principles of the agreement. First, as stated in sub-paragraph (iv) of Article I.1, for a subsidy to be proved it is not sufficient that government intervention has led to a particular result. A financial contribution must still be shown, by reference to a distinct act of the government. A restriction on exports alone is not sufficient to satisfy this condition.[48] Second, while the Panel agreed that the purpose of the SCM Agreement was to curtail market distortions caused by sovereign intervention, not every intervention which might in theory distort trade would necessarily comprise a 'subsidy'. Taking such a broad approach would result in the replacement of the 'financial contribution' requirement altogether with any government action that could be understood to be a trade-distorting

[44] Benitah, 'China's Fixed Exchange Rate for the Yuan'.
[45] The converse case is that in *Canada – Measures Affecting the Export of Civilian Aircraft*, Appellate Body Report, WT/DS70/AB/R, 20 August 1999 (hereafter, 'Canada – Aircraft'), para.154, where the Appellate Body ruled that 'cost to Government' alone does not establish a benefit, which must be independently established.
[46] *United States – Measures Treating Exports Restraints as Subsidies*, Panel Report, WT/DS194/R, 29 June 2001 (hereafter *US – Export Restraints*).
[47] See L. Rubini, *The Definition of Subsidy and State Aid: WTO and EC Law in Comparative Perspective* (Oxford University Press, 2009), at 109ff.
[48] *US – Export Restraints*, para. 8.34.

subsidy.[49] Finally, when looking at the negotiation history of the SCM Agreement, the Panel noted that the term 'financial contribution' had been included precisely in order to prevent the countervailing of benefits from any and all government measures. Hence the panel rejected an approach that would merely focus on conferred benefits at the expense of giving an independent meaning to the term 'financial contribution'.[50]

Let us assume that the argument can be made out that there is a financial contribution via an exchange subsidy, and that there is also a benefit. Even so, a subsidy must either be (1) *prohibited* such as where it is *contingent upon export performance* or upon the use of domestic over imported goods (Art. 3.1), or (2) *actionable* where it causes adverse effects to the interests of other members (Art. 5). In the latter case – i.e. actionable subsidies – the subsidy must also be *specific enough* for the purposes of Article 2 of the SCM Agreement, although an export subsidy is automatically deemed under Article 2.3 of the SCM Agreement to be specific.

In seeking to show a *prohibited export subsidy*, it also needs to be shown that the PBC's policies are *'contingent upon'* in the sense of being 'conditional' or 'dependent' upon export performance.[51] This would be the case even if what we would be looking for is so-called de facto contingency – i.e. *evidence* that the policy has a 'close connection with' export performance, in the absence of a written measure which defines the recipients of the 'subsidy'.[52] As we shall see, the mere fact that an undervalued currency may have helped China boost its exports during the recent global economic recession, and may even have been intended to do so, would not automatically make such policies contingent in the sense of being dependent upon export performance. Putting aside the difficulty of proving the motivations underlying the PBC's policies, footnote 4 to the SCM Agreement states that: 'The mere fact that a subsidy is granted to enterprises which export shall not for that reason alone be considered to be an export subsidy.'

Thus, aside from the need to show that there has been the grant of a subsidy (i.e. the requirements of a 'financial contribution' and ensuing

---

[49] *Ibid.*, paras. 8.62–8.63.   [50] *Ibid.*, para. 8.73.
[51] Trachtman, 'Yuan to Fight about It?'. For the WTO jurisprudence, see e.g. *Canada – Aircraft*, para. 166.
[52] *Australia – Subsidies Provided to Producers and Exporters of Automotive Leather*, Panel Report, WT/DS126/R, 16 June 1999, para. 9.55.

'benefit'), the subsidy must be 'tied to'[53] a certain 'actual or anticipated exportation or export earnings'.[54] The meaning of this requirement was clarified in the *Canada - Aircraft* case. There, the Appellate Body ruled that such subsidy must be *limited to, or restricted to* certain export conditions.[55] Herein lies the real difficulty. It would seem that, at best, the case against China is the other way round; the commercial (i.e. export) performance of Chinese manufacturers is dependent upon PBC policies. The Appellate Body added the following qualifier: 'It does not suffice to demonstrate solely that a government granting a subsidy *anticipated* that exports would result.'[56] In a later phase in that litigation, the Appellate Body reiterated that view: 'we have...stated that it is not sufficient to show that a subsidy is granted in the *knowledge*, or with the anticipation, that exports will result', but that at most the 'export orientation of the recipient' may be taken into account as a relevant fact.[57]

Any attempt to pursue a claim against China on this ground, or to defend countervailing duties, must therefore show *more than* that the PBC anticipated or knew that its policies would (also) result in higher export earnings. However, the subsidy is also available to other persons holding dollars. This raises the question of whether the subsidy so far as exporters are concerned is, as a result, non-contingent. We return to this in the discussion of the *US - FSC* case, below.

Alternatively, the claim could be made that the PBC's policies would constitute an *actionable* subsidy, whether or not it is an export subsidy. Here, the SCM Agreement requires a subsidy to be 'specific', in order for it to be actionable. The difficulty lies in saying that the PBC's currency policies are specific to an enterprises or industry, or group of enterprises and industries.[58] Indeed, the allegation is that it boosts all Chinese exports of whatever kind. It is precisely this specificity rule which the proposed Currency Exchange Rate Oversight Reform Act 2011 (s. 1619) targets as an unnecessary 'bright line' rule, in the apparent belief that the US Commerce Department has been too conservative in its reading of

---

[53] *US - Subsidies on Upland Cotton*, Appellate Body Report, WT/DS267/AB/R, para. 572.

[54] *Canada - Aircraft*, para. 169.   [55] *Ibid.*, para, 171.   [56] *Ibid.* (my emphasis).

[57] *Canada - Aircraft (Article 21. 5 - Brazil)*, WT/DS70/AB/RW, paras. 48, 51 (my emphasis).

[58] Trachtman, 'Yuan Fight About It?'; *US - Final Countervailing Duty Determination with respect to Certain Softwood Lumber from Canada*, Panel Report, WT/DS257/R, 29 August 2003, paras. 7.119–7.122.

the specificity rule.[59] Specificity must be proved in the case of actionable subsidies, but is assumed where it can be said that an export subsidy is involved. We have already seen that it would, on the face of it, be difficult to argue that the PBC's policies amount to an export subsidy, *even* if it could be said to amount to a subsidy. The framers of the Currency Exchange Rate Oversight Reform Act 2011 have, in this regard, mounted a further argument; relying instead on the Appellate Body's ruling in the *US – FSC* case.[60] While there are no specifics on their precise thinking, there is mention of such reliance and we may surmise what the argument would actually look like.

In the *US – FSC* case, the Appellate Body did not discuss specificity as such, but the United States had argued that, in order to be contingent upon export performance, the impugned measure – the US Foreign Sales Corporation (FSC) Tax – cannot benefit exporters and non-exporters alike which in that case it did.[61] The Appellate Body ruled that this, however, did not preclude the tax from being a prohibited export subsidy where it applies to exporters.[62] Thus, reasoning further from that conclusion, just because the PBC's policies benefit exporters and non-exporters alike does not make it non-specific. This ruling weighs in favour of treating the PBC's policies as an exchange subsidy to exporters.

However, the Obama administration – without entering into specific details – has urged caution stating that it wanted 'to make sure the legislation wouldn't violate World Trade Organization rules'.[63] Similarly, the views expressed by international economic lawyers have been sceptical. That is probably correct, on balance. Even if the point about the *US – FSC* case is correct, it does not get around the need to establish a subsidy – i.e. a financial contribution.

The jury is out on whether an anti-subsidy argument will succeed. A 'financial contribution' needs to be found, and it may or may not be found through arguing that what the PBC has done is to provide such a contribution through an exchange subsidy. Specificity needs to be established, and if it is to be done by saying that specificity is to be deemed to exist because what is involved is an export subsidy, then the subsidy

---

[59] 'Currency Exchange Rate Oversight Reform Act 2011 (S. 1619) Legislative Bulletin', DPCC press release, 3 October 2011.
[60] *Ibid.*   [61] *US – FSC*, paras. 110, 114–115.   [62] *Ibid.*, para. 119.
[63] J. A. Favole, 'Obama urges caution on Currency Bill', *Wall Street Journal*, 7 October 2011; A. Beattie, 'China Currency Bill on path to conflict after Senate vote', *Financial Times*, 7 October 2011.

would still have to be shown to be an export subsidy over and above the fact that exporters benefit. It may not suffice to point out that the law does not preclude the argument from succeeding just because non-exporting industries also benefit. It certainly does not suffice to show, merely, that the PBC could have anticipated the benefit to exporters. Doubt about whether anti-subsidy action can be taken against China counsels rule-based 'tolerance' towards the PBC's policies.

V. Disciplinary fragmentation and 'rule-tolerance', distinguished from disciplinary fracture and rule abdication

During the pre-Judicature Act era in Ireland, Lord Killanin, then Chief Justice of the Common Pleas, advised plaintiffs who had technicality on their side but no merit to bring themselves before the Barons of the Exchequer; for these barons were very technical. If a plaintiff has merit instead but not technicality, they should go to the Common Pleas. But if plaintiffs have neither, they should just proceed to the Queen's Bench for there is no knowing what the judges there will do.[64] Were His Lordship alive today to comment on the Chinese currency, the first category would have suggested the IMF as the right forum, the second category would have suggested the WTO, and the third would have suggested unilateral sovereign action.

Alan Greenspan has called the PBC's policies 'the definition of currency manipulation',[65] suggesting that the issue falls within the purview of the IMF.[66] Recall that Article IV's 'anti-manipulation' rule is effectively the only 'hard law' rule which is framed in imperative terms (i.e. 'shall...avoid...'). In the absence of any other equally hard rule, the Chinese currency issue must be forced within it. But this has, understandably, not been the position of the Obama administration, even if observers have argued that it should not be inferred that the administration does not consider China a currency manipulator simply because it has avoided calling it such.[67] The real reason may be that while China devalued the yuan from 2009 to the first half of 2010 – i.e. at the height of the crisis – from the summer of 2010 onwards, the yuan was allowed to

---

[64] E. Marjoribanks, *Edward Carson QC* (Edinburgh: Emslie, 2011), at 25.

[65] M. Drajem, 'Greenspan says China currency mistakenly used to boost jobs', *Bloomberg*, 17 June 2011.

[66] Sanford, 'Currency Manipulation'.

[67] 'US Declines to say China manipulates its currency', *New York Times*, 27 November 2012.

rise again in the wake of inflationary pressures in China. The IMF too has shifted its stance, by reclassifying the Chinese currency as being merely 'moderately undervalued' in contrast with its conclusion that the currency was 'substantially undervalued' at the start of the crisis.[68] This fact was observed by Barack Obama when expressing caution over passage of the proposed Currency Exchange Rate Oversight Reform Act during 2011.[69] It seems that moral suasion behind the scenes may have had an effect, just as a similar problem with Japan two decades ago had led to the Plaza and Louvre Accords.

Trachtman also suggests taking the issue out of the WTO altogether – i.e. to the IMF, although he does not say so expressly – yet Bhala damns the IMF with faint praise and only counsels seeking a formal decision of the IMF Executive Board as that can only help but could hardly hinder subsequent WTO litigation.[70] Staiger and Sykes have also pointed out the IMF's bias against confrontation,[71] but more importantly the ineffectiveness of its primary sanction – i.e. cutting a People's Republic of China, which already has trillions of reserves, off from access to IMF funding.[72] They also argue that there is no precedent for the application of IMF rules in such a situation, although this is probably not strictly true.[73]

As for taking the issue to the WTO, Brazil has raised the issue before the Working Group on Trade, Debt and Finance. In contrast, Bhala has counselled WTO litigation as an action befitting a responsible nation which believes in – and ought to promote – the rule of law in international affairs:[74]

> Is it not the duty of a courageous trade empire to assume the risks of legal uncertainty, litigate key issues, and thereby enhance the rule of law?

Trachtman counsels against this, saying the United States will likely lose (a view apparently shared in the White House);[75] or that litigation would just take too long, even assuming the United States wins.

What Trachtman, An Hertogen and Bhala all seem to accept is that trade rules do not clearly weigh against China. But, in the heat of public political debate, that message should not be confused with the total absence of trade rule regulation – i.e. that 'anything goes'. Instead, the

---

[68] 'Renminbi (yuan)', *New York Times*.   [69] Favole, 'Obama urges caution'.
[70] Bhala, 'Virtue', 224–8.
[71] Staiger and Sykes, '"Currency Manipulation" and World Trade', 27.   [72] *Ibid.*, 28.
[73] *Ibid.*, 27–8. For the 'Swedish case', in 1980, see Lowenfeld, *International Economic Law*, 636.
[74] Bhala, 'Virtue', 221.   [75] Beattie, 'China Currency Bill'.

ambiguity of trade rules means that while some such as Hertogen have highlighted the importance of discussions at the WTO,[76] others like Trachtman have gauged the strength of any proposed litigation which will inevitably follow American trade remedy action accordingly. Yet others such as Staiger and Sykes question the assumed correlation between currency policies and their assumed trade effects; like Bhala and Trachtman, they are critical of suggestions for unilateral trade remedy action not simply because of the rules, but because there is no normative justification for doing so.

It may be argued, however, that trade rule tolerance of China's currency policies is accompanied by the very opposite of one importance sense of disciplinary fragmentation. Fragmentation is typically viewed as involving overlapping and competing sites of rule governance – of too many regulators, as opposed to too little regulation. In the present case, not only is trade regulation ineffectual, so too is the regime for international monetary cooperation. But we need not be pessimistic about trade law. Anti-dumping action is one answer, and more will be said in the Conclusion below. It is also unclear why such little credence has been given to the IMF's role in the writings surveyed.

The Currency Exchange Rate Oversight Reform Act 2011 rightly envisages a role for the IMF in the context of national trade remedy action. According to the proposed Act, trade remedy action will be premised on the IMF's views about currency misalignment. The reason for scepticism, according to Staiger and Sykes, is that the sort of currency misalignment addressed by the IMF is not what GATT–WTO rules contemplate. If true, the picture that emerges is not fragmentation in the sense of competing and overlapping regimes, but of a *fractured international economic order*, with gaps in between, disassociated and mismatched parts. But this is not the case. GATT Article XV.4, mentioned earlier, is a provision which clearly contemplates a strong linkage between the IMF's work and the WTO's.

Trachtman has drawn an analogy with the nullification and impairment clause, and applies a specific assumption about the correct benchmark for measuring a denial of the legitimate expectation of China's trading partners. First, Article XV:4 speaks of a frustration of the intent of the GATT provisions not (or at least, not directly of) the legitimate

---

[76] Hertogen, 'The Forgotten GATT Articles'.

expectations of China's trading partners.[77] But even if that is what is meant, and Trachtman may yet be correct, saying the benchmark is the yuan rate in 2001 may be difficult. It could be like saying the benchmark for showing a surge of imports justifying safeguard action is the tariff rate of the safeguard user in 1947. There is at least a question about the appropriate, normative benchmark. China's dollar peg was removed in 2005, the yuan rose, then in 2009 to 2010 it was considered to have been significantly undervalued before rising again. While the currency issue has been a live issue since China's accession, the crisis and ensuing devaluation is what has most recently reignited the controversy in the run-up to an election year. What the Currency Exchange Rate Oversight Reform Act 2011 seems to do is different, which is to signify the role of the IMF in taking any trade action but it does not appear to hinge on GATT Article XV:4 which prohibits exchange action which frustrates the intention of the GATT, and trade action which frustrates the intention of the IMF Articles.

We should not underestimate the central role of the IMF. In the context of GATT Article XV:4 especially, the relationship between the IMF and the then stillborn ITO was discussed in earnest at the Geneva Conference. This led to the delegates at Havana choosing substantial deference to the IMF.[78] Notwithstanding the accuracy of Bhala's view that if that provision is disputed, the WTO panel or Appellate Body would appear to have the final word on its legal interpretation, and to that extent is not 'bound' by the IMF's views.[79] Article XV: 4's difficulty, particularly when read in the context of its Ad Note, is as follows.

---

[77] That the nullification and impairment clause may have independent force of application to the currency issue is another matter. See GATT art. XXIII:1(b), and art. 26.1 of the Dispute Settlement Understanding. One argument may be that currency devaluations affect *ad valorem* tariffs and thereby nullify or impair benefits under GATT art. II (tariff bindings).

[78] D. A. Irwin, P. C. Mavroidis and A. O. Sykes, *The Genesis of the GATT* (Cambridge University Press, 2008), 155–6; J. H. Jackson, *World Trade and the Law of GATT* (Charlottesville, VA: Michie, 1969), 693ff.

[79] In other words, in the case of true conflict/regime fragmentation in the sense of overlapping and competing international authorities (Bhala, 'Virtue', 224–5). However, it might be asked if art. XV:2 imposes an obligation on all contracting parties (i.e. WTO members) to accept the determinations of the Fund as to whether an exchange action violates the IMF Articles. If so, a true conflict would arise only where trade action is involved which is said to violate the intent of the IMF Articles under art. XV:4. An exchange action which violates the intent of the GATT falls squarely within the WTO's jurisdiction.

Assuming that the PBC's policies constitute exchange action, could they also comprise trade action? Arguably, it is only where they do that the IMF Articles are brought into the interpretation of Article XV:4. What is beyond doubt is that the GATT framers contemplated, and GATT practice confirms the application of IMF disciplines even to those GATT Contracting Parties who were not IMF members – i.e. the IMF Articles would somehow apply to GATT Contracting Parties where the 'trade' action of a Contracting Party violates the intent of the IMF Articles.[80] What remains uncertain is the role of the IMF when 'exchange' action violates the GATT–WTO. It would appear from its drafting history, that the intention was to carve out the respective spheres of the GATT's and the IMF's authority where an 'exchange' (as opposed to trade) action is involved.

Yet the question concerning the IMF and GATT–WTO relationship extends beyond interpreting Article XV:4. As we have seen in discussing the anti-dumping option, is 'fairness' in Article 2.4 of the Anti-Dumping Agreement to be read in conjunction with Article IV(1)(iii) of the IMF Articles' anti-manipulation rule?

VI. Conclusion

Franciscus de Victoria was one of the earliest international lawyers to argue that when the rules run out, states are free to do what they like.[81] In the early part of the twentieth century, the Permanent Court of International Justice also had occasion to decide that in the absence of a prohibitive rule, states are at liberty to act.[82] The danger today is that where trade regulation and the rules on monetary cooperation fall somewhat short, the impression created is that of a regulatory free-for-all. This would be misleading. Countervailing subsidies as a response to

---

[80] Jackson, *World Trade*, 486ff. art. XV:2 appears to impose an obligation on the contracting parties as a whole, and does not specifically proscribe exchange action which violates the intent of the GATT and trade action which violates the intent of the IMF Articles.

[81] de Victoria, First Reflectio, 151 ('everything is lawful which is not prohibited or which is not injurious or hurtful to others in some other way').

[82] 'The Case of the S.S. Lotus', PCIJ Reports, Series A(1927), No. 10, 18 ('The rules of law binding upon States . . . emanate from their own free will as expressed in conventions or by usages generally accepted as expressing principles of law and established in order to regulate the relations between these co-existing independent communities or with a view to the achievement of common aims. Restrictions upon the independence of States cannot therefore be presumed').

the PBC's policies will most likely be unlawful. Anti-dumping action which takes currency misalignment (and therefore the linkages between IMF and WTO regulation) into account could yet survive WTO scrutiny.

Attempts to invoke provisions like GATT Article XV:4 or to peg trade action against IMF surveillance findings of currency misalignment speak against the view that a regulatory free-for-all results when the rules run out. Broader principles, sometimes more implicit than we like, play a role. At the very least, they indicate, even if they do not compel,[83] how the legal–professional viewpoint should address situations of legal uncertainty.

Recent writing on the history of international law has tried to cast light on how the discipline competed with an eighteenth-century rival – economic science as a competing body of understanding about the management of international affairs.[84] It serves as a useful reminder that 'we are not alone'. Imagine a conversation between an economist working in the WTO and a lawyer. Imagine the reactions of the economist to the assertion that unilateral sovereign action is permissible in the absence of prohibitive international rules; and that this is so even if we accept that unilateral action is generally to be shunned. The economist might ask if the international trade lawyer does not believe in Smith and Ricardo anymore, or if the lawyer has some special insight which the economist proclaims does not yet exist in how currency misalignment disadvantages trade.[85]

I have sought to argue that, here at least, the normative prescriptions of international law do not run out so easily. While recognizing that economists would generally find the notion of unilateral action against China in the absence of trade rule violation abhorrent for its welfare-reducing effect, international lawyers too are not so unaware of these dangers of unilateral action. It is probably no coincidence that the writers surveyed in this chapter have invariably weighed against unilateral action. Why?

---

[83] In an 'all-or-nothing' fashion (see R. Dworkin, *Taking Rights Seriously* (London: Duckworth, 1977), 24–5).

[84] M. Koskenniemi, 'The Advantage of Treaties: International Law in the Enlightenment', *Edinburgh Law Review*, 13(2009), 64–7.

[85] See 'The Relationship between Exchange Rates and International Trade: A Review of Economic Literature'. Note by the Secretariat, WT/WGTDF/W/57, 27 September 2011; 'The Relationship between Exchange Rates and International Trade: A Short Update of Recent Economic Literature. Note by the Secretariat, WT/WGTDF/W/65, 18 July 2012.

Unilateral action in light of legal uncertainty is abhorrent because even if anti-subsidy or anti-dumping action against China were to be lawful, trade lawyers know to look not only for rules, but the best view of the rules – i.e. their normative justification.[86]

We can test this thought further.

Let us just assume, for the sake of illustration, that it would be harder to make out an anti-subsidy argument than an anti-dumping argument, and that anti-dumping action would most likely be lawful whereas anti-subsidy action would most likely be unlawful. We can then point out that since WTO members have also chosen to recognize that dumping is unfair, it would probably be 'inappropriate' to calculate a dumping margin which took no account of currency interventions. But if that were all, that normative justification would *in principle* apply to anti-subsidy action too. We might then reason further that since even 'harmful' forms of unilateral action could incentivize the trading nations of the world to 'repair' any 'gaps' in the law through further litigation or lawmaking, unilateral, countervailing duties too would be justifiable on the basis that using countervailing duties would end up improving the scope and depth of trade law regulation. Particularly if there is already an accepted moral–political justification – a fairness-based consideration – for anti-dumping and anti-subsidy action, then does it really matter if the law supports one form of unilateral action, but probably not another? Such an argument goes too far, for it would involve illegality under the present rules, as well as welfare-reducing effects. 'Rule tolerance', in the sense of admitting gaps in legal regulation, is therefore different from countenancing harmful rule-breaking. The reason we have rule tolerance, or admit that the currency issue involves reading the darker pages of the GATT text, is because global law matters. Nineteenth-century fears of Russian circumvention of US. sugar tariffs by subsidizing Russian exporters led to the first anti-subsidy rules,[87] but – still relying on our hypothesis that anti-subsidy law does not, today, permit action against China – decisions about unilateral trade remedy action at that time did not have to contend with global rule-breaking. The situation is different today, with the existence of the SCM Agreement. Assuming that such countervailing duty action would be unlawful, proposing unilateral action would be to propose conscious law-breaking.

---

[86] R. Dworkin, *Law's Empire* (Cambridge MA: Belknap, 1986).
[87] P. D. Ehrenhaft, 'Remedies Against Unfair Int'l Trade Practices', SF24 ALI-ABA 203.

In contrast, anti-dumping action – we are still assuming its legality – would not be 'unilateral' sovereign action at all but 'legally permissible' action. To the extent that anti-dumping action based on fair value comparisons is a familiar part of trade law regulation – i.e. how we justify the rules of trade regulation – it is also to that extent normatively justifiable. Put simply, if global anti-dumping rules allow for trade remedy action against China, then the conventional political–morality of the GATT–WTO also supports it.[88]

In the end, rule tolerance and the fragmented nature of the discipline suggests that we do not ignore evaluations of the best moral–political course of action when venturing into virgin areas of regulation, drawing from our experience of trade law's past. Doing so here suggests a response under anti-dumping law, which appears clothed in sufficient legal permission and grounded in fairness-based considerations. If this impression proves to be incorrect in later litigation brought by China, greater rule clarity will only result. Indeed, China itself could consider taking similar action against its trading partners, if not now then possibly in the future. That is how our system works, and how trade law works itself pure.[89]

---

[88] I am therefore not engaging those who would say that anti-dumping action is never morally justified; see Hudec, 'Mirror, Mirror'.

[89] *Omychund* v. *Barker* (1744) 26 Eng. Rep. 15, 24; 1 A. and K. 22, 23 (*per* Lord Mansfield).

PART II

Trade and some of its linkages

7

Roadblocks and pathways towards inter-state cooperation in increasing interdependence

AN HERTOGEN

This chapter argues that imbalances in international rules and principles governing the exercise of sovereignty block effective cooperation in response to problems of increasing interdependence. The argument is illustrated through the example of monetary management policies, i.e. policies through which states manage the supply of money to their economies. As the global financial crisis (GFC) has made clear, states' monetary management policies can adversely affect other states. Despite lofty pronouncements at the G20 about the need for cooperation, states have so far agreed on few effective limits on their monetary sovereignty to avoid these negative effects.

Section I outlines the instances of interdependence central to the discussion. Section II performs a reality check of the traditional narrative of international law as a liberal system of states. It will be argued that imbalances have arisen due to overly restrictive limits on states' ability to protect their domestic affairs against the negative externalities of other states' monetary management policies combined with only few limits on how they exercise their monetary sovereignty. Section III advocates reinterpretation as a pathway to correct the imbalances in the exercise of sovereignty. Section IV discusses the substantive drivers of reinterpretation and outcomes thereof. Section V concludes.

I. Economic interdependence central to this chapter

States manage the money supply in their economies through their monopoly over the monetary base,[1] through capital adequacy ratios for banks, and, in states operating a fractional reserve banking system, through

---

[1] The 'monetary base' consists of cash and the central bank reserves of commercial banks (M. Burda and C. Wyplosz, *Macroeconomics: A European Text* (4th edn, Oxford University Press, 2005), 203).

reserve ratios.[2] Both ratios determine how much credit banks can create. Capital adequacy ratios define the amount of capital banks need to maintain relative to their risk-weighted assets, such as the loans they extend. A requirement to hold more capital acts as a brake on their ability to extend credit. Reserve ratios require banks to hold a certain amount of cash or other liquid assets, defined as a percentage of their deposit liabilities, in reserve to ensure sufficient liquidity when depositors call in their funds. As a result, reserve ratios limit the aggregate money supply.[3]

Due to the liberalization of capital, trade in services and investment, financial institutions now provide credit beyond their home state and companies borrow from financial institutions in other states. This has intensified interdependence between states with monetary management policies increasingly causing negative externalities for other states. For example, when Iceland deregulated its banks without an appropriate supervisory infrastructure in place,[4] its banks went on a borrowing spree. In the process, they built up considerable currency and maturity mismatches. When they could no longer refinance their loans after the GFC hit, a bank run occurred, including on their branches in other European Economic Area (EEA) states where they had offered high-interest on-call savings accounts.[5]

Further, trade liberalization has created a collective action problem with respect to regulation of financial institutions, because states can inflict a competitive externality on other states by adopting more lenient regulation than other states.[6] Competitive pressures have already resulted in low reserve ratios.[7] Capital adequacy ratios pose a similar collective action problem.[8]

---

[2] 'Fractional Reserve Banking', in J. Black, N. Hashimzade and G. Myles (eds.), *A Dictionary of Economics* (Oxford University Press, 2009).

[3] W. A. Baumol and J. S. Blinder, *Economics: Principles and Policy* (12th edn, Ohio, OH: South-Western Cengage Learning, 2012), 630, 654.

[4] J. Danielsson and G. Zoega, 'Entranced by banking' (*VoxEU*, 2009) www.voxeu.org/index. php?q=node/3029

[5] A. Sibert, 'The Icesave dispute' (*VoxEU*, 2010) www.voxeu.org/index.php?q=node/4611; M. Waibel, 'Iceland's financial crisis – *quo vadis* international law' (*ASIL Insights*, 2010) www.asil.org/insights100301.cfm

[6] J. P. Trachtman, 'The International Law of Financial Crisis: Spillovers, Subsidiarity, Fragmentation and Cooperation', *Journal of International Economic Law*, 13(2010), 719, 723.

[7] Burda and Wyplosz, *Macroeconomics*, 205, 209.

[8] R. Kreitner, 'The Jurisprudence of Global Money', *Theoretical Inquiries in Law* 11 (2010), 177, 199; D. K. Tarullo, *Banking on Basel: The Future of International Financial Regulation* (Washington, DC: Peterson Institute for International Economics, 2008), 45–6.

II.   International law's response to externalities: theory and practice

International law is often described as a liberal system of sovereign states.[9] Under this narrative, states have the ultimate legal authority to decide, free from external interference, over their domestic affairs. The concept of 'monetary sovereignty' expresses this idea of sovereignty with respect to monetary management policies.[10]

Since sovereignty is applied in a world of about 200 states, it is limited by other states' equal sovereignty.[11] To this end, and reflecting its liberal nature, international law has long known 'rules of abstention', such as the principle of non-intervention and the no harm principle.[12] If the 'rules of abstention' are insufficient to deal with the transboundary effects of a state's actions, the traditional thinking is that states will consent to agreements determining how sovereignty can be exercised.

In practice, few rules of abstention or specialized rules of international law limit monetary sovereignty, making it easier to inflict externalities on other states, as section 1 discusses. Section 2 describes how limitations in trade liberalization agreements on states' ability to regulate financial services offered within their territory exacerbate this situation.

---

[9] L. Henkin, *International Law: Politics and Values* (Leiden: Nijhoff, 1995), 100–1; M. Koskenniemi, *From Apology to Utopia: The Structure of International Legal Argument* (Cambridge University Press, 2005), 93–4; G. Simpson, 'Two Liberalisms', *European Journal of International Law* 12 (2001), 537, 540–1.

[10] Case Concerning the Payment of Various Serbian Loans Issued in France and Case Concerning the Payment in Gold of the Brazilian Federal Loans Issued in France (1929) PCIJ Series A 20/21, 44; F. Gianviti, 'Current Legal Aspects of Monetary Sovereignty', in International Monetary Fund (ed.), *Current Developments in Monetary and Financial Law*, vol. IV (2004), 4–5; R. M. Lastra, *Legal Foundations of International Monetary Stability* (Oxford University Press, 2006) 16–18, 22–3.

[11] M. R. Fowler and J. M. Bunck, *Law, Power, and the Sovereign State: The Evolution and Application of the Concept of Sovereignty* (Pennsylvania State University Press, 1995), 44–5; U. K. Preuss, 'Equality of States – Its Meaning in a Constitutionalized Global Order' *Chicago Journal of International Law* 9 (2008), 17, 27.

[12] B. Fassbender, 'Sovereignty and Constitutionalism in International Law', in Walker (ed.), *Sovereignty in Transition* (Oxford: Hart Publishing 2003), 117; W. Friedmann, *The Changing Structure of International Law* (New York: Columbia University Press, 1964), 60–2.

1. A lack of limits on states' exercise of their monetary sovereignty

(i)   Difficulties applying the rules of abstention

The principle of non-intervention prohibits states from intervening in the internal or external affairs of other states.[13] 'Intervention' is however narrowly defined; it must be coercive,[14] with the intention of forcing policy change in the target state.[15] Coercion is broader than the use of armed force,[16] and could thus exist when states use monetary management policies to effect structural change elsewhere. Instances thereof are, however, uncommon.[17]

Second, the no harm principle, as currently understood, is ill equipped to deal with economic interdependence. When discussing its Draft Principles on Allocation of Loss and on its Draft Principles on Prevention, the International Law Commission considered the inclusion of economic harm too delicate.[18] Special Rapporteur Quentin-Baxter added that although the principle could be useful to balance 'liberty of action' and 'freedom from adverse effects' in the economic area,[19]

> there is no possibility of proceeding inductively from the evidence of State practice in the field of the physical uses of territory to the formulation of rules or guidelines in the economic field.

To invoke the no harm principle successfully, affected states must establish a causal link between the harm experienced and the policies of the

---

[13] UN General Assembly, *Declaration on Principles of International Law concerning Friendly Relations and Co-operation among States in accordance with the Charter of the United Nations*, GA Res. 2625, UN GAOR, 25th sess., 1883rd plen. mtg (1970) ['Friendly Relations Declaration']; Case Concerning Military and Paramilitary Activities in and against Nicaragua (*Nicaragua* v. *United States of America*) (Merits) (27 June 1986), *ICJ Reports* 14, para. 205 [*Nicaragua*].

[14] *Nicaragua*, para. 205.

[15] M. Jamnejad and M. Wood, 'The Principle of Non-Intervention', *Leiden Journal of International Law* 22 (2009), 345, 348.

[16] The Friendly Relations Declaration prohibits 'armed intervention and all other forms of interference'; *Nicaragua*, para. 209.

[17] See J. Kirshner, 'Currency and Coercion in the Twenty-First Century', in D. Andrews (ed.), *International Monetary Power* (New York: Cornell University Press, 2006), 142–7 for an example from Iraq in 1993.

[18] ILC, *Fourth Report on International Liability for Injurious Consequences Arising out of Acts Not Prohibited by International Law*, by Mr. Robert Q. Quentin-Baxter, UN Doc. A/CN.4/373 (1983), 204–5, para. 212.

[19] *Ibid.*, 205, para. 215.

affecting state.[20] There is no prescribed standard of causation,[21] but a traditional test is a 'but for' test.[22] This test does not work well in the multilateral context of financial stability where causal links are often insufficiently understood and where adverse effects often result from complex interactions between the actions of states and those of private economic actors.

(ii)   A lack of specialized international agreements

The obligations regarding members' monetary management policies in Article IV(1) of the Articles of Agreement of the International Monetary Fund (IMF)[23] are only 'best effort obligations'.[24] The IMF exercises bilateral surveillance,[25] but has few tools available to address non-compliance, particularly against members that are its creditors rather than borrowers.[26]

The Basel Committee on Banking Supervision ('Basel Committee') has developed minimum capital adequacy ratios for internationally active banks.[27] Strictly speaking, however, the Basel Accords are only gentlemen's

---

[20] H. Xue, *Transboundary Damage in International Law* (Cambridge University Press, 2003), 86–7.

[21] C. Voigt, 'State Responsibility for Climate Change Damages', *Nordic Journal of International Law* 77(2008), 1, 16.

[22] P. Barton, 'State Responsibility and Climate Change: Could Canada Be Liable to Small Island States?', *Dalhousie Journal of Legal Studies*, 11(2002), 83.

[23] Articles of Agreement of the International Monetary Fund, 22 July 1945, 2 UNTS 39, art. IV(1)(i) and (iii) ['IMF Articles of Agreement'].

[24] B. Mercurio and C. Z. N. Leung, 'Is China a "Currency Manipulator"?: The Legitimacy of China's Exchange Regime under the Current International Legal Framework', *International Lawyer* 43(2009), 1257, 1282.

[25] IMF, *Bilateral Surveillance over Members' Policies – 2007 Decision* (15 June 2007), at www.imf.org/external/pubs/ft/sd/index.asp?decision=13919-(07/51), para. 5 ['2007 Surveillance Decision']. Its successor, the *Integrated Surveillance Decision*, was adopted on 18 July 2012, and entered into force on 18 January 2013, see International Monetary Fund, *IMF Executive Board Adopts New Decision on Bilateral and Multilateral Surveillance* (30 July 2012), at www.imf.org/external/np/sec/pn/2012/pn1289.htm

[26] C. Herrmann, 'Don Yuan: China's "Selfish" Exchange Rate Policy and International Economic Law', in C. Herrmann and J. P. Terhechte (eds.), *European Yearbook of International Economic Law 2010* (Heidelberg: Springer, 2010), 45; A. Mattoo and A. Subramanian, 'Currency Undervaluation and Sovereign Wealth Funds: A New Role for the World Trade Organization', Peterson Institute for International Economics Working Paper Series, 7.

[27] The latest version is Basel Committee on Banking Supervision, *Basel III: A Global Regulatory Framework for More Resilient Banks and Banking Systems* (December 2010), at www.bis.org/publ/bcbs189.pdf

agreements between the Basel Committee's members.[28] Nevertheless, pressure from the IMF, the World Bank, Basel Committee members,[29] and financial markets[30] has led to their adoption by more than one hundred states. Thus, while not constituting formal international obligations, the Basel Accords' minimum requirements constrain states' monetary management policies. Nevertheless, states retain some freedom because what constitutes 'capital' has not been harmonized.[31] Moreover, competitiveness is not determined solely by capital adequacy ratios, but is also affected by tax laws, accounting standards and by the alternative safety nets for financial institutions, which have not yet been harmonized.[32]

2. Limits on affected states' ability to protect domestic affairs

A second factor in our reality check of the traditional narrative of international law as a liberal system are the limits on states' domestic regulatory autonomy in trade liberalization agreements. WTO members' obligations under the General Agreement on Trade in Services (GATS)[33] limit states' ability to restrict inflows of foreign money or to impose minimum regulatory requirements on all banks active within their territory, whether through a branch or a subsidiary (sections (i)–(iii)), shifting the weight of protecting states' domestic affairs to the exceptions (section (iv)).

(i)   Restrictions on qualitative measures

To protect their domestic affairs against the negative externalities of insufficient regulation in another state, states could consider, for example, restricting the remote supply of financial services to financial

---

[28] For a list, see Bank for International Settlements, *About the Basel Committee*, www.bis.org/bcbs/index.htm

[29] R. Bismuth, 'Financial Sector Regulation and Financial Services Liberalization at the Crossroads: The Relevance of International Financial Standards in WTO Law", *Journal of World Trade* 44(2010), 489, 490.

[30] K. Alexander, R. Dhumale and J. Eatwell, *Global Governance of Financial Systems: The International Regulation of Systemic Risk* (Oxford University Press, 2006), 36, 41; C. Brummer, 'How International Financial Law Works (and How It Doesn't)', *Georgetown Law Journal*, 99(2011), 257, 284–90.

[31] Trachtman, 'Spillovers', 739.   [32] Tarullo, *Banking on Basel*, 211.

[33] General Agreement on Trade in Services, 15 April 1994, Marrakesh Agreement Establishing the World Trade Organization, Annex 1B, 1869 UNTS 183, 33 ILM 1167 (1994) ['GATS']. The obligations are replicated in bilateral free trade agreements. Given the space constraints, the discussion below focuses on the GATS only.

service providers physically present within their market. States may also want to exclude the offer of new financial services until the risks involved have been assessed. Regulation could also subject foreign financial service providers to specific reporting obligations, different reserve requirements or specific qualification standards.

Under the GATS qualitative measures have to comply with the national treatment obligation.[34] There are two important components to the national treatment obligation: 'likeness' as the trigger for its application, and 'less favourable treatment' as the substantive standard. 'Likeness' has not yet been interpreted in the context of trade in services.[35] Important questions are whether differences in the mode of supply, or in the methods or means of supply, affect 'likeness'. The question about cross-modal likeness arises when a member restricts the supply of a financial service to providers incorporated within its territory (mode 3) and excludes natural persons (mode 4) from offering this service. If the latter are considered 'like' incorporated suppliers, members will have to treat all foreign suppliers no less favourably than their domestic counterparts, regardless of the mode of supply. Similarly, if services are considered like despite differences in the method of supply, e.g. a savings account offered by internet-only banks or by 'brick and mortar' banks, members cannot regulate these services differently.

The determination of likeness is further complicated by Article XVII's reference to 'like services and service suppliers'. Three interpretations are possible. First, both the service supplier and the service offered have to be like before the national treatment obligation applies.[36] Second, likeness of either the service or the service supplier is required, depending on what the domestic measure relates to.[37] Third, both the service and its provider need to be *unlike* to exclude the application of the national treatment obligation.[38] The latter results in the broadest obligation of national treatment, because it will apply as

---

[34] *Ibid.*, art. XVII:1.

[35] N. Diebold, *Non-Discrimination in International Trade in Services: 'Likeness', in WTO/ GATS* (Cambridge University Press, 2010), 120.

[36] *Ibid.*, 205; M. Krajewski and M. Engelke, 'Article XVII GATS', in Wolfrum, Stoll and Feinäugle (eds.), *WTO – Trade in Services* (Leiden: Nijhoff, 2008), 408.

[37] Krajewski and Engelke, 'Article XVII GATS', 409. This approach is advocated by J. P. Trachtman, 'Lessons for the GATS from Existing WTO Rules on Domestic Regulation', in Sauvé and Mattoo (eds.), *Domestic Regulation and Services Trade Liberalization* (Washington, DC: World Bank, 2003), 63.

[38] Krajewski and Engelke 'Article XVII GATS', 408.

soon as either the service or the service supplier is like its domestic counterpart. WTO Panels seem to have chosen the third interpretation by asserting that 'to the extent that entities provide . . . like services, they are like service suppliers'.[39] As a result, trade liberalization is prioritized over regulatory autonomy.[40]

Once 'likeness' has triggered the national treatment obligation, a violation occurs when foreign services and service suppliers are treated, de jure or de facto,[41] less favourably than their domestic counterparts. Additional reporting requirements for foreign financial service providers are de jure discriminatory. But it is really the prohibition on de facto discrimination that is crucial to determining the limits on WTO members' ability to protect their domestic affairs.[42] The Appellate Body confirmed, in the context of Article 2.1 TBT Agreement,[43] the asymmetric impact test described in an *obiter dictum* in *EC – Asbestos*.[44] According to this test, less favourable treatment depends on a comparison between the treatment of the group of imported products and that of the group of like domestic products. A comparison at the 'group' level implies that de facto discrimination exists if domestic services or service suppliers are comparatively overrepresented in the group of like services or service suppliers that are subject to a lesser regulatory burden.[45] In contrast, the diagonal test finds discrimination as soon as a 'like' domestic product is treated more favourably than a 'like'

---

[39] Panel, *European Communities – Regime for the Importation, Sale and Distribution of Bananas, Complaint by Ecuador*, WT/DS27/R/ECU (1997), para. 7.322; Panel, *Canada – Certain Measures Affecting the Automotive Industry*, WT/DS139/R, WT/DS142/R (2000), para. 10.248; Diebold, *Non-Discrimination*, 188–95; Krajewski and Engelke, 'Article XVII GATS', 408–9.

[40] Diebold, *Non-Discrimination*, 204; Krajewski and Engelke, 'Article XVII GATS', 409.

[41] GATS, art. XVII(3); Diebold, *Non-Discrimination*, 123.

[42] J. Pauwelyn, 'Comment: The Unbearable Lightness of Likeness', in Panizzon, Pohl and Sauvé (eds.), *GATS and the Regulation of International Trade in Services* (Cambridge University Press, 2008), 359.

[43] Appellate Body, *United States – Measures Affecting the Production and Sale of Clove Cigarettes*, WT/DS406/AB/R (2012), para. 175.

[44] Appellate Body, *European Communities – Measures Affecting Asbestos and Asbestos-Containing Products*, WT/DS135/AB/R (2001), para. 100.

[45] Diebold, *Non-Discrimination*, 44; L. Ehring, '*De Facto* Discrimination in World Trade Law: National and Most-Favoured-Nation Treatment – or Equal Treatment?', *Journal of World Trade*, 36(2002), 921, 943–4, 964–5; E. Vranes, *Trade and the Environment: Fundamental Issues in International Law, WTO Law, and Legal Theory* (Oxford University Press, 2009) 235, 238.

imported product. In effect, a member will be discriminating unless its regulation is more lenient than that of its trading partners.[46]

In addition to prohibiting discriminatory qualitative measures, various GATS provisions restrict non-discriminatory qualitative measures. Article XVI:2(e) prohibits imposing a specific legal form on financial service providers within a WTO member's territory, unless a reservation has been scheduled. Regulation requiring foreign financial service providers to operate through subsidiaries rather than branches could thus be contrary to a WTO member's market access obligations.[47] The difference between branches and subsidiaries is crucial, because host states typically only regulate and supervise subsidiaries, while branches remain within the jurisdiction of the parent company's home state.[48] If members have made commitments in accordance with the Understanding on Financial Services,[49] the commercial presence provisions therein oblige them to grant financial service suppliers of another member market access through a branch rather than through a subsidiary.[50]

Until the Council for Trade in Services develops disciplines under Article VI:4, Article VI:5 requires that members' qualification requirements and procedures, technical standards and licensing requirements ('QTL-requirements') do not nullify or impair their specific commitments by being 'more burdensome than necessary to ensure the quality of the service'.[51] Relevant examples are capital adequacy ratios or minimum qualifications of board members of financial institutions. This obligation can restrict WTO members' regulatory autonomy, particularly when a measure's necessity for the quality of the service is debated.[52]

---

[46] Diebold, *Non-Discrimination*, 40–1.

[47] Committee on Trade in Financial Services, *Communication from Barbados: Unintended Consequences of Remedial Measures Taken to Correct the Global Financial Crisis: Possible Implications for WTO Compliance*, JOB/SERV/38 (18 February 2011), para. 12 ['Communication from Barbados']; P. Delimatsis and P. Sauvé, 'Financial Services Trade after the Crisis: Policy and Legal Conjectures', *Journal of International Economic Law* 13 (2010), 837, 841–2.

[48] Delimatsis and Sauvé, 'Financial Services Trade', 841–2.

[49] *Understanding on Commitments in Financial Services*, LT/UR/U/1 (15 April 1994) ['Understanding']. The Understanding is only binding if, and to the extent that, members have integrated it into their Schedule. See A. von Bogdandy and J. Windsor, 'Understanding on Commitments in Financial Services', in Wolfrum, Stoll and Feinäugle (eds.), *WTO – Trade in Services* (Ledien: Nijhoff, 2008), 650–2.

[50] Understanding, A.   [51] GATS, art. VI:5(a)(i) *jo.* art. VI:4(b).

[52] Trachtman, 'Lessons', 68.

Finally, members that have scheduled commitments in accordance with the Understanding cannot adopt certain non-discriminatory qualitative measures. They have to endeavour to remove any obstacles to market access that financial service providers from other members may experience,[53] and have to allow foreign financial service suppliers established within their territory to offer new financial services[54] that are already offered in the territory of another member.[55] The latter is not necessarily limited to financial services offered in the supplier's home state applies even if the host state, the home state and the state in which the financial service is already supplied have a different regulatory framework and the new financial service is not suited for the host state's one.

(ii)   Restrictions on quantitative measures

Article XVI prohibits specific quantitative restrictions on services and service suppliers. Unless exceptions have been scheduled, members cannot, in sectors where market access commitments have been undertaken, impose limits on the number of service suppliers, service operations or natural persons that can be employed, on the value of service transactions or assets, or on the maximum foreign capital participation.[56]

Financial service providers who want to stand out in a crowded marketplace often seek to increase the yield on their investments to attract potential investors. A higher yield can however be a reward for higher risks taken rather than reflecting superior investment skills. Because it can encourage higher-risk activities,[57] Members may want to reduce excessive competition between financial service providers through a cap on the number of financial service providers. However, Article XVI:2(a) restricts their ability to do so.

The restriction on quantitative measures was broadened by the Panel's decision in *US – Gambling* to morph qualitative into quantitative measures when it held, and the Appellate Body confirmed, that a non-discriminatory ban on remote gambling was a 'zero quota' because the ban in effect limited imports of remote gambling services to a maximum

---

[53] Understanding, B(10)–B(11).   [54] *Ibid.*, D(3).   [55] *Ibid.*, B(7).

[56] GATS, art. XVI:2(a)–(d) and (f).

[57] E. J. Kelsey, 'Legal Analysis of Services and Investment in the CARIFORUM–EC EPA: Lessons for Other Developing Countries' www.southcentre.org/index.php?option=com_docman&task=doc_download&gid=1860&Itemid=182&lang=en, 85.

of zero.[58] This conclusion was reached despite the recognition that Article XVI exhaustively lists prohibited measures and does not include limits based on how a service is supplied.[59] It shows a preference for liberalized trade over members' regulatory autonomy,[60] as the Panel confirmed when it held that members' right to regulate under Article VI GATS, 'ends whenever rights of other Members under the GATS are impaired'.[61] Various qualitative responses to the GFC as a result come within the scope of Article XVI if members have made commitments to grant market access to financial service providers. In a communication to the Committee on Trade in Services, Barbados invoked the examples of bans on the use of hedge funds.[62]

(iii)   Obligations to liberalize the current and the capital account

WTO members might want to impose capital controls on hot money inflows, triggered by another state's monetary management policies. However, Article XI GATS prohibits restrictions on transfers and payments relating to current and capital transactions inconsistent with specific commitments. Members must also allow capital transfers that are an essential part of a cross-border service and capital inflows relating to a commercial presence.[63]

(iv)   Limited exceptions on the broad obligations to liberalize

As shown in sections (i)–(iii), the scope of WTO members' obligations under the GATS is very broad. Often, therefore, the legality of members' domestic regulation hinges upon the availability of an exception.

First, members could attempt to justify their domestic measures under the public order exception in Article XIV(a). Although members have

---

[58] Panel, *United States – Measures Affecting the Cross-Border Supply of Gambling and Betting Services*, WT/DS285/R (2004), paras. 6.330 and 6.335 ['*US – Gambling (Panel)*']; Appellate Body, *United States – Measures Affecting the Cross-Border Supply of Gambling and Betting Services*, WT/DS285/AB/R (2005), paras. 238 and 251 ['*US – Gambling (AB)*'].

[59] *US – Gambling (Panel)*, paras. 6.298 and 6.318; N. J. King and K. Kalupahana, 'Choosing between Liberalization and Regulatory Autonomy under GATS: Implications of *US – Gambling* for Trade in Cross Border E-Services', *Vanderbilt Journal of Transnational Law* 40 (2007), 1189, 1240.

[60] D. H. Regan, 'A *Gambling* Paradox: Why an Origin-Neutral "Zero-Quota" Is Not a Quota under GATS Article XVI', *Journal of World Trade* 41 (2007), 1297, 1315.

[61] *US – Gambling (Panel)*, para. 6.316.   [62] Communication from Barbados, para. 9.

[63] GATS, art. XVI:1.

some freedom to define 'public morals' and 'public order' in accordance with their own values, the Panel in *US – Gambling* referred to other members' practices on gambling.[64] This comparative approach limits members' ability to define public morals unilaterally.[65] A member aiming to justify financial regulation that is otherwise contrary to its GATS commitments will need to argue that financial instability is a genuine and sufficiently serious threat to a fundamental interest of society.[66] Successfully clearing this threshold is only a first step. Trade restrictive measures also need to be necessary and must be applied consistently with Article XIV's *chapeau.*

To determine necessity, the Panel and the Appellate Body in *US – Gambling*[67] applied the weighing and balancing test developed under Article XX GATT in *Korea – Beef.*[68] The Appellate Body has asserted that 'necessity' is an objective standard.[69] While it may be objective in the sense of not self-judging, such assertions create the impression that necessity can be established using objective means. The weighing and balancing test, however, requires a judgement on the relative merit of trade compared to competing social values, and thus involves inherently subjective assessments of the importance of the values pursued, the seriousness of the impact on trade, and the strength of the domestic measure's contribution to the non-trade goal.[70] A Panel, subject to review by the Appellate Body, ultimately makes this decision.[71] This interpretation of 'necessity' limits members' ability to protect their domestic affairs against the adverse effects of other members' actions or omissions.

Second, Article XII's exception for balance-of-payments purposes is theoretically available, e.g. when a sudden in- or outflow of capital threatens to destabilize an economy. In practice, the requirements that restrictions not exceed those necessary to address the balance-of-payments problems and

---

[64] *US – Gambling (Panel)*, para. 6.473.

[65] J. Marwell, 'Trade and Morality: The WTO Public Morals Exception after *Gambling*', *NYU Law Review* 81 (2006), 802, 817–19.

[66] GATS, art. XIV(a), fn. 5.

[67] *US – Gambling (Panel)*, para. 6.477; *US – Gambling (AB)*, paras. 305–8.

[68] Appellate Body, *Korea – Measures Affecting Imports of Fresh, Chilled and Frozen Beef*, WT/DS161/AB/R, WT/DS169/AB/R (2000), para. 164.

[69] *US – Gambling (AB)*, para. 304.

[70] C. Doyle, 'Gimme Shelter: The "Necessary" Element of GATT Article XX in the Context of the *China-Audiovisual Products* Case', *Boston University International Law Journal*, 29 (2011), 143, 166.

[71] M. M. Du, 'Autonomy in Setting Appropriate Level of Protection under the WTO Law: Rhetoric or Reality?', *Journal of International Economic Law* 13(2010), 1077, 1097.

that unnecessary damage to the commercial, economic and financial interests of other states be avoided restrict its availability. While these requirements may sound reasonable, necessity may be difficult to establish,[72] particularly given the prevailing belief that balance-of-payments problems should be adjusted through exchange rate depreciation or devaluation, rather than through trade restrictions.[73] Thomas attributes the negative attitude towards trade restrictions to a belief that balance-of-payments problems are due to policy mistakes by the affected states that can be solved by adopting trade liberalization policies.[74] Yet, financial instability does not necessarily stem from misguided domestic policies. This is particularly so for smaller economies that cannot rely on a sizable domestic financial market for all their funding needs.[75] An overly restrictive interpretation of the balance-of-payments exception thus limits members' ability to protect their domestic affairs through restrictions on the trade that channels the negative impact other members' policies.

Finally, members could invoke the prudential carve-out in paragraph 2(a) of the GATS Annex on Financial Services.[76] However, uncertainties regarding the prudential carve-out's scope hamper members' ability of justifying their trade restrictive unilateral regulatory measures.

A first area of uncertainty relates to the meaning of 'prudential'. WTO jurisprudence has yet to answer, for example, whether prudential measures can be preventive (ex ante) or only protective (ex post facto) measures to remedy financial instability,[77] or whether the prudential

---

[72] K. P. Gallagher, *Policy Space to Prevent and Mitigate Financial Crises in Trade and Investment Agreements* (May 2010), at www.ase.tufts.edu/gdae/Pubs/rp/KGCapControlsG-24.pdf, 8.

[73] M. Matsushita, T. J. Schoenbaum and P. C. Mavroidis, *The World Trade Organization: Law, Practice, and Policy* (2nd edn, Oxford University Press, 2006), 463, 65; P. van den Bossche, *The Law and Policy of the World Trade Organization: Text, Cases, and Materials* (2nd edn, Cambridge University Press, 2008), 714.

[74] C. Thomas, 'Balance-of-Payments Crises in the Developing World: Balancing Trade, Finance and Development in the New Economic Order', *American University International Law Review*, 15(2000), 1275.

[75] S. Ishii and K. Habermeier, 'Capital Account Liberalization and Financial Sector Stability', IMF Occasional Paper No. 211, Washington, DC, 2002, 13.

[76] Annex on Financial Services, General Agreement on Trade in Services, 15 April 1994, Marrakesh Agreement Establishing the World Trade Organization, Annex 1B, 33 ILM 1189 (1994).

[77] B. de Meester, 'The Global Financial Crisis and Government Support for Banks: What Role for the GATS?', *Journal of International Economic Law* 13(2010), 27, 57.

objective can be incidental or has to be the measure's main objective of the measure.[78]

Second, the implications of the prudential carve-out's second sentence are unclear. The sentence stipulates that

> where [measures taken for prudential reasons] do not conform with the provisions of the Agreement, they shall not be used as a means of avoiding the Member's commitments or obligations under the Agreement.

Some argue that it requires prudential regulation to comply with Articles VI, XVI and XVII or, in case of non-compliance with Article XIV.[79] This position is problematic, because it makes the prudential carve-out redundant. As the Appellate Body held in the context of the GATT, treaty interpretation should not result in a provision's redundancy.[80] Instead, the anti-avoidance provision should be interpreted as a limit to avoid abuse of the right to regulate under the prudential carve-out.[81] The implication of this test will be further explored in section IV.

(v)   Conclusion

Section 1 has revealed that international law does not restrict states' ability to inflict externalities upon other states through the exercise of their monetary sovereignty. Moreover, as section 2 discussed, the GATS limits WTO members' ability to regulate financial services and service

---

[78] L. E. Panourgias, *Banking Regulation and World Trade Law: GATS, EU and 'Prudential' Institution-Building* (Oxford: Hart, 2006), 70–1 gives the example of excluding foreign branches from the domestic payment and settlement system to ensure the efficiency of this system.

[79] A. Gkoutzinis, 'International Trade in Banking Services and the Role of the WTO: Discussing the Legal Framework and Policy Objectives of the General Agreement on Trade in Services and the Current State of Play in the Doha Round of Trade Negotiations', *International Lawyer* 39(2005), 877, 903; C. Kaufmann and R. H. Weber, 'Reconciling Liberalized Trade in Financial Services and Domestic Regulation', in Alexander and Andenas (eds.), *The World Trade Organization and Trade in Services* (Leiden: Nijhoff, 2008), 426; T. Tucker and L. Wallach, *No Meaningful Safeguards for Prudential Measures in World Trade Organization's Financial Service Deregulation Agreements* (September 2009), at www.citizen.org/documents/PrudentialMeasuresReportFINAL.pdf, 3, 5.

[80] Appellate Body, *United States – Standards for Reformulated and Conventional Gasoline*, WT/DS2/AB/R (1996), 23.

[81] Key, 'Financial Services', in Macrory, Appleton and Plummer (eds.), *The World Trade Organization: Legal, Economic and Political Analysis*, vol. I (New York: Springer, 2005), 964; Leroux, 'Trade in Financial Services under the World Trade Organization' *Journal of World Trade* 36 (2002),413, 430–1.

suppliers when this regulation affects trade in financial services, unless one of the narrow exceptions justifies the restrictions. This inability to restrict trade means that affected states cannot respond when other states cause negative externalities. It also creates a situation in which affecting states have nothing to gain from international cooperation.

This reality check contradicts the traditional narrative of international law as a liberal system of states, in which states are free from external interference with their domestic affairs and in which states consent to cooperation in response to global problems. The remainder of this chapter focuses on how to address the imbalances, procedurally and substantively.

III. Proposed pathway of reinterpretation

Many pathways are open to address the problems of increasing interdependence discussed in this chapter. The traditional pathway of negotiating a formal international agreement on the exercise of monetary sovereignty is however unlikely to be successful because existing imbalances create hurdles for consent to effective responses. Fortunately, a 'big bang' creation of international agreements is not the only option. Instead, I argue for the reinterpretation of existing rules and principles governing the exercise of sovereignty. As this does not require the wholesale development of new legal provisions, it avoids the need to secure states' consent.

A first advantage of reinterpretation is pragmatism; it works with what already exists. Reinterpretation is possible because many rules and principles governing the exercise of sovereignty depend for their application on concepts, such as 'like' or 'necessity', whose meaning is contingent upon the context, circumstances and community in which they are used.[82] There is room for flexibility in their interpretation to ensure that the rules and principles are applied in ways that are more compatible with the fundamental requirements of a liberal system than they currently are.

---

[82] A. Lang, *World Trade Law after Neoliberalism: Reimagining the Global Economic Order* (Oxford University Press, 2011), 164. More generally, see A. Bianchi, 'Textual Interpretation and (International) Law Reading: The Myth of (In) Determinacy and the Genealogy of Meaning', in Bekker, Dolzer and Waibel (eds.), *Making Transnational Law Work in the Global Economy: Essays in Honour of Detlev Vagts* (Cambridge University Press, 2010), 49–50.

Second, reinterpretation is a flexible process that allows for continuous adaptation of states' rights and obligations, should the underlying conditions of interdependence change. Sandholtz and Stiles describe the dynamic, cyclical process of normative change as follows:[83]

> The cycle begins with the constellation of existing norms, which provides the normative structure within which actors decide what to do, decide how to justify their acts, and evaluate the behaviour of others. Because rules cannot cover every contingency and because conflicts among rules are commonplace, actions regularly trigger disputes. Actors argue about which norms apply and what the norms require or permit. As actors seek to resolve disputes, they reason by analogy, invoke precedents, and give reasons, whether their audience is a judge or a set of other governments. The outcome of such discourses is always to change the norms under dispute, making them stronger or weaker, more specific (or less), broader or narrower … The process of disputing reveals the extent to which states and other actors agree on the international rules in question. The crucial point, however, is that the cycle of normative change has completed a turn and modified the norms underlying the dispute.

To lawyers, the term 'dispute' may conjure up images of a formal judicial proceeding. Formal litigation, for better or for worse, has a lawmaking function.[84] However, in the current context 'dispute' refers to any form of contestation or debate due to a lack of clarity of the rules, uncertainty about their applicability in a given context, or a conflict between rules.[85]

A wide variety of processes exist in international law to enable contestation and interaction. International institutions provide fora for informal or formal state interaction. Formal interactions are, for example, the negotiation of new international agreements, the adoption of disciplines on domestic regulation by the Council for Trade in Services, or formal dispute settlement. Examples of informal interactions are the discussions in the WTO's Committee on Trade in Financial Services or the Committee on Balance-of-Payments Restrictions.

Normative change through dispute settlement is an incremental process that can at times move slowly and in various directions. However, it

---

[83] W. Sandholtz and K. W. Stiles, *International Norms and Cycles of Change* (Oxford University Press, 2009), 6–7. The role of engagement between actors in shaping international law is also central in J. Brunnée and S. J. Toope, *Legitimacy and Legality in International Law: An Interactional Account* (Cambridge University Press, 2010).

[84] V. Lowe, 'The Function of Litigation in International Society', *International and Comparative Law Quarterly* (2012), 209, 214–20.

[85] W. Sandholtz, 'Dynamics of International Norm Change: Rules against Wartime Plunder', *European Journal of International Relations* 14(2008), 105.

is not necessarily as slow as one might expect. An advantage of dispute settlement as a locus for contestation and interaction is that it allows for the immediate testing of the tension that arises when one state's exercise of its sovereignty causes negative externalities for another state. The affected state does not need to wait until other states wake up to the importance of an issue, commit resources to international negotiations, and develop new rules or principles. Instead, the affected state can raise the issue as soon as a negative externality occurs. Obviously, claiming a violation of international law does not guarantee a solution, but the ensuing debate will illustrate tangible problems with the existing rules and principles, and provide an opportunity to fine-tune these rules and principles through the exchange of arguments.

A state's motives for selecting one process over another can vary, and states are not necessarily limited to one. Often these processes can be combined in a multi-pronged strategy that involves other states, international institutions or non-state actors. Specific combinations of processes will depend on the strategies chosen and the resources available to the different sides in a debate about the meaning of a norm. Given that the availability of resources determines the choice of processes, not all options will be available to all states.

Power asymmetries between states can hinder less powerful states' ability to influence international negotiations or to enforce international judgments, particularly if their desired outcome is incompatible with that of more powerful states. However, these asymmetries do not leave less powerful states completely unable to influence the development of international law.[86] For example, in trade negotiations, developing states have successfully used various negotiating tactics to improve their chances of being heard and achieving their desired outcomes.[87] Moreover, powerful states do not automatically dominate this cyclical process of normative change.[88]

There is no silver bullet for the obstacles small or otherwise vulnerable states face to meaningful participation in international processes of normative change. However, normative change can occur despite these

---

[86] Brunnée and Toope, *Legitimacy and Legality*, 84–5, 353.
[87] T. Cottier, 'A Two-Tier Approach to WTO Decision Making', in Steger (ed.), *Redesigning the World Trade Organization for the Twenty-First Century* (Waterloo, Ont.: Wilfrid Laurier University Press, 2010), 48–9; J. S. Odell, 'Negotiating from Weakness in International Trade Relations', *Journal of World Trade* 44 (2010), 545.
[88] Sandholtz, 'Dynamics', 108.

obstacles. Importantly, externalities are not only experienced by developing states, but also by developed states. If the exercise of sovereignty
needs to be balanced against other states' sovereignty, the outcome of
normative change does not only affect the relationship between the
acting and affected states, but relationships generally among all other
states subject to the changed rule or principle concerning the exercise of
their sovereignty. For example, if the Appellate Body expands its interpretation of the prudential carve-out, this new interpretation will inform
not only the trade relations between the applicant and the respondent in
the particular case, but also similar relations between other members due
to the de facto *stare decisis* of their decisions.[89]

Non-state actors, such as NGOs, lobbyists and academics, play an
important role in shaping the outcome of normative change. They
identify problems, analyse different interpretations, or persuade states,
international adjudicators and public opinion of the appropriateness of
the proposed new norms.[90] Once a norm has been modified, its evaluation by non-state actors can highlight the implications of this modification and set in motion a new cycle of change.[91]

IV.   Substantive drivers and outcomes of the dynamic
processes of reinterpretation

The dynamic process of reinterpretation is rudderless without substantive guidance about what its outcome ought to be. 'Interstitial norms',
which operate 'in the interstices between ... primary rules' when these
rules compete for application to a specific set of facts, can provide that
guidance.[92] I advance three.

The first is *locality*, which holds that states should be able to regulate
when their domestic affairs are adversely affected, regardless of whether
the regulated act takes place within their territory. Since an act and its

---

[89] R. Bhala, 'The Precedent Setters: *de facto stare decisis* in WTO Adjudication (*Part Two of a Trilogy*)', *Journal of Transnational Law and Policy* 9 (1999), 1, 3–4.

[90] Brunnée and Toope, *Legitimacy and Legality*, 60–5; M. Finnemore and K. Sikkink, 'International Norm Dynamics and Political Change', *International Organization* 52 (1998), 887, 895–901.

[91] W. Sandholtz and A. Stone Sweet, 'Law, Politics, and International Governance', in Reus-Smit (ed.), *Politics of International Law* (2004), 268.

[92] V. Lowe, 'The Politics of Law-making: Are the Method and Character of Norm Creation Changing?', in Byers (ed.), *The Role of Law in International Politics* (Oxford University Press, 2000), 213–14.

effects do not necessarily occur within the same territory, even actions in accordance with locality can have an adverse impact on other states. Therefore, two additional norms – *reasonableness* and *good neighbourliness* – further limit the exercise of states' sovereignty to avoid situations whereby states adversely affect their 'neighbours', which is understood broadly and therefore not limited to states that physically border each other. If an adverse effect on other states is inevitable, states should ensure that the adverse effects of their actions remain within reasonable bounds.

Interstitial norms can first be used to reinterpret the rules of abstention. The best option is to reinterpret the no harm principle, and particularly its standard for causation. The 'but for' test allows states to hide behind the complexity of increasing interdependence to avoid accountability for their actions or omissions. Reasonableness dictates that causation should instead be based on the contribution of an action or omission to the overall adverse effects on other states. Another useful reinterpretation of the no harm principle would be to apply a precautionary approach to test whether a state's actions or omissions were diligent. This approach is useful when there is scientific uncertainty about the precise consequences of an action or omission.[93] So far, the precautionary approach has been limited to the risk of physical harm in the broader context of protecting the environment or health, although domestically the USA and the UK have argued for a precautionary approach in the context of counterterrorism.[94] The GFC has illustrated that irresponsible monetary policy or inadequate regulation of credit creation by financial institutions carries 'tail risks'[95] similar to those related to ultra-hazardous activities that can harm the environment. Moreover, the GFC has laid bare the limits of macroeconomic models. A precautionary approach would not expose states to liability claims whenever their economic policies have an adverse effect abroad, but only when their actions or omissions are not those of a diligent state acting as a good neighbour.

---

[93] G. Hafner and I. Buffard, 'Obligations of Prevention and the Precautionary Principle', in J. Crawford, A. Pellet and S. Olleson (eds.), *The Law of International Responsibility* (Oxford University Press, 2010), 525.

[94] J. B. Wiener, 'Precaution', in Bodansky, Brunnée and Hey (eds.), *The Oxford Handbook of International Environmental Law* (Oxford University Press, 2007), 611.

[95] International Monetary Fund, 'The Acting Chairman's Summing up – 2008 Triennial Surveillance Review – Overview Paper, Executive Board Meeting 08/84, September 26, 2008', Selected Decisions and Selected Documents of the IMF, 42.

Reinterpretation of the principle of non-intervention is, however, not advised. This principle was already significantly transformed during the second half of the twentieth century, when it was extended to include instances of coercion not involving the use of armed force.[96] Removing the coercion requirement would make any state action that affects another state an intervention, leaving states exposed to claims of violation of the principle of non-intervention almost every time they exercise their sovereignty, which would hardly be reasonable.

In addition to guiding the reinterpretation of limits on the exercise of sovereignty, locality, good neighbourliness and reasonableness can guide the reinterpretation of WTO members' trading obligations under the GATS so as to enable states affected by their trading partners' actions or omissions to protect their domestic affairs. The reinterpretation should focus on both the obligations and the exceptions that together determine the scope of members' regulatory autonomy.

As for the obligations, reinterpretation should temper existing restrictions on domestic regulation. To start, qualitative measures should not be examined under Article XVI as in the *US – Gambling* 'zero quota' jurisprudence. The conditionality of a qualitative measure cannot be equated to the numerical conditionality of a quota.[97] Likewise, the Scheduling Guidelines'[98] equation of nationality requirements to zero quota does not imply that origin-neutral qualitative restrictions qualify as 'zero quota'.[99] Instead, prohibitions on the supply of a sub-standard service or by an unqualified service supplier should be assessed under the national treatment obligation of Article XVII, if discriminatory, or under the domestic regulation obligation of Article VI, if non-discriminatory.

---

[96] T. Mitrovic, 'Non-Intervention in the Internal Affairs of States', in Milan Sahovic (ed.), *Principles of International Law Concerning Friendly Relations and Cooperation* (New York: Dobbs Ferry, 1972), 224, 27.

[97] See Regan, 'A *Gambling* Paradox', 1302–3, 06, 12.

[98] Group of Negotiations on Services, *Scheduling of Initial Commitments in Trade in Services*, MTN.GNS/W/164 (3 September 1993), para. 6(a) ['*1993 Scheduling Guidelines*'], repeated in Council for Trade in Services, *Guidelines for the Scheduling of Specific Commitments under the General Agreement on Trade in Services (GATS)*, S/L/92 (28 March 2001), para. 12(a).

[99] Regan, 'A *Gambling* Paradox', 1313; F. Ortino, 'Treaty Interpretation and the WTO Appellate Body in *US – Gambling*: A Critique', *Journal of International Economic Law* 9(2006), 117, 144 points out that the *1993 Scheduling Guidelines* (para. 4) clearly state that the criteria of art. XVI:2(a)–(d) 'do not apply to the quality of the service supplied or to the ability of the supplier to supply the service'.

This interpretation is consistent with the three interstitial norms advanced here. First, it is consistent with locality because it would allow members to decide which services or service suppliers they consider too objectionable to be offered or present within their market. Second, the result is consistent with good neighbourliness and reasonableness. Qualitative trade restrictions would still be subject to the requirements of Articles VI and XVII, and, if contrary to either of these articles, to the requirements of the exceptions. At the same time, members that avoid a negative impact on other members when exercising their monetary sovereignty will be rewarded with trading opportunities for their private economic actors because their services or service suppliers will pass muster in the importing jurisdiction.

Reinterpretation should also reduce the broad scope of the national treatment obligation. The current situation in which the obligation applies unless the service and the supplier are 'unlike' reduces WTO members' ability to restrict the supply of a service to a specific type of service supplier subject to regulatory supervision. Thus, it restricts their ability to protect their domestic affairs when their trading partners insufficiently regulate their internationally active financial institutions.

The standard for de facto discrimination further determines the national treatment obligation.[100] The confirmation of the asymmetric impact test is to be welcomed, and is in line with the interstitial norms. This test allows each member to regulate at its chosen level, while prohibiting regulation that disproportionately affects foreign services and service suppliers as a group. The latter type of regulation would be incompatible with reasonableness and good neighbourliness, because it enables members to engage in protectionist behaviour under the guise of regulation. In contrast, the diagonal test allows the most deregulated trading partner to set the ceiling for domestic regulation in other members even if its regulation negatively affects other members and is thus contrary to good neighbourliness.

So far the discussion on the reinterpretation of GATS obligations has focused on the legality of qualitative measures. There are good reasons for this. Article XVI clearly prohibits specific quantitative measures. Reinterpreting restrictions on these measures is thus much harder, because reinterpretation cannot be inconsistent with the GATS text or WTO members' commitments. Quantitative restrictions within the

---

[100] Pauwelyn, 'Comment', 359.

scope of Article XVI thus rely on the availability of an exception for their legality.

There is scope for reinterpretation of the exceptions. First, the 'weighing and balancing' test to analyse a measure's necessity is incompatible with the interstitial norm of locality, because the Appellate Body ultimately determines the balance between the protected value and the trade restrictions, despite assertions that members decide individually on the appropriate level of protection.[101] Regan suggests correcting this inconsistency by focusing not on the balance between a measure's underlying goal and its trade costs, but between the goal and the additional administrative costs for the regulating member of a less trade restrictive alternative.[102] This interpretation is compatible with the interstitial norms. By allowing members to decide on the appropriate level of protection of a societal value, locality is respected. However, the comparison of the measure's costs for the regulating member and the costs for trade ensure reasonableness and good neighbourliness.

Second, the availability of the balance-of-payments exception and the prudential carve-out can be improved by a more critical approach to traditional neo-liberal economic models and their preference for exchange rate responses to balance-of-payments problems[103] and against capital controls as prudential measures.[104] Indications of a more critical approach are visible in the aftermath of the GFC.[105] Even at the IMF, the pendulum has swung from aiming for full capital account liberalization fifteen years ago to a willingness to consider the darker side of capital account liberalization.[106]

---

[101] *US – Gambling (AB)*, paras. 305–8.

[102] D. H. Regan, 'The Meaning of 'Necessary', in GATT Article XX and GATS Article XIV: The Myth of Cost–Benefit Balancing', *World Trade Review*, 6(2007), 347, 349–50.

[103] See section II 2 (iv).

[104] See statements of US officials quoted in K. P. Gallagher, 'Reforming United States Trade and Investment Treaties for Financial Stability: The Case of Capital Controls', *Investment Treaty News*, 10 www.iisd.org/pdf/2011/iisd_itn_april_2011_en.pdf In contrast, B. Christ and M. Panizzon, 'Article XI GATS', in Wolfrum, Stoll and Feinäugle (eds.), *WTO – Trade in Services* (Leiden: Nijhoff, 2008), 54 argue that the prudential carve-out is available as an exception to art. XI GATS.

[105] Delimatsis and Sauvé, 'Financial Services Trade', 840.

[106] S. Hagan, 'Enhancing the IMF's Regulatory Authority', *Journal of International Economic Law*, 13(2010), 955, 967; J. D. Ostry *et al.*, 'Capital Inflows: The Role of Controls', *IMF Staff Position Note SPN/10/04* (19 February 2010), www.imf.org/external/pubs/ft/spn/2010/spn1004.pdf, 4; IMF, *Recent Experiences in Managing Capital Inflows – Cross-Cutting Themes and Possible Policy Framework* (5 April 2011), www.imf.org/external/np/pp/eng/2011/021411a.pdf. See also J. D. Ostry *et al.*, 'Managing Capital Inflows:

These improved understandings of the macroeconomic dynamics are important to guide the process of normative change. The first possible outcome is a broader scope for the balance-of-payments exception. In line with the norm of locality, members should be allowed to decide for themselves whether to rely on capital controls or on other policies, such as exchange rate adjustment, to address a balance-of-payments problem. Once again, reasonableness and good neighbourliness act as a counterweight to locality by requiring that the measures are reasonable and do not unduly harm other members. Thus, members would not be allowed to use capital controls to offload the adjustment costs of policy mistakes on trading partners. In the assessment of reasonableness and good neighbourliness, the specific characteristics of the member imposing the capital controls need to be considered. Developing member should, for example, be given more flexibility than developed members to impose capital controls.

A second possible outcome of the change in attitude towards capital controls would be a different interpretation of the prudential carve-out, particularly of the measures qualifying as 'prudential'. As argued by Panourgias, 'prudential' is a 'dynamic and evolutionary' concept.[107] In the context of the prudential carve-out in NAFTA, Trachtman has argued that the term 'for prudential reasons', which is also used in the prudential carve-out, can be given a 'post-financial crisis evolutionary interpretation' to include capital controls.[108]

A reinterpretation of the prudential carve-out does not necessarily have to be limited to permitting capital controls. Lamy has stated that the prudential carve-out is not restricted to specific measures, as long as the chosen measures have a prudential objective.[109] Likewise, the WTO Secretariat has confirmed that 'any measure adopted for prudential reasons is covered *a priori*', even if contrary to specific commitments on financial services.[110]

What Tools to Use?', *IMF Staff Discussion Note SDN/11/06* (5 April 2011), www.imf.org/external/pubs/ft/sdn/2011/sdn1106.pdf

[107] Panourgias, *Banking Regulation*, 17.

[108] J. P. Trachtman, 'Applicability of the NAFTA "Prudential Carveout" to Capital Controls' (2011) http://worldtradelaw.typepad.com/ielpblog/2011/01/applicability-of-the-nafta-prudential-carveout-to-capital-controls.html

[109] Trade Policy Review Body, *Report to the TPRB from the Director-General on the Financial and Economic Crisis and Trade-Related Developments*, WT/TPR/OV/W/2 (15 July 2009), para. 54.

[110] Council for Trade in Services and Committee on Trade in Financial Services, 'Financial Services'. Note by the Secretariat, S/C/W/312, S/FIN/W/73 (3 February 2010), paras. 28–9.

Finally, the anti-avoidance provision of the prudential carve-out should be interpreted as an obligation of good faith,[111] requiring a reasonable relationship between a domestic measure and its prudential objective.[112] This requirement can accommodate situations in which prudential objectives combine with non-prudential objectives. If the prudential objective is only added to give a non-prudential trade restriction the veneer of legality, the measure is not reasonable. In making this determination, attention should be paid to the tail risks of insufficient prudential regulation and to the imbalance between the short-term benefits of liberalized trade and the long-term risks for financial stability, which 'may lead to a strong bias in favour of inaction'.[113]

This reinterpretation does not result in the redundancy of the prudential carve-out. Moreover, it gives effect to the anti-avoidance provision in which the reference to 'used' can be seen as implying a member's intention behind the allegedly prudential measure.[114] This reinterpretation allows members to protect their domestic affairs against the externalities of their trading partners' more lenient prudential regulation, such as financial instability or a loss in competitiveness. Admittedly, this could be seen as a limit on the trading partner's right to determine the desired level of prudential regulation. However, nothing stops the latter from setting lower prudential regulation for financial institutions active within its market. Moreover, the reinterpretation would create the incentives to develop a sound regulatory framework for internationally active financial institutions that are currently lacking in WTO law.[115]

---

[111] De Meester, 'The Global Financial Crisis', 59; Delimatsis and Sauvé, 'Financial Services Trade', 850; A. van Aaken and J. Kurtz, 'Prudence or Discrimination? Emergency Measures, the Global Financial Crisis and International Economic Law' *Journal of International Economic Law* 12(2009), 859, 876.

[112] De Meester, 'The Global Financial Crisis', 61; Delimatsis and Sauvé, 'Financial Services Trade', 850.

[113] Financial Stability Board *et al.*, *Macroprudential Policy Tools and Frameworks: Update to G20 Finance Ministers and Central Bank Governors*, www.bis.org/publ/othp13.pdf, 11.

[114] J. Kelsey, 'How the Trans-Pacific Partnership Agreement Could Heighten Financial Instability and Foreclose Governments' Regulatory Space', *New Zealand Yearbook of International Law*, 8(2010), 3, 36.

[115] T. Cottier and M. Krajewski, 'What Role for Non-Discrimination and Prudential Standards in International Financial Law?', *Journal of International Economic Law* 13 (2010), 817, 829.

V.   Conclusion

This chapter evaluated how international law is thought to respond when a state's actions or omissions in the exercise of its monetary sovereignty inflict externalities on other states and how international law responds to these externalities in practice. It concluded that, contrary to expectations, international law does not ensure a liberal system of sovereign states, in which states have the authority to determine their domestic affairs free from interference by other states. In reality, states' domestic affairs are exposed to the external adverse effects of other states' actions due to a lack of limits on states' exercise of their monetary sovereignty, combined with limits resulting from the GATS on affected states' ability to regulate unilaterally when this regulation restricts trade.

In many instances the problem arises out of the interpretation of the rules and principles on the exercise of monetary sovereignty and of the provisions on regulatory autonomy in trade liberalization agreements. Therefore, the pathway of reinterpretation was suggested as part of the dynamic processes through which normative change is achieved in international relations and international law. This process of reinterpretation would be guided by interstitial norms that can alleviate conflicts between competing exercises of state sovereignty.

The reinterpretations advanced can help to correct the existing imbalances in the exercise of sovereignty, by requiring states to internalize the costs of their policies. Having to take into account costs that they could previously inflict upon other states may alter states' cost–benefit analysis when making policy decisions. Better internalization of a policy's costs also has the potential to remove disincentives that currently exist towards cooperation because states will have less to give up when consenting to formal international agreements. At the very least, more lenient limits on affected states' regulatory autonomy in trade liberalization agreements will safeguard their ability to protect their domestic affairs through trade restrictions.

8

The industrial policy of China and WTO law: 'the shrinking policy space' argument as sterile fragmentation

JUNJI NAKAGAWA

I. Introduction: fragmentation of international trade law and international development law?

Joining the WTO provides both opportunities and challenges to a new member. While the new member enjoys an improved access to the markets of other members of the WTO on an MFN basis (as one of the substantive trade benefits of WTO membership), it has to constrain its regulatory power within the confines of the rules of the WTO Agreements and its accession commitment. This means that some policies of the new member that were available before its accession to the WTO are no longer available because of their inconsistency with the rules of the WTO Agreements or with its accession commitment.

Critics of WTO law, most notably those within the 'anti-globalization' camp, call this challenge "the challenge of shrinking policy space" (i.e. for economic development).[1] Robert Hunter Wade, for instance, argues that the TRIPs Agreement, TRIMs Agreement, and the GATS limit the options of developing country governments to constrain the choices of companies operating within their borders in pursuit of their economic development strategies.[2] He asserts that WTO law should be relaxed for developing country members (and for those members in transition from planned to market economy); so that they may adopt the policy

---

[1] See for instance, K. P. Gallagher, 'Globalization and the Nation-State: Reasserting Policy Autonomy for Development,' in K. P. Gallagher (ed.), *Putting Development First: The Importance of Policy Space in the WTO and IFIs* (London and New York: Zed Books, 2005), 1.

[2] R. H. Wade, 'What Strategies are Viable for Developing Countries Today? The World Trade Organization and the Shrinking of "Development Space,"' *Review of International Political Economy* 10 (2003), 621, 622.

instruments for economic development (and/or transition) that were adopted by the developed countries when the latter achieved economic development in the late nineteenth century (e.g., Great Britain, Germany, and the other Continental European countries), the early twentieth century (e.g., the USA) or during the early to mid-twentieth century (e.g. Japan, Korea, and the other East Asian countries).[3]

Although the cry for the New International Economic Order (NIEO) and 'droit international de développement' lost traction by the 1990s, it has resurged in the new name of 'the shrinking policy space' argument, demanding the expansion of policy space for development, in the sense that international trade law should be relaxed for the sake of international development law.

Setting aside the adequacy and the legitimacy of the 'shrinking policy space' argument, under the current WTO law, a new member – whether it be a developing country or a country in transition from a planned to market economy – must redesign its development and/or transition strategy within the contracted policy space according to WTO law, namely, the WTO Agreements and its accession commitments. This is particularly prominent in the formation and implementation of industrial policy of the new member, because it generally entails a broad range of policy instruments for governmental intervention in the market, such as planning, subsidization, and protective tariffs. They may violate the rules of the WTO Agreements or may even exceed the new member's accession commitments.

Although the 'shrinking policy space' argument may sound like a plausible argument, this chapter does not support it, *at least as a general argument*, for the following reasons. First, the adoption of public policies similar to those adopted by the developed countries in the past may not prove to be effective under contemporary circumstances, especially within the more globalized international economy of the late twentieth and early twenty-first centuries. Second, given the diversity in the internal factor endowments of each country and its external environment, industrial policy should be designed and implemented on a case-by-case basis, taking into account each country's specific internal factors and external environment, including the rules of the WTO Agreements and each country's accession commitments. Third, relaxing the application of WTO law to developing country members

---

[3] H.-J. Chang, *Kicking Away the Ladder: Development Strategy in Historical Perspective* (London: Anthem, 2002).

beyond the existing formal mechanisms (such as waiver, S&D, and Article XVIII of the GATT 1994) entails revision of the rules of WTO law. This is highly unlikely, given the stringent procedural requirements for such revision set out in the Marrakesh Agreement Establishing the WTO.[4]

Instead, this chapter argues that a new member *may* successfully achieve economic development and/or transition by redesigning its industrial policy within the confines of the rules of the WTO Agreements and its accession commitments. The 'shrinking policy space' argument, or the twenty-first version of the NIEO or 'droit international de dével-oppement', *should be dismissed as a general argument,* as it would result in sterile fragmentation between international trade law and international development law.

As an illustration, this chapter will analyze how China has managed to meet the challenge of a 'shrinking policy space'; a challenge it faced when acceding to the WTO. In this regard, the chapter will examine how China has successfully managed to redesign its industrial policy within the confines of WTO law and its accession commitments, focusing on its automotive sector. The automotive industrial policy is taken up as a typical example of the industrial policy of China which had to be substantively redesigned when China joined the WTO.

Section II briefly explains the definition of industrial policy and enumerates its major policy instruments. Section III traces the historical development of China's automotive industrial policy since its inception in the early 1950s up until China's accession to the WTO. Section IV analyzes how China redesigned the automotive industrial policy after it joined the WTO, and evaluates the compatibility of the new automotive industrial policy with WTO law and China's accession commitments. Also, it points out how China's recent automotive industrial policy has the alarming tendency to violate WTO law and its accession commitments. A brief conclusion follows in section V.

---

[4] Arts. X.2 and X.3 of the Marrakesh Agreement provide that proposals to amend the major WTO Agreements (Marrakesh Agreement and the Multilateral Trade Agreements in Annexes 1A and 1C) shall be adopted by the General Council either by consensus or by a two-thirds majority, and they shall take effect for the Members that have accepted them upon acceptance by two-thirds of the Members. There has so far been no amendment to the major WTO agreements.

II. Industrial policy and its major instruments

In a broad sense, industrial policy refers to the policies implemented for raising the welfare level of a given economy when the defects of a competitive market system – market failures – create problems for resource allocation and income distribution through free competition. It includes the totality of policies that are designed to attain this objective either (1) through intervention in the allocation of resources between industries or sectors, or (2) through intervention in the industrial organization of individual industries.[5]

The former (i.e. (1)) can be divided into: (1a) policies that affect the industrial infrastructure in general (e.g., roads, ports, industrial water supplies, and electric power supply, etc.); and (1b) policies that affect inter-industry resource allocation.

The latter (i.e. (2) above) can be divided into: (2a) policies aimed at regulating the internal organization of particular industries (e.g., industrial restructuring, consolidation of firms, output restriction, etc.); and (2b) policies affecting cross-industry organization, such as measures to support small and medium enterprises (SMEs). Of these groupings, (1b) is what would be thought of as industrial policy in the narrow sense.[6] However, this chapter uses the term 'industrial policy' in a broader sense, encompassing all the above four categories of policies.

Governments seeking to implement an industrial policy may adopt some or all of the following policy instruments:

(1) legislation or a plan to support a particular industry for a specific period;
(2) administrative guidance;
(3) infrastructure building;
(4) special taxation measures (e.g., tax incentives on depreciation, etc.) to provide incentives to targeted industries;
(5) government subsidies;
(6) policy-based lending;[7]

---

[5] M. Itoh et al. (eds.), *Economic Analysis of Industrial Policy* (San Diego, CA: Academic Press, 1991), 8; R. Komiya, 'Introduction,' in R. Komiya et al. (eds.), *Industrial Policy of Japan* (Tokyo and New York: Academic Press, 1988), 3. Industry refers to manufacturing industry, and does not include agriculture and service industry. It is normally unclear whether mining is to be considered a targeted industry.

[6] See Komiya, 'Introduction,' 3.

[7] The fourth, fifth, and sixth items may be defined as 'subsidies' under the WTO Agreement on Subsidies and Countervailing Measures, insofar as they entail 'a financial contribution by a government' under its art. 1.1(a)(1). However, they are enlisted here as separate items in order to clarify the variety of the policy instruments available.

(7) tariff measures (e.g., high protective tariffs, tariff escalation, etc.) and quantitative import restriction to protect targeted industries;

(8) establishment and management of state enterprises to directly enhance targeted industries; and

(9) promoting inward foreign direct investments (FDIs) in targeted industries.[8]

Not all of these policy instruments have been adopted by a country in its pursuit of industrial policy. In the case of Japan's post-war industrial policy, items (1), (4), and (6) listed above were particularly important.[9] The government enacted sector-specific special laws that set the goals of sector-specific industrial development in a fixed time-frame, and enlisted policy instruments to achieve them, most important of which were special taxation measures and policy-based lending. In the case of Japan's automotive sector, items (3) and (7) were also important, because the government intended to promote its domestic automotive industry by constructing roads and by shielding the domestic automotive industry from competition with foreign auto manufacturers.[10] After its accession to the GATT in 1955, however, the protective tariffs were gradually reduced. The protective commodity tax rates were also gradually reduced.[11]

The success of Japan's industrial policy has been well researched, and mimicked by other countries, notably those in East Asia,[12] including China. However, the policy instruments adopted by China relating to its automotive industrial policy were different from those adopted by Japan, reflecting, inter alia, China's peculiar internal factor endowments and its external environment before and after its accession to the WTO.

---

[8] Nihon Kaihatsu Ginko [Japan Development Bank], *SeisakuKin'yu: Sengo Nihon no Keiken* [Policy-based Finance: The Experience of Post-War Japan] (Tokyo: Nihon Kaihatsu Ginko, 1993), 36–43, enumerates items (1)–(6) in the list; (7)–(9) added by the author.

[9] A. Suehiro, *The Trajectory and Prospects of East Asian Economies* (Singapore: NUS Press, in association with Kyoto University Press, 2008), 140.

[10] As a general account of Japan's post-war industrial policy in automotive sector, see H. Mutoh, 'The Automotive Industry,' in Komiya, *et al.* (eds.), *Industrial Policy of Japan* (Tokyo and New York: Academic Press, 1988), 307–331.

[11] *Ibid.,* 313–317.

[12] See for instance, World Bank, *The East Asian Miracle: Economic Growth and Public Policy* (Oxford University Press, 1993).

III. China's automotive industrial policy before its accession to the WTO

The history of China's industrial policy in the automotive sector can be divided into four periods:[13]

(1) the era of planned economy (early 1950s–early 1980s);
(2) the period from the early 1980s to 1992;
(3) the period from 1993 to 2001; and
(4) the period following China's accession to the WTO (2001–to date).

This section analyzes the first three periods of China's industrial policy in the automotive sector before its accession to the WTO.

1. China's automotive industrial policy during the era of planned economy (early 1950s–early 1980s)

China's automotive industrial policy started in 1953, when the construction of a factory of the First Automotive Works (FAW, 第一汽車) – a state enterprise – began in Changchun (長春).[14] It started production of medium trucks in 1955, and produced 16,000 units in 1958. However, the production of automobiles did not grow substantively during this period. In 1978, twenty years after the first production of automobiles in China, the total production of automobiles was fewer than 150,000 units.[15]

China's automotive industrial policy during this period consisted of tariffs and other trade policies, as well as investment and financing policies. China introduced its first tariff schedule in 1951. The tariff rates were: 60 percent for passenger cars (which were solely imported for use by high rank members of the Communist Party); 20 percent for medium and small trucks; and 25 percent for buses. While they were not prohibitively high, China's automotive industry was practically immune from competition with imported automobiles by other means, for the following reasons.

---

[13] Y. Takayama and T. Marukawa, 'Jidoshosangyo no sangyoseisaku' [Industrial Policy of Automotive Industry] in Y. Takayama and T. Marukawa, *Shinban global kyosojidai no Chuugokujidoshasangyo* [China's Automotive Industry in the Era of Global Competition] (Tokyo: Sososha, 2005), 60–61.

[14] T. Marukawa, 'Jidoshasangyo' [Automotive Industry], in T. Marukawa (ed.), *IkokiChuugoku no Sangyo seisaku* [Industrial Policy of China in Times of Transition] (Chiba: Institute of Developing Economies, Japan Export Trade Organization, 2000), 365.

[15] *Ibid.*

First, import trade was monopolized by a small number of state trading companies that were supervised by the Chinese Ministry of External Trade, so that the central government could control the volume of imports lest it should damage the domestic automotive industry. Second, after 1964, the government set the domestic price of imported cars not according to the imported c.i.f. (cost, insurance, and freight) price plus tariffs, but according to the level which was higher than the prices of like domestic automobiles, most of which were trucks and buses. Through these means, China's domestic automotive industry was not exposed to competitive pressures from imported automobiles.[16]

During the era of planned economy, investment in the automotive industry was monopolized by the central government and local governments. The ratio of investment in the automotive industry was persistently low during the era and tough, ranging from between 0.28 percent to 2.31 percent of the total investment in manufacturing and mining industries.[17] While the investment by the central government was concentrated in the production of medium trucks, local governments invested in the production of small trucks. Both the central and local governments made only a marginal investment in the production of passenger cars.[18] Marukawa explained the low ratio of the public investment in the automotive sector during this period as being a result of the continuation of the development strategy which was introduced in China (by borrowing from the USSR in the 1950s), under which heavy, input industries such as iron and steel industry took priority over manufacturing industries, including the automotive industry.[19]

2. China's automotive industrial policy from the early 1980s to 1992

China's automotive industry grew rapidly during this period under the Chinese economic reform (改革開放) policy led by Deng Xiao Ping (鄧小平). From 1982 to 1992, the production of automobiles increased five-fold. Foreign automotive companies started production of automobiles in China in the form of a joint venture (合弁) with Chinese

---

[16] *Ibid.*, 365–366.

[17] *Ibid.*, 368 (Table 1). This was in contrast to a much higher ratio of investment in the automotive industry in manufacturing industries in Japan during the 1960s. It was 13.9 percent in 1965 (*ibid.*).

[18] *Ibid.*, 369–373.   [19] *Ibid.*, 368–369.

domestic automotive companies.[20] While the direct control by the central government of imports and investments diminished, the central government began to make more use of tariff and tax policies for the purpose of protecting and promoting the domestic automotive industry.[21]

Tariff policy became one of the major instruments of China's automotive industrial policy during this period. The monopoly of state trading companies which was under the supervision of Chinese Ministry of External Trade was abolished in 1981, and the other ministries of the central government and local governments entered the import market. From 1984 to 1986, the pricing policy of imported automobiles shifted from the one based on the price of like domestic products to the one based on the cost of imports (import c.i.f. price plus tariffs and other charges). As a result of these policy changes, the government of China came to rely more heavily on tariff policy as a means of protecting the domestic automotive industry. Tariffs on imported passenger cars and trucks were substantively raised from 60 percent and 20 percent to 120 percent and 50 percent respectively, by 1985. In addition, import adjustment taxes were levied at 80 percent for passenger cars and 50 percent for trucks. In total, import charges for passenger cars and truck were 200 percent and 100 percent, respectively.[22] Imports of passenger cars was further restricted by the introduction of a special consumption tax on passenger cars in 1988, with a higher rate applied to imported cars and auto parts. The rate was 40,000 yuan on imported complete cars, 15,000 to 20,000 yuan on cars assembled with imported auto parts and 1,000 yuan on domestic cars.[23]

The ratio of investment in the automotive industry steadily increased during this period, from 1.50 percent of total investment in manufacturing and mining industries in 1981–1985 to 4.47 percent in 1991–1995.[24] However, the central government and local governments were no longer the sole investors. Instead, domestic automotive companies raised capital mainly from bank financing, retained earnings, and foreign automotive

---

[20] The first joint venture agreement with AMC (American Motors Corporation, which was bought by Chrysler in 1987) was signed in 1983 to set up the Beijing Jeep Company, followed by Shanghai Auto Industry Corporation – VW (Volkswagen) in 1984 and Guangzhou – Peugeot in 1985. See W.-W. Chu, 'How the Chinese Government Promoted a Global Automotive Industry,' *Industrial and Corporate Change*, 20 (2011), 1235, 1243.

[21] Marukawa, 'Jidoshasangyo' [Automotive Industry], 373–374.

[22] *Ibid.*, 376.   [23] *Ibid.*, 377.   [24] *Ibid.*, 368 (table 1).

companies. The government of China promoted investment in the automotive industry through these non-governmental channels by position-
ing the automotive industry among the 'pillar industries' (支柱産業) for
the first time under the Seventh Five-Year Plan (1986–1991).[25]

Under the Seventh Five-Year Plan, the government placed emphasis on
promoting domestic production of passenger cars. Two policies were
adopted to achieve this goal. First, the government tried to limit the
number of production bases, as this was deemed necessary to promote a
small number of domestic passenger car manufacturers with economy of
scale. Second, it tried to promote domestic production of passenger car
parts. However, the former was not much successful. Due to strong
pressure from domestic car manufacturers to enter the domestic passenger
car production market, the target number of the companies was increased
from the original 'three majors (三大)' in 1987 to 'three majors, three
minors (三大三小)' in 1988, to 'three majors, three minors and two
micros (三大三小二微)' in 1992 and to ten in 1998.[26] However, in fact,
the number of companies exceeded one hundred by the end of the 1990s.

In order to promote the domestic production of passenger car parts,
the government introduced a tariff escalation policy in 1988. The tariff
rates of passenger car parts were set gradually lower according to the
ratio of the domestic content of complete passenger cars.[27] The government also introduced a surcharge for promoting the domestic production
of passenger car parts in 1988. The surcharge was imposed on the sales
price of complete cars, and the collected surcharge was provided to the
manufacturers of domestic passenger car parts in the form of loans at low
interest rates. As a result of these policies, the local content of passenger
cars steadily increased and reached 80 percent in major domestic passenger car manufacturers by the early to mid 1990s.[28]

3.   China's automotive industrial policy from 1993 to 2001

The State Council of China published a Formal Policy on Development
of Automotive Industry (汽車工業産業政策, hereafter 'the 1994 Policy')

---

[25] *Ibid.*, 379.

[26] *Ibid.*, 382–384. The government's policy to promote a small number of automotive
manufactures has not been successful. As of 2004, 131 companies manufactured automobiles in China (T. Marukawa, *Gendai Chuugoku no sangyou* [Industry of Contemporary China] (Tokyo: Chuo Kouronsha, 2007), 193–194).

[27] *Ibid.*, 386.   [28] *Ibid.* (table 5).

in 1994.[29] It was the first systematic pronouncement of China's industrial policy in the automotive sector. It consisted of the following major policies. First, it aimed at consolidating the domestic automotive industry to achieve economy of scale. About 120 existing automotive companies were planned to be consolidated into eight to ten groups by the year 2000, and to three to four groups by the year 2010. Second, it promoted purchasing automobiles by individuals, and it put passenger car production in the center place of the automotive industry. Third, new automotive production companies were to be permitted subject to minimum production requirements (annual production of 150,000 units for passenger cars with an engine size of 1,600 cc or smaller, and annual production of 100,000 units for small trucks).Fourthly, with respect to foreign investment in the production of complete cars and engines, maximum capital requirement was set at less than 50 percent. Fifth, it did not permit knock-down production, and it maintained the tariff escalation policy for passenger car parts of 1988.[30] All in all, the 1994 Policy aimed at promoting a domestic automotive industry which was internationally competitive.

The 1994 Policy was not fully implemented, however, for two main reasons. First, the domestic demand for automobiles did not grow as envisioned in the 1994 Policy. The Chinese Ministry of Machinery Industry had estimated that the size of domestic automotive market would become three million units in the year 2000, half of which were passenger cars.[31] However, the production of automobiles was slightly over two million units in the year 2000, of which only about 600,000 units were passenger cars.[32] Marukawa explains the reason for the slow growth of the demand for automobiles as follows: (1) the surcharges imposed by local governments on the purchase and the use of passenger cars discouraged domestic consumption; (2) banks were not allowed to enter the market of auto loans (payments in installments) until 1998.[33]

Second, as a result of its drastic restructuring since the late 1990s, the global automotive industry became highly oligopolized. The overall goal

---

[29] The English translation is available at: http://english.mofcom.gov.cn/aarticle/lawsdata/chineselaw/200211/20021100053370.html (accessed May 17, 2013)

[30] Marukawa, 'Jidoshasangyo' [Automotive Industry], 390–391.   [31] Ibid., 397.

[32] T. Marukawa, Y. Takayama, W. Baoning, and L. Jingnan, 'Jidoshashijo no Kozo to Doko' [Structure and Trends of Automotive Industry], in Takayama and Marukawa, Shinban global kyosojidai no Chuugokujidoshasangyo [China's Automotive Industry in the Era of Global Competition], 17 (table 1-1).

[33] Marukawa 'Jidoshasangyo' [Automotive Industry], 397–398.

of the 1994 Policy, namely, to promote a domestic automotive industry which was internationally competitive, turned out to be less feasible under this situation.[34]

The advancement of China's accession negotiation to the GATT (and later the WTO) put additional burden on the achievement of the goal of the 1994 Policy. In anticipation of the accession to the GATT/WTO, China began to lower its tariffs and other import charges on automobiles in 1992.[35] Although this would gradually expose the Chinese domestic automotive industry to intense competition from imported cars, the government of China prioritized the goal of joining the GATT/WTO over the goal of promoting domestic automotive industry.

IV.   China's automotive industrial policy under the WTO

1.   The WTO Agreements and China's accession commitment relevant to China's automotive industrial policy

China joined the WTO in November 2001 after sixteen years of prolonged and tough negotiation. In its accession document, China assumed a number of obligations that were relevant to its automotive industrial policy. First, China assumed a significant reduction of tariffs on automobiles. The tariffs on automobiles (buses, passenger cars, and trucks), which were from 40 percent to 55.0 percent at the time of China's accession to the WTO, would be reduced to 25 percent in stages.[36] The tariffs on auto parts would also be reduced to 10 percent in stages.[37] Moreover, in the Report of the Working Party on the Accession of China, China confirmed that it would set the tariff rates of completely knocked-down kits (CKD) and semi-knocked down kits (SKD) for automobiles at no more than 10 percent, if China was to create independent tariff lines

---

[34] *Ibid.*, 399–400.

[35] The import adjustment tax was abolished in 1992. Although tariff rates were raised in the same year, the total rate of import charges was lowered from 200 percent to 180 per cent for passenger cars, and from 100 percent to 70 percent for trucks. The tariffs were gradually lowered to 100 percent for passenger cars and 50 percent for trucks by 1996 (*ibid.*, 392).

[36] While the tariffs on buses and trucks with GVW (gross vehicle weight) below 5 tons would be reduced to 25 percent by January 1, 2005, those on passenger cars would be reduced to 25 percent by July 1, 2006. Those on trucks over GVW 5 tons would be reduced to 15 percent to 20 percent by January 1, 2004 or January 1, 2005. See China's goods schedule, WT/ACC/CHN/49/Add.1. October 1, 2001.

[37] *Ibid.*

for them.[38] Second, in its services schedule, China opened its market of auto loans to foreign non-financial institutions.[39] It also confirmed that it would progressively accord trading rights to foreign enterprises in three years.[40] Third, China undertook a commitment to phase out its import license and import quota scheme on automobiles and auto parts by 2005.[41] During the phase-out period, the initial quota for automobiles and auto parts was set at US$6bn., with the annual growth rate of 15 per cent.[42] Fourth, on technical barriers to trade (TBT), China confirmed that it would bring into conformity with the TBT Agreement all of its technical regulations, standards and conformity assessment procedures. It also ensured that the same technical regulations, standards, and conformity assessment procedures were applied to both imported and domestic products.[43] Fifth, on trade-related investment measures (TRIMs), China ensured that, upon accession, it would comply with the TRIMs Agreement, assuming non-application of the general phase-out period for developing countries.[44] It would, thus, instantaneously eliminate foreign-exchange balancing and trade-balancing requirements, local content requirements, and export performance requirements.[45] Specifically, China confirmed that the 1994 Policy would be amended to ensure compatibility with WTO rules and principles.[46] China confirmed that amendments would be made to ensure that measures applicable to automotive manufacturers restricting the categories, types, or models of vehicle permitted for production, would gradually be lifted.[47] China also agreed to gradually raise the limit within which investments in automotive manufacturing could be approved at the level of provincial governments.[48] Finally, China committed itself toward removing the 50 percent equity limit for joint ventures for the manufacture of automotive engines upon accession.[49]

All of these commitments were incorporated in China's Protocol of Accession and shall be deemed to be an integral part of the WTO Agreement.[50] In order to monitor the implementation of these

---

[38] WT/ACC/CHN/49, October 1, para. 93.

[39] See China's services schedule, WT/ACC/CHN/49/Add 2. October 1, 2001.

[40] WT/ACC/CHN/49, October 1, 2001, paras.83 to 84.

[41] *Ibid.*, Annex 3, serial Nos. 248–318.   [42] *Ibid.*, Annex 3, table 2.

[43] Protocol on the Accession of the People's Republic of China, WT/L/432, 23 November 2001, pt 1, section 13.

[44] *Ibid.*, section 7.   [45] WT/ACC/CHN/49, October 1, 2001, para.203.

[46] *Ibid.*, para. 204.   [47] *Ibid.*, para. 205.   [48] *Ibid.*, para. 206.   [49] *Ibid.*, para. 207.

[50] *Ibid.*, para. 342. Also see Protocol on the Accession of the People's Republic of China, WT/L/432, November 23, 2001, pt 1, section 1, para. 2.

commitments by China, a Transitional Review Mechanism was introduced. The subsidiary bodies of the WTO[51] and the General Council
would review the implementation by China of the WTO Agreements and
the provisions of its accession Protocol each year for eight years,[52] and
there would be a final review in year 10 or at an earlier date decided by
the General Council.[53]

2. The Automotive Industry Development Policy of 2004

Although China confirmed in its accession document that the 1994 Policy
would be amended to ensure compatibility with the rules and principles
of the WTO, it was not until May 2004 that the new Automotive Industry
Development Policy (汽車産業発展政策, hereafter 'the 2004 Policy')
was promulgated by the National Reform and Development Commission.[54] The 2004 Policy formally replaced the 1994 Policy.[55]

The preamble of the 2004 Policy set out the overall goal of promoting
China's automotive industry to make it into a pillar industry of China's
national economy by 2010.[56] The 2004 Policy enumerated various policy
measures to achieve this goal, but they were generally within the confines
of the rules of the WTO Agreements and China's WTO commitment.
For instance, the local content requirement and the export-balancing
requirement for the import of auto parts, which had been adopted under
the 1994 Policy, were not adopted by the 2004 Policy.

One exception is Article 57. It provides that those auto parts which
would be imported for knock-down production would be deemed as
characterized as complete vehicles.[57] As the 2004 Policy did not provide
for the specific treatment on the imports of these auto parts, China issued
Administrative Rules on Verification of Imported Auto Parts Characterized as Complete Vehicles[58] and Rules on Verification of Imported Auto

---

[51] They were the thirteen bodies of the WTO including the Council for Trade in Goods, Council
     for Trade-Related Aspects of Intellectual Property Rights, Council for Trade in Services and
     Committees on Trade-Related Investment Measures (*ibid.*, pt 1, section 18, fn. 1).

[52] *Ibid.*, paras. 1–2 and 4.   [53] *Ibid.*, para. 4.

[54] The Chinese text of the Policy is available at: www.chinanews.com/auto/news/2007/03-
     20/895703.shtml (accessed May 17, 2013).

[55] The preamble of the 2004 Policy announced that the 1994 Policy had suspended its
     implementation upon the date of the promulgation of the 2004 Policy (*ibid.*).

[56] *Ibid.*   [57] *Ibid.*

[58] Decree of the People's Republic of China, No. 125, entered into force April 1, 2005
     (hereafter, 'Decree of April 1, 2005').

Parts Characterized as Complete Vehicles[59] in April 2005. According to these Rules, if a vehicle model is manufactured using imported parts that exceed specified quantity or value thresholds,[60] all imported parts are considered as auto parts characterized as complete vehicles. If a vehicle manufacturer produces a vehicle that uses imported parts which are characterized as complete vehicles, the manufacturer will be required to pay a charge on all imported parts incorporated into the vehicle. The charge equates to a 10 percent tariff on auto parts and an additional 15 percent internal charge, which is equivalent to the amount of the tariff rate on complete vehicles (25 percent). Charges are levied not at the border but at a later date after the parts have been incorporated into manufactured vehicles, depending on the use to which they are put into in China. If imported parts used in the manufacturing of automobiles are not characterized as complete vehicles, the tariff rate applicable to auto parts (10 percent) will be levied.[61]

In March 2006, the EC and the USA filed a complaint against China with respect to these measures pursuant to Article 4 of the Understanding on Rules and Procedures Governing the Settlement of Disputes (DSU).[62] Canada followed suit in April 2006.[63] A dispute Panel was

---

[59] Public Announcement of the Customs General Administration of the People's Republic of China, No.4 of 2005, entered into force April 1, 2005.

[60] Art. 21 of the Administrative Rules on Importation of Auto Parts Characterized as Complete Vehicles (Decree of April 1, 2005) sets out the following thresholds of the imported auto parts that would make those used to produce or assemble a motor vehicle to be characterized as complete motor vehicles:

(1) imports of CKD or SKD kits for the purpose of assembling vehicles;
(2) (a) imports of a body (including cabin) assembly and an engine assembly for the purpose of assembling vehicles;
    (b) imports of a body (including cabin) assembly or an engine assembly, plus at least three other assemblies (systems), for the purpose of assembling vehicles;
    (c) imports of at least five assemblies (systems) other than the body (including cabin) and engine assemblies for the purpose of assembling vehicles, or
(3) the total price of imported parts accounts for at least 60% of the total price of a complete vehicle.

(Cited in *China – Measures Affecting Imports of Automobile Parts*, Reports of the Panel, WT/DS339/R, WT/DS340/R, WT/DS342/R, 18 July 2008, para. 7.32.)

[61] *Ibid.*, paras. 7.24–38.

[62] *China – Measures Affecting Imports of Automobile Parts*, Request for Consultations by the European Communities, WT/DS339/1, April 3, 2006; *China – Measures Affecting Imports of Automobile Parts*, Request for Consultations by the United States, WT/DS340/1, April 3, 2006.

[63] *China – Measures Affecting Imports of Automobile Parts*, Request for Consultations by Canada, WT/DS342/1, April 19, 2006.

established in October 2006, and the Panel circulated its reports to the members in July 2008. The reports held that the measures at issue were inconsistent with Article III:2, first sentence of the GATT 1994 (the principle of national treatment) in that they accorded imported auto parts to an internal charge in excess of that applied to like domestic auto parts.[64] The reports also held that China violated its commitment under para. 93 of the China's Working Party Report, that it would apply tariff rates of no more than 10 percent to CKD and SKD kits if China creates tariff lines for CKD and SKD kits.[65] In the alternative, they held, assuming that the measures at issue are tariffs which fall within the scope of the first sentence of Article II:1(b) of the GATT 1994, that they were inconsistent with Article II:1(a) and Article II:1(b), first sentence of the GATT 1994 (obligation of tariff binding) in that they exceeded China's WTO commitment on tariffs on auto parts.[66]

China appealed in September 2008. The reports of the Appellate Body, circulated in December 2008, upheld the Panel's finding that the charge imposed under the measures at issue was an internal charge within the meaning of Article III:2 of the GATT 1994, and not an ordinary customs duty within the meaning of Article II:1(b), first sentence.[67] They also upheld the Panel's finding that the measures were inconsistent with Article III:2, first sentence of the GATT 1994 in that they subjected imported auto parts to an internal charge that was not applied to like domestic auto parts.[68] On the other hand, they reversed the Panel's finding that China violated its commitment under para. 93 of the Working Party Report, because the Panel had not established that the charge to CKD and SKD kits was not an internal charge, but a customs duty.[69] China repealed the measures at issue in August 2009.[70]

---

[64] *China – Measures Affecting Imports of Automobile Parts*, Reports of the Panel, WT/DS339/R, WT/DS340/R, WT/DS342/R, July 18, 2008, VIII. Conclusions and recommendations, A.(a)(i), B.(a)(i), and C.(a)(i).

[65] *Ibid.*, para. 7.758.

[66] *Ibid.*, VIII, Conclusions and recommendations, A.(b)(i), B.(b)(i), and C.(b)(i).

[67] *China – Measures Affecting Imports of Automobile Parts*, Reports of the Appellate Body, WT/DS339/AB/R, WT/DS340/AB/R, WT/DS342/AB/R, December 15, 2008, para. 253(a).

[68] *Ibid.*, para. 253(b).

[69] *Ibid.*, para. 253(e). The Appellate Body reports found it unnecessary to rule on the Panel's alternative finding that the measures at issue were inconsistent with art. II:1(a) and (b) of GATT 1994, because the measures at issue were not a customs duty, but an internal charge (*ibid.*, para. 253(d)).

[70] *China – Measures Affecting Imports of Automobile Parts*, Agreement under Article 21.3(b) of the DSU, WT/DS339/15, WT/DS340/15, WT/DS342/15, March 3, 2009.

3. Assessment of the Automotive Industry Development Policy of 2004

The measures at issue were aimed at promoting the domestic auto parts industry in China by discouraging the so called 'knock-down' production. Although this goal itself might be legitimate under WTO law, the measures adopted to pursue it were held inconsistent with the rules of WTO law. The Panel reports presented two alternative interpretations on the legal character of the measure at issue: it was either (1) an excessive internal charge (15 percent) that was not applied to like domestic auto parts in violation of the principle of national treatment, or (2) an excessive tariff duty (25 percent) tantamount to those on complete vehicles in violation of China's tariff commitment on auto parts (10 percent). The Appellate Body reports upheld the first interpretation of the Panel reports, for the following reason: in light of the method of calculation and the timing of imposition, the charge (15 percent) imposed on the auto parts in addition to the ordinary tariff (10 percent) was deemed not as a customs duty, which shall be charged "on their importation" (Article II:1(b), first sentence of the GATT 1994), but as an internal charge, which were charged after the products had been "imported" (Article III:2, first sentence of the GATT 1994).[71] This was based on the precedent under the GATT dispute settlement jurisprudence.[72]

This was the second WTO dispute case where China was a respondent,[73] and the first one where China appealed and lost.[74] One interesting question is why China did not reach an amicable settlement before a Panel was established. Kawashima explains this was because the National Reform and Development Commission, which promulgated the 2004 Policy, had paid less attention to the compatibility of its automotive industrial policy with WTO law and China's accession commitment than the other agencies of the central government which were directly

---

[71] China - Measures Affecting Imports of Automobile Parts, Reports of the Appellate Body, WT/DS339/AB/R, WT/DS340/AB/R, WT/DS342/AB/R, December 15, 2008, paras. 153, 161-165.

[72] See EEC - Regulation on Imports of Parts and Components, Report by the Panel adopted May 16, 1990, L/6657, BISD 37S/132, paras. 5.3-5.8.

[73] The first WTO dispute case where China was a respondent was China - Value-added Tax on Integrated Circuits (WT/DS309).

[74] In the first case, China reached settlement with the USA, the complainant, before a panel was established (ibid.).

responsible for implementing WTO law and China's WTO commitment, notably the Ministry of Commerce.[75]

Kawashima also points out that WTO disputes multiplied on account of the subsidies China provided to various industrial sectors since 2007.[76] They were, namely: *China – Certain Measures Granting Refunds, Reductions or Exemptions from Taxes and Other Payments* (WT/DS358, 359); *China – Grants, Loans and Other Incentives* (WT/DS387, 388, 390); and *China – Measures concerning wind power equipment* (WT/DS419). In all these cases, China abolished the subsidies either at the consultation stage (in the first and the third cases) or during the Panel proceeding (in the second case). At first glance, this suggests that the WTO dispute settlement mechanism has been effective in securing China's compliance with WTO law and its accession commitments. However, as Kawashima emphasizes,[77] this also means that China has recently been introducing a number of industrial policy instruments which clearly violate WTO law and its accession commitment, and it abolishes them only after the other WTO members bring them into question and the WTO dispute panels and the Appellate Body condemn them as violations of WTO law and China's accession commitment. Kawashima concludes that China's governmental agencies in charge of industrial policy take almost no account of the rules of WTO law, particularly the SCM Agreement.[78]

4. China's post-crisis stimulus package for the automotive industry

There is another example of China's recent disregard of WTO law and its accession commitments. In the wake of the global economic crisis triggered by the Lehman shock in September 2008, many countries in the world adopted measures to rescue their domestic economic downturn. China was not an exception. Although China was not directly hit by the financial crisis in the USA and Europe, China experienced a sharp decline in its export and import trade in early 2009. As part of the stimulus package to boost domestic consumption, China adopted the following measures to support its domestic automotive industry.

---

[75] See F. Kawashima, 'WTO kameigo 10 nenwohetaChuugokuniokeruhouseidooyobijigyoukankyou' [The Legal System and Business Environment of China 10 Years After its Accession to the WTO], *Soshiki Kagaku*, 45 (2011), 16, 18–19.
[76] *Ibid.*, 21.   [77] *Ibid.*, 21–22.   [78] *Ibid.*, 22.

First, it lowered the purchase tax of automobiles with engine capacity under 1,600 cc from 10 to 5 percent.[79] Second, it subsidized the purchase of eco cars as replacement of old cars ('scrap initiative (以旧换新)'). Third, it subsidized the purchase of light trucks and minivans with engine capacity under 1,300 cc in rural areas ('sell automobiles to peasants (汽車丈鄉)'), totaling 5 billion yuan.[80] Fourth, it subsidized the purchase of electric vehicles (EVs) at a maximum of 60,000 yuan per unit and plug-in hybrid vehicles (PHVs) at a maximum of 50,000 yuan per unit.[81] As a result of these measures, the domestic sales of automobiles increased 46 percent and that of small automobiles increased 71 percent in 2009.[82]

The consistency of some of these measures with WTO law is, at least, suspicious. First, the 'sell automobiles to peasants (汽車丈鄉)' subsidy program flatly excluded imported trucks and minivans from the category of eligible automobiles, regardless of their engine capacity. It clearly violates the principle of national treatment under Article III:4 of the GATT 1994.[83] Second, the subsidy program for the purchase of EVs and PHVs also excluded imported EVs and PHVs in violation of Article III:4. In addition, it restricted the eligibility to those vehicles whose major components (e.g., batteries) are domestically produced. Accordingly, this is a subsidy contingent upon the use of domestic over imported goods, which is prohibited under Article 3.1(b) of the SCM Agreement.[84]

It must be noted that China was not the only WTO member that adopted suspicious measures to rescue domestic economic downturn. The global economic crisis had a huge negative impact on the global automotive market, and a number of WTO members, including the USA,

---

[79] 'China issues stimulus package for auto sector: state media', AFP, January 14, 2009, www.google.com/hostednews/afp/article/ALeqM5gBBAzDcp4XtPPUMYgRBEyR_iNqpA (accessed May 17, 2013).

[80] See Y. Hong and Y. Mu, 'China's Automobile Industry: An Update' (2010), *EAI Background Brief, No. 500*, East Asian Institute, National University of Singapore, 7, 15, at www.eai.nus.edu.sg/BB500.pdf (accessed May 17, 2013); T. Kawase, 'Sekaikin'yukikika no kokkaenjo to WTO hojokinkiritsu' [State Aid under the Global Financial Crisis and the WTO Discipline on Subsidies] (2011) RIETI Discussion Paper Series 11-J-65, 70–71.

[81] See F. Kawashima, 'Chuugokuniyoruhojokinkyouyo no tokuchou to jitsumutekikadai–Beichuukanfunsouwosozaini' [The characteristics and the issues of China's subsidies – focusing on US–China disputes], RIETI Discussion Paper Series 11-J-067, 3 (fn. 6).

[82] See 'Understanding China's Automobile Industry (1) rapidly booming China's Automobile Market', Electro to Auto Forum, Industry Trend, Theme 08, January 25, 2010, at: http://e2a.jp/trend/100125.shtml (accessed May 17, 2013).

[83] *Ibid.*, 3 (fn. 5).   [84] *Ibid.*, 3 (fn. 6).

Japan, Korea, and various European countries, introduced support pro-
grams and scrapping schemes which were similar to those adopted by
China.[85] The compatibility of some of these programs and schemes with
WTO law is also suspicious.[86]

As many members adopted similar subsidy programs whose consistency with WTO law is suspicious, each member might refrain from
making a WTO dispute complaint against a program of another member,
including that of China, for fear of being complained against by other
members on account of its own program.[87] This might result in a
situation where a number of programs and schemes in the automotive
sector whose consistency with WTO law is suspicious will remain intact.
Although, politically speaking, this might be a sensible solution to deal
with the emergent rescue measures adopted during the global economic
crisis, this might also infringe the rules of WTO law, notably those on
subsidies.[88]

V. Conclusion

China became the world's largest automobile-producing country for the
first time in 2009, with 13,790,934 units (of which 10,383,831 were
passenger cars (75.3 percent) and 3,407,163 buses and trucks (24.7
percent)). This was a remarkable growth, in light of China's automobile
production in 2001, with 2,330,000 units.[89] We can conclude that the
overall goal of the 2004 Policy – namely, to transform the automotive
industry into a pillar industry of China's national economy by the year
2010 – was achieved.

---

[85] For the details of the support programs and scrapping schemes adopted by the G20
member countries, see Kawase, 'Sekaikin'yukikika no kokkaenjo to WTO hojokinkiritsu',
48–90; OECD, 'Responding to the Economic Crisis: Fostering Industrial Restructuring
and Renewal' (Paris: OECD, 2009), 20–21, 25–27.

[86] See Kawase, 'Sekaikin'yukikika no kokkaenjo to WTO hojokinkiritsu', 77–78, 85.

[87] See e.g. R. J. Ahear, 'The Global Economic Downturn and Protectionism' (2009) CRS
Report for Congress, R40461 (Washington, DC: Congressional Research Service), 8.

[88] Kawase suggests introducing a 'peace clause' to automotive sector, so that non-recourse
to the WTO dispute settlement procedure with respect to the support programs and
scrapping schemes may be justified under the WTO law ('Sekaikin'yukikika no kokkaenjo
to WTO hojokinkiritsu', 117).

[89] See Japan Automobile Information Center, Country Share of Automobile Production,
2008 and 2009, http://autoinfoc.com/seisan/sekaiseisan/s-sekaiseisan-2.html (accessed
May 17, 2013).

We must note that this rapid growth was achieved in spite of the fact that China had substantively contracted the policy space for its automotive industrial policy. China had to give up a number of policy measures that had been available before its accession to the WTO, as they might have violated the rules of the WTO Agreements and China's WTO commitments. On the other hand, accession to the WTO brought in a number of opportunities and benefits to China's automotive industry. A substantive reduction of tariffs on automobiles and auto parts resulting from China's accession commitment significantly lowered the domestic sales prices of automobiles in China. The purchasing power of China's domestic population significantly increased due to the rapid economic growth led by the rapid growth in trade after its accession to the WTO.[90] These factors contributed to the rapid growth in China's domestic demand for automobiles, notably for passenger cars. Foreign automobile manufacturers came to enjoy the benefits of doing business in China in a more transparent and foreseeable regulatory environment that was secured by the rules of the WTO and China's WTO commitment. This enabled them to accelerate their investment in automobile manufacturing and in research and development (R&D) in the automotive sector. All of these were the developments resulting either directly or indirectly from China's accession to the WTO, which contributed to the significant growth of China's automotive industry.

The case of China suggests that the argument which refutes WTO law as having the effect of shrinking the policy space for development (and/or transition) does not hold true for *all* developing countries. Accession to the WTO brings in both opportunities and challenges including 'the shrinking policy space'. The case of China shows us that the former prevailed a great deal over the latter. However, it may be too much to say that accession to the WTO will guarantee better performance in economic growth and development *in all cases*. The WTO law and WTO members' commitments are only part of the many factors, both internal and external, to be taken into account in working out an optimal industrial policy, which may differ from country by country. The real challenge for a new WTO member is, therefore, how to make full use of the opportunities provided by the WTO membership (e.g., improved market access), while constricting the negative effects of 'the shrinking policy

---

[90] China's per capita real GDP more than tripled from US$1,038 in 2001 to US$3,739 in 2009. See IMF, World Economic Outlook Database, October 2010, www.imf.org/external/pubs/ft/weo/2010/02/weodata/index.aspx (accessed May 17, 2013).

space'. By accumulating case studies, of both successful cases and failed ones, we may clarify the possibilities and limits of WTO membership in working out an optimal set (or, more precisely, *sets*) of industrial policy for developing countries and transition countries.

On the other hand, there has recently been an alarming tendency on the part of China to adopt industrial policy instruments, notably subsidies, whose compatibility with WTO law and China's accession commitments is suspicious.[91] As is shown by the recent surge of the WTO cases where the compatibility of China's industrial policy measures with WTO law is disputed,[92] the WTO dispute settlement mechanism has been effective in controlling such deviation of China's industrial policy from WTO law. We may conclude that, ten years after its accession to the WTO, China's attitude toward WTO law has shifted from that of unconditional obedience to that of occasional disobedience for the sake of a wider space for industrial policy. Whether this observation is correct or not, and whether this should bring us to the reconsideration of the role of WTO law as a regulator of the policy space available for economic development (and transition), will be a topic for further research.

[91] See Kawashima, 'WTO kameigo', 22–25.   [92] *Ibid.*, 20 (table 2).

9

The first condition of progress? Freedom of speech and the limits of international trade law

TOMER BROUDE AND HOLGER HESTERMEYER

[T]he first condition of progress is the removal of all censorships.

George Bernard Shaw[1]

I. Introduction

When economic operators trade internationally, not only goods and services cross national boundaries, but also the culture, opinions, information, and ideas that they carry.[2] This creates complex links between the regulation of international trade and international human rights law. Measures that restrict the freedom of speech may concurrently interfere with international trade, while barriers to trade may encroach upon the freedom of expression,[3] which under international law applies "regardless of frontiers."[4]

The link between these two regimes is more than theoretical. A WTO complaint brought by the European Union against China in

---

* We thank the University of Virginia for permission to reprint this chapter, which originally appeared in 54(2) *Virginia Journal of International Law* 295–321 (2014).

[1] G. B. Shaw, *The Author's Apology from Mrs. Warren's Profession* (Brentanos, 1905: 41): "All censorships exist to prevent any one from challenging current conceptions and existing institutions. All progress is initiated by challenging current conceptions, and executed by supplanting existing institutions. Consequently the first condition of progress is the removal of censorships."

[2] As an indication of the economic scale of international trade in cultural goods and services, the Motion Picture Association of America (MPAA) reported $13.5 billion earned in audio-visual services exports and a solid trade surplus for the USA of $11.9 billion (*The Economic Contribution of the Motion Picture & Television Industry to the United States* (2012)).

[3] "Everyone shall have the right to freedom of expression; this right shall include freedom to seek, receive and impart information and ideas of all kinds" (International Covenant on Civil and Political Rights, art. 19, para. 2, Dec. 16, 1966, 999 UNTS 171 [hereafter ICCPR]).

[4] The right applies "regardless of frontiers, either orally, in writing or in print, in the form of art, or through any other media of his choice" (ICCPR).

2008 challenged regulations that required all foreign financial information service providers to act, in essence, through China's central news
agency, Xinhua.[5] While these regulations quite clearly violated international trade agreements, they simultaneously restricted the freedom
of expression and access to information.[6] In 2009, a complaint by the
USA showed that China had reserved the distribution of films, audiovisual entertainment products, sound recordings and certain publications
to state-designated and -owned enterprises – again posing not only a
trade problem but also a restriction on the freedom of expression (the
Audiovisual Products case).[7] In the same year, a WTO panel ruled partly
against China despite its invocation of public order exceptions (the *IPR
Enforcement* case),[8] because its copyright legislation denied protection
from works that had not been authorized for public circulation by
government censors, suggesting yet another interaction between trade
and the freedom of expression.[9]

What is striking in these cases is that international trade law and
human rights seem to be mutually reinforcing, in contrast to the more
familiar narrative in which trade liberalization somehow negates or

---

[5] See Request for Consultations by the European Community, *China – Measures Affecting
Financial Information Services and Foreign Financial Information Suppliers*, WT/DS372/1
(Mar. 3, 2008); see Request for Consultations by the United States, WT/DS373/1 (Mar. 3,
2008); see Request for Consultations by Canada, WT/DS378/1 (Jun. 20, 2008). The parties
to the dispute reached a mutually agreed solution.

[6] The EU and China settled this dispute by way of a mutually agreed solution notified to the
WTO (see Joint Communication from China and the European Communities, 'China –
Measures Affecting Financial Information Services and Foreign Financial Information
Suppliers,' WT/DS372/4 (Dec. 9, 2008)), in which China made certain commitments
relating to the regulation of financial information services, though notably subject to the
Chinese regulator's authority to require all service providers "to comply with all relevant
Chinese laws, regulations, and departmental rules" (2).

[7] See Appellate Body Report, 'China – Measures Affecting Trading Rights and Distribution
Services for Certain Publications and Audiovisual Entertainment Products,' WT/DS363/
AB/R (Jan. 19, 2010). We deal with this case in greater depth in section IV.2.

[8] See Panel Report, 'China – Measures Affecting the Protection and Enforcement of
Intellectual Property Rights,' WT/DS362/R (Jan. 26, 2009) (unappealed). This case is
analyzed below in section IV.1.

[9] It should be noted that the trade–expression nexus is not exclusive to the WTO or trade
agreements, and can also arise in human rights tribunals. For example, the European
Court of Human Rights (ECtHR) has recognized cross-border commercial activities as
covered by the freedom of expression. See *Groppera Radio AG and others v. Switzerland*
(App. No. 10890/84), 173 Eur. Ct HR (Ser. A) (1990); *Informationsverein Lentia and
others v. Austria* (No. 36/1992/381/455-459), 276 Eur. Ct HR (Ser. A) (1993). However,
our focus here is on the capacity of trade law and international economic institutions to
promote the freedom of speech, not vice versa.

overrides human rights. The fragmentation of international law is often considered a source of normative and institutional conflict. With respect to trade and the freedom of expression, could the strengths of one regime actually promote the goals of another? More specifically, could a 'Google case' (i.e., a WTO complaint aimed against China's internet-filtering laws and practices, of the type that ultimately forced Google to significantly downscale its commercial presence in China, and relocate its servers to Hong Kong in 2010)[10] promote the freedom of speech? The relevance of this question has in fact risen over recent years, as the extent to which internet-based communications companies such as Skype, must adjust their commercial and technological operations to Chinese censorship requirements, is exposed.[11]

Could trade law tear down the great 'cyberwall' of China? The First Amendment Coalition (FAC), a US non-profit public interest organiza-tion, seems to think so. They have lobbied in favor of a Google case, touting their initiative (grounded in academic writing)[12] as "the biggest access-to-information and free speech case in history."[13] To this end, they have retained international trade law counsel, presenting a legal case against Chinese media control to the US Trade Representative (USTR) and the US–China Economic and Security Review Commission.[14] This

---

[10] Google took the decision after cyber attacks on its websites were traced back to China. The difficulties posed by Chinese censorship have also been cited, however, as grounds for the move (*BBC News*, 'China Condemns Decision by Google', http://news.bbc.co.uk/2/hi/asia-pacific/8582233.stm (March 23, 2010); B. Powell, 'Who will profit when Google exits from China?,' *Time*, Mar. 9, 2010, www.time.com/time/business/article/0,8599,1973410,00.html

[11] Researchers have, for example, only recently revealed how Skype text-messaging is subject to surveillance in China, with respect to politically sensitive words such as 'Tiananmen' and 'Amnesty International,' requiring the cooperation of Microsoft (owner of Skype). See V. Silver, 'Cracking China's Skype Surveillance Software,' *Bloomberg Business Week*, Mar. 8, 2013, www.businessweek.com/articles/2013-03-08/skypes-been-hijacked-in-china-and-microsoft-is-o-dot-k-dot-with-it

[12] In particular, see T. Wu, 'The World Trade Law of Censorship and Internet Filtering,' *Chi. J. Int'l. L.* 7(2006), 263. For an earlier reference see M. C. Rundle, 'Beyond Internet Governance: The Emerging International Framework for Governing the Networked World,' Berkman Center Research Publication No. 2002-16 (2005); M. Panizzon, 'How Human Rights Violations Nullify and Impair GATS Commitments,' *GATS and the Regulation of International Trade in Services: World Trade Forum*, 534 (2008).

[13] See P. Scheer, *Acting Globally and Locally: From Internet Censorship in China to a TRO against Atherton, CA*, First Amendment Coalition (January 20, 2008), http://firstamend-mentcoalition.org/2009/06/report

[14] See Testimony of Gilbert Kaplan, partner, King & Spalding LLP, Access to Information and Media Control in the People's Republic of China (June 18, 2008), www.uscc.gov/

even led USTR to pose substantial questions on internet restrictions to Chinese authorities,[15] although no request for consultations on the issue, let alone for the establishment of a dispute settlement panel, has been brought to the WTO so far.

The idea of trade and free speech marching in lockstep can be highly appealing to both the trade community and international human rights advocates. For the sake of simplicity, we will refer to this concept as the 'confluence thesis.' However, in this chapter we skeptically assert that despite the intuition of a natural synergy between free trade and free speech, the real capacity of WTO law to promote free speech is significantly restricted, casting more than a shadow of doubt on the confluence thesis.

Section II locates the notion of confluence between trade liberalization and free speech in the broader 'trade and human rights' debate. Section III explains the legal and functional differences between a human rights law approach to a restriction on free speech and a trade law approach, with particular reference to trade in goods, as analysis illustrative of the systemic obstacles to confluence that cut across all areas of WTO law. Section IV presents two case studies that demonstrate the weakness of the confluence in practice, in the areas of trade in services and trade-related intellectual property rights. Section V concludes with general observations.

II.   Trade liberalization and free speech: five configurations

Confluence between trade liberalization and human rights in general (and free speech in particular) is but one of several configurations of the trade law and human rights relationship. As one of us has elaborated elsewhere,[16] there are essentially five types of international trade law–human rights linkages that have been contemplated, discussed and indeed played out, at least since the establishment of the WTO. They

---

hearings/2008hearings/written_testimonies/08_06_18_wrts/08_06_18_kaplan_state-ment.php

[15] See press release, 'USTR, United States seeks detailed information on China's internet restrictions (Oct. 22, 2011) (www.ustr.gov/about-us/press-office/press-releases/2011/october/united-states-seeks-detailed-information-china's-i).

[16] See T. Broude, 'From Seattle to "Occupy": Trade, Human Rights and the Shifting Focus of Social Protest,' in Daniel Drache and Les Jacobs (eds.), *The Changing Global Landscape for International Trade and Human Rights Linkages* (Cambridge University Press, 2013).

are (1) *conflict*, (2) *conditionality*, (3) *constitutionalism*, (4) *conformity*, and (5) *confluence*.

Conflict is the basic idea that trade liberalization can contradict human rights, in principle or in practice. The GATT/WTO regime is built on the premise that trade liberalization stimulates economic growth and creates wealth. Such wealth generation might enable governments and societies to better fulfill their human rights objectives (and obligations). However, mere economic growth does not necessarily translate into greater and more equitably distributed wealth for the populace at large, and certainly does not imply that human rights conditions are automatically improved.[17] Critics argue that trade liberalization conflicts with human rights by eroding the ability of states to provide social rights protections and/or by creating economic and social unrest that drives governments to wholesale violations of civil and political rights.[18] In many circles there exists a general perception that trade law 'trumps' human rights.[19] Indeed, concerns over specific legal conflicts between trade disciplines and international human rights law and policy have been raised and analyzed, such as between patent protection for pharmaceuticals required by the WTO agreement on Trade Related Aspects of Intellectual Property (TRIPs),[20] on the one hand, and the right to health,[21] on the

[17] See 'Trade Liberalization and Poverty: A Handbook,' in N. McCulloch, L. A. Winters, and X. Cirera (eds.) (2001) in which a series of studies demonstrates that the effects of trade liberalization on poverty vary among states, sectors and areas of regulation, sometimes positive, sometimes negative.

[18] For a general survey of the literature on this aspect, see Andrew T. F. Lang, 'The Role of the Human Rights Movement in Trade-Policy Making: Human Rights as a Trigger for Policy Learning,' *N.Z. J. Pub. & Int'l. L.* 5 (2007), 77. For an analysis aimed especially at economic, social and cultural rights, see R. Howse and R. G. Teitel, 'Beyond the Divide: The Covenant on Economic, Social and Cultural Rights and the WTO,' in F. Kirchmeier (ed.), Occasional Paper No. 30 (2007). For a useful graphic depiction of the diverging views of the effects of economic liberalization on human rights, see M. R. Abouharb and D. Cingranelli, *Human Rights and Structural Adjustment* 68 (2007).

[19] A rhetorical question posed by Pascal Lamy shows as much: "Is not the World Trade Organization for many the symbol of a globalization in which mercantile pursuits have precedence over human beings, the market over individuals, and might over right?" (remarks after receiving the title of Doctor Honoris Causa at the University of Geneva 450th Anniversary Celebration, Jun. 5, 2009).

[20] Agreement on Trade-Related Aspects of Intellectual Property Rights, Apr. 15, 1994, Marrakesh Agreement Establishing the World Trade Organization, Annex 1C, Legal Texts: The Results of the Uruguay Round of Multilateral Trade Negotiations 320 (1999), 1869 UNTS 299, 33 ILM 1197 (1994) [hereafter TRIPS Agreements].

[21] See International Covenant on Economic, Social and Cultural Rights art. 12, Dec. 16, 1966, 993 UNTS 3 [hereafter ICECSR].

other.[22] Conflicts between trade law and the freedom of expression have not been focal points of debate, although they undoubtedly exist (e.g., in intellectual property rules, as will be discussed below in our study of the IPR Enforcement case in section 4(i) below).

Conditionality refers to the creation of explicit links of legal contingency between trade liberalization disciplines and compliance with international human rights norms.[23] Conditionality as a means of promoting international human rights may have its proponents, although empirical research casts doubt both on the real motivations for the establishment of human rights conditionality and on the extent of its effectiveness, given the low degree of political willingness and capability to enforce it.[24] It is surely possible to consider the promotion of the international right to freedom of expression by conditionality, through measures that impose restrictions on or deny preferences from goods and services originating in states with a deficient free speech environment. Arguably, the inclusion of the ICCPR and ICESCR in the qualification criteria of the EU's 'GSP+' program does just that.[25] However, the effectiveness of this framework is ultimately an empirical question on which little actual knowledge exists.

Constitutionalism, perhaps the most controversial strand of the trade and human rights debate, contemplates market freedoms as additional human rights.[26] Critics have vociferously argued that this approach misconstrues the foundations of human rights law, and threatens to erode them.[27]

---

[22] See H. P. Hestermeyer, *Human Rights and the WTO: The Case of Patents and Access to Medicines* (Oxford University Press, 2007.) For a series of case studies of trade law's relations with particular human rights in specific contexts, see T. Cottier, J. Pauwelyn, and E. Bürgi (eds.), *Human Rights and International Trade* (Oxford University Press, 2012), 245–504.

[23] The literature on human rights conditionality is extensive. Important milestones in this literature are P. Alston, 'International Trade as an Instrument of Positive Human Rights Policy,' *Human Rights Quarterly* 4(1982) 155; L. Bartels, *Human Rights Conditionality in the EU's International Agreements* (2005).

[24] See E. M. Hafner-Burton, *Forced to Be Good: Why Trade Agreements Boost Human Rights* (Ithaca, NY: Cornell University Press, 2009).

[25] See Lorand Bartels, 'The WTO Legality of the EU's GSP+ Arrangement', *J. Int'l. Econ. L.* 10 (2007).

[26] For a central exposition of this thesis, see E.-U. Petersmann, 'Time for a United Nations "Global Compact" for Integrating Human Rights into the Law of Worldwide Organizations: Lessons from European Integration,' *Eur. J. Int. L.* 13(2002), 621

[27] For discussion, see R. Howse, 'Human Rights in the WTO: Whose Rights, What Humanity? Comment on Petersmann,' *Eur. J. Int. L.* 13 (2002), 651; P. Alston, 'Resisting the Merger and Acquisition of Human Rights by Trade Law: A Reply to Petersmann,'

Constitutionalism in this vein[28] is a distinctive interpretation of the political philosophy of ordoliberalism,[29] and as such represents a particular normative understanding of global social order, in which market-oriented rules are elevated to the level of human rights. Although the constitutional approach seeks conceptual harmony between trade disciplines and human rights, its impact upon human rights in general and the freedom of expression in particular is difficult to divine.

Conformity is the functional idea that international trade law should be interpreted in light of human rights, not only in cases of potential conflict between trade and human rights, but also more generally. Sometimes this interpretative notion is advanced with respect to a particular human right, or a cluster of rights, such as the right to development.[30] This is a very attractive approach, both normatively and doctrinally, serving a potential role in providing positive interactions between trade and other fields. Regarding the freedom of expression, it would expect international trade law to be interpreted in conformity with international human rights law. To date, WTO law's tendency toward compartmentalization has not allowed this to happen.[31]

In contrast to these configurations, the *confluence* thesis is both more modest and simultaneously more presumptuous. It proposes that trade law has sufficient overlaps with human rights law that it can, at least in certain cases, spontaneously enhance traditional human rights. Yet the idea of confluence neither establishes a new category or class of human rights, as would forms of constitutionalism, nor relies on a particular

Eur. J. Int. L. 13 (2002), 815; E.-U. Petersmann, 'Taking Human Dignity, Poverty and Empowerment of Individuals More Seriously: A Rejoinder to Alston,' *Eur. J. Int. L.* 13 (2002), 845.

[28] There are, surely, other uses of the term 'constitutionalism,' in the international context. See Deborah Cass, *The Constitutionalization of the World Trade Organization* (Oxford University Press, 2005); J. L. Dunoff and J. P. Trachtman (eds.), *Ruling the World? Constitutionalism, International Law, and Global Governance* (Cambridge University Press, 2009).

[29] R. Ptak, 'Neoliberalism in Germany: Revisiting the Ordoliberal Foundations of the Social Market Economy,' in P. Mirowski and D. Plehwe (eds.), *The Road From Mont Pelerin: The Making of the Neoliberal Thought Collective* (Cambridge, MA: Harvard University Press, 2009), 89–138.

[30] For one expression of such an approach, see R. L. Howse, 'Mainstreaming the Right to Development into International Trade Law and Policy at the World Trade Organization' (Study, UN Doc. E/CN.4/Sub.2/2004/17, 2004).

[31] See T. Broude, 'It's Easily Done: The China – Intellectual Property Rights Enforcement Dispute and the Freedom of Expression,' *J. of World Intellectual Property* 13 (2010), 660

justification or formulation of either trade law or human rights law, as would the frames of conditionality and conformity. Rather, the confluence thesis considers economic liberalization as a veritable handmaiden of a human right. Instead of conflict, it posits a comfortable mutual reinforcement between two separate regimes of law, that appear to somehow "point in the same direction,"[32] in the sense that the removal of restrictions to trade may also promote the freedom of speech. In the following section we turn to examine the validity of the confluence thesis in the particular context of the freedom of expression.

III.   The confluence thesis examined

1.   The divergent rationales of international trade law and human rights with respect to the freedom of speech

Both trade law and human rights value speech, but confluence's weakness is soon exposed by the gaps between their respective reasoning. Two fundamentally different rationales for free speech exist: the utilitarian, justifying it as an instrument in the advancement of efficiency, truth and democracy;[33] and the deontological, looking at the intrinsic value of human beings. While human rights law is shaped by both of these, trade law is, at best, informed by a narrow version of the former.

The utilitarian rationale theory goes back to John Stuart Mill: "complete liberty of contradicting and disproving our opinion is the very condition which justifies us in assuming its truth for purposes of action."[34] Oliver Wendell Holmes concurred through the metaphor of the marketplace of ideas.[35] One need not believe, however, in absolute truths to accept that better outcomes may be reached through the

---

[32] ILC, 'The Fragmentation of International Law: Difficulties Arising from the Diversification and Expansion of International Law,' A/CN.4/L.682 (Apr. 13, 2006) noted that in some cases norms that hold a *lex generalis–lex specialis* relationship do not conflict with each other but rather "point in the same direction" (at 52). Such non-conflictual relations between fragmented norms can exist in a broader set of "multi-sourced equivalent norms" (see T. Broude and Y. Shany, *The International Law and Policy of Multi-Sourced Equivalent Norms* (Cambridge University Press, 2010); under the confluence thesis, freedom of expression and trade liberalization maintain such an equivalence.

[33] See T. Scanlon, 'A Theory of Freedom of Expression,' *Philosophy and Public Affairs* 1 (1972), 204–206; E. Chemerinsky, *Constitutional Law Principles and Policies* (3rd edn, New York: Kluwer, 2006), 924–930.

[34] J. S. Mill, *On Liberty* (London: Pearson College Div. 2006) (1878), 11 This logic can also be detected in J. Milton, *Areopagitica* (Elibron Classics, 2000) (1644).

[35] See *Abrams* v. *United States*, 250 US 616 (1919) (dissent, Holmes, J.).

comparison of various imperfect ideas.[36] Democratic systems vitally depend on the test of ideas in the public sphere, the free confrontation of government with the speech of its citizens and, most prominently of all, the press.[37] Furthermore, open discourse may itself legitimate the outcome.[38]

In contrast, the deontological rationale views freedom of expression as "an essential function of self-identity: the ability to express oneself as a means of constructing the self."[39] In international human rights law, this approach is manifest in the idea that all civil and political rights, including the freedom of expression "derive from the inherent dignity of the human person."[40] The freedom of expression is the extension of the freedom to "hold opinions without interference" (Article 19(1) ICCPR)) and is closely related to the deontologically based freedom of conscience (Article 18 ICCPR).[41]

However, the trade scope of free speech pursues only particular utilitarian goals: economic efficiency and market perfection. Free speech is promoted as a derivative of market freedom, or as one of its conditions, instead of an end goal in itself.[42] As John Jackson has written, "[s]ome of these [human rights] are even necessary in order for markets to work. A particular example is free speech."[43]

Thus, we find only partial, weak support for a conceptual confluence between liberal trade and the human right of free speech. Trade law views the freedom of speech as an instrument to promote economic market efficiency. The human rights rationale is much broader, including

---

[36] C. E. Baker, *Human Liberty and Freedom of Speech* (Oxford University Press, 1989), 17.

[37] This line of thinking is associated with Alexander Meiklejohn. See E. Barendt, *Freedom of Speech* (Oxford University Press, 1987), 20–23.

[38] See generally J. Habermas, *Theorie des Kommunikativen Handelns* (Suhrkamp, 2006). As A. Sen notes: "informed and unregimented formation of our values requires openness of communication and arguments, and political freedoms and civil rights can be central for this process. Furthermore, to express publicly what we value and to demand that attention be paid to it, we need free speech and democratic choice" (*Development as Freedom* (Oxford University Press, 1999), 152).

[39] See D. E. Guinn, 'Philosophy and Theory of Freedom of Expression,' *Encyclopedia of American Civil Liberties* (2006); Barendt, *Freedom of Speech*, 14–20.

[40] See ICCPR.

[41] *Ibid.*

[42] M. Friedman, *Capitalism and Freedom* (University of Chicago Press, [1962] 2002).

[43] See J. H. Jackson, 'Reflections on the Possible Research Agenda for Exploring the Relationship between Human Rights Norms and International Trade Rules,' in F. M. Abbott, C. B. Kaufmann, and T. Cottier (eds.), *International Trade and Human Rights: Foundations and Conceptual Issues* (Cambridge University Press, 2006), 19, 26.

political freedoms as a good in and of themselves. The functional economic justification ends where expressions and information no longer have a market-perfecting contribution. In turning to the legal analysis of confluence, we must bear in mind the difference in the goals of international trade and human rights law with respect to free expression.

2. The human rights law framework

For confluence with the freedom of expression to be tested, an international trade element must be apparent, such as a limitation on international commerce. To examine the human rights side of the confluence thesis, let us assume a restriction on trade that may be considered an infringement on the freedom of expression, such as a restriction on importing speech-containing goods and services (e.g., a ban on the importation of a foreign book title or music album). An initial question in analyzing such trade restrictions with respect to international free speech law is whether states are at all under an obligation to respect the freedom of expression of foreign authors. The freedom of expression, like other human rights,[44] is a universal and effectively transnational human right.[45] It applies to everyone, regardless of frontiers, therefore including all authors of expressions irrespective of their nationality or domicile.[46] An author of information or of an idea expressed in one country has generally not exhausted her freedom of expression, which continues to apply in all other countries.[47] This is consonant with both instrumental and deontological human rights rationales for the freedom of expression.

Further supporting this conclusion, rights protected under Article 19 ICCPR include not only the author's freedom of expression but also the right of 'everyone' to *access* information – the corollary freedom to 'seek' and to 'receive' information and ideas.[48] This freedom of access to

---

[44] *Inter alia*, the right to non-discrimination, equality and fairness, the right to freedom of thought, conscience and religion, the right to be presumed innocent, the right to freedom from slavery, the right to freedom of torture.

[45] See also Universal Declaration of Human Rights, GA Res. 217A (III), UN Doc. A/810 pmbl. (1948); see ICCPR.

[46] UN Human Rights Committee (HRC), ICCPR General Comment No. 34, CCPR/C/GC/ 34 (Sept. 11, 2011).

[47] *Ibid.*, para. 6.

[48] ICCPR: "Everyone shall have the right to freedom of expression; this right shall include freedom to seek, receive and impart information and ideas of all kinds, regardless of

information is an important complement to the freedom to impart information. The same government measure may violate both freedoms. If a newspaper is banned from circulation, both the journalists' expression and readership's freedoms of access have been curtailed. This effectively emphasizes that the freedom of expression is of general public interest, not only individual concern. Generally, 'everyone' has the right to hear 'everyone.' While the party imparting an opinion may be intimidated from pursuing her individual freedom of expression, or lack the will to overcome the barriers to expression in a given jurisdiction, the resolve of a larger audience interested in hearing her opinion might be more difficult to repress, ultimately satisfying the same goals. Conversely, the removal of a restriction of the freedom of access to information would have little real impact if the freedom of expression were not upheld.

The ICCPR expansively protects ideas and information expressed orally, in writing, in print, as art, or 'through any other media.' Thus, all goods or services that are themselves an expression of ideas or information, or are physical media of such, should normally lie within the scope of the protection of the freedom of expression. Indeed, the UN Human Rights Committee has held this protection to also include commercial speech.[49] The substantive range of international human rights protections of the freedom of expression therefore is very broad, albeit subject to exceptions and limitations, which will be addressed briefly below.

3.   The international trade law framework

In this section we highlight some of the fundamental incongruities that emerge when a restriction on the freedom of expression is analyzed as a trade measure. WTO provisions hinge on several technical factors that diminish or even annul the functional confluence between trade rules and human rights law. To demonstrate this, we will focus on the area of trade in goods and its regulation under the GATT.[50]

---

frontiers, either orally, in writing or in print, in the form of art, or through any other media of his choice."

[49] *Ballantyne, Davidson and McIntyre* v. *Canada*, Communications Nos. 359/1989 and 385/ 1989, UN Doc. CCPR/C/47/D/359/1989 and 385/1989/Rev.1 (1993), para. 11.3.

[50] Undoubtedly, similar issues arise under additional WTO agreements, such as the TBT, and in section IV below we will address real disputes that have arisen under the GATS and TRIPS. Agreement on Technical Barriers to Trade, Jan. 1, 1995, 1868 UNTS 120

Quantitative restrictions: Consider first a deceptively simple hypothetical that encapsulates some of the complexities of our inquiry: a ban instituted by a WTO member on the importation of foreign-printed copies of a particular book title, that is otherwise readily available on the domestic market from local publishers.

To begin with, the book title import ban would likely be considered a quantitative restriction prohibited under Article XI GATT, since it is implemented only at the border, on the importation of the book, and is not complemented by a ban on the production and distribution of the same book in the domestic market.[51] Because Article XI:1 GATT refers to "prohibitions or restrictions... of any product," it would be immaterial if the ban did or did not apply to other book titles. So long as the 'product' is the particular title in question, the ban constitutes a 'prohibition'; and if one considers instead the relevant product to be books in general or some sub-category thereof, the ban is a 'restriction,' which is similarly GATT inconsistent, subject to certain general exceptions, that will be discussed below.[52]

Interestingly, in such a case GATT actually limits governmental measures more than human rights law does, reflecting its economic goals. The measure in question violates a GATT rule – indeed, a rule that is considered to be "one of the cornerstones of the GATT system"[53] – but because the book is, in our hypothetical, in fact available on the domestic market, the right of access to information as well as the author's freedom of expression remain intact. The only freedom of expression that is impaired is that of the foreign publishers – whose interest is primarily, if not exclusively, commercial. Even this might not be the case, if the foreign publishers were not prevented from publishing the book within the domestic market, so that their right to publish the book's content would not be precluded.

[hereafter TBT]; General Agreement on Tariffs and Trade 1994, Apr. 15, 1994, Marrakesh Agreement Establishing the World Trade Organization, Annex 1A, Legal Texts: The Results Of The Uruguay Round Of Multilateral Trade Negotiations 17 (1999), 1867 UNTS 187, 33 ILM 1153 (1994) [hereafter GATT 1994]; TRIPS Agreements.

[51] Report, 'European Communities – Measures Affecting Asbestos and Asbestos – Containing Products,' WT/DS135/R, paras. 8.83–8.100 (Sept. 18, 2000).

[52] Appellate Body Report, 'United States – Import Prohibition of Certain Shrimp and Shrimp Products,' WT/DS58/AB/R (Oct. 12, 1998).

[53] Report, 'Turkey – Restrictions on Import of Textile and Clothing Products,' WT/DS34/AB/R (Oct. 22, 1999).

The (in this respect) stricter protection by trade law exists even though, as we have seen, human rights law protects foreign and domestic expressions alike, but in contrast, the terms of Article XI:1 GATT apply only to a "product *of the territory* of any other contracting party." This qualification draws a distinction between foreign and domestic products, which human rights law does not. Quite, simply, GATT does not grant privileges to domestic products. That does not pose a difficulty, to say the least, for the domestic publishers in our hypothetical, because the book ban in that hypothetical does not prevent the local production and distribution of the book, and indeed, prefers local publishers over the foreign. This, indeed, is the basis for applying Article XI:1 GATT (on quantitative restrictions) in the first place. The economic goal of the GATT/WTO in the removal of the ban is clear: the ban merely reserves the local market to locally printed editions, and this creates economic inefficiency. On the other hand, the human rights interest in the removal of the restriction is minimal. The interests protected by Art. XI:1 GATT and the freedom of expression diverge significantly in this case, in the sense that, generally speaking, human rights would be quite indifferent to a removal of the trade barrier.

A second, alternative, hypothetical confirms this analysis. Let us now imagine that a WTO member bans the domestic sale and distribution of a particular book title across the board, and not just the importation of its foreign produced physical copies. Arguably, such a law is no longer a border measure, but a rule applying to imported and domestic products alike and hence is to be analyzed under the non-discrimination clause of Article III GATT, and not under Article XI:1 GATT.[54] Clearly, freedom of speech as well as access to information are infringed in this example, yet Article XI:1 GATT, which does not apply, cannot be relied upon to prevent the infringement.

Article XI:1 GATT hence diverges significantly from the protection of the freedom of expression. If, on one hand, the expressive good is banned for import but is nonetheless available domestically, the prohibition of quantitative restrictions may apply but human rights are generally fulfilled regardless of the import ban or its removal. If, on the other hand, the good is banned entirely on the domestic market, Article XI:1 is arguably not the relevant GATT provision.

---

[54] See H. P. Hestermeyer, 'Article III,' in Rüdiger Wolfrum *et al.* (eds.), *WTO – Trade in Goods* (Leiden: Nijhoff, 2011), para. 110.

This hypothetical analysis is upheld by jurisprudence related to similar, though technically more complicated, problems relating to expressive goods. A 1984 GATT panel[55] found that restrictions instituted by the USA on the importation of printed material under the (now defunct) 'Manufacturing Clause' were violations of Article XI GATT. Much of the panel report revolved on temporal issues with no bearing on the free speech–free trade nexus, and the substantive inconsistency of the Manufacturing Clause with Article XI:1 GATT was not even contested by the US.[56] The Manufacturing Clause prohibited the importation into the USA and public distribution therein of copyrighted, non-dramatic, literary works in the English language authored by US domiciliaries, unless they had been manufactured in the USA or Canada. The Manufacturing Clause had implications in the area of international intellectual property (well before intellectual property rights were introduced to the GATT system under the TRIPs), because copyright protection was denied to works imported in contravention of the Manufacturing Clause. More fundamentally, however, the US measure was simply a ban on the importation of a particular class of foreign published books, deliberately aimed at nurturing and sustaining the domestic US publishing industry.[57] Like the hypothetical book ban above, the Manufacturing Clause did not preclude the freedom of expression of US (or indeed foreign) authors or publishers, although it did restrict the US commercial activity of foreign publishers. The Manufacturing Clause was clearly protectionist from a trade viewpoint, and the panel report is faultless in its application of GATT law. However, the finding that US legislation was not GATT consistent could have had no appreciable effect on the freedom of expression.

In the 1997 WTO *Canada – Periodicals* case,[58] Canada was challenged for prohibiting the importation of so-called 'split-run' periodicals – magazines with the same or similar editorial content as those available abroad, but containing advertisements directed to the Canadian market. Periodicals domestically produced with the same advertising material

---

[55] See Report, 'The United States Manufacturing Clause' (L/5609, BISD 31S/74 para. 34) (May 15, 1984) [hereafter the 'Manufacturing Clause' report].

[56] *Ibid.*

[57] H. J. Boyd and W. S. Lofquist, 'New Interests in Old Issues: Antiprotection and the End of the Manufacturing Clause of the US Copyright Law,' *Publishing Research Quarterly* 7 (1991).

[58] Appellate Body Report, 'Canada – Certain Measures Concerning Periodicals,' WT/DS31/AB/R (Jun. 30, 1997).

were not prohibited.[59] This ban was straightforwardly found to be a violation of Article XI GATT, shifting the discussion to the GATT's general exceptions.[60] *Periodicals* clearly related to the commercial interests – and commercial speech – of media and advertisers. Yet even this commercial speech, in the form of advertisements directed at the Canadian market, would have been available to the public through Canadian advertising media, in Canadian printed periodicals, which were not restricted by the measure. The removal of the disputed legislation would hardly have had an effect on the freedom of expression or access to information in Canada.[61]

There is, however, one scenario in which the removal of an import ban relating to a book title promotes the freedoms of expression and access to information in a manner that makes available information that was not available before: if the title were not banned from publication or distribution within the country, but simply not available in the market e.g. for economic reasons (such as insufficient market size). The import ban would then effectively prevent access to the book's content, and a successful challenge under Article XI GATT could allow such access from foreign sources. However, the importing country could avoid this outcome by extending the ban to domestic production (leading into a national treatment analysis, discussed below).

Overall, the analysis of Article XI GATT shows that it might have some limited parallels with the freedom of expression, but also, more clearly, that there exists significant divergence, and in practice the prohibition of quantitative restrictions does not promote speech to a significant extent. The divergence is also apparent in an analysis of an import ban on a good that does not incorporate an expression but rather facilitates it – such as a computer or telephone. Consider a case in which a WTO member bans the importation of camera-equipped cellphones, of the type that has recently proven very effective in increasing access to information (in the Arab Spring, for example).[62] If the regulation allowed domestic production of such telephones, but banned the importation of such products from abroad, this would, prima facie, constitute an Article XI GATT issue, especially if telephones were in fact domestically

---

[59] *Ibid.*, para. 5.5.   [60] *Ibid.*

[61] C. Carmody, 'When Cultural Identity Was Not at Issue: Thinking about Canada – Certain Measures concerning Periodicals,' *Law & Pol'y Int'l Bus.* 30 (1998–1999), 231.

[62] R. Srinivasan, 'Taking power through technology in the Arab Spring', Al Jazeera (Oct. 26, 2012), www.aljazeera.com/indepth/opinion/profile/ramesh-srinivasan.html

produced; but, then, this would not create a restriction of the freedom of expression. In contrast, restrictions on the use of cellphones would restrict speech, but generally might not restrict trade.

National treatment: As we have argued, a complete domestic ban on the distribution of a book title (including imports) would have to be analyzed under Article III GATT, i.e. the national treatment principle. National treatment generally provides that all taxes and regulations affecting the internal sale of products "shall not be applied to imported and domestic products so as to afford protection to domestic production."[63] This pertains even if the tax is collected or the regulation applied to the foreign product at the time or point of importation.[64] Taxation applied to "like" domestic products should not be "in excess of" taxation applied to domestic products (Article III:2 GATT). Any other regulations applied to imported products shall be "no less favourable" than the treatment accorded to the "like" domestic product (Article III:4 GATT). If the domestic and imported products being compared are not 'like' and yet belong to the broader category of "directly competitive or substitutable products," differential treatment would still run afoul of the GATT if the tax afforded protection to the domestic product.[65]

In this brief, schematic, description of the national treatment principle in Article III GATT we find its chief weaknesses in promoting the freedom of expression, revealing significant divergence rather than confluence. First, by definition the national treatment principle aims at 'leveling the playing field' between foreign and domestic producers and goods. This is a market-oriented principle, but one that does not have the capacity to remove regulatory restrictions that are non-discriminatory. A restriction on free speech or access to information that is equally intolerant, even repressive, of expressions embedded in or facilitated by foreign and domestic goods will be unmoved by national treatment. Second, a measure that violates national treatment by granting a preference to a local product may contravene trade law, but not human rights law, at least to the extent that the freedom of expression is allowed through the domestic product, similarly to what we have shown with respect to import bans. Third, as a general matter, national treatment, with its focus on the source of products and the nebulous concept of

---

[63] GATT 1994, art. 3, para. 1.
[64] *Ibid.*; Report, 'European Communities', paras. 8.83–8.100.
[65] Appellate Body Report, 'Chile – Taxes on Alcoholic Beverages,' WT/DS87/AB/R (Dec. 13, 1999).

product 'likeness,' is a comparative rule. The freedom of expression is not – it applies without comparison to the treatment of others, and regardless of nationality.[66]

To see how these gaps play out in practice, consider the same book title ban we discussed with respect to the prohibition on quantitative restrictions, except that now it applies not only toward imports (either internally or at the point of importation), but is augmented by a complementary and equivalent ban on domestic production and distribution of the same book title. Such a ban is more clearly aimed at preventing the expression embedded in the book from gaining public purchase in the territory of the restricting member, and from a human rights perspective, it would undoubtedly be a restriction on the freedom of expression. From a trade viewpoint, however, there would be, at least prima facie, no violation of national treatment because the same product is being granted the same (negative) regulatory treatment.

Under a different scenario, if a book title were banned or otherwise prevented from local publication, but not for import, trade law would have nothing to say in this respect, since there would be no restriction of imports or discrimination against foreign producers. Conversely, however, if national regulations granted a preference to domestic production, sales and distribution of the book – not as an import ban (which would constitute a quantitative restriction), but as a tax preference, for example – there might be a violation of trade law, but the restriction on the freedom of expression would be minimal. In the *Canada – Periodicals* case, the measure, under which an 80 percent excise tax was levied only on the value of foreign printed 'split-run' periodicals, was found to violate Article III:2 GATT.[67] Yet the discriminatory tax could hardly have been considered a violation of international human rights law.

International trade lawyers will quickly note that this discussion of the book ban simplifies the issues by treating the foreign and domestic editions of the banned book as the only relevant products. In practice, national treatment in GATT/WTO law depends on the scope of 'like' products that WTO jurisprudence has likened to an accordion that "stretches and squeezes in different places."[68] The foreign-printed,

---

[66] Although the freedom of expression is subject to the general norm of non-discrimination in political rights (ICCPR, art. 2).
[67] Appellate Body Report, 'Canada,' at para. 5.30.
[68] Appellate Body Report, 'Japan – Taxes on Alcoholic Beverages,' WT/DS11/AB/R (Oct. 4, 1996).

restricted title is surely 'like' its domestically produced version, but is it also 'like,' domestically manufactured editions of *other* book titles that are *not* restricted or banned in any way?

On one hand, the products whose treatment should be compared might include all books of all sorts, but this would ignore the underlying issue of substitutability and competition that informs the question of 'likeness.' Telephone books and motorcycle maintenance manuals,[69] both printed and bound, are not in competition with each other, regardless of their place of publication, any more than are law reviews and suspense novels. On the other hand, the general ban of particular titles while permitting the domestic distribution of domestically published books of similar content but different authorship seems to enter the domain of product likeness.[70] Further increasing the resolution of the inquiry into likeness along these lines is a slippery slope potentially leading *ad absurdum*, to queries such as whether Voltaire and Balzac, or Shakespeare and Marlowe are 'like';[71] or whether different translations of the Bible are directly competitive or substitutable.

The established WTO tests of product likeness relate to the good (the book, in this case), seemingly with little regard to its expressive content. The cumulative tests are physical properties, consumer preferences, end-uses, and a sufficiently detailed tariff classification.[72] These tests might be helpful in some narrow circumstances, at least if clear differences in consumer preferences were shown (e.g., hardcover vs. paperback editions), but generally they are not appropriate for the purpose of defining categories of expression. Books of similar character or genre would be aimed at the same audiences and might be considered 'like.' Indeed,

---

[69] See 'Certain Automotive and Motorcycle Repair Manuals from the United Kingdom', Inq. No. AA1921-Inq.-19, USITC Pub. 913 (September 1978); FR Doc. No. 78-28019, 43 Fed. Reg. 193 (Oct. 4, 1978) (investigation terminated due to applicability of the Florence Agreement).

[70] This hypothetical borders on copyright protection, but can also be viewed from a national treatment perspective. Consider, for example, the case of *The Adventurous Prince*, a book of Chinese authorship (by Zhou Yiwen) intended for Chinese readership, but reportedly accused of bearing a strong resemblance to J. K. Rowlings's *Harry Potter* novels (http://english.people.com.cn/90001/90782/90873/6680948.html). While this is clearly a copyright issue, had *Harry Potter* been banned in China, but the *Adventurous Prince* permitted, regardless of the copyright question, the similarity between the works could be the basis for a national treatment claim, especially as *Harry Potter* books would be imported, while *Adventurous Prince* books are mainly printed locally.

[71] D. R. Williams, *Shakespeare, Thy Name is Marlowe* (New York: Philosophy Library, 1966).

[72] *Ibid.*

the *Canada – Periodicals* panel, in comparing imported 'split-run' periodicals and domestic non-'split-run' periodicals for the purpose of determining 'likeness', made clear that it was not its mandate to consider the likeness of 'periodicals in general.'[73] In that case, however, the panel could fall back on a market distinction that did not relate to the substantive content of the foreign and domestic periodicals. If one is to seriously pursue the path of likeness in comparing foreign and domestic expressive products, some reference to their content would appear to be necessary.

In any case, what emerges is that where different books (or indeed other expressive media, including digital products) are similar enough for national treatment requirements to apply, trade law can be useful in promoting the freedom of expression of the relevant authors as well as (foreign) publishers. However, several paradoxes reduce the potential human rights effect of this seeming confluence. Most clearly, none of the substantive distinctions that inform the question of product likeness under Article III GATT matter as far as human rights law is concerned. Subject to specific exceptions, a book ban is a restriction of the freedom of expression, regardless of the book's similarity or dissimilarity to other expressions, by other authors, whatever its comparative basis or scope. Furthermore, the more similar the domestic and foreign expressive products are to each other (and hence, the greater the potential for applying national treatment rules), the smaller the ban's impact on the availability of the different ideas on the 'marketplace of ideas,' as the same expression and information would already be available. Clearly, the ban of an author's expression remains an infringement of the freedom of expression even though the idea is already available in the market from another source. However, one cannot fail to notice that the likelihood of an application of Article III GATT decreases, the more vulnerable the right to freedom of expression is.

In general, the national treatment requirements of international trade law have little direct impact on the freedom of expression, if at all. They clearly promote only foreign-produced products that embed or facilitate expression. They rely on comparative issues, such as the 'like product' test, that are much more detailed than those of human rights law, and are irrelevant to substantive human rights. When they do apply, they do so in situations where the freedom of expression is not particularly

---

[73] Appellate Body Report, 'Canada,' para. 5.22.

vulnerable. In some cases a trade cause might parallel a human rights one, but there is little basis to claim consistent substantive confluence.

This analysis of interactions between basic GATT provisions and the freedom of speech is by no means exhaustive. We have not, for example, set out the relationship between exceptions to the freedom of expression in human rights law, on one hand, and exceptions to GATT obligations. Here too, however, the absence of confluence is evident. In a nutshell, while both legal regimes allow for public morals exceptions,[74] among others, and examine their validity through tests of necessity and proportionality, they entail very different balancing exercises. In human rights, the justification for a restriction on the freedom of expression is assessed directly in comparison with the burden caused to the individual whose speech has been restricted.[75] In trade, the public morals exception of Article XX(a) GATT has indeed been invoked to justify censorship, with no reference to human rights considerations – a policy that is anathema to freedom of expression.[76] While a claim to justify all censorship under Article XX(a) GATT is clearly exaggerated, the comparison in that provision is (very roughly stated), not with the restriction on speech, but rather with the extent to which the measure restricts trade.[77] This clearly could lead to disparate results, such as a book ban found to be justified under trade law but not under human rights.

Turning full circle, we see that the separate rationales of the two areas of law underlie their different coverage of the same measure, making confluence uncertain, arbitrary and sporadic, rather than systematic. In the next section we demonstrate the absence of confluence in two actual cases, beyond physical goods such as books and beyond the GATT, in trade and services and intellectual property-related issues.

---

[74] See ICCPR, art. 19(3)(b); GATT, Report, 'European Communities,' paras. 8.83–8.100, art. XX(a).

[75] See e.g. *Kivemaa* v. *Finland*, Communication No. 412/1990, UN Doc. CCPR/C/50/D/412/ 1990 (1994) and *Faurisson* v. *France*, Communication No. 550/1993, UN Doc. CCPR/C/ 58/D/550/1993 (1996).

[76] Panel Report, 'China – Publications and Audiovisual Products,' WT/DS363/R, para. 7.727.

[77] See e.g. Appellate Body Report, 'Brazil – Measures Affecting Imports of Retreaded Tyres', WT/DS332/AB/R (Dec. 3, 2007) specifying (in the context of art. XX (b) necessity test) that a measure will be assessed taking account of "the importance of the interests or values at stake, the extent of the contribution to the achievement of the measure's objective, *and its trade restrictiveness*" (para. 178).

IV. Confluence in action? The impact of WTO cases on the freedom of speech

1. The China – IPR Enforcement dispute

The *China – IPR Enforcement* case[78] was the first WTO complaint that included a direct challenge to a national measure whose non-trade related aim was at least in part to restrict an internationally recognized human right – the freedom of expression.[79] It therefore provides an excellent testing ground for the confluence thesis. One measure at issue in the dispute was the first sentence of Article 4 of China's Copyright Law, whereby "works the publication and/or dissemination of which are prohibited by law shall not be protected by this Law."[80] The USA argued that this provision constituted a violation of Article 5(1) and 5(2) of the Berne Convention[81] as incorporated by Article 9.1 of TRIPS,[82] and of Articles 14, 61 (first and second sentences) and Article 41.1 TRIPS. We will focus on the claim under Article 5(1) of the Berne Convention, which is the most relevant here. The claim was, in essence, that by depriving copyright protection from works that could not legally be published in China under its censorship laws,[83] China was in violation of its WTO obligations. Although not addressed in the dispute, for our present purposes, one can consider that a trade–human rights confluence would have occurred if the removal of the trade law (i.e., TRIPS) violation had promoted the freedom of expression.

Indeed, the denial of copyright protection was certainly part of China's overall system of censorship. It referred to rules and regulations that established which expressions were considered illegal in China, and

---

[78] Appellate Body Report, *China – Measures*; G. R. Butterton, 'Pirates, Dragons and US Intellectual Property Rights in China,' *Ariz. L. Rev.* 38(1996), 1081; K. K. Athanasakou, 'China IPR Enforcement: Hard as Steel or Soft as TOFU – Bringing the Question to the WTO under TRIPS,' *Geo. J. Int'l. L.* 39 (2008), 217

[79] For detailed analysis of the dispute, see Ptak, 'Neoliberalism in Germany.'

[80] Appellate Body Report, 'China – Measures,' para.7.1.

[81] Art. 5(1) Berne establishes a national treatment obligation and an obligation to respect author's minimum rights "specially granted" by the Convention, which include the substantive rights of copyright. The Berne Convention for the Protection of Literary and Artistic Works, September 9, 1886, as revised at Paris on July 24, 1971 and as amended in 1979, 102 Stat. 2853, 1161 UNTS 3 [hereafter Berne Convention] (did not enter into force with respect to the United States until March 1, 1989).

[82] TRIPS Agreements.

[83] For the precise category of works for which the Panel considered that the USA successfully shows that protection was denied, see Ptak, 'Neoliberalism in Germany.'
    Appellate Body Report, 'China – Measures,' para.7.103.

deferred to the governmental system of 'content control.' That China's copyright law was in fact aimed at reinforcing the repressive effect of Chinese censorship is made abundantly clear by China's claim that the denial of copyright from unauthorized works was covered by the Article 17 Berne defense, which states that the Convention "cannot in any way affect the right of governments to permit, to control, or to prohibit the circulation, presentation or exhibition of any work or production in regard to which the competent authority may find it necessary to exercise that right."[84] China was essentially arguing that its authority to censor expression overrode its trade obligations.

The USA, as complainant in the case, and subsequently the WTO Panel in its Report, agreed that Article 17 Berne allowed interference in the enjoyment of rights in protected works, but, as the Panel stated, "there is no reason to suppose that censorship will eliminate those rights entirely with respect to a particular work."[85] In other words, in the copyright context, a government may choose to ban the circulation of certain works, but that is not relevant to the question of whether those works are eligible for copyright protection. Hence, the Panel determined that copyright should be protected in any case. The Panel's approach seems doctrinally sound. If China's denial of copyright was part of its censorship system, one might assume that the Panel's ruling against this denial of copyright is pro-free speech, supporting the confluence thesis. By removing the TRIPS violation and ensuring that copyright is enforceable, the negative effects on the freedom of expression might also be cured.

However, the Panel's decision is at best a pyrrhic victory for freedom of speech. First, it protects material that does not necessarily fall under the protection of freedom of expression under international law. The ruling means that the vilest of child pornography material or hate speech – content whose censorship would have been justified by the human rights exceptions of Article 19(3) ICCPR – can still enjoy copyright, even if the state (China, in this case) determines that it is illegal to publish and disseminate it. Second, however, even the most pedestrian educational content, or the most elevated and universally accepted moral content can be absolutely banned, as far as the narrow TRIPS framework is concerned, so long as its copyright is protected under trade law – even if the ban were not justifiable under human rights law. Third, Article 5(1) Berne Convention as incorporated by TRIPS only relates to the rights of authors "in countries ... other than their country of origin," and hence

---

[84] See Berne Convention, TRIPS Agreements.   [85] 'China – Measures,' para. 7.132.

the decision applies only to China's treatment of non-Chinese rights holders. The Panel report thus technically applies only to non-Chinese authors and their works. A banned Chinese work can still be denied copyright on the basis of its content, with all the derivative, negative effects on the freedom of expression.

What is worse, arguably, is that the direct impact of the Panel report on the freedom of speech of foreign authors and the freedom of access to information in China is negative. China is now bound by a WTO Panel report that requires it to grant copyright protection to content it censors. In addition to censorship laws, the full weight of copyright enforcement – criminal and administrative – must now be brought to bear on unauthorized works. In other words, copyright can – indeed, must – now be used to stifle expressions and their dissemination.

Indeed, China itself, in its statements before the Panel, acknowledged the mutually reinforcing effect of copyright protection and censorship. At one point China argued that a content ban is itself an effective protection against violation of copyright, and is "in a sense, an alternative form of enforcement against infringement."[86] In another context China referred to the negative rights of copyright holders as "private censorship."[87] These comments aptly capture the paradoxical power of copyright enforcement to restrict the freedom of speech – ironically harking back to one of the origins of copyright law in 'stationer's copyright,' – rights granted to members of the book trade seeking to protect their monopoly and granted by a government trying to police the press.[88]

In sum, although the *China – IPR Enforcement* dispute dealt with a measure that both violated WTO law and was aimed at restricting the freedom of expression, the operation of WTO dispute settlement was to remove the trade law violation, without promoting the human right – epitomizing the absence of confluence.

2.   The China – Audiovisual Products case

The difficult relationship between free speech and free trade is further illustrated by the *China – Publications and Audiovisual Products* case.[89]

---

[86] Appellate Body Report, 'China – Measures,' para. 7.180.   [87] *Ibid.*, para. 7.61.

[88] L. R. Patterson, *Copyright in Historical Perspective* (Nashville, TN: Vanderbilt University Press, 1968).

[89] Appellate Body Report, 'China – Measures'; see also E. A. Mangin, 'Market Access in China – Publications and Audiovisual Materials: A Moral Victory With a Silver Lining,' *Berkeley Tech. L. J.* 25 (2010), 279; P. K. Yu, 'From Pirates to Partners: Protecting Intellectual Property in China in the Twenty-First Century,' *Am. UL Rev.* 50 (2000), 131.

The USA challenged a series of Chinese measures (ranging from foreign investment regulations to film distribution and exhibition rules) as they related to the importation and distribution of reading material, audio-visual home entertainment products, sound recordings, and films for theatrical release. The Chinese regulations were complex, differing from product to product and according to the foreign involvement, forcing us to oversimplify the facts. In general the effect of the Chinese regulation was as follows: China maintained a content review process for these products. Imports and distribution of them into China were channeled, in the case of imports, through selected Chinese state-owned importers (which in some cases conducted the 'content review' in-house), and in the case of domestic distribution, through a number of normally lesser restrictions.[90] The USA considered these restrictions as violations of China's commitment in the Accession Protocol[91] to provide all enter-prises in China and all foreign enterprises and individuals the right to trade in all goods, and as a violation of China's GATS commitments to national treatment and market access as well as a violation of Article III:4 GATT.

One of China's defenses related to the special nature of the products and services concerned: "Cultural goods and services have in common the fact of being vectors of cultural identity and values and, as such, of justifying the implementation of specific, yet WTO compliant regulatory measures."[92] China claimed its measures were justified, stating that its importation regime "is designed to guarantee an effective and efficient application of the content review decided by China."[93]

---

[90] The complaint is described in much more detail in the dispute settlement reports and the US submissions. The US submissions are available on the website of the USTR at www.ustr.gov/trade-topics/enforcement/dispute-settlement-proceedings. The facts of the case are presented in the Panel Report, 'China – Measures Affecting Trading Rights and Distribution Services for Certain Publications and Audiovisual Entertainment Products,' para. 2.1–3, 4 WT/DS363/R (Aug. 12, 2009); and in the Appellate Body Report, Joint Communication from China and the European Communities, 'China – Measures,' at para. 1–5, Annex III.

[91] See Accession Protocol, 'Accession of the People's Republic of China,' Part 1 paras. 1.2, 5.1–5.2 WT/L/432 (Nov. 23, 2001); Report, 'Working Party on the Accession of China,' paras. 83–84 WT/ACC/CHN/49 (Oct. 1, 2001).

[92] Panel Report, 'China – Measures Affecting Trading Rights and Distribution Services for Certain Publications and Audiovisual Entertainment Products,' para. 4.89 WT/DS363/R (Aug. 12, 2009).

[93] *Ibid.*, para. 4.107.

The Panel found several infringements of WTO law. China violated its Accession Protocol commitment to allow the right to trade in all goods to all enterprises in China (including foreign enterprises)[94] by discriminating between foreign and domestic services, and between imported and like domestic products. Some market access commitments under Article XVI GATS were also violated.

The decisive issue was whether the infringing measures were justifiable. The trading rights commitment came without prejudice to China's right to regulate trade in a WTO-consistent manner, meaning it could subject imports or exports to governmental control and restrictions[95] and regulate importers or exporters of the relevant goods – but only in a WTO-consistent manner.[96] Article III GATT is subject to Article XX GATT exceptions, and GATS violations can be justified under Article XIV GATS exceptions. The Panel did not rule on the question of whether Article XX(a) GATT could be directly invoked as a defense to a breach of China's trading rights commitments under the Accession Protocol.[97] Instead, the Panel referred generally to the notion of "public morals" as defined in the *US – Gambling* decision, as "standards of right and wrong conduct maintained by or on behalf of a community or nation" giving members "some scope to define and apply for themselves the concept of 'public morals' … in their respective territories, according to their own system and scales of value."[98] With an almost palpable sigh of relief the Panel noted that it did not have to address the issue of whether the materials at issue really could impact negatively on 'public morals' in China – after all the USA had not argued the issue and the Panel's ruling on the necessity prong of Article XX made a decision on 'public morals' unnecessary.[99] On necessity the Panel repeated the familiar definition taken from prior jurisprudence requiring first a thorough analysis of the interests and values at stake and of the contribution to the achievement of the measure's objective and its trade restrictiveness[100] and in addition that no WTO-consistent alternative measure was reasonably available.[101]

---

[94] *Ibid.*, para. 7.249.   [95] *Ibid.*, para. 7.258.   [96] *Ibid.*, para. 7.275.
[97] *Ibid.*, para. 7.745. The Appellate Body found that China may invoke art. XX(a) GATT to justify provisions found to be inconsistent with China's trading rights commitments under its Accession Protocol and Working Party Report, WT/DS363/AB/R, at para. 415.
[98] *Ibid.*, para. 7.759, see also Appellate Body Report, 'United States – Measures Affecting the Cross-Border Supply of Gambling and Betting Services,' WT/DS285/AB/R (Apr. 7, 2005).
[99] *Ibid.*, para. 7.763.   [100] *Ibid.*, paras. 7.783–786.   [101] *Ibid.*, para. 7.870–871.

The Panel held that 'public morals' rank "among the most important values or interests pursued by Members"[102] and that each member can determine the level of protection it provides for.[103] But despite this importance the measures fell through: some were held not necessary when weighing the interests involved and their trade restrictiveness,[104] others when considering a reasonably available alternative measure, namely sole responsibility for content review of the Chinese government.[105] China appealed three aspects of the Panel's report, including various elements of the necessity analysis[106] and the USA, too, had its squabbles with the interpretation.[107] The Appellate Body addressed a few issues. Despite finding fault with the Panel, the Appellate Body ended up confirming that the Chinese measures were not "necessary" to protect public morals.[108]

At first glance the USA seems to have achieved a major breakthrough for free speech: China's restrictive import and distribution rules for speech-related products and services were held to be in violation of WTO law. But the victory in this respect is superficial at best. The USA did not challenge Chinese censorship rules, nor even "specifically argue that the measures at issue are not measures to protect public morals,"[109] or even the notion that the material at issue "could have a negative impact on public morals in China."[110] Appearing to accept GATT justifications of censorship, the USA instead attacked the necessity of linking content review with importation. Indeed, at certain points, the USA appeared to be explaining to China how to censor properly (i.e. in a WTO-consistent manner). The WTO cases did not rule on the legality of Chinese censorship per se, they rule on the way the censorship was administered.

But leaving the matter of principle and the specific legal technicalities of the holding aside, import restrictions of speech-related products were indeed declared in violation of WTO law. This might have been a triumph for free speech if China were consequently to abolish its content review system rather than rearranging it along the lines proposed by the USA. China indeed alleged in its appeal that "the cost of the 'tremendous

---

[102] Ibid., para. 7.817.   [103] Ibid., para. 7.819.
[104] Ibid., paras. 7.849, 7.863, 7.868.   [105] Ibid., para, 7.908.
[106] Joint Communication from China and the European Communities, 'China – Measures,' para. 14.
[107] Ibid., para. 91.   [108] Ibid., para. 415 (e).
[109] Panel Report, 'China – Measures,' para. 7.756.   [110] Ibid., paras. 7.762–763.

restructuring' that would be required to implement the alternative [ways of doing content review] proposed by the United States would result in an 'undue financial burden' for China,"[111] suggesting that a rearrangement of the content review system would have been impossible and that losing the case in the WTO would deal a death blow to its censorship system. However, to the surprise of few, the Chinese system of censorship has survived.[112]

Even more than in the *China – IPR Enforcement* case, the *Audiovisual Products* case shows that a removal of a measure that both violates trade rights and restricts the freedom of expression may easily result in more liberalized trade, without in any way promoting the freedom of expression.

V.   Conclusion: be careful what you wish for

Our analysis of the relationship between international trade law (focusing on the law of the WTO in goods, services, and intellectual property) and the freedom of expression (and its corollary, the freedom of access to information) effectively refutes the confluence thesis. Indeed, the international legal regimes of human rights law as to free speech and world trade law do overlap in various respects. However, they clearly do not march in lockstep towards a brighter future for both free trade and free expression. The goals of the two legal systems, when applied to the same restrictive governmental measure, are fundamentally different in their utilitarian and deontological dimensions. The applicable substantive rules operate in very different ways; in some scenarios, trade law applies stricter standards, at times it is human rights law that is the more demanding. These rules, and the public policy exceptions and derogations that accompany them, apply significantly different balancing tests, reflecting the diverging goals of the two systems.

Thus, any commonality between the fields is arbitrary, inconsistent, and unforeseeable, rather than systematic and mutually reinforcing. WTO law has no methodical, free-speech-enhancing effect. It is aimed at trade liberalization. While this objective does, at times, seem to point in a similar direction as the protection of the freedom of expression, the

---

[111] Joint Communication from China and the European Communities, 'China – Measures,' para. 32.
[112] I. Bennett, *Media Censorship in China*, Council on Foreign Relations (updated Jan. 24, 2013), www.cfr.org/china/media-censorship-china/p11515

relationship is uneasy and disharmonious. It can even regress to the conflictual: a complaint based on trade law aimed at measures that restrict both trade and speech may result in more liberal trade but more restrictive censorship. We have seen this occur both in theory and in practice, in the case studies of the *China – IPR Enforcement* and *China – Audiovisual Products* cases. Even when a WTO case has been won by a member, a triumph for the freedom of expression might prove elusive or even counterproductive.

These conclusions do not bode well for the human rights aspects of a prospective 'Google case.' A WTO challenge to China's internet censorship system might prove successful in promoting the access of non-Chinese internet businesses to the Chinese market (although this is also questionable, as others have analyzed in detail),[113] but the effects on the exercise of the freedom of expression and access to information in China would likely be marginal, at best, harmful at worst.

This analysis ultimately provides a somber cautionary tale for both trade law and international human rights. For the WTO, and indeed for other trade agreements, taking up the cause of the freedom of speech would be too heavy a burden, and one that would merely be harmful to their overarching legitimacy. No less importantly, for human rights, and especially for rights advocates, it is clearly dangerous to make instrumental use of trade law for the promotion of the freedom of expression.

---

[113] H. Gao, 'Google's China problem: a case study on trade, technology and human rights under the GATS', AJWH 6 (2011), 346

10

Emergency safeguard measures for trade in services: a case study of intradisciplinary fragmentation

SHIN-YI PENG

I. Introduction

The authors of other chapters in this volume argue that international economic law is ill-served by excess disciplinary fragmentation. But clearly this dimension of fragmentation exists within the WTO itself as well. To be more specific, the multiplicity of trade regime is not only of interdisciplinary (e.g., IP v. trade, investment v. trade, or climate change v. trade), but also of intradisciplinary (i.e., between different areas of trade law within the WTO regime) discourse. This chapter reviews the negotiations on services emergency safeguard measures (ESM) with a view to offering a critical assessment of the main systematic issues within the WTO – that goods and services are often not subject to common forms of governance. There are many interactions between fragmented regulatory approaches between goods and services worthy of exploration,[1] but in this chapter I will dwell only on the question of to what extent the GATT provisions can be borrowed to establish services ESM. I will take an intradisciplinary approach by analogizing whether and how goods-type safeguards could be adjusted to make it workable in the services context. In doing so, I will take an intradisciplinary focus to examine the issues of normative fragmentation within the WTO. I will argue that in the case the ESM, it is necessary for the GATS to operate as separate and somewhat insular disciplines.

---

[1] So far little attention has been paid to the distinction between goods and services (and the intra-disciplinary fragmentation–integration between them). See e.g. P. Delimatsis, *International Trade in Services and Domestic Regulations* (Oxford University Press, 2007), 31; F. Smith *et al.*, 'A Distinction without A Difference: Exploring the Boundary between Goods and Services in the World Trade Organization and the European Union,' *Colum. J. Eur. L.* 12 (2006), 1; J. Pauwelyn, 'Rien Ne Va Plus? Distinguishing Domestic Regulation from Market Access in GATT and GATS,' Duke Law School Working Paper Series 25 (2005).

II.   Negotiations on ESM under GATS Article X

At the time of concluding the General Agreement on Trade in Services (GATS), notwithstanding the existence of a precedent in the goods area, emergency safeguard measures (hereafter ESM) in services could not be agreed since the question of their "feasibility" and "desirability" was not solved.[2] This explains the language used by Article X.[3] Article X:1 of the GATS states that "there shall be multilateral negotiations *on the question of emergency safeguard measures* based on the principle of non-discrimination. The results of such negotiations shall enter into effect on a date not later than three years from the date of entry into force of the WTO Agreement" (emphasis added). Regardless of conflicting inter-pretations of Article X of the GATS,[4] most members, especially develop-ing countries, consider ESM as a part of the balance struck under the Uruguay Round services negotiations and therefore should be an integral component of the GATS.[5]

Negotiations under the mandates of GATS Articles X started shortly after the Uruguay Round under the auspices of the Working Party on GATS Rules (WPGR).[6] In particular, during the years between 2000 and 2005, there have been intensive discussions among WTO members for and against an ESM.[7] The main proponents of a Services ESM are most of the members of the ASEAN, which have submitted several negotiating

---

[2] See generally F. Pierola, 'A Safeguards Regime for Services,' in M. Panizzon *et al.*, *GATS and the Regulation of International Trade in Services* (Cambridge University Press, 2008), 434–465. P. Sauvé, 'Been There, Not Yet Done That: Lessons and Challenges in Services Trade,' *ibid.*, 617–620; M. Marconini, 'Emergency Safeguard Measures in the GATS: Beyond Feasible and Desirable,' United Nations Conference in Trade and Development 1–28 (9 March 2005); G. Gauthier *et al.*, 'Déjà vu, or New Beginning for Safeguards and Subsidies Rules in Services Trade?,' in P. Sauvé *et al.*, *GATS 2000: New Directions in Service Trade Liberalization* (Washington, DC: Brookings Institute, 2000), 165–183.

[3] Art. X, GATS: Emergency Safeguard Measures.

[4] The wording of this mandate has given rise to different meanings regarding the scope of the ESM negotiations. Some WTO members argued that the GATS merely calls for "negotiations on the question of emergency safeguard measures" based on the principle of non-discrimination; on the other hand, some members argued that Article X:1 impli-citly acknowledges that negotiations must lead to results as referred to in the second sentence. See R. Adlung, 'Negotiations on Safeguards and Subsidies in Services: A Never-ending Story?,' *Journal of International Economic Law* 10 (2007), 235, 265.

[5] Pierola, 'A Safeguards Regime,' 435.   [6] Adlung, 'Negotiations on Safeguards,' 235.

[7] Discussions on emergency safeguard measures are reflected in WPGR meeting minutes e.g. paras. 4–41 of S/WPGR/M/53, paras. 2–16 of S/WPGR/M/54, paras. 3–21 of S/WPGR/M/55, and paras. 2–26 of S/WPGR/M/56.

papers. On the other hand, a number of WTO members are strongly opposed to the introduction of such a mechanism.[8]

The negotiating momentum has been slowed down since 2005. However, various views continued to be expressed on ESM. For example, at the meeting of 30 March 2009, delegations continued to exchange views on the communication from the delegations of Brunei Darussalam, Cambodia, Indonesia, Malaysia, Myanmar, the Philippines, Thailand, and Vietnam on a draft Annex on Article X Emergency Safeguard Measures, as contained in JOB (07)/155. At the meeting of June 22, 2009, delegations discussed a communication from China on the issue of the definition of domestic industry.[9] In May 2010, the delegation of the Philippines urged the Working Party to take advantage of the lull in the negotiations to conduct "further technical discussions."[10] At the same meeting, the representative of the United States, however, continued to question the need for and the feasibility of an ESM in services.[11] In November 2010, members agreed to postpone the presentation on ESM-relevant data until after an updated background note on international trade statistics can be provided.[12] Generally speaking, the meetings of WPGR, to some degree, helped to clarify certain concepts and concerns with regard to the application of an ESM, however, the technical discussions apparently are endless and going nowhere towards the goal.

As of to date, although no agreement has yet been reached at the negotiating table, much has been written about ESM for services trade,[13] and the aspects of these studies vary greatly. This chapter does not intend to look at all technical details nor analyze all economic arguments advanced in the negotiations. The first part of this chapter will give a short review of the unfinished business of GATS and an overview of the general

---

[8] *Ibid.*

[9] WPGR, Report of the Meeting held on July 1, 2010, Note by the Secretariat, S/WPGR/M/69.

[10] WPGR, Report of the Meeting held on 27 April 2010, Note by the Secretariat S/WPGR/M/68.

[11] *Ibid.*

[12] WPGR, Report of the Meeting held on October 1, 2010, Note by the Secretariat TN/S/M/38.

[13] See generally Pierola, 'A Safeguards Regime,' 434–465. Sauvé, 'Been There, Not Yet Done,' 617–620; Marconini, 'Emergency Safeguard Measures,' 1–28; Gauthier *et al.*, 'Déjà vu, or New Beginning,' 165–183; M. Krajewski, 'Services Liberalization in Regional Trade Agreements: Lessons for GATS Unfinished Business?,' in Lorand Bartels *et al.* (eds.), *Regional Trade Agreements and the WTO Legal System* (Oxford University Press, 2006), 175, 196–199.

issues arising in the context of GATS negotiations on an ESM for services.[14] The second part will examine the safeguard-type provisions in economic integration agreements. In spite of the fact that ESM in existing trade agreements are rare,[15] it is nevertheless of practical significance to discuss the recent trends of the GATS-plus provisions in the post-crisis era. The main part of the chapter will discuss the key questions of whether we should look at GATT Article XIX as a possible template for services. The distinction between goods and services at a generic level allows us to identify the necessary differences between GATT and GATS rules (and their interrelationship). I will argue that basing a GATS ESM on a goods-type model raises complications, and therefore members should look for simpler ways to revolve the most fundamental issues. Having said that, the chapter will examine the evolving GATS jurisprudence with an aim to seeking guidance for constructing the concept of services ESM. Based on the finding of the analysis, the final section of this chapter will conduct a case study of the Economic Cooperation Framework Agreement (ECFA) between China and Taiwan so as to explore alternative approaches which would help to take the negotiations forward.

III.   Working party on GATS rules

1.   The need for an ESM – link to progressive liberalization

As mentioned, after the Uruguay Round, negotiations under GATS continued in several rule-making areas, including ESM. The negotiations pursuant to Article X:1 of the GATS have been taking place since 1995. However, there have been divergent views among WTO members for and against services ESM,[16] and there is so far very little consensus on most of the issues.

According to the ASEAN WTO members,[17] given the binding and largely irrevocable nature of services commitments, some form of ESM

---

[14] This chapter will not focus on specific technical issues. Nevertheless, some revisiting and repetition are necessary in an effort to gather relevant considerations and to propose solutions.

[15] Krajewski, 'Services Liberalization,' 182.

[16] See also P. Poretti, *The Regulation of Subsidies within the General Agreement on Trade in Services of the WTO: Problems and Prospects* (New York: Kluwer Law International, 2009), 17–18.

[17] WPGR, 'Further Thoughts on an Emergency Safeguard Mechanism,' communication from Brunei Darussalam, Indonesia, Malaysia, Myanmar, the Philippines and Thailand, JOB 04/4 (Feb. 2004).

would be needed to address adverse consequences that may arise in the course of implementing services commitments on a temporary basis. The ASEAN also argue that an ESM will help governments in developing country members to address some of their domestic concerns over making commitments under the GATS. In other words, ESM can be seen as an "essential safety net" for services liberalization.[18] These members are concerned that once commitments are made, market liberalization and regulatory reform are generally "locked in," and therefore an adjustment may be necessary to allow the domestic industry to catch up with a more competitive environment.[19] In the context of services trade, the possibility to impose ESM would allow members confronted with an unforeseen surge in imports which have caused injury to domestic suppliers to temporarily depart from their legally binding GATS commitments.[20] Following the same logic, safeguards are also seen by many as facilitators of trade liberalization, encouraging the conclusion of binding commitments.[21] If the mechanism were put in place, trade liberalization would be deeper, as WTO members would be more willing to make new commitments.[22]

However, some members consider that the GATS already has the built-in flexibility to accommodate the interests of any member intending protecting a particular sector.[23] There are no clear reasons why such a mechanism is needed.[24] In particular, some of these members wonder whose interests an ESM would protect and in what particular circumstances it would apply.[25] They also question to what extent the introduction of a safeguard mechanism can contribute to the liberalization of services.[26]

2.   How it might operate in practice – possible elements for an ESM

Even if an ESM were desirable, a number of members consider that the implementation of an ESM mechanism raises serious problems as to

---

[18] *Ibid.*

[19] Panizzon *et al.*, *GATS and the Regulation*, 438–439. As argued, an ESM would allow these members some level of comfort in knowing that if they have somehow misjudged the impact of liberalization, a safety net is available to them.

[20] Poretti, *Regulation of Subsidies*, 18–19.   [21] *Ibid.*

[22] Panizzon *et al.*, *GATS and the Regulation*, 438–443. As argued, an ESM can encourage members to consider certain requests for trade liberalization which would not otherwise have even considered in the absence of an ESM, and as a result offers incentives for members to bind their liberalization measures earlier.

[23] *Ibid.*   [24] *Ibid.*, 437.   [25] *Ibid.*

[26] WPGR, note from the chairperson, JOB(01)/122 (Aug. 7, 2001).

feasibility.[27] In 2000, ASEAN submitted a paper on possible elements of an ESM.[28] In general, the ASEAN tries to use existing and established agreements and terms as much as possible.[29] For example, the preamble, object and purpose and definitions are mostly based on the Agreement on Safeguards (hereafter SG Agreement) and GATS, with the belief that using familiar language would provide more comfort for WTO members than would the use of altogether new wording.[30] Having been criticized as borrowing too much from the SG Agreement, the ASEAN defended the transplantation on the grounds that much of the goods model remain relevant for services.[31]

The ASEAN proposal is the main blueprint for applying ESM to services. However, for many WTO members, the ASEAN proposal does not remove doubts about the feasibility of an ESM in services.[32] Nor has it addressed the question of enforceability and the applicability of the ESM to the different modes of supply.[33] Some delegations even felt that the document, rather than resolving issues previously raised, had generated more queries about why and how an ESM might be needed.[34]

---

[27] See Panizzon et al., GATS and the Regulation, 437, 445; JOB 3449, paras. 14–18; JOB 3449/Add.2, paras. 9–13; JOB 6943, paras. 35–36; JOB(01)/26, paras. 3–8; JOB(01)/108, paras. 6–9.

[28] WPGR, Non-Paper from ASEAN, Draft Agreement on Emergency Safeguard Measures for Trade in Services, JOB 6830 (Oct. 31, 2000). Further discussions on the ASEAN proposal can be found in paras. 2–30 of S/WPGR/M/57, paras. 12–14 of S/WPGR/M/58 and paras. 2–5 of S/WPGR/M/59.

[29] Annual Report of the WPGR to the Council for Trade in Services, S/Wpgr/152, September 2005.

[30] ASEAN Interventions at WPGR Meeting, May 13, 2003.

[31] WPGR, 'Further Thoughts on an Emergency Safeguard Mechanism,' communication from Brunei Darussalam, Indonesia, Malaysia, Myanmar, the Philippines and Thailand, Job(04)/4, February 2004.

[32] Such as the modalities for the introduction of services ESM, the definitions of 'domestic industry' and 'locally established foreign suppliers,' the determination of whether there is an import surge in services, the determination of injury, 'likeness,' in the context of services trade, and the form and level of the ESM in the light of the different modes of supply, etc., see WPGR, note from the chairperson, JOB(01)/122, 7 August 2001; WPGR, 'Communications from the European Communities and their Member States, Scope for Emergency Safeguard Measures (ESM) in the GATS,' S/WPGR/W/41, March 2003.

[33] M. Bosworth et al., 'Emergency Safeguard Measures on Services: Where to Now?,' Taiwanese Journal of WTO Studies 93 (2006).

[34] Ibid.

IV. GATS-plus rules in economic integration agreements – services safeguards?

1. General observation

A feature of the new generation RTAs has been the inclusion of chapters on trade in services. Services are now a necessary component of RTAs.[35] In light of the generally low level of progress concerning the GATS ESM negotiations, studying how these aspects have been treated in RTAs could provide useful lessons for the GATS context.[36] Given that comparisons between regional and multilateral liberalization of services trade have so far predominantly focused on issues such as market access, this section will discuss the treatment of ESM in selected RTAs.

Tables 10.1–3 show an overview of the selected RTAs. Even a glance reveals the issue is treated similarly in the various agreements, with few going beyond the existing rules of the GATS and some even less ambi-

Table 10.1 *Type I: A mandate to negotiate ESM with a specific timeframe*

Provisions:	Japan–Malaysia FTA Article 106 Emergency Safeguards Measures
	1. The Countries shall initiate discussions within one year from the entry into force of this Agreement to develop mutually acceptable guidelines and procedures for the application of emergency safeguard measures within five years of the entry into force of this Agreement.
	2. (a) Notwithstanding the provision of paragraph 1 of this Article, if a Country deems itself to be affected by the negative impact caused by its specific commitments in Annex 6, the Country may request to hold a consultation with the other Country to deal with such situation and the other Country shall respond to the request in good faith.
	(b) In the consultation, the Countries shall endeavour to reach a mutually acceptable solution within a reasonable time.
Examples	Japan–Malaysia FTA, Article 106 Japan–Thailand FTA, Article 84

---

[35] WTO Website, http://rtais.wto.org/UI/PublicMaintainRTAHome.aspx (last visited 2012/10/02).

[36] Krajewski, 'Services Liberalization,' 175, 196–199.

Table 10.2 *Type II: Pending until the conclusion of the GATS Article X negotiations*

Provisions:	China–Pakistan FTA Article 9 Emergency Safeguards Measures 1. The Parties note that the multilateral negotiations pursuant to Article X of the GATS on the question of emergency safeguard measures are based on the principle of non-discrimination. Upon the conclusion of such multilateral negotiations, the Parties shall conduct a review for the purpose of discussing appropriate amendments to this Agreement so as to incorporate the results of such multilateral negotiations. 2. In the event that the implementation of this Agreement causes substantial adverse impact to a service sector of a Party before the conclusion of the multilateral negotiations referred to in paragraph 1 of this Article, the affected Party may request for consultations with the other Party for the purposes of discussing any measure with respect to the affected service sector. Any measure taken pursuant to this paragraph shall be mutually agreed by the Parties concerned. The Parties concerned shall take into account the circumstances of the particular case and give sympathetic consideration to the Party seeking to take a measure.
Examples	China–Pakistan FTA, Article 9 ASEAN–China FTA, Article 9 ASEAN–Australia/New Zealand FTA, Article 19 ASEAN–Korea FTA, Article 10 China–New Zealand FTA, Article 121 Japan–Indonesia FTA, Article 89 Japan–Viet Nam FTA, Article 73 China–Singapore FTA, Article 71

tious than the GATS. The following tables analyze the provisions in greater detail.[37]

Type I covers cases in which the mandate for the negotiations on ESM in services emanates from the text of the RTA. This type of RTAs foresees the development of guidelines and procedures for the application of

---

[37] This part will not attempt to provide a comprehensive analysis of all present negotiations involving ESM in services chapters of the RTAs, but will seek to identify whether there is any common approach toward ESM in the RTAs which could be used as a raw model in the GATS negotiations.

Table 10.3 *Type III: Expressly forbidding the imposition of safeguards measures*

Provisions:	Korea–India FTA Article 6.11 Safeguard Measures 1. Neither Party shall take safeguard action against services and service suppliers of the other Party from the date of entry into force of this Agreement. Neither Party shall initiate or continue any safeguard investigations in respect of services and service suppliers of the other Party. 2. The Parties shall review the issue of safeguard measures in the context of developments in international fora of which both Parties are party.
Examples	Korea–India FTA, Article 6.11 Singapore–Australia FTA, Article 13 India–Singapore FTA, Article 7.14

ESMs within certain years of the entry into force of the agreement. The second type of RTAs as listed in Table 10.2 consist of commitments that reproduce in part or in full GATS commitments. The undertakings did not go beyond (a country's) GATS commitment, which means that those RTAs have not established services ESMs either. The third type of RTAs as listed in Table 10.3 consists of undertakings which expressly forbid the initiation of safeguards investigations and the imposition of safeguards measures.

2. Critical innovations?

There are a few exceptions such as the safeguard provision in the CARICOM Agreement,[38] the NAFTA and the EU Gas Directive, which under certain circumstances seem to allow ESM actions by member states. Among them, Article 47 of CARICOM of the revised treaty of Chaguaramas directly addresses ESM for services,[39] which in the first

---

[38] Krajewski, 'Services Liberalization,' 96.
[39] Caribbean Community (CARICOM) Secretariat, Revised Treaty of Chaguaramas establishing the Caribbean community including the CARICOM single market and economy, Chapter Three, Establishment, Services, Capital And Movement Of Community Nationals, Article 47 Restrictions to Resolve Difficulties or Hardships Arising from the Exercise of Rights.

paragraph indicates that "where the exercise of rights granted under this Chapter creates serious difficulties in any sector of the economy of a member state or occasions economic hardships in a region of the Community, a member state adversely affected thereby may, subject to the provisions of the Article, apply such restrictions on the exercise of the rights as it considers appropriate in order to resolve the difficulties or alleviate the hardships." This to some degree demonstrates that some countries considered that the possibility of using ESM was necessary and did find concrete ways to implement such provisions.[40]

In addition, in NAFTA, a safeguard is established in Section 3.6b[41] for financial services. Thus, the NAFTA parties even with regard to a "foreseen situation," considered it necessary to have a safeguard mechanism in place. The NAFTA provisions, which only relate to one sector, has also provided a sectoral example that features safeguard-type characteristics.[42]

Another example is the EU energy integration. Article 26 of the EU Gas Directive[43] states that member states may temporarily take the necessary safeguard measures in the event of a "sudden crisis" in the energy market in which the system's integrity is threatened. The inclusion of the safeguard instrument within the Directive, which should be temporary and apply to the extent needed to prevent or remedy serious injury, indicates the special economic and security sensitivities associated with the energy sector.[44]

Are there any lessons to be drawn from RTAs? Which of these might be of value in the GATS context? This section considers whether there is any common approach toward ESM in the RTAs which could serve as a

---

[40] See A. Mattoo and P. Sauvé, 'Regionalism in Service Trade,' in A. Mattoo, R. M. Stern and G. Zanini (eds.), *A Handbook of International Trade in Services* (Oxford University Press, 2008), 221, 245.

[41] NAFTA contains an ESM mechanism limited to financial services under Annex 1413.6, a provision that would have enabled Mexico to unilaterally freeze new entries by NAFTA-based banks for a period of three years starting from January 1, 2000. A market share of foreign commercial banks in excess of 25 percent of the banking sector's net capital would have triggered the ESM mechanism. See Annex 1413.6, Section B Payments System Protection.

[42] Mattoo and Sauvé, 'Regionalism in Service Trade,' 245.

[43] Directive 2003/55/EC of the European Parliament and of the Council of 26 June 2003 concerning common rules for the internal market in natural gas and repealing Directive 98/30/EC, Chapter VIII, Final Provisions, Article 26 safeguard measures.

[44] P. C. Evans, 'Strengthening WTO Members Commitments in Energy Services: Problems and Prospects,' in Sauvé and Mattoo, *Domestic Regulation and Services Trade Liberalization*, 167–189.

model in the GATS negotiations. At present the answer seems to be quite clear: little progress has been made in tackling the issue in the context of the RTAs.[45] They generally do not go beyond in substantial way the GATS in disciplining services ESM. With a few exceptions, RTAs have made little headway in dealing with the issues of services ESM, where governments confront similar political sensitivities and legal complexity at the regional level as they do in the WTO. However, it should be noted that there are RTAs that have produced some innovations with regard to the sectoral ESM disciplines.[46]

V. Constructing the concept of services ESM – differentiating economic activity

1. Goods-type safeguard measures – an impossible model

As indicated, the debate on feasibility has largely focused on how to 'replicate' relevant categories of the safeguard regime for goods in the services context. However, it is questionable whether the focus on a goods-type mechanism for services would be appropriate. At the core of the issues is whether it makes sense to replicate the goods approach. Does this approach fail to take into account the differences between goods and services? Furthermore, whether and how goods-type safeguard measures could be adjusted to make it workable in the services context fall to be considered. And, if not, what alternatives would address the policy concerns for services ESM?

There are fundamental differences between goods and services.[47] In the view of some commentators, a service is essentially an act even though the result of the service may be embodied in a person, a thing, or data.[48] A good, on the other hand, is clearly a thing even though it may result from an act, i.e. its production.[49] These significant distinguishing characteristics of services affect the way in which trade in services occurs. They also shape the "trade barriers" specific to the services context.[50]

---

[45] C. Fink et al., 'East Asian Free Trade Agreements in Services: Key Architectural Elements,' *J. Int'l Econ. L.* (2008), 263.

[46] It is extremely interesting to note that the countries of ASEAN, which have been among the most vocal proponents of an ESM in the GATS, have not adopted such a provision under the ASEAN framework agreement on services.

[47] See generally Poretti, *Regulation of Subsidies*, 9; M. Krajewski, *National Regulation and Trade Liberalization in Services* (The Hague: Kluwer, 2003), 98–106.

[48] *Ibid.*   [49] *Ibid.*   [50] *Ibid.*

Only a limited part of services transactions, namely, the 'mode 1' trade, involves crossing boundaries similarly to what occurs in goods trade[51] Given their inherent characteristics, goods and services should be treated differently. Indeed, in most jurisdictions distinctions are made between goods and services with different regimes applying to each of them.[52]

Under the WTO regime, in the absence of guidance as to how a multilateral legal framework governing trade in services should be drafted, the GATS essentially borrowed the core concepts of the GATT and applied them to the services trade.[53] This chapter argues that basing a services ESM on a goods-type model will raise serious complications. The nature of 'trade in services' and the differences in the design of the legal frameworks regulating goods and services make the elaboration of services ESM a complex exercise. It is impossible to simply translate the existing multilateral regimes governing industrial and agricultural goods safeguards into the services context. It may thus be advisable to consider other options. The following section will examine the systemic implications of evolving GATS jurisprudence and discuss whether the dispute settlement cases offer some guidance as to the construction of the concept of services ESM.

2. GATS dispute settlement cases – implications for constructing ESM

(i)   Domestic industry/foreign services suppliers
(EC – Bananas, Canada – Autos)

As discussed, the most problematic aspect of applying an ESM relates to mode 3. GATS Article XXVIII provides a basis for distinguishing between national and foreign-established suppliers. The definition of 'domestic industry' includes only national suppliers (natural and juridical persons defined in accordance with GATS Article XXVIII) of the invoking member.[54] It should also be noted that the ASEAN in its position paper stressed the importance of the explicit guidance provided by the definitions already multilaterally agreed to by all members in GATS Article XXVIII.

---

[51] A. K. Abu-Akeel, 'Definition of Trade in Services under the GATS: Legal Implications,' *Geo. Wash. J. Int'l L. & Econ* 32(1999), 189; S. Wunsch-Vincent, *The WTO, The Internet and Trade in Digital Products: EC–US Perspectives* (Oxford: Hart, 2006).

[52] Smith *et al.*, 'A Distinction without A Difference,' 1; K. Lapid, 'Outsourcing and Off-shoring under the GATS,' *Journal of World Trade* 40 (2005), 341–364.

[53] Delimatsis, *International Trade in Services*, 31.   [54] JOB(01)/67, para. 14.

The Panel in *EC – Bananas*[55] and *Canada – Autos*[56] touched upon the issues of how to define "service suppliers of any other Member." In *EC – Bananas*, the Panel examined whether the EU[57] measures adversely modify the conditions between "foreign" and "domestic" suppliers. In doing so, the Panel first considered whether there are non-EU owned or controlled service suppliers that provide wholesale trade services in bananas in and to the EU.[58] The Panel found that the complainants submitted sufficient evidence to show that companies registered in the complainants' countries provide wholesale trade services in respect of bananas in and to the EU through commercially present owned or controlled subsidiaries, within the meaning of Article XXVIII(n).[59] In *Canada – Autos*,[60] the Panel noted that Article XXVIII(m) of the GATS provides the definition of a "juridical person of another Member." In its view, DaimlerChrysler Canada Inc. is a service supplier of the USA within the meaning of Article XXVIII(m)(ii)(2) of the GATS because it is controlled by DaimlerChrysler Corporation, a juridical person of the USA according to subparagraph(i) of Article XXVIII(m). The Panel also indicated that in order to define a "juridical person of another Member," Article XXVIII(m) of the GATS does not require the identification of the ultimate controlling juridical or natural person.[61]

It is apparent that the relevant definitions referred to in Article XXVIII remain legally valid and binding as a general rule in the GATS. However, the reality is, members appear to have varying definitions of the term 'domestic industry.' In other words, notwithstanding the GATS provisions and practices, their domestic laws, even their constitutions, contained specific definitions of what would constitute 'domestic industry.' Therefore the question remains as to whether each member can use its own definition of domestic industry, as opposed to having a multilaterally agreed definition when applying ESM. In fact, a large number of

---

[55] Appellate Body Report, 'European Communities – Regime for the Importation Sale and Distribution of Bananas,' WT/DS27/AB/R. Panel Report, 'European Communities, Regime for the Importation Sale and Distribution of Bananas,' WT/DS27/R.

[56] Appellate Body Report, 'Canada – Certain Measures Affecting the Automotive Industry,' WT/DS139/AB/R. Panel Report, 'Canada – Certain Measures Affecting the Automotive Industry,' WT/DS139/R.

[57] For the purpose of this chapter, the terms 'EC' and 'EU' are interchangeable.

[58] W. Zdouc, 'WTO Dispute Settlement Practice Relating to the GATS,' in E.-U. Petersmann *et al.* (eds.), *The WTO Dispute Settlement System* (The Hague: Kluwer, 2004), 382, 402; see also Wolfrum *et al.*, *WTO – Trade in Goods*, 540–564.

[59] Panel Report, 'EC – Bananas', paras. 7.329–331.

[60] Panel Report, 'Canada – Autos,' paras. 7.329–331.   [61] *Ibid.*, paras. 6.884.

WTO members are of the view that the concept of 'domestic industry' under the services ESM should include both national and foreign-established suppliers. Action under mode 3 should thus be possible, including action in the event of injury caused by foreign-established suppliers.[62]

(ii)   Likeness/like services (*EC – Bananas, Canada – Autos, US – Gambling*)

The determination of 'like domestic service' poses more challenges than in the context of goods trade. Once an imported service has been defined, the next question is how to determine whether it is 'like' or 'directly competitive' with the service provided by the domestic industry.[63] In the WPGR meetings, some delegations stressed that 'like services' or 'directly competitive services' is the key concept for the ESM.[64]

The text of GATS does not provide guidance as to which criteria should be taken into account to determine likeness. To date, Panels and the Appellate Body have addressed the issue of 'likeness' in the GATS in two disputes (*EC – Bananas III* and *Canada – Autos*). In both disputes the Panels accepted that foreign and domestic services and services suppliers were 'like' and reference was made to the nature and characteristics of the services at issue without justifying its decision in great detail.[65] In *US – Gambling*,[66] the parties developed detailed arguments on 'likeness' in the gambling industry but the Panel exercised judicial economy with respect to the complaint of national treatment violation made by Antigua and Barbuda under Article XVII.[67] Some commentators suggest that requiring a complaining party to demonstrate likeness for the services and the suppliers may make the burden of proof

---

[62] WPGR, Note from the Chairperson, JOB(01)/122, August 7, 2001. See also JOB(01)/26, paras. 11–35; JOB(01)/45, paras. 24–26; JOB(01)/74, paras. 17–19; JOB(01)/108, paras. 15–21.

[63] See generally M. Cossy, 'Determining "likeness" under the GATS: squaring the circle?' WTO Economic Research and Statistics Division' (MS, September 2006).

[64] WPGR, 'Further Thoughts on an Emergency Safeguard Mechanism, Communication From Brunei Darussalam, Indonesia, Malaysia, Myanmar, the Philippines and Thailand,' JOB(04)/4, February 2004.

[65] Panel Report, 'EC – Bananas III (US),' para. 7.322; Panel Report, 'Canada – Autos,' paras. 10.247–10.248.

[66] Panel Report, 'United States – Measures Affecting the Cross-Border Supply of Gambling and Betting Services,' WT/DS285/R.

[67] Appellate Body Report, 'United States – Measures Affecting the Cross-Border Supply of Gambling and Betting Services,' WT/DS285/AB/R (April 7, 2005).

more difficult.[68] However, in *EC – Bananas*, the Panel found that "to the extent that entities provide these like services, they are like service suppliers."[69] The Panel in *Canada – Autos* applied the same reasoning as the *EC – Bananas* Panel.[70] In addition, the text of GATS Article XVII does not suggest that the mode of supply is relevant for defining likeness. The Panel, therefore, introduced the concept of likeness across modes in *Canada – Autos*.[71] There must at least be a presumption that the fact that the services are provided by cross-border supply cannot, standing alone, make a service 'unlike' a domestically provided service.[72] There is also a strong argument that if the use of a different 'mode of supply' were sufficient for a WTO member to escape the obligations of national treatment on the basis of 'unlikeness,' this would seriously undermine the effectiveness of the GATS.[73]

Should the responsibility of showing 'likeness' or the 'directly competitive' nature of the services concerned should be on the member invoking the ESM? Is there any reason to distinguish between the notion of likeness with respect to the national treatment principle and that of likeness for the purpose of an ESM?[74] The limited GATS case law does not provide much clarification on the interpretation of likeness, and it is perhaps more appropriate to leave this issue to future WTO Panels and the Appellate Body on a case-to-case basis.

(iii) Additional commitments (*Mexico – Telecom, US – Gambling, China – Audiovisual Services*)

As mentioned earlier, different views have been expressed regarding the modalities for the introduction of a GATS ESM. Some advocates argued that a more flexible approach to including ESM provisions in the GATS might be the negotiation of a reference paper on ESM. This way, members would attach, individually, to their schedule of specific commitments, in the way as was done for financial and telecommunication services during the Uruguay Round.[75] In fact, a 'Reference Paper'-type model through the adoption by individual

---

[68] See e.g. M. Krajewski, *National Regulation*, 95–117; Cossy, 'Determining "likeness,"' 37.

[69] Panel Report, 'EC – Bananas III,' para. 7.322.

[70] Panel Report, 'Canada – Autos,' para. 10.283.   [71] *Ibid.*, para. 10.307.

[72] Cossy, 'Determining "likeness,"' 37.

[73] See generally N. F. Diebold, *Non-Discrimination in International Trade in Services: 'Likeness' in WTO/GATS* (Cambridge University Press, 2010).

[74] Panizzon *et al.*, *GATS and the Regulation*, 450.

[75] Marconini, 'Emergency Safeguard,' 18.

members as additional commitments under Article XVIII has proven attractive for some members.[76]

The Panels in *Mexico – Telecom*,[77] *US – Gambling*, and *China – Audiovisual Services* touched upon the interpretation issues concerning the relationship between Article XVIII Additional Commitments, Article XVI Market Access, and XVII National Treatment. In *Mexico – Telecom*, the Panel held that a limitation inscribed in the market access or the national treatment column can limit the applicability of an additional commitment under Article XVIII.[78] In *US – Gambling*, the Panel stressed that the conception of Article XVIII was linked to that of Article VI:4 which establishes a work program for the development of disciplines to ensure that measures relating to qualification requirements and procedures, technical standards, and licensing requirements and procedures do not constitute unnecessary barriers to trade in services.[79] Moreover, in footnote 428 of the Panel Report of *China – Audiovisual Services*, the Panel further indicated that "nothing in Article XVIII of the GATS suggests that by undertaking additional commitments Members could diminish its other WTO obligations."

The existing interpretations of Article XVIII offer very little indication as to how to bring new rules through additional commitments. For future negotiations, a positive outcome might well depend on a critical mass of members being prepared to cooperate. One option could be that a core group of interested members develop ESM disciplines that would then be left for adoption by individual members as additional commitments under Article XVIII.[80] In any event, a 'Reference Paper'-type model through the adoption by individual members as additional commitments would amount to something which would be attached to national schedules. It would be subject to bilateral or plurilateral negotiations and therefore depends on the bargaining power of each individual member.[81] If so, more questions will arise as to whether a 'Reference Paper'-type model would start from a horizontal level that specifies minimum obligations for all members.[82] From this aspect, it seems that the systemic

---

[76] R. Adlung, 'Services Negotiations in the Doha Round: Lost In Flexibility?,' *J. Int'l Econ. L.* 9(2006), 865

[77] Panel Report, 'Mexico – Measures Affecting Telecommunications Services,' WT/DS204/R.

[78] *Ibid.*, para.7.368.   [79] *Ibid.*, para. 6.312.

[80] Marconini, 'Emergency Safeguard,' 11–13.

[81] See generally UNCTAD paper, www.unctad.org

[82] *Ibid.* See also, R. Adlung, 'Negotiations on Safeguards and Subsidies in Services: A Never-Ending Story?,' *J. Int'l Econ. L.* 10(2007), 235, 263.

implications of evolving GATS jurisprudence cannot offer any direct guidance on constructing the concept of services ESM.

(iv) Modification of schedules (*US – Gambling 22.6*)

There have been proposals regarding other available options of services ESM. Some believe that a simplified GATS Article XXI-like procedure or an amendment to Article XXI may be an alternative.[83] Under the current procedure, a modification or withdrawal of commitment pursuant to Article XXI can only take place after compensatory adjustments to affected members have been made.[84] A feature of an Article XXI-like ESM procedure could be the temporary nature of the withdrawal of modification of commitments until the domestic industry resolves its problems.[85]

In *US – Gambling* arbitration under Article 22.6 of the DSU,[86] the EU argued that its substantial interest in the arbitration proceedings derives from the fact that the arbitration decision may affect its WTO rights in the context of ongoing procedures under Article XXI:1(b) of GATS relating to the modification of US commitments on "Other recreational Services." The Arbitrator declined the EU request to be accorded third-party status in these proceedings, with the view that its mandate in these proceedings is defined in Article 22.7 of the DSU and is limited to matters arising from Antigua and Barbuda's request for suspension of concessions and other obligations and the US challenge to this request, in accordance with Articles 22.6 and 22.7 of the DSU. By contrast, proceedings under Article XXI:1(b) of GATS, which arise from an intent to modify or withdraw a scheduled commitment under GATS, involve a negotiation process among members concerned, "with a view to reaching agreement on any necessary compensatory adjustment." The Arbitrator saw no basis for assuming that its determination under Article 22.7 of the DSU would adversely affect the EU's rights in the context of the separate proceeding under Article XXI:1(b) of GATS, which has both a distinct legal basis and a distinct object.

---

[83] Gauthier *et al.*, 'Déjà vu, or New Beginning,' 174–176.
[84] Bosworth *et al.*, 'Emergency Safeguard Measures,' 68.
[85] Panizzon *et al.*, *GATS and the Regulation*, 459–462.
[86] Decision by the Arbitrator, United States – Measures Affecting the Cross-Border Supply of Gambling and Betting Services – Recourse to Arbitration by the United States under Article 22.6 of the DSU, WT/DS285/ARB, December 21, 2007.

Is amendment to Article XXI an alternative? The above arbitration reasoning to some degree support an Article XXI-like ESM procedure in the sense that agreeing on mutually acceptable compensation under Article XXI is cumbersome in practice and difficult to use.

To conclude, the current GATS jurisprudence provides only limited guidance to negotiators addressing the issues of services ESM. Dispute settlement cases offer some but very little indication as to how to construct the concepts of services ESM. Key questions remained unanswered and were left open for future discussions, which, indeed, required more creativity. It is necessary to look for simpler ways to conceptualize services ESM.

3. Exploring alternative approaches – the China – Taiwan Treaty

(i) Revisiting the question of 'desirability' – a case study on ECFA

The Economic Cooperation Framework Agreement (ECFA), signed in June 2010, is an interim FTA between China and Taiwan. The purposes of the ECFA, as propounded by its advocates, would help to stabilize and eventually increase Taiwan's presence in the global market.[87] Under ECFA, among all items eligible for service trade liberalization across the Taiwan Strait, the financial service sector has become a major focus of attention. The commitments for the banking sector in the early-harvest list of ECFA are as set out in Tables 10.4 and 10.5.

Recently, the Financial Supervisory Commission (FSC) in Taiwan announced that Taiwan will relax conditions for mainland Chinese banks to set up offices in Taiwan and set a timetable for them to buy into Taiwanese banks, in exchange for reciprocal concessions made by the Chinese counterpart, including earlier allowance for Taiwanese-invested banks to undertake renminbi-denominated businesses, ahead of the original schedule. Although this rapid development of trade and investment liberalization under ECFA may greatly benefit Taiwanese businesses, increasing concerns and anxieties have been voiced that it could also harm the Taiwanese market.

Generally speaking, Taiwan is overbanked. The country has long been Asia's most saturated banking market.[88] With almost seventy banks

---

[87] P. L. Hsieh, 'The China–Taiwan ECFA, Geopolitical Dimensions and WTO Law,' *Journal of International Economic Law* 14 (2010), 121–156.

[88] Gavin Bowring, 'Waiting for China,' *The Banker* (July 1, 2010).

Table 10.4 *The commitments of the Taiwan side on liberalization of financial services sector*

Sector	Specific commitments
Banking and other financial services (excluding securities, futures and insurance)	The Mainland's banks which have been permitted to incorporate representative offices in Taiwan and whose representative offices have so incorporated for one full year, may apply for incorporation of branches in Taiwan.

serving a population of 23 million, the streets of central Taipei are testament to this cut-throat environment, where there are often three or more banks directly facing each other. Given the intense competition, Taiwan's banks have among the lowest return on equity, return on assets, dividend yields, and interest margins in Asia.[89] The government has been trying to encourage more bank mergers, as overcrowding in the domestic market leads to intense competition that erodes profitability.[90] To survive in the increasingly competitive local market, several domestic banks are looking to expand their operations abroad, and especially to mainland China.[91]

Although developing a presence in the Chinese market is potentially lucrative for Taiwan's banks, it will also increase their exposure to risk. Under the ECFA, Taiwan is also opening its banking sector to mainland Chinese banks and investors. Mainland banks will be able to convert their representative offices in Taiwan into branches after a year of operation. Banks on both sides can also tap into each other's markets by buying stakes in each other's financial institutions.[92] In addition, given

---

[89] Taiwan's Mainland Affairs Council, www.mac.gov.tw/mp.asp?mp=1 (last visited 2012/10/25).

[90] *Ibid*. The number of domestic banking institutions fell from 53 in 2001 to 38 in early 2012. Banks' profitability was boosted in 2012 by low credit costs, but the ratio of net income before tax to average assets was still modest in 2011, at 0.54.

[91] *Ibid*.

[92] Taiwan's professionals are in demand in China's growing financial sector also because they come from the same culture and speak the same language. Chinese banks will also invest in Taiwan mainly to acquire talent and the knowledge, particularly because Taiwan has trained many world-class professionals especially in business development and wealth management. See generally www.itrade.usc.edu.tw

Table 10.5 *The commitments of the China side on liberalization of financial services sector*

Sector	Specific commitments
Banking and other financial services (excluding securities, futures and insurance)	1. For Taiwan banks to set up wholly owned banks or branches (not branches affiliated to a wholly owned bank) in the Mainland with reference to the Regulation on Administration of Foreign-funded Banks, they shall have representative offices in the Mainland for more than one year before application.
	2. For the operating branches of Taiwan banks in the Mainland to apply to conduct RMB business, they shall have been operating in the Mainland for more than two years and be profitable in the preceding year before application.
	3. For the operating branches of Taiwan banks in the Mainland to apply to conduct RMB business for Taiwan corporates in the Mainland, they shall fulfill the following conditions: they should have been operating in the Mainland for more than one year and been profitable in the preceding year.
	4. The operating branches of Taiwan banks in the Mainland may set up special agencies providing financial services to small businesses, the specific requirements of which shall follow relevant rules in the Mainland.
	5. Fast tracks shall be established for Taiwan banks applying to set up branches (not branches affiliated to wholly owned banks) in central and western, as well as northeastern regions of the Mainland.
	6. In conducting profitability assessment on the branches of Taiwan banks in the Mainland, the relevant authorities shall take into account the overall performance of the Taiwan bank under assessment.

that Taiwan has almost seventy banks, consolidation would seem a natural evolutionary step. Chinese banks will be allowed to take larger strategic stakes, and this could pave the way for larger Chinese banks to swallow much smaller Taiwanese banks. Several mainland banks have currently chosen to expand in Taiwan via branch networks. For example,

Bank of China, which is one of China's big four state-owned commercial banks,[93] opened an operating branch in June 2012 in Taipei. Concerns exist that mainland firms may use their size and funding advantages to out-muscle local competitors. The banking industry in Taiwan began to worry that the four giant state-owned banks in mainland China might come to Taiwan and buy out all banks in Taiwan, if Taiwan opens the banking industry to mainland China, without any essential safety net for services liberalization.[94] Taiwanese regulators should be alert to the danger and may take action to curb expansion by Chinese banks if it occurs too rapidly.[95]

An ESM is now on the negotiating table. From a pragmatic perspective, an ESM will help the Taiwanese government to address some of its domestic constituents' concerns and anxieties over making financial services commitments under the ECFA. An ESM would allow Taiwan some level of comfort in knowing that if it had somehow misjudged the extent or the pace of liberalization or reform Taiwan ought to have committed to, or failed to anticipate certain consequences or other circumstances which may cause loss to certain domestic private stakeholders, a safety net is available to Taiwan, even if only on a temporary basis.[96] It remains to be seen whether consensus will be obtained between China and Taiwan. The Need for an ESM is evident (at least from the Taiwan perspective), but how to make it work in practice?

(ii) Differentiating economic activity–the specificity of the sectoral elements

At the moment the draft provision proposed by China is identical to that of the China–Pakistan FTA, which is categorized as 'Type II' (see section III, 1 above). The provision simply notes that the multilateral negotiations pursuant to Article X of the GATS on the question of emergency safeguard measures are based on the principle of non-discrimination, and parties agree that upon the conclusion of such multilateral negotiations, they shall conduct a review for the purpose of discussing

---

[93] W. Wang, 'The GATS and the Legal Framework of the Chinese Banking Sector,' in Kern Alexander et al. (eds.), *The World Trade Organization and Trade in Services* (Leiden: Nijhoff, 2008), 713–744.

[94] JOB(01)/105. See also JOB(01)/67, paras. 8–9.

[95] Financial Services Forecast, Economist Intelligence Unit, July 11, 2012.

[96] C. Manduna, 'The WTO Services Negotiations: An Analysis of the GATS and Issues of Interest for Least Developed Countries,' Trade-Related Agenda, Development And Equity Working Papers, 23 (December 2004).

appropriate amendments to the Agreement so as to incorporate the results of such multilateral negotiations. As explained earlier, this type of provision essentially does not go beyond GATS commitments.

In the case of ECFA, how to build up a meaningful ESM for banking services remains a high priority on the negotiating agenda. At the core of the issue is the extent to which any ESM discipline should be horizontal in application – across the board for all sectors, or developed on a sector-specific basis. In fact, similar issues have been raised under the WTO. In the WPGR meetings, some members were of the view that ESM application could not exclude any sector *a priori* or be confined to certain sectors only.[97] Their position is that an ESM is usually considered to be a cross-cutting issue that is not dependent on sectoral specificities, and therefore should be generally applicable.[98] Irrespective of the final form of an ESM, some kind of horizontal framework has to be in place.[99] There is a need to sequence disciplines, starting first with horizontal discussions, and then to engage in sectoral discussions as appropriate.[100]

It is nevertheless possible to explore non-horizontal options.[101] The ECFA negotiations are now at a crossroad, and discussions on various alternative approaches, including an operational sector-specific ESM, would help to take the negotiations forward. This chapter takes the position that an ESM should be tailored to the particularities of specific sectors. Services differ significantly, and therefore an attempt should be made to explore the scope for developing sector-specific ESMs rather than generic all-encompassing instruments. Looking back to the negotiating history of the GATS, the sectoral discussions to date have been useful in the sense of facilitating the participation of capital-based sectoral experts, seeking more information about sectoral regulations and highlighting the specificity of the sectoral elements.

[97] WPGR, Report of the Meeting of June 21, 2006, Note by the Secretariat, S/WPGR/M/56, 4 July 2006.
[98] JOB No. 6830.
[99] JOB(01)/81. S/WPGR/M/10, para. 5; S/WPGR/M/11, para. 9; S/WPGR/M/19, paras. 3–6; S/WPGR/M/20, paras. 4–9; S/WPGR/M/21, paras. 7–11. A number of delegations have strongly expressed the view that a horizontal mechanism would be based on generally applicable criteria and would be applicable whenever the situation in given sector meets the relevant criteria. In their opinions, sectoral specificities should be dealt with on a case-by-case basis. Petitioning industries (and the governments) would be responsible for introducing relevant sectoral specificities in their application of ESM so as to prove their case (Marconini, 'Emergency Safeguard Measures,' 15).
[100] Marconini, 'Emergency Safeguard Measures,' 15.
[101] See generally Sauvé, 'Been There, Not Yet Done,' 617–618.

In addition, to develop a workable ESM, the measures need not apply to all modes of transacting services.[102] From a mode application perspective, the goods model is not appropriate for services, since trade in goods is equivalent only to cross-border supply of services (mode 1). The enforceability of an ESM under different modes may vary, and it may appear more difficult to enforce a safeguard measure in certain modes of supply for particular sectors.[103]

In fact, examples of sector-specific and mode-specific ESM can be found in Taiwan's domestic law. To illustrate, Article 50 *bis* of the Motion Picture Act of Taiwan stipulates that, "when imported foreign motion pictures have caused or might cause severe damage to our motion picture enterprises, the central authority in charge shall establish relevant measures to maintain the development of the domestic motion picture industry."[104] Indeed, services sectors themselves may be highly diverse. Priorities for which measures should be addressed by what type of disciplines may also differ among sectors. It is better to include specific rules than to develop general disciplines for ESM, especially considering the fact that not all service sectors are traded to the same extent and not all encounter the same degree of problems with lack of ESM.[105] To conclude, while arguments remain supporting the cross-sectoral application of an ESM, tailor-made solutions may indeed be more practically developed on a sector- and mode-specific basis than through a generic catch-all instrument.[106]

4. A step towards 'feasibility' – an ESM for commercial presence of banking services under ECFA

This chapter therefore concludes that a sectoral approach would provide for a less complex, more targeted and easier domestic consultation process as compared to what an all-encompassing horizontal approach would demand. The long overdue GATS ESM negotiations have shown that it is extremely difficult to establish ESM disciplines which are uniform across sectors because of the nature of the sectors themselves. In the case of ECFA, Taiwan and China should focus their attention on work priorities and ways to carry them through, and to develop an ESM

---

[102] Gauthier, 'Déjà vu, or New Beginning,' 173.   [103] *Ibid.*
[104] The provision was deleted by Presidential Order on January 7, 2004.
[105] Pierola, 'A Safeguards Regime,' 617–620.
[106] Sauvé, 'Been There, Not Yet Done,' 618.

for *commercial presence (mode 3) of banking services* before seeking a generic horizontal solution. The parties could subsequently decide, based on such experimentation,[107] to extend the logic of the approach to other sectors or to develop a generic safeguards instrument after several years' practice.

With respect to the banking sector, as indicated in section III of this chapter, RTAs have produced some innovations with regard to the sectoral ESM disciplines, such as the NAFTA provisions for financial sector and the EU energy sector directive. In the case of ECFA, it is possible to develop meaningful regulatory disciplines for banking services sectors. In practice, individual services sectors in most countries are typically regulated by ministries other than the ministry of trade.[108] The more complicated a sector, the fewer people will be able to understand that sector.[109] It would be natural for the specialists to structure the negotiations along sectoral approaches, and this is particularly true for the banking sector. A sectoral approach would provide greater detail and a more limited scope for trade negotiations between China and Taiwan, thus allowing for the identification of elements of crucial importance to the sector and for effective domestic consultations to address particular sectoral sensitivities.

With respect to mode 3 (*commercial presence*), one might argue that with the advent of new technologies and the resulting possibilities of remote transactions, mode 1 cross-border trade is becoming more and more common in the supply of banking services, as compared to mode 3. However, for certain types of financial services, in particular private banking, which involves, e.g., long-term contracts or personal attention, direct contact between the consumer and the supplier is still necessary. Therefore, mode 3 will still be the predominant mode for the supply of banking services,[110] and is most likely to generate significant injurious dislocations in domestic services markets. Mode 2 does not seem particularly relevant to the discussion, and the limited mobility of mode 4 makes it an unlikely source of serious unanticipated injury.

To conclude, how to build up a meaningful ESM for services remains a high priority on the ECFA negotiating agenda, and a step toward

---

[107] P. Sauvé, 'Completing the GATS Framework: Addressing Uruguay Round Leftovers,' *Aussenwirtschaft* 57. Jahrgang (2002), Heft III, Zürich: Rüegger, S. 301–341.

[108] H. Gao, 'Evaluating Alternative Approaches to GATS Negotiations: Sectoral, Formulate and Others,' in Panizzon *et al.*, *GATS and the Regulation*, 183, 198–201.

[109] *Ibid.*   [110] WTO Secretariat, *Guide to the GATS* (Geneva, 2005), 339.

feasibility is to develop an ESM for mode 3 of banking services. By taking such approaches cross-strait sectoral experts would be able to highlight the specificity of the banking sector and focus on the questions, e.g., how could it be determined whether serious injury, or threat of serious injury, was being caused by liberalization undertaken in a party's schedule of commitments, as opposed to other factors? What type of information would be considered in making a determination of injury or threat thereof? With respect to mode3, how could such increase be sudden if the banks causing the injury had been established in the market for some time? How to determine the element of suddenness for banking activities? Should it be evaluated in the context of its effect on the affected domestic industry? Indeed, targeted and tailor-made solutions to the above technical questions can be more fruitfully deployed on a sector-specific and mode-specific basis.

VI. Concluding remarks

This chapter has focused on the questions of whether – within the WTO – the inherent characteristics of goods and services (should) reflect differences in the structures of the two legal orders, i.e., the GATT and GATS. After identifying the main challenges that arise from the negotiations on services ESM, I conclude that although the meetings of WPGR helped to clarify certain concepts with regard to the application of an ESM, the technical discussions appear endless and we are nowhere near our intended goal. Such complexity is detrimental to an ESM in services. While arguments remain supporting the cross-sectoral application of an ESM, there is a need to consider sectoral specificities. The lack of movement on developing horizontal disciplines suggested that there could be a greater chance of reaching agreement on sectoral disciplines. Recognizing that there were many complex issues in relation to ESM, a sectoral approach might be a more practical way to go. Differentiating economic activities is the first step toward solving many of the intractable legal and policy issues raised in the last fifteen years.

As articulated in this book, an important common challenge to the international economic order is the disciplinary fragmentation of global economic regulation into separate disciplines without much thought to regulatory issues that are common to all systems of regulation. This chapter demonstrates that intradisciplinary fragmentation, like interdisciplinary fragmentation, is also an important aspect as far as normative fragmentation is concerned, and that intradisciplinary dialogue is almost as difficult.

We are now facing an increasingly complex legal environment that requires an understanding of both intradisciplinary and interdisciplinary issues of international economic law. In this volume the comparative experiences recounted in other chapters confirm the dangers of disciplinary fragmentation of the international economic regulation. This chapter supports that general fear.

11

The schizophrenia of countermeasures in international economic law: the case of the ASEAN Comprehensive Investment Agreement

MARTINS PAPARINSKIS

I. Introduction

The interrelated operation of different regimes of international economic law (IEL) may involve the presence of mutually contradictory or inconsistent elements.[1] It would not be unreasonable to expect a further sharpening of these considerations during and after crises. This chapter addresses a tangle of rules, regimes, and paradigms, exploring the limits of the consistency of countermeasures in international economic law, on the basis of a case study taken from the Association of Southeast Asian Nations (ASEAN).

The starting point of the discussion on countermeasures is that rules of international law on the issue display considerable tensions, wavering between recognition of their conceptual and practical importance and nothing the structural inevitability of abuse. Kelsen famously considered the presence and effectiveness of countermeasures an appropriate benchmark for evaluating the validity of international law as a legal order;[2] other authors have emphasised the great possibilities for abuse inherent

---

[1] The *Oxford English Dictionary* explains the figurative meaning of 'schizophrenic' as 'with the implication of mutually contradictory or inconsistent elements', www.oed.org. It is probably the case that editors, when using this term do not intend to suggest that the literal meaning of the concept may illuminate the intellectual operation of international law(yers), although some authors might have welcomed that suggestion (H. Morgenthau, 'Positivism, Functionalism and International Law', *American Journal of International Law* 260 (1940) 260, particularly 260-1).

[2] H. Kelsen, 'Théorie du droit international public', RCADI 84 (1953), 1, 32–34; H. Kelsen, 'Théorie générale du droit international public: problèmes choisis', RCADI 42 (1932), 117, 135–7.

in a regime permitting decentralised breaches of law (even with wrong-fulness precluded).[3]

In the last decade, elaboration of the law of countermeasures has, somewhat unexpectedly, taken place through adjudication in inter-national economic law. The immortal trio of cases[4] which have shaped the modern law[5] have been supplemented by the reports of the World Trade Organization Dispute Settlement Body (WTO DSB) and by three awards given by investment treaty Tribunals.[6] The twists and pulls of these different regimes – investor-state and inter-state – provide a fascinating case study of the operation of international economic law, permitting an exploration of uncertainties within and between trade and investment regimes, and raising the question of the possibility of certainty at the 'meta-level' of legal reasoning.

The operation of countermeasures in international economic law has been addressed in legal writings, both regarding the *lex specialis* countermeasures in WTO law[7] and the general international law coun-termeasures in investment protection law.[8] Their possible interplay has

---

[3] D. Alland, 'The Definition of Countermeasures', in J. Crawford, A. Pellet, and S. Olleson (eds.), *The Law of International Responsibility* (Oxford University Press, 2010), 1127, 1129.

[4] To borrow the expression from P. Birnie, A. Boyle, and C. Redgwell, *International Law and the Environment* (3rd edn, Oxford University Press, Oxford, 2009), v.

[5] *Responsabilité de l'Allemagne à raison des dommages causés dans les colonies portugaises du sud de l'Afrique (sentence sur le principe de la responsabilité)* (*Portugal* v. *Allemagne*) (1928) 2 RIAA 1011, 1025–8; *Air Service Agreement of 27 March 1946 between the United States of America and France* (1978) 18 RIAA 417, 443 (para. 81); *Gabčíkovo–Nagymaros Project* (*Hungary/Slovakia*) [1997] ICJ Rep. 7, 56.

[6] *Archer Daniels Midland Company and Tate & Lyle Ingredients Americas, Inc.* v. *Mexico* (ICSID AF Case No. ARB(AF)/04/5, Award of 21 November 2007) 146 ILR 439, paras. 110–84; *Corn Products International, Inc.* v. *Mexico* (ICSID AF Case No. ARB/(AF)/04/1, Decision on Responsibility of 15 January 2008) 146 ILR 581, paras. 144–92; *Cargill, Inc.* v. *Mexico* (ICSID AF Case No. ARB(AF)/05/2, Award of 13 August 2009) 146 ILR 642, paras. 379–430. The argument of countermeasures was also considered in a recent ICJ case, yet in a manner so brief as to provide little illumination to the legal issues, *Applica-tion of the Interim Accord of 13 September 1995* (*FYRM* v. *Greece*) [2012] ICJ Rep., para. 164.

[7] C. P. Brown and J. Pauwelyn, *The Law, Economics and Politics of Retaliation in WTO Dispute Settlement* (eds.) (Cambridge University Press, 2010); J. Gomula, 'Responsibility and the World Trade Organization', in Crawford *et al.*, *Law of International Responsibility*, 791, 797–801.

[8] M. Paparinskis, 'Investment Arbitration and the Law of Countermeasures', *British Year-book of International Law* 79 (2008), 264; J. Kurtz, 'The Paradoxical Treatment of the ILC Articles on State Responsibility in Investor-State Arbitration', *ICSID Review – Foreign Investment Law Journal* 25 (2010), 200, 214–16; H. Lesaffre, 'Circumstances Precluding

also been dealt with.[9] This chapter does not seek to reargue the theoretical issues discussed elsewhere, but will consider the mechanics of their application from the perspective of one particular treaty instrument: the ASEAN Comprehensive Investment Agreement (ACIA).[10] The analysis will be undertaken in two steps, exploring the applicability of countermeasures in different situations of 'multi-sourced equivalence' between primary obligations of trade and investment law; that is, situations where obligations, while having identical or similar normative content, have been created through different international instruments.[11] The first case study below will consider the manner in which a suspension of concessions by a WTO arbitrator could be applied to equivalent obligations of the ACIA (I). Second, the opposite scenario will be considered, concerning a suspension of concessions authorised under the ASEAN dispute settlement regime (II). In both cases, the interplay of legal rules and regimes will be considered from multiple perspectives, including the WTO, the ACIA, and the investor.

The argument advanced in this chapter is that the problem does not lie, or does not chiefly lie, in the formulation of the particular regimes. It also does not lie, despite appearances to the contrary, in deficiencies of a trans-systemic rule of law on the matter,[12] if that is meant to suggest the absence of a legal vocabulary that would permit the articulation of consistent solutions. There also does not seem to be any particular

Wrongfulness in the ILC Articles on State Responsibility: Countermeasures', in Crawford *et al.*, *Law of International Responsibility*, 469, 473; Z. Douglas, 'Other Specific Regimes of Responsibility: Investment Treaty Arbitration and ICSID', *ibid.*, 815, 821; R. O'Keefe, 'Proportionality', *ibid.*, 1157, 1161–2, 1165; N. J. Calamita, 'Countermeasures and Jurisdiction: Between Effectiveness and Fragmentation', *Georgetown Journal of International Law* 42 (2011), 233.

[9] P.-J. Kuijper, 'Does the World Trade Organization Prohibit Retorsions and Reprisals? Legitimate "Contracting Out" or "Clinical Isolation" Again?', in M. E. Janow and others (eds.), *The WTO: Governance, Dispute Settlement, and Developing Countries* (New York: Juris, 2008), 707; G. Marceau and J. Watt, 'Dispute Settlement Regimes Intermingled: Regional Trade Agreements and the WTO', *Journal of International Dispute Settlement* 1 (2010), 67, 73–95; M. Paparinskis, 'Equivalent Primary Rules and Differential Secondary Rules: Countermeasures in WTO and Investment Protection Law', in Broude and Shany, *Multi-Sourced Equivalent Norms*, 259.

[10] ASEAN Comprehensive Investment Agreement (adopted 26 February 2009, entered into force 29 March 2012), www.asean.org; M. Paparinskis, *Basic Documents on International Investment Protection* (Oxford: Hart, 2012), 401.

[11] On multi-sourced equivalent rules, see generally T. Broude and Y. Shany, 'The International Law and Policy of Multi-Sourced Equivalent Norms', in Broude and Shany, *Multi-Sourced Equivalent Norms*, 1.

[12] F. Fontanelli, 'Book Review', *European Journal of International Law* 23 (2012), 597, 602.

political will to resist synchronisation of countermeasures across regimes. At the end of the day, the buck may have to stop at the doors of the invisible college of lawyers.[13] WHO may have been insufficiently imaginative in providing the regime-builders with the right tools and bricks to build bridges between the moving islands of international law.[14]

II.   *Lex specialis* WTO countermeasures and equivalent obligations of the ACIA

Trade law has a different scope from the law of investment. At the same time, the factual overlap of trade and investment may lead to situations where particular conduct is required by obligations under both trade and investment law or, to put it conversely, where particular conduct would be wrongful under both trade and investment law.[15] Since the WTO suspension of concessions may authorise conduct that is, in principle, in breach of WTO obligations, it is similarly possible that a suspension of concessions authorised by the WTO would be in breach of equivalent obligations under investment protection law.[16] Hence, the question: what is the legal situation of a state party to the ACIA that has been authorised to suspend its concessions under the WTO Agreements vis-à-vis another

[13] O. Schachter, 'Invisible College of International Lawyers', *Northwestern University Law Review* 72 (1977–8), 217.

[14] J. Pauwelyn, 'Bridging Fragmentation and Unity: International Law as a Universe of Inter-Connected Islands', *Michigan Journal of International Law* 25 (2003–4), 903.

[15] This is precisely what happened in the cases against Mexico regarding its treatment of soft drinks, where Mexico was found to have breached both investment protection obligations under NAFTA, *ADM*, paras. 193–213; *CP*, paras. 103–43; *Cargill*, paras. 185–223, and trade law obligations, WTO, *Mexico – Tax Measures on Soft Drinks and other Beverages*, Panel Report (7 October 2005), WT/DS308/R, paras. 8, 9.2. On trade and investment see further references in Paparinskis 'Equivalent Obligations', nn. 20–1; and L. Guglya, 'The Interplay of International Dispute Resolution Mechanisms: The Softwood Lumber Controversy', *Journal of International Dispute Settlement* 2 (2011), 175; A. Davies, 'Scoping the Boundary between the Trade Law and Investment Law Regimes: When Does a Measure Relate to Investment?', *Journal of International Economic Law* 15 (2012), 793. A further (or perhaps rather anterior) layer of equivalence that will not be directly addressed in this chapter may be caused by a 'double breach' of equivalent trade obligations expressed at the universal and regional levels (W. Davey and A. Sapir, 'The *Soft Drinks* Case: The WTO and Regional Agreements', *World Trade Review* 8 (2009), 5, 23).

[16] For example, the suspension of concessions under GATT, GATS and TRIPS that Brazil was found to be entitled to could conceivably raise issues under investment protection obligations on non-discrimination as well as certain aspects of fair and equitable treatment and expropriation, WTO, *US – Subsidies on Upland Cotton*, Decision by the Arbitrator (31 August 2009) WT/DS267/ARB/2, paras. 6.1–5.

ACIA party if this suspension would be in a prima facie breach of the ACIA? One might engage with the question from four perspectives: the WTO, the ACIA, a conflict between the WTO and ACIA, and an investor. These perspectives will be considered in turn.

1. WTO

The WTO perspective may be disposed of relatively briefly. The suspension of obligations that may be requested from the Dispute Settlement Body (DSB) and determined by the arbitrator under Article 22.6 of the Dispute Settlement Understanding (DSU) relates to obligations 'under the covered agreements'. An equivalent obligation formulated in a different and unrelated rule of international law is not one 'under the covered agreements', and therefore authorisation of the DSB does not apply to such obligations. Of course, States and international organisations are entitled to agree under a treaty A on the suspension of a separately existing treaty B (and that is precisely what WTO parties have done in Article 22.3(g)(iii) DSU regarding the IP treaties incorporated by TRIPS).[17] However, ACIA is not referenced in this way, so the *pari materia* obligations under it remain unaffected. Since WTO parties have agreed on the WTO as the exclusive forum for settlement of disputes regarding breaches of WTO Agreements,[18] they cannot unilaterally choose to apply countermeasures in response to its breach that would be in breach of other rules of international law. Consequently, to the extent that the *pari materia* ACIA investment obligations cannot be taken care of by another legal argument, the state party to the ACIA would be entitled to suspend WTO concessions but would not be able to exercise this right in compliance with ACIA.[19]

---

[17] WTO parties, even though they remain bound by those treaties, have agreed *inter se* on *lex specialis* countermeasures to the extent of incorporation. An alternative reading would be to say that if a breach of WIPO obligations does take place, TRIPS might operate to preclude either wrongfulness by consent or the invocation of responsibility for wrongfulness by other WTO parties, in the latter sense in terms of an estoppel or an *ex ante* waiver of the right of invocation, C. Tams, 'Waiver, Acquiescence, and Extinctive Prescription', in Crawford *et al.*, *Law of International Responsibility*, 1035.

[18] WTO, *US/Canada – Continued Suspension of Obligations in the EC–Hormones Dispute, Report of the Appellate Body* (14 November 2008) WT/DS320/AB/R, WT/DS321/AB/R, para. 382.

[19] Paparinskis 'Equivalent Primary Rules', 270–4.

2. ACIA

It may not be entirely surprising that the 1994 WTO regime does not coordinate the application of countermeasures with equivalent obligations of investment protection law – after all, the great NAFTA arbitrations of the late 1990s that reminded everybody of the importance of investment protection law were still a few years in the future. One might expect more explicit *ex ante* coordination from the ACIA, drafted in 2009 and against the background of the WTO. In technical terms, States can synchronise the application of the countermeasures against equivalent rules, for example by providing that measures authorised regarding rule A will not be in breach of rule B (or the authorisation will be treated as an *ex ante* consent, or a waiver of the right to invoke responsibility). The ACIA drafters were clearly aware of the possible overlap of investment and trade rules and provided for some limited synchronisation. Article 7 states that (otherwise unmentioned and unqualified) provisions of TRIMs 'shall apply, mutatis mutandis, to this Agreement'; presumably, since the scope and content of the primary obligation is established by reference to another regime, a suspension of TRIMs under the WTO would necessarily result in a *mutatis mutandis* suspension of the 'appl[icable]' rules of the ACIA.[20] Other references to the WTO would probably not synchronise the legal rules in cases of suspension.[21] The challenge of creating rules that could appropriately take into account the procedural regimes regarding equivalent rules is not trivial, and careful drafting would be necessary to capture the idea of the different scope of regimes in general, even if their rules are equivalent in particular circumstances. Nevertheless, taking the ACIA as it stands, an interpretation of the primary obligations, particularly against the contextual background of rare explicit

---

[20] Art. 14(5) defines the scope of expropriation as not applying 'to the issuance of compulsory licences granted in relation to intellectual property rights in accordance with the TRIPS agreement'. The direct impact of the rule would be to condition the scope of primary investment obligations by compliance with primary trade obligations, but it is not inconceivable that it could apply to appropriately suspended primary trade obligations.

[21] Art. 9(5) defines the scope of national and MFN treatment by reference to exceptions and derogations in TRIPS but is explicitly limited to exceptions provided in the primary rules of TRIPS (arts. 3–5), most likely excluding the derogation by way of suspension. Art. 17(2) incorporates GATS rules on the general exceptions regarding financial services, see also 17(1)(d).

references to WTO, suggests that they remain, in principle, unaffected
by the suspension in the latter forum.

3.   WTO v. ACIA

Even if WTO and ACIA rules do not sufficiently take into account the
effect of countermeasures regarding one of the equivalent primary obligations, the situation where WTO-authorised conduct cannot be exercised due to investment protection obligations suggests the possible
presence of a conflict. Identification and resolution of the conflict raise
a number of complex questions that will be merely indicated and not
pursued here. Could one say that there is no conflict between a WTO
right and an ACIA obligation because the state can act in compliance
with international law by electing not to exercise its right? Or should one
read the concept of conflict more broadly, and say that the obligation and
exceptional right point in different directions and pursue different purposes? And in terms of taxonomy of state responsibility,[22] could not one
say that 'there is no conflict between' a primary rule and a secondary rule
relating to a breach of a different primary rule because '[t]he two sets of
rules address different matters'?[23] In any event, if a conflict can be
identified, how should it be resolved? Should one apply the rule of *lex
posterior* from Article 30 of the VCLT and analogous customary law,[24]
resolving the conflict between the 1994 WTO and 2009 ACIA in favour
of the latter? Or could the *lex specialis* maxim provide the right tool, and
would then a special secondary rule be more special than an equivalent
primary rule? These inquiries raise broader theoretical questions about
the nature and operation of the international legal order, and require
some careful thinking on the matter.[25]

---

[22] E. David, 'Primary and Secondary Rules', in Crawford *et al.*, *Law of International Responsibility*, 27.

[23] As the ICJ concluded regarding substantive prohibitions and procedural rules on state immunity, *Jurisdictional Immunities of the State* (*Germany* v. *Italy: Greece Intervening*) [2012] ICJ Rep., para. 93. Albeit from a perspective different from that in the present chapter, Talmon has noted that the (procedural) rules on countermeasures are unaffected by the nature of the (substantive) primary prohibitions (S. Talmon, *'Jus Cogens* after *Germany* v. *Italy*: Substantive and Procedural Rules Distinguished', *Leiden Journal of International Law*, 25 (2012), 979, 993).

[24] A. Orakhelashvili, 'Article 30: Convention of 1969', in O. Corten and P. Klein (eds.), *The Vienna Convention on the Law of Treaties: A Commentary* (Oxford University Press, 2011), vol. I, 764, 774.

[25] Paparinskis, 'Equivalent Primary Rules', 274–7.

4. Investor state

It is conceivable that an ACIA investor-state tribunal might forgo the fine theoretical points noted above and articulate its unease about seemingly schizophrenic interplay of WTO and ACIA between the same parties by prioritising the former over the latter. Where would that leave an investor that has brought a case before the Tribunal regarding its mistreatment by a host state, where the complaint relates to conduct that falls within the WTO-authorised suspension of concession? The view expressed in legal writings,[26] and adopted in the three investment arbitrations to address the issue,[27] has focused on the legal nature of the investor and its rights in investment protection law and investment arbitration as the determinative factor. To somewhat simplify the argument, the architecture of investment protection treaties permits two readings. It is intuitively more plausible to say that investment protection rules provide for legal rights of the investor, and investor-state arbitration embodies invocation of state responsibility by the injured investor. However, substantive investment protection obligations may also be owed only on the inter-state level (similarly to the traditional perception of friendship, commerce and navigation treaties), with investment arbitration embodying a delegated invocation of inter-state responsibility. If the host state's obligations are owed only to the home state, they can be suspended with precluded wrongfulness as a countermeasure; the investor's claim fails *in limine*.[28] If the host state's obligations are owed also to the investor, due to its structural incapability to trigger the precondition of breaching an obligation owed to the state the countermeasures argument fails akin to one directed against a third party;[29] the investor's claim proceeds.

---

[26] Paparinskis, 'Investment Arbitration and the Law of Countermeasures', 317–51; Douglas, 'Investment Treaty Arbitration and ICSID', 821; Kurtz, 214–16; Paparinskis, 'Equivalent Obligations', 264–8, 277–80.

[27] *ADM*, paras. 110–84; *CP*, paras. 144–92; *Cargill*, paras. 379–430.

[28] The 2001 ILC Articles leave the question of compensation in cases of precluded wrongfulness open, ILC, '2001 Draft Articles on Responsibility of States for Internationally Wrongful Acts with Commentaries', in *Official Records of the General Assembly, Fifty-Sixth Session*, Supplement No. 10, UN Doc. A/56/10 20 art. 27(b), but it is generally agreed that it would not be required for countermeasures (S. Szurek, 'The Notion of Circumstances Precluding Wrongfulness', in Crawford *et al.*, *Law of International Responsibility*, 427, 436–7); see further references in Paparinskis, 'Equivalent Obligations', 267.

[29] A further question, not directly relevant for analysing countermeasures but of importance for other aspects of state responsibility, is whether the investor's international law rights

The choice between the direct rights and agency approaches is ultimately a matter of treaty interpretation. The most authoritative guidance regarding the determination of individual treaty rights was probably provided by the International Court of Justice in the *LaGrand* case where it addressed the rights of consular notification under the Vienna Convention on Consular Relations. The Court noted that:

> Article 36, paragraph 1 *(b)*, spells out the obligations the receiving State has towards the detained person and the sending State. It provides that, at the request of the detained person, the receiving State must inform the consular post of the sending State of the individual's detention 'without delay'. It provides further that any communication by the detained person addressed to the consular post of the sending State must be forwarded to it by authorities of the receiving State 'without delay'. Significantly, this subparagraph ends with the following language: 'The said authorities shall inform the person concerned without delay of *his rights* under this subparagraph' [emphasis added]. Moreover, under Article 36, paragraph 1 (c), the sending State's right to provide consular assistance to the detained person may not be exercised 'if he expressly opposes such action'. The clarity of these provisions, viewed in their context, admits of no doubt. It follows, as has been held on a number of occasions, that the Court must apply these as they stand . . . Based on the text of these provisions, the Court concludes that Article 36, paragraph 1, creates individual rights.[30]

As *per LaGrand*, the two considerations weighing in favour of the direct nature of the rights seem to be: first, formulation of the treaty rule in the manner that its application is conditional upon the individual's conduct ('at the request of the detained person', 'any communication by the detained person'); second, the formulation of unconditional obligations by the state in the language of individual 'rights'.[31]

---

are akin to human rights or rather to third-party rights under the law of treaties (M. Paparinskis, 'Investment Arbitration and the (New) Law of State Responsibility', *European Journal of International Law* 24(2) (2013), 617–47).

[30] *LaGrand (Germany* v. *US)* [2001] ICJ Rep. 466, para. 77 (emphasis in the original).

[31] The broader context and preparatory materials that might have pointed in the opposite direction persuaded only two judges (*ibid.*), Separate Opinion of Vice-President Shi, 518, paras. 3–16; Dissenting Opinion of Judge Oda, 525, paras. 23–5. If the formulation and expression of treaty rules is the right (and perhaps exclusive) way of determining the presence of individual rights, an interesting implication is that disputes regarding individual treaty rights might have already been *sub silentio* dealt with by the Court, precisely in the context of the protection of foreign investment and aliens. In the *ELSI* case, the Court used the language of 'rights' of nationals when interpreting and applying the FCN Treaty, *Elettronica Sicula S.p.A. (ELSI) (US* v. *Italy)* [1989] ICJ Rep. 15, paras. 68–71,

For the investor, the question of its rights is linked with the question
whether its claims may succeed. When reading the ACIA, one might
point to arguments both in favour and against direct investor's rights. In
the former category of arguments, the investor-state arbitration procedure is formulated as an elective right of the investor to submit a claim
against the state,[32] and generally described as applying to disputes about
'loss or damage by reason of an alleged breach of *any rights conferred by
this Agreement*'.[33] There are other statements that suggest in a similarly
contextual manner that ACIA perceives the investment protection rules
as investors' rights.[34] The provision on expropriation gives a right to the
investor to request compensation in a freely reusable currency.[35] At the
same time, the investment protection rules are otherwise consistently
formulated in terms of obligations to provide certain treatment, rather
than grant rights.[36] The primary obligations[37] and general exceptions[38]
more or less directly borrowed from the WTO would also provide

74–6, 94, 99, 120, 133, 135 (and at one point even described the question as 'whether or
not certain acts could constitute a breach of *the treaty right to be permitted to control and
manage*' (*ibid.*, para. 74, emphasis added), similarly para. 99). Indeed, even the Permanent Court of International Justice was perfectly content to formulate a provisional
measure in a Belgium–China dispute in terms of 'a right on the part of any Belgian' or
'of physical or moral persons of Belgian nationality', *Denunciation of the Treaty of
2 November 1865 between China and Belgium* (*Belgium* v. *China*) (Order) [1927] PCIJ
Rep. Ser. A 8 6, 7–8. These cases are not usually read as involving individuals' international rights, and the resolution of the schizophrenic uneasiness might suggest either
increased scepticism about the criteria of *LaGrand*, or a rethinking of the openness of the
traditional international legal order to individuals, perhaps much greater than is usually
thought to be the case e.g. K. Parlett, *The Individual in the International Legal System*
(Cambridge University Press, 2011), 10–26. Conversely, it is less obvious that the
dominant reading of the *Danzig* advisory opinion as accepting that treaties may create
individual rights under international law is necessarily accurate. While its language is not
a model of clarity, the opinion is better read as making a much finer and subtler point
that international law may be used to determine the content of rights already created
under domestic law, *in casu*, contractual rights, *Jurisdiction of the Courts of Danzig*
(Advisory Opinion) [1928] PCIJ Rep. Ser. B no 15 1, 17–21 (and Gidel on behalf of
Danzig was perfectly explicit that the question about direct international rights of
individuals played no role in the dispute, PCIJ Rep. Ser. C no. 14/1 24).
[32] ACIA, art. 32.   [33] *Ibid.*, art. 29(1) (emphasis added).
[34] Special formalities were not permitted to 'materially impair the *rights afforded by a
Member State to investors of another Member State and investments pursuant to this
Agreement*' (*ibid.*, art. 20(1) (emphasis added)).
[35] *Ibid.*, art. 14(3)–(4).   [36] *Ibid.*, arts. 5, 6, 7, 8, 11, 12, 13, 14(1)–(2).
[37] *Ibid.*, arts. 7, 9(5), 14(5).
[38] *Ibid.*, art 17; cf. General Agreement on Tariffs and Trade (adopted 30 October 1947,
applied provisionally 1 January 1948) 55 UNTS 194 art. XX(a), (b), (d), (f), (g).

contextual support for reading ACIA in the same inter-state terms as the universal free trade regime.[39] Finally, the rule on 'denial of benefits', both by describing investment protection rules as 'benefits', rather than rights, and by requiring notification in particular circumstances to the home state, fits more comfortably within a legal relationship that is not expressed in terms of rights opposable between the investor and the state.[40] Overall, while the procedural autonomy of the investor makes the reading of direct rights more intuitively attractive,[41] the Court in *LaGrand* did not have to address the issue and therefore could not provide any guidance, and the textual and contextual expression of ACIA permits plausible arguments to be made on both sides. One might imagine that the investor, having followed the tangled path of reasoning up to this point, could characterise the manner in which trade and investment rules take into account each other's existence and functioning as schizophrenic.

III. ACIA countermeasures and equivalent obligations of the WTO

The assumption underlying the analysis of the previous section was that trade law and investment law may be equivalent. The previous section sketched the implications of the equivalence for the applicability of WTO *lex specialis* countermeasures. This section will consider the opposite side of the normative coin: the applicability of ACIA countermeasures in light

---

[39] The submission of the inter-state disputes to settlement in accordance with the 2004 ASEAN Protocol on Enhanced Dispute Settlement Mechanism, ACIA, art. 27, with the possibility of suspension of concessions, also fits more comfortably within an inter-state paradigm, where the applicability of particular rules is a matter of inter-state concern (adopted 29 January 2004, entered into force 29 November 2004), www.asean-sec.org; M. Paparinskis, *Basic Documents on International Investment Protection* (Oxford: Hart, 2012), 387, art. 16.

[40] ACIA, art. 19. There is some disagreement whether denial of benefit clauses has only prospective or also retrospective effect: two Energy Charter Treaty Tribunals have adopted the former position, *Plama Consortium Limited* v. *Bulgaria* (ICSID Case No. ARB/03/24, Decision on Jurisdiction of 8 February 2005), paras. 159–65; *Veteran Petroleum Ltd.* v. *Russia* (PCA Case No. AA 228, Interim Award on Jurisdiction and Admissibility of 30 November 2009), para. 514, while a DR–CAFTA Tribunal has recently accepted retrospective effect, *Pac Rim Cayman LLC* v. *El Salvador* (ICSID Case No. ARB/09/12, Decision on Jurisdictional Objections of 1 June 2012), paras. 4.83–4.92. The idea of retrospective withdrawal of benefits would also fit more easily within a legal regime that is not based on investors' rights.

[41] Z. Douglas, 'The Hybrid Foundations of Investment Treaty Arbitration', *British Yearbook of International Law* 74 (2003), 151, 167–84.

of the equivalent primary rules of the WTO law. Again, one might engage
with the issue from multiple perspectives: the ACIA, the WTO, and the
investor. These perspectives will be considered in turn.

1. ACIA

Countermeasures against ACIA obligations might conceivably be applied
in a number of situations. First, the inter-state ACIA disputes are settled
in accordance with the ASEAN Protocol on Enhanced Dispute Settlement Mechanism ('Protocol') that provides for a WTO-like suspension
of concessions under the covered agreements.[42] While the 2009 ACIA is
(understandably) not listed in the 2004 Protocol, it is plausible to read the
ACIA reference to the Protocol as fully subjecting ACIA to the regime of
the Protocol, including to the *lex specialis* countermeasures by suspension of obligations in a prospective manner. Second, if the Protocol-based
system were to become inoperative (say, in a manner similar to that
alleged by Mexico regarding the NAFTA Chapter 20 in *Mexico - Soft
Drinks*),[43] the right to apply general international law countermeasures
could become active again, certainly for the purpose of implementing the
obligations in the dispute settlement process,[44] and possibly regarding
the original underlying dispute as well.[45] Third, the Protocol does not
require its *lex specialis* countermeasures to be reciprocal (although there
is a WTO-like preference for reciprocity),[46] therefore an obligation under
ACIA could be suspended in response to a breach of another ASEAN

---

[42] ACIA, art. 27; Protocol, art. 16.

[43] WTO, *Mexico - Tax Measures on Soft Drinks and Other Beverages*, Appellate Body
Report (24 March 2006) WT/DS308/AB/R, para. 19 fn. 33. The dispute settlement regime
of the Protocol, see art. 5, would seem to preclude the possibility of blocking the dispute
settlement process by wrongful non-appointment of panellists, alleged to have happened
in NAFTA (North American Free Trade Agreement (adopted 17 December 1992, entered
into force 1 January 1994) (1993) 32 ILM 612, art 2009).

[44] A state may commit an internationally wrongful act in failing to cooperate in the
formalised settlement of disputes, *Interpretation of Peace Treaties (Second Phase)* (Advisory Opinion) [1950] ICJ Rep. 221, 226-9.

[45] Simma and Pulkowski have argued that the general international law right to take
countermeasures may be reactivated, if the special regimes on dispute settlement and
enforcement fail to implement the responsibility (B. Simma and D. Pulkowski, 'Of
Planets and the Universe: Self-Contained Regimes in International Law', *European
Journal of International Law* 17 (2006) 483, esp. 509-29); B. Simma and D. Pulkowski,
'*Leges Speciales* and Self-Contained Regimes', in Crawford *et al.*, *Law of International
Responsibility*, 139, 148-62.

[46] Protocol, art. 16(3).

obligation subject to dispute settlement in accordance with the Protocol. Fourth, it might be possible that a *lex specialis* ASEAN countermeasure applies both to an ACIA obligation and an equivalent trade obligation under another ASEAN treaty (just as the Mexican countermeasure in *Mexico – Soft Drinks* was in breach of NAFTA investment protection obligations and also, one imagines, its trade obligations). One imagines that equivalence would be taken into account in considering the proportionality elements. Finally, since countermeasures under general international law do not have to be reciprocal,[47] it is perfectly possible that an ACIA party may apply a countermeasure to an ACIA obligation in order to implement responsibility for breach entirely unrelated to international economic law (regarding, say, alleged infringements in territorial or maritime disputes). Depending on the legal setting, the legal nature of countermeasures may differ: they may be *lex specialis* or *lex generalis*, adopted through the third-party system of the Protocol or in a (procedurally) self-judging manner, and be intended to ensure cessation of the wrongful act or full reparation. The legal nature of countermeasures has to be taken into account in considering their effect.

2. WTO

The WTO perspective on countermeasures adopted for the breach of non-WTO rules and purportedly applied to non-WTO rules (that are, however, equivalent to WTO rules) may be considered in three steps. As a matter of primary rules, the Appellate Body in *Mexico – Soft Drinks* rejected the argument that countermeasures fell under the general exception of Article XX(d) of GATT regarding measures 'necessary to secure compliance with laws and regulations', *inter alia* because deciding upon it 'would entail a determination whether the United States has acted consistently or inconsistently with its NAFTA obligations. We see no basis in the DSU for panels and the Appellate Body to adjudicate non-WTO disputes.'[48] While the breadth of the language may be excessive and one might imagine how non-WTO legal issues may be brought within the four corners of WTO legal reasoning,[49] the Appellate Body

---

[47] Alland, 'Definition of Countermeasures', in Crawford *et al.*, *Law of International Responsibility*, 1132–4; O'Keefe, 1158–9.

[48] *Mexico – Soft Drinks* AB, para. 56.

[49] Paparinskis, 'Equivalent Obligations', 281–2; see the classic argument in J. Pauwelyn, *Conflict of Norms in Public International Law* (Cambridge University Press, 2003),

was right on the particular issue. The peculiarity – perhaps even unique-
ness – of the formulation of the legal criteria for precluded wrongfulness
of countermeasures is that it depends, in a *sine qua non* manner, on
the determination of an anterior wrongful act. It should not be
possible for an adjudicator with a limited jurisdiction to conclusively
decide upon the international responsibility regarding a rule that it has
no jurisdiction over.

Marceau and Watt have viewed the applicability of non-WTO countermeasures in WTO through the lenses of GATT Article XXIV, suggesting that a Regional Trade Agreement (RTA)-based countermeasure
would comply with the WTO law if the RTA itself, its general regime
on countermeasures as well as the particular countermeasures complied
with Article XXIV.[50] For the purposes of the present chapter, the argument may be relevant only for the third and the fourth hypotheticals
suggested in the previous section, where the *lex specialis* countermeasure
may be taken in the context of ASEAN trade rules. ACIA is not an RTA.
To the extent that countermeasures may be plausibly viewed as coming
from an RTA, to adopt GATT Article XXIV as the analytical perspective
is not an attractive solution, since it has been eroded through the
constant relaxation of its substantive and procedural safeguards and the
almost general absence of meaningful litigation.[51]

Whatever the impact of countermeasures as a matter of primary rules
of WTO law, their role as a matter of secondary rules still needs to be
considered. *Mexico – Soft Drinks* case leaves the issue open since Mexico
curiously did not rely on the fallback argument of countermeasures as a
circumstance precluding wrongfulness in case if its initial argument of
countermeasures as an interpretative criterion for the primary rule got
rejected. The issue has been subject to some discussion in the legal
writings, and the legal arguments of both sides are finely balanced (or,
perhaps more accurately, lead to equally unattractive solutions). One

---

456–86; J. Pauwelyn, 'How to Win a World Trade Organization Dispute Based on Non-
World Trade Organization Law?: Questions of Jurisdiction and Merits', *Journal of World
Trade* 37 (2003), 997, and an argument from a perspective of incidental norms, L. Bartels,
'Jurisdiction and Applicable Law: Where does a Tribunal find the Principal Norms
Applicable to the Case before It?', in Broude and Shany, *Multi-Sourced Equivalent Norms*,
115, 117–20, 137–41.

[50] Marceau and Watt, 'Dispute Settlement Regimes Intermingled', 80–93.
[51] For a summary of the state of affairs, see P. Mavroidis, 'WTO and PTAs: A Preference for
Multilateralism? (or, the Dog that Tried to Stop the Bus', *Journal of World Trade* 44
(2010), 1145, 1148–50.

might either construct a waiver out of the teleology of effectiveness of the WTO law (despite the *a contrario* textual indication that States knew how to limit countermeasures and chose not to draft a general waiver); or permit the application of countermeasures with all the procedural challenges that non-reciprocal countermeasures bring to adjudicators with limited jurisdiction.[52] Neither of these solutions is intuitively appealing.

Marceau and Watt have argued in an explicitly pragmatic, common-sense manner that it would be distinctly odd if a WTO party invoking a GATT Article XX general exception had to satisfy the DSB that it had complied with the requirements of the particular paragraph and the *chapeau*, while a similar argument framed as a countermeasure would be subject to different criteria and would not be considered by the DSB.[53] They are certainly right about the aesthetically unpleasant feel of the situation but one might query with the legal implications that they drew from the normative uneasiness. If treaty-makers create a regime that seems slightly disharmonious (no rules on countermeasures in breach *of* WTO law), yet do not resolved the uneasiness in legal terms (while expertly articulating legal solutions regarding similar subject matters: countermeasures *for* the breach of the WTO law), the right conclusion seems to be that they were, as a matter of law, content with the disharmonious elements of the regime.

3. *Investor state*

It was suggested at section II.(iv) above that the effect of a WTO-authorised countermeasure on an ACIA investor may depend on the nature of its ACIA rights: if the ACIA host state owes obligations also to the investor, an inter-state countermeasure is not opposable to it; if the obligations run only on the inter-state level, a countermeasure may preclude wrongfulness for the breach of an investment-related obligation. Is this conclusion affected by the fact that the *lex specialis* countermeasure is taken in accordance with the ACIA and the Protocol? To some extent, the mere existence of the Protocol supports the latter reading by positing the applicability of particular rules as a matter of inter-state concern. However, countermeasures remain countermeasures, whether expressed in terms of general or special rules, and whether implemented in the traditional unilateral manner or through a particular third-party

---

[52] Paparinskis, 'Equivalent Obligations', 283–7.
[53] Marceau and Watt, 'Dispute Settlement Regimes Intermingled', 76–7.

structure. The right question to ask is whether States act to preclude wrongfulness for a breach of a primary obligation – where the distinction between direct and agency models suggested above applies – or go further and tinker with the primary rules as such, with the investor being necessarily affected as well.[54]

IV. Conclusion

Is the international legal regulation of countermeasures regarding equivalent rules in international economic law schizophrenic? It certainly does not provide intuitively plausible and straightforward solutions. However, it is useful to consider the precise reasons for such a state of affairs. The problem does not lie, or does not chiefly lie, in the formulation of the particular regimes. The WTO and ACIA seem internally perfectly coherent. It is also not the case that no legal vocabulary exists that would permit the articulation of consistent solutions. The problem rather seems to lie at the relatively technical level of both accurately identifying the potential legal relationships and articulating the concerns in appropriate legal terms. It is not a trivial challenge – the discussion of the relatively easier and somewhat related case of forum shopping between the WTO and the RTA illustrates some of the complexities and pitfalls[55] – but one that the invisible college should be able to resolve by a clear-headed identification of challenges as well as the treaty- or non-treaty-based legal rules for their solution. So, at the end of the day, no inescapable inconsistencies to be found here, only more work to be done.

---

[54] For example, by invoking a denial of benefit clause (see n. 40), or by prospectively suspending parts of a treaty as a matter of law of treaties, Softwood Lumber Agreement www.international.gc.ca/controls-controles/assets/pdfs/softwood/SLA-en.pdf   (adopted 12 September 2006), art. X(1)(a), XI(2); Guglya, 'Interplay of International Dispute Resolution Mechanisms', 195–207.

[55] See a summary of the different positions in Marceau and Watt, 'Dispute Settlement Regimes Intermingled', 68–73.

PART III

Investment law and intellectual property protection

12

Multilateral convergence of investment company regulation

ANITA K. KRUG[*]

I. Introduction

As economies worldwide have sought to emerge from the global finan-cial crisis, laws and regulations governing investment advisers and investment funds have been a policymaking and regulatory focus. That attention is a product of, among other things, the speculation that funds' activities, such as those involving derivative instruments or leverage, might have exacerbated the systemic weaknesses leading to the crisis. Different jurisdictions have taken different approaches to addressing perceived regulatory deficiencies in the investment indus-try. A common thread among these regulatory reforms has been a general concern with both systemic risk mitigation and heightened protection of investors, the latter being a longstanding objective of financial industry and securities market regulation. However, in the push for increased oversight and transparency, little consideration has been given to the prospect that global laws and norms governing investment companies (that is, *public* investment funds, such as UCITS in Europe and mutual funds in the United States) are begin-ning to adhere to a common model or share a number of characteris-tics. Nor, for that matter, has there been any discussion of whether global laws and norms can or should follow similar patterns. In other words, the topic of multilateral convergence in the investment company

* The author thanks C. L. Lim, Robert B. Ahdieh, and Faith Stevelman for helpful com-ments on earlier drafts. The author wrote this chapter in early 2011. She has previously published portions of sections III and IV, including much of section IV.1., in Anita K. Krug, 'Investment Company as Instrument: The Limitations of the Corporate Governance Regulatory Paradigm' (2013) 86(2) *Southern California Law Review*, and has previously published much of the substance and certain specific components of section II in Anita K. Krug, 'Discerning Public Law Concepts in Corporate Law Discourse,' in Kit Barker and Darryn Jensen (eds.), *Private Law: Key Encounters with Public Law* (Cambridge University Press, 2013).

regulatory context has not, as yet, been addressed, either as a descriptive or as a normative matter.[1]

This lacuna becomes all the more apparent when we consider the literature concerning multilateral convergence in other corporate and regulatory contexts. For example, many scholars have elucidated, from a descriptive standpoint, the extent to which global corporate governance laws and norms have been converging over time and whether that convergence is efficient (that is, centered on the most efficient laws and norms). Indeed, the scholarship evinces strong positions on both sides of the discussion. For some, convergence has effectively already occurred, with the US 'shareholder-centered' model having become dominant worldwide, in function if not through formal rules. For others, the pronouncement that convergence has occurred and, in particular, that laws and norms have converged around the US model, is misinformed at best and narcissistic at worst. Some scholars have further observed that, to the extent convergence is evident, there are compelling reasons why that convergence may, in fact, be inefficient. Scholars have also, from a normative perspective, evaluated whether multilateral convergence is desirable.

However, the particular observations and arguments made in discussions about convergence of corporate governance laws and norms do not squarely apply to the investment company context. In particular, given the role of investment companies as sources of financial services, the laws and norms governing them necessarily must *assume* the paramount importance of shareholders. Consequently, even for investment companies organized as corporations, the convergence question centers not on the proper governance focal point but, rather, on the particular modes of regulation to which investment companies are subject.

Why think about convergence, whether in the corporate law context or any other? In the corporate law context, the inspiration behind serious thinking about convergence arguably has been the importance of the

---

[1] This chapter does not address the regulation of private investment funds, such as hedge funds and private equity funds, even though private funds, which use a wide array of investment strategies and many of which employ substantial leverage, are generally deemed to have been greater contributors than were public funds to the conditions that caused the financial crisis. This chapter focuses on public funds because, as part of the investment industry, regulation of them was part of policymakers' post-crisis reform analyses and because only they (and not private funds) are subject to comprehensive regulation. Private funds, by definition, are able to avail themselves of exemptions from public fund regulation, which renders the prospect of private fund regulatory convergence less pronounced an issue, as compared with convergence in the public fund context.

corporate structure as an efficient means of organizing production. That same inspiration is readily transferable to the investment company regulatory context: The growth of investment companies, and their role as intermediaries between shareholders and corporations, is a worldwide phenomenon, as these 'intermediating' institutions have come to replace individuals and other smaller investors as participants in the capital and securities markets. In other words, investment companies have come to serve as a dominant means of capital formation and investment and, hopefully, an efficient one at that. Accordingly, the laws and norms that structure investment companies and their operations and management give rise to another important locus of convergence analysis.

This chapter extends multilateral convergence analysis to the investment company regulatory context and, in so doing, shows its limitations and its promise. In section II, it introduces the literature surrounding convergence in the corporate law context. Largely setting forth descriptive analyses, scholars addressing the topic have reached markedly divergent conclusions. Taken together, the literature sets the stage for an extension of the analysis to other contexts, an exercise that becomes increasingly important as both economic activity and politics become more global. Section III considers, through focusing on the United States and the European Union, diversity and convergence in the context of investment company regulation – in particular, laws and norms governing public investment funds. This section posits that entrenched interests and practices may explain the substantial heterogeneity that characterizes prevalent approaches to investment company regulation but asserts that convergence of these disparate laws and norms may be normatively desirable. Starting with that premise, section IV considers what model of investment company regulation may be 'better,' in the sense of being more coherent and more effective. Because the normative force behind multilateral convergence of laws and norms in any context derives, at least in part, from the extent to which that convergence is efficient, the chapter also assesses what 'efficiency' might mean in the investment company regulatory context.

II.   Globalization and convergence

We live in an increasingly global investment arena. Investment companies, regardless of the jurisdictions in which they are based and, therefore, by which they are regulated, are increasingly pursuing investment opportunities in other countries and seeking foreign investors.

In those transnational activities, regulatory regimes may collide to the extent that investment advisers are permitted to market the investment companies they manage in foreign jurisdictions and supposing that investors may be more or less attracted to an investment company based on protections afforded by applicable regulatory requirements. To the extent that differences in regulatory norms governing investment companies hinder or preclude transnational investment, then investors are less able to allocate assets in a manner suiting their investment needs, which in turn redounds to the detriment of capital market efficiency. Beyond that, of course, to the extent that particular jurisdictions' regulatory regimes hinder or preclude transnational investment more than do others, then certain investors and investment companies are disproportionately disadvantaged, even though those investors may have relatively more capital to invest globally and even though those investment companies may offer relatively superior services.

Investment company globalization, therefore, opens many rich avenues of analysis. In particular, globalization naturally raises consideration of different regulatory regimes and the norms that inform them, and a comparative analysis is the almost-ineluctable next step. One question in that analysis concerns which regulatory regime is 'best,' a question that itself turns on analyses of regulatory objectives and conceptions of efficiency. An associated question is whether, if there is a 'best' model of investment company regulation, we might reasonably expect that, over time, and with the ongoing forces of globalization, there will be multilateral convergence around that best model. In other words, might we hope for or expect a 'convergence' of laws and norms around those that are most efficient, however that might be defined? Even if that does not seem likely, further questions are whether convergence of any kind is normatively desirable, regardless of whether it is efficient or inefficient, and what factors might be most important in indicating the occurrence of convergence.[2] But, first, it is worth considering the recent history of convergence analysis.

Globalization has made a deep imprint on corporate governance reform and scholarship, as a result of its implications both for the relative performance of national economies in international capital markets, products markets, and labor markets and for the competitive success of

---

[2] These types of questions, of course, also arise from the vast contemporary discourse on legal and regulatory competition. See e.g. Larry E. Ribstein and Erin O'Hara, *The Law Market* (Oxford University Press, 2009).

business enterprises as they pursue their activities in those markets. First, political decision makers have been forced to contemplate the performance of local firms against the performance of firms globally and, toward that end, have been compelled to evaluate their local corporate governance regimes against alternatives, looking to whether the local regime adversely affects local firms' global competitiveness.[3] Second, decision makers for firms expanding into the global arena and seeking to attract public capital have had to evaluate whether local corporate governance structures are conducive to attracting investors, on the premise that investors may prefer investing in firms whose governance structures they understand and with which they feel comfortable.[4] With globalization of economic activity becoming an increasingly important factor in corporate governance questions, comparative analysis of corporate governance structures has become a focal point of analysis and reform proposals, and an inevitable question has emerged: Will global economic or political forces, or combinations of them, lead to a global convergence of corporate governance structures?

Not surprisingly, then, on and off throughout the past fifteen years or so, the prospect of convergence of corporate governance laws and norms has been the subject of academic discussion, including as to whether convergence will occur, the means through which it will occur, the forces that might impede it, the laws and norms around which it likely will occur, and the extent to which those laws and norms will be the best or most efficient ones. As this list suggests, scholars have come at the subject from diverse perspectives. Some, embracing a neoclassical framework, have asserted that convergence on the US shareholder-centered model of corporate governance, as the hands-down most efficient model, will, through competitive forces, come to be adopted as the universal model. Many other scholars have assumed a considerably less teleological stance and have focused on some other facets of the diversity among corporate governance regimes and relative pressures toward and against convergence. Their scholarship highlights that convergence may be only partial or may be brought about formally (through national adoption of new regimes or rules) or functionally (through firm-by-firm changes based on competitive pressures or evolving notions of best

---

[3] See Jeffrey N. Gordon and Mark J. Roe (eds.), *Convergence and Persistence in Corporate Governance* (Cambridge University Press, 2004), pp. 1–2.
[4] See *ibid.*, p. 2.

practices).[5] It also proposes that convergence on some norms, such as public share ownership, may foster convergence on others, such as heightened managerial accountability,[6] and asserts that the best norms of each governance model cannot be cobbled together into a hybrid model of governance because each model is a system unto itself.[7] Further, this scholarship contends that convergence on a particular corporate governance regime, whether efficient or inefficient, may be helped or impeded as a result of the interests of political elites and interest groups[8] and the extent to which countries recognize strong property rights.[9] A few of these arguments are elaborated below.

Henry Hansmann and Reinier Kraakman have put forth perhaps the most emphatic position regarding convergence and divergence in corporate law, arguing that we have reached the 'end of history' for corporate law. By that, the authors mean that law in developed markets is converging – at least ideologically and in governance practices (function), if not through actual legal reform (form) – on a single 'standard model' of corporate governance.[10] That model, they proclaim, is the shareholder-oriented model, which, as they define it, gives primacy to the notions that shareholders hold ultimate control over corporations, that managers are to manage in furtherance of shareholders' interests, that other corporate stakeholders (employees, creditors, suppliers, etc.) should be protected 'through contractual and regulatory means rather than through participation in corporate governance,' that controlling shareholders should be prevented from exploiting non-controlling shareholders, and that the value of shareholders' interests should be based on the market value of their shares.[11] The convergence toward the shareholder-oriented model, Hansmann and Kraakman observe, was the product of several factors: competitive forces' revealing the model's

---

[5] See Ronald J. Gilson, 'Globalizing Corporate Governance: Convergence of Form of Function,' in Gordon and Roe, *Convergence and Persistence*, pp. 128–158.

[6] See *ibid.*, p. 3.

[7] See William W. Bratton and Joseph A. McCahery, 'Comparative Corporate Governance and the Theory of the Firm: The Case against Global Cross Reference,' (1999) 38 *Colum. J. Transnat'l L.* 213, 219.

[8] See Jeffrey N. Gordon, 'The International Relations Wedge in the Corporate Convergence Debate,' in Gordon and Roe, *Convergence and Persistence*, p. 161.

[9] See Curtis J. Milhaupt, 'Property Rights in Firms', *ibid.*, p. 211.

[10] See Henry Hansmann and Reinier Kraakman, 'The End of History for Corporate Law,' (2001) 89 *Geo. L. J.* 439, 439.

[11] See *ibid.*, pp. 440–441.

saliency;[12] the failure of other possible models, such as manager-oriented, labor-oriented, state-oriented, and stakeholder-centric models;[13] and, rather more dubiously, the rise of 'a public shareholder class as a powerful interest group in both corporate and political affairs across jurisdictions.'[14]

Of those three factors, the effect of competitive forces would seem dominant – at least insofar as convergence of corporate governance laws and norms is, or should be, *efficient* convergence. The authors at least point toward that conclusion in disposing of the possibilities that either efficient divergence or inefficient convergence is sustainable. The former, which might arise as a result of extant social structures or through happenstance, cannot survive indefinitely because globalization or, more precisely, 'the network efficiencies of a common standard form in global markets' militate against divergence and toward convergence.[15] The latter, which derives from market failures or flaws in widely shared political institutions that are reinforced by transnational competition,[16] likewise cannot survive indefinitely because those persons adversely affected by inefficient conver-gence are incentivized, through their contractual relationships with cor-porations, to 'establish[] efficient law' or because the political process ultimately will provide redress.[17] In other words, competition appears to be both a *sufficient* condition for the occurrence of convergence but a *necessary* condition for that convergence to be efficient.

Convergence analysis in the mode of Hansmann and Kraakman has had its detractors, as one might expect. The normative message from many scholars, distilled, might be that we should not get too caught up with the prospect or hope of corporate governance convergence. These scholars' work relies on a number of positive observations that are at odds with the occurrence and/or possibility of meaningful convergence. One of the more prominent analyses has been that of Lucian Bebchuk and Mark Roe, who are skeptical of convergence on the basis that differences among corporate governance structures, including in the world's more advanced econ-omies, may persist because of path dependence – the notion that 'the corporate structures that an economy has at any point in time are likely to depend on those that it had at earlier times.'[18] According to Bebchuk and Roe, both initial ownership structures and early corporate rules hinder

---

[12] *Ibid.*, pp. 449–452.   [13] *Ibid.*, pp. 443–449.   [14] *Ibid.*, p. 452.
[15] *Ibid.*, p. 466.   [16] *Ibid.*   [17] *Ibid.*, p. 467.
[18] Lucian Arye Bebchuk and Mark J. Roe, 'A Theory of Path Dependence in Corporate Ownership and Governance', (1999) 52 *Stan. L. Rev.* 127, 129–131.

288 ANITA K. KRUG

global movement toward common structures and rules.[19] More specifically, corporate governance structures persist because they are efficient,
relatively speaking, in that the high costs of moving toward other structures (such as a block-shareholding regime's moving toward a dispersed-
shareholding regime) outweigh the efficiency benefits of those new structures.[20] They persist also because they are supported by self-interested
actors, such as corporate management and interest groups, who benefit
from existing structures and rules.[21]

Reinhard Schmidt and Gerald Spindler build on Bebchuk's and Roe's
analysis, adding to the mix the notion of complementarity. For Schmidt and
Spindler, complementarity characterizes the 'elements' of any system,
including a corporate governance system, and the elements of any particular
system are complementary to one another 'if there is the potential that they
fit together well,' mutually increasing their benefit or reducing their costs
vis-à-vis the system's function.[22] Some of the complementary elements of a
corporate governance system, according to Schmidt and Spindler, include
'the distribution of ownership and residual decision rights,' the composition
and structure of the board, the 'role and function of the stock market,' and
the nature of applicable market regulation.[23] Complementarity in systems
means both that making partial changes, such as by importing elements
from more (globally) efficient systems, is difficult because those changes
disrupt the locally efficient system and that more comprehensive changes
are difficult because of 'switching costs.'[24] More than that, however, because
there is 'complementarity between the different elements of an economic,
social, and legal system in which governance is embedded,' it is difficult to
discern 'where the limits of a corporate governance system must be drawn
and which other elements of an economic and legal system' would also need
to change in the process of fundamentally altering an existing governance
system.[25]

John Coffee, for his part, acknowledging the role of ideology, culture,
and politics in hindering convergence of corporate law,[26] rejects Hansmann's and Kraakman's and others' neoclassical economic view of corporate governance and, specifically, the conclusion that 'efficiency

---

[19] *Ibid.*   [20] *Ibid.*   [21] *Ibid.*
[22] Reinhard H. Schmidt and Gerald Spindler, 'Path Dependence and Complementarity in
Corporate Governance,' in Gordon and Roe, *Convergence and Persistence*, p. 119.
[23] *Ibid.*, p. 121.   [24] *Ibid.*, pp. 115–119.   [25] *Ibid.*, p. 124.
[26] See John C. Coffee, Jr., 'The Future as History: The Prospect for Global Convergence in
Corporate Governance and its Implications,' (1999) 93 *Nw. L. Rev.* 641, 646.

considerations ultimately prevail and determine corporate structure."[27] Nonetheless, Coffee discerns the possibility of functional convergence, if not formal convergence, thanks to national securities laws.[28] In particular, for Coffee the primary models of corporate structure are 'market' systems, characterized by dispersed share ownership and liquid and robust trading markets, on the one hand, and 'blockholder' systems, characterized by controlling stakes held by wealthy families and insider coalitions and limited trading of non-controlling stakes, on the other.[29] That the former model is dominant in the United States, the United Kingdom, and certain other countries, Coffee supposes, is a product of legal rules in those countries that protect small, dispersed shareholdings.[30] As foreign firms increasingly participate in US equity markets, whether through 'the integration of markets, the harmonization of standards across markets,' or firms' migration to US and UK markets, 'a substantial degree of convergence seems predictable.'[31]

Most recently, Franklin Gevurtz has articulated convergence skepticism from a couple of interrelated perspectives. For one thing, according to Gevurtz, corporate norms are evolving such that, at best, they are in continuous process of diverging and re-converging and diverging once again.[32] As Gevurtz describes it, this is a process of fluid imitation and transplanting of laws and norms, as governance regimes react differently to crises and other events and gradually move from 'one globally followed norm to another.'[33] Gevurtz also posits that, where convergence occurs, it may be quite enduring even if inefficient and regardless of whether there exist competitive forces.[34] For example, the 'global spread of the prohibition on insider trading' is perhaps best explained as a 'fad' or a 'fashion' that garnered global popularity despite the prohibition's debatable utility.[35] Gevurtz also questions what is meant by 'convergence,' observing that the important yardsticks for measuring convergence are the 'tough policy questions' of whether corporate governance

---

[27] *Ibid.*   [28] *Ibid.*, pp. 705–706.
[29] *Ibid.*, p. 645 (citing Bratton and McCahery, 'Comparative Corporate Governance').
[30] *Ibid.*, p. 647. Absent those rules, 'shareholders' primary protective response to the risk of exploitation is to invest only through the protective medium of a substantial block' (*ibid.* p. 647). Coffee summarizes his position thus: '[S]trong regulation permits "weak" owners, while "weak" regulation necessitates "strong" owners' (*ibid.*, p. 648).
[31] *Ibid.*, p. 650.
[32] See Franklin A. Gevurtz, 'The Globalization of Corporate Law: The End of History or a Never-Ending Story?,' 86 (2011), *Washington Law Review* 475 485–486.
[33] *Ibid.*, p. 486.   [34] *Ibid.*, at 496–500.   [35] *Ibid.*, at 497.

laws and norms should be mandatory or permissive and whether the driving principle of corporate law, even in the shareholder-oriented model, should be managerial accountability or managerial authority.[36] However, he notes, these questions mark the areas where convergence has been most elusive (and/or illusory).[37]

We can extrapolate few overarching principles or conclusions from these divergent approaches to corporate governance diversity and convergence. Indeed, the literature seems both scattered and overlapping as to each of the facets of convergence noted above, which is hardly surprising, given the myriad lenses – economics, politics, law, psychology, biology, or a combination thereof – through which different scholars have viewed the subject. Take, for example, the neoclassical argument, and the path-dependency approach. With one supporting the ineluctable forces of global competition and the other emphasizing the historical and localized factors that challenge those forces, the arguments are very different in their conclusions about the prospect of convergence. Yet both arguments presume that the emergence or persistence of corporate governance structures is a product of efficiency considerations (at a local level, for Bebchuk and Roe, or at a global level, for Hansmann and Kraakman).[38] Moreover, since Bebchuk's and Roe's focus on concentrated versus diversified ownership structures seems to take as a given a system 'oriented' around share ownership, both arguments seem to agree, if only implicitly, on the primacy of the shareholder-centered model.[39] From that perspective, the two arguments may, by some metric, be more closely aligned than, say, Bebchuk's and Roe's path-dependency, on the one hand, and Schmidt's and Spindler's complementarity, on the other, as the latter entertains the possibility of not only convergence but also (indeed, especially) *inefficient* convergence.[40]

The counterarguments and alternative viewpoints regarding diversity among corporate governance systems (or portions thereof) and whether convergence has occurred or may occur, whether it is desirable, and whether it is efficient instruct us to be careful in carrying out the project of comparative corporate governance and admonish us against sweeping pronouncements about the global evolution of laws and norms. However,

---

[36] *Ibid.*, pp. 511–520.   [37] *Ibid.*

[38] See Gordon and Roe, *Convergence and Persistence*, p. 13.   [39] *Ibid.*

[40] According to Schmidt and Spindler, inefficient convergence might emerge as a result of 'myopic' and 'chaotic' decisions made in times of crisis (Schmidt and Spindler, 'Path Dependence,' 124–126).

they do not undermine the project itself or the value of thinking about the ultimate interrelationship among laws and norms developed over time, in different countries. In a similar vein, convergence analysis can elucidate investment company laws and norms – and, conversely, from a comparativist's perspective, those laws and norms provide another arena for considering convergence: Like 'operating' companies (the business enterprises that are the subject of traditional corporate governance concerns), investment companies operate in an ever more boundary-free world, and much as operating companies are fairly universally recognized as an efficient means of organizing production, investment companies serve as a means (ideally an efficient one) of achieving capital formation and investment returns.

III.   Multilateral convergence and investment company regulation

Given the competing approaches to convergence and divergence in corporate governance literature, how to begin thinking about similar considerations in the investment company regulatory context may not seem obvious. However, the literature suggests a few points of departure. First, there is the question of what models of regulation may be deemed candidates for a 'standard model,' to draw on Hansmann's and Kraakman's terminology, around which convergence might occur. Presumably the better model is the most efficient model – that which, perhaps, entails lower transaction costs or better promotes investor confidence. Second, there is the question of what forces or factors stand as the most formidable obstacles to any possible convergence process. Here, we draw on considerations articulated by Bebchuk and Roe ('path dependence' and the notion that continuing on a worn path has its own efficiencies) and by Schmidt and Spindler ('complementarities'), as well as the recurring themes of interest group politics and rent-seeking behavior. If another rule or norm is preferable to the existing one in any particular jurisdiction and if policymakers are aware of that fact, then should movement to that rule or norm not occur, the reason must lie in a certain 'stickiness' of the existing rule or norm. It remains an open question, however, what factors in the investment company context might give rise to that stickiness. Interest group behavior and the associated notion of rent-seeking presumably play a role in any conception or explanation of dominant rules and norms in any context. The question that remains is the particular role they play in the subject at hand.

1. Competing models of regulation

Accordingly, we begin with the standard model of investment company regulation and, more precisely, plausible candidates for that label. Perhaps not intuitively, that question and the answer that this chapter ultimately poses are effectively the inverse of the question asked and answer posed in the corporate law context. In particular, in the latter context we ask what model of power relationship as among participants in the corporate enterprise is 'standard,' in the sense of being the one that is most efficient and/or the one on which corporate governance regimes the world over are converging. In other words, the question assumes a corporate governance paradigm and the answer supplies the particular type: one in which shareholders have primacy. In the investment company regulatory context, by contrast, we start by assuming shareholder primacy, because, certainly in name and hopefully also in fact, the exclusive purpose of an investment company is to advance the pecuniary interests of its shareholders or otherwise to play a role in its shareholders' achieving financial betterment. Shareholder primacy therefore is the basis of our question: What model of regulation – a model based on corporate governance paradigms or one based on something else – best promotes the primacy of shareholders and their interests, as opposed to the interests of 'management' (meaning directors and investment advisers)?

Two candidates for the standard model appear to have emerged so far, although, presumably, they are not the only conceivable possibilities. These models govern in two of the most prominent jurisdictions for investment companies, the United States and the European Union.[41] The first model is the 'corporate governance' model, which characterizes US investment company regulation. This model relies on the circumstance that investment companies are formally structured like operating companies, in that they are governed by boards of directors. An investment company's directors, who are fiduciaries to its shareholders, represent the investment company in negotiating the advisory contract with the company's investment adviser and in overseeing the adviser's activities and monitoring its potential conflicts of interest relating to the company. Regulation in this model specifies how directors' monitoring

---

[41] That status is likely attributable to the fact that some of the largest investment advisory firms are based in these jurisdictions. In the United States, those firms include Fidelity Investments, Franklin Templeton Investments, and T. Rowe Price Co.

functions are to be carried out and the constraints on investment advisers' discretionary activities, all with a view toward ensuring that, in this assumed business enterprise, those in control are adequately accountable to those in the position of passive owner.

The second model could be called the 'financial services' model. In that model, which prevails in the European Union, the structure of the investment company – and whether it has a board of directors – is irrelevant. The model instead focuses on the position of the investment adviser vis-à-vis the investment company's shareholders and, more importantly, the nature of the adviser's relationship to the investment company. Ultimately, the model regards that relationship as just one type of relationship among many in which an investment adviser provides services to 'clients,' with the clients in this case (functionally, if not formally) being the shareholders that invest, collectively, in a 'pool' that the adviser then manages as a single account. With that understanding of the adviser's role as the basis of the model, regulatory requirements are directed almost exclusively toward the investment adviser and specify what is to be done and what is not to be done in connection with the adviser's managing the investment company's assets, communicating with shareholders, engaging in personal securities transactions, managing other client accounts, and so forth.

To be sure, EU and US laws and regulations governing investment companies may embody various pockets of convergence. For example, both jurisdictions recognize and impose on investment advisers certain transaction-related restrictions designed to mitigate conflicts of interest. However, divergence arguably dominates, given that US regulation relies on oversight by boards of directors, while EU regulation provides no role for board governance. And, whereas US regulation and reform center on how boards might better pursue and achieve their oversight function and ensuring the independence of board members, EU regulation concerns itself with requirements governing the activities of investment advisers, in their capacities as the parties responsible for investment companies' existence and most aspects of their operations.

2.   Obstacles and entrenched patterns

That there are divergent governing models in two prominent jurisdictions for investment company and financial industry regulation leads to consideration of the extent to which convergence of those models – the

'imitation and transplant[ing]' of the laws and norms they comprise[42] –
is a reasonable prospect, leaving aside for the moment the question of
whether it is normatively desirable. In that regard, the following discussion focuses on the obstacles that might confront and hinder the US
adoption of model similar to the EU's financial services model of regulation. That focus is a product of two unrelated factors: First, this author
has substantially more familiarity not only with the US model of investment company regulation but also with the US legislative and regulatory
processes and the participants in the US investment company industry.
Second, and as discussed further below, there are reasons to believe that
the financial services model is the superior one and that, if convergence
of governing EU and US norms were to occur, the primary changes
would (or, at least, should) take place on the US side. Those considerations, in turn, lead to the question of what would be the consequences
for the US regulatory regime if a broad convergence were to occur
around the financial services model and supposing the United States
wished (whether expressly or implicitly) to be part of that convergence.
Would, or could, the US regulatory structure be transformed?

Answering that question logically begins with investment companies
themselves or, more precisely, the investment company industry. We
need not proceed too far to discern some of the implications of a possible
US regulatory transformation, many of which stem from the fact that the
financial services model contemplates no role for a board of directors
or other management voice apart from that of the investment adviser.
Most starkly, eliminating the board of directors entails rethinking an
investment company's modes of operation, including what it means for
the company and its investment adviser to be in 'compliance' with
applicable laws and regulations. Under the US statute governing investment companies, the Investment Company Act of 1940 (the ICA), an
investment company's board of directors plays a role in all aspects of the
company's operations, including – indeed, especially – its regulatory
obligations. Among other things, the board approves and monitors the
company's compliance with its operating policies and procedures, and
the board's consent is a precondition to the company's entering into
various types of transactions, such as those deemed to involve conflicts of
interest. The (presumed) operational efficiency that derives from the

---

[42] See Gevurtz, *Globalization of Corporate Law*, 484.

continued reign of the current regulatory structure would, of course, be lost if that structure were replaced wholesale.

Certainly, then, it is reasonable to suppose that path dependence and structural entrenchment might play a role in connection with any proposed movement toward a new regulatory regime in the United States.[43] That conclusion is buttressed by additional factors appearing throughout the convergence literature, namely, interest group politics and rent-seeking behavior. As an initial matter, through the industry associations that it has spawned, the US investment company industry has, over the years, sought to promote its 'interests', however they might be defined. Most notably, the Investment Company Institute, an association of US-based investment companies, advocates on behalf of and represents the industry in litigation and in addressing regulatory proposals. One might reasonably suppose that such an association would be inclined to favor the regulatory approach with which it is intimately familiar. Moreover, beyond the 'investment company industry', taken as a whole, are groups and interests that are integral to it. In this regard, the investment advisers who manage investment companies – and who may well have an even greater interest in continuing the status quo – come to mind. Of all the constituencies that may be affected by a regulatory overhaul, investment advisers could have the most to lose, at least to the extent they have benefited from their close relationships to (and influence on) investment company boards of directors.

As one example, an investment company's directors effectively determine the amount of the investment adviser's compensation (although that determination ultimately must be approved by the investment company's shareholders when they approve the investment advisory agreement). To the extent an investment company's board of directors is, in effect, 'captured' by the company's investment adviser, the adviser is effectively able to set its own compensation. Under the financial services model of investment company regulation, by contrast, the investment adviser would not be able to rely on an independent (albeit controlled) board of directors' approval of the fees the investment adviser desired to charge the investment company. Rather, the investment adviser would be forced to adhere to applicable laws and regulations regarding compensation and excessive fees. In other words, the adviser would not be able to

---

[43] In the European Union, that prospect arguably is somewhat less acute, given the relative newness of the UCITs regulatory system – although, to be sure, it has been in place now for over a quarter century.

hide behind the shield of authorization by purportedly independent fiduciaries.

Finally, one might reasonably anticipate political resistance from still other constituencies, including firms that provide transfer agent and distribution services to investment companies. Each of those firms might be expected to support the status quo, whether based on the high costs of changing operating systems or the lower amount of compensation that could be extracted from investment companies under an alternative model. At this stage, it is not necessary to provide a detailed accounting of those parties and their likely motivations. The point is simply that the financial services model of investment company regulation is sufficiently different from the model that currently governs US investment companies that a number of constituencies would likely regard themselves disadvantaged by, and could be candidates to resist, any legal and regulatory reform that substantially transforms that latter model.

3. Does multilateral convergence matter?

As discussed above, at least anecdotally, investment company laws and norms may be characterized by divergence rather than convergence. The explanations for that circumstance may be varied, to be sure. To the extent that the strength of early structures and rules and the costs of adopting alternatives ('entrenched patterns,' for the sake of expediency) help perpetuate the laws and norms of today's regulatory regimes or affect the extent to which convergence may occur in the future, their influence becomes a possible (albeit very preliminary) explanation. At the time the ICA was enacted, the corporate governance paradigm served as the basis for investment company regulation presumably because the line between 'operating company' and 'investment company' was not particularly distinct. In that environment, it may have made sense that the board of directors would continue to play a significant role in the regulatory structure fashioned by the ICA.

However, as described in greater detail below, much has changed in the intervening seventy-five years in terms of investment company activities and relationships, with the most important change being the adoption of a structure in which an outside investment adviser dominates an investment company's activities, from the decision to bring the company into existence to the decisions about director nominees to decisions about who will be the company's administrator, auditor, transfer agent, and brokers to the decisions about what securities the company will buy and sell. So much has changed, from a structural perspective, that the corporate governance model seems outdated indeed, and yet in policy-making and regulatory circles there has been scant, if any, discussion about law reform that would bring the regulatory framework to reflect the ways in which today's investment companies operate (such as the adoption of a structure similar to the financial services model of regulation). One basis for that apparent oversight may well be the costs that such a transformation would entail.

With these considerations in mind, an obvious question is whether ongoing regulatory divergence is problematic. Returning to the discussion above about convergence analysis in the traditional, corporate law context, might divergence in the investment company context be *efficient* divergence, based on the unique social structures and entrenched modes of operation of the United States versus the European Union? If investment company activity were not becoming globalized, that prospect might be a sufficiently satisfactory stopping point in the analysis. However, investment activity is, of course, no longer an intra-jurisdictional activity, whether because of companies' pursuit of investment opportunities or foreign investors or because of investors' desire to diversify their portfolios through investing in companies in other world regions. That means that 'efficient divergence' cannot be an answer because investment companies are (or wish to be) operating outside their local regulatory structures. In effect, the apples are trying to become oranges, and vice versa. Accordingly, even if we assume divergence is efficient, it will become only more problematic.

That conclusion becomes evident, for example, when we consider that US investment advisers often desire to market the investment companies they manage to investors in non-US jurisdictions, and, on that front, EU countries are often regarded as promising arenas for seeking new capital. However, in order to offer securities in EU countries, a US investment company must meet the applicable EU securities law requirements. That might entail, among other things, complying with application and approval requirements, which might involve the relevant EU member country's evaluating the investment company, the types of marketing activities in which it proposes to engage, and the regulatory regime to which it is subject. Conversely, under the ICA, a non-US investment company is expressly prohibited from offering its securities within the United States, unless it obtains express permission from the US Securities and Exchange Commission (SEC) to register with the SEC under the ICA – permission that may be based in part on the nature of the non-US company's 'home' regulation. These transnational regulatory hurdles may not be insurmountable, to be sure, but they are likely more than mere speed bumps in the growth of transnational flows of investment capital.

IV. Toward a 'standard' model of investment company regulation

Despite the challenges presented by the prospect of global norm-shifting in the context of investment company regulation, the intuition that the phenomenon is normatively desirable at least warrants considering the direction in which it should occur. Comparing the EU and US approaches to regulation, this section considers what model of investment company regulation is better equipped to effectively protect shareholders while allowing investment companies and their advisers to effectively pursue their activities. It takes as a starting point an evaluation of the US approach, on the basis that it perhaps warrants greater skepticism: Regulatory frameworks tend to become outdated with time, as regulatory subjects and the surrounding industry in which they operate evolve, and the US model is considerably older than its EU counterpart.

1. Tailoring regulation to reality

As suggested above, at the time the US Congress turned to establish a regulatory regime governing investment companies, most incarnations of 'investment company' in lawmakers' view were derivative of operating companies.[44] Some, for example, were operating companies that deployed their assets to purchase capital equipment, pay suppliers, and compensate employees but that also held ownership interests in other companies for investment purposes.[45] The investment company was entity-centric, moreover, not only in the sense that investment companies emerged from operating companies but also in the sense that the SEC (and perhaps Congress, as well) evaluated them and their perceived shortcomings by asking, first, about what types of investment companies existed and what were their activities and, second, about the sponsors, brokers, investment advisory firms, banks, and others that were

---

[44] See SEC, Investment Trusts and Investment Companies Report, Pt 1, HR Doc. No. 707, pp. 65–97.
[45] *Ibid.*, pp. 76–83.

involved in their operations.[46] If the entity (rather than its organizers) was lawmakers' starting point, it should not be surprising that investment company regulation assumed the flavor of corporate codes specifying the roles and responsibilities of boards of directors vis-à-vis shareholders.

The prospect that corporate law may not be the appropriate model for investment company law, however, becomes evident when we evaluate how investment companies have shed their operating company roots and today hardly resemble their predecessors. Perhaps most important is the relatively straightforward matter of how an investment company comes to be, particularly as compared with the inception process for operating companies. In the operating company context, one or more entrepreneurs determine to organize production through a corporation, which, governed by corporate law, generally involves one or more shareholders, whether they be active participants in the business or passive investors, and governance through a board of directors. From that basic determination almost naturally derives corporate governance concerns and decisions, involving maintaining a balance between the firm's ability to adapt to new circumstances and its accountability to shareholders.[47] On an ongoing basis, shareholders evaluate their continued holdings in the company based on its particular activities – the services it provides or the products it produces – and management's ability to exploit those activities to the company's best financial advantage. Shareholders' analyses revolve around what the company is and does that sets it apart from its competitors or from other potential investments.

In the investment company context, whether in the United States, the European Union, or other jurisdictions, the 'entrepreneur' is typically the investment adviser, with hopes of managing an investment company with substantial assets and, therefore, the ability to generate sizable fees. In the United States, that investment adviser typically forms the investment company and effectively sets the terms under which the investment company will operate. Among other things, therefore, the investment adviser chooses the company's name, selects the members of its board of directors, determines its share class structure, and dictates the content of its certificate of incorporation or other constitutive document. Beyond that, the adviser also selects the other service providers to

---

[46] *Ibid.*, pp. vi–vii.
[47] See, e.g., Charles R. O'Kelley, Jr., 'Filling the Gaps in the Close Corporation Contract: A Transaction Cost Analysis,' 87 (1992) *Northwestern University Law Review* 216, 218–220.

the company – the company's auditor, distributor, and administrator, for example – negotiates the services contracts on behalf of the company, and oversees the performance of the service providers' responsibilities. However, the adviser has no real role *within the enterprise*, meaning that it does not occupy one of the three defining roles within an operating company: It is neither a director, nor an officer, nor a shareholder. Rather, its relationship with the company is merely contractual in nature, governed by the investment advisory agreement between the adviser and the company, the terms of which are largely proposed by the adviser and formally approved by the board of directors.

Moreover, the relationship between the entrepreneur and shareholders in the investment company context differs from that in the operating company context. Shareholders' evaluation of an investment company does not depend on what the company does or produces, as it neither does anything nor produces anything that is not reducible to the controlling influence of the investment adviser. The investment company's success depends on the ability of the investment adviser to make decisions that increase, rather than reduce, the value of the assets that shareholders have invested or otherwise to achieve the goals established for the investment company. That means that the entity itself is subordinate to the role of the investment adviser. Shareholders invest their capital in an investment company because of the investment adviser, whether on the basis of its reputation or its performance or, perhaps, its popularity, and the investment adviser, in turn, provides services to those shareholders. To be sure, those services are provided indirectly, through an intermediating entity (the investment company) but the entity serves merely a facilitating function.

A shareholder's investing in an investment company, then, effectively establishes a services relationship between the shareholder and the investment adviser that manages the company. Accordingly, it is worth considering the implications of this characterization for establishing the best regulatory regime, one that might be a suitable standard model around which global laws and norms might reasonably converge. As an initial matter, with that characterization, one might be less inclined to think that an approach based on the legacy of operating companies is an ideal approach. Indeed, it would seem that regulation of investment companies should perhaps pay greater attention to investment advisers' responsibilities, including, among others, to manage client assets in accordance with the relevant investment objectives, to place client interests ahead of the advisers' own interests, to manage and mitigate conflicts of interest, to disclose material facts to clients, and to provide clients with information about their services on an ongoing basis.

If those responsibilities should be the focus of investment company regulation, then we might have a form of regulation that substantially resembles the regulation governing investment advisers' relationships with clients that are *not* investment companies (or investment company shareholders) but that instead are individuals or entities that have engaged the adviser to directly manage their assets, in a non-pooled manner, separately from the assets of any other client. This sort of regulatory regime, focusing on the role and responsibilities of the adviser, is, as noted above, more or less the approach the European Union has adopted. That is perhaps most evident in the fact that the European Union's regulation of UCITS (essentially, publicly offered, open-end investment companies)[48] makes no mention of directors, nor does it suggest that investment companies themselves – through a board of directors or other governance mechanism – play a role in management-type activities. Indeed, the Council Directive setting forth investment company regulation ('Directive') notes that investment companies need not even be structured as 'companies.' Rather, '[s]uch undertakings may be constituted according to law, either under the law of contract (as common funds managed by management companies) or trust law (as unit trusts) or under statute (as investment companies).'[49]

The Directive speaks in terms of the 'management company' – that is, the investment advisory firm that manages the investment company – the investment company itself, and the unitholders (shareholders) of the investment company. The management company, which must be authorized as such by its member country,[50] bears the primary regulatory compliance obligations, as specified by the relevant member country. Those obligations must, among other things, require the management company to maintain adequate administrative and accounting procedures and trading policies governing transactions by its affiliates and to take steps to minimize conflicts of interests between the management company and its clients.[51] The obligations to which the investment companies themselves are subject, by contrast, consist largely of investment restrictions – for example, requirements that an investment

---

[48] See Council Directive of 20 December 1985 on the coordination of laws, regulations and administrative provisions relating to undertakings for collective investment in transferable securities (UCITS) (85/611/EEC), art. 2 § 1.

[49] *Ibid.*, art. 1 § 3.   [50] *Ibid.*, art. 5 § 1.   [51] *Ibid.*, art. 5f § 1.

company invest only in transferable securities and certain other instruments, concentration limitations, and prohibitions on borrowing.[52] However, those activities are, by definition, controlled by the relevant management company; accordingly, it is effectively the management company's responsibility to ensure the investment company's compliance with its regulatory obligations.

2. *Efficiency and investment company regulation*

The European Union's regulation of UCITS and the management companies controlling them reflects a recognition that the regulation of investment companies is *financial services* regulation and not a matter of corporate governance. The management company is obligated to carry out its activities relating to an investment company in compliance with the Directive, which sets forth obligations not unlike those governing its management of accounts held by individuals, foundations, endowments, pension plans, and others who are not investment companies and does not attribute to the investment company a management 'voice' independent of the investment adviser's. In light of these considerations, the financial services model is more streamlined and possibly more coherent than the corporate governance model. That, in turn, may suggest that, to the extent the forces of competition push investment company regulation toward convergence, that convergence should push toward the financial services model.

However, if there were to emerge global convergence on the 'financial services model,' rather than the corporate governance paradigm, would we be able to call that convergence 'efficient'? On this question, too, it may seem helpful to begin the analysis with the operating company context and, in particular, what it means to evaluate whether the convergence of corporate governance laws and norms is efficient. In that context, efficiency – though often viewed through the lens of agency costs – by most accounts revolves around economic performance.[53] Put another way, inefficient convergence is regarded as such because it has no

---

[52] *Ibid.*, art. 19.
[53] See Gevurtz, *Globalization of Corporate Law*, p. 507. Agency–cost analysis is, of course, relevant in that it addresses the extent to which corporate managers are accountable to shareholders (or other stakeholders) and working in furtherance of shareholders' interests. Low agency costs signify efficiency in individual firm performance. Achieving that efficiency, however, is part of the larger goal of promoting shareholder value and, beyond that, economic performance, more broadly.

(or insufficient) relationship to performance. The challenge, then, is to discern what it is about certain rules that produce better overall performance by companies operating in accordance with those rules. A few things come to mind: Rules might enhance performance if they create disincentives for managers to engage in self-interested activities or to focus on objectives other than achieving earnings or profit or to focus on constituencies other than shareholders. Rules might also enhance performance by rewarding more socially beneficial risk–reward analysis, reducing externalities and losses due to moral hazard.

Performance may seem a robust yardstick of efficiency in the investment company context. After all, performance – which we might conceptualize as aggregate net return to investors – is the essence of investing. However, it is worth evaluating that prospect further, given the realities of today's (intermediated) investment landscape and, more importantly, the goals of investment company regulation. Answering the question (how do we measure efficiency?) in both the operating company and the investment company context requires consideration of what makes aspects of companies' operations economically beneficial. In the operating company context, 'performance' comes to the fore because it is both indicative of productivity and a precondition for creating shareholder value – and, beyond that, improved overall economic well-being. Consistent with that notion, investors buy shares of operating companies primarily in the hopes of selling at a price that is higher than the price at which they purchased the shares. That is the case in the investment company context as well, although investment company investors also tend to view investment companies as means of achieving long-term financial growth or stability based on their particular financial needs.

That additional objective, which is not necessarily present in the operating company context, may mean that one marker of a 'successful' investment company, as much as or more than performance, is reward relative to the amount of risk taken (measured by the so-called Sharpe ratio) or to volatility experienced. Risk-relative-to-reward, to be sure, is also prominent in investors' analyses in the operating company context. However – and this is merely a supposition based on anecdotal observations – it is conceivable that investors elevate that consideration when it comes to their investment company allocations. If so, that could be a product of another marker of what investors seek in an investment company – namely a tool of diversification that, in any period, may 'hedge' losses from investments in other investment companies. Consistent with that suggestion, investors often choose investment companies for the role they play in a larger bundle of portfolio assets and/or for mere 'preservation' of investment capital.

These considerations on 'efficiency,' preliminary though they are, ultimately may be little more than a red herring, at least to the extent that efficiency for investment company regulation is something different altogether. After all, the laws and regulations governing investment companies necessarily are of a different kind than corporate governance laws and norms. The former are regulatory – limiting what market actors can and cannot do – whereas the latter are structural, setting forth a framework for private actors to deploy to their own best use. Thus, whereas the objectives of corporate governance are, in a sense, open-ended, the ends of investment company regulation are, as noted in section III, focused on protecting investors and fostering their confidence. Viewed in that light, the efficiency to be sought with any investment company regulatory regime is the somewhat amorphous concept of *regulatory* efficiency, which, in turn, connotes conceptions of correcting market failures or minimizing transaction costs or some combination thereof. To be sure, as suggested previously, investment companies help fuel capital formation and, in turn, economic growth, but, at base, the regulation of them centers on protecting and bolstering the confidence of those who invest capital in them.

Based on the history of investment company regulation, one might surmise that the primary market failure that regulation exists to remedy is investment advisers' using the investment companies they manage for their own advantage through, among other things, engaging in self-interested transactions with them. If that is so, then presumably an efficient investment company regulatory regime would eliminate the ability of investment advisers to engage in rent-seeking behavior (or otherwise to take action based on conflicted interests) and promote the flow of information both to investment company shareholders and to regulators – and possibly also encourage more shareholder activism and interest in managerial accountability. From that perspective, it is questionable whether a requirement that investment companies be formally governed by an 'independent' body along the lines of a board of directors is efficiency-promoting. Indeed, the corporate governance paradigm has given rise to a number of regulatory weaknesses stemming from investment advisers' relationships with boards of directors – including boards' failure to dissent meaningfully to advisers' activities and requests. That, in turn, suggests that the financial services approach may better serve regulatory efficiency, though, of course, it may also require a more robust regulator, one that has the means to pursue effective investigation and enforcement.[54]

V. Conclusion

Perhaps more than in the corporate governance context and other contexts in which legal and regulatory 'convergence' has traditionally been evaluated, greater consistency among the laws and norms governing investment companies worldwide could bolster global investment activity and capital formation. Beyond universalist efficiency considerations are the more provincial ones: Countries left out of the forces of convergence could be at a disadvantage in attracting capital beyond domestic sources. Moreover, if it is the case that multilateral imitation and transplanting of laws and norms is a normative good, regulation should tend to follow the financial services paradigm, both to avoid the infirmities of governance by a board of directors and to foster greater coherence in financial services regulation.[55]

---

[54] However, the financial services model is perhaps assisted by the more direct relationship between shareholders and investment advisers that it at least permits, if not expressly contemplates.

[55] Although this chapter advocates a particular model of investment company regulation, it makes no claims about what the substance of that regulation should be – either regarding substantive regulatory requirements governing investment advisers or the types of activities in which investment companies are able to engage.

13

Greek debt restructuring, *Abaclat* v. *Argentina* and investment treaty commitments: the impact of international investment agreements on the Greek default

JULIEN CHAISSE

I. Introduction: the emergence of a new international economic issue

The crisis in Greece emerged in 2007–2008, when it became obvious that Greece was not in a situation to meet its repayment obligations to its creditors. At that time, the budget deficit of Greece was in the range of 13 per cent of its gross domestic product (GDP).[1] The stock of debt was equivalent to 115 per cent of the GDP.[2] The debt problem was further compounded by the fact that nearly three-fourths of the government debt was held by foreign institutions, particularly foreign banks.[3] This led Greece to a painful sovereign debt crisis. Such a scenario means that the Greek government's borrowing from domestic and external markets was in excess of its capacity to repay, resulting in loan defaults requiring rescheduling of loans or bailout packages from other countries or multilateral institutions.[4] In 2008, Greece reached an agreement with the International Monetary Fund (IMF), the European Commission and the European Central Bank (ECB) on a rigorous programme to stabilize

---

[1] See M. Lynn. *Greece, the Euro, and the Sovereign Debt Crisis* (New York: Wiley, 2011), 3–4.
[2] *Ibid.*
[3] Not only was the high fiscal deficit a problem, it was also camouflaged by derivative hedging. Reportedly, investment banks misled investors into investing in Greek government bonds by being secretive about the actual state of affairs. The rating agencies played accomplice and allegedly 'failed' to assess the correct fiscal position.
[4] For a comprehensive account of the empirical evidence on the outcomes of SDR negotiations and the mechanisms at work, see M. Wright 'Restructuring Sovereign Debts with Private Sector Creditors: Theory and Practice', in C. P. Braga and G. Vincelette, *Sovereign Debt and the Financial Crisis* (Washington, DC: World Bank Press 2011), 296–303.

its economy with the support of a $145 billion financing package, against which the Greek government was required to implement fiscal measures, structural policies and financial sector reforms.[5] Essential points of the reform package were: reducing the fiscal deficit to 3 per cent by 2014; pensions and wages to be reduced for three years; government entitlement programmes had to be curtailed and social security benefits cut.[6]

The German law firm Gröpper-Köpke announced in the wake of the reform package that it was preparing lawsuits against banks and the Greek state on behalf of holders of Greek bonds who have been forced to take part in the €206bn debt swap that occurred in 2012,[7] the biggest sovereign restructuring in history.[8] Such a move makes a lot of sense in the wake of the most recent developments.[9] Indeed, in the 2011 award, the Abaclat Tribunal made at least two novel findings: first, that a claim based on a sovereign debt default falls within ICSID's jurisdiction;[10] and, second, that mass claims can be adjudicated before an ICSID tribunal. Both findings expose sovereign debtors to potential claims,[11] as in the

---

[5] See E. Favaro, Y. Li, J. Pradelli and U. Panizza, 'Europe's Crisis: Origins and Policy Challenges', in Braga and Vincelette, *Sovereign Debt and the Financial Crisis*, 221–5; C. Paulus, 'A Standing Arbitral Tribunal as a Procedural Solution for Sovereign Debt Restructurings', *ibid.*, 317–31.

[6] Arguably, what makes sovereign debt a distinctively important issue is not its size, since private debts can be rather huge, too. Rather, it is, as the 'austerity' measures hitting Europe Union at the moment show, that efforts to repay 'troubled' sovereign debt can have major impacts on all areas of society. See Lynn, *Greece, the Euro, and the Sovereign Debt Crisis*, 93–111.

[7] It is reported that 'a German law firm is seeking to challenge the Greek state for breaching the German–Greece BIT . . . the law firm Gröpper-Köpke intends to file a class action suit on behalf of small investors who have been forced to take part in the recent €206 billion debt swap, arguing that the bond swap amounts to expropriation of investors who did not volunteer' (International Institute for Sustainable Development, 'German law firm eyes case over sovereign debt restructuring', *Investment Treaty News*, 13 April 2012). See also J. Wilson and G. Wiesmann, 'Germans seek lawsuits over Greek debt swap, *Financial Times*, 12 March 2012.

[8] See Wright 'Restructuring Sovereign Debts', 295–316.

[9] Such a claim echoes the Serbian loans and Brazilian loans cases (Payment of Various Serbian Loans Issued in France (*France* v. *Yugoslavia*), 1929 PCIJ (Ser. A) No. 20 (12 July), Payment in Gold of Brazilian Federal Loans Contracted in France (*France* v. *Brazil*), 1929 PCIJ (Ser. A) No. 21 (12 July), or when the League of Nations proposed the creation of an International Loans Tribunal with the power to adjudicate lending contracts (1938). See Paulus, 'A Standing Arbitral Tribunal', 317–30.

[10] See S. Wordsworth, '*Abaclat and others* v. *Argentine Republic*: Jurisdiction, Admissibility and Pre-conditions to Arbitration', *ICSID Review* 27 (2012), 255–60.

[11] Mass investment arbitration would probably only arise when other methods of redress are actually or effectively unavailable. See H. van Houtte and Bridie McAsey, '*Abaclat and*

sovereign debt context, creditors seeking enforcement of sovereign debt instruments may prefer to litigate, since arbitration clauses in sovereign debt instruments are relatively rare. Also, after Abaclat, filing a claim before ICSID might be perceived as preferable to exhausting the remedies provided for in the debt instruments. ICSID awards are automatically enforceable in any member state.[12]

Historically conceived as an instrument to be used by developed countries to protect their firms' investments against political risks, the role of IIAs has, over the years, undergone a mutation. With growing FDI flows, the last decade has witnessed an exponential surge of investment disputes between foreign investors and host country governments. Arbitral panels have been charged with the task of applying the rules of IIAs in specific cases, a task not often straightforward, given the broad and sometimes ambiguous terms of these arrangements. This new phenomenon of investment litigation has brought about a number of decisions from different arbitral fora, contributing to investment law 'system' by giving meaning to its provisions – the 2011 Abaclat award being a good case in point.[13] As a result, the international law of foreign investment is an illustration of the fragmentation in an important area of international economic law.[14] This fragmentation has grown over time with a

---

others v. *Argentine Republic*: ICSID, the BIT and Mass Claims', *ICSID Review*, 27 (2012), 231–6.

[12] Subject only to rules of sovereign immunity protecting state assets from execution. See J. Ostrander, 'The Last Bastion of Sovereign Immunity: A Comparative Look at Immunity from Execution of Judgements', *Berkeley Journal of International Law* 22 (2004), 541–82.

[13] The cumulative number of treaty-based cases had risen to more than 300 by 2013, with more than 200 brought before the International Centre for Settlement of Investment Disputes (ICSID).

[14] Fragmentation is caused by the fact that international law consists of diverse polycentric legal systems eclipsing the former Westphalian system of nation states. The post-war propensity towards accelerated cooperation has led to intensive inter-state treaty-making and the emergence of autonomous legal orders beyond the nation-state model. See ILC, *Fragmentation of International Law: Difficulties Arising from the Diversification and Expansion of International Law*. Report of the Study Group of the ILC Finalized by Martii Koskenniemi, 13 April 2006, UN Doc. A/AC.4/L.682. Various factors are responsible for the increased fragmentation: The proliferation of international regulations, increasing political fragmentation (juxtaposed with growing regional and global interdependence in such areas as, economics, the environment, energy, resources, health, and the proliferation of weapons of mass destruction), the emancipation of individuals from states and the specialization of international regulations. See P.-M. Dupuy, 'The Danger of Fragmentation or Unification of the International Legal System and the International Court of Justice', *New York University Journal of International Law & Policy* 31 (1999), 791; P.-M. Dupuy, 'A Doctrinal Debate in the Globalisation Era: On the "Fragmentation"

continuously increasing number of treaties (bilateral investment treaties, preferential trade agreements with investment chapters and other multilateral agreements), actors (public and private investors) and fora (ICSID, UNCTAD, WTO, OECD) dealing with cross-border capital issues.[15]

This chapter further explains the Greek crisis and sets the scene for the subsequent analysis. Section I reviews the existing Greek treaties, while section II reviews their coverage of sovereign debt-related issues in terms of scope of application. Section III explains key features of the Greek–foreign IIAs and their significance for sovereign debt restructuring (SDR), namely the scope of Greek–foreign IIAs in terms of substantial rights of investors under IIAs. Section IV summarizes the main points of contention for the future of SDR in light of the Abaclat decision, but also the litigation prospects as for the Greek SDR.

II.   Greek investment treaty practice

This section aims at giving a brief overview of the existing and evolving investment regime that is available to investors, to ensure a high degree of protection for their operations abroad. There are generally two main types of IIAs that foreign investors, such as private bondholders, need to know to enforce their rights in a foreign state: bilateral investment treaties and preferential trade agreements with investments chapters. In the case of Greece, there is not free trade agreement but a significant set of bilateral investment agreements which were concluded before the EU member states transferred FDI to the European Union in 2009.[16] As of February 2013, Greece had concluded forty-three BITs which focus on the protection of foreign investors (Annex 12.1).

of International Law', *European Journal of Legal Studies* 1 (2007); see *contra* T. Cottier, P. Delimatsis, K. Gehne and T. Payosova, 'Fragmentation and Coherence in International Trade Regulation: Analysis and Conceptual Foundations', in T. Cottier and P. Delimatsis (eds.), *The Prospects of International Trade Regulation – From Fragmentation to Coherence* (Cambridge University Press, 2011).

[15]   Chaisse Julien *et al.*, 'The Regulatory Framework of International Investment: The Challenge of Fragmentation in a Changing World Economy', in Cottier and Delimatsis, *Prospects of International Trade Regulation*, 420.

[16]   On the competence transfer and implementation of national investment treaties, see J. Chaisse, 'Promises and Pitfalls of the European Union Policy on Foreign Investment', *Journal of International Economic Law* 15 (2012), 51–84.

Annex 12.1 *Total number of Greek bilateral investment agreements concluded; February 8, 2013*

Partner	Signature	Entry into force
Albania	1-Aug-91	4-Jan-95
Algeria	20-Feb-00	21-Sep-07
Argentina	26-Oct-99	—
Armenia	25-May-93	28-Apr-95
Azerbaijan	21-Jun-04	3-Sep-06
Bosnia & Herzegovina	12-Dec-00	15-Jun-07
Bulgaria	12-Mar-93	29-Apr-95
Chile	10-Jul-96	27-Oct-02
China	25-Jun-92	21-Dec-93
Congo	26-Apr-91	—
Croatia	18-Oct-96	21-Oct-98
Cuba	18-Jun-96	18-Oct-97
Cyprus	30-Mar-92	26-Feb-93
Czech Republic	3-Jun-91	31-Dec-92
Egypt	16-Jul-93	6-Apr-95
Estonia	17-Apr-97	7-Jul-98
Georgia	9-Nov-94	3-Aug-96
Germany	27-Mar-61	15-Jul-63
Hungary	26-May-89	1-Feb-92
India	26-Apr-07	10-Apr-08
Iran, Islamic Republic	13-Mar-02	9-Jan-09
Jordan	21-Feb-05	8-Feb-07
Kazakhstan	26-Jun-02	—
Korea, Republic	25-Jan-95	4-Nov-95
Latvia	20-Jul-95	9-Feb-98
Lebanon	24-Jul-97	17-Jul-99
Lithuania	19-Jul-96	10-Jul-97
Mexico	30-Nov-00	26-Sep-02
Moldova, Republic of	23-Mar-98	27-Feb-00
Morocco	16-Feb-94	28-Jun-00
Poland	14-Oct-92	20-Feb-95
Romania	23-May-97	11-Jun-98
Russian Federation	30-Jun-93	23-Feb-97
Serbia	25-Jun-97	13-Mar-98
Slovakia	3-Jun-91	31-Dec-92
Slovenia	29-May-97	11-Feb-00
South Africa	19-Nov-98	5-Sep-01
Syrian Arab Republic	23-Feb-03	27-Feb-04

Annex 12.1 (*cont.*)

Partner	Signature	Entry into force
Tunisia	31-Oct-92	21-Apr-95
Turkey	20-Jan-00	24-Nov-01
Ukraine	1-Sep-94	4-Jan-97
Uzbekistan	1-Apr-97	8-May-98
Vietnam	13-Oct-08	—

Sources: Compiled by author based on ICSID database of bilateral investment treaties; UNCTD database of investment agreements; national ministries of foreign affairs public information.

It is a significant number of international treaties which places Greece in the world top thirty countries with the greatest number of BITs. The oldest BIT was signed with Germany in 1961 while the majority of treaties was negotiated and concluded in the early 1990s. Out of these numerous BITs, only four treaties have not yet entered into force (Argentina, Congo, Kazakhstan, Vietnam).

These preliminary quantitative observations show that private bond-holders could find several instruments to support their claims before an international tribunal. Indeed, BITs concluded by Greece with other European countries (Germany, Poland, Croatia, Slovenia) or potential foreign investors (China, Lebanon, Turkey) offer a dense network of international commitments which may be used per se or through the most-favoured national treatment clause they entail.[17]

These forty-three Greek BITs maintain some important reservations on some key guarantees towards foreign investment, such as national treatment, measures against unlawful expropriation and access to international arbitration. This is however the core of Greece's investment policy and the essential legal framework applicable to SDR under the international of foreign investment.

III. The scope of Greek treaty commitments

The provisions concerning the scope of an IIA are of key importance, since they delimit the cases where the IIA will apply or fail to apply. In

---

[17] One can however note that some major investment partners of Greece are missing such as the UK, France, Italy and Spain.

particular, the definitions of *investor* and *investment* determine the subject matter of an IIA. Countries may choose to provide ample coverage and permit the broadest set of investors to benefit from the IIA, or restrict it to certain qualified investors. Importantly, the scope of the IIA may be one of the few substantial matters – if not the only one – that escapes the reach of the principle of most-favoured nation. Indeed, the examination of the applicability of the IIA comes logically before the application of its substantial obligations.[18] The broader or narrower scope of the IIA – especially as determined by the definitions of *investor* and *investment* – constitutes one of the fundamental elements for granting more or less preferences to investors of one particular country vis-à-vis other investors of other countries. A review of the investment definitions will help to determine whether the Greek bonds are covered by the forty-three BITs (III.1) while the review of the definitions of investor will help to determine whether the Greek creditors are investors covered by the same BITs (III.2). In order to provide a mapping of the investor and investment clauses in Greek treaty practice, I have used the BITSel Index.[19]

1. Greek sovereign bonds as foreign investments

For Greek foreign bondholders to enjoy the benefits under an IIA, one of the preconditions is that they qualify as 'investors', i.e. that they have made an 'investment'. The question therefore is what *type* of investments are covered by an IIA.

Typically, IIAs adopt a broad definition of 'investment' that refers to 'every kind of asset' of a foreign investor in a host country, suggesting that any economic value is covered by the agreement.[20] This asset-based definition is usually followed by an illustrative list of assets covered.

---

[18] For this reason, for instance, persons that do not qualify as 'investors', in the terms of the IIA that applies to them, may not resort to the MFN principle, to other more liberal definitions found in other IIAs. See A. F. Rodriguez, 'The Most-Favored-Nation Clause in International Investment Agreements – A Tool for Treaty Shopping?', *Journal of International Arbitration* 25 (2008), 89–102.

[19] BITSel (2012) Bilateral Investment Treaties Selection Index, Version 3.00, www.cuhk.edu.hk/proj/BITsel (8 February 2013). For a commentary on this Index, see J. Chaisse and C. Bellak 'Do Bilateral Investment Treaties Promote Foreign Direct Investment? Preliminary Reflections on a New Methodology', *Transnational Corporations Review* 3 (2011), 3–11.

[20] See R. J. Hunter, 'Property Risks in International Business', *International Trade Law Journal* 15 (2006), 26. See also D. R. Sieck, 'Confronting the Obsolescing Bargain: Transacting around Political Risk in Developing and Transitioning Economies through

Alternatively, some IIAs that have been concerned primarily with foreign direct investment have focused on foreign investment in an 'enterprise' rather than in a variety of assets.[21] This enterprise-based definition gives attention to the investor's objective of establishing a long-term relation with the economy of the host country, through the acquisition of a lasting interest in the ownership or management control of an enterprise. None of the Greek IIAs under review feature a definition of investment of this kind, but rather, as explained above, a broad asset-based definition which encompasses foreign direct investment as well as portfolio investment.

All BITs concluded by Greece, reviewed for this chapter, feature a broad, asset-based definition of investment that is very favourable to Greek foreign investors. Although the definition of *investment* has varied in terms of language through the many IIAs signed by Greece, differences in drafting in Greece's BITs do not seem to alter the broad scope of that definition. For instance, the Greece–China BIT says in Art. 1.1 that 'investment means every kind of assets intenced [*sic*] to be invested by an investor of a contracting party and admitted by the other Contracting party'. The Greece–Germany BIT drafted in German, indicates in Art. 8.1 that 'der Ausdruck "kapitalanlagen" umfasst alle Vermoegenswerte'. The Greece–Algeria BIT, drafted in French, indicates in Art. 1.1 that 'le terme d'investissement désigne tout élément d'actif détenu par un investisseur d'une Partie Contractante, investi sur le territoire de l'autre Partie contractante'. The term 'every kind of asset' sets off the open-ended definition, followed by an illustrative list of assets that are expressly covered by the agreement.[22] All categories of assets described above fall either expressly or implicitly under the disciplines of the agreement. The categories covered by all Greek BITs remain substantially identical, namely:

(a) movable and immovable property and other property rights;
(b) interests in the property of companies;
(c) claims to money and claims to a performance;
(d) intellectual property rights; and
(e) concession rights conferred by law or contract.

Renewable Energy Foreign Direct Investment', *Suffolk Transnational Law Review* 33 (2010), 319–45.
[21] See C. Lévesque, '*Abaclat and Others* v. *Argentine Republic*: The Definition of Investment', *ICSID Review* 27 (2012), 247–54.
[22] *Ibid.*

Although an increasing number of IIAs expressly exclude sovereign debt instruments from the treaty's definition of *investment*, none of the Greek BITs do the same. Of the forty-three BITs entered into by Greece, the notion of investment is broad, always encompassing portfolio investment and also, implicitly, these types of sovereign bonds. Following the private-sector involvement (PSI)[23] the Greek government intended to adopt legislation that would retroactively introduce Collective Action Clauses (CACs) to those bonds covered under Greek law. As it stands, 90 per cent of these bonds are governed by Greek law and the limits of the state in cases of acute crises may justify certain measures. The remaining 10 per cent are governed by English law and are covered by CACs.[24] Since ICSID accepted its jurisdiction in 2011 in respect of Argentina's debt restructuring,[25] investment arbitration jurisdiction would seem viable for most bonds.[26]

2. Bondholders as foreign investors

IIAs apply to investments made by 'investors' of one of the contracting parties in the territory of the other party. Together with the concept of 'investment', the definition of the 'investor' delimits the subject matter of the agreement. Investments made by persons not covered under that definition will not be covered by the terms of the agreement. IIAs normally apply to investments made by both natural and juridical persons and Greek BITs follow this rule.

First, in the case of juridical persons, the definition of 'investor' specifies what types of legal entities are covered by the agreement. Additionally, given the preferential nature of BITs, the definition of 'investor' features the link between the investor and one of the

---

[23] The private-sector involvement (PSI) is also called the 'haircut' of bonds. Part of the Greek SDR in 2012 was a PSI agreement, whereby private investors were asked to accept to write off 53.5 per cent of the face value of their Greek sovereign bonds. See Lynn, *Greece, the Euro, and the Sovereign Debt Crisis*, 282. If not enough private-sector bondholders had agreed to participate in the bond swap, per the PSI requirement, the Greek government had threatened to retroactively introduce a collective action clause to enforce participation.

[24] A collective action clause allows a supermajority of bondholders to agree to a debt restructuring that is legally binding on all holders of the bond, including those who vote against the restructuring. See T. Matsuda and S. Thompson, 'Return of the CAC: collective Action Clauses in Sovereign Bond Restructurings', BJIB & FL 27 (2012), 118.

[25] Wordsworth, '*Abaclat and Others*', 255–60.   [26] See section 3 below.

contracting parties required by the agreement to cover some investors, and exclude others, from the benefits granted by the agreement.

Second, as far as natural persons are concerned, it must be assessed whether investments made by *which* natural persons are covered by the respective IIAs. The great majority of IIAs extend the benefits of the agreement to the natural persons who are deemed to have the nationality of one of the contracting parties. The key criteria applied in this regard are: the nationality of the natural persons; the residency, which would include foreigners present in the home country of the investment but exclude nationals residing abroad, and the centre of economic interest. The application of an IIA in regard to investments made by juridical persons requires the identification of the different types of legal entities that may be considered to be 'investors' under the respective IIA. IIAs may exclude certain types of juridical persons based on their legal form, purpose or ownership structure. The legal form adopted by the company determines, *inter alia*, which assets may be reached by the creditors or to what extent a juridical person can be legally prosecuted under its own name.

In terms of treaty practice, definitions of 'investor' as a juridical person commonly seek to encompass all types of legal entities, independently of the legal form adopted, whether or not for profit, or whether or not privately owned. For instance, in the Greece–Azerbaijan BIT, Art. 1.3 reads 'the term "investor" means with regards to either Contracting party: a) any natural person who is a national of either Contracting Party in accordance with its laws; or b) any legal person such as company, corporation, firm, business association, institution, or other entity constituted in accordance with the laws and regulations of that Contracting Party and having *its seat* within the territory of that Contracting Party'. While the seat is the key criteria in some BITs, it can alternatively be the 'substantive business interest' as in the Greece–India BIT which states at Art. 1.3 that 'the term "investor" means … any legal person such as company, corporation, firm, business association, institution, or other entity constituted in accordance with the laws and regulations of that Contracting Party and have their *substantive business activities* in the territory of that same Contracting Party' (emphasis added).

All BITs concluded by Greece, reviewed for the purpose of this chapter, subscribe to this trend and provide coverage for investments made by all sorts of juridical persons. Language in Greek IIAs, however, varies greatly, although they all seek to set a broad and all-encompassing coverage.

IV. Bondholders' procedural rights under Greek treaties

If Greek bondholders want to enforce their rights under an IIA, they have to initiate legal proceedings against the host state. As states may bring claims against private investors arising out of interpretation or application disputes, investors may bring claims against the states arising out of treaty violations. A series of questions arise then such as: are public debt obligations covered by IIAs? Can private bondholders file arbitral claims under IIAs to pursue their financial interests? To these questions it is possible to answer positively. First, private bondholders may have access to investor-state dispute settlement procedures (section IV.1); second, they can bring investment treaty claims which are collective in nature (section IV.2). Advance planning, specialized staff and technology and information sharing are three of the many measures that facilitate mass claims and that may not be readily available to international investment arbitration – yet.

1. Investor-state dispute settlement procedures

In principle, foreign investors may choose to initiate legal proceedings in the domestic courts of the host country, a right they never lose. Alternatively, they may initiate international arbitration proceedings that can be more favourable to them, since it is easier to know international law and practice, and international tribunals are not subject to political domestic pressure.

Where foreign investors face discrimination in a state with a weak legal system, it is highly recommended that they initiate international arbitration proceedings as a priority. International arbitration is the process by which neutral arbitrators settle disputes concerning bilateral IIAs between sovereign states and foreign investors. In order to avoid multiple proceedings on the same matter, however, IIAs often establish that, once a dispute has been brought to one forum – or, in some cases, a decision has been reached – the dispute may not be pursued in another venue.

Most IIAs further allow the foreign investor to choose the venue for the arbitration. Ad hoc arbitration allows the parties to agree on the procedural rules for the dispute, although countries commonly rely on the established UNCITRAL arbitration rules.[27] The Investor-State

---

[27] The parties may also resort to organizations that provide a venue and have developed their own arbitral procedures. The ICSID, established in 1967 under the umbrella of the

Dispute Settlement (ISDS) clause constitutes a major instrument in the hands of foreign bondholders, as they can force host states to comply with international law. Statistics show that investment arbitral awards are respected, i.e. enforced by states even if the financial cost may be very high.

Nearly all Greek–foreign IIAs provide for ISDS procedures and refer to both ad hoc procedures and institutional arbitration. Also, Greece signed the ICSID convention on 16 March 1966, and ratified the said treaty which entered into force on 21 May 1969.[28] Such a scenario shows that most of the foreign bondholders, who are investors within the meaning of the relevant BIT concluded by Greece, will also be granted the right to bring a claim before investment tribunals. However, a hurdle to over-come in the case of German potential bondholders wishing to initiate arbitral proceedings against Greece is the lack of an investor–state arbi-tration clause in the 1961 Greece–Germany BIT. Since there is no ISA clause in that BIT, the key legal issue relates to the difficulties of importing such clause on the ground of the most-favoured national (MFN) treatment clause.

More generally, claimants against Greece might rely on some special-ties of the relevant BIT. Its article on expropriation contains (a) a clause saying that the legality etc. and the amount can be reviewed by a court and (b) a special MFN *Maffezzini*-like clause[29] stating that in 'all matters

World Bank, specialized in investor-state disputes, and has received the most attention, totalling well over half the investor-state claims brought today. For the most part, IIAs feature more than one option for international arbitration. Most IIAs allow resorting to ICSID, and to ad hoc arbitration under UNCITRAL rules. Some agreements additionally allow the claim to be brought to other institutions, such as the Stockholm Chamber of Commerce or the International Chamber of Commerce.

[28] See List of Contracting States and Other Signatories of the ICSID Convention as of 25 July 2012, https://icsid.worldbank.org/ICSID/FrontServlet?requestType=ICSIDDocRH and actionVal=ShowDocument and language=English

[29] The tribunal decided that by virtue of the MFN clause of the 1991 Argentine–Spain Bilateral Investment Treaty, the claimant had the right to import the more favourable jurisdictional provisions of the 1991 Chile–Spain Agreement. Tribunal stated: 'it can be concluded that if a third-party treaty contains provisions for the settlement of disputes that are more favorable to the protection of the investor's rights and interests than those in the basic treaty, such provisions may be extended to the beneficiary of the most-favored nation clause as they are fully compatible with the *ejusdem generis* principle. Of course, the third-party treaty has to relate to the same subject matter as the basic treaty, be it the protection of foreign investments or the promotion of trade, since the dispute settlement provisions will operate in the context of these matters; otherwise there would be a contravention of that principle. This operation of the most-favored nation clause does, however, have some important limits arising from public policy considerations that

relating to this article', MFN would be due. It would seem that Art. 2 of the Greece–Germany BIT enshrines the broad MFN provision.[30]

2. Do Greek BITs give consent to mass claims?

The key question is whether Greek BITs encompass mass arbitration. For instance, the Greece–Slovakia BIT, by providing that 'Any dispute between either Contracting Party and *an investor* of the other Contracting Party concerning investments including disputes on expropriation or nationalization of an investment' and further that '*the investor* concerned may submit the dispute either to the competent court of the contracting party, or to an international arbitration tribunal', does seem to restrict access to ISA to one investor per claim as opposed to mass claims.[31] In other words, by giving its consent to arbitration in a BIT, does Greece (in most of its BITs) also give its consent to mass arbitration, in which it would be faced by hundreds or thousands of investors? This issue was raised and answered in *Abaclat v. Argentina*.

The claimant strategy of acting together in a mass claims proceeding raised new questions about ICSID's willingness and ability to decide mass claims.[32] ICSID had to address a 'mass claims' case that joined the claims of many small investors. This issue in particular divided the Abaclat majority from the dissenters.[33] The majority found that:

will be discussed further below' (*Emilio Augustín Maffezini v. Kingdom of Spain*, Decision on Jurisdiction, Case No. ARB/97/7 (25 Jan. 2000), para. 56).

[30] Art. 2 Greece–Germany BIT (German version): 'Kein vertragsstaat wird die Staatsange-hoerigen und Gesellschaften des anderen Vertragsstaates hinsichtlich ihrer beruflichen und wirtschaftlichen Betaetigung, soweit sie im Zusammenhang mit Kapitalanlagen in seinem Hoheitsgebiet ausgeuebt wird, und hinsichtlich des Verwaltung, des Gebrauchs und der Nutzung ihrer Kapitalanlagen in seinmen Hoheitsgebiet ungunstigen Bedingun-gen unterwerfen als seine eigenen Staatsangehoerigen und Gesellschaften dritter Staaten hinsichtlich einer gleichartigen beruflichen und wirtschaftlichen Betaetigung'.

[31] See H. van Houtte and Bridie McAsey, '*Abaclat and others*', 231–6.

[32] See generally J. B. U. Chrostin, 'Sovereign Debt Restructuring and Mass Claims Arbitra-tion before the ICSID: The *Abaclat* Case', *Harv. Int'l LJ* 53 (2012), 505.

[33] And prompted a request by Argentina for the disqualification of President Pierre Tercier and Arbitrator Albert Jan van den Berg. See *Abaclat v. Argentine Republic*, ICSID Case No. ARB/07/5, Request for the Disqualification of President Pierre Tercier and Arbitrator Albert Jan van den Berg (Motion by Argentina), 15 September 2011, para. 19 ('In an unprecedented move and in the absence of any urgency, the majority of the Tribunal transmitted its Decision on Jurisdiction: (a) without the dissenting opinion of the other arbitrator (b) without his consent, and (c) without even waiting for a draft of said opinion').

[a]ssuming that the Tribunal has jurisdiction over the claims of several individual Claimants, it is difficult to conceive why and how the Tribunal could lose such jurisdiction where the number of Claimants outgrows a certain threshold. First of all, what is the relevant threshold? And second, can the Tribunal really 'lose' a jurisdiction it has when looking at Claimants individually? In addition ... it would be contrary to the purpose of the BIT and to the spirit of ICSID, to require in addition to the consent to ICSID arbitration in general, a supplementary express consent to the form of such arbitration. In such cases, consent to ICSID arbitration must be considered to cover the form of arbitration necessary to give efficient protection and remedy to the investors and their investments, including arbitration in the form of collective proceedings.[34]

In a nutshell, the Tribunal found that where the BIT covers bonds and where collective relief is required to provide effective protection, it would be contrary to the purpose of the BIT and the spirit of ICSID to require an additional expression of consent as to the form of the arbitration. Thus the relevant question was not whether Argentina consented to mass proceedings, but whether ICSID arbitration can be conducted in such a form, which the Tribunal confirmed was the case.[35]

In contrast, Prof. Georges Abi-Saab dissented and found the majority's re-characterization of the issue (as one of admissibility rather than jurisdiction) to be conceptually wrong[36] as it adopts an

extremely narrow, in fact partial, concept of jurisdiction, limiting it to the ambit within which jurisdiction is exercised. But ... jurisdiction is first and foremost a power, the legal power to exercise the judicial or arbitral function. Any limits to this power, whether inherent or consensual, i.e. stipulated in the jurisdictional title (consent within certain limits, or

---

[34] *Abaclat v. Argentine Republic*, ICSID Case No. ARB/07/5, Decision on Jurisdiction and Admissibility (4 Aug. 2011), para. 490.

[35] The Tribunal considered that 'the relevant question is not – has Argentina consented to the mass proceedings?, but rather – can an ICSID arbitration be conducted in the form of mass proceedings' considering that this would require an adaptation and/or modification by the Tribunal of certain procedural rules provided for under the current ICSID framework? If the answer is in the affirmative, then Argentina's consent to ICSID arbitration includes such mass aspect. If the answer is in the negative, then ICSID arbitration is not possible, not because Argentina did not consent thereto but because mass claims as the ones at stake are not possible under the current ICSID framework' (*Abaclat v. Argentine Republic*, ICSID Case No. ARB/07/5, Decision on Jurisdiction and Admissibility (4 Aug. 2011), para. 491). See also, S. Strong, 'Mass Procedures in *Abaclat v. Argentine Republic*: Are They Consistent with the International Investment Regime?', *Yearbook on International Arbitration* (2012).

[36] *Abaclat and others v. Argentina*, Dissenting Opinion, Georges Abi-Saab, 28 October 2011, para. 126.

subject to reservations or conditions relating to the powers of the organ)
are jurisdictional by essence. They are no less jurisdictional, in fact more
so, than the limits relating to one of the four dimensions of the ambit
within which jurisdiction is exercised.

The dissenter, relying in part on the US Supreme Court's decision in
Stolt – Nielsen SA, argued that consent to mass arbitration cannot be
imputed from a simple agreement to arbitrate.[37]

Coming back to the lessons of the *Abaclat* decision on the mass claims
aspect of the decision, at the very least *Abaclat* makes it more likely than
not that future classes of creditors will bring collective investment arbitration claims against sovereign debtors.[38] As stated above, a German law
firm is already preparing an investment arbitration claim on behalf of a
class of 200 investors, alleging that Greece's actions expropriated their
investment in violation of the Germany–Greece BIT.[39] That response to
Greece's debt restructuring is an early example.

V.   Bondholders' substantial rights under Greek treaties

IIAs enshrine a series of obligations on the parties, aimed at ensuring a
stable and favourable business environment for foreign investors. These
obligations pertain to the treatment that foreign investors and their
investments are to be afforded in the host country by the domestic
authorities. They are also aimed at ensuring foreign investors' ability to
perform certain key operations related to their investment. The types of
IIA obligations are more or less consistent in the majority of IIAs.[40] The
core provisions found in an IIA typically include a most-favoured nation
treatment obligation, the granting of national treatment, obligation
to provide fair and equitable treatment – as well as protection and

---

[37] In the first of these cases, *Stolt-Nielsen SA* v. *Animal Feeds International Corp.*, the Court held: 'An implicit agreement to authorize class-action arbitration . . . is not a term that the arbitrator may infer solely from the fact of the parties' agreement to arbitrate. This is so because class action arbitration changes the nature of arbitration to such a degree that it cannot be presumed the parties consented to it by simply agreeing to submit their disputes to an arbitrator' (*Abaclat* v. *Argentine Republic*, ICSID Case No. ARB/07/5, Decision on Jurisdiction and Admissibility (4 Aug. 2011), paras. 150–3).

[38] See H. van Houtte and Bridie McAsey, '*Abaclat and others*', 231–6.

[39] See IISD, 'German law firm eyes case over sovereign debt restructuring'; Wilson and Wiesmann, 'Germans seek lawsuits'.

[40] See J. W. Salacuse, 'The Treatification of International Investment Law', *Law and Business Review of the Americas* 13 (2007), 155.

security – to foreign investors and an obligation to allow international transfers of funds (Table 13.1).

However, while the substance of these principles remains the same in the majority of investment agreements, the precise scope and reach of each obligation depends on the precise wording in each case.[41] Because BITs are very diverse in their provisions and the way the existing provisions are drafted – giving rise to a broad *kaleidoscope* of legal obligations and, hence, regulatory effects – we have developed an index which allows a better analysis of the likely effect of a BIT on the FDI flows between two countries. These general principles are well reflected in Greek BIT rule making. Indeed, classical provisions are found in all forty-three BITs but differ in scope in the same treaties. This chapter focuses on the two standards which are the most likely as a result of SDR: first the fair and equitable treatment (V.1); second, the national treatment (V.2).

1. *The absolute standard of 'fair and equitable treatment'*

All the Greek BITs under review include a provisions dealing with fair and equitable treatment. For instance, the Greece–India BIT indicates in Art. 3.2 that 'investment and returns of investors of a Contracting party shall, at all times, be accorded fair and equitable treatment and shall enjoy full protection and security in the territory of the other Contracting party.' Greece's BITs with Germany or China employ a similar broad (and vague) wording.

The fair and equitable treatment (FET) standard is sometimes understood to be an independent standard that embodies the concept of the rule of law (minimum standard of treatment). The 'ordinary meaning' of the 'fair and equitable treatment' standard can only be defined by terms of almost equal vagueness. In *MTD Equity* v. *Chile*, the tribunal stated that 'in their ordinary meaning, the terms "fair" and "equitable" ... mean "just", "even-handed", "unbiased", 'legitimate"'.[42] On the basis of such and similar definitions, one cannot say more than the tribunal did in *S. D. Myers* by stating that an infringement of the standard requires 'treatment in such an unjust or arbitrary manner that the treatment rises to a

---

[41] See R. Dolzer and S. Christoph, *Principles of International Investment Law* (Oxford University Press, 2008), 360–429.
[42] ICSID, *MTD Equity* v. *Chile* (2004) Case No. ARB/01/07, para. 105.

Table 13.1 *Matrix of BITs' legal drafting variations*

Key investment provision	Description and scope for variation
Definition of investment	Subject matter of the investment agreement
Admission vs. establishment	Allows the host country to apply any admission and screening mechanism for foreign investment that it may have in place and therefore to determine the conditions on which foreign investment will be allowed to enter the country
National treatment	Requires that countries not discriminate against foreign investors in favour of domestic investors
Most-favoured nation	Requires that a government does not discriminate between foreign investors from different countries
Expropriation and indirect expropriation	Seizure of actual physical taking of property, effective loss of management, use or control, or a significant depreciation of the value of the assets of a foreign investor
Fair and equitable treatment	Relates to the concept of investors' legitimate expectations, which heavily depends on arbitrators' analysis. Repeatedly raised questions before arbitrators include: (1) To what extent may an investor legitimately rely on the stability of the legal and factual conditions under which he made his investment? and (2) What sort of changes in the host state must the investor have anticipated?
Transfer of investment-related funds out of the host state	Guarantee to allow outward transfers ensures foreign investors the ability to repatriate the amounts derived from their investment
Non-economic standards	Any protection offered to non-eco standards (be they environmental, labour, etc.)
Investor-state dispute mechanism	Disputes between a state party and an investor national of the other state are settled by international arbitration, rather than by the domestic courts of the host state (as would be the case otherwise)
Umbrella clause	Umbrella clause extends the scope of the application of a BIT: it offers more protection to the investor
Temporal scope of application	Either the treaty protection is extended to investments made before the entry into force of the agreement, or the coverage is restricted to the future

Source: Author's elaboration.

level that is unacceptable from an international perspective'.[43] Past litigation shows that the FET standard which seeks to address this situation is closely related to the concept of investors' legitimate expectations and it has resulted in questions repeatedly raised before arbitrators, such as: (1) to what extent may an investor legitimately rely on the stability of the legal and factual conditions under which he made his investment? (2) What sort of changes in the host state must the investor anticipate?[44]

In substance, an investor's investment decision is not made solely on the basis of the legal situation in a given host state at the time of the investment, but also on the expectation that he/she will, in the future, be treated fairly and equitably which can address two kinds of situation and potential violations.

First, it is important to quote the *Abaclat* tribunal which said that the 'arbitrary promulgation and implementation of regulations and laws can, under certain circumstances, amount to an unfair and inequitable treatment. It may even further constitute an act of expropriation where the new regulations and/or laws deprive an investor from the value of its investment or from the returns thereof.'[45]

---

[43] See PCA, *Saluka Investment BV (Netherlands)* v. *Czech Republic* (2006) Partial Award, at para. 297. For more information on FET in foreign direct investment, see T. Ioana, *The Fair and Equitable Treatment Standard in International Foreign Investment Law* (Oxford University Press, 2008) 300; Chaisse, 'Promises and Pitfalls', 51–84.

[44] One can easily observe that the meaning of the 'fair and equitable treatment' standard may not necessarily be the same in all investment agreements. The ordinary meaning of the 'fair and equitable treatment' standard can only be defined by terms of almost equal vagueness. In *MTD Equity* v. *Chile*, the tribunal stated that 'in their ordinary meaning, the terms "fair" and "equitable" … mean "just", "even-handed", "unbiased", "legitimate"' (ICSID, *MTD Equity* v. *Chile* (2004) Case No. ARB/01/07, para. 105). On the basis of such and similar definitions, one cannot say more than the tribunal did in *S. D. Myers* by stating that an infringement of the standard requires 'treatment in such an unjust or arbitrary manner that the treatment rises to a level that is unacceptable from an international perspective'. In substance, the FET is sometimes understood to be an independent standard that embodies the concept of the rule of law (minimum standard of treatment). Some other commentators try to dock FET to the customary international law minimum standard of treatment that has developed in the arbitral practice of various claims commissions in the inter-war period (beyond the minimum standard of treatment). Others again see it as an independent self-contained treaty standard. For an extensive analysis of arbitrators' approaches, see I. Tudor, *The Fair and Equitable Treatment Standard in International Foreign Investment Law* (Oxford University Press, 2008), 300.

[45] *Abaclat* v. *Argentine Republic*, ICSID Case No. ARB/07/5, Decision on Jurisdiction and Admissibility (4 Aug. 2011), paras. 314 and 315.

Second, in the specific context of SDR, the question to be addressed is what are the protected legitimate expectations of the private bondholders vis-à-vis the Greek state? Logically, any investor purchasing sovereign debt expects some sort of restructuring, discount or even default. However, the existence of a secondary market for sovereign bonds and, even more importantly, the role of hedge funds and the like in buying sovereign debt at a fraction of face value and then attempting collection, signal the acceptance of the risks associated with sovereign debts. If governments are not willingly defaulting on their sovereign bonds, the likelihood of default/discount/restructuring is present at the time of purchase, or even some worsening economic conditions that signal a future economic crisis. In this scenario, the task of a tribunal will be to balance the traditional 'legitimate expectations' of the investors with the specific nature of sovereign bonds market in order to assess the extent of 'breach' by the government of its obligations under the relevant BIT.

2.   The relative standard of 'national treatment'

The principle of national treatment (NT) prohibits discrimination between investors and investments produced domestically and those from other countries. Together with the MFN obligation, it forms the fundamental principle of non-discrimination in investment law.[46] Essentially, national treatment requires that countries not discriminate against foreign investors in favour of domestic ones.

The standard of treatment can be defined in two ways: 'same' or 'as favourable as' treatment or 'no less favourable' treatment. The difference is subtle, but the 'no less favourable' formulation leaves open the possibility that investors may be entitled to treatment that is more favourable than that accorded to domestic investors, in accordance with international standards. Often the definition of NT is qualified by the inclusion of the provision that it only applies in 'like circumstances' or 'similar circumstances'. With the situations of foreign and domestic investors

---

[46] The scope and practical relevance of NT is to a large extent dependent on the reading of the term 'like circumstances'. Its definition essentially sets the benchmark for national regulatory freedom to treat certain imported products differently from domestically produced. Indeed, often the definition of national treatment is qualified by the inclusion of the provision that it only applies in 'like circumstances' or 'similar circumstances'. As the situations of foreign and domestic investors are often not identical, this language obviously leaves room for interpretation.

often not being identical, this language obviously leaves room for interpretation.

Generally, not all BITs address the NT scope in the same manner. The first group does not deal with the issue at all. The second group – that of the majority – provides NT, but limits its coverage to established investments only (admission). A third group of agreements provides NT to the investors in the pre- and post-establishment phase (right of establishment). The legal situation with regard to Greek BITs is simpler as (except the Greece–China BIT without NT) they all provide national treatment, which coverage is classically limited to established investments only. For instance, Art. 3.1 of the Greece–Estonia BIT states: 'Each Contracting Party shall accord to investments, made in its territory by investors of the other Contracting Party, treatment not less favourable than that which it accords to investments of its own investors or to investments of investors of any third State, whichever is more favourable.'

It is perhaps in relation to the NT that potential claimants may strengthen their claim against Greece. Indeed, when scrutinizing the *Abaclat* dispute, it is important to note that the claimants alleged that Argentina afforded preferential treatment to local pension funds in violation of national treatment.

In *Abaclat*, the tribunal stated that the 'allegations by Claimants with regard to different treatment afforded to domestic investors, such as Argentine pension funds, are susceptible of constituting a discriminatory treatment in breach of the obligation to refrain from discriminatory measures and to provide for national treatment'. In this connection, the majority decision suggests that these facts, if established, may show a violation of the Argentina–Italy BIT.[47] From this, we can conclude that any claims against Greece supported by similar evidence could prove to be successful before international arbitration.

VI.   Concluding remarks: the crisis that turned debt restructuring from a national to an international issue

Our first conclusion relates to the technical application of investment treaties to SDR. From the viewpoint of holders of Greek sovereign bonds, existing BITs are important for the following three main reasons:

---

[47] *Abaclat v. Argentine Republic*, ICSID Case No. ARB/07/5, Decision on Jurisdiction and Admissibility (4 Aug. 2011), paras. 314 and 315.

- Investment agreements are meant to be broad and encompass a wide range of situations. Obligations of fair and equitable treatment and in respect of unlawful expropriation have starred in investment arbitration as the main guarantees against mistreatment of foreign investments.
- Greece's BITs provide outbound investors with investor-state dispute settlement procedures that constitute an efficient instrument in the hands of bondholders.
- In order to promptly evaluate whether BIT provisions are engaged and the nature of any potential claim, a set of six preliminary questions must be answered: was the alleged BIT breach by the state after its entry into force or is it a continuing breach? Is there an investor? There is a very broad definition in Greek BITs. Is there an investment? '*Every kind of asset*' is the very broad concept used in Greece's BITs. Has there been an absence of fair and equitable treatment? Has there been expropriation of the investment? What is the damage suffered by the foreign bondholders?

This first basic level of conclusion is confirmed by the most recent developments. In May 2013, a first claim was formally filed with ICSID by a bank from Slovakia under the Greece–Slovakia BIT of 1992.[48] A little earlier another notice had been filed by the Popular Bank of Cyprus under the Cyprus–Greece BIT of 1993.[49] Finally, although the notice had not been filed at the time of writing, the Gropke law firm is expected to proceed to litigation soon under the Germany–Greece BIT 1963. This will bring the number of disputes against Greece to three.

Second, a new question that has emerged is whether investment tribunals are in general – and ICSID especially – the right fora for handling the growing numbers of loan disputes? As a matter of public policy, *Abaclat* could significantly complicate future sovereign debt restructurings. As the *Abaclat* dissent had observed, 'the ramifications of the decision open a Pandora's box for sovereign debt'.[50] Arguably,

---

[48] *Poštová banka, a.s. and Istrokapital SE* v. *Hellenic Republic* (ICSID Case No. ARB/13/8).

[49] 'A Greek company filed a notice of dispute under the Greece–Cyprus bilateral investment treaty shortly after Cyprus' recent banking crisis began, citing its unfair and inequitable treatment as a result of the effective takeover by Cyprus of the ailing Cyprus Popular Bank' (William Kirtley, 'The Cypriot debt crisis and recourse to international arbitration', International Arbitration Girard Gibbs LLP (2013)), www.internationalarbitrationlaw. com/cypriot-debt-crisis-and-recourse-to-international-arbitration

[50] *Abaclat and others* v. *Argentina*, Dissenting Opinion, Georges Abi-Saab, 28 October 2011, para. 271.

facilitating creditor claims against a defaulting sovereign is a good thing, in that it protects investors, discourages default and promotes trust in the sovereign debt market. Moreover, the public nature of ICSID awards may afford creditors some leverage against the sovereign debtor. Perhaps, most importantly, violating ICSID Convention Art. 53 ('each party shall abide by and comply with the terms of the award') could jeopardize a sovereign respondent's future access to World Bank, IMF or other public funding. For these reasons, at least until the Argentinian financial crisis, ICSID awards enjoyed a high rate of voluntary compliance. However, when a sovereign experiences a financial crisis, there is no international bankruptcy regime to provide the sovereign with automatic stay protection against individual creditors. In the absence of such a regime, in order to be successful, sovereign debt restructurings need the participation of as many creditors as possible, and creditors to voluntarily refrain from enforcing the debt. The 'hold out' non-participating creditors (including hedge funds that purchase sovereign debt for a fraction of its face value) may then bring lawsuits or investment arbitration claims against the sovereign debtor, seeking to recover the full face value of the debt with interest. If a sufficient number of creditors were to seek full enforcement, it could risk derailing the restructuring. Also, the point is that the enforcement advantages of ICSID awards could be perceived as making it worth the uncertainties and costs of bringing a mass investment arbitration claim, either after – or possibly even before – exhausting other options.[51] This set of new questions offer a rich canvass against which researchers and policy makers should reflect on the increasing fragmentation of international investment and monetary law and policies.

Finally, on a more conceptual level, this chapter acknowledges that encouraging investor claims may not be desirable from the policy

---

[51] Another systemic question which, however, goes beyond the scope of this chapter is whether there would be any advantages of using state-to-state arbitration and diplomatic protection to deal with mass investor claims. Perhaps the involvement of the investors' home state reduces political pressure on the part of the host state to make it more amenable to more creative and efficient procedural solutions. Such a positive side must be put in balance with the fact that the traditional drawbacks of diplomatic protection might emerge (requirement to exhaust local remedies, substitution of private right for political discretion, loss of control over the process and an enhanced risk of politicization of the dispute). See the conference records 'State-to-State Investment Treaty Arbitration: Dead End or New Frontier?', Columbia Law School, 29 November 2012, http://media.law. columbia.edu/valecenter/State-to-State_Investment_Treaty_Arbitration_121129.mp4

perspective of promoting orderly debt restructuring. Additionally, when dealing with a financial crisis, a sovereign debtor may, for legitimate policy reasons, adopt measures that violate national treatment. The *Abaclat* decision and Greek SDR incident show that there is a variety of ways of addressing the various aims. However, the key lesson that can be drawn from the recent investment jurisprudence and the Greek crisis is that whether the *Abaclat* tribunal has it precisely right as a general matter is less important than the way in which *Abaclat* is forcing policy makers to think through these concerns on an international and comparative – rather than national – basis. After the crisis, SDR has become a true international issue which can only be properly addressed and regulated at the international level.

14

Chinese bilateral investment treaties: a case of 'internal fragmentation'

JUAN IGNACIO STAMPALIJA

I. Introduction: the 'fragmentation' of investment law and Chinese BIT policy

The whole international investment law discipline as it exists today is inevitably fragmented. Two undisputable factors contribute to such state of affairs. First, international investment agreements (IIAs) are the main sources of investment law and most of them are bilateral investment treaties (BITs).[1] Today there are more than 2,800 BITs,[2] and there is an increasing trend to include investment provisions in other treaties, such as free trade agreements (FTAs). In total we can find more than 3,100 IIAs.[3] Second, those treaties are applied and interpreted by one-off arbitral tribunals. Although tribunals have made relatively similar interpretations of investment treaties, there are still several important questions that have brought about divergent solutions, even regarding very similarly worded BITs.[4] These two factors show that the main sources of investment law are in themselves fragmented, so it seems difficult to deny the fragmentation of this particular area of international law.

In this context, China's BIT policy is particularly interesting. Since the establishment of the People's Republic of China in 1949, the country has experienced a changing attitude towards foreign investment, from

---

[1] The concept of 'international investment agreements' is comprehensive of BITs, and other international investment instruments, such as investment chapters in free trade agreements. Therefore, when we mention IIAs, BITs are included.

[2] UNCTAD, 'World Investment Report 2012: Towards a New Generation of Investment Policies,' 84, www.unctad-docs.org/files/UNCTAD-WIR2012-Full-en.pdf (last visited March 1, 2013).

[3] Ibid.

[4] See S. W. Schill, 'W(h)ither Fragmentation? On the Literature and Sociology of International Investment Law,' Eur. J. Int'l L. 22 (1985), 890–894.

economic isolation in the first thirty years of the PRC,[5] to the open door policy launched in 1978, which led to numerous changes in the country's economic and legal system.[6] For the purpose of this chapter, it is relevant to mention that China started concluding BITs with several investment partners, in order to enhance and protect their investments in China. The first BIT was concluded with Sweden in 1982,[7] and then other developed countries followed, such as Germany and France.[8] The Chinese government engaged in those BITs in order to show its investment partners the seriousness of the commitment with the open door policy.[9] From 1991 on, foreign investment in China increased dramatically. Furthermore, in the last decade, the open door policy was complemented by a "Going Abroad" strategy. Mainly due to its massive accumulation of foreign exchange reserves, China started stimulating outward investments in both developed and developing countries.[10] This phenomenon also explains Chinese interest in concluding IIAs in order to provide those investments in foreign countries with a higher level of protection.

China has negotiated more BITs than most countries. In fact, as of January 2012, China had signed 130 BITs.[11] In addition, China has entered into several FTAs, many of which contain chapters related to investment protection, in similar terms as BITs.[12] These treaties are far from identical, and there has been a clear evolution in China's position. Initial treaties were somehow limited, regarding both standards of

---

[5] See S.W. Schill, 'Tearing Down the Great Wall: The New Generation Investment Treaties of the People's Republic of China', *Cardozo J. Int'l & Comp. L.* 15 (2007), 77.

[6] *Ibid.*, 78.   [7] China–Sweden BIT (1982).

[8] China–Germany BIT (1983) and China–France BIT (1984).

[9] See N. Gallagher and W. Shan, *Chinese Investment Treaties: Policy and Practice* (Oxford University Press, 2009), 35–36.

[10] *Ibid.*, 49.

[11] By June 2008, Gallagher and Shan found 126 BITs concluded by China (*ibid.*, 31). From then on, China has concluded four more BITs according to MOFCOM's website: new China–France BIT (entered into force in 2010); new China–Uzbekistan BIT (2011); China–Malta BIT (2009); China–Mali BIT (2009). Information available at http://tfs. mofcom.gov.cn/aarticle/Nocategory/201111/20111107819474.html (last visited March 1, 2013).

[12] China–Pakistan FTA (2007), Chapter IX 'Investments'; China–New Zealand FTA (2009) Chapter 11 'Investment'; China–ASEAN Agreement on Investment of the Framework Agreement on Comprehensive Economic Co-operation (2009); China–Peru FTA (2010), Chapter 10 'Investment'; China–Costa Rica FTA (2011), Chapter 9 'Investment, Trade in Services and Temporary Entry of Business Persons.' China and Chile are holding negotiations to conclude an Investment Agreement to add to their FTA. See G. Wang, 'China's FTAs: Legal Characteristics and Implications,' AJIL 105 (2011), 493.

treatment and dispute resolution clauses. However, further economic opening and acceptance of international law led to more progressive BITs, which followed the most well-established practices in international investment law. In this respect, we can observe that the definitions of investments and investors in most Chinese IIAs are quite standard.[13] Besides, Chinese IIAs follow international patterns in granting investors a fair and equitable treatment,[14] except those with Japan, Korea, Turkey, Romania and Belarus.[15] As for non-discrimination standards, China has abandoned a history of rejection to pass to a permissive posture, including most-favored-nation clauses in most of its IIAs,[16] and even national treatment in many of them.[17] Those treaties also afford an appreciable degree of protection against expropriation.[18] Finally, China has historically adopted a restrictive approach towards investment arbitration, and only relatively recently has this posture been changed.

The existence of diverse Chinese BITs does not make China different from other countries, as most of them usually update or change their negotiating models. For example, the United States made several updates to their model BIT,[19] including one in 2012.[20] The particular issue arising from Chinese IIAs is their divergent approach to investor-state dispute settlement, especially since many of them provide for it in a very limited way. Former Soviet countries adopted a similar approach.[21] However, taking into consideration the central role that China has gained both as a capital importer and exporter, combined with the existence of 130 Chinese BITs, we should understand the importance of studying the implications of this approach to investor-state dispute settlement.

---

[13] K. Qingjiang, 'Bilateral Investment Treaties: The Chinese Approach and Practice,' *Asian Y.B. Int'l L.* 8 (1998–1999), 116–119.

[14] *Ibid.*, 123.   [15] Gallagher and Shan, *Chinese Investment Treaties*, 127.

[16] Qingjiang, 'Bilateral Investment Treaties,' 123

[17] For a complete analysis of different types of national treatment clauses in Chinese IIAs, see Gallagher and Shan, *Chinese Investment Treaties*, 165–171.

[18] *Ibid.*, 296–298.

[19] See generally, K. S. Gudgeon, 'United States Bilateral Investment Treaties: Comments on their Origin, Purposes, and General Treatment Standards', *Int'l Tax and Bus. Law.* 4 (1986).

[20] Available at www.ustr.gov/sites/default/files/BIT%20text%20for%20ACIEP%20Meeting. pdf (last visited March 1, 2013).

[21] See Gallagher and Shan, *Chinese Investment Treaties*, 313.

Furthermore, despite having concluded many BITs, China has not played a very important role arbitrating investment disputes. Only once has an investor brought a complaint against China before ICSID. The case was *Ekran Berhad* v. *People's Republic of China*,[22] and was started by a Malaysian investor. However, the Chinese government settled the case very quickly. Only one case involving a Chinese BIT reached an award, and that was *Tza Yap Shum* v. *Republic of Peru*,[23] in which a Chinese investor sued before ICSID for breach of the China–Peru BIT. Two other cases filed by Chinese companies against the Republic of Mongolia and Belgium are still pending.[24] That is why Wei Shen maintains that there is a "China disequilibrium" in investment arbitration: China has concluded numerous IIAs but has been party in only one investment dispute.[25] The author considers restrictive dispute resolution clauses as the main cause for such imbalance.[26]

The purpose of this chapter is to analyze dispute resolution clauses in Chinese IIAs in order to establish whether their diversity and restrictive nature justifies such disequilibrium, or if those clauses give investors enough possibilities to settle their disputes through investment arbitration. We believe that dispute settlement provisions in Chinese BITs cannot be deemed an unsurpassable obstacle for investors seeking a remedy for breaches of those treaties. That will be the focus of section II; in section III we will see how the *Tza Yap Shum* case illustrates that point. Finally, the last section will show that Chinese IIAs are not only an adequate way to protect investors' rights, but also a powerful instrument to deal with problems regarding enforcement of judgments or arbitral awards in China. Since the country's judiciary is not usually trusted by foreign investors, and enforcement obstacles are a common difficulty, Chinese IIAs emerge as a very useful tool that investors should seriously take into consideration.

---

[22] *Ekran Berhad* v. *People's Republic of China*, ICSID Case No. ARB/11/15.

[23] *Tza Yap Shum* v. *Republic of Peru*, ICSID Case No. ARB/07/6.

[24] *China Heilongjiang International & Technical Cooperative Corp, Qinhuangdaoshi Wilong International Industrial, and Beijing Shougang Mining Investment* v. *Republic of Mongolia*, Ad hoc arbitration under the UNCITRAL Arbitration Rules and China–Mongolia BIT, pending; *Ping An Life Insurance Company of China, Limited and Ping An Insurance (Group) Company of China, Limited* v. *Kingdom of Belgium*, ICSID Case No. ARB/12/29, pending.

[25] W. Shen, 'The Good, the Bad or the Ugly? A Critique of the Decision on *Jurisdiction and Competence in Tza Yap Shum* v. *Republic of Peru*,' *Chinese J. Int'l L.* 10 (2011), 55–56.

[26] *Ibid.*, 56–57.

II.   Investor-state dispute resolution in Chinese IIAs

1.   Importance and evolution

This is arguably the most relevant aspect of Chinese IIAs. Foreign investors tend to have a certain level of distrust toward Chinese courts. And such distrust could also justify recourse to investor-state arbitration, especially if the defendant is the Chinese government itself. However, China has always had a restrictive approach to investor-state dispute resolution, which has started to relax quite recently. We will now consider the evolution of the Chinese treaty practice with regard to investor-state arbitration and the problems that may arise.

Early Chinese BITs usually established that investor-state disputes related to the amount of compensation for expropriation that could be submitted by investors to an ad hoc tribunal, whereas all other disputes were subject to jurisdiction of the local courts.[27] There was no reference to institutional arbitration, and the jurisdiction of the ad hoc tribunals was consented to only in disputes over the amount for expropriation. After China's accession to ICSID in 1990, this approach started changing and China included reference to ICSID arbitration in several BITs. Its BIT with Lithuania was the first to do so.[28] Nonetheless, China kept a restrictive approach to investor-state arbitration, which was limited to disputes about compensation for expropriation.[29] This restriction was included in BITs using different but very similar wording, such as: disputes "involving the amount of compensation for expropriation";[30] or disputes "concerning the amount of compensation" for expropriation.[31] There is little doubt that China's intention behind this wording was to exclude most disputes from investment arbitration.

Another element that reaffirms this restrictive approach is China's notification under Article 25 paragraph (4) of the ICSID Convention,[32] which affirmed that China would only consider submitting to the

---

[27] See Gallagher and Shan, *Chinese Investment Treaties*, 37.
[28] China–Lithuania BIT (1993), art. 8, para. (2)(b).
[29] See Gallagher and Shan, *Chinese Investment Treaties*, 37.
[30] China–Peru BIT, art. 8, para. 3.   [31] China–Japan BIT, art. 11, para. 2.
[32] Art. 25, para. (4), ICSID Convention: "Any Contracting State may, at the time of ratification, acceptance or approval of this Convention or at any time thereafter, notify the Centre of the class or classes of disputes which it would or would not consider submitting to the jurisdiction of the Centre. The Secretary-General shall forthwith transmit such notification to all Contracting States. Such notification shall not constitute the consent required by para. (1)."

jurisdiction of ICSID those disputes over compensation resulting from expropriation and nationalization.[33] The effect of this type of notifications is not completely clear. Most commentators agree that these notifications are neither reservations to the ICSID Convention, nor do they limit consent under Article 25.[34] In other words, if a country ratifies the ICSID Convention, it then consents to its jurisdiction under Article 25. Obviously, specific consent is also necessary in an IIA or an investment contract before an investor can bring a claim against a country which is party to the ICSID Convention and, therefore, consented to its jurisdiction under Article 25. However, notifications under Article 25, paragraph (4) could be used, for example, to reveal parties' intentions when interpreting the wording of particular IIAs.[35] Consequently, China's notification proves its restrictive approach toward investment arbitration during the initial years of its BIT program, but does not imply that China cannot submit other types of disputes to ICSID arbitration.[36]

A major breakthrough in China's investment treaty practice was the China–Barbados BIT (1998), which granted all investor-state disputes access to ICSID arbitration.[37] After this treaty, Chinese IIAs started following the same pattern. China–Botswana BIT (2000), China–Netherlands BIT (2001), and new China–Germany BIT, for instance, all contain broad investor-state dispute settlement clauses.[38] Nevertheless, in some treaties those clauses refer to ad hoc arbitration, but not ICSID arbitration. For example, China–Mali BIT (2009).[39] The reasons for this change in paradigm are not clear. Some Chinese commentators are especially critical of this move. They consider it an unnecessary sovereignty renunciation, since China was receiving huge amounts of foreign investment without making those commitments. However, it should be noted that many of those IIAs were concluded with developing countries, especially in Asia and Africa. That fact may show that the

---

[33] See J. Y. Willems, 'The Settlement of Investor State Disputes and China: New Developments on ICSID Jurisdiction,' S.C. J. Int'l L. & Bus. 8 (2011).
[34] Ibid.   [35] Ibid.   [36] Ibid.   [37] China–Barbados BIT (1998), art. 9.
[38] A complete list of Chinese BITs and FTAs with broad investor-state dispute resolution clauses by July 2008 can be found in Gallagher and Shan, Chinese Investment Treaties, 42. The authors count forty-four IIAs with these dispute resolution clauses. However, since July 2008 some new IIAs were signed with broad investor-state dispute resolution clauses: new China–France BIT (entered into force in 2010); new China–Uzbekistan BIT (2011); China–Malta BIT (2009); China–Mali BIT (2009). Information available at http://tfs.mofcom.govcn/aart./Nocategory/201111/20111107819474.html and http://fta.mofcom.govcn/ (last visited September 30, 2012).
[39] China–Mali BIT (2009), art. 9.

underlying reason for the adoption of broader investor-state resolution clauses could be the necessity to protect Chinese investors in those countries.

There are three main questions that arise from Chinese IIAs' investor-state dispute settlement clauses. The first is the need to exhaust local remedies. The second is the effect of the restrictive clauses contained in older Chinese BITs. Finally, the third relates to whether investors limited by those clauses could rely on most-favored-nation clauses so as to benefit from broad dispute settlement clauses in China's most recent IIAs.

2.   Exhaustion of local remedies

Although most modern IIAs do not require exhaustion of local remedies as a condition to bring a claim to arbitration, Chinese BITs do require it. In international treaty practice, the most common approach is to require that the dispute be submitted to local remedies for a certain period of time, after which the investor may submit the dispute to investment arbitration if he has not obtained adequate relief.[40] Almost all Chinese BITs require the exhaustion of local remedies, mainly through domestic administrative review process in the national courts.[41] Most of them include a time limit, usually three months.[42] In several cases, investors have avoided the requirement to exhaust local remedies by relying on the most-favored-nation clause: if some BITs do not require exhaustion of local remedies, then they are more favorable and the benefits should be extended to investors under BITs that do require such exhaustion. We will analyze those cases below.

3.   Effect of restrictive clauses in first- and second-generation BITs

As mentioned, older Chinese BITs limit the scope of consent to arbitration to disputes relating to the amount of compensation for expropriation. These clauses were usually interpreted as leaving the determination of existence and legality of expropriation to local courts. Only if dissatisfied with the amount of compensation granted by those courts, could investors take their claim to international arbitration, so as to obtain the

---

[40]   See Vandevelde, *Bilateral Investment Treaties* (New York: Oxford University Press, 2010), 441.
[41]   See Gallagher and Shan, *Chinese Investment Treaties*, 364.   [42]   *Ibid.*, 366.

amount that they consider appropriate. The local courts' decision should be considered final on other issues, such as existence or legality of the expropriation.[43] If this interpretation is maintained, investors under those BITs would have a very narrow chance of accessing investment arbitration. However, it has been argued that tribunals should not be limited to deciding only the amount of the expropriation, but also its existence and legality.

The jurisprudence on this issue offers both alternatives. On the one hand, in *Saipem* v. *Bangladesh*,[44] and in *Telenor Mobile Communications* v. *Republic of Hungary*,[45] among others, tribunals interpreted similar restrictive dispute settlement clauses and they considered that they could decide not only the quantification of compensation, but also any other issues related to the expropriation. The same criterion was followed in *Czech Republic* v. *European Media Ventures SA*,[46] where the Queen's Bench Division (England) dealt with a decision relating to the execution of an arbitral award issued by a tribunal under the UNCI-TRAL Arbitration Rules. On the other hand, the tribunals in *Berschader* v. *Russia*[47] and *RosInvest UK Ltd* v. *Russia*,[48] reached the opposite conclusion.

4. Most-favored-nation treatment and dispute settlement clauses

The interaction between most-favored-nation treatment and dispute settlement clauses has been one of the most debated issues in investment law. The question that arises is whether investors can rely on most favorable dispute resolution clauses based on most-favored-nation treatment. Both commentators and jurisprudence are divided on this issue. This could become particularly relevant in the case of China, because older IIAs have limited dispute resolution clauses, whereas third-generation treaties include broad ones.

---

[43] See J. W. Salacuse, *The Law of Investment Treaties* (Oxford University Press, 2010), 385.

[44] *Saipem S. p. A* v. *Bangladesh*, ICSID Case No. ARB/05/07, Decision on Jurisdiction, March 21, 2007.

[45] *Telenor Mobile Communications AS* v. *Hungary*, ICSID Case No. ARB/04/15, Decision on Jurisdiction, September 13, 2006.

[46] *Czech Republic* v. *European Media Ventures SA*, Court of Appeal – Commercial Court, December 5, 2007 (2007) EWHC 2851 (Comm.).

[47] *Berschader* v. *Russian Federation*, SCC Case No. 080/2004, Award, April 21, 2006.

[48] *RosInvest UK Ltd* v. *Russian Federation*, SCC Case No. V079/2005, Award, October 2007.

The first case that brought this issue into consideration was *Maffezini* v. *Spain*.[49] Maffezini was an Argentine investor which had filed a claim against Spain based on the Argentina–Spain BIT. According to that BIT, an investor should first pursue a claim in local courts for eighteen months before resorting to arbitration. Maffezini did not do so, but alleged that the Chile–Spain BIT did not contain that requirement, and based on the most-favored-nation clause in the Argentina–Spain BIT, he could rely on the Chile–Spain BIT to avoid that requirement. The tribunal accepted Maffezini's argument, mainly due to the wording of the most-favored-nation clause in the Argentina–Spain BIT, which was particularly broad. Other tribunals followed the same criteria in very similar cases involving most-favored-nation clauses used to avoid the exhaustion of local remedies.[50]

Other cases have rejected the application of most-favored-nation treatment to dispute resolution clauses. In *Plama* v. *Bulgaria*,[51] the plaintiff tried to rely on a most-favored-nation clause to submit the dispute to a different forum (ICSID, instead of ad hoc arbitration as provided in the Cyprus–Bulgaria BIT). In this case, the tribunal rejected Plama's argument. The approach was different from *Maffezini*. The tribunal stated that consent to arbitration must be unequivocal. Since the most-favoured-nation clause did not refer to dispute resolution explicitly, a tribunal could not find such consent in the most-favored-nation clause.[52]

Most commentators pointed out that these two lines of cases were not actually contradictory, but based on different factors. While those following the *Maffezini* doctrine were cases in which the most-favored-nation clause was being used to avoid resort to local courts before bringing

[49] *Maffezini* v. *Kingdom of Spain*, ICSID Case No. ARB/97/7, Decision on Objections to Jurisdiction, January 25, 2000.

[50] For example, *Siemens AG* v. *Argentine Republic*, ICSID Case No. ARB/02/8, Decision on Jurisdiction, August 3, 2004; *Gas Natural SDG, SA* v. *Argentine Republic*, ICSID Case No. ARB/03/10, Decision on Preliminary Questions on Jurisdiction, June 17, 2005, among others. For a complete review of these cases, see G. S. Tawil, 'Most Favoured Nation Clauses and Jurisdictional Clauses in Investment Treaty Arbitration,' in Christina Binder *et al.* (eds.), *International Investment Law for the 21 Century: Essays in Honour of Christoph Schreuer* (Oxford University Press, 2009), 13–20.

[51] *Plama Consortium Limited* v. *Republic of Bulgaria*, ICSID Case No. ARB/03/24, Decision on Jurisdiction, February 8, 2005.

[52] Another case with a similar approach is *Berschader et al.* v. *Russia* (see n. 47), among others. For a complete review of these cases, see Tawil, 'Most Favoured Nation Clauses,' 21–27.

a dispute to arbitration, the *Plama* line of cases involved cases in which investors invoked the most-favored-nation clause to start claims under different forums or to expand the tribunal's jurisdiction.[53] However, other new cases led to increasing confusion. In *Rosinvest* v. *Russia*, for example, the tribunal did not follow the *Plama* doctrine and stated that most-favoured-nation treatment must also apply to dispute resolution clauses. Therefore, the tribunal extended its jurisdiction *ratione materiae* from the limits of the dispute resolution clause. In the case, the UK–Russia BIT allowed investors to submit to arbitration only disputes related to the amount of compensation for expropriation. The tribunal, by applying the most-favoured-nation clause, expanded its jurisdiction based on the Denmark–Russia BIT, which established that all disputes could be settled in arbitration. This case shows that the interaction between most-favored-nation treatment and dispute resolution clauses is far from over,[54] but we can also see that most-favored-nation clauses may play an important role in dealing with fragmented investors' protection.[55]

5. *Summary*

The possibility of resolving disputes against the Chinese government before international arbitration tribunals would be of paramount importance for foreign investors, since it would let them avoid the risks and uncertainties they would have to face in Chinese courts, or even arbitrating in China. In this respect, we should differentiate between those investors protected by Chinese IIAs with broad dispute resolution clauses, and those under restrictive ones. The former will be in a good position to pursue investment arbitration without serious limitations. This alternative is preferable to dealing with the Chinese government in local courts or arbitration commissions. Hence, they should consider resorting to international arbitration to solve their investment disputes against the Chinese government. As for investors under older BITs, which have a restrictive dispute resolution clause, they face a more difficult challenge, but that does not mean that arbitral tribunals will adopt literal interpretation of those clauses, as we will see below in the *Tza Yap Shum* case. The best alternative might be to structure their investment in China in such a way that they

---

[53] See Tawil, 'Most Favoured Nation Clauses,' 20.   [54] *Ibid.*, 25.
[55] See S. W. Schill, *The Multilateralization of International Investment Law* (Cambridge University Press, 2009), 121–196.

would fall under the scope of IIAs with broad dispute resolution clauses, so as to take advantage of them.

III. *Tza Yap Shum* v. *Peru*

The *Tza Yap Shum* case is relevant in several aspects. To begin with, it was the first case in which an arbitral tribunal interpreted and applied a Chinese BIT. Furthermore, it deals with many of the issues that arise from older Chinese BITs. That is why it is important to see how arbitral tribunals may address those questions, and whether that can be positive or negative for investors protected by older BITs.

1. *Facts of the case*

The dispute arose from some measures taken by the Peruvian tax administration (SUNAT) against TSG Peru. The latter was a Peruvian company which produced fish-based products and exported them to Asia. In 2004, SUNAT carried out an audit of TSG and concluded that there were inconsistencies in TSG's books, which led to an imposition of back taxes and fines. In addition, SUNAT also adopted interim measures and froze TSG's bank accounts in Peru. TSG challenged both SUNAT's audit determinations and its imposition of interim measures via administrative and judicial procedures available under Peruvian law, but obtained no relief. Due to its impossibility to operate its bank accounts, TSG's sales fell dramatically and led the company to a debt restructuring proceeding.

Mr. Tza Yap Shum was indirectly one of the owners of the company and claimed that SUNAT destroyed TSG by illegally freezing the company's bank accounts. He started an arbitration procedure before ICSID, based on the China–Peru BIT. According to the claimant, Peru breached several obligations under the BIT, namely, those related to fair and equitable treatment, protection to investments, compensation for expropriation and allowing free transfer of capital and earnings.[56]

2. *Decision on jurisdiction*

Peru reacted to Mr. Tza Yap Shum's claim by objecting the jurisdiction of ICSID and the arbitral tribunal. Such objection led to a decision on

---

[56] See *Tza Yap Shum* v. *Republic of Peru*, ICSID Case No. ARB/07/6, Decision on Jurisdiction, June 19, 2009, para. 31.

jurisdiction issued by the arbitral tribunal, which dealt with many relevant issues arising from older Chinese BITs.

(i)   Covered investors

The first objection to jurisdiction brought by Peru was that Mr. Tza Yap
Shum was not an investor under the China–Peru BIT. To begin with,
Peru alleged that the claimant must be a Chinese citizen and that
nationality must be proved with a birth certificate.[57] In the case,
Mr. Tza Yap Shum was a Hong Kong resident, but could not produce
a Chinese birth certificate. However, he had his Hong Kong passport,
which stated that he was born in Fujian Province, China, and documents
from local authorities saying that birth records had been destroyed
during the Chinese civil war, among other documents. Besides, Peru
alleged that even if he were a Chinese national, Hong Kong residents
are excluded from the China–Peru BIT, because Hong Kong has autonomy to sign its own IIAs, and those usually include Hong Kong residents
under the scope of application.[58] Besides, under the Basic Law Act of
Hong Kong SAR, BITs signed by China were not applicable to Hong
Kong.[59]

The tribunal rejected Peru's objection. According to the tribunal, the
China–Peru BIT established that it applied to persons "who have nation-
ality of the People's Republic of China in accordance with its laws."[60] The
Chinese Nationality Act is in force in Hong Kong and the Standing
Committee of the People's Congress found that Hong Kong residents
of Chinese descent and born in Chinese territories (including Hong
Kong) are Chinese nationals.[61] The tribunal considered that the claimant
proved that he was born in Fujian province from Chinese parents, and
therefore he was a Chinese national.[62] The tribunal explained that the
Nationality Act did not require the production of a birth certificate to
prove Chinese nationality, so it was unreasonable to require it for the
purpose of the arbitration.[63] The tribunal found that the claimant was
protected under the China–Peru BIT, as the only requirement was
holding Chinese nationality, and there was nothing in the treaty meant
to exclude Hong Kong residents from the scope of application.[64] In other
words, the China–Peru BIT is applicable to Chinese nationals regardless
of their place of residence.

---

[57] *Ibid.*, para. 44.   [58] *Ibid.*, para. 45.   [59] *Ibid.*, para. 47.
[60] China–Peru BIT, art. 1 (2).   [61] See *Tza Yap Shum* v. *Republic of Peru*, para. 60.
[62] *Ibid.*, para. 61.   [63] *Ibid.*, para. 64.   [64] *Ibid.*, para. 71.

This interpretation seems reasonable, because the China–Peru BIT, as most Chinese IIAs, establishes that it covers those who are Chinese nationals under Chinese law. Consequently, it takes into consideration the nationality of the investor and not his residence.

(ii) Covered investments

Peru's second objection to jurisdiction was that Mr. Tza Yap Shum did not have an investment in Peru when the dispute arose and that the China Peru–BIT did not cover indirect investments.[65] Peru argued that the dispute arose when SUNAT conducted an audit on TSG in May 2004, which then led to the measures on the banks accounts in January 2005.[66] The problem was that until February 2005, 90 percent of TSG shares were owned by Linkvest International Ltd, which was a company incorporated in the British Virgin Islands. The only shareholder of Linkvest was Mr. Tza Yap Shum. Then, in February 2005, after the dispute arose, the claimant acquired directly 90 percent TSG shares, previously owned by Linkvest.[67] In short, Peru's argument was that until that time, the investor was Linkvest and not Mr. Tza Yap Shum. The tribunal considered that it was proved in the case that Mr. Tza Yap Shum was the sole shareholder of Linkvest. Besides, he started his project in Peru in 2001 and behaved as its owner when signing contracts and dealing with third parties. Therefore, the tribunal found that the investment was done in 2001 and not before the dispute arose, the fact that he bought TSG shares personally in 2005 being irrelevant.[68]

Then the tribunal had to determine whether the China–Peru BIT protected indirect investments of Chinese nationals in Peru. In other words, whether the claimant's decision to invest through Linkvest excluded him from the scope of application of the ICSID Convention and the BIT. The tribunal found that Article 25 (1) of the ICSID Convention did not differentiate between direct and indirect investments.[69] In addition, many arbitral tribunals have maintained that indirect investments should not deter tribunals from exercising jurisdiction unless the BIT expressly excluded them from the scope of protection.[70] The tribunal should look at the investors' nationalities and not the corporate schemes through which the investment had been channeled.[71] As for the China–Peru BIT, the tribunal pointed out that the purpose of the treaty as stated in the preamble was to promote and protect

---

[65] *Ibid.*, para. 78.   [66] *Ibid.*, para. 86.   [67] *Ibid.*, para. 88.   [68] *Ibid.*, para. 90.
[69] *Ibid.*, para. 96.   [70] *Ibid.*, para. 97.   [71] *Ibid.*, para. 100.

investments, and that nothing in the wording of the treaty excluded expressly indirect investments from the scope of application. Instead, the parties adopted a broad formulation which protected all kind of investments.[72] If parties had intended excluding indirect investments, they would have done so explicitly in the BIT.[73] Thus, the tribunal considered that the China–Peru BIT protects indirect investments from Chinese nationals in the Peruvian territory.[74]

(iii) Interpretation of restrictive dispute settlement clauses

The tribunal had the opportunity to interpret the dispute settlement clause in the China–Peru BIT. Article 8 established:

> 2. If the dispute cannot be settled through negotiations within six months, either party to the dispute shall be entitled to submit the dispute to the competent court of the Contracting Party accepting the investment.

> 3. If a dispute involving the amount of compensation for expropriation cannot be settled within six months after resort to negotiations as specified in Paragraph 1 of this Article, it may be submitted at the request of either party to the international arbitration of the International Center for Settlement of Investment Disputes (ICSID) . . . Any disputes concerning other matters between an investor of either Contracting Party and the other Contracting Party may be submitted to the Center if the parties to the dispute so agree. The provisions of this Paragraph shall not apply if the investor concerned has resorted to the procedure specified in Paragraph 2 of this Article.

This is a typical dispute resolution clause of an old Chinese BIT, which provides for arbitration in disputes involving compensation for expropriation.

Peru argued that the arbitration clause was meant to limit the consent to ICSID jurisdiction and that the tribunal could only intervene in disputes regarding the amount of compensation for expropriation. As the plaintiff initiated no procedure before local courts to determine the existence of expropriation, then the ICSID tribunal had no jurisdiction in the case. Peru maintained that the wording of Article 8 (3) was clear and that according to Articles 31 and 32 of the Vienna Convention such wording should be respected.[75] Besides, it relied on an expert witness and the negotiators from both China and Peru who apparently agreed that such restrictive interpretation was the intention of the parties when the

---

[72] *Ibid.*, para. 106.   [73] *Ibid.*, para. 107.   [74] *Ibid.*, para. 111.   [75] *Ibid.*, para. 130.

treaty was concluded.[76] Finally, Peru mentioned that China's notification under Article 25 (4) of the ICSID Convention was in line with such interpretation. The plaintiff answered that this clause allowed the tribunal not only to decide on the amount of compensation due for expropriation, but also to determine the existence of expropriation and its legality. He rejected the respondent's view and requested that the clause should be interpreted taking into account the context and the purpose of the BIT, namely, the promotion and protection of investments and investors.[77] He argued that Peru's interpretation would leave investors defenseless in case of indirect expropriation, because the Peruvian legal system offers no actions against indirect expropriation.[78]

The tribunal adhered to the plaintiff's position. First, the tribunal affirmed that the interpretation given to the phrase "involving the amount of compensation for expropriation" is the main question under analysis.[79] The tribunal relied on Article 31 of the Vienna Convention and stated that the word "involving," according to the *Oxford English Dictionary*, means "to enfold, envelope, entangle, include."[80] So a bona fide interpretation leads one to conclude that the "dispute must 'include' the determination of the amount of a compensation, and not that the dispute must be restricted thereto."[81] The tribunal pointed out that other language was possible, "such as 'limited to' or 'exclusively,' but the wording used in this provision reads 'involving.'"[82] Consequently, the tribunal concluded that any potential dispute arising from expropriation could be settled under ICSID arbitration.[83]

Furthermore, the tribunal explained that following the interpretation proposed by Peru, investors would never have access to arbitration,[84] because the last sentence of Article 8 (3) states that investment arbitration will not apply if the investor has resorted to the local courts. In other words, the tribunal considers that sentence as a 'fork in the road' clause. In the tribunal's view, Peru cannot require investors first to file expropriation claims to local courts, because then the last sentence of Article 8 (3) would mean that they would not be able to access ICSID afterwards.[85] In addition, the tribunal analyzed the expert witness's statement and other testimonies from negotiators on both parties, but did not find conclusive support for the restrictive interpretation proposed by Peru.[86] Then the tribunal reviewed different cases that had posed similar questions,

---

[76] *Ibid.*, paras. 131 and 135.   [77] *Ibid.*, para.140.   [78] *Ibid.*, para. 142.
[79] *Ibid.*, para. 149.   [80] *Ibid.*, para. 151   [81] *Ibid.*   [82] *Ibid.*   [83] *Ibid.*, para. 152.
[84] *Ibid.*, para. 154.   [85] *Ibid.*, para. 157.   [86] *Ibid.*, paras. 171–172.

alleging that there was no uniform jurisprudence on this issue, but praised those awards that had granted a broad interpretation of dispute resolution clauses. Finally, the tribunal expressed the view that China's notification under Article 25 (4) of the ICSID Convention had little legal effect and did not limit its consent to arbitration.[87]

It is not the purpose of this chapter to assess the merits of the award,[88] although we should admit that this is its most questionable point. The tribunal made a serious effort to conclude that it could hear disputes related to any issues arising from expropriation, not only the amount of compensation. In order to reach that conclusion, the tribunal did take a few problematic steps in the course of its reasoning. First, the tribunal adopted a textual interpretation of Article 8. The tribunal found that the phrase "disputes involving the amount of compensation for expropriation" was the same as saying "disputes including the amount of compensation for expropriation." Even if that were true, the conclusion of the tribunal was contradictory. If it is enough that the claim 'includes' a dispute about the amount of compensation for expropriation for the tribunal to have jurisdiction, it is not clear why that jurisdiction must be restricted to expropriation issues and not to others, such as violation of fair and equitable treatment. In other words, if 'involving' is the same as 'including,' there is no reason to limit the tribunal's jurisdiction to expropriation claims. It is enough to 'include' an expropriation claim in the dispute to resort to arbitration. Obviously, this idea leaves the reference to 'other disputes' that can be arbitrated under Article 8 as totally irrelevant, and thus cannot be accepted. The only differentiation expressly admitted by Article 8 is between disputes that refer to "the amount of compensation for expropriation" and "other disputes."

Second, not only is the interpretation questionable from a textual point of view, but also because it somehow ignores the intention of the parties when they concluded the BIT, saying that they were not clear, even when negotiators from both parties were witnesses in the case and agreed their intention was to follow a restrictive approach. The tribunal seems to require such a high standard of proof of the parties' intention that would be almost impossible to achieve. Besides, the tribunal gave no effect to China's notification under Article 25 (2) of the ICSID Convention. Although most commentators agree that those notifications are not reservations to the Convention or limitations to the consent under

---

[87] *Ibid.*, para. 165.
[88] For a complete analysis of the award, see Shen, 'The Good, the Bad or the Ugly?'

Article 25, they can surely be considered as a sign of China's position toward investment arbitration in early 1990s, especially taking into account that China's accession to ICSID and the China–Peru BIT were relatively close in time.

Maybe the most convincing point is the reference to the 'fork in the road' clause included in Article 8. If investors could not bring their expropriation claims to local courts and then resort to arbitration where they are not satisfied with the amount of compensation for expropriation, it would seem that reference to ICSID arbitration in Article 8 made no sense, and investors would not be able to bring any kind of disputes to arbitration. Nonetheless, we consider that the 'fork in the road' clause could be interpreted as applicable once a local court has determined the existence of expropriation. This interpretation looks more respectful of the intention of the parties and preserves the underlying balance of Article 8.

(iv)   Most-favored-nation and dispute resolution clauses

Finally, the tribunal analyzed the question concerning the possibility of relying on the most-favoured-nation clause of the BIT to broaden the scope of the ICSID arbitration established in the treaty. In the case, as we mentioned, the plaintiff not only requested compensation for expropriation, but also alleged violations of the fair and equitable treatment, the requirement of protection of investments and the free transfer of funds and earnings.[89] Article 8 (2) of the China–Peru BIT only provided for arbitration in disputes involving compensation for expropriation. The plaintiff argued that Peru had several BITs with broad dispute resolution clauses, such as the Colombia–Peru BIT, and according to the most-favored-nation treatment established in Article 3 of the China–Peru BIT, he should be able to rely on the Colombia–Peru BIT's broad dispute settlement provision.[90]

When addressing this issue, the tribunal maintains that it is not possible to give a general answer to the interaction between most-favored-nation and dispute resolution clauses. Instead, it was particularly important to pay attention to the BIT itself and, especially, to the wording of the clauses under discussion.[91] In this respect, the tribunal pointed out that Article 8 of the China–Peru BIT specifically provided that expropriation disputes could be settled by ICSID arbitration, and

---

[89]   See *Tza Yap Shum* v. *Republic of Peru*, para. 133.
[90]   *Ibid.*, paras. 190–191.   [91]   *Ibid.*, para. 198.

"any disputes concerning other matters ... may be submitted to the Center if the parties to the dispute so agree."[92] According to the tribunal, the parties clearly established the possibility of ICSID arbitration in "other matters," and this was a specific provision that showed the intention of the parties on the issue. Consequently, this specific provision should prevail over the generality of the most-favored-nation clause.[93] Based on this argument, the tribunal refused to extend its jurisdiction to matters other than expropriation. As we have mentioned before, this interpretation is in line with the intention of the parties, but not with the tribunal's own argument about disputes "including" the amount of compensation for expropriation, as the key element for the tribunal to assert jurisdiction in the case. It should be noted that this interpretation is mostly based on the wording of the treaty, which may differ in other Chinese BITs. Thus, this interpretation may not be possible under other Chinese IIAs.[94]

Moreover, the tribunal went through the different cases on this issue, and distinguished them from the *Tza Yup Shum* case. In short, all of them dealt with dispute resolution clauses referring to "any disputes," instead of limited clauses such as the one under the China–Peru BIT.[95] The tribunal found some similarities with *Plama* v. *Bulgaria*, where the claimant wanted to skip preliminary stages and change the arbitral proceeding agreed in the BIT based on the most-favored-nation clause. In that case, the tribunal found that the dispute resolution clause was more specific and should therefore prevail over the general most-favored-nation clause.[96] Once again we find uncertainties for investors, though some of them can be used in the investors' interests, avoiding literal interpretation of the BITs' provisions.

3. Final award

The tribunal rendered its final award on the merits on July 2011. This award is not pertinent to our subject of inquiry, compared to the tribunal's decision on jurisdiction. Whereas the latter dealt with specific issues that could be highly relevant in determining the effects of several

---

[92] *Ibid.*, para. 214.   [93] *Ibid.*, para. 216.

[94] See N. Eliasson, 'Chinese Investment Treaties: A Procedural Perspective,' in V. Bath and L. Nottage (eds.), *Foreign Investment and Dispute Resolution Law and Practice in Asia* (Abingdon, Oxon.: Routledge, 2011), 98.

[95] See *Tza Yap Shum* v. *Republic of Peru*, para. 217.   [96] *Ibid.*, para. 220.

provisions under Chinese BITs, the former focused on the merits of the expropriation claims which are not substantially different under Chinese and other IIAs.

The tribunal found that the interim measures imposed on TSG by SUNAT were arbitrary and could therefore be considered as a case of indirect expropriation. The tribunal did not consider the audit itself as expropriatory, because it could be acceptable within the state's administrative powers,[97] and the results of the audit were not arbitrary.[98] However, the measures imposed by SUNAT, which froze TSG's bank account, constituted an indirect expropriation for several reasons. First, they prevented TSG from operating in Peruvian banks, which was absolutely necessary for its business. Therefore, these measures had an extremely serious impact on TSG's business and its sales dropped dramatically.[99] Second, the tribunal stated that the imposition of such measures was arbitrary, because SUNAT did not follow its own guidelines and procedures, which regarded interim measures as an exceptional remedy that could only be adopted with strong evidentiary support and trying to avoid affecting the debtor's business operations.[100] Third, the tribunal considered that the administrative and judicial organs where TSG challenged the interim measures, violated due process standards, since they simply adopted SUNAT's positions without reasoned argumentation.[101] Hence, they were not an effective legal recourse.

As for the amount of compensation, the tribunal noted that the measure of damages is the amount needed to place the claimant in the same position he would have been without the expropriatory act. Both parties agreed that the amount should be based on the value of TSG, but disagreed on how to calculate such value: the claimant requested damages based on the discounted cash flow of TSG, while Peru believed that the company's adjusted book value was preferable. The tribunal rejected the claimant's position, based on the fact that TSG had been in operation for only two years before the alleged expropriation, and its cash flow was negative.[102] Besides, the company was highly leveraged. Other factors taken into account were that the fishing industry was risky and that the company started losing market share well before the measures adopted by SUNAT.[103] That is why the tribunal considered that TSG's adjusted

---

[97] See *Tza Yap Shum v. Republic of Peru*, ICSID Case No. ARB/07/6, Award, 7 July 2011, para. 103.

[98] *Ibid.*, para.113.   [99] *Ibid.*, para.155.   [100] *Ibid.*, paras. 172, 177, and 210.

[101] *Ibid.*, para. 230.   [102] *Ibid.*, para. 262.   [103] *Ibid.*, paras. 264 and 265.

book value was a more appropriate method to determine the value of the company, and awarded the damages based on that value.[104]

4. Summary

The tribunal, especially in its Decision on Jurisdiction, referred to many of the issues that we mentioned in the first part of this chapter. Despite the lack of binding character of precedents in investment arbitration, we can draw some significant conclusions from the case.

Chinese BITs will most certainly protect Chinese nationals, regardless of their place of residence. This fact could become important if we take into consideration the high number of Chinese nationals residing over-seas. Even more significant, structuring investments through companies incorporated in other countries would not exclude Chinese investors from the protection of Chinese BITs, though that possibility would depend on the drafting of the treaty. These two points altogether, afford Chinese investors a great deal of protection under those treaties.

As for the interpretation of restrictive dispute resolution clauses, it must be noted that the tribunal really forced the interpretation of Article 8 of the BIT, and somehow disregarded the parties' intentions to make a broad interpretation. Although the jurisprudence on this issue is not settled, we can point out that this case shows that even restrictive dispute resolution clauses can be interpreted in a wide manner, which means that investors under those older BITs may have more access to dispute resolution under those treaties that initially expected. In this respect, tribunals could decide not only on the amount of compensation for expropriation, but also on its existence and legality. It seems quite unlikely that tribunals will extend their jurisdiction to matters other than expropriations, solely based on the most-favored-nation clause. Hence, the restrictions established in older BITs may actually limit investors' possibilities in investment arbitration claims. Nonetheless, in this case, that position was based on the exact wording of the China–Peru BIT, which may differ from that in many BITs.

IV.   Enforcement issues in the Chinese legal system and IIAs

The Chinese legal system has certain known flaws, especially regarding the enforcement of judgments and arbitral awards. IIAs

---

[104] *Ibid.*, para. 273.

could offer investors certain mechanisms to address such enforcement problems. The first question that arises is whether judgments or arbitral awards actually fall under the protection of IIAs. In this respect, jurisprudence has been quite unanimous in answering the question in an affirmative way. Tribunals considered that when an award refers to a contract or some other right that falls under the scope of the IIAs, then the award is part of that original investment and is therefore protected by the IIA. In *White Industries v. India*, for example, the tribunal affirmed that the original contract that led to an ICC arbitration was an investment covered by the Australia–India BIT (1999),[105] and that the rights under the ICC award were part of that contract, as they were "a crystallization of its rights under the contract."[106] Similar approaches were adopted in *Mondev v. US*[107] and *Chevron et al. v. Ecuador*.[108] In short, we can say that there is certain unanimity in investment arbitration in considering arbitral awards protected under IIAs, provided that they refer to an investment covered by them.

Once it has been established that an award can be an investment, the second question is how an IIA can be infringed by a state when an award is not duly enforced. An analysis of existing cases shows three main standards that must be considered: denial of justice, expropriation and effective means standard.

1. Denial of justice

Protection against denial of justice is a principle of international law. As for investment law, it has been included in the fair and equitable treatment standard.[109] As far as China is concerned, it could be particularly relevant to point out that the denial of justice can be produced by excessive judicial delays, also regarding enforcement of awards. Some Chinese IIAs expressly mention the protection against denial of justice as part of the fair and equitable treatment standard.

---

[105] *White Industries Australia Limited* v. *Republic of India*, Ad Hoc tribunal, Award, November 30, 2011, para. 7.4.19.
[106] *Ibid.*, para. 7.6.10.
[107] *Mondev International Ltd.* v. *United States*, ICSID Case No. ARB (AJ)/99/2, Award, October 11, 2002.
[108] *Chevron Corporation and Texaco Petroleum Company* v. *Ecuador*, Partial Award on the Merits, March 30, 2010.
[109] See Schill, 'Tearing Down the Great Wall,' 105.

For example, Article 143, paragraph 2 of the China–New Zealand FTA states that "fair and equitable treatment includes the obligation to ensure that, having regard to general principles of law, investors are not denied justice or treated unfairly or inequitably in any legal or administrative proceeding affecting the investments of the investor."[110] A similar provision can be found in the China–Peru FTA.[111] Since almost all Chinese IIAs contain an exception to most-favored-nation treatment relative to customs unions and FTAs, it will be difficult for investors not covered by the China–New Zealand or China–Peru FTAs to take advantage of them. Having said that, it is somehow unanimously accepted that the protection against denial of justice is part of the fair and equitable treatment, which is included in almost all Chinese IIAs.

It should be noted that this is a really stringent standard. In *Chevron et al. v. Ecuador* the tribunal explained that "the test for establishing a denial of justice sets … a high threshold."[112] In order to determine whether judicial delays may lead to denial of justice, several elements must be taken into account. In *White Industries v. India*, for instance, the tribunal mentioned "the complexity of the proceedings, the need for swiftness, the behavior of the litigants involved, the significance of the interest at stake and the behavior of the courts themselves."[113] The specific analysis of those elements should show some degree of bad faith, or "egregious conduct that shocks or at least surprises a sense of judicial propriety."[114]

Clear proof of the difficulty of invoking denial of justice can be seen in *White Industries v. India*. In that case, the investor spent nine years trying to enforce an arbitral award without success. The tribunal admitted that the Indian courts were undoubtedly inefficient, but found that there was no bad faith or such serious shortcoming to consider it a case of denial of justice.[115] An interesting remark made by the tribunal, which could become useful for China, was that it should take into account the fact that India is a developing country, with 1.2 billion people and a "seriously overstretched judiciary."[116]

---

[110] China–New Zealand FTA (2009), Chapter 11 'Investment,' art. 143, para. 2.
[111] China–Peru FTA (2010), Chapter 10 'Investment,' art. 132, para. 2 (c).
[112] *Chevron Corporation and Texaco Petroleum Company v. Ecuador*, Partial Award on the Merits, March 30, 2010, at para. 244. In similar terms, see *White Industries v. India*.
[113] See *White Industries v. India*, para. 10.4.10.
[114] *Ibid.*, para. 10.4.23.   [115] *Ibid.*   [116] *Ibid.*, para. 10.4.18.

2. Expropriation

If an arbitral award is considered part or continuation of an investment, as we have already seen, we might also wonder if it is covered by protection against expropriation. It may be quite difficult to find a direct expropriation of an arbitral award, i.e., a case in which the state directly assumes the title of the award. Nevertheless, it is possible to cite cases in which the state deprives the investor of the rights under an arbitral award, which would constitute a measure tantamount to expropriation.

The award in *Saipem v. Bangladesh* is of particular importance.[117] In the context of an ICC arbitration between Saipem, an Italian company, and Petrobangla, the latter filed an action in the court of Dhaka requesting the court to revoke the authority of the ICC tribunal due to arbitrator misconduct and violation of Petrobangla's procedural rights. The Dhaka court granted the motion and revoked the authority of the ICC tribunal. Besides, Petrobangla obtained several injunctions restraining Saipem from continuing with the ICC arbitration. The ICC tribunal, however, did not stop the proceedings and finally reached a decision in favor of Saipem. After the award, Petrobangla requested the High Court Division of the Supreme Court of Bangladesh to set aside the award. The Court refused such request considering that the ICC award was rendered without authority and against the injunctions issued by Bangladeshi courts. Therefore, it was an inexistent award according to Bangladeshi law, and could neither be enforced nor set aside.

Saipem started an ICSID arbitration alleging the violation of the Italy–Bangladesh BIT. From Saipem's point of view, the ICC award should be considered part of its investment and the decisions by Bangladeshi courts illegally deprived Saipem of its rights under the ICC award. The ICSID tribunal maintained that the ICC arbitration had its seat in Dhaka and so Bangladeshi law was applicable and its courts had supervisory jurisdiction over the ICC award. However, the Bangladeshi courts had exceeded their supervisory function by revoking the arbitrators' authority without justification, since there was no proof of error or misconduct. The tribunal found that the ICC award was virtually unenforceable due to the decisions taken by the Bangladeshi courts, which implied a substantial deprivation of Saipem's rights, equivalent to an expropriation.

In *White Industries v. India*, a similar argument was made by the plaintiff, who alleged that the undue delay of the enforcement of its ICC

---

[117] See *Saipem v. Bangladesh*.

award by the Indian courts was conduct tantamount to expropriation. In its award, the tribunal rejected this argument. According to the tribunal, since the award was not set aside but was pending for enforcement, the substantial deprivation of the investor's rights had not actually occurred.[118] Nonetheless, the tribunal admitted that if the ICC award were to be set aside, it could eventually lead to an expropriation claim.

This kind of approach can be particularly risky for China for many reasons. First, almost all Chinese BITs contain expropriation clauses. Second, the vast majority of Chinese IIAs also agree to the settlement of disputes regarding expropriation claims in investment arbitration, as we have already observed. Therefore, Chinese IIAs provide both for the substantive and procedural mechanisms to file complaints based on uncompensated expropriation.

3. Efficient means standard

The efficient means standard is a less popular but powerful standard that has been quite recently been invoked successfully by investors in *Chevron et al.* v. *Ecuador* and *White Industries* v. *India*. This standard is found in some IIAs, in which states agree to provide investors with effective means of asserting claims and enforcing rights with respect to investments.[119] In both cases, the tribunals found that this standard was less stringent than denial of justice, and that possible defenses such as systemic problems of the courts or lack of bad faith have less weight in the court's decision, because the state made a specific compromise in the BIT to permit enforcement of rights, so it would not be reasonable to rely on its own faults to deny such enforcement. Both tribunals denied the existence of denial of justice, but found that the states had breached the effective means standard. As we can see, this standard can be of great help for investors against undue delays in judicial proceedings or lack of timely enforcement in China, not only related to arbitral awards, but also to other rights, such as intellectual property rights.

An analysis of numerous Chinese IIAs,[120] reveals that just one Chinese IIA contains such a standard, namely the China–United Arab Emirates

---

[118] See *White Industries* v. *India*, para. 12.3.6
[119] For example, India–Kuwait BIT (2001), art. 4 (5); and US–Ecuador BIT (1993), art. II (7).
[120] The study included all those treaties referred to in note 11 (above), which were available in English.

BIT, which states that "each Contracting State shall in accordance with its laws and regulations provide effective means of asserting claims and enforcing rights with respect to investments."[121] The wording is identical to the first part of the Kuwait–India BIT's provision applied in *White Industries v. India*.[122] The inclusion of the effective means standard in the China–United Arab Emirates BIT, combined with the most-favored-nation clause contained in most Chinese IIAs, can become extremely useful for foreign investors in China, as a means of seeking relief when they face serious obstacles to enforcing their rights in Chinese courts. As we have already mentioned, this standard is less tight than the protection against denial of justice, and can be invoked even without need to prove an expropriation.

Another relevant provision is that of Article 5 of the China–Australia BIT, which determines that

> a Contracting Party shall in accordance with its law: (a) provide nationals of the other Contracting Party who have made investments within its territory ... full access to its competent judicial or administrative bodies in order to afford means of asserting claims and enforcing rights in respect of disputes with its own nationals; (b) permit its nationals to select means of their choice to settle disputes relating to investments and activities associated with investments with the nationals of the other Contracting Party, including arbitration conducted in a third country; and (c) provide for the recognition and enforcement of any resulting judgment or awards.

This article proclaims that investors should be granted full access to competent judicial or administrative bodies so as to assert claims and enforce their rights. Although the reference to 'effective means' is not mentioned, it would be difficult to maintain that access to judicial or administrative bodies does not mean that such access must provide effective means of making claims and enforcing rights, because that interpretation would render the whole provision completely meaningless.

---

[121] China–United Arab Emirates (1994), art. 2, para. 8.
[122] Article 4, para. (5) of the India–Kuwait BIT (2001) establishes that "Each Contracting State shall in accordance with its applicable laws and regulations provide effective means of asserting claims and enforcing rights with respect to investments and ensure to investors of the other Contracting State, the right of access to its courts of justice, administrative tribunals and agencies, and all other bodies exercising adjudicatory authority, and the right to employ persons of their choice, for the purpose of the assertion of claims and the enforcement of rights with respect to their investments."

Why would somebody start a judicial or administrative proceeding if such is not assumed to be an effective way to protect their rights?

As far as judgments or awards are concerned, paragraph (c) is completely clear in establishing that contracting parties ought to provide for its recognition and enforcement. This means that the Chinese government has assumed an undisputable commitment to grant enforcement, and any undue restriction or obstacle found by investors in Chinese courts to obtain it can lead to a BIT breach by China, which could trigger dispute resolution mechanisms under those IIAs. We consider that Article 5 of the China–Australia BIT can be invoked by investors from other countries other than Australia, based on most-favored-nation clauses included in their IIAs with China.

4. Summary

Enforcement problems and improper interventions have been considered some of the main deficiencies of China's legal system. The cases we analyzed provide a basis for investors to challenge those problems by resorting to investment arbitration. Protection against denial of justice and expropriation are available in most Chinese IIAs and can be useful for foreign investors. Although both are relatively stringent standards, expropriation allows investors to access international arbitration under most Chinese IIAs, and therefore should not be neglected.

Moreover, the most important findings come from the China–United Arab Emirates and the China–Australia BITs. The first includes a typical effective means standard clause and the second also establishes China's commitment to provide for recognition and enforcement of judgments and awards. These two provisions, combined with most-favored-nation clauses included in numerous Chinese IIAs, give foreign investors a solid ground to start claims against China when they find unjustified obstacles to such enforcement.

V. Conclusion

Foreign investors have only exceptionally relied on China's IIAs in order to settle their investment disputes, despite the fact that China has one of the most extensive – but fragmented – IIAs networks in the world. The evolution of China's investment treaty practice no longer justifies that conduct. IIAs offer an interesting level of protection to foreign investors in China, who should start taking advantage of that.

As for investor-state dispute resolution, older Chinese BITs contain certain limitations and the possibility of avoiding them is not at all clear in the present state of discussions over the interpretation of restrictive dispute resolution clauses and the possible application of most-favored-nation clauses to dispute resolution ones. However, there is enough jurisprudence to have at least a little hope that those limitations could be overcome, especially where reliance on the wording of the dispute resolution clause is possible. When an investor is trapped and cannot seek relief by other means, there may yet be hope. Furthermore, almost half of Chinese IIAs nowadays contain broad dispute resolution clauses, so investors can easily avoid limitations by structuring their investment in such a way that they come within the scope of one of the newer IIAs.

IIAs could also become extremely important when Chinese authorities resist or somehow affect the enforcement of investors' rights arising from arbitral awards or judgments. In limited cases, where such governmental action leads to denial of justice or expropriation, investors will find reasonable protection contained in Chinese IIAs, since almost all of them provide both for fair and equitable treatment standard and for protection against expropriation. In the latter, access to international arbitration is usually granted. Finally, the most significant protection is given by those clauses contained in the China–United Arab Emirates and the China–Australia BITs, which provide for an effective means standard and ascertain China's obligation to recognize and enforce judgments and awards, respectively. Extended to other investors by means of the most-favored-nation clauses included in most Chinese IIAs, those provisions give investors an important course of action when Chinese courts unduly refuse recognition and enforcement of judgments and awards.

In conclusion, dispute resolution clauses diverge in their content, leading to the 'internal fragmentation' of foreign investment protection in China. Most of them contain certain limitations, but this fact does not justify the existence of a "China disequilibrium," as such. Foreign investors have numerous ways to protect their investments under Chinese IIAs and access international investment arbitration if necessary. They can even use these treaties to fight many of the well-known flaws of the Chinese judicial system, such as enforcement issues. Such protection can be achieved especially from the diversity of Chinese BITs and from the effect of the most-favored-nation treatment established in most of them. Hence, fragmentation becomes a problem and a solution at the same time. That is why investors should start taking advantage of these treaties and the protection they offer.

15

A post-global economic crisis issue:
development, agriculture, 'land grabs,'
and foreign direct investment

ANTOINE MARTIN

I. Introduction

Following the 2008 food crisis, sovereign and private investors have engaged in a race for land acquisition and food production, especially in Eastern Africa and Eastern Europe where significant areas of land have been made available. As a result of a drop in food stocks and a mechanical rise in food prices, capital owners have increasingly thought of agriculture as a means to invest in speculative deals while worldwide land development has significantly emerged as a long-term business opportunity. As a result, many land-rich developing countries in need of capital nowadays seem to favor leasing land to foreign investors instead of developing food production schemes for domestic and export purposes. This phenomenon – involving the interface between investment law and the international economic regulation of agricultural production and trade – is extremely difficult to quantify,[1] but is

The author would like to thank Mulugeta M. Ayalew, Research Fellow at the African Climate Policy Centre of the UN Economic Commission for Africa for his participation to the early draft of this work. The author is also grateful to Belachew Fikre, lecturer at Addis Ababa University Centre for Human Rights and East African Research Fellow, British Institute in Eastern Africa for his critical and constructive feedback and for the numerous discussions throughout.

[1] Guesstimates vary significantly. The Land Coalition concluded that 50–60 million hectares might have been traded as of 2010. See for instance J. Vidal, 'How food and water are driving a 21st-century African land grab,' *Observer* (7 March 2010), http://goo.gl/gniw (accessed September 2012); the Landportal database also documented more than 1,000 land deals accounting for 58.5 million hectares (2000–10), http://landportal.info/land-matrix; Cotula however suggested that figures for 2004–9 might have been much lower than those suggested by Media reports, even using top-end figures (L. Cotula, 'Land Deals in Africa: What Is in the Contracts?', International Institute for Environment and Development, 12 March 2011). The International Food Policy Research Institute similarly

356

increasingly commented on in NGO and press reports where large-scale foreign investment projects in agriculture are frequently denounced as neo-colonial 'land grabs' and criticized for their effects on water and food security, biodiversity protection, jobs, and population expulsions.[2]

In addition to their widely documented controversial impact on populations and the environment, foreign investment in land development also constitutes a new trend in international economic relations and international economic law. This is one characteristic of the period following the global crisis which host states seem unable to regulate.

On the one hand, governments facing rocketing food prices have started being involved in transnational food production schemes aimed at bypassing unaffordable international food markets. In doing so, they have not only pushed developing economies to rely on foreign capital as the engine of their agricultural development policies; they have also initiated a radical shift in the way food production is transferred from producers to consumers. On the other hand, this evolution in transnational economic relations is making waves in contemporary international economic law because of potential conflict with current investment and trade rules. Given the increasing nature of food security and climate change concerns, long-term investment projects falling under the international investment protection framework might, at some point, lead to significant clashes between foreign investors entitled to stability rights under customary international law and host states in need of productive lands, productive capacity, and food stocks for their basic survival. In addition to potentially numerous international arbitration claims, attempts by various governments to avoid traditional food markets might also lead to significant disputes under WTO law principles aiming at facilitating, liberalizing, and increasing international trade. In practice, it looks as if new categories of import substitution measures aimed at bypassing international trade channels have replaced

suggested that between 15 and 20 million of hectares, amounting to one-fifth of the EU's farmland, might have been subject to transactions worth US$20–30 billion since 2006 ('Buying farmland abroad: outsourcing's third wave,' *The Economist* (London, May 21, 2009)), http://goo.gl/KPf9i (accessed September 2012).

2 See for instance http://farmlandgrab.org or the Landportal map available at http://landportal.info/landmatrix. For major contributions, see C. Smaller and H. Mann, 'A Thirst for Distant Lands: Foreign Investment in Agricultural Land and Water,' International Institute for Sustainable Development, May 2009, 1; L. Cotula, 'Land Grab or Development Opportunity? International Farmland Deals in Africa,' 8 (June 22, 2009) *Columbia FDI Perspectives*; Cotula, 'Land Deals in Africa: What Is in the Contracts?'

the red-flagged export substitution policies devised in the 1960s and 1970s to develop domestic capacity building.

This chapter briefly summarizes the various criticisms formulated against foreign investments in agriculture (section II) before considering why developing countries suffering from hunger problems, including being dependent on food aid – especially in Africa – are making thousands of hectares available to foreign investors while they could in theory initiate agricultural policies on their own and use their land to produce food (section III.1). The chapter then considers the trend's future potential impact in terms of international economic law, particularly against the backdrop of the fragmented regimes of international economic law (section III.2), and concludes by examining the argument that this trend amounts to a form of neo-colonialism (section IV).

II.   Questioning current practices

Foreign investments in land and agriculture are widely commented upon and documented in the media. Therefore, it is relevant to briefly summarize the main criticisms formulated against them at this stage, and to focus on legal issues in the next section.

The impact on local food and water security of land development projects by foreign investors are controversial. Although it is suggested that large investments in agriculture could help to increase worldwide cereal production by 10 to 18 percent,[3] many commentators for instance fear that the ability of most investors to repatriate crops to their home markets might not guarantee that local populations will ever benefit from potential food stock increases.[4] Some furthermore argue that new

---

[3] *The Economist*, 'Buying farmland abroad.'

[4] Some data for instance suggest that Sudan allowed foreign investors to repatriate 70 percent of their production (*ibid.*). NGOs for instance suspect that rice produced in Mali, Liberia, and Mozambique was destined to Libyan markets (S. Haidara, 'Interview with Amadou Kante dit Bany', Representative of the Libya Africa Investment Portfolio and Charge de mission for the Presidency of the Republic of Mali, translated from French – Les investissements libyens sont une aubaine pour le Mali L'independant (May 15, 2008), http://goo.gl/WH9KW (accessed September 2012); 840,000 hectares leases signed in favor of Egyptian firms for the production of wheat and maize might have been fully sent to Cairo ('Seized! The 2008 Land Grab for Food and Financial Security,' GRAIN Briefing, October 2008), http://goo.gl/pqR2q. Allegedly, the produce from the 20,000 hectares of Mauritius-owned land in Mozambique were similarly exported to the home state ('The New Farm Owners: Corporate Investors Lead the Rush for Control Over Overseas Farmland,' GRAIN, October 2009), http://goo.gl/zbxmH (accessed September 2012). The produce of a 80,400-hectare Chinese deal in Russia were partly returned to China

agricultural methods developed for large-scale farming could have a significant impact on local producers since the increasing recourse to hybrid seeds (deemed more productive) could be incompatible with traditional farming methods.[5] Palm oil and biofuel production is criticized for destroying biodiversity while diverting significant amounts of crops from local populations.[6]

The use of land for mining purposes is denounced for confiscating large spaces previously used by local populations and generating intense blasting and vibration while increasing waste abandon, which in turn endangers people's access to land and pollutes water.[7]

Water is in fact a major area for discussion, if only because the right given to foreigners to exploit "unused" lands tends to give them privileged access to water resources described as a "water grab."[8]

The low rent – or absence of rent – paid by foreign investors to host states is an additional ground of criticism.[9] A possible explanation for

as well (A. Bokhari, 'Buying Foreign Land for Food Security,' DAWN Media Group, December 15, 2008), http://goo.gl/zoRF4 (accessed September 2012).

[5] A. Martin and M. M. Ayalew, 'Acquiring Land Abroad for Agricultural Purposes: "Land Grab" or "Agri-Fdi?,"' Report of the Surrey International Law Centre and Environmental Regulatory Research Group, Surrey Law Working Papers, 08/2011, March 2011, 1.1; 'Rice Land Grabs Undermine Food Sovereignty in Africa,' GRAIN, January 2009, 3, http://goo.gl/VydDu (accessed September 2012); 'Mauritius Leads Land Grabs for Rice in Mozambique,' GRAIN, September 2009, http://goo.gl/a1CLN (accessed September 2012); the argument is however questioned. Ikisan, a think-tank specialized in agricultural technologies notes that hybrids are at best to achieve food sufficiency, and China – where rice production was increased nearly by 200 million tons from 1976–1991– is given as an example (www.ikisan.com). The FAO and the UNDP similarly emphasize the ability of hybrid rice seeds to yield about 15–20 percent more than the best varieties (*Hybrid Rice for Food Security* (FAO, 2004)).

[6] For instance, the EU's commitment to produce 10 percent of its energy through biofuel by 2015 implies that 17.5 million hectares of land could be diverted from food production In fact, European companies might have already negotiated 3.9 million of hectares for this purposes (Martin and Ayalew, 'Acquiring Land Abroad,' 1.1 and 2.2).

[7] Because of their structuring role, international financial organizations are also criticized. See for instance the Iduapriem mine scandal, co-developed with the IFC (World Bank branch) which holds US$2.5 million in the mine and has provided about 45 million in loans since 1990s to the mine ('Ghana: Gold Mining Company Cuts off More than 700 People from Their Farms (FIAN, January 2010)).

[8] Some for instance question the granting of priorities in water allocations to investors in seasons when the general level of the Niger River is low ('Rice Land Grabs Undermine Food Sovereignty in Africa,' 2). As Nestlé's chairman emphasized, land deals "weren't about land, but water, for with the land comes the right to withdraw the water linked to it, in most countries essentially a freebie that increasingly could be the most valuable part of the deal," (*The Economist*, 'Buying farmland abroad').

[9] Data indicate important differences in land price from one country to another. Ethiopian land could for instance be negotiated from US$1–10 (135 birr) per hectare per year but

this is that virtually non-existent costs for the use of the land could allow foreigners investing more money in African land or exploiting more hectares with optimized funding.[10] Nothing indicates, however, that the cash flows invested in making the land productive genuinely benefit the economy: if part of the investment was used to acquire the necessary equipments in the home states, the capital effectively directed toward the host would indeed be sensibly reduced.

The losses suffered by inhabitants and local people are often considerable, yet difficult to assess in financial terms. In the absence of formal records in many countries, it is indeed generally complicated to identify which land is owned or used and to determine to what extent populations may be dispossessed from their property: while investors claim that the land is unused – either because it is vacant, under-utilized and uncultivated or because it is under the control of the host government[11] – issues arise in relation to land tenure because the right to use the land is often transferred in a customary fashion without any formal registry in place.[12]

some deals might not require any rent (Vidal, 'How food and water are driving'); X. Rice, 'Ethiopia – country of the silver sickle – offers land dirt cheap to farming giants. Addis Ababa sells vast fertile swaths to international companies in effort to introduce large-scale commercial agriculture,' *Guardian* (January 15, 2010), http://goo.gl/i4Z7R (accessed September 2012). Cotula similarly notes that rents from US$2–$13 might be paid in Africa but suggests that the rent paid for the land does not help establish whether a deal is fair, if only because local market values may vary ('Land Deals in Africa,' 24). Although the land value in Ethiopia is below US$100 per hectare, the average land value in Africa is US$800–1,000, much lower than in Europe where hectares can be worth US$18,000 (UK) or US$22,000 (Germany) (K. Hunt, 'Africa investment sparks land grab fear,' *BBC News* (5 August, 2009), http://goo.gl/Lkqer; 'Land prices in Africa,' Biopact (September 15, 2006), http://goo.gl/ifTVc

[10] For instance, a 500,000-hectare development project in Ethiopia allegedly created 10,000 jobs and generated US$2 billion in investments (Vidal, 'How food and water are driving'). For a similar argument, see 'Land Deals in Africa.'

[11] Ethiopian government officials for instance defend their foreign investment policies by arguing (1) that vast reserves of land (i.e. about 80 percent) are underdeveloped or underexploited and (2) that the land allocated to foreign investors only represents a minority 3–4 percent of the available land. Thus, 60 million hectares of the country's 74 million hectares suitable for agriculture are allegedly not cultivated (Rice, 'Ethiopia – country of the silver sickle').

[12] Two to 10 percent of the land would be privately held in Africa, the rest is customarily held in commons (K. Sharife, 'Africa: Land Grabs – New "Resource Curse"?,' Norwegian Council for Africa, December 1, 2009), http://goo.gl/DOUcm (accessed September 2012). Thus, NGOs claim that unused lands are not desert but used to graze livestock or deliberately left fallow, so that "there is no land in Ethiopia that has no owners and users" (Vidal, 'How food and water are driving'). The IIED adds that most developing countries have no sufficient mechanisms to protect their people's rights, so that local communities are generally unable to oppose their governments' policies (Sharife, 'Africa: Land Grabs')

Large agriculture development projects furthermore tend to cause significant forest destruction which is not without consequences since these generate a wide range of non-timber forest products generally consumed at the household level and have an important cultural and symbolic value to local populations.[13] Finally, many commentators denounce significant and recurrent population displacement/resettlement as well as the inability of host governments to provide populations with acceptable solutions.[14]

III. Trends in contemporary political economy and potential international economic law issues

The questionable aspects of land deals by worldwide investors are largely available in media reports and thus do not merit further comment here. What seems interesting, however, is to understand (1) why host governments do get involved in land trading instead of putting in place domestic agricultural and land policies capable of generating economic and social development on local, domestic, and regional scales; and (2) what impact such policies may have in terms of international economic law. Section III.1, therefore, attempts to clarify why host authorities in various countries would in practice rely on foreign investment in land as the engine of their domestic development policies in relation to agriculture, employment, or poverty reduction. Section III.2 looks at the potential legal issues surrounding this trend.

---

[13] It is estimated that forests might cover at least 45 percent of arable lands (FAO Economic and Social Development Department, *World Agriculture: Towards 2015/2030: An FAO Perspective* referring to Alexandratos (1995) (London: Earthscan, 2003); J. Falconer, *The Major Significance of 'Minor' Forest Products: The Local Use and Value of Forests in the West African Humid Forest Zone* (FAO, Rome 1990); as some research notes, "hundreds of millions of people in Sub-Saharan Africa obtain a major share of their subsistence from a large and diverse set of forest products, even though the work to gather them is not their main economic activity. Of these people, an estimated fifteen million earn some cash income from forest-related activities. Rural Africans use plants and animals from natural forests and woodlands as well as planted trees for food, energy, medicine, fodder, housing, furniture, baskets, mats, dyes . . . they also use them for windbreaks and to reduce erosion, restore soil fertility, pollinate crops, control weeks, pests and diseases and maintain water quality' (T. Oksanen, B. Pajari, and T. Tuomasjukka, 'Forests in Poverty Reduction Strategies: Capturing the Potential,' EFI Proceedings, 2003).

[14] As many as 25,000 villages might have been dislocated due to a Qatari project in Pakistan (Bokhari, 'Buying Foreign Land').

1. Leasing land rather than producing: the new trend

Reliance on international markets is commonly used to satisfy domestic
needs, but the idea of generating development by leasing land to foreigners instead of developing agricultural sectors for local and export use
seems relatively new. Many countries have actually made this choice,
especially in Africa where the demand for agricultural land (by private
and sovereign investors alike) is high and increasing. Such demand,
indeed, provides an opportunity to optimize the use of apparently unused
areas of arable land, while offering a major opportunity to modernize
agricultural production and escape subsistence agriculture.

On the one hand, it is regularly said that African states (among other
developing countries) have immense areas of land not currently used
productively. FAO research conducted since the 1970s for instance
suggests that less than 19 and 30 percent of land was used in Latin
American and sub-Saharan Africa respectively in 1997–1999. By contrast, 60–94 percent of the land was used in Asia and North Africa/Near
East.[15] Thus, African land represents a significant opportunity for countries lacking agricultural space and productive capacity. On the other
hand, African countries have long relied on subsistence agriculture at the
household level for the day-to-day survival of important populations, but
this self-sufficiency-based model has not brought prosperity and comfort
to farmers. Offer and demand for food products as well as the added
value per farmer on the local market are low in the subsistence-based
model and the contribution of agriculture to supporting the economy at
the local and domestic levels is thus limited. At the domestic level,
moreover, subsistence agriculture tends to act as a barrier against trade
exchanges because production is not sufficient to allow food exports.[16] As
a result, many governments which have long failed to develop medium or
large-scale agricultural sectors are increasingly perceiving the quest for
arable land as a unique opportunity to generate economic growth by

[15] The exact estimate is 63–94 percent in Asia, 87 percent in North Africa and the Near East.
The notion of 'land used' is not limited in this case to agricultural use but includes
manipulations to obtain material (cereals, livestock) and immaterial benefits (erosion
prevention) (H. George, *Statistics on Land Use* (FAO Land and Water Development
Division, 2003)).

[16] G. Meijerink and P. Roza, 'The Role of Agriculture in Economic Development, Markets,
Chains and Sustainable Development,' Strategy and Policy paper 4, http://goo.gl/wV350
(accessed September 2012). See also O. Cadot, L. Dutoit, and M. Olarreaga, 'Barriers to
Exit from Subsistence Agriculture,' CEPREMAP paper, June 2009, http://goo.gl/SILQx
(accessed September 2012).

multiplying food production, creating jobs, developing national demand for food, increasing exports and eventually creating new markets unreachable until then.

The idea of transforming subsistence agriculture into an industrial springboard generating employment and stimulating local and national economies has actually been considered by economists for decades. In the 1970s, Thorbecke for instance described the need to develop sophisticated "dual-economy models" in which growth depended on whether the agricultural and industrial sectors were sufficiently "interdependent" to escape small-scale farming and give domestic production access to international markets.[17] During the same period, economies in South America (such as Brazil) developed their agricultural sector with the objective of exporting food produce to international markets to restore equilibrium to their balance of payments.[18] First, a developed agricultural sector acted as a "saver of foreign exchange" when increased domestic production of food allowed limiting imports by substituting local goods for traded necessities. Two, agriculture also became a "provider of foreign exchange" when surpluses and tradable products became exportable on foreign markets.[19]

Surprisingly, current foreign investment in agriculture does not correspond to the industrialization trend of the 1960s and 1970s. Nowadays, some governments rather seem to favor the option of letting their land in exchange for economic compensation (in the form of low rents or large investments). At the same time, such governments refrain from developing their domestic industries.[20] A reason for this could be the difficulty

[17] E. Thorbecke, *The Role of Agriculture in Economic Development* (UMI, 1970), 4. For Meijerink and Roza, similarly, while subsistence models make employment dependent on small-size farming generating limited wealth, large-scale agriculture would therefore have the ability to increase employment by developing further industrial sectors, but it would also help developing national, regional, and local economies by permitting the import of value-added goods which cannot be normally produced domestically. Agriculture is thus described as "the key sector for nearly all poverty analysis" because trade liberalization affects the rural poverty through distribution, business profits, employment and wages, as well as by improving the government's fiscal position ('Role of Agriculture,' 2, 12).

[18] D. H. Graham, H. Gauthier, and J. R. Mendonça de Barros, 'Thirty Years of Agricultural Growth in Brazil: Crop Performance, Regional Profile, and Recent Policy Review,' *Economic Development and Cultural Change* 36 (1987), 1–34.

[19] Thorbecke, *Role of Agriculture in Economic Development*, 5.

[20] Commentators thus denounce an increasing contradiction between the offering of vast arable land to foreign investors and the persistent inability of some host states to ensure food and water security to their population. For instance, while the World Food Programme provided US$116 million worth 230,000 tonnes of food aid to Ethiopia

for hosts to fund land development and method-improvement policies. Most South American development policies in the 1960s, indeed, were largely financed through important subsidies which countries cannot afford at the moment,[21] especially in Africa where agriculture is under-developed as a result of years of disinvestment in agriculture.[22] Given that about US$1,500–2,000 might be needed to make 1 hectare of land profitable in Africa and Eastern Europe,[23] 'small' 20,000–50,000 hectares deals could require US$30–75 million in investment against US$150–600 million for larger 100,000–400,000-hectare deals. For governments, foreign investors and the increasing demand for land could therefore constitute essential assets in the move from subsistence agriculture to larger-scale farming and constitute key parts of the country's develop-ment strategy. As an official of the Ethiopian Agriculture Ministry puts it, "there is no crop that won't grow in Ethiopia but we cannot produce quantity and quality. Why? It's a vicious cycle of the lack of capital and technology," so that overall, "leasing land is a real opportunity."[24]

This inability of many developing states to finance costly activities is actually the reason why developing countries have long relied on foreign investors to set up large energy or telecommunications infrastructures

(2007–2011), the Ethiopian government concluded in parallel a US$100 million deal with Saudi Arabia to grow wheat, barley and rice eventually repatriated to Saudi Arabia's domestic markets (*The Economist*, 'Buying farmland abroad'). See also Vidal, "Ethiopia is one of the hungriest countries in the world with more than 13 million people needing food aid [but] paradoxically the government is offering at least 3m hectares of its most fertile land to rich countries and some of the world's most wealthy individuals to export food for their own populations" ('How Food and Water are Driving). Bokhari thus deplores that "instead of arranging food for its population, the government of Sudan was at some point discussing with Asian and Middle Eastern governments the opportun-ity to raise US$3 billion in exchange for millions of hectares in land concessions" ('Buying Foreign Land'). Some also question land-leasing practices in Cambodia and in Darfur where the World Food Programme respectively supports 100,000 families (US$35 mil-lion) and feeds 5.6 million refugees. For instance, deals for 690,000 and 400,000 hectares amounting to one-fifth of the Sudan's arable land are allegedly let to South Korea, the Emirates, and Egypt (*The Economist*, 'Buying farmland abroad'). Deals were also made in exchange for a US$600m. premium ('Seized! The 2008 Land Grab for Food and Financial Security,' 6).

[21] On the subsidization of South American development policies, see Graham, Gauthier, and de Barros, 'Thirty Years of Agricultural Growth,' 10.

[22] On disinvestments, see A. Spieldoch, 'Global Land Grab,' *Foreign Policy in Focus* (June 18, 2009), http://goo.gl/pSdvJ (accessed September 2012).

[23] A. Bakr, 'Interview – Gulf sovereign funds show interest in farmland fund,' Reuters (January 21, 2010), http://goo.gl/cuXjX (accessed September 2012).

[24] Rice, 'Ethiopia – country of the silver sickle.'

and the right to explore and exploit natural resources, either on their behalf or in exchange for a share in profits and production.[25] For instance, although Nigeria is oil rich, the country was recently described as being unable to finance the structures necessary to exploit and process oil and is thus known to import 70 percent of its related needs.[26]

The potential parallel markets and future contracts brought by foreign capital (such as roads, ports, and other infrastructures) could also explain why developing states increasingly trade land.[27] As the 2009 UNCTAD World Investment Report notes, openness to foreign capital is often promoted for increasing technology transfers, improving productive methods and skills, giving better access to credit and markets and improving the productivity of local industries and economies as a whole.[28] In theory, foreign capital could thus act as an alternative to traditional public financing and play an increasing role in infrastructure development,[29] especially since aid funds are not sufficient to cope with underdevelopment issues worldwide.[30] As a result, official comments suggest that Arab states' farming investments in Sudan were expected to raise from US$700 million in 2007 to US$7.5 billion in 2010,[31] while

---

[25] On the evolution of host governments involvement in oil exploitation agreements, see for instance C. Duval and others, 'International Petroleum Agreements – Politics, Oil Prices Steer Evolution of Deal Forms,' *Oil & Gas Journal*, http://goo.gl/sOqQb (accessed April 2012).

[26] See for instance Malgwi, 'Fraud as Economic Terrorism: The Efficacy of the Nigerian Economic and Financial Crimes Commission,' JFC 12 (2004).

[27] See for instance Spieldoch, 'Global Land Grab.'

[28] UNCTAD, *World Investment Report 2009: Transnational Corporations, Agricultural Production and Development* (New York and Geneva, 2009), xviii.

[29] UNCITRAL, *Legislative Guide on Privately Financed Infrastructure Projects* (Document A/CN9/SERB/4, New York, 2001), 56. FDIs are increasingly considered "as important as trade in terms of delivering goods and services to foreign markets [as well as in terms of] integrating developing states into the world economy" (Kwakwa, 'Institutional Perspectives on International Economic Law,' in A. Qureshi (ed.), *Perspectives in International Economic Law* (The Hague: Kluwer, 2002)); UNCTAD, *Global Investment Trends Monitor No. 1* (Second and Third Quarters of 2009, December 1, 2009); UNCTAD, *Best Practices in Investment for Development: How to Utilise FDI to Improve Infrastructure – Electricity – Lessons from Chile and New Zealand* (Document UNCTAD/DIAE/PCB/2009/1, Investment Advisory Series, Series B, No. 1, 2009); UNCTAD, *Best Practices in Investment for Development: How to Utilize FDI to Improve Transport Infrastructure – Roads – Australia and Peru* (Investment Advisory Series, Series B, No. 2, 2009).

[30] Governments provided US$120 billion in development aid in 2008, whereas worldwide FDI, at US$1.070 billion, were nine times higher (*That's Right! Corporate Responsibility for Human Rights: Concepts, Examples, Approaches. Summary Report* (January 21, 2010)).

[31] *The Economist*, 'Buying farmland abroad.'

important deals with Chinese investors were officially justified by technologies transfer negotiations, workforce training schemes, infrastructure constructions, access to development funds, and research programs.[32] The Libyan LIA fund's project in Mali was also presented as part of a gigantic investment scheme encompassing oil and gas equipment, hotel resorts, canal enlargements, multiple local infrastructures, and local banking, while a deal for 2.47 million hectares of land was reportedly concluded against oil and gas contracts.[33]

2. Economic law issues

In addition to being a new phenomenon in international economic relations, large-scale foreign investments in agriculture – in their current shape – are also worth considering for their potential impact in terms of contemporary economic law.

Disputes relating to recent deals have not been witnessed yet, but land investments have generated disputes in the past and could well lead to significant investment treaty arbitrations in the future. It is worth recalling at this stage that transnational investment projects are generally set up under specific frameworks offering stability guarantees to foreign capital owners and which could prevent host governments from reclaiming land and water stocks in the future.

On the one hand, bilateral investment treaties (BITs) grant foreign investors the benefit of internationally recognized standards of treatment guaranteeing that investors shall enjoy the benefit of their investments at all times and be protected against expropriations.[34] In particular,

---

[32] 'Seized! The 2008 Land Grab for Food and Financial Security,' 3; *The Economist*, 'Buying farmland abroad.'

[33] Martin and Ayalew, 'Acquiring Land Abroad,' 1.1.b; S. Haidara, 'Interview with Amadou Kante dit Bany.'

[34] "Relative" and "absolute" standards adapt various principles of customary international law attached to the treatment and protection of aliens into an FDI-specific set of rules also known as *lex specialis*. For instance, states may grant foreign investors the benefit of minimum standards deemed higher than local standards, "National" and "Most Favoured Nation" treatments guaranteeing that foreign capitals will be treated 'no less favourably' than domestic or third-state investors, due process of law guarantees, the right to a Fair and Equitable treatment, the right not to be expropriated in an inappropriate manner, transparency guarantees, free transfer of funds rights, full protection and security or the right to benefit from dispute settlement mechanisms at the international level. See for instance I. Brownlie, *Principles of Public International Law* (7th edn, Oxford University Press, 2008), 525. For a complete survey of the various standards of treatment see for

"prompt, adequate, and effective" compensation is commonly recognized as a legal requirement of a lawful expropriation under public international law (from which investment treaties and standards are derived), which generally admits that "reparation must, as far as possible, wipe out all the consequences of the illegal act and re-establish the situation which would, in all probability, have existed if the act had not been committed."[35] On the other hand, specific investment contracts known as host-government agreements (HGAs) may also provide specific arrangements negotiated between foreign investors and host authorities.[36] In addition to the technical details, these tend to reiterate at a contractual level non-expropriation guarantees, the granting of jurisdiction to international arbitral tribunals (should any dispute arise between the investor and the host state) while providing various types of stability commitments deemed particularly constraining for host states.[37] For instance, various comments show that leasing contracts tend to grant foreign investors freehold rights over the land for extensive 99-year periods,[38] but stabilization clauses altering the contracting authorities' ability to unilaterally modify the existing economic, social, or environmental rules (freezing clauses), or at creating an obligation to compensate investors for changes in the economic equilibrium of the contract (economic balancing clauses) are another key feature of investment contracts.[39] Both types of arrangement are commonly relied upon (especially in large oil and gas or infrastructure

instance, *Bilateral Investment Treaties 1995–2006: Trends in Investment Rulemaking* (UNCTAD/ITE/IIA/2006/5 edn, 2007), 28ff.

[35] ILC Draft Articles on Responsibility of States for Internationally Wrongful Acts (2001), Article 31; on the definition of "prompt, adequate and effective" compensations, see Lowenfeld, *International Economic Law* (2nd edn, Oxford University Press, 2008), ch 15; on reparation and substitution, see also M. Shaw, *International Law* (6th edn, Cambridge University Press, 2008), 802; Brownlie, *Principles of Public International Law*, 436, 463–464; Sornarajah, *The International Law on Foreign Investment* (2nd edn, Cambridge University Press, 2007), 414–415, 447. On the Hull formula, see Brownlie, *Principles of Public International Law*, 533; R. Wallace and O. Martin-Ortega, *International Law* (6th edn, London: Sweet & Maxwell, 2009), 213; C. Yannaca-Small, 'Indirect Expropriation and the Right to Regulate in International Investment Law' (OECD Working Papers on international investments, September 2004).

[36] BIT standards adapt various principles of customary international law attached to the treatment and protection of aliens into a FDI-specific set of rules also known as a *lex specialis*. See for instance Brownlie *Principles of Public International Law*, 525.

[37] Cotula, 'Land Deals in Africa,' 23.

[38] Bakr, 'Interview – Gulf sovereign funds show interest in farmland fund.'

[39] A. Maniruzzaman, 'Damages for Breach of Stabilisation Clauses in International Investment Law: Where Do We Stand Today?,' 11–12 IELTR (2007) 11–12, 246.

projects spread over decades) and are perfectly legal under many investment laws. Thus, although contractual terms surrounding agricultural
investments are not available publicly, it is reasonable to suggest that
recourse to such contractual terms most likely takes place in practice.[40]
Investment rules would thus give significant protection to foreign capital
owners which can foster foreign investment, but they would also most
likely lead to investment disputes when, in time, host governments need to
recuperate their land for domestic food production purposes.

The point here is not to question the merits and legitimacy of investment protection standards. Rather, the question is whether the decision
of several host governments to allow large-scale foreign investment in
land is a major policy move which might become problematic if host
governments do not plan their land development programs carefully and
leave their development opportunities in the hands of foreign funds. For
instance, what would happen in a decade or two if, in a climate-changed
world, host countries (where agriculture depends on foreign capital)
faced food scarcity and had no choice but to interrupt agreements which
permit investors to use land to export significant quantities of crops to
foreign populations? As an investment tribunal recalled in 2009 in a
farmland-related case,[41] international standards regarding investment
protection would prevail over lawful domestic measures allowing land
dispossession[42] and would typically lead to recognizing any policy aimed
at taking land rights back as expropriation, thus forcing host governments to pay significant compensation equivalent to the genuine value
market value of the property (taking soil quality, production types, and
equipments into account) at the time of the dispossession.[43] In addition,
long-lasting contractual obligations might possibly prevent host states
from protecting their populations' interests in time. For instance, while
climate change could in the future force host governments to review their
food production policies to secure their populations' access to crops, food

---

[40] Cotula, 'Land Deals in Africa.'
[41] *Bernardus Henricus Funnekotter and others* v. *Republic of Zimbabwe* (*ICSID Case No.
Arb/05/6*) – *Award* [April 22, 2009], http://goo.gl/K7Dpg. It is important to mention that
the case did not relate to a matter of legitimate public policy but to violent and uncompensated expropriation following an invasion by nationals. In this case, the authorities
eventually enacted a law (the Rural Land Occupiers Act of 2001) protecting the invaders
and preventing domestic tribunals from ordering the recovery of the farms by their
owners. Nevertheless, the legal principles emphasized by the tribunal would typically
apply to any land investment dispute.
[42] *Ibid.*, paras. 103, 107.   [43] *Ibid.*, paras. 123, 130–132.

products, or water, the legal arrangements surrounding foreign investments in agriculture could become a source of dispute because interrupting a 99-year lease, even for public interest purposes, would most likely be in breach of contract breach, amounting to expropriation, and thus triggering compensation.

Large-scale investments in agriculture might alternatively have an impact in terms of international trade and could possibly lead to disputes under WTO law. Indeed, various sovereign or institutional investors have acknowledged being involved in foreign land development programs to avoid relying on international food markets. In particular, the Saudi Agriculture Minister seems to have admitted that food production and import schemes developed since 2008–2009 are aimed at compensating for declining domestic production following a decision to reduce domestic production in times of growing water scarcity.[44] Also, the King Abdullah Initiative for Saudi Agricultural Investment Abroad invested US$100 million in Ethiopia to raise wheat, barley, and rice to then be entirely repatriated to local markets.[45] In addition, these repatriation schemes are often characterized by a marked tendency to bring in a migrant workforce, thereby minimizing any involvement of the host's productive forces; some client countries attempt to transform their agricultural experiments abroad into a form of internationalized domestic food production.[46]

---

[44] *FAO Food Outlook Global Market Analysis* (June 2011). It was admitted that "the goal [was] to support supply of main goods which [could] not be produced locally like rice and sugar or which require[d] a lot of water in production like wheat, malt and fodder' as well as fish and livestock" (U. Laessing, 'Saudi Arabia Eyes Overseas Farmland Investments'), arabianbusinesscom (March 16, 2010), http://goo.gl/Edlir (accessed September 2012.

[45] *The Economist*, 'Buying farmland abroad.'

[46] India was for instance criticized for sending Indian farmers in Burma in order to grow crops shipped back afterwards ('Seized! The 2008 Fand Grab for Food and Financial Security,' 5). Similarly, although China denied having farmland investment projects abroad at all, Chinese corporations controlled by Chinese authorities might have set up large infrastructures and relied on Chinese farmers, workers and scientists to conduct agricultural work in Africa. See Martin and Ayalew, 'Acquiring Land Abroad,' 2.3(a). In Mozambique where US$800 million was invested to 'modernise' the local agriculture, China allegedly signed a memorandum of understanding allowing the settlement of 3,000 Chinese farmers, see 'Mauritius Leads Land Grabs for Rice in Mozambique.' Some also mention Chinese projects in Cameroon initiated in 2006 in which Chinese farmers constituted the essential workforce, although day-to-day local farmers subjected to strict working conditions were used for "assistance" (C. Nforgang, 'Chinois au Cameroun: une incompréhension foncière,' Syfia Info (December 18, 2009), http://goo.gl/0qkDO (accessed September 2012). An article by *The Economist* overall estimates that one million Chinese farmers might have been sent to Africa around 2010 ('Buying farmland abroad').

As a result, one might question whether large-scale foreign investments in agriculture which take the form of institutional schemes deliberately established to avoid reliance on international food markets are
compatible with current rules on international trade. In particular, it is
difficult to say whether the current trend relies on traditional import and
export trade transactions or whether the notions of growing and taking
could be more adequate. According to the *Collins English Dictionary*,
"trade" refers to the "buying" and "selling" of goods and services, while
the notions of import and export similarly imply a "sale" of goods and
services to a foreign country. Official WTO documentation similarly
emphasizes that goods or services are being traded, exported, or imported
when economic relations occur between residents and non-residents,
which would thus characterize "trade" as a matter of balance of payments.[47] In practice, however, land development and production
schemes involving foreign institutional investors appear to be based upon
the more or less total autonomy of the visiting state (providing capital,
seeds, equipment, workforce, and repatriating food products) together
with the minimum involvement of the host, serving as a mere investment
platform. Interpreting South Korea's farmland expansion abroad, the
Korea Times thus suggested that the country no longer "import[ed]"
food grown overseas but rather rendered foreign lands "effectively
Korean" thereby practicing "agricultural imperialism."[48]

The 'imperialism' argument requires to be considered cautiously, but it
seems realistic to suggest that the economic model might, in such
circumstances, constitute an externalized form of domestic production
aiming at overriding international trade dependencies. Therefore, while
the Marrakesh Declaration clearly emphasizes that states parties under
the WTO regime ought "not to take any trade measures that would
undermine or adversely affect" the results of the negotiations promoting
trade liberalization and a progressively more open world trading environment,[49] institutional/sovereign foreign investments intended to avoid
market dependency could clearly conflict with worldwide "trade facilitation" efforts.[50] The WTO Agreement on Agriculture is not very helpful in

---

[47] WTO, 'GATS training modules,' http://goo.gl/9jRm4 (accessed September 2012).
[48] D. Durbach, 'Korea's overseas development backfires,' *Korea Times* (December 4, 2009)
http://goo.gl/VHAFW (accessed September 2012).
[49] Agreement Establishing the World Trade Organization (1994), 2.
[50] WTO, 'Trade Facilitation: A New High Profile,' http://goo.gl/EtXX9 (accessed
September 2012).

assessing whether current foreign investments in agriculture are compatible with WTO rules but it nonetheless indicates possible incompatibil-
ities.[51] For instance, Article 9.1(b) stipulates that host governments shall
not sell or dispose of non-commercial stocks of agricultural products at a
price lower than the comparable price of like products in domestic
markets.[52] Thus, allowing foreign partners to repatriate foodstuffs outside of the scope of normal commercial transactions could possibly
amount to disposing of non-commercial food stocks and contradict
Article 9.1(b). Producing abroad to limit recourse to international
markets could also conflict with the Agreement for which the "long-
term objective is to provide for substantial progressive reductions in
agricultural support and protection sustained over an agreed period of
time."[53] In practice, schemes aiming at substituting food produced
abroad to food bought on international markets could indeed be associated with import-substitution subsidies described as "prohibited – red
light – subsidies" under Article 3 of the WTO Agreement on Subsidies
and Countervailing Measures.[54]

The point is worth considering because this recourse to import-
substitution strategies points toward two emerging trends in contemporary international economic relations. First, recourse to import-
substitution schemes seems to have resurfaced several decades after their
progressive abandonment. Defined as the process of developing domestic
production facilities to manufacture goods which were formerly
imported,[55] import-substitution policies were indeed heavily relied upon
by developed and developing economies alike in the past. Governments
in Europe and the United States used them in the second half of the

[51] WTO Agreement on Agriculture.
[52] "(b) the sale or disposal for export by governments or their agencies of non-commercial stocks of agricultural products at a price lower than the comparable price charged for the like product to buyers in the domestic market."
[53] WTO Agreement on Agriculture, Preamble.
[54] "Except as provided in the Agreement on Agriculture, the following subsidies ... shall be prohibited ... (b) subsidies contingent, whether solely or as one of several other condi-tions, upon the use of domestic over imported goods" (WTO Agreement on Subsidies and Countervailing Measures); see UNCTAD, *Dispute Settlement, World Trade Organ-isation, 3.7 Subsidies and Countervailing Measures*, para. 2.2. On the prohibition of import substitution policies under the Washington Consensus, see also H. J Bruton, 'A Reconsideration of Import Substitution,' *Journal of Economic Literature* 36 (1998), 903–936, 930.
[55] W. Baer, 'Import Substitution and Industrialization in Latin America: Experiences and Interpretations,' *Latin American Research Review* 7 (1972), 95–122; Bruton, 'A Reconsideration,' 904.

nineteenth century and many Latin American governments followed this pattern from the 1960s as their principal method for establishing large industrial diversification schemes. Such methods preserved national interests and achieved economic growth.[56] In both cases, recourse to import-substitution measures was at the heart of economic growth strategies, but ideological patterns differed. Developed economies intended to encourage their "initial industrialization" by protecting their infant industries, while developing economies clearly intended to avoid the influence of international economics and achieve greater independence through self-sufficiency in manufactured goods.[57] Thus, import-substitution development strategies had a strong nationalist and ideological orientation.[58] As Bruton noted, import-substitution measures in the 1960s was an answer to the idea that "the division of labour between the rich countries and the poor ones seemed to doom the latter to permanent poverty [thus] the appropriate strategy for development was to replace imports from the rich North with their own domestic production."[59] However, although some authors have emphasized "substantial early success" in increasing a country's industrialization, the inability of import-substitution policies to produce sustained growth was generally recognized by 1970:[60] industries depending on significant subsidies were overall unable to increase productivity so as to achieve efficient economies of scale and to give access to international export markets to those economies.[61]

[56] W. Baer, 'Import Substitution,' 96; on the difference between "excessive diversification" and greater specialization, see *ibid.*, 104–105.

[57] *Ibid.*, 98; in Argentina and Brazil, for instance, import substitution aimed at developing domestic metallurgical industries, but agriculture was also sometimes targeted specifically (see S. Teitel and F. E. Thoumi, 'From Import Substitution to Exports: The Manufacturing Exports Experience of Argentina and Brazil,' *Growth Reform, and Adjustment: Latin America's Trade and Macroeconomic Policies in the 1970s and 1980s Economic Development and Cultural Change* 34 (1986), 455–90, 457–462); Graham, Gauthier, and de Barros, 'Thirty Years of Agricultural Growth.'

[58] S. Maxfield and J. H. Nolt, 'Protectionism and the Internationalization of Capital: U.S. Sponsorship of Import Substitution Industrialization in the Philippines, Turkey and Argentina,' *International Studies Quarterly* 49–81; 'Thirty Years of Agricultural Growth in Brazil,' 4.

[59] Bruton, 'A Reconsideration,' 905–907.

[60] Teitel and Thoumi, 'From Import Substitution to Exports,' 465–466; Bruton, 'A Reconsideration,' 920.

[61] Diverging views can be found. For Teitel and Thoumi, 'From Import Substitution to Exports,' 486, protectionism and import substitutions have in time led to increase exports

Having said this, recourse to import-substitution measures is not only interesting because it constitutes a resurfacing trend adapted to agriculture. It is also significant because the role of import-substitution policies seems to be changing. Since the goal in the 1960s was to develop competing 'initial' domestic industries by limiting imports, most debates on import substitutions in the 1970s focused on whether the policies had succeeded in developing competitive domestic industries and constituted sustainable development strategies. In the 2010s, by contrast, states involved in foreign food production aim at reducing their dependency on international food markets, but they do not aim at improving the competitiveness of local food producers or at protecting domestic industries. Given the lack of arable land in Gulf countries and the diminishing food-producing populations in China or South Korea, investing states merely aim at providing populations with goods they cannot produce on their own, without buying those on international markets. This shift shows that some states' economic growth, increasing financial means, and export capacities cannot compensate for food import prices any more, but the trend could nonetheless create significant problems in relation to international trade rules in the future. In addition to possibly breaching WTO principles, development schemes aiming at preventing imports would essentially be anti-competitive and prevent other countries whose economies depend on food sales from export their produce.

IV.   Conclusion

Current foreign investment in agriculture constitutes a significant trend in contemporary international economic relations and law which remains difficult to assess.

On the one hand, foreign capital is recurrently presented as a significant source of development funding at a reduced cost to taxpayers, especially in relation to energy or telecommunication

---

because they have helped to absorb technology progress worldwide. For Bruton, these policies rather created economic distortions detrimental to domestic and global economies alike ('A Reconsideration,' 915–917). For Baer, "Given small markets, limited capital, and a dearth of skilled manpower, autarkic industrial growth leads to the development of inefficient and high-cost industries" ('Import Substitution,' 102–106). For Graham, Gauthier, and de Barros, the cost of local production became unsustainably more important than the cost of importing ('Thirty Years of Agricultural Growth in Brazil,' 6).

infrastructures.[62] Thus, it is fair to suggest that foreign capital, if regulated and used to protect local populations, could similarly contribute to improving living conditions in food-insecure countries. On the other hand, numerous comments suggest that foreign investment in agriculture does not serve or preserve local interests in practice, at least not in their current form. Clearly, the idea of shifting from a subsistence agriculture to larger-scale methods of production could justify relying on foreign capital, but only one the condition that local populations effectively benefit from increasing food stocks and employment. As Bruton noted, "the basic objective is not to attract foreign investment as such, but to create an internal social and economic environment within which the national knowledge-accumulating process profits from the presence of foreign firms."[63] Given that important quantities of food are either repatriated into foreign markets or diverted for biofuels production, and given that many investors bring in their own workforce instead of providing jobs for the local workforce, it is difficult to ascertain at this stage whether local economies genuinely benefit from changes in the existing model. Moreover, the liberty left to foreign investors could have a significant impact on water supplies and the effects on biodiversity of recourse to hybrid seeds and improved agricultural methods are unclear. The low rents (if any) paid to local authorities for the land is understandable considering the necessary investments, but they remain questionable when compared to what the land is worth elsewhere.[64] Poor land tenure and insufficient public participation methods lead to the destruction of forests as well as to the loss of grazing areas and traditions while increasing population resettlements.

Finally, this chapter argues that land-letting countries clearly take the risk of facing investment treaty disputes in the future considering the absence of clear investment frameworks and policies for agriculture development at the moment. At the same time, the habit of 'taking' the food to home markets instead of relying on international trade gives cause for concern and could also lead to significant disputes in time.

---

[62] See for instance UNCTAD, *Best Practices in Investment for Development: How to Utilise FDI to Improve Infrastructure – Electricity – Lessons from Chile and New Zealand*. See also UNCTAD, *Best Practices in Investment for Development: How to Utilize FDI to Improve Transport Infrastructure – Roads – Australia and Peru*.

[63] Bruton, 'A Reconsideration,' 929–930; Graham, Gauthier, and de Barros, 'Thirty Years of Agricultural Growth in Brazil,' 6.

[64] See the guesstimates provided at n. 9.

Several other remarks may be formulated at this stage.

First, the suggestion that foreign investment in agriculture is about speculation might be partly misleading. Commentators frequently blame corporate investors for making money on the back of the food crisis and it is clear that some speculation is taking place,[65] but the research conducted prior to drafting this chapter concluded that major deals might be concluded by developing states on a government-to-government basis.[66] Thus, it seems fair to suggest that the focus here should not be so much on greedy investors; rather, the focus should be on why so many states increasingly get involved in such economic and agricultural policies.

It also seems important to emphasize that foreign investments in agriculture reflect key food security issues on a global scale involving client and host countries at the same time. Host states are land rich but remain among the least developed countries, while land-seeking states could be defined as land-poor wealthy economies using their growing influence to produce abroad what they cannot afford to acquire on traditional international food markets. Thus, the trend is not merely a matter of domination, it clearly points towards a complex situation in which both land seekers and land letters face food insecurity, one way or another. Although investing governments and host states are both criticized for aggravating the issues they are actually trying to solve,[67] various voices thus suggest that improving land occupation in Africa could be a significant way to fight poverty and food insecurity worldwide. While it is admitted that there is no land left available for agricultural expansion in South Asia and the Near East/North Africa,[68] studies conducted by the

---

[65] On US universities investing in foreign land, see 'The New Farm Owners: Corporate Investors Lead the Rush for Control over Overseas Farmland'; J. Vidal and C. Provost, 'US universities in Africa land grab,' *Guardian* (June 8, 2011), http://Goo.Gl/T4hxl (accessed September 2012); 'Seized! The 2008 Fand Grab for Food and Financial Security,' 7.

[66] Martin and Ayalew, 'Acquiring Land Abroad,' 15.

[67] "The failure of the government to protect the community's access to its fertile lands or to provide replacement land or adequate compensation violates the community's right to food. In addition, the failure of the state authorities to mitigate the loss of access to surface water sources and break down of boreholes constitutes a violation of the human right to water" ('Ghana: Gold Mining Company, Financed by the World Bank, Cuts off More than 700 People in Teberebie from Their Fields,' FIAN, January 2010).

[68] In these regions, according to the FAO, the land balance is actually negative, meaning that "some land classified as not suitable is made productive through human intervention such as terracing of sloping land, irrigation of arid and hyperarid land" (*World Agriculture: Towards 2015/2030: An FAO Perspective*).

FAO since the 1970s for instance indicate that only 36 percent of the land estimated to be to some degree suitable for crop production is actually so used at the moment, and that 90 percent of such land in Latin America and sub-Saharan Africa.[69] Therefore, although the trend is questionable as it is,[70] this suggests that there might still be some scope for further agricultural land expansion.[71]

Large-scale foreign investment in agriculture could be sustainable and mutually profitable if properly regulated and managed.[72] So far, however, it seems clear that states and the international community are totally incapable of regulating the trend. In 2010, the World Bank proposed various principles on responsible agricultural investment susceptible to influencing investors' conduct in relation to social responsibility,[73] while the UN Special Rapporteur on the Right to Food presented a set of minimum principles on the right to food.[74] More recently, the FAO also released guidelines for responsible governance in relation to the tenure of land, fisheries, and forests,[75] but all these initiatives are voluntary and thus have possibly limited effects since they merely rely on the good will of investors.

Nonetheless, various mechanisms could be put in place to frame land investments and agricultural activities by foreigners. The amount of land left to foreign investors could for instance be restricted to ensure that domestic food production will not fall under foreign control, especially given that climate change is anticipated. Concerned by increasing land

---

[69] According to the report, more than half of the total might be concentrated in just seven countries (Brazil, the DRC, the Sudan, Angola, Argentina, Colombia, and Bolivia)

[70] Grain claims that "if left unchecked, this global 'land grab' could spell the end of small-scale farming, and rural livelihoods, in numerous places around the world" ('Seized! The 2008 Fand Grab for Food and Financial Security'). Alternatively, Durbach deplores that "unless global measures are put in place to stop this new colonialism ... other nations will simply step into the breach" ('Korea's overseas development backfires').

[71] *World Agriculture: Towards 2015/2030.*

[72] Rather than reducing the trend to imperialism, Rodney Cooke, Director at the UN International Fund for Agricultural Development therefore concludes: "I would avoid the blanket term 'land-grabbing.' Done the right way, these deals can bring benefits for all parties and be a tool for development" ('How Food and Water Are Driving'). On FDI regulation, see Sornarajah, *International Law on Foreign Investment*, 132.

[73] *Principles for Responsible Agricultural Investment (RAI) that Respects Rights, Livelihoods and Resource*, http://goo.gl/GVyKo

[74] 'Large-Scale Land Acquisitions and Leases: A Set of Minimum Principles and Measures to Address the Human Rights Challenge,' presented to the HRC (A/HRC/13/33/Add.2), March 2010, http://goo.gl/4sxxB

[75] FAO and CFS, *Guidelines on the Responsible Governance of Tenure of Land, Fisheries and Forests in the Context of National Food Security*, http://goo.gl/VPvyn

acquisition by foreigners, Brazil for instance recently reinstated in August 2010 a 1970s rule which limited land deals with foreign investors to 5,000 hectares.[76] The use of land also requires to be regulated and host authorities ought to ensure public participation and public involvement in future development projects, especially when forests and traditional habitats are potentially at stake.[77] Where resettlements are inevitable, relocation schemes must be set up to accompany, support, and compensate affected populations. Local authorities must ensure that access to water, food, and biodiversity are preserved, but also that the production methods employed will not exclude local farmers from the food production industry. Interestingly, food repatriation to the investor-state markets are not inherently incompatible with local food security requirements: as long as the food products left to the local population is significantly superior to what used to be produced on a subsistence basis, the model could guarantee that local food markets are supplied and help developing local economies. In practice, host governments could for instance protect the interests of its population by putting in place contract-farming schemes under which investors would have legal obligations to rely on local farmers;[78] production sharing agreements normally used in the oil production industry could also be adapted in the largest contracts to ensure that both the local population and entrepreneurs (private or institutional) obtain a fair share of the food produced, whatever the quantities produced. Similarly, recourse to foreign workforce should be regulated to ensure that local farmers are being involved in the food production process and get priority access to employment opportunity over foreigners. Given the risk posed by future investment arbitration disputes, public authorities must ensure that investment contracts are drafted specifically to delimit investors' expectations. In all situations, specific policies must be set up by host governments to ensure that their populations will effectively benefit from foreign capital and investment projects.

---

[76] 'Le Brésil restreint l'achat de terres par des étrangers' (AFP, August 24, 2010).

[77] Spieldoch interestingly suggests that "Governments should articulate a national vision . . . All investment measures should be transparent, participatory and accountable to those who will be most impacted, such as smallholder producers. A mandatory review of land use and land rights would be essential to understanding the potential impact and how to promote investment that makes sense for communities and their culture and environment. All national investment plans should be assessed based on international human rights obligations' ('Global Land Grab').

[78] UNCTAD, *World Investment Report 2009: Transnational Corporations, Agricultural Production and Development.*

Finally, the tendency of foreign investors to pay low prices for the land, to displace/resettlement populations, to rely on imported workforce rather than providing jobs to local populations, and to 'take' food rather than importing it from international markets has led to serious neo-colonialism allegations which need to be considered carefully. Denouncing "foreign private corporations getting new forms of control over farmland to produce food not for the local communities but for someone else," Grain for instance suggested that "colonialism" might not be a relic of the past.[79] The term 'colonialism' was also used in a major article by *The Economist*,[80] as well as in an FAO and UN press release commented on by various other sources.[81] Elsewhere, the *Korea Times* described the trend as "a global power struggle for food security that threatens the sovereignty of poorer nations and the livelihoods of rural communities in Africa, South East Asia and South America."[82] The relationship between foreign investments in agriculture and 'colonialism' must however be considered carefully to avoid polemical shortcuts. Associating all foreign investments in agriculture with neo-colonialism is possibly far reaching because the concept – which describes a situation in which domestic policies are directed from outside[83] – does not adequately describe the current trend. The current model of foreign investment in agriculture may well distort international markets and might not serve the development of host economies,[84] but they hardly aim at creating or maintaining colonial forces overriding local governance. Not so far, at least. Host

---

[79] The article concludes "did someone say colonialism was a thing of the past?" ('Seized! The 2008 Fand Grab for Food and Financial Security,' 3).

[80] 'Buying farmland abroad.'

[81] Bokhari, 'Buying Foreign Land'; Spieldoch, 'Global Land Grab'; J. Blas, 'Welcome fades for wealthy nations,' *Financial Times* (London, November 20, 2008), http://goo.gl/4AKUH (accessed September 2012).

[82] Durbach, 'Korea's overseas development backfires.'

[83] For Kwame Nkrumah, "[T]he essence of neo-colonialism is that the State which is subject to it is, in theory, independent and has all the outward trappings of international sovereignty. In reality its economic system and thus its political policy is directed from outside" (*Neocolonialism: The Last Stage of Imperialism* (New York: International Publishers, 1965)). Yew alternatively describes neo-colonialism as the "continued control of former colonies through ruling native elites compliant with neo-colonial powers" (L. Yew, 'Political Discourse: Theories of Colonialism and Postcolonialism' (2002), University of Singapore, http://goo.gl/nLBwn (accessed September 2012).

[84] "The result of neo-colonialism is that foreign capital is used for the exploitation rather than for the development of the less developed parts of the world. Investment under neo-colonialism increases rather than decreases the gap between the rich and the poor countries of the world" (Nkrumah, *Neocolonialism*).

states remain sovereign and deliberately allocate the land to foreign capital owners in order to develop larger-scale industries and replace current subsistence-based agricultural practices. The notion of "contemporary form of economic or political influence,"[85] by contrast, is extremely relevant and the various excesses highlighted previously suggest that some have largely benefited from unregulated areas to impose their influence. That said, most investment projects considered in this chapter involve developing states in need of long-term strategies, which suggests that such investment in agriculture does not correspond to the North–South domination paradigm to which the neo-colonialism concept generally refers.[86]

Overall, one may therefore disapprove of the excesses of the trend as it is currently conducted, but it remains fair to say that – if well regulated – such developments in international economic relations could lead to significant development-oriented partnerships in which foreign capital, expertise, and know-how could serve many. In the best of all possible worlds, that is.

---

[85] Yew, 'Political Discourse.'   [86] See Martin and Ayalew, 'Acquiring Land Abroad.'

16

Intellectual property rights in international investment agreements: striving for coherence in national and international law

TANIA VOON, ANDREW MITCHELL, AND JAMES MUNRO

I. Introduction

The investment arbitration launched by Philip Morris Asia (PMA) against Australia in 2011[1] in relation to Australia's mandatory plain packaging of tobacco products is a recent reminder of the significant protections for intellectual property rights (IPRs) in international investment agreements. Given its focus on trademarks, the *Philip Morris* dispute provides a useful case study for exploring the relationship between intellectual property and international investment law. The parallel legal challenges brought by various tobacco companies against Australia in the High Court of Australia[2] on constitutional grounds and by Ukraine,[3] Honduras,[4] the Dominican

We acknowledge the generous funding from the Australian National Preventive Health Agency and the Australian Research Council (2012–15) for research conducted in collaboration with the Cancer Council Victoria. The views expressed here are our own personal views as academics, and do not necessarily reflect those of any employer or other entity. Any errors or omissions are ours.

[1] Philip Morris Limited, 'News Release: Philip Morris Asia Initiates Legal Action against the Australian Government over Plain Packaging' (27 June 2011). See also e.g. Chris Kenny, 'Big tobacco ignites legal war', *The Australian*, 27 June 2011; International Centre for Trade and Sustainable Development, 'Philip Morris Launches Legal Battle Over Australian Cigarette Packaging' 15(24) *Bridges Weekly Trade News Digest* (29 June 2011). This chapter was written in September 2013.

[2] *JT International SA* v. *Commonwealth of Australia; British American Tobacco Australasia Limited* v. *Commonwealth of Australia* [2012] HCA 43.

[3] *Australia – Certain Measures Concerning Trademarks and other Plain Packaging Requirements Applicable to Tobacco Products and Packaging: Request for the Establishment of a Panel by Ukraine*, WT/DS434/11 (17 August 2012) (*Ukraine Panel Request*).

[4] *Australia – Certain Measures Concerning Trademarks, Geographical Indications and Other Plain Packaging Requirements Applicable to Tobacco Products and Packaging: Request for the Establishment of a Panel by Honduras*, WT/ DS435/16 (17 October 2012).

Republic,[5] Cuba[6] and Indonesia[7] against Australia in the World Trade Organization (WTO) also make this a valuable case for demonstrating the fragmenting nature of intellectual property law at the domestic and international levels. That fragmentation poses challenges for international trade and investment law, raising questions concerning the relationship between intellectual property rights conceived at the domestic level with the protections available in international fora. For example, what significance does the High Court's conception of intellectual property under Australian law have for the claims against plain packaging under the Agreement between the Government of Hong Kong and the Government of Australia for the Promotion and Protection of Investments ('Hong Kong–Australia BIT')[8] and the WTO's Agreement on Trade-Related Aspects of Intellectual Property Rights (TRIPS Agreement)?[9]

By using the *Philip Morris* case study, this chapter aims to explore the complex interaction between intellectual property and international investment agreements (IIAs), meaning bilateral investment treaties (BITs), plurilateral investment treaties such as the Energy Charter Treaty, and preferential trade agreements containing investment provisions. After explaining the background to the *Philip Morris* dispute in its various forms, we consider the protection of intellectual property as an 'investment' under IIAs. We then examine three substantive investment obligations in connection with intellectual property: most-favoured-nation obligations, expropriation, and so-called 'umbrella clauses'. This chapter reveals the high degree of uncertainty permeating the relationship between intellectual property and international investment law.

---

[5] *Australia – Certain Measures Concerning Trademarks, Geographical Indications and Other Plain Packaging Requirements Applicable to Tobacco Products and Packaging; Request for the Establishment of a Panel by Dominican Republic*, WT/DS441/15 (9 November 2012).

[6] *Australia – Certain Measures Concerning Trademarks, Geographical Indications and Other Plain Packaging Requirements Applicable to Tobacco Products and Packaging: Request for Consultations by Cuba*, WT/DS458/1 (7 May 2013).

[7] Indonesia is reported to have requested consultations with Australia on 20 September 2013: Daniel Pruzin, 'Indonesia joins WTO Dispute Complaint Against Australian Plain Packaging Rules (20 September 2013), *BNA International Trade Daily* (online). Official documents are not publicly available at the time of writing.

[8] Agreement between the Government of Hong Kong and the Government of Australia for the Promotion and Protection of Investments, signed 15 September 1993, 1748 UNTS 385 (entered into force 15 October 1993) ('Hong Kong–Australia BIT').

[9] Marrakesh Agreement Establishing the World Trade Organization, opened for signature 15 April 1994, 1867 UNTS 3 (entered into force 1 January 1995) annex 1C.

382 TANIA VOON, ANDREW MITCHELL, AND JAMES MUNRO

In particular, intellectual property poses conceptual difficulties concerning when intellectual property protections might be considered more favourable, the objective meaning of intellectual property if not delineated by domestic law, and the impact on an investor's overall investment of restrictions on the use of intellectual property rights.

II. Plain tobacco packaging in Australia

The *Philip Morris* dispute concerns Australia's world first legislation mandating the 'plain packaging' of tobacco products, which must be sold in packets of a specified colour ('drab dark brown'), without graphic logos, and with graphic health warnings covering 75 per cent of the front of the pack and 90 per cent of the back.[10] Following the Australian government's announcement of the scheme on 29 April 2010[11] and the introduction of the legislation into Parliament on 6 July 2011,[12] Australia's Tobacco Plain Packaging Act 2011 (Cth) received royal assent on 1 December 2011. Prohibitions on the manufacture and packaging of non-compliant tobacco products applied from 1 October 2012, and on the retail sale of such products from 1 December 2012.[13]

The Australian legislation has two express objectives: to improve public health, for example by discouraging smoking initiation, encouraging smoking cessation, discouraging relapse, and reducing exposure to second-hand smoke; and to implement certain of Australia's obligations as a party to the World Health Organization (WHO) Framework Convention on Tobacco Control (FCTC). Guidelines agreed by the Conference of the Parties to the WHO FCTC specify that Parties 'should consider adopting . . . plain packaging'.[14] The legislation aims to achieve these objectives by reducing the attractiveness and appeal of tobacco products to consumers, increasing the effectiveness of health warnings,

[10] Competition and Consumer (Tobacco) Information Standard 2011 (Cth) ss. 9.13.1, 9.19.1; Tobacco Plain Packaging Regulations 2011 (Cth) regs. 2.2.1(2), 2.2.1(3), 2.3.4(1).
[11] Prime Minister of Australia, 'Media release: anti-smoking action' (29 April 2010).
[12] Tobacco Plain Packaging Bill 2011 (Cth). See also Trade Marks Amendment (Tobacco Plain Packaging) Bill 2011 (Cth), introduced into the House of Representatives on the same day.
[13] Tobacco Plain Packaging Act 2011 (Cth), s. 2.
[14] WHO, *Guidelines for Implementation of Article 11 of the WHO Framework Convention on Tobacco Control (Packaging and Labelling of Tobacco Products)*, [46]; WHO, *Guidelines for Implementation of Article 13 of the WHO Framework Convention on Tobacco Control (Packaging and Labelling of Tobacco Products)*, 17.

and reducing the ability of the retail packaging to mislead consumers about the harmful effects of smoking.[15]

On 23 February 2011 (well after the announcement of plain packaging in Australia), Philip Morris Asia Limited (PMA) purchased Philip Morris (Australia) Limited (PML),[16] which manufactures, markets, and distributes tobacco products in Australia. PMA issued a notice of claim concerning the legislation shortly thereafter, on 27 June 2011,[17] under the Australia–Hong Kong Bilateral Investment Treaty (BIT).[18] This was followed by a notice of arbitration under the Arbitration Rules of the United Nations Commission on International Trade Law 2010 on 21 November 2011, claiming that the plain packaging legislation 'manifestly deprives' it of its intellectual property and the commercial utility of its brands.[19] PML claims to own intellectual property in Australia including trademarks, copyright, designs, know-how, trade secrets, the overall get-up of product packaging, and the 'substantial goodwill' generated from the use of this intellectual property in relation to its products.[20]

On 20 December 2011, PML joined other tobacco companies in launching a claim against the legislation within Australia's highest court, alleging a breach of section 51(xxxi) of the Australian Constitution, which precludes the acquisition of property by the Australian government other than on just terms. The High Court of Australia rejected that claim on 15 August 2012,[21] issuing its reasons for the decision (by a 6:1 majority) on 5 October 2012.[22] The Australian case provides insights on the nature of intellectual property and the impact of the

---

[15] Tobacco Plain Packaging Act 2011 (Cth), s. 4.

[16] Philip Morris (Australia) Limited, *Financial Report 2010*; IBISWorld, *IBISWorld Company Report: Philip Morris (Australia) Limited – Premium Report* (31 December 2010, with update as at 11 April 2011), 14.

[17] *Written Notification of Claim by Philip Morris Asia Limited to the Commonwealth of Australia Pursuant to Agreement between the Government of Hong Kong and the Government of Australia for the Promotion and Protection of Investments* (27 June 2011) (PMA Claim).

[18] *Agreement between the Government of Hong Kong and the Government of Australia for the Promotion and Protection of Investments*, 1748 UNTS 385 (signed 15 September 1993, entered into force 15 October 1993).

[19] *Notice of Arbitration from Philip Morris Asia Limited to the Commonwealth of Australia* (21 November 2011) (PMA Arbitration).

[20] PMA Claim, 9.

[21] *JT International SA v. Commonwealth of Australia; British American Tobacco Australasia Limited v. Commonwealth of Australia* [2012] HCA 30 (15 August 2012).

[22] *JT International SA v. Commonwealth of Australia; British American Tobacco Australasia Limited v. Commonwealth of Australia* [2012] HCA 43 (5 October 2012).

legislation on that property, factors that are relevant in the investment law context as discussed further below.

III. Intellectual property as an investment

Intellectual property almost always falls within the definition of an 'investment' in IIAs; hence, investors may in principle utilize IIAs to protect and enforce their intellectual property rights. However, the precise boundaries of this definition may depend on both the particular wording of the IIA in question and the arbitration rules the IIA authorizes; these boundaries may be further informed by certain ongoing disputes. Below, we apply to intellectual property first the variable or subjective criteria for defining an investment (based on the specific IIA) and second the fixed or objective criteria for defining an investment (potentially applicable to all IIAs).[23]

1. Variable criteria of investments: specific to each IIA

Many recent IIAs expressly include intellectual property in a non-exhaustive list of items falling within the scope of the term 'investment'. As an example, the 2012 United States Model BIT defines an 'investment' as 'every kind of asset that an investor owns or controls ... Forms that an investment may take include: ... (f) intellectual property rights'.[24] Some IIAs also specify the kinds of intellectual property covered. For example, the Energy Charter Treaty defines intellectual property as including 'copyrights and related rights, trademarks, geographical indications, industrial designs, patents, layout designs of integrated circuits and the protection of undisclosed information'.[25] A similar but slightly different formulation is found in the Agreement between the Republic of Turkey and Australia on the Reciprocal Promotion and Protection of Investments, which omits 'geographical indications' and 'layout designs

---

[23] See Mahnaz Malik, 'Definition of Investment in International Investment Agreements' 1 (August 2009) *International Institute for Sustainable Development Best Practice Series*, 5–10.

[24] 2012 United States Model BIT, art. 1, www.state.gov/e/eb/ifd/bit/index.htm. For further examples, see Rachel A. Lavery, 'Coverage of Intellectual Property Rights in International Investment Agreements: An Empirical Analysis of Definitions in a Sample of Bilateral Investment Agreements and Free Trade Agreements', (2009) 6(2) *Transnational Dispute Management*, 1, 4.

[25] Energy Charter Treaty, signed 17 December 1994, 2080 UNTS 95 (entered into force 16 April 1998), art. 1(12).

of integrated circuits' but includes 'know-how' and 'goodwill'.[26] The Canadian Model BIT omits 'know-how' and 'goodwill' but covers 'plant breeders' rights'.[27] While some debate or difference between agreements might arise with respect to areas such as folklore, traditional knowledge, and genetic resources, the more common forms of intellectual property are generally clearly covered within all these definitions.

Intellectual property will also usually fall within the definition of investment even in agreements that do not explicitly refer to intellectual property as such. For example, the investment chapter in the Agreement between Japan and the United Mexican States for the Strengthening of the Economic Partnership defines investment to include 'real estate or other property, tangible or intangible...',[28] which would include intellectual property as intangible property. The Agreement between the Belgo-Luxembourg Economic Union and the Government of the Republic of India for the Promotion and Protection of Investments states that an 'investment' is 'any kind of asset and any direct or indirect contribution in cash, in kind or in services, invested or reinvested in any sector of economic activity'.[29] Intellectual property would likely be considered an 'asset of any kind', since the term 'asset' has been broadly interpreted as 'property of any kind'[30] and 'everything of economic value, virtually without limitation'.[31]

Some IIAs expressly restrict the intellectual property rights protected to those conferred under municipal law.[32] Where the agreement is silent

---

[26] Agreement between the Republic of Turkey and Australia on the Reciprocal Promotion and Protection of Investments, signed 16 June 2005, [2010] ATS 8 (29 June 2009), art. 1(1)(a)(iv).

[27] 2004 Canadian Model BIT, art. 1, italaw.com/documents/Canadian2004-FIPA-model-en.pdf

[28] Agreement between Japan and the United Mexican States for the Strengthening of the Economic Partnership, signed 17 September 2004 (not yet in force), art. 96(i)(GG).

[29] Agreement between the Belgo-Luxembourg Economic Union and the Government of the Republic of India for the Promotion and Protection of Investments, signed 31 October 1997, UNTS 2136 (entered into force 8 January 2001), art 1(b).

[30] *Romak SA* v. *Uzbekistan (Award)* (Permanent Court of Arbitration, Case No. AA280, 26 November 2009), 177.

[31] *Mytilineous Holdings SA* v. *Serbia and Montenegro, Serbia (Partial Award on Jurisdiction)* (Ad Hoc Arbitral Tribunal, UNCITRAL Rules, September 8 2006), 106.

[32] See e.g. ASEAN Comprehensive Investment Agreement, signed 26 February 2009 (entered into force 29 March 2012) art. 4(c), which limits an 'investment' to 'intellectual property rights which are conferred pursuant to the laws and regulations of each Member State'. For further examples, see Lavery, 'Coverage of Intellectual Property Rights in International Investment Agreements', 1, 12.

on this question, municipal law may still influence the scope of protection of intellectual property: an IIA might not protect a particular intellectual property right where the host state has rejected an application for its registration or simply does not recognize that form of intellectual property. Without a touchstone in municipal law, terms such as 'intellectual property' are 'empty concepts'.[33] For example, an IIA might protect investments in the form of copyright, but it would not normally deal with issues such as whether copyright subsists in phonograph records and for how long it continues after the death of the author.[34]

Thus, in *Saipem SpA* v. *Bangladesh*,[35] Bangladesh argued that certain rights were not recognized as property under Bangladeshi law and accordingly did not fall within the definition of an investment in its BIT with Italy. However, the tribunal rejected this argument, stating: 'If one were to follow Bangladesh's approach, this would lead to a different interpretation and thus a different scope of protection under the BIT depending on the country in which the investment is made. This cannot be the meaning of the BIT.'[36] According to this reasoning, the scope of protection of an IIA cannot vary for different parties to the treaty, and therefore an investor may be able to claim protection under an IIA for intellectual property even within a host state that does recognize the existence of that property. Such a conclusion seems counter-intuitive, potentially undermining the regulatory sovereignty of the host state and raising unanswerable questions about the source of intellectual property protections. Given that even multilateral treaties such as the TRIPS Agreement and WIPO-administered intellectual property agreements leave some scope for members/parties to determine their own intellectual property laws and systems, domestic law must ultimately determine the meaning of intellectual property in a given jurisdiction.

In the context of the *Philip Morris* dispute, this debate may have little impact. Under the Hong Kong–Australia BIT, an investment means 'every kind of asset, owned or controlled by investors of one Contracting Party and admitted by the other Contracting Party subject to its law and investment policies applicable from time to time', including in specified

---

[33] Sasson, *Substantive Law in Investment Treaty Arbitration*, 66.

[34] These are cited as a lack of uniformity in WIPO, 'Fields of Intellectual Property Protection', in *WIPO Intellectual Property Handbook: Policy, Law and Use* (2nd edn. 2008) [2.227], [2.177]; www.wipo.int/export/sites/www/about-ip/en/iprm/pdf/ch2.pdf.

[35] *Saipem SpA* v. *People's Republic of Bangladesh (Decision on Jurisdiction)* (ICSID Arbitral Tribunal, Case No. ARB/05/07, 21 March 2007).

[36] *Ibid.*, 121.

forms such as trademarks.[37] The extent to which Australian law recognizes a positive right to use trademarks (for example) may be relevant in assessing Australia's substantive investment obligations as discussed further below. However, the fact that Australian law recognizes trademarks as intellectual property may be sufficient to conclude as an initial matter that, if confirmed, PMA's claimed indirect ownership or control of PML's owned and licensed trademarks relating to brands such as Marlboro, Alpine, and Peter Jackson[38] satisfies the subjective criteria of investments.

2. Fixed criteria of investments: applicable to all IIAs?

Intellectual property may also need to meet certain fixed or objective criteria of investments in order to receive protection under an IIA. These objective indicia are sometimes found explicitly in the definition of investment, such as the requirement in the 2012 United States Model BIT that a protected asset must have 'the characteristics of an investment, including such characteristics as the commitment of capital or other resources, the expectation of gain or profit, or the assumption of risk'.[39] Moreover, a discernible trend exists[40] among tribunals convened under the Convention on the Settlement of Investment Disputes between States and Nationals of Other States (ICSID)[41] to identify objective indicia as a threshold requirement for the exercise of jurisdiction. These criteria usually include: a capital contribution, a certain duration, participation in the risks of the operation, and contribution to the development of the host state.[42] Some non-ICSID tribunals have adopted a similar approach.[43] The jurisprudence suggests that not all indicia need to be present in every investment. Instead, the identification of an investment

---

[37] Hong Kong–Australia BIT, art. 1(e).   [38] *PMA Arbitration*, 23–25.
[39] 2012 United States Model BIT, art. 1.
[40] See also Andrew D. Mitchell and Sebastian M. Wurzberger, 'Boxed In? Australia's Plain Tobacco Packaging Initiative and International Investment Law', (2011) 27 *Arbitration International*, 623, 629–33.
[41] 575 UNTS 159, concluded 18 March 1965 (entered into force 14 October 1966), art. 25(1).
[42] See e.g. *Salini Costruttori SPA v. Kingdom of Morocco (Decision on Jurisdiction)* (ICSID Arbitral Tribunal, Case No. ARB/00/4, 23 July 2001), 52, 54; *Joy Mining Machinery Ltd v. Egypt (Award on Jurisdiction)* (ICSID Arbitral Tribunal, Case No. ARB/03/11, 6 August 2004), 53; *Biwater Gauff (Tanzania) v. Tanzania (Award)* (ICSID Arbitral Tribunal, Case No. ARB/05/22, 24 July 2008), 312–17.
[43] See e.g. *Romak SA v. Uzbekistan (Award)* (Permanent Court of Arbitration, Case No. AA280, 26 November 2009), 207; *Mytilineous Holdings SA v. Serbia and Montenegro, Serbia (Partial Award on Jurisdiction)* (Ad Hoc Arbitral Tribunal, UNCITRAL Rules,

is a holistic exercise using a 'flexible and pragmatic approach' adapted to the particular circumstances of a case.[44]

Whether particular intellectual property rights meet these criteria is determined on a case-by-case basis. Simply owning intellectual property rights, without actively using them for any commercial purpose, assuming any risk, or generating any returns, may not satisfy the objective criteria. This question has arisen in the ongoing *Apotex* dispute.[45] In that case, the investor, Apotex, has argued that the marketing rights, goodwill, know-how, and intellectual property rights associated with the products it imports into the United States qualify as 'investments' within the United States that attract the protection of the applicable IIA.[46] The United States, by contrast, has argued that Apotex does not have an investment in the United States but instead engages in cross-border commercial sales of its products, which it manufactures in Canada and markets in the United States.[47] This dispute could potentially shape the contours of when intellectual property, in and of itself, can be considered an 'investment' under objective criteria.

The *Philip Morris* dispute presents a different conceptual difficulty. Unlike Apotex, PMA may be seen as using its intellectual property rights[48] as part of a broader in-country manufacturing and marketing

---

8 September 2006), 115–20; cf. *White Industries Australia Ltd* v. *India (Final Award)* (Ad Hoc Arbitral Tribunal, UNCITRAL Rules, 30 November 2011), rejecting this argument.

[44] *Biwater Gauff (Tanzania)* v. *Tanzania (Award)* (ICSID Arbitral Tribunal, Case No. ARB/05/22, 24 July 2008), 312. See also Emmanuel Gaillard, 'Identify or Define? Reflections on the Evolutions of the Concept of Investment in ICSID Practice', in Christina Binder *et al.* (eds.), *International Investment Law of the 21st Century: Essays in Honour of Christoph Schreuer* (Oxford University Press, 2009), 407–10.

[45] *Apotex Holdings, Inc. and Apotex, Inc.* v. *United States of America (Pending)* (ICSID Arbitral Tribunal, UNCITRAL Rules, Case No. ARB(AF)/12/1); *Notice of Arbitration under the Arbitration Rules of the United Nations Commission on International Trade Law and the North American Free Trade Agreement from Apotex Inc. to the Government of the United States of America* (10 December 2008), www.state.gov/documents/organization/115447.pdf

[46] *Request for Arbitration by Apotex Holdings and Apotex Inc with the United States of America under the North American Free Trade Agreement* (29 February 2012), 2, 7.

[47] Jarrod Hepburn and Luke Eric Peterson, 'As United States is hit with another arbitration claim, pharma companies are growing creative in their use of investment treaties', *Investment Arbitration Reporter* (13 March 2012); Jarrod Hepburn, 'Parties in NAFTA pharmaceuticals arbitration trade arguments on jurisdiction, as tribunal rejects amicus participation', *Investment Arbitration Reporter* (1 December 2011). See also USA's arguments in earlier related proceedings (*Reply on Objections to Jurisdiction of Respondent United States of America*, 32–39: www.state.gov/s/l/c27648.htm).

[48] PMA Claim, 9.

operation in Australia.[49] In doing so, it contributes capital, assumes risk, and generates returns from the commercial use of its intellectual property. However, does PMA's investment in the form of intellectual property contribute to Australia's economic development? Australia could argue that, by promoting tobacco consumption, PMA's investment causes considerable net harm to Australian society. Indeed, Australia estimates the social costs of smoking in Australia at $31.5 billion each year.[50] Whether such an argument would succeed is an open question. Some tribunals have placed substantial weight on the 'economic development' criterion,[51] but others have cast doubt over whether it can, on its own, determine the existence of an investment pursuant to the objective criteria.[52]

IV. Intellectual property and most-favoured-nation treatment

1. MFN obligations in IIAs

IIAs commonly require host states to accord most-favoured-nation (MFN) treatment to covered foreign investors. The Draft Articles on Most-Favoured-Nation Clauses of the International Law Commission (ILC) describes the typical content of such provisions:[53]

> Most-favoured-nation treatment is treatment accorded by the granting State to the beneficiary State, or to persons or things in a determined relationship with that State, not less favourable than treatment extended by the granting State to a third State or to persons or things in the same relationship with that third State.

---

[49] Philip Morris International, 'Australia', www.pmi.com/marketpages/pages/market_en_au.aspx
[50] Parliament of the Commonwealth of Australia, House of Representatives, Tobacco Plain Packaging Bill 2011, Explanatory Memorandum (6 July 2011),1. See also David J. Collins and Helen M. Lapsley, *The Costs of Tobacco, Alcohol and Illicit Drug Abuse to Australian Society in 2004/05* (Australian Government, University of New South Wales, 2008), xi.
[51] See e.g. *Joy Mining Machinery Limited v. Arab Republic of Egypt* (ICSID Arbitral Tribunal, Case No. ARB/03/11, August 6 2004), 53, 58; *Malaysian Historical Salvors v. Malaysia (Award on Jurisdiction)* (ICSID Arbitral Tribunal, Case No. ARB/05/10, 10 May 2007), 113–24.
[52] See also *Consortium Groupement LESI-Dipenta v. People's Democratic Republic of Algeria (Award)* (ICSID Arbitral Tribunal, Case No. ARB/03/8, 10 January 2005), 13; *Phoenix Action Ltd v. Czech Republic (Award)* (ICSID Arbitral Tribunal, Case No. ARB/06/5, 15 April 2009), 85; Gaillard, 'Identify or Define?', 412–13.
[53] ILC, *Draft Articles on Most-Favoured-Nation Clauses*, Report of the ILC on Its Thirtieth Session (1978) 2 YBILC 8 (pt 2) (UN Doc. A/33/10), art. 5.

MFN treatment in IIAs thus precludes discrimination between foreign investors or their investments where those investors or investments share the same relationship with the relevant host state. This 'same relationship' criterion is usually textually expressed in IIAs as 'in like circumstances' or 'in a like situation'.[54] Most IIAs provide MFN protection in relation to the 'post-establishment' period of investment only, such that the initial registration or establishment of intellectual property rights would not be covered.[55] However, more recent IIAs tend to provide MFN protection in respect of the pre-establishment phase as well, preventing a host state from conditioning the acquisition by a foreign investor of intellectual property rights on reciprocal access to such rights for its own nationals in the investor's home state.[56]

PMA has not specifically claimed a violation of this obligation in its case against Australia pursuant to the Hong Kong–Australia BIT. In that sense, the relationship between intellectual property and MFN treatment is not directly relevant to the *Philip Morris* case. However, in its WTO claim, Ukraine has raised MFN obligations,[57] which could therefore become relevant to the investment dispute pursuant to the umbrella clause as discussed further below. Moreover, the MFN treatment obligation gives rise to important systemic questions regarding the interaction between IIAs and international intellectual property law.

With varying degrees of success, investors have used MFN provisions to claim the benefit of more favourable procedural and substantive protections contained in the host state's IIAs with other countries.[58]

---

[54] Andrew Newcombe and Lluís Paradell, *Law and Practice of Investment Treaties* (The Hague: Kluwer, 2009), 225.

[55] Carlos M Correa, 'Bilateral Investment Agreements: Agents for New Global Standards for the Protection of Intellectual Property Rights?' (2004) GRAIN Study, 11–12, www.grain. org/briefings/?id=186; Marie Louise Seelig, 'Can Patent Revocation or Invalidation Constitute a Form of Expropriation', (2009) 6(2) *Transnational Dispute Management*, 1, 3–4.

[56] Bryan Mercurio, 'Awakening the Sleeping Giant: Intellectual Property Rights in International Investment Agreements', (2012) 15 *Journal of International Economic Law*, 871, 885.

[57] Ukraine Panel Request, 4.

[58] See e.g. *Emilio Agustín Maffezini v. Kingdom of Spain (Decision of the Tribunal on Objections to Jurisdiction)* (ICSID Arbitral Tribunal, Case No. ARB/97/7, 25 January 2000); *MTD Equity Sdn. Bhd. and MTD Chile SA v. Ecuador (Award)* (ICSID Arbitral Tribunal, Case No. ARB/01/7, 25 May 2004); *Bayindir Insaat Turizm Ticaret Ve Sanayi AS v. Pakistan (Decision on Jurisdiction)* (ICSID Arbitral Tribunal, Case No. ARB/03/29, 14 November 2005) [227]–[32]. Cf. *Plama Consortium v. Republic of Bulgaria (Decision on Jurisdiction)* (ICSID Arbitral Tribunal, Case No. ARB/03/24, 8 February 2005); *Salini Costruttori SPA v. Hashemite Kingdom of Jordan (Decision on Jurisdiction)* (ICSID Arbitral Tribunal, Case No. ARB/02/13, 1 November 2004).

A successful MFN claim of this nature results in the de facto incorporation of the higher standards of treatment into the subject IIA. In the
intellectual property context, a key question is whether investors may use
MFN provisions to effectively incorporate into an IIA more favourable
intellectual property protections from the host state's international intellectual property agreements with other countries and claim the benefit of
these through investor-state dispute settlement. Relevant international
agreements could include the TRIPS Agreement, preferential trade agreements containing higher levels of intellectual property protections (e.g.
so-called TRIPS-plus agreements), and intellectual property treaties
administered by the World Intellectual Property Organization (WIPO).[59]
The answer to this question may lie in the *ejusdem generis* principle,
according to which MFN provisions apply only to 'those rights which fall
within the limits of the subject-matter of the clause'.[60] *Maffezini* v. *Spain*
provides an example of an extremely broad application of that principle.
In that dispute, under an IIA between Argentina and Spain, the claimant
successfully invoked, pursuant to the MFN provision, the investor-state
dispute settlement procedures contained in another IIA. This allowed the
claimant to avoid the requirement in the IIA between Argentina and
Spain to submit the dispute to local courts for a period of eighteen
months before commencing arbitration.[61] According to the tribunal,
'even if not strictly a part of the material aspect of the trade and investment policy pursued by treaties of commerce and navigation', dispute
settlement arrangements are 'inextricably related to the protection of
foreign investors'.[62] Applying this reasoning, even if the protection of
intellectual property is not a 'material aspect' of an IIA, it could nevertheless be characterized as related to the protection of foreign investors'
investments and therefore potentially brought in through the MFN
clause.

[59] Bertram Boie, 'The Protection of Intellectual Property Rights through Bilateral Invest-
ment Treaties: Is There a TRIPS-plus Dimension' (2010), World Trade Institute Working
Paper No. 2010/19, 12–13; Correa, 'Bilateral Investment Agreements', 11–12;
Lahra Liberti, 'Intellectual Property Rights in International Investment Agreements: An
Overview' (2010) OECD Working Papers on International Investment, 9; Henning
Grosse Ruse-Khan, 'Investment Law and Intellectual Property Rights', in Mare Bungen-
berg, Jöm Griebel, Stephan Hobe and August Reinisch (eds.), *International Investment
Law* (Oxford: Hart, 2013), 8–9.
[60] ILC, *Draft Articles on Most-Favoured-Nation Clauses*, art. 9(1).
[61] *Emilio Agustín Maffezini v. Kingdom of Spain (Decision of the Tribunal on Objections to
Jurisdiction)* (ICSID Arbitral Tribunal, Case No. ARB/97/7, 25 January 2000), 38–63.
[62] *Ibid.*, 54.

Importantly, however, the tribunal in *Maffezini* v. *Spain* stated:

> Of course, the third-party treaty has to relate to the same subject matter as the basic treaty, be it the protection of foreign investments or the promotion of trade, since the dispute settlement provisions will operate in the context of these matters; otherwise there would be a contravention of [*ejusdem generis*].[63]

An intellectual property treaty would not necessarily be seen as relating to the 'same subject matter' as an IIA, although a preferential trade agreement including both investment and intellectual property obligations might fit that description.

The approach of the tribunal in *Maffezini* v. *Spain* has sparked considerable debate, and a number of subsequent tribunals have opted for less generous readings of MFN provisions.[64] The tribunal in *Plama* v. *Bulgaria*, for example, raised a question of significance to intellectual property: by what standard can a tribunal determine when an unorthodox subject matter involves more or less favourable treatment?[65] This is a particularly difficult question in the context of intellectual property, because the answer depends on the particular perspective of each investor. For some investors, particularly owners of intellectual property, more stringent intellectual property protections such as longer periods of patent protection are more favourable. However, for other investors, such as those seeking to access and exploit intellectual property held by other actors, the opposite is true: less stringent intellectual property protections are more favourable. This dichotomy could militate against the extension of MFN provisions in IIAs to intellectual property treaties.

2. MFN under TRIPS

According to Article 4 of the TRIPS Agreement:

> With regard to the protection of intellectual property, any advantage, favour, privilege or immunity granted by a Member to the nationals of

---

[63] *Ibid.*, 56.

[64] See e.g. *Telenor Mobile Communications AS* v. *Republic of Hungary (Award)* (ICSID Arbitral Tribunal, Case No. ARB/04/15, 13 September 2006), 90; *Plama Consortium* v. *Republic of Bulgaria (Decision on Jurisdiction)* (ICSID Arbitral Tribunal, Case No. ARB/03/24, 8 February 2005), 219, 223; *Salini Costruttori SPA* v. *Hashemite Kingdom of Jordan (Decision on Jurisdiction)* (ICSID Arbitral Tribunal, Case No. ARB/02/13, 1 November 2004), 115.

[65] *Plama Consortium* v. *Republic of Bulgaria (Award)* (ICSID Arbitral Tribunal, Case No. ARB/03/24, 27 August 2008), 208.

any other country shall be accorded immediately and unconditionally to the nationals of all other Members.

Unlike other key WTO agreements, the TRIPS Agreement contains no explicit exception for MFN treatment with respect to advantages accorded under bilateral arrangements such as preferential trade agreements.[66] Thus, more favourable intellectual property protections accorded by a member to the nationals of another country must arguably be accorded to the nationals of all members, without exception.

Although a national will not necessarily favour stronger intellectual property protections, depending on his or her circumstances (as discussed above), at least in some circumstances stronger intellectual property protections may amount to more favourable intellectual property protections. To the extent that a WTO member's IIA provides stronger intellectual property protections to the nationals of a given country, the MFN provision in the TRIPS Agreement may therefore require the member to accord those protections equally to nationals of all WTO members. Equally, with respect to investments in the form of intellectual property, an obligation imposed under a member's IIA concerning expropriation, fair and equitable treatment, or unreasonable impairment could be regarded as an 'advantage, favour, privilege or immunity' granted by that member to the nationals of the corresponding party with respect to intellectual property protection. On that basis, in a WTO complaint brought against that member, the TRIPS MFN provision might conceivably be argued to allow invocation of those investment protections. Going even further, if the IIA contains an investor-state dispute settlement mechanism, one might even contend that the TRIPS MFN provision requires the member to provide investor-state dispute settlement to the nationals of all members with respect to intellectual property protections.

In our view, the WTO Appellate Body is unlikely to interpret the TRIPS MFN provision as extending to investor-state dispute settlement[67]

[66] Marrakesh Agreement Establishing the World Trade Organization, opened for signature 15 April 1994, 1867 UNTS 3 (entered into force 1 January 1995), annex IA ('GATT 1994'), art. XXIV; Marrakesh Agreement Establishing the World Trade Organization, opened for signature 15 April 1994, 1867 UNTS 3 (entered into force 1 January 1995), annex IB ('GATS'), art. V. See also Tania Voon and Andrew D. Mitchell, 'Patents and Public Health in the WTO, FTAs and Beyond: Tension and Conflict in International Law', (2009) 43 *Journal of World Trade*, 571, 596–9.
[67] Ruse-Khan, 'Investment Law and Intellectual Property Rights', 11–12.

or even substantive investment protections with respect to intellectual property. Without delving into the details of the correct interpretation of the language of TRIPS Article 4, pursuant to the *ejusdem generis* principle discussed earlier, investor-state dispute settlement, prohibitions against expropriation, and other substantive investment protections appear to fall outside its scope, being only indirectly related to intellectual property protection of the kind envisaged in the TRIPS Agreement. Furthermore, bringing substantive investment obligations into the TRIPS Agreement through the MFN provision would be likely to raise jurisdictional difficulties given the limited scope of WTO disputes. The Appellate Body (and hence WTO Panels) would also be reluctant to rule on these non-WTO obligations.[68] Finally, an overly broad interpretation and application of the TRIPS MFN provision would be mirrored in other WTO agreements, in particular the General Agreement on Trade in Services, which contains an MFN provision protecting services and service suppliers,[69] including those operating through a commercial presence in a foreign WTO member.[70] Such a sudden and dramatic expansion in the scope of WTO law would be astonishing.

V.   Intellectual property and expropriation

A typical example of the prohibition on unlawful expropriation in IIAs is found in the Australia–Chile Free Trade Agreement:[71]

> 1. Neither Party may expropriate or nationalise a covered investment either directly or indirectly through measures equivalent to expropriation or nationalisation ('expropriation'), except:
>
> (a) for a public purpose;
> (b) in a non-discriminatory manner;
> (c) on payment of prompt, adequate, and effective compensation . . .; and
> (d) in accordance with due process of law

The inclusion in this provision of the words 'or indirectly through measures equivalent to expropriation' reflects the widespread recognition in international investment law that expropriation is not limited to seizure of property or formal transfer of title, but extends to

---

[68] Appellate Body Report, *Mexico – Taxes on Soft Drinks*, 56.
[69] GATS, art. II:1.   [70] GATS, art. I:2(c).
[71] Australia – Chile Free Trade Agreement, signed 30 July 2008, [2009] ATS 6 (entered into force 6 March 2009), ch. 10 art. 11.10.1.

deprivation of the meaningful use of an investment.[72] This recognition is significant because challenged measures affecting intellectual property rights are more likely to be designed to protect public health or the environment than to effect outright seizure of such rights,[73] as discussed further below.

1. Significance of domestic law in defining intellectual property

In relation to the *definition* of investment, we concluded above that intellectual property can be protected in an IIA with a given host state only to the extent that that state recognizes that form of intellectual property. Similarly, in assessing a substantive claim of *expropriation* of intellectual property, IIAs must arguably defer to municipal law in defining the scope and content of protected intangible rights including intellectual property rights.[74] Accordingly, the tribunal stated in *EnCana Corp* v. *Ecuador*: 'For there to have been an expropriation of an investment or return (in a situation involving legal rights or claims as distinct from the seizure of physical assets) the rights affected must exist under the law which creates them, in this case the law of Ecuador.'[75] The majority therefore held that Ecuador had not expropriated the investor's right to tax refunds because no such right existed under Ecuadorian law.[76]

In *Waste Management Inc.* v. *Mexico*, the tribunal held that the 'mere non-performance of a contractual obligation' is not tantamount to expropriation; in that case the claimant 'did not lose its contractual rights, which it was free to pursue before the contractually chosen forum'.[77] By emphasizing that the municipal legal system allowed the

---

[72] See e.g. Newcombe and Paradell, *Law and Practice of Investment Treaties*, 322.

[73] See Christopher Gibson, 'A Look at the Compulsory Licence in Investment Arbitration: The Case of Indirect Expropriation', *Transnational Dispute Management* 6(2009), 1, 18–19; Valentina Vadi, 'Global Health Governance at a Crossroads: Trademark Protection v Tobacco Control in International Investment Law', (2012) 48 *Stanford Journal of International Law*, 93, 105; Ruse-Khan, 'Investment Law and Intellectual Property Rights', 12; Correa, 'Bilateral Investment Agreements'.

[74] See e.g. Ruse-Khan, 'Investment Law and Intellectual Property Rights', 6; Monique Sasson, *Substantive Law in Investment Treaty Arbitration: The Unsettled Relationship between International Law and Municipal Law* (The Hague: Kluwer, 2010), 77–96.

[75] *EnCana Corporation* v. *Republic of Ecuador (Award)* (London Court of International Arbitration, Case No. UN3481, 3 February 2006), [184].

[76] *Ibid.*, [184]–[197].

[77] *Waste Management Inc* v. *Mexico (Award)* (ICSID Arbitral Tribunal, Case No. ARB(AF)/98/2, 30 April 2004), 174.

claimant to enforce its contractual rights, the tribunal was effectively relying on municipal law to determine the contours of the claimed rights and whether they had been substantially deprived.

In contrast, some tribunals have placed much less importance on the role of municipal law in determining the existence and scope of intangible rights for the purposes of an expropriation claim. In *Pope & Talbot* v. *Canada*, the tribunal accepted that a 'right to access the U.S. market' could be expropriated, even though neither United States law nor the IIA itself expressly protected such a market access or property right.[78] By distilling and protecting the 'true interest at stake', the tribunal implicitly rejected the notion that municipal law determines the content of intangible rights.[79] Similarly, the majority in *Eureko* v. *Poland* accepted that a suite of intangible rights was capable of being expropriated, without assessing whether these rights actually existed under Polish law.[80] (The dissenting opinion noted that only one of the claimed rights was enforceable under Polish law.)[81] As discussed earlier, though, if domestic law does not determine the scope and content of intellectual property rights, what does? Under this broader approach, property rights risk morphing into 'floating rights ungoverned by any set of rules'.[82]

In the *Philip Morris* dispute, PMA asserts that Australia's plain packaging legislation amounts to an 'unlawful expropriation' because it 'substantially deprives' PMA of: (1) the value of its shares, 'which is heavily dependent upon the ability to *use*' its intellectual property on its products; and (2) its intellectual property and 'the goodwill derived from the *use* of that intellectual property'.[83] In making out this claim of expropriation, PMA is likely to need to establish (among other things) either that Australian law confers a right to use the intellectual property in question, or that the scope and content of the intellectual property of Hong Kong investors protected under the Hong Kong–Australia BIT does not depend on Australian law.

---

[78] *Pope & Talbot* v. *Canada (Interim Award)* (Ad Hoc Arbitral Tribunal, UNCITRAL Rules, 26 June 2000), 87–99.

[79] *Ibid.*, 98.

[80] *Eureko* v. *Poland (Partial Award)* (Ad Hoc Arbitral Tribunal, 19 August 2005). For a discussion of this point, see Sasson, *Substantive Law in Investment Treaty Arbitration*, 83–5.

[81] *Eureko* v. *Poland (Dissenting Opinion of Partial Award)* (Ad Hoc Arbitral Tribunal, 19 August 2005), 10.

[82] Sasson, *Substantive Law in Investment Treaty Arbitration*, 81.

[83] *PMA Arbitration*, 7.3, 7.5 (emphasis added).

In the constitutional challenge to the legislation before the High Court of Australia, the sole dissenting judge, Heydon J, suggested that Australian trademark law, as an example, provides trademark owners with a positive right to use their trademarks.[84] However, judges in the majority tended to emphasize the negative aspects of trademark rights in Australia: 'It is a common feature of the statutory rights asserted in these proceedings that they are negative in character';[85] '[s]trictly speaking, the right subsisting in the owner of a trade mark is a negative and not a positive right'.[86] Thus, a trademark owner has the right to exclude others from using its trademarks. As the plain packaging legislation does not affect the trademark owner's negative rights (for example, the right to 'seek relief for infringement . . . is not disturbed'),[87] a 'logical gap' arose in asserting that the government had effectively acquired those rights.[88] This conclusion with respect to the plain packaging legislation is consistent with the fact that 'trade mark registration systems ordinarily do not confer a liberty to use the trade mark, free from what may be restraints found in other statutes or in the general law',[89] for example with respect to passing off, copyright infringement, or consumer protection.[90]

2. Indirect expropriation of intellectual property

Assuming that the impugned measure does affect something within the bounds of intellectual property as protected by an IIA, the next question is whether that measure can be properly characterized as an unlawful expropriation. Absent outright seizure or the formal transfer of title, the key task in most cases affecting intellectual property will be to ascertain whether the measure is a non-compensable regulation, for example a health regulation, or whether it amounts to an indirect expropriation. Tribunals have identified a number of relevant factors in determining whether a measure constitutes an indirect expropriation.[91]

---

[84] *JT International SA* v. *Commonwealth of Australia; British American Tobacco Australasia Limited* v. *Commonwealth of Australia* [2012] HCA 43 (5 October 2012) [208] (Heydon, J., dissenting).

[85] *Ibid.*, 36 (French CJ).   [86] *Ibid.*, 348 (Kiefel, J.).

[87] *Ibid.*, 258 (Crennan, J.).   [88] *Ibid.*, 43.

[89] *Ibid.*, 78 (Gummow, J.); see also 88, 137 (Gummow, J.).   [90] *Ibid.*, 266 (Crennan, J.).

[91] See *Técnicas Medioambientales Tecmed* v. *Mexico (Award)* (ICSID Arbitral Tribunal, Case No. ARB(AF)/00/2, 29 May 2003), 113–50; *Saluka Investments* v. *Czech Republic (Partial Award)* (Permanent Court of Arbitration, 17 March 2006), 253–64. For an in-depth

First, the measure must result in a substantial and lasting deprivation of the protected investment.[92] This may involve, for example, the destruction of the value of the investment,[93] the effective loss of control of the investment,[94] or the effective neutralization of the benefit of the investment.[95] Substantial deprivation is a high threshold to meet. Even where an investment is impaired to the point of making a loss, no substantial deprivation arises if the investor continues to exert overall control over the investment.[96] In addition, intellectual property rights will typically comprise only one small part of a broader investment in the form of a commercial operation involving manufacture, marketing and distribution. In such circumstances, a tribunal may be reluctant to characterize a measure impairing intellectual property as expropriation or even partial expropriation of the investment.[97]

Second, the character of the measure is relevant, particularly whether it entails an exercise of the state's sovereign regulatory or police powers. As stated by one tribunal, '[i]t is well established that the mere exercise by government of regulatory powers that create impediments to business or entail the payment of taxes or other levies does not of itself constitute expropriation'.[98] Thus, measures that protect public order and morality,

discussion of these factors, see Newcombe and Paradell, *Law and Practice of Investment Treaties*, 321–70.

[92] See e.g. *Alpha Projektholding v. Ukraine (Award)* (ICSID Arbitral Tribunal, Case No. ARB/07/16, 20 October 2010), 408; *AES Summit Generation v. Hungary (Award)* (ICSID Arbitral Tribunal, Case No. ARB/07/22, 17 September 2010), 14.3.1, 14.3.3; *Suez v. Argentina (Decision on Liability)* (ICSID Arbitral Tribunal, Case No. ARB/03/17, 30 July 2010), 122–3, 134.

[93] *CME Czech Republic v. Czech Republic (Partial Award)* (Ad Hoc Arbitral Tribunal, UNCITRAL Rules, 13 September 2001), 599, 609.

[94] *Sempra Energy v. Argentina (Award)* (ICSID Arbitral Tribunal, Case No. ARB/02/16, 18 September 2007), 285.

[95] *CME Czech Republic v. Czech Republic (Partial Award)* (Ad Hoc Arbitral Tribunal, UNCITRAL Rules, 13 September 2001), 604.

[96] See e.g. *Sergei Paushok and others v. Mongolia (Award on Jurisdiction and Liability)* (Ad Hoc Arbitral Tribunal, UNCITRAL Rules, 28 April 2011,) 334.

[97] See e.g. *Marvin Feldman v. Mexico (Award)* (ICSID Arbitral Tribunal, Case No. ARB (AF)/99/1 (NAFTA) December 16, 2002), 52, 111, 142, 209; *Telenor Mobile Communications AS v. The Republic of Hungary (Award)* (ICSID Arbitral Tribunal, Case No. ARB/04/15, 13 September 2006), 67. Cf. *SD Myers v. Canada (First Partial Award)* (Ad Hoc Arbitral Tribunal, UNCITRAL Rules, 13 November 2000), 283; *Waste Management Inc v. Mexico (Award)* (ICSID Arbitral Tribunal, Case No. ARB(AF)/98/2, 30 April 2004), 141.

[98] *Telenor Mobile Communications AS v. The Republic of Hungary (Award)* (ICSID Arbitral Tribunal, Case No. ARB/04/15, 13 September 2006), 64.

human health or the environment, or that impose taxation, will not usually meet the standard of substantial deprivation.[99] Recent practice in IIAs is even to embed this principle in the treaty text. For example, the 2012 United States Model BIT states that, '[e]xcept in rare circumstances, non-discriminatory regulatory actions by a Party that are designed and applied to protect legitimate public welfare objectives, such as public health, safety, and the environment, do not constitute indirect expropriations'.[100]

The exercise of sovereign regulatory power in the pursuit of the public interest must often be balanced by a third factor: the proportionality between the public interest pursued and the measure's degree of interference with the investment. If the measure is 'obviously disproportionate to the need being addressed', it is more likely to be an indirect expropriation.[101] The 'legitimate expectations' of the affected investors are also relevant.[102] Ultimately, the assessment of whether a measure results in an indirect expropriation is context and fact specific, requiring a case-by-case analysis.[103] Different factors may be relevant in specific cases, with varying weight and priority apportioned among the range of considerations.

In the *Philip Morris* case, PMA alleges that the plain packaging legislation: will 'significantly impai[r]' the enterprise of PML; will 'destro[y] the commercial value' of its intellectual property and goodwill; and 'is not for a proven public purpose related to the internal needs of Australia'.[104] As acknowledged by some judges in the High Court of

---

[99] See e.g. *Suez v. Argentina (Decision on Liability)* (ICSID Arbitral Tribunal, Case No. ARB/03/17, 30 July 2010), 128, 147–8; *SD Myers v. Canada (First Partial Award)* (Ad Hoc Arbitral Tribunal, UNCITRAL Rules, 13 November 2000), 281–282; *Saluka Investments v Czech Republic (Partial Award)* (Permanent Court of Arbitration, 17 March 2006), 254–5, 257–8, 261–2, 275–6.

[100] 2012 United States Model BIT, annex B, www.state.gov/e/eb/ifd/bit/index.htm

[101] *LG&E Energy Corp v. Argentina (Decision on Liability)* (ICSID Arbitral Tribunal, Case No. ARB 02/1, 3 October 2006), 195.

[102] *Fireman's Fund Insurance Company v. Mexico (Award)* (ICSID Arbitral Award, Case No. ARB(AF)/02/01, 17 July 2006), 176(k); Anne Hoffmann, 'Indirect Expropriation', in August Reinisch, *Standards of Investment Protection* (Oxford University Press, 2008), 162–3; Campbell McLachlan, Laurence Shore, and Matthew Weiniger, *International Investment Arbitration: Substantive Principles* (Oxford University Press, 2007), 8.104–8.105; Jeswald Salacuse, *The Law of Investment Treaties* (Oxford University Press, 2010), 311–12.

[103] *Saluka Investments v. Czech Republic (Partial Award)* (Permanent Court of Arbitration, 17 March 2006), 264–5; *Generation Ukraine Inc. v. Ukraine (Award)* (ICSID Arbitral Tribunal, Case No. ARB/00/9, 16 September 2003), 20.29.

[104] *PMA Arbitration*, 7.3–7.4.

Australia, the legislation might ultimately reduce the value of the relevant intellectual property rights[105] and harm the plaintiffs' businesses by reducing their sales.[106] However, in the absence of evidence that PML has lost or will lose the ability to manufacture, distribute and trade its products, the legislation is unlikely to meet the threshold for substantial deprivation. In the High Court, only Heydon J in dissent considered that the plain packaging legislation 'deprive[s]' the plaintiffs of 'control of their property, and of the benefits of control'.[107] The 6:1 majority decision that the legislation does not effect an acquisition of property is consistent with a conclusion that the legislation does not substantially deprive PMA of its investment: in the words of Crennan J, the legislation 'does not involve any diminution in or extinguishment of any property'.[108]

The fact that both the WHO and the Convention Secretariat of the WHO Framework Convention for Tobacco Control[109] have expressed support for Australia's initiative with reference to that treaty and associated guidelines,[110] enhances Australia's position that plain packaging is a proportionate response to the adverse health effects of tobacco products. Further, for a number of reasons, PMA cannot be regarded as having a legitimate expectation that a measure such as plain packaging would not be introduced in Australia at the time it made its investment: Australia made no specific assurances to PMA regarding plain tobacco packaging or the stability of the regulatory environment for tobacco products more generally;[111] PMA cannot reasonably have expected that the regulatory environment for its tobacco

---

[105] *JT International SA* v. *Commonwealth of Australia; British American Tobacco Australasia Limited* v. *Commonwealth of Australia* [2012] HCA 43 (5 October 2012), 44 (French CJ), 139 (Gummow, J.), 356 (Kiefel, J.), 214 (Heydon, J, dissenting).
[106] *Ibid.*, 295 (Crennan, J), 372 (Kiefel, J).   [107] *Ibid.*, 212 (Heydon, J, dissenting).
[108] *Ibid.*, 301 (Crennan, J).
[109] Adopted 21 May 2003, 2302 UNTS 166 (entered into force 27 February 2005).
[110] WHO, *Submission re Australia Plain Packaging Legislation* (June 2011); Convention Secretariat WHO FCTC, *Submission in Respect of Australia's Draft Tobacco Plain Packaging Bill 2011* (6 June 2011).
[111] See e.g. *GEA Group* v. *Ukraine (Award)* (ICSID Arbitral Tribunal, Case No. ARB/08/16, 31 March 2011), 283; *Total* v. *Argentina (Decision on Liability)* (ICSID Arbitral Tribunal, Case No. ARB/04/1, 21 December 2010), 116, 117, 119, 121; *AES Summit Generation* v. *Hungary (Award)* (ICSID Arbitral Tribunal, Case No. ARB/07/22, 17 September 2010), 9.3.17–9.3.18, 9.3.31; *EDF (Services)* v. *Romania (Award)* (ICSID Arbitral Tribunal, Case No. ARB/05/13, 2 October 2009), 217; *Glamis Gold* v. *United States (Award)* (Ad Hoc Arbitral Tribunal, UNCITRAL Rules, 14 May 2009), 620, 622.

products would remain *frozen* as at the time of its investment;[112] more-over, PMA's investment in Australia took place almost one year after the Australian government announced that mandatory plain packaging of tobacco products would be implemented.[113]

In recent IIAs (and particularly in investment chapters in preferential trade agreements), drafters have attempted to harmonize the standard for expropriation with intellectual property-specific treaties and obliga-tions.[114] For example, Article 10.11.5 of the Australia–Chile Free Trade Agreement and Article 11.6.5 of the United States–Korea Free Trade Agreement provide:[115]

> This Article [on expropriation] does not apply to the issuance of compul-sory licences granted in relation to intellectual property rights in accord-ance with the TRIPS Agreement, or to the revocation, limitation, or creation of intellectual property rights, to the extent that such revocation, limitation, or creation is consistent with Chapter 17 (Intellectual Property).

This is an important development in mitigating the potential for fragmentation between international investment law and intellectual property-specific obligations under WTO law, preferential trade agreements, and intellectual property treaties. It establishes the pri-macy of specific disciplines on intellectual property over general expropriation protections, such that expropriation claims cannot be used to undermine the balance between intellectual property owners and users in the TRIPS Agreement and other intellectual property treaties.

---

[112] See e.g. *Impregilo* v. *Argentine Republic (Award)* (ICSID Arbitral Tribunal, Case No. ARB/07/17, 21 June 2011), 290–1; *Total* v. *Argentina (Decision on Liability)* (ICSID Arbitral Tribunal, Case No. ARB/04/1, 21 December 2010), 120; *AES Summit Gener-ation* v. *Hungary (Award)* (ICSID Arbitral Tribunal, Case No. ARB/07/22, 17 September 2010), 9.3.34; *EDF (Services)* v. *Romania (Award)* (ICSID Arbitral Tribunal, Case No. ARB/05/13, 2 October 2009), 217.

[113] Philip Morris (Australia) Limited, *Financial Report 2010*; IBISWorld, *IBISWorld Com-pany Report: Philip Morris (Australia) Limited – Premium Report* (31 December 2010, with update as at 11 April 2011) 14; PM of Australia, 'Media release: anti-smoking action'.

[114] See Boie, 'Protection of Intellectual Property Rights', part 3.2.

[115] Australia–Chile Free Trade Agreement, signed 30 July 2008, [2009] ATS 6 (entered into force 6 March 2009), ch. 10, art. 10.11.5; Free Trade Agreement between the United States of America and the Republic of Korea, signed 30 June 2007 (entered into force 15 March 2012), art. 11.6.5.

VI.   Intellectual property and umbrella clauses

The so-called 'umbrella clause' is a regular feature of IIAs, with one estimate suggesting that forty percent of IIAs contain such a clause.[116] The usual function of these clauses is to bring within the ambit of the IIA obligations of the host state outside the IIA, such as pursuant to a specific investment authorization or contract with the relevant investor. In this way, an aggrieved investor could arguably pursue as a breach of the IIA through investor-state dispute settlement a breach of contract or other undertaking by the host state.[117]

Examples of umbrella clauses include:

> Each Party shall observe any other obligation it has assumed with regard to investments in its territory by investors of the other Party.[118]

> A Contracting Party shall, subject to its law, do all in its power to ensure that a written undertaking given by a competent authority to a national of the other Contracting Party with regard to an investment is respected.[119]

The outside obligations covered by an umbrella clause may be variously described as 'obligations',[120] 'undertakings',[121] 'commitments',[122] and 'legal frameworks'.[123] The obligations may have to relate to specific

---

[116] Judith Gill, Matthew Gearing, and Gemma Birt, 'Contractual Claims and Bilateral Investment Treaties: A Comparative Review of the SGS Cases', (2004) 21 *Journal of International Arbitration*, 397.

[117] See Katia Yannaca-Small, 'What about this "Umbrella Clause"?', in Yannaca-Small (ed.), *Arbitration under International Investment Agreements: A Guide to the Key Issues* (Oxford University Press, 2010), 479, 486–93, 502–3.

[118] Agreement between the Swiss Confederation and the United Mexican States on the Promotion and Reciprocal Protection of Investments, signed 10 July 1995 (entered into force 15 March 1996), art. 10(2).

[119] Agreement between Australia and the Republic of Poland on the Reciprocal Promotion and Protection of Investments, signed 7 May 1991, [1992] ATS 10 (entered into force 27 March 1992), art. 10.

[120] Agreement between the Swiss Confederation and the United Mexican States on the Promotion and Reciprocal Protection of Investments, signed 10 July 1995 (entered into force 15 March 1996), art. 10(2).

[121] Agreement between Australia and the Republic of Poland on the Reciprocal Promotion and Protection of Investments, signed 7 May 1991, [1992] ATS 10 (entered into force 27 March 1992), art. 10.

[122] Agreement between the Government of the People's Republic of China and the Government of the Republic of Singapore on the Promotion and Protection of Investments, signed 21 November 1985, art. 15.

[123] Agreement between the Government of the Hashemite Kingdom of Jordan and the Government of the Italian Republic on the Promotion and Protection of Investments, signed 21 July 1996, art. 2(4).

things: some umbrella clauses refer to obligations 'assumed with regard to investments',[124] 'entered into with regard to investments',[125] or 'entered into with regard to specific investments'.[126] The host state may be required to 'observe',[127] 'ensure',[128] 'respect',[129] or 'constantly guarantee'[130] the protected obligations.

These different permutations can lead to wide variations in the scope and content of the protection offered by umbrella clauses across different IIAs. At one end of the spectrum, umbrella clauses might cover only specific contracts concluded between a host state and a particular investor. At the other end, umbrella clauses could potentially extend to domestic legal and administrative acts, unilateral undertakings or assurances by a host state.[131] The meaning of a particular clause may not be evident from the words of the clause alone; rather, the same words may be interpreted differently by different tribunals depending on the broader context of the clause or other factors. While one tribunal found that the use of the words 'obligations entered into' in an umbrella clause largely limited its application to specific undertakings to particular investors,[132]

---

[124] Agreement between the Swiss Confederation and the United Mexican States on the Promotion and Reciprocal Protection of Investments, signed 10 July 1995 (entered into force 15 March 1996), art. 10(2).

[125] Agreement between the Government of Hong Kong and the Government of Australia for the Promotion and Protection of Investments, signed 15 September 1993, 1748 UNTS 385 (entered into force 15 October 1993), art. 2.

[126] Agreement between the Kingdom of the Netherlands and the Republic of the Philippines for the Promotion and Protection of Investments, signed 27 February 1985, UNTS 1488 (entered into force 1 October 1987), art. 3(3).

[127] Agreement between the Swiss Confederation and the United Mexican States on the Promotion and Reciprocal Protection of Investments, signed 10 July 1995 (entered into force 15 March 1996), art. 10(2).

[128] Agreement between Australia and the Republic of Poland on the Reciprocal Promotion and Protection of Investments, signed 7 May 1991, [1992] ATS 10 (entered into force 27 March 1992), art. 10.

[129] Agreement between the Government of the Hellenic Republic and the Federal Government of the Federal Republic of Yugoslavia for the Reciprocal Promotion and Protection of Investments, signed 25 June 1997, art. 2(4).

[130] Agreement between the Government of the Hashemite Kingdom of Jordan and the Government of the Italian Republic on the Promotion and Protection of Investments, signed 21 July 1996, art. 2(4).

[131] *Société Générale du Surveillance SA* v. *Pakistan (Decision on Objections to Jurisdiction)* (ICSID Arbitral Tribunal, Case No. ARB/01/13, 6 August 2003), 166; *Enron* v. *Argentina (Award)* (ICSID Arbitral Tribunal, Case No. ARB/01/3, 22 May 2007), 269–77.

[132] *Noble Ventures, Inc.* v. *Romania (Award)* (ICSID Arbitral Tribunal, Case No. ARB/01/11, 5 October 2005), 42–62.

another tribunal read the words 'commitments entered into' as sufficiently broad to cover commitments embedded in general domestic law.[133] The umbrella clause in the Hong Kong–Australia BIT provides that '[e]ach Contracting Party shall observe any obligation it may have entered into with regard to investments of investors of the other Contracting Party'.[134] In the *Philip Morris* dispute, PMA contends that this clause extends beyond 'specific obligations or representations made by the host State to investors from the other Contracting State' to 'other international obligations binding on the host State'. Thus, Philip Morris contends that Australia has violated the umbrella clause by violating (*inter alia*) Australia's obligations under the TRIPS Agreement. On its face, the term 'any obligation' might seem broad enough to encompass international obligations: "'[a]ny" obligations is capacious; it means not only obligations of a certain type, but "any" – that is to say, all – obligations'.[135] However, Australia's obligations under the TRIPS Agreement are arguably not specific enough to PMA's investment, investments of Hong Kong investors, or foreign investment generally, to engage the umbrella clause. Assuming the umbrella clause could be engaged in this way, PMA would also need to overcome jurisdictional difficulties with an investment tribunal ruling on a WTO claim,[136] not to mention the substantive hurdles involved in that WTO claim, as we have discussed elsewhere.[137]

VII. Conclusion

The relationship between international investment law and intellectual property is complex, fragmented, and largely unsettled. Continuing

---

[133] *Société Générale du Surveillance SA* v. *Pakistan (Decision on Objections to Jurisdiction)* (ICSID Arbitral Tribunal, Case No. ARB/01/13, 6 August 2003), 166.

[134] Agreement between the Government of Hong Kong and the Government of Australia for the Promotion and Protection of Investments, signed 15 September 1993, 1748 UNTS 385 (entered into force 15 October 1993), art. 2(2).

[135] *Eureko* v. *Poland (Partial Award)* (Ad Hoc Arbitral Tribunal, 19 August 2005). See also *Enron* v. *Argentina (Award)* (ICSID Arbitral Tribunal, Case No. ARB/01/3, 22 May 2007) [274]. See also Newcombe and Paradell, *Law and Practice of Investment Treaties*, 459. Cf. *Noble Ventures, Inc* v. *Romania (Award)* (ICSID Arbitral Tribunal, Case No. ARB/01/11, 5 October 2005), 51.

[136] *Philip Morris Asia Limited* v. *Commonwealth of Australia: Australia's Response to the Notice of Arbitration* (21 December 2011), 33, 35.

[137] Tania Voon and Andrew Mitchell 'Implications of WTO Law for Plain Packaging of Tobacco Products', in Tania Voon, Andrew Mitchell, and Jonathan Liberman with Glyn Ayres (eds.), *Public Health and Plain Packaging of Cigarettes: Legal Issues* (Cheltenham: Edward Elgar, 2012), 136.

puzzles include the role of municipal law in determining the contours of intellectual property rights protected by IIAs, the ability of umbrella clauses to de facto incorporate intellectual property obligations from other treaties, and the extent to which the use of intellectual property must positively benefit a host state in order to qualify as a protected investment. Nevertheless, some recent steps suggest a deliberate attempt at constructive integration between international investment law and intellectual property. These include in some recent IIAs the effective subordination of expropriation standards to rights under intellectual property treaties and the explicit tying of protected intellectual property rights to their subsistence at domestic law. Such efforts are still relatively piecemeal and may provide clarity only at the margins. In that context, it will be interesting to observe whether treaty drafting and practice responds decisively to the challenges presented by the *Philip Morris* dispute.

17

The Anti-Counterfeiting Trade Agreement: less harmonization, further fragmentation

BRYAN MERCURIO

I. Introduction

The field of international intellectual property (IP) law is one of if not the most fragmented areas of international economic law. Such fragmentation of IP occurs in trade law, investment law and in pure IP agreements. Thus, the fragmentation of international IP law occurs not only inter-disciplines, as is the case of say trade and investment or trade and human rights (or, of course, IP and trade and IP and investment), but also intra-discipline as between the multilateral (at both the World Trade Organization (WTO) and World Intellectual Property Organization (WIPO)), bilateral/regional and stand-alone agreements.

In trade, with the WTO's Doha Round of trade negotiations in a moribund state, governments have increasingly turned to bilateral and regional agreements in an attempt to liberalize trade and spur economic growth. These agreements not only go beyond the standard set out in the WTO's Agreement on Trade-Related Aspects of Intellectual Property (TRIPS Agreement) in both depth and scope, but also differ between and among the vast array of agreements. In so doing, IP law moves beyond the harmonized system of minimum standards set out in the TRIPS Agreement and does so in a fragmented, disorganized manner.

In terms of investment agreements, without any multilateral architecture the treatment of IP in investment agreements is left solely to bilateral and regional agreements. While until recently IP has been underemphasized in the field of investment law and is treated fairly similarly in most international investment agreements, the regulation of

With permission of the publisher, sections of this chapter are drawn from B. Mercurio, 'The Anti-Counterfeiting Trade Agreement: Ambitious Aims vs. Political Reality', *KLRI Journal of Law and Legislation* 3 (2012), 315–43.

IP as it relates to international investment law is now recognized to be fragmented and unsettled.[1]

Finally, and in response to the failure of the multilateral system to continue 'legislating', some countries have sought to fragment the system even further through a new stand-alone agreement focusing on enforcement where IP cannot be traded off for gains in other sectors. Designed to increase cooperation among countries and establish standards in the area of IP enforcement,[2] the Anti-Counterfeiting Trade Agreement (ACTA) adds an additional layer of complexity to an already fragmented system.

Attempting to build upon domestic, international and regional standards, the now seemingly abandoned the ACTA perfectly illustrates both the fragmented nature of international IP as well as its complexity. This chapter argues that the ACTA is a failed agreement, not as a result of its rejection, but because the final text does not meet the aims and objectives set out by the negotiating countries. This argument is coupled with a more systemic analysis of the field of contemporary international IP law in light of the complex and sometimes contradictory aims of global lawmakers of increased harmonization and the exportation of national IP regimes. While it is true that an unsatisfactory or failed attempt at harmonization does not necessarily result in greater fragmentation, these negotiations produce a stand-alone agreement in competition with the already fragmented international IP regime. In addition, the ACTA neither adopts nor mandates an existing international standard but is more of a hybrid of existing domestic law alongside slightly amended versions of relevant existing international standards.

---

[1] See Chapter 16 of this volume. See also B. Mercurio, 'Awakening the Sleeping Giant: Intellectual Property Rights in International Investment Agreements', *Journal of International Economic Law* 15(2012), 871–915; T. Voon and A. Mitchell, 'Implications of International Investment Law for Plain Tobacco Packaging: Lessons from the Hong Kong-Australia BIT', in T. Voon, A. Mitchell, J. Liberman and G. Ayres (eds.), *Public Health and Plain Packing of Cigarettes: Legal Issues* (Cheltenham: Edward Elgar, 2012), 137–72.

[2] The global economic costs of counterfeiting and piracy are difficult to measure and estimates range from US$250 billion (as per the OECD in 2009, see World Intellectual Property Organization, 'Counterfeiting and Piracy Endangers Global Economic Recovery Say Global Congress Leaders', WIPO PR/2009/621, 3 December 2009, http://tinyurl.com/yd9edmq) to over US$600 billion (as per the International AntiCounterfeiting Coalition, www.iacc.org/about-counterfeiting/), with the latter also estimating that counterfeiting results in a loss of US$250 billion and 750,000 US jobs. For analysis of the claims, see P. Chaudhry and A. Zimmerman, *The Economics of Counterfeit Trade* (Heidelberg: Springer, 2009), esp. 13. See also M. Blakeney, *Intellectual Property Enforcement: A Commentary on the Anti-Counterfeiting Trade Agreement (ACTA)* (Cheltenham: Edward Elgar, 2012), ch. 1.

Section II introduces the ACTA, including the background to the negotiations, the controversial nature of the negotiations and ultimately its rejection by the European Parliament in July 2012. Section III contains the core argument of the chapter; that is, that the ACTA failed to meet its negotiating objectives. With the focus on the failure to deliver any meaningful international standards, section III provides several examples where a negotiating party or parties proposed harmonized standards but ultimately the final text fails to adopt such standards. In maintaining the status quo, most of the negotiating parties were thus able to defend their role in the ACTA negotiations to domestic constituencies by insisting that the agreement does not require any legislative amendments. Of course, such a result does nothing to harmonize an increasingly fragmented area of international economic law. One also wonders how an agreement which requires no legislative amendments and simply maintains the status quo could possibly play any meaningful role in combating piracy and counterfeiting. Section IV concludes.

II. Negotiating the ACTA

The genesis of the ACTA is a proposal by Japan in July 2005 at the Group of Eight (G8) meeting at Gleneagles, Scotland, which the G8 published as its own in a four-paragraph statement entitled 'Reducing IPR Piracy and Counterfeiting through More Effective Enforcement'.[3] The statement essentially recognizes the ills brought about by piracy and counterfeiting and sets out a number of steps which countries could take to 'reduc[e] substantially global trade in pirated and counterfeit goods, and efficiently combat[] the transnational networks that support it'.[4] The statement also calls for future action to implement the identified steps.[5] In November 2005, Japan followed up on the G8 statement and call for action by proposing a 'Treaty on Non-Proliferation of Counterfeits and Pirated Goods'.[6] Japan's call for a treaty was met by virtual indifference by most governments and onlookers, including the USA.[7]

---

[3] G8 (Gleneagles 2005), 'Reducing IPR, piracy and counterfeiting through more effective enforcement', post-meeting statement, www.g7.utoronto.ca/summit/2005gleneagles/ipr_piracy.pdf

[4] Ibid., para. 3.   [5] Ibid., para. 4.

[6] See T. I. S. Gerhardsen, 'Japan proposes new IP enforcement treaty', Intellectual Property Watch, 15 November 2005, www.ip-watch.org/weblog/index.php?p=135 (reporting that the Japanese originally envisaged either Interpol or the World Customs Organization overseeing the treaty).

[7] Ibid.

Despite the lack of response to Japan's proposal in 2005 the issue remained on the G8 agenda and in July 2006 at a meeting in St Petersburg, Russia, the G8 issued a statement announcing a comprehensive IP rights enforcement strategy entitled 'Combating Intellectual Property Rights Piracy and Counterfeiting'.[8] The focus of this statement continued to be combating counterfeiting and piracy through increased cooperation among governmental agencies and international organizations. Interestingly, the statement also mentioned concern for the 'public health and safety' effects from counterfeiting and piracy and the possibility for 'technical assistance pilot plans' to be developed in cooperation with WIPO, WTO, the Organisation for Economic Co-operation and Development (OECD), Interpol and the World Customs Organization (WCO).[9] The G8 also issued a lengthy document entitled 'Fight against Infectious Diseases', which among other things calls for increased access to medicines through reduced costs.[10] More specifically, the statement calls for the elimination of tariffs and non-tariff barriers on medicines and devices as well as noting the possibility of countries to make use of the flexibilities existing in the TRIPS Agreement.[11]

Japan followed the G8 efforts the next year when on 23 October 2007 its Ministry of Foreign Affairs announced its intention to bring about 'a new international legal framework to strengthen the enforcement of intellectual property rights'.[12] This time, the European Commission and the US Trade Representative (USTR) supported the initiative. In February 2008, the European Commission published a Recommendation to the Council to authorize the Commission to begin negotiations on a plurilateral anti-counterfeiting trade agreement[13] while at the same time

---

[8] G8, 'Combating Intellectual Property Rights Piracy and Counterfeiting', 16 July 2006, http://en.g8russia.ru/docs/15.html. See also T. I. S. Gerhardsen, 'G8 Outcome Has IP Implications for Enforcement, Trade and Health', *Intellectual Property Watch*, 19 July 2006, www.ip-watch.org/2006/07/19/g8-outcome-has-ip-implications-for-enforcement-trade-and-health

[9] *Ibid.*, paras. 1 and 5.

[10] G8, 'Fight against Infectious Diseases', 16 July 2006, http://en.g8russia.ru/docs/10.html

[11] *Ibid.*, paras. 37 and 32.

[12] Ministry of Foreign Affairs of Japan (2007), PR, 'Framework of the Anti-Counterfeiting Trade Agreement (ACTA)', Ministry of Foreign Affairs of Japan, 23 October 2007, www.mofa.go.jp/announce/announce/2007/10/1175848_836.html. For more background on the initial stages of the ACTA negotiations, see M. Kaminski, 'The Origins and Potential Impact of the Anti-Counterfeiting Trade Agreement (ACTA)', *Yale Journal of International Law* 34 (2009), 247, 250–1.

[13] Recommendation from the Commission to the Council to authorize the Commission to open negotiations of a plurilateral anti-counterfeiting trade agreement (SEC(2008) 255 final/2), Brussels, 27 February 2008, http://ec.europa.eu/transparency/regdoc/rep/2/2008/EN/2-2008-255-EN-F2-0.Pdf.

the USA began publishing official requests for comments and notices of public meetings.[14]

In the end, thirty-seven countries (Australia, Canada, EU (twenty-seven member states), Japan, Mexico, Morocco, New Zealand, Singapore, South Korea, Switzerland and the USA) were involved in the ACTA negotiations. The negotiations purported to enhance international cooperation regarding both the civil and criminal enforcement of IP and to establish a new best practice enforcement framework in order to better combat global counterfeiting and piracy. Covering enforcement processes involving purely domestic procedures and also those requiring international cooperation, eleven formal negotiating rounds were held and the agreement was concluded in late 2010.

The agreement was officially adopted on 15 April 2011. At a signing ceremony held in Tokyo, Australia, Canada, Japan, South Korea, Morocco, New Zealand, Singapore and the USA signed ACTA[15] The Council of the EU unanimously adopted the agreement in December 2011 and 22 member states signed the ACTA at a ceremony held on 26 January 2012. The agreement, however, is not in force and will only come into force following ratification of six negotiating parties.[16] To date, only Japan has ratified the ACTA. With widely publicized protests across Europe in 2012,[17] followed by the EU Parliament rejecting the ACTA,[18] ratification remains unlikely not only for the EU but also for many of the other negotiating parties, including Switzerland, Australia and Mexico.[19] Moreover, as negotiations on other more comprehensive trade

---

[14] See www.regulations.gov/#!documentDetail;D=USTR-2008-0007-0001; and www.regu-lations.gov/#!documentDetail;D=USTR-2008-0030-0001

[15] See 'Joint press statement of the Anti-Counterfeiting Trade Agreement Negotiating parties', PR, October 2011, available at www.ustr.gov/about-us/press-office/press-releases/2011/october/joint-press-statement-anti-counterfeiting-trade-ag

[16] ACTA, art. 40.

[17] On the large-scale protests against the ACTA in Europe, see D. Lee, 'ACTA protests: thousands take to streets across Europe', BBC News, 11 February 2012, www.bbc.co.uk/news/technology-16999497

[18] The European Parliament voted on 4 July 2012 to reject the treaty, with 478 MEPs votes against, 39 votes in favour of ACTA and 165 abstentions. For background and commentary on the EU parliamentary process, see D. Matthews, 'The Rise and Fall of the Anti-Counterfeiting Trade Agreement (ACTA): Lessons for the European Union' Queen Mary University of London, School of Law, Legal Studies Research Paper No. 127/2012, 3–6, www.ssrn.com

[19] See 'Uncertainty Looms over EU Ratification of Anti-Counterfeiting Pact', 16(6) (15 February 2012) Bridges Weekly Trade Digest 5; 'Anti-counterfeiting Pact Referred to European Court of Justice', 16(7) (22 February 2012) Bridges Weekly Trade Digest 10.

agreements gather momentum, the ACTA has been virtually ignored by supporters and critics alike.

The protests against the ACTA were not unexpected, as the negotiations were plagued by criticism almost from the beginning. More specifically, the negotiations were heavily criticized for lacking legitimacy and transparency,[20] for encroaching upon territory traditionally viewed exclusively in the purview of domestic legislatures and authorities, for being excessively industry driven[21] and for attempting to shift the forum for IP enforcement away from existing multilateral organizations, most notably the WIPO and the WTO.[22] Critics also claimed that the ACTA threatened everything from civil liberties (such as freedom of speech) – with some even warning that customs authorities at airports would individually inspect every incoming passenger's iPod and computer for

---

[20] Draft texts were released in April (http://trade.ec.europa.eu/doclib/docs/2010/april/tradoc_146029.pdf) and November 2010 (http://commondatastorage.googleapis.com/leaks/Anti-Counterfeiting%20Trade%20Agreement.pdf), following repeated requests from NGOs and interested observers (including a rejected request for a copy of the ACTA discussion draft and related materials under the US Freedom of Information Act (FOA) on the grounds that the documents are 'classified in the interest of national security') and following EU Parliament Resolution of 10 March 2010 on the Transparency and State of Play of the ACTA Negotiations [2010] OJ C 349E/46). Draft texts were also leaked in July 2010 (http://publicintelligence.net/anti-counterfeiting-trade-agreement-acta-july-2010-draft) and August 2010 (http://publicintelligence.net/anti-counterfeiting-trade-agreement-acta-august-2010-draft). On the FOA and the secrecy surrounding the ACTA negotiations, see D. Levine, 'Transparency Soup: The ACTA Negotiating Process and "Black Box" Lawmaking', *American University Journal of International Law and Policy* 26 (2011), 811.

[21] The fact that several industry representatives had access to and influenced the USA as private sector advisers increased the discontent. See e.g. J. Love, 'Who Are the Cleared Advisors That Have Access to Secret ACTA Documents?', KEI blog posting, 13 March 2009, www.keionline.org/blogs/2009/03/13/who-are-cleared-advisors

[22] 'WTO Members at Odds over Anti-Counterfeiting Pact', 16(9) (7 March 2012) *Bridges Weekly Trade Digest* 6; Blakeney, *Intellectual Property Enforcement*, 44–54. While such an assertion is technically true, several attempts to even discuss increased enforcement standards at the WTO (TRIPS Council) and WIPO (Advisory Committee on Enforcement) have been rejected out of hand by a large contingent of developing countries as not appropriate for discussion in that particular forum. In such an environment, if neither the WTO's TRIPS Council nor WIPO's Advisory Committee on Enforcement are the appropriate forum to discuss norm-setting in the area of IP enforcement, it follows that those countries desiring to establish a global standard had no choice but to move to different, more suitable forum. Moreover, several WTO members complained about several provisions contained in the ACTA which match their own domestic law. See US Second Intervention made at the WTO TRIPS Council Meeting held on 28 February 2012 under agenda item Agenda item N 'IP enforcement trends', http://keionline.org/node/1379

possible IP infringements[23] – to access to information (i.e. the 'right' to use the internet) to access to medicines.[24]

These well-known criticisms have been subjected to scrutiny in academic scholarship and in the online blogosphere.[25] This chapter posits, however, that while the (mostly overblown or patently incorrect) criticisms and protests did likely ultimately 'kill' the ACTA (in that they caused the EU Parliament to reject the agreement),[26] internal negotiating difficulties plotted its downfall by slowly draining the agreement of any ambition and usefulness. In the end, the urgency to conclude *an* agreement became more important than to conclude a *meaningful* agreement. Thus, while the ACTA was promoted as a 'twenty-first century' agreement aimed at deepening international cooperation and promoting strong enforcement practices,[27] the final text of the ACTA accomplishes neither objective. Section III argues this point in some detail.

III. The undelivered objectives of the ACTA

The main aims for negotiating the ACTA were: increased international cooperation and a new standard of international enforcement. These aims were often publicly repeated during the negotiations. For instance, the website of the United States Trade Representative (USTR) states that the ACTA includes 'innovative provisions to deepen international

---

23 See Professor M. Geist, www.michaelgeist.ca/index.php?option=com_tags&task=view& tag=acta&Itemid=408. Negotiating countries countered by releasing press releases and negotiating summaries. See the summary of negotiations released on USTR website, 'ACTA: Summary of Key Elements under Discussion' (April 2009), www.ustr.gov/ webfm_send/1479. The governments of Canada, EU, Japan, New Zealand and the UK released identical summaries on the same day.

24 See e.g. Oxfam, 'Secret Plans to Criminalize Generic Medicines Could Hurt Poor Countries and People', 15 July 2009, www.oxfam.org/en/pressroom/pressrelease/2009-07-15/ criminalize-generic-medicines-hurt-poor-countries

25 See e.g. P. K. Yu, 'Enforcement, Enforcement, What Enforcement?', *IDEA: The Journal of Law and Technology* 52 (2011).

26 Despite this and misinformation regarding the obligations contained in the ACTA persist and even intensified following the successful movement to defeat a recent legislative attempt in to strengthen penalties for IP infringers via the Stop Online Piracy Act (SOPA). For a basic review of the SPOA, see J. Pepitone, 'SOPA Explained: What It Is and Why It Matters', *CNN Money*, 20 January 2012, http://money.cnn.com/2012/01/17/ technology/sopa_explained/index.htm

27 See USTR, ACTA webpage, www.ustr.gov/acta; Anti-Counterfeiting Trade Agreement, opened for signature 31 March 2011 (not yet in force), http://trade.ec.europa.eu/doclib/ docs/2011/may/tradoc_147937.pdf, preamble.

cooperation and to promote strong enforcement practices'.[28] Likewise, the USTR website succinctly claims the 'negotiations aim to establish a state-of-the-art international framework that provides a model for effectively combating global proliferation of commercial-scale counterfeiting and piracy in the 21st century'.[29] Another page of the USTR website elaborates:

> ACTA aims to establish a comprehensive international framework that will assist Parties to the agreement in their efforts to effectively combat the infringement of intellectual property rights, in particular the proliferation of counterfeiting and piracy, which undermines legitimate trade and the sustainable development of the world economy. It includes state-of-the-art provisions on the enforcement of intellectual property rights, including provisions on civil, criminal, border and digital environment enforcement measures, robust cooperation mechanisms among ACTA Parties to assist in their enforcement efforts, and establishment of best practices for effective IPR enforcement.[30]

Judged against this standard, the ACTA fails as an instrument in international lawmaking. Quite simply, as will be demonstrated below, the agreement fails to produce any 'state-of-the-art provisions' which would meaningfully assist in the fight against piracy and counterfeiting. While there are a number of reasons for this result, the primarily reason is the failure to realize and adequately account for wide differences between the laws and regulations among the negotiating parties. In other words, even though the negotiating parties all maintain high levels of IP protection and enforcement standards, the particulars of each regime significantly differs in a number of areas and as incredible as it seems several of the parties genuinely believed they could 'harmonize' without any domestic legislative and/or administrative modifications.

Unsurprisingly, the objective of harmonization through the exportation of one's own law and regulations proved problematic as multiple negotiating parties (including Australia, Canada, the EU, Switzerland and the USA) publicly announced that the ACTA would not require any domestic legislative modifications. Surprisingly, the fact that the

---

[28] USTR, ACTA webpage, www.ustr.gov/acta. See also USTR, 'ACTA: meeting US objectives', fact sheet, October 2011, www.ustr.gov/about-us/press-office/fact-sheets/2011/september/acta-meeting-us-objectives

[29] USTR, ACTA webpage.

[30] USTR, 'US participants finalize Anti-Counterfeiting Trade Agreement text' (November 210) PR, www.ustr.gov/about-us/press-office/press-releases/2010/november/us-participants-finalize-anti-counterfeiting-trad

domestic laws of one party were not in sync with the laws of all other negotiating parties seemed to continuously befuddle negotiators and stymie progress. Again, if harmonization in the form of a 'gold standard' of norm setting was one of the aims to be achieved, the parties would have had to agree on a position and set a single international standard. This did not occur, however, and in several areas the final text of the ACTA simply allows for multiple positions to be maintained. This is despite the fact that these issues were heavily negotiated, which itself indicates both the intent of the parties to export their own laws and unwillingness to agree to a standard which requires a legal change. Taken together, the resulting agreement simply maintains the status quo of all of the negotiating parties to the detriment of harmonization and international standard setting.

It is important to note, however, that this failure to harmonize does not mean that the ACTA does not contain any provisions which advance the agenda beyond the TRIPS Agreement. On the contrary, the ACTA contains several provisions which go beyond what is required in the TRIPS Agreement.[31] While some criticize the ACTA for advancing beyond the standards set out in the TRIPS Agreement, such criticism is unwarranted as there simply would have been no point even to begin negotiations if the aim was to repeat existing international obligations. Any agreement which now addresses IP will be its very nature advance beyond the TRIPS Agreement. But even here, most if not all of the advancements beyond TRIPS already form part of the domestic law in most of the negotiating parties. So while the provisions advance beyond what is required in TRIPS in practice they merely codify existing domestic law of the respective negotiating parties. Thus, the fact that the ACTA contains some TRIPS-Plus provisions does not detract from the broader point that the ACTA maintains the status quo of the negotiating parties to the detriment of harmonization and international standard setting.

Having provided this necessary background information, the remainder of this section will provide examples of the broader point: the ACTA fails to provide for meaningful standards which advance beyond existing domestic law of the negotiating parties. Moreover, the failure to do so not only fails to harmonize international IP law but further adds to the intra-disciplinary and inter-disciplinary fragmentation in the field.

---

[31] See ACTA, art. 8 (injunctions applying to imports and exports whereas art. 44(1) of TRIPS only applies to imports); and art. 9 (potential calculation of damages is more prescriptive than art. 24(1) of TRIPS).

The first example of the provision relates to damages. While it seems clear from the negotiations that the issue of damages was widely discussed and debated, it is also clear that at least some of the parties favoured a harmonized approach which would set a clear and unambiguous standard. As the current approach to damages differs widely among the negotiating parties, such an approach would have forced domestic legislative changes on a number of countries. Ultimately, the parties failed to compromise and the resulting provision seriously fails as an instrument of harmonization and international standard setting. Article 9(3) relating to damages, states:

> At least with respect to infringement of copyright or related rights protecting works, phonograms, and performances, and in cases of trademark counterfeiting, each Party shall also establish or maintain a system that provides for one or more of the following: (a) pre-established damages; or (b) presumptions for determining the amount of damages sufficient to compensate the right holder for the harm caused by the infringement; or (c) at least for copyright, additional damages.

Article 9(3) therefore allows for a variety of different methods in line with existing practice of the ACTA negotiating parties. Moreover, and perhaps for the better, the provision is limited to 'at least' copyright and trademark, which allows each party to determine whether to establish or maintain any of the three options (pre-established damages, presumptive damages or additional damages) for other IP rights (IPRs). More damning, the article does not even attempt to harmonize the rationale behind the three options. To illustrate, whereas both the USA and EU utilize 'pre-established damages' their respective reasons for doing so differ quite radically: in the USA, pre-established damages are used in part to punish infringers and as a deterrent the EU uses them only against unintentional infringers as a way of compensating IP owners. Similarly, the rationale for including 'additional damages' in Australia (compensation awarded following the principles of aggravated and exemplary damages at common law) differs from that of England and Wales (restitution through the use of aggravated damages). Given such varying interpretations of the terms in the domestic setting of each of the parties, it will be difficult if not impossible to find a common meaning of the language used in the treaty text. While this will cause obvious interpretative difficulties, the main point for our purposes is the attempt by each party to allow for the continuation of its own laws and correspondingly the failure of the parties to harmonize or set an international standard.

Likewise, the parties heavily negotiated section 3 of the ACTA relating
to border measures. This aspect of the negotiations received worldwide
media coverage, as many in the public health community worried that
the ACTA would destabilize the hard-fought gains of developing countries and public health campaigners in the area of access to essential
medicines. While there were numerous worries and criticisms, they
essentially centred on whether the terms 'counterfeiting' and 'piracy'
would be extended to include the manufacture, sale and import/export
of generic pharmaceuticals and thus potentially severely curtail trade in
generic pharmaceuticals and add significant costs to the procurement of
essential medicines.[32]

Such concerns were legitimate given the ACTA negotiations coincided
with the seizure/detention of several shipments of generic pharmaceuticals while transiting through the EU on their way from and to developing countries where a patent was not in place.[33] While the legality of the
customs measures with WTO[34] and EU law[35] continues to evoke considerable debate, the relevant point for this chapter is that the negotiation of
ACTA could have opened up a separate avenue to legitimize the seizures/

---

[32] See 'Consumer groups fear ACTA could encourage generic drug seizures', *Inside US
    Trade* (30 April 2010); P. K. Yu, 'Six Secret (and Now Open) Fears of ACTA', *Southern
    Methodist University Law Review* 63 (2010), 84; H. G. Ruse-Khan, 'A Trade Agreement
    Creating Barriers to International Trade? ACTA Border Measures and Goods in Transit',
    American University International Law Review 26 (2011), 645.
[33] From late 2008 to 2009 the EU (primarily the Netherlands) detained at least nineteen
    shipments of generic pharmaceuticals exported from India and other developing coun-
    tries transiting through the EU on their way to other developing countries. Following
    months of heated exchanges between European, Brazilian and Indian diplomats, India
    and Brazil filed complaints at the WTO over the matter. A final settlement was reached in
    July 2011. See B. Mercurio, 'Drugs Seized in Transit: The Case that Wasn't', *International
    and Comparative Law Quarterly* 61(2012), 389.
[34] On the measures' consistency with TRIPS, see *ibid.*
[35] A recent ECJ decision held that in normal circumstances EU IPRs do not apply, but in
    some cases (i.e. destination of goods not declared, false information submitted, lack of
    cooperation with customs or proven risk of diversion) the EU rules can apply. The
    availability of the suspension is clearly intended to enable a domestic court in the member
    concerned to conduct a proper examination of whether there is sufficient evidence of
    infringement of an IPR. Judgment in Joined Cases C-446/09 *Koninklijke Philips Electron-
    ics NV* v. *Lucheng Meijing Industrial Company Ltd and others* and C-495/09 *Nokia
    Corporation* v. *Her Majesty's Commissioners of Revenue and Customs*, www.eulaws.eu/?
    p=1165 (visited 31 December 2011). Interestingly, Indian law includes in-transit goods
    within the meaning of 'importation'. See *Gramophone Company of India* v. *Birendra
    Bahadur Pandey* AIR 1984 SC 66 (interpreting import as 'bringing into India . . . that it is
    not limited to importation for commerce only but includes importation for transit across
    the country').

detentions. For instance, the definitions of 'counterfeit' and/or 'piracy' could have been drafted or interpreted in an expensive manner so as to clearly allow for the seizure of generic pharmaceuticals transiting through the territory of ACTA members. Additionally, the ACTA could have been drafted in such a manner so as to *require* the seizure of transiting goods which violate the IPRs in the country of transit.

Neither concern materialized and the final text of the ACTA represents far less of a threat to the trade in generic pharmaceuticals for a number of reasons. First, while the ACTA continues to include all of the TRIPS-covered areas of IPRs in its mandate[36] it restricts the definitions of both 'counterfeit' and 'piracy' to trademark in the former and copyright in the latter. Thus, infringements of patents are not included in the terms 'counterfeit' or 'piracy'. Second, the language of Article 16.2 provides that parties *may*, but are not required to, adopt or maintain procedures leading to the suspension of release with respect to in-transit goods. Finally, a footnote to Article 13 (which provides for the scope of border measures and calls for enforcement in a manner that does not discriminate unjustifiably between IPRs and in a manner which avoids the creation of barriers to legitimate trade) excludes patents and protection of undisclosed information from the scope of Section 3 of ACTA.[37]

Thus, while the ACTA does not require parties to enforce domestic IPRs with respect to goods in transit it takes an equivocal position by maintaining the status quo. Through silence, the ACTA thus allows parties to adopt such procedures if and when they see fit and in so doing does not depart very far from the position taken in Part IV of the TRIPS Agreement.[38]

While public health campaigners would have preferred the ACTA to prohibit the seizures/detentions of generic pharmaceuticals in transit the final text is perhaps the best realistic outcome for such interested observers given the (then) ongoing dispute between the EU/Netherlands and India and Brazil at the WTO. What is more, the result could have been

---

[36] ACTA, art. 5 (General Definitions), defining IP as 'all categories of intellectual property that are the subject of Sections 1 through 7 of Part II of the TRIPS Agreement'.
[37] ACTA, s. 3, fn. 6.
[38] It should be noted that Article 5 of the ACTA defines counterfeiting and piracy 'under the law of the country in which the procedures ... are invoked'. This clarifies the uncertain standard set out in the TRIPS Agreement and prevents customs officials in one country being forced to interpret the laws of another country which could occur under a possible reading of the relevant language of the TRIPS Agreement. See Mercurio, 'Drugs Seized in Transit'.

far more threatening as it appears the issue of border measures was among the most contentious negotiating topics, and one that threatened to derail the entire agreement.[39] Moreover, the early drafts of the negotiating text were expansive in scope and covered all forms of IPRs contained in the TRIPS Agreement (including patents) and provided for the possibility of mandatory injunctions for IPR infringements of in-transit goods.[40]

In the end, the aims of harmonization and an international standard gave way to a political compromise which allowed the EU to claim victory through the inclusion of at least a portion of its domestic regulations regarding the seizure/detention of in-transit goods suspected of patent infringement into the ACTA and for extending Section 4 to cover all IPRs (less patents and undisclosed information), which potentially allows for enhanced the recognition and protection of geographical indications through the ACTA.[41] At the same time, the compromise allowed the US, EU, Australia and others to announce that nothing in these provisions will require amending domestic law.[42] While many are content with this result, the point for our purposes is that the provision again fails to harmonize laws or set any meaningful standard. Thus, the fragmentation within the field of international IP law is maintained.

This pattern of an issue being heavily negotiated – and potentially containing provisions which would have caused significant shifts in the law of several negotiating parties – before being whittled down to little more than the status quo repeats to a certain extent in almost every section of the ACTA, and certainly can be further illustrated in the sections on civil enforcement (Section 2) and the digital environment (Section 5).

Section 5 received considerable attention in the media (and on the streets), and it is worth highlighting a few provisions which illustrate the significant backtrack in the negotiations and ultimate agreement which allows for countries to maintain their existing regime without

---

[39] See 'De Gucht Lashes out at US over ACTA, Geographical Indications', 28 (16 July 2010) *Inside US Trade*.

[40] Bracketed language, with 'may' being the alternative. Thus, discussion revolved around whether seizure of in-transit goods should be mandatory of discretionary. See Draft ACTA (July 2010 version), art. 2.2.

[41] See 'De Gucht Lashes Out'.

[42] K. Weatherall argues this point while claiming the ACTA does not represent any new, clear international standard ('Politics, Compromise, Text and the Failures of the Anti-Counterfeiting Trade Agreement', *Sydney Law Review* 33 (2011), 248–9).

amendment. For example, it is clear that for some time the negotiations included the possibility of requiring a graduated response (also referred to as 'three strikes law'), notice-and-takedown provisions and other measures relating to copyright violations over the internet which potentially encroach on civil liberties.[43] Intense negotiations over these issues, however, produced a final text which is much more restrained. All of the provisions some saw as being nefarious in nature have not been retained in the final text. Again, while most onlookers view this backtrack as a positive result the point here is simply that the agreement fails to produce a coherent standard or harmonize the laws of the negotiating parties.

Another example of this backtrack can be seen in the inclusion of a number of general 'safeguards'[44] in the text generally as well as several specific safeguards included in Section 5. Thus, and unlike all of the leaked draft texts, while Section 5 extends the enforcement proceedings mandated in Sections 2 (Civil Enforcement) and 4 (Criminal Enforcement) to the digital environment,[45] it also calls for implementation 'in a manner that avoids the creation of barriers to legitimate activity, including electronic commerce, and, consistent with that Party's law, preserves fundamental principles such as freedom of expression, fair process, and privacy'.[46] Article 27.4 provides another example of the flexibility of ACTA in providing:

> A Party *may* provide, *in accordance with its laws and regulations*, its competent authorities with the authority to order an online service provider to disclose expeditiously to a right holder information sufficient to identify a subscriber whose account was allegedly used for infringement, where that right holder has filed a legally sufficient claim of trademark or copyright or related rights infringement, and where such information is being sought for the purpose of protecting or enforcing those rights. These procedures shall be *implemented in a manner that avoids the creation of barriers to legitimate activity, including electronic commerce, and, consistent with that Party's law, preserves fundamental principles such as freedom of expression, fair process, and privacy.* [emphasis added][47]

---

[43] Draft ACTA (January 2010 version), section 4.
[44] See ACTA, preamble, arts. 1, 2.3, 4, 6.2, 6.3.   [45] *Ibid.*, art. 27.1.   [46] *Ibid.*, art. 27.2.
[47] Despite such permissive language, some commentators still seem to be under the illusion that the ACTA requires signatories to adopt a graduated response approach. See e.g. M. Horten, 'Final ACTA Puts Europe under More Pressure for Graduated Response', posted on IPtegrity.com, 10 October 2010, www.iptegrity.com/index.php/acta/569-final-acta-puts-europe-under-more-pressure-for-graduated-response

While the provision calls on parties to order online service providers to disclose information which could identify the identity of a subscriber alleged to have infringed IPRs, the provision is discretionary; that is, parties are not required to implement the provision. Moreover, where a party chooses to implement the provision, Article 27.4 explicitly states that such implementation is subject to existing laws and regulations of the party. Finally, the Article repeats the language used in Article 27.2 as a general safeguard and nod to civil liberties. While such drafting may be preferable to harmonization and setting a mandatory international standard in this emerging and important area, it perfectly illustrates the failure of the parties to meet their negotiating objectives and instead agreeing to text which requires few (or in this case, no) change of practice.[48] Again, fragmentation is maintained.

It is important to conclude this section with a disclaimer – the point of illustration through these examples is not that the agreement failed as it did not contain maximalist IP provisions but that the agreement failed to meets its objectives of harmonization and international standard setting due to its ambiguous and permissive text. This is a disappointing result from an international lawmaking perspective but inevitable when the stated intention of several parties was harmonization and standard setting through the export of its domestic law. Given that no party wanted to actually amend its own law, the negotiators simply drafted treaty language to allow for positions and interpretations suitable to all parties current law. For this reason, the ACTA is a failure as an instrument in international lawmaking. More disappointingly, the ACTA does not serve to bring together any strand of international IP but only serves to further imbed both intra- and inter-disciplinary fragmentation.

IV.   Future trend: the continued fragmentation of international IP

Negotiated to address a gap in the existing international legal architecture, the ACTA serves as a strong signal that certain members believe the TRIPS Agreement does too little to effectively enforce its norms and standards.[49] It could also be a signal that certain members do not believe

---

[48] See also art. 27.8 (exceptions) and its limiting effect on the substantive provisions relating to the circumvention of effective technological measures (art. 27.5–6) and electronic rights management information (art. 27.7).

[49] EU negotiators expressed this sentiment at a public briefing session held in April 2009. See M. Ermert, 'European Commission on ACTA: TRIPS Is Floor Not Ceiling',

that the WTO has the institutional capacity to correct the perceived deficiencies; that is, that the consensus could never be reached at the WTO to amend the TRIPS Agreement in a manner supportive of efforts to increase IP enforcement. That being said, the ACTA is not the first sign of a (temporary) abandonment of the multilateral trading system, but more so an evolution of a trend that began following the collapse of the Cancun Ministerial Conference in 2003.[50] The failure to progress the Doha Round in Cancun made it clear to certain developed countries that the WTO was no longer the 'can do' forum for trade liberalization, including progress in the area of IPRs. The efforts of several developing countries from the late 1990s onwards to reverse what they viewed as maximalist IPR policies further cemented the notion among some developed country members that progress in the area of IPRs would have to be accomplished outside the WTO.[51] This push-back culminated in developing countries securing a significant victory in the form of the much of the final text of the Doha Declaration on TRIPS and Public Health.[52] The

---

Intellectual Property Watch, 22 April 2009, www.ipwatch.org/weblog/2009/04/22/european-commission-on-acta-trips-is-floor-not-ceiling. See also P. K. Yu, 'TRIPS and Its Achilles' Heel', *Journal of Intellectual Property Law* 18(2011).

[50] See L. Elliott, C. Denny and D. Munk, 'Blow to world economy as trade talks collapse', *Guardian*, 15 September 2003, www.guardian.co.uk/world/2003/sep/15/business.politics (reporting then-US Trade Representative Robert Zoellick 'would redouble its efforts to reach bilateral trade deals with favored nations' and quoting him as stating: 'Whether developed or developing, there were "can do" and "can't do" countries here. The rhetoric of the "won't do" over whelmed the concerted efforts of the "can do". "Won't do" led to impasse'). See also R. B. Zoellick, 'America will not wait', *Financial Times*, 21 September 2003.

[51] See D. Gervais, 'TRIPS and Development', in D. Gervais (ed.), *Intellectual Property, Trade and Development: Strategies to Optimize Economic Development in a TRIPS-Plus Era* (Oxford University Press, 2007), xv–xvi, 13–15. See also *Brazil – Measures Affecting Patent Protection* – Request for the Establishment of a Panel by the United States, WT/DS199/3 (9 January 2001); art. 68 of Brazil's industrial property law (Law No. 9,279 of 14 May 1996; effective May 1997); art. 27.1 of the TRIPS Agreement. See generally, B. Mercurio and M. Tyagi, 'Treaty Interpretation in WTO Dispute Settlement: The Outstanding Question of the Legality of Local Working Requirements', *Minnesota Journal of International Law* 19 (2010).

[52] See generally Draft Ministerial Declaration, 'Proposal from a Group of Developed Countries', IP/C/W/313 (4 October 2001) (submitted by Australia, Canada, Japan, Switzerland and USA); Draft Ministerial Declaration, 'Proposal from a Group of Developing Countries' IP/C/W/312, WT/GC/W/450 (4 October 2001) (submitted by African Group, Bangladesh, Barbados, Bolivia, Brazil, Cuba, Dominican Republic, Ecuador, Haiti, Honduras, India, Indonesia, Jamaica, Pakistan, Paraguay, Philippines, Peru, Sri Lanka, Thailand and Venezuela).

Doha Declaration received worldwide notoriety for clarifying the TRIPS Agreement, prioritizing public health and emphasizing the 'flexibilities' existing in the Agreement.

Of note, paragraph 6 'recognize[s] that WTO with insufficient or no manufacturing capacities in the pharmaceutical sector could face difficulties in making effective use of compulsory licensing under the TRIPS Agreement', but the paragraph leaves the issue unresolved, instead instructing the Council for TRIPS to find an 'expeditious solution' to the problem.[53] The Implementation Decision, reached until 30 August 2003, provides a 'waiver' to obligations under Article 31(f) and thus allows any member to export pharmaceutical products made under compulsory licences to others with insufficient or no manufacturing capabilities within the terms set out in the decision. The decision has been criticized for being too cumbersome,[54] and to date has only once been utilized.[55] Despite this, members agreed to transform the waiver into the TRIPS' first ever amendment.

Despite the criticism, the Implementation Decision marked the watershed of momentum in favour of developing countries on the issue of TRIPS and public health. Since that time, developed countries have once again gained the upper hand and through a forum shift to bilateral and regional trade agreements (and to a lesser extent, BITs) are incorporating obligations which build upon the standards of the TRIPS Agreement.[56] Attempts by developing countries to once again shift the forum back to WIPO via the 'WIPO Development Agenda' have largely been unsuccessful.[57]

---

[53] Doha Declaration on TRIPS and Public Health, at para. 6.
[54] See MSF, 'Neither Expeditious, Nor a Solution: The WTO August 30th. Decision Is Unworkable' (2006), www.msfaccess.org/content/neither-expeditious-nor-solution-wto-august-30th-decision-unworkable
[55] For details, see M. Rimmer, 'Race against Time: The Export of Essential Medicines to Rwanda', *Public Health Ethics* 89(1) (2008); M. Rimmer, 'The Jean Chretien Pledge to Africa Act: Patent Law and Humanitarian Aid', *Expert Opinion on Therapeutic Patents* 15 (2005).
[56] In relation to access to essential medicines, the most notable TRIPS-Plus provisions include limits on compulsory licensing, the linkage of market approval to patent status, patent term extension, limits on parallel importation and the aforementioned test data protection. See M. Handler and B. Mercurio, 'Intellectual Property', in S. Lester and B. Mercurio (eds.) *Bilateral and Regional Trade Agreements: Commentary and Analysis* (Cambridge University Press, 2009), 325–8. All of these provisions have the potential to significantly impede access to essential medicines.
[57] In 2007, the WIPO General Assembly adopted forty-five recommendations which aim to address the interests and needs of developing countries and ensure the balance between

One of the most ardent drivers of this shift has been the USA. Although the US position relating to FTAs, pharmaceuticals and TRIP-Plus provisions began being formulated with the conclusion of the US–Jordan FTA (2001), its position subsequently hardened and later agreements produced more meaningful and wide-ranging TRIPS-Plus provisions. Such provisions can be seen in US agreements with Singapore (2004), Australia (2005), Morocco (2006), CAFTA–DR (2006) and Bahrain (2006).[58] It is also noteworthy that the recently approved FTA with Korea (2011) further strengthens IPR protection and the presence of TRIPS-Plus provisions.[59] After initially demanding fewer (and for the most part less onerous) TRIPS-Plus provisions in its FTAs, the EU announced it would 'revisit [its] approach to the IPR chapter of bilateral agreements'[60] and now similarly demand significant TRIPS-Plus provisions be included in all of its recent FTAs.[61]

The negotiations leading to the ACTA represent a further forum shift away from the WTO.[62] Negotiated among a group of (mainly) like-minded group of countries, each with significant IP interests the plurilateral setting of the ACTA seemed to be the perfect setting to formulate and internationalize ambitious IP norms and standards. In such a setting, decoupled from the 'single undertaking' of the WTO, the parties could negotiate an agreement free of trade-offs involving non-IPR issues and concerns. Furthermore, the agreement could be negotiated among a select group of invited participants, free of interference from Brazil, India, China and other vocal opponents of strengthened IP enforcement

creators/owners and users/public interest is maintained. To date, members are still implementing the Development Agenda and although they have agreed to some implementation projects, progress has generally been postponed or stalled. For a recent update, see J. de Beer and S. Bannerman, 'Foresight into the Future of WIPO's Development Agenda', *WIPO Journal* 2 (2010).

[58] See Handler and Mercurio, 'Intellectual Property', 325–8.

[59] See also letter from Ron Kirk, US Trade Representative, to Ron Wyden, US Senator, 28 January 2010, 2, www.ustr.gov/webfm_send/1700

[60] *Strategy for the Enforcement of Intellectual Property Rights in Third Countries*, Official Journal of the European Union (2005/C 129/03).

[61] See the recently signed EU–South Korea Free Trade Agreement, http://eur-lex.europa.eu/JOHtml.do?uri=OJ:L:2011:127:SOM:EN:HTML

[62] See M. Blakeney and L. Blakeney, 'Stealth Legislation? Negotiating the Anti-Counterfeiting Trade Agreement (ACTA)', *International Trade Law and Regulation* 16 (2010), 90–1.

efforts (and coincidently, the source of the vast majority of the world's counterfeit and pirated products).[63]

The negotiation of the ACTA thus continues a long tradition of the fragmentation of international IP. Indeed, international IP has always been highly fragmented, both before and subsequent to the creation of the TRIPS Agreement. In fact, the negotiation of the WIPO Internet Treaties (concluding in December 1996) prove not only that TRIPS was outdated at the time of its coming into force,[64] but also that other organizations extraneous to the WTO continue to have a role to play in standard setting and the development of legal norms.[65] Continued activity and treaty-making at WIPO (including, for instance, the WIPO Development Agenda and the copyright initiative for the blind)[66] and the above-mentioned proliferation of FTAs containing IP chapters are further illustrations of the fragmentation.[67]

At this point, the question becomes what short and long-term effect the ACTA will have on the multilateral and bilateral system. This is an especially important question given the difficulties the 'like-minded' group of countries has in concluding the ACTA and the 'significant differences in philosophy and approach' which emerged between the negotiating parties.[68] An answer is already beginning to emerge – the ACTA's effect will be limited. The reason for this answer centres on the fact that so many demands from each of the major negotiating parties were not included in the final version of the ACTA. Thus, far from becoming the 'gold standard' of enforcement,[69] negotiators are

---

[63] On the opposition to the strengthening of IPRs, see P. K. Yu, 'Access to Medicines, BRICS Alliances, and Collective Action', *American Journal of Law & Medicine* 34 (2008), 349–52.

[64] For a prescient article on the future of online activities, see M. A. Hamilton, 'The TRIPS Agreement: Imperialistic, Outdated, and Overprotective', *Vanderbilt Journal of Transnational Law* 29(1996).

[65] WIPO Copyright Treaty, 20 December 1996, S. Treaty Doc. No. 105–17, at 1 (1997); WIPO Performances and Phonograms Treaty, 20 December 1996, S. Treaty Doc. No. 105–17, 18 (1997).

[66] Further information on the WIPO Standing Committee on Copyright and Related Rights is available at www.wipo.int/meetings/en/topic.jsp?group_id=62

[67] Seventy-nine of the 202 agreements notified to the WTO contain provisions on IPRs, including 34 of the 75 agreements coming into force since 1 January 2005. Statistics compiled by the author using the WTO RTA Database, http://rtais.wto.org/UI/Public-MaintainRTAHome.aspx

[68] Weatherall, 'Politics, Compromise, Text' 10.

[69] See H. G. Ruse-Khan, 'From TRIPS to ACTA: Towards a New "Gold Standard" in Criminal IP Enforcement', Max Planck Institute for Intellectual Property and Competition Law Research Paper No. 10-06 (2010), http://papers.ssrn.com/sol3/papers.cfm?

simply ignoring the ACTA and reaching back to the proposals which were submitted, discussed and ultimately rejected by the other negotiating parties to the ACTA.

This can be illustrated by the Trans Pacific Partnership (TPP) negotiations, currently ongoing between countries as diverse as Brunei, Canada, Chile, Japan, Mexico, New Zealand, Singapore, Australia, Malaysia, the US, Vietnam and Peru.[70] While most negotiating parties to the TPP are already parties to the ACTA, it is clear from a leaked draft text that the ACTA is not being used as a standard to be negotiated into FTAs. On the contrary, the ACTA is virtually being ignored in the negotiations. The leaked text, which for the most part is the model US text, uses these negotiations not to merely incorporate the standards of ACTA but rather to incorporate substantive provisions that were rejected or not even raised in the context of the ACTA.[71] For example, the USA has sought, *inter alia*, statutory damages in copyright and for violations of the anti-circumvention provisions, mandatory seizure of infringing goods while in transit, criminal liability for private non-commercial activities involving copyright, a mandatory offence for camcording and detailed safe harbour provisions for online service providers.[72] These issues were negotiated by the parties to the ACTA but ultimately not incorporated into the final text. Moreover, the leaked draft chapter contains few of the safeguards that form part of the ACTA, such as specific reference to Articles 7 and 8 of the TRIPS Agreement and the requirement that procedures be fair, equitable and proportionate.[73] It is doubtful that the

---

abstract_id=1592104 (arguing the 'ACTA will become the next international "gold standard in IPR enforcement", it will replace the flexible minimum standard of art. 61 TRIPS with a set of more detailed and comprehensive rules on criminal offenses, liability and penalties as well as other specific remedies').

[70] The TPP negotiations began as an extension of a trade agreement known as the P4 between Brunei, Chile, New Zealand and Singapore. The text of the P4 is available at www.worldtradelaw.net/fta/agreements/TransPac_SEP_FTA.pdf

[71] A leaked version of the US Draft TPP IP Chapter (February 2011) is at http://keionline. org/sites/default/files/tpp-10feb2011-us-text-ipr-chapter.pdf; another draft was leaked in September 2011 at www.citizenstrade.org/ctc/wp-content/uploads/2011/10/TransPacifi-cIP1.pdf

[72] See *ibid.*, arts. 12.2, 12.4, 14.4, 15.1, 15.3 and 16.3, respectively. For commentary, see Knowledge Ecology International, 'The complete Feb 10, 2011 text of the US proposal for the TPP IPR chapter', 10 March 2011, http://keionline.org/node/1091

[73] See ACTA, arts. 2.3 and 6.2–3. For analysis of the US Draft, see S. Flynn, M. Kaminski, B. Baker and J. Koo, 'Public interest analysis of the US TPP proposal for an IP chapter', paper produced for the Program on Information Justice and Intellectual Property at the American University Washington College of Law, 6 December 2011, http://infojustice. org/tpp-analysis-december2011

final IP chapter of the TPP will resemble the leaked draft, but for our purposes that is irrelevant. The point is simply that the US starting point is not the ACTA but the position it unsuccessfully put forward in negotiating the ACTA. To some extent, the US position is understandable as, even though like-minded countries negotiated the ACTA, the result was less than optimal from a trade negotiator point of view. The final text of the ACTA provided much weaker obligations than the USA (and many others) desired and the TPP is another opportunity to reach a more comprehensive agreement which stretches the international legal framework.

V. Conclusion

One the one hand, the failure of the ACTA to achieve its objectives is unfortunate as counterfeiting and piracy has rapidly expanded over the past decade and in certain cases represents a serious threat to public health and safety. On the other hand, the failure of the ACTA is not necessarily an undesirable result. Beyond the rhetoric, the negotiating objectives of the Agreement were ill-defined and the negotiating parties never fully committed to negotiating an agreement which harmonized enforcement standards or truly engaged in serious standard setting. Instead, all of the major negotiating parties simply sought to 'harmonize' through the exportation of their own laws to the other parties.

With domestic laws diverging in several respects between and among the negotiating parties, the Agreement's original aims slowly faded into the background and the priority became simply to conclude *an* agreement as opposed to conclude a *meaningful* agreement. The result is a patchwork of vague legal standards allowing for multiple approaches and interpretations. Rather than harmonize laws and set standards, the ACTA thus only serves to add to the fragmentation of international IP law. For these reasons, perhaps it would be better for the discipline if the ACTA never comes into force.

PART IV

Aspects of climate change regulation

18

The WTO legality of the application of the EU's emissions trading system to aviation

LORAND BARTELS

I. Introduction

Aviation accounts for around 3 percent of global carbon emissions.[1] In an effort to reduce these emissions, the EU emissions trading system (ETS) was extended to cover aviation on 1 January 2012.[2] All airlines must now acquire and 'surrender' allowances for the carbon emissions produced by their flights, failing which the airline will be fined €100 per allowance and must make up the shortfall the following year.[3] The scheme applies to virtually all[4] passenger and cargo flights operated by EU[5] and non-EU airlines (subject to a potential exemption), and it applies not only to flights between EU airports, but also – and

---

[1] According to 2005 figures, aviation is responsible for around 2.5 per cent of global carbon emissions. Taking into account other emissions and effects (e.g. on clouds), aviation is responsible for 4.9 per cent of total anthropogenic climate effects (D. S. Lee et al., 'Aviation and Global Climate Change in the 21st Century', Atmospheric Environment 43 (2009), 3520. A commonly quoted but now out-of-date figure, deriving from a 1999 IPCC Report, is 3.5 per cent of global carbon emissions (J. Penner et al. (eds.), Aviation and the Global Atmosphere: Summary for Policymakers (Cambridge University Press, 1999), 8).

[2] Dir. 2008/101/EC amending Dir. 2003/87/EC so as to include aviation activities in the scheme for green-house gas emission allowance trading within the Community, OJ (2008) L8/3. A consolidated version of Dir. 2003/87/EC ('the Directive') is available at: http://eur-lex.europa.eu/LexUriServ/LexUriServ.do?uri=CON SLEG:2003L0087:20090625:EN:PDF

[3] Ibid., art. 16(3).

[4] There are exceptions for special flights, listed in Annex I (ibid.).

[5] In fact, the scheme extends beyond the EU to the EEA EFTA countries (Iceland, Norway, and Liechtenstein): EEA Joint Committee Dec. No. 6/2011, OJ (2011) L93/35 and Dec. No. 43/2011, OJ (2011) L171/44; see also Dec. No. 87/2011 and Dec. No. 93/2011 (not yet published). Switzerland is reportedly negotiating an agreement on aviation emissions ('Second round of Swiss–EU negotiations on linking emissions trading systems', Swiss Federal Office for the Environment, PR, 20 Sept. 2011, www.bafu.admin.ch/dokumentation/medieninformation/00962/index.html?lang=en&msg-id=41297).

controversially – to the last leg of international flights between EU and non-EU airports.[6]

The EU's aviation scheme has been highly controversial, largely because it raises a number of difficult legal questions in several areas of international law. One is whether the EU has the power to regulate airlines in respect of emissions produced outside the EU, given restrictions under international law on the extent to which states are permitted to regulate activities taking place outside their territorial jurisdictions. Another is whether the EU's scheme is consistent with its obligations under applicable bilateral and multilateral agreements governing air transport service agreements. And a third – the subject of this chapter – is whether the aviation scheme is compatible with the EU's WTO obligations.

The controversy provoked by the scheme also points to a wider failing of international regulation – the question of appropriate forum. To date, both at the international level and in academic commentary, the EU's aviation scheme has been discussed in the context of the International Civil Aviation Organization (ICAO), where the main issue is whether the EU should be able to regulate air transport unilaterally in the absence of an international agreement. This makes perfect sense as far as air transport services are concerned. But the ICAO is clearly incompetent to deal with the trade implications of measures regulating air transport services, a matter that is (or should be) the preserve of the WTO. In an ideal world, these respective competences should be allocated to the ICAO and the WTO at the level of primary law. In fact, as this chapter shows, while there has been some attempt to do this within the WTO, the results are at best ambiguous. This makes it difficult to arrive at legal conclusions in any given case, such as the present case. But it also means that there is a need for a more wide-ranging discussion on how to bring greater coherence to the regulation of international transportation at the international level.

---

[6] Annex I to the Directive, refers to '[f]lights which depart from or arrive in an aerodrome situated in the territory of a Member State to which the Treaty applies'. Commission Dec. 2009/450/EC, OJ (2009) L149/69, giving a detailed interpretation of Annex I, states '[t]he term "flight" means one flight sector that is a flight or one of a series of flights which commences at a parking place of the aircraft and terminates at a parking place of the aircraft'. The Directive itself apparently leaves it open to consider 'flights' more broadly, perhaps based on the total journey taken by a single aeroplane with a single flight code.

II. The EU'S aviation scheme in detail

1. Structure of the scheme

The EU ETS – of which the EU's aviation scheme is now a part – is a 'cap and trade' scheme for reducing emissions of carbon dioxide (and some other gases). These schemes set a 'cap' on total overall emissions by establishing a fixed number of emissions 'allowances', distribute these to industries according to a given benchmark, and permit industries to trade these allowances according to their needs. In the case of the EU ETS, the allowances are distributed initially by a combination of free allocation and auction. The EU ETS also envisages agreements for the mutual recognition of allowances issued by other countries participating in the Kyoto Protocol system.[7]

The EU has created emissions allowances for aviation operators corresponding to 97 percent[8] of a benchmark calculated as the industry's average carbon emissions[9] during the three years 2004–2006.[10] In 2012, 85 percent of these allowances are allocated for free[11] (according to the airlines' respective 2010 market shares[12]), and the remaining 15 per cent are available for purchase by auction.[13] From 2013, when the so-called ETS Phase III commences, the total quantity of allowances drops to 95 percent of the 2004–2006 benchmark,[14] and 3 percent of this new total will be reserved for 'new entrants' and rapidly growing airlines.[15] Airlines are also able to purchase a certain number of additional allowances from other industries covered by the EU ETS[16] but this is not

---

[7] *Ibid.*, art. 25.   [8] *Ibid.*, art. 3c(1).
[9] Emissions are calculated according to tonne–kilometres, calculated by multiplying the payload transported (cargo, mail and passengers) by the mission distance (great-circle-distance plus an additional fixed factor of 95 km) (*ibid.*, Annex IV Part B).
[10] The total number of these allowances was determined by Commission Dec. 2011/389/EU, OJ (2011) L173/13.
[11] Art. 3e of the Directive.
[12] The benchmarks used to calculate the freely allocated allowances are set out in Commission Dec. 2011/638/EU, OJ (2011) L252/20. EU member states were obligated to calculate the actual free allowances allocated to each operator, based on their reported and verified tonne-kilometre figures, by the end of 2011. These figures are available at: http://ec.europa.eu/clima/policies/transport/aviation/ allowances/links_en.htm
[13] Art. 3d of the Directive.   [14] *Ibid.*, art. 3c(2).
[15] *Ibid.*, art. 3f. Rapidly growing means growth at a rate of more than 18 per cent annually (*ibid.*).
[16] *Ibid.*, art. 11a.

reciprocal: operators of stationary installations are not permitted to purchase allowances issued to airlines.[17]

2. Economic impacts of the scheme

The economic impacts of the EU's scheme are somewhat uncertain, and vary according to the actors involved.[18] In theory, airlines can stay within their free allowance by developing greater fuel efficiency, or by using biofuels, these not being counted for purposes of the scheme.[19] In practice, and given the overall growth in the aviation industry of around 5 percent annually,[20] and projected growth in overall emissions,[21] this seems unlikely. In fact, it is generally agreed that the EU's scheme will come at a direct cost to the aviation industry. The estimates of costs vary significantly, and are inherently unstable, as they depend on the state of the carbon market. A number of recent academic studies have estimated total annual costs at around €3–4 billion.[22] On the other hand, Thomson Reuters Point

---

[17] *Ibid.*, art. 12(3). This is because allowances issued for airlines are not considered within the Kyoto Protocol allowances nor included within Kyoto targets (A. Anger, 'Including Aviation in the European Emissions Trading Scheme: Impacts on the Industry, CO_2 Emissions and Macroeconomic Activity in the EU', *J. Air Transport Management* 16 (2010), 101).

[18] The European Commission's assessment is contained in its Proposal for a directive of the European Parliament and of the Council amending Dir. 2003/87/EC so as to include aviation activities in the scheme for greenhouse gas emission allowance trading within the Community, Brussels, COM(2006)818 final, 20 Dec. 2006, 5, and the accompanying impact assessment of the inclusion of aviation activities in the scheme for greenhouse gas emission allowance trading within the Community, SEC(2006)1684, 20 Dec. 2006. Academic studies include Anger, 'Including Aviation in the European Emissions Trading Scheme'; and S. G. Pentelow and D. Scott, 'Aviation's Inclusion in International Climate Policy Regimes: Implications for the Caribbean Tourism Industry', *J. Air Transport Management* 17(2011), 199. See also PricewaterhouseCoopers, *Aviation Emissions and Policy Instruments*, 23 Sept. 2005, at 43 and Ernst & Young, *Inclusion of Aviation in the EU ETS: Cases for Carbon Leakage*, 31 Oct. 2008, at 72; and J. Faber and L. Brinke, *The Inclusion of Aviation in the EU Emissions Trading Scheme: An Economic and Environmental Assessment*, Trade and Sustainable Energy Series, Issue Paper 5 (Sept. 2011).

[19] Pt B of Annex IV to the Directive.

[20] IATA, '2011 Ends on a Positive Note – Capacity, Economy Loom as Issues in 2012', 1 Feb. 2012, available at: www.iata.org/pressroom/facts_figures/traffic_results/Pages/2012-02-01-01.aspx. This is an aggregate figure. It does not correspond exactly to flights subject to the EU's aviation scheme.

[21] Standard & Poor's, 'Airline Carbon Costs Take off as EU Emissions Regulations Reach for the Skies', 18 Feb. 2011, 6 (chart 3).

[22] J. Vespermann and A. Wald, 'Much Ado about Nothing? – An Analysis of Economic Impacts and Ecologic Effects of the EU-Emission Trading Scheme in the Aviation

Carbon estimated in February 2012 that, because of economic stagnation and falling carbon prices, the cost would be €505 million, and only €360 million if the industry makes full use of Kyoto allowances.[23] But even if there are costs, this does not mean that the aviation industry will suffer. It is generally assumed that virtually all of the increased cost will be passed on by airlines to consumers.[24] Indeed, it is quite likely that, far from suffering losses to their profitability, individual airlines may make a windfall profit.[25] As for consumers, the effects are also small, at around 4 percent of average passenger ticket prices.[26] And, while this may have some impact on demand,[27] this is mitigated by expected industry growth.

Even taking into account a small reduction in demand, the European Commission estimated that the effect of its scheme would be that instead

Industry', *Transportation Research Part A: Policy and Practice* 45 (2011), 1066, 1072 (€2.98 billion); Standard & Poor's, 'Airline Carbon Costs', 2 (€2.6–€3.9 billion), both assuming a carbon price of €25/tCO$_2$. Similar costs are estimated by J. D. Scheelhaase and W. G. Grimme, 'Emissions Trading for International Aviation – an Estimation of the Economic Impact on Selected European Airlines', *J. Air Transport Management* 13 (2007), 253, 262.

[23] McGarrity, 'Airlines to save up to 150 mln euros through EU offset concession', Point Carbon, Thomson Reuters, 14 Feb. 2012, www.pointcarbon.com/news/1.1753718

[24] CAPA, Centre for Aviation, 'Like Dominos: Airlines Globality Raise Fares after EU Emissions Trading Scheme Starts' (10 Jan. 2012), available at: www.centreforaviation. com/blogs/aviation-blog/like-dominos-aviation-globally-raise-fares-after-eu-emission-trading-scheme-starts-65856

[25] Malina *et al.*, 'The Impact of the European Union Emissions Trading Scheme on US Aviation', *J. Air Transport Management* 19 (2012), 36. Andrew Charlton has calculated that in 2012 Ryanair will make a profit of €10.8 million: 'Green Taxes – A Nice Little Earner for Some', Economist Blog, 6 Feb. 2012, avail able at: www.economist.com/blogs/gulliver/2012/02/airlines-and-emissions-permits.

[26] This figure is estimated by Faber and Brinke, *Inclusion of Aviation*, 7. See also the European Commission's impact assessment, SEC(2006)1684, and Pentelow and Scott, 'Aviation's Inclusion in International Climate Policy Regimes', 204, put the additional cost of a ticket from the UK to the British Virgin Islands at between $US6 and $US23, depending on carbon allowance prices.

[27] COM(2006)818 final, 5, and SEC(2006)1684, para. 20, which states, '[f]or an allowance price of €30 and a geographic coverage of all departing flights, by 2020 revenue tonne kilometres decrease by 1.7% for domestic flights, 1.9% for flights between Member States, and 1.5% for flights to and from third countries compared to business as usual levels. This breaks down into reductions of 1.6%, 1.9% and 1.6% respectively for passenger demand, and 3.1%, 2.0% and 1.4% respectively for cargo demand.' For a clear explanation of price elasticities in passenger travel, see Pierce, 'What Is Driving Travel Demand? Managing Travel's Climate Impacts', in J. Blanke and T. Chiesa (eds.), *The Travel & Tourism Competitiveness Report 2008: Balancing Economic Development and Environmental Sustainability* (World Economic Forum, Geneva, 2008).

of growing by 145 percent over this period, the aviation industry would grow instead by 138 percent.[28] On these figures, one might wonder why the scheme has proved so controversial.

One economic answer is that these figures conceal certain more significant impacts on particular stakeholders. First of all, the projected reduction in demand is an aggregate figure, and it is likely that its effects on airlines will depend on their business models. There has also been some discussion on whether there will be negative effects on EU airports, which because of the 'last leg' rule become less attractive as hubs, compared to airports in, for example, Switzerland, Turkey, or the Middle East.[29] Finally, and of particular importance from the perspective of this chapter, the reduction in demand is much higher for price-sensitive travel, such as travel for tourism, with estimates ranging from 2.4 to 7 percent.[30] For countries heavily dependent on tourism, such as Barbados,[31] this is no trivial matter.[32] Effectively, the EU's scheme could cost a country like Barbados 1–2 percent of its GDP.

The controversy provoked by the scheme cannot, however, be explained solely in terms of its economic impact. Rather, it has to be understood in the context of more general political considerations and parallel efforts to deal with the climate effects of aviation in other international fora, principally the ICAO.

III.   The EU'S aviation scheme in the international context

1.   The ICAO dimension

The EU's aviation scheme did not emerge out of the blue, but came as a unilateral response to failed efforts to reach international agreement

---

[28] COM(2006)818 final, 5.

[29] See Albers, Bühne, and Peters, 'Will the EU–ETS Instigate Airline Network Reconfigurations?', *J. Air Transport Management* 15(2009), 1.

[30] Pentelow and Scott, 'Aviation's Inclusion in International Climate Policy Regimes', 203 (flights to the Caribbean based on a hypothetical EU-style ETS operated by the EU, the US, and Canada). Faber and Brinke estimate a decrease in tourist travel of 2.4 per cent (*Inclusion of Aviation*, 14–15). Even the European Commission, in its impact assessment, considered that inbound tourism to the EU would decrease by up to 5 per cent (SEC (1006)1684).

[31] Tourism has been estimated to contribute 59 per cent of Barbados's GDP (Pentelow and Scott, 'Aviation's Inclusion in International Climate Policy Regimes', 202).

[32] *Ibid.*, 203, estimate total revenue losses to the Caribbean region at US$1.3 billion from 2012 to 2020, based on a 7 per cent reduction (though based on a much more general hypothetical ETS: see n. 18).

on the issue within the ICAO.[33] In 2007, the ICAO Assembly adopted Resolution A36–22 which '[u]rged Contracting States not to implement an emissions trading system on other Contracting States' aircraft operators except on the basis of mutual agreement between those States'.[34] However, in a 2010 Resolution A37–19 the Assembly recognized that 'some States may take more ambitious actions prior to 2020, which may offset an increase in emissions from the growth of air transport in developing States'.[35] It also implicitly endorsed unilateral measures, '[u]rg[ing] States to respect the guiding principles listed in the Annex, when designing new and implementing existing MBMs [market-based measures] for international aviation', even as it also urged them 'to engage in constructive bilateral and/or multilateral consultations and negotiations with other States to reach an agreement'.[36]

The ICAO heralded Resolution A37–19 as a 'historic breakthrough'.[37] However, this is an overstatement. A number of ICAO Contracting States lodged reservations expressly denying that unilateral measures were permitted.[38] Perhaps most belligerently, the Russian Federation warned that it 'does not rule out the introduction of adequate retaliatory measures by other Contracting States in respect of the operators of Contracting States which introduce market-based measures unilaterally'. Furthermore, even to the extent that Resolution A37–19 can be said to

[33] Truxal, 'The ICAO Assembly Resolutions on International Aviation and Climate Change: An Historic Agreement, a Breakthrough Deal and the Cancun Effect', *Air and Space L.* 36 (2011), 217.
[34] Consolidated Statement of Continuing ICAO Policies and Practices Related to Environmental Protection, ICAO Assembly Res. A36-22, 28 Sept. 2007, para. 1(b)(1), www.icao.int/env/A36_Res22_Prov.pdf
[35] Consolidated Statement of Continuing ICAO Policies and Practices Related to Environmental Protection, ICAO Assembly Res. A37-19, 8 Oct. 2010, para. 6(c), www.icao.int/icao/en/assembl/A37-Docs/a37_res_prov_en.pdf
[36] *Ibid.*, para. 14.
[37] 'Icao Member States Agree to Historic Agreement on Aviation and Climate Change', ICAO news release PIO 14/10, 8 Oct. 2010, www2.icao.int/en/Assembly37newsroom-public/Documents/ICAO%20Member%20States%20Agree%20To%20Historic%20Agreement%20On%20Aviation%20And%20Climate%20Change.pdf. See Truxal, 'The ICAO Assembly Resolutions', and, more sceptically, Adam, 'ICAO Assembly's Resolution on Climate Change: A 'Historic' Agreement?', *Air and Space L.* 36 (2011), 23.
[38] Reservations to the EU's scheme were lodged by the Russian Federation, the United States, China, and Argentina on behalf of a number of other countries. The reservations are available in an untitled compilation document at: www.icao.int/icao/en/assembl/A37-Docs/10_reservations_en.pdf

endorse unilateral measures, it is not clear on the question whether unilateral measures may be applied to non-national airlines. Obviously those countries that do not accept the premise deny that this is possible. But the legal situation was evidently sufficiently uncertain to prompt the EU and forty-four European states[39] to lodge a reservation setting out their view:

> The Chicago Convention contains no provision which might be construed as imposing upon the Contracting Parties the obligation to obtain the consent of other Contracting Parties before applying . . . market-based measures . . . to operators of other States in respect of air services to, from or within their territory.

The very fact that the EU and these other states felt it necessary to stress this point in a reservation, of all things, indicates that the issue is not as straightforward as one might otherwise be led to believe. And this is also supported by the fact that, on 2 November 2011, the 36-member ICAO Council – by a vote of 16 to 8 (all EU member states) and with 2 abstentions[40] – endorsed a working paper presented by 26 ICAO members, containing a 'New Delhi' Declaration which, *inter alia*, 'urge[d] the EU and its Member States to refrain from including flights by non-EU carriers to/from an airport in the territory of an EU Member State in its emissions trading system'.[41]

---

[39] The 44 states comprise the 27 EU member states and an additional 17 other states members of the European Civil Aviation Conference (ECAC) (*ibid.*).

[40] The votes were twenty-six in favour (Argentina, Brazil, Cameroon, China, Dominican Republic, Ecuador, Egypt, El Salvador, Ghana, India, Japan, Malaysia, Mexico, Namibia, Nigeria, Republic of Korea, Russian Federation, Saudi Arabia, Singapore, South Africa, Switzerland, Tunisia, Uganda, United States, Uruguay, Venezuela), eight against (Austria, France, Germany, Iceland, Italy, Romania, Spain, UK), and two abstentions (Australia and Canada): see 'States opposed to Europe's emissions trading scheme win ICAO Council backing but EU remains defiant', www.greenaironline.com/news.php?viewStory=1366 (states' votes have been calculated based on the ICAO Council membership).

[41] ICAO Working Paper, 'Inclusion of International Civil Aviation in the European Union Emissions Trading Scheme (EU ETS) and Its Impact' (presented by Argentina, Brazil, Burkina Faso, Cameroon, China, Colombia, Cuba, Egypt, Guatemala, India, Japan, Malaysia, Mexico, Morocco, Nigeria, Paraguay, Peru, Republic of Korea, Russian Federation, Saudi Arabia, Singapore, South Africa, Swaziland, Uganda, the United Arab Emirates, and the United States), C-WP/13790, 17 Oct. 2011. The New Delhi Declaration itself, annexed to the Working Paper, was adopted by twenty-three countries, including those presenting the paper plus Chile and Qatar but minus Burkina Faso, Cameroon, Guatemala, Morocco, and Peru.

2. Challenges in other fora

There has also been a significant reaction outside the ICAO. Domestic-ally, China has blocked US$4 billion worth of orders from Airbus,[42] and both China and India have prohibited their national carriers from com-plying with the EU's scheme.[43] In the United States, a bipartisan bill to equivalent effect awaits Senate approval after being passed by the House of Representatives on 24 October 2011.[44] The bill is supported by the US Secretary of State, who has warned the EU that the USA would be 'compelled to take action' if the EU did not abandon its scheme.[45] On 16 January 2012, the European Commission wrote back vowing to retain its scheme.[46]

The airlines have also taken the dispute directly to the EU. In 2010, a consortium of US airlines, supported by the International Air Transport Association (IATA) and the National Airlines Council of Canada, initi-ated a legal action in which they argued that the EU violated its obliga-tions under customary international law and various international agreements, including the Chicago Convention.[47] On 21 December 2011, following an Opinion by Advocate General Kokott,[48] the CJEU

---

[42] Wall, 'China's Objection to EU ETS Hits A380 Order', *Aviation Week*, 28 June 2011, www.aviationweek.com/aw/generic/story_generic.jsp?channel=comm.&id=news/avd/2011/06/28/08.xml&headline=China%27s%20Objection%20To%20EU%20ETS%20Hits%20A380%20Order

[43] Kotoky, 'India Joins China in Boycott of EU Carbon Scheme', Reuters, 22 Mar. 2012, http://www.reuters.com/article/2012/03/22/uk-india-eu-emissions-idUSLNE82L02220120322

[44] HR 2594 'European Union Emissions Trading Scheme Prohibition Act of 2011', http://hdl.loc.gov/loc.uscongress/legislation.112hr2594. The bill is currently being considered by the Senate Committee on Commerce, Science, and Transportation.

[45] 'EU tells Clinton it won't abandon carbon limits for airlines', *Bloomberg Businessweek*, 17 Jan. 2012, http://news.businessweek.com/article.asp?documentKey=1376-LXXZVY1A74 E801-7RN4RU7HKN5492BA60E0BF88HF

[46] *Ibid.*

[47] Case C-366/10, *Air Transport Association of America, American Airlines, Inc, Continental Airlines, Inc, United Airlines, Inc v. The Secretary of State for Energy and Climate Change*, OJ (2010) C260/9 (including the claims). The reference was made in *R. (Air Transport Association of America, Inc.) v. Secretary of State for Energy and Climate Change* [2010] EWHC 1554 (Admin.), 27 May 2010. For a transcript of the proceedings, see www.casetrack.com/ct4plc.nsf/items/8-503-3384

[48] *Ibid.*, Case C-366/10 (AG's Opinion), 6 Oct. 2011, http://curia.europa.eu. AG Kokott found that only certain provisions in the Open Skies Agreement had direct effect in EU law, such that the applicants could rely on it. She also found, in the alternative, that the EU's scheme would not violate these obligations in any case.

held that the EU's scheme was consistent with all relevant rules on international law and, in particular, with international legal obligations restricting the power of states to regulate extraterritorially.[49]

Against the background of this failed litigation strategy, on 22 February 2012, twenty-three countries adopted a 'Moscow' Declaration denouncing the EU's aviation scheme, and threatening a range of measures in response. These include litigation under Article 84 of the Chicago Convention, the prohibition of domestic airlines and operators from participating in the EU's scheme, and countermeasures, such as reviewing air transport service agreements, mandating EU carriers to submit flight details and other data, and imposing additional charges on EU carriers and aircraft operators. In addition, and relevantly for this chapter, the participating states invoked the possibility that the EU's scheme might violate its WTO obligations.[50]

3. The WTO dimension

As mentioned, the EU's aviation scheme may have real economic consequences for WTO members, especially in the area of services.[51] And this assumes that airlines will comply with the scheme. If they do not, and are either charged a penalty or cease to operate flights to the EU, the impact will be much more dramatic.

But, particularly given the political context, it is perhaps even more important that WTO law may be violated even in the absence of any

---

[49] *Ibid.*, judgment of 21 Dec. 2011, http://curia.europa.eu/juris/document/document.jsf? text=&docid=117193&pageIndex=0&doclang=en&mode=doc&dir=&occ=first&part=1& cid=107836

[50] Joint Declaration of the Moscow meeting on inclusion of international civil aviation in the EU–ETS, 22 Feb. 2012, adopted by Armenia, Argentina, Republic of Belarus, Brazil, Cameroon, Chile, China, Cuba, Guatemala, India, Japan, Republic of Korea, Mexico, Nigeria, Paraguay, Russian Federation, Saudi Arabia, Seychelles, Singapore, South Africa, Thailand, Uganda and USA, available at http://images.politico.com/global/2012/02/ 120222.pdf

[51] There is trade in services under Mode 2 (consumption abroad) when a service consumer travels to a service supplier in another WTO member's territory (art. I:1 GATS). In her Opinion in *ATAA*, Case C-366/10, para. 229, AG Kokott said that 'the purpose [of the EU emissions trading scheme] is environmental and climate protection and it has nothing to do with the importing or exporting of goods'. This does not of course mean that the scheme has no effects on imports or exports of goods (or services).

trade effects.[52] Thus, in *EC – Bananas*, the United States won a victory despite the fact that it exported not a single banana to the EU.[53]

The following assesses the legality of the EU's scheme in terms of the most applicable obligations under the GATT. It begins by considering its character as a fiscal or non-fiscal measure. Next, it looks at whether, at least in part, the EU's scheme might constitute a quantitative restriction on trade in goods in violation of Article XI:1, or a discriminatory internal measure under Article III:4 GATT. It then considers the relevance of the most-favoured-nation obligation in Article I:1, which applies to certain measures affecting the importation and domestic sale of products, and Article V, which governs goods in transit. A final section discusses the possible application of Article XX, which provides for certain exceptions to the GATT for measures adopted, among other things, for environmental reasons.

The analysis then turns to the GATS. In this context, the first major issue concerns the applicability of the agreement, given the carve-out in the Annex on Air Transport Services, which purports to carve out a range of measures from the scope of the GATS. On the tentative basis that this Annex does not, in all cases, apply to measures affecting services dependent on air transport services, this section considers various GATS obligations, and then the applicability of available defences.

The overall conclusion is that the EU's scheme is likely to violate a number of GATT and GATS obligations, but that virtually all violations can be justified on environmental grounds under the general exceptions

---

[52] See WTO Panel Report, *Argentina – Hides and Leather*, WT/DS155/R, adopted 16 Feb. 2001, para. 11.20, for a concise statement that 'Article XI:1, like Articles I, II and III of the GATT 1994, protects competitive opportunities of imported products not trade flows'. Further statements to similar effect are found in WTO Appellate Body Report, *Korea – Beef*, WT/DS161/AB/R, adopted 10 Jan. 2001, para. 146 (on art. III:4 GATT), and see the statements of the parties in WTO Appellate Body Report, *China – Raw Materials*, WT/DS394/AB/R, adopted 22 Feb. 2012, paras. 59, 97, 192 (on art. XI:1 GATT). The Appellate Body has interpreted the scope of GATS in a similar way (WTO Appellate Body Report, *EC – Bananas III*, adopted 25 Sept. 1997, para. 220).

[53] WTO Appellate Body Report, *EC – Bananas III*, para. 136, where the Appellate Body even stated that the USA had standing not only because it might be a future exporter of bananas but also because '[t]he internal market of the United States for bananas could be affected by the EC banana regime, in particular, by the effects of that regime on world supplies and world prices of bananas'. See also WTO Appellate Body Report, *US – Bananas III (Article 21.5 – US)*, WT/DS27/AB/RW/USA, adopted 22 Dec. 2008, at para. 469. Trade effects do, however, have an effect on the value of retaliatory measures than may be adopted by a complainant against an unsuccessful recalcitrant defendant (art. 22.4 of the WTO Dispute Settlement Understanding (DSU)).

in these agreements. That there are certain anomalies, interestingly, has more to do with the desirability (and perhaps even correctness) of certain WTO jurisprudence, a point that is addressed in the final remarks concluding the chapter.

IV. The EU'S aviation scheme and the General Agreement on Tariffs and Trade

1. The character of the EU's scheme

One of the basic distinctions made by the GATT is between fiscal measures, namely duties, taxes, and other charges, and other regulatory measures affecting trade in goods. In order to determine the EU's WTO obligations regarding its aviation scheme, it is therefore necessary to analyse the legal character of the scheme.

The first question is whether the EU's scheme can be considered a fiscal measure within the meaning of Article III:2 GATT.[54] On this point, the recent *ATAA* case is relevant, even though it dealt with provisions of other international agreements.[55] In this case, Advocate General Kokott considered whether the EU's aviation scheme violated Article 15 of the Chicago Convention, which governs the imposition of 'fees, dues or other charges' on transit, entry and exit of aircraft, or persons or property thereon.[56] She held that the EU's scheme constituted neither a charge nor a tax:

[54] For a recent analysis of this issue, and the opposite conclusion, see Meltzer, 'Climate Change and Trade – The EU Aviation Directive and the WTO', *J. Int' l Economic L.* 15 (2012), 111. Earlier general discussions are found in J. Pauwelyn, 'US Federal Climate Policy and Competitiveness Concerns: The Limits and Options of International Trade Law', Nicholas Institute for Environmental Policy Solutions, Working Paper 02/07, Apr. 2007, 21; de Cendra, 'Can Emissions Trading Schemes be Coupled with Border Tax Adjustments? An Analysis vis-à-vis WTO Law', *Rev. European Community & Int' l Environmental L.* 15(2006), at 136; R. Ismer and K. Neuhoff, *Border Tax Adjustments: A Feasible Way to Address Non-Participation in Emission Trading*, Cambridge Working Papers in Economics (CMI Working Paper 36, 2004), 11; W. H. Maruyama, 'Climate Change and the WTO: Cap and Trade versus Carbon Tax', *J. World Trade* 45 (2011), 695; R. Quick, '"Border Tax Adjustment" in the Context of Emission Trading: Climate Protection or 'Naked' Protectionism?', *Global Trade and Customs J.* 3(2008), 166.

[55] Case C-366/10, *ATAA*, concerned obligations under the Chicago Convention and the EU–US Open Skies Agreement. However, for reasons to be explained, the description of the EU's aviation scheme is still relevant to its characterization under the GATT.

[56] On this sentence, see A. Macintosh, 'Overcoming the Barriers to International Aviation Greenhouse Gas Emissions Abatement', *Air and Space L.* 33 (2008), 403, 415. See also

Charges are levied as consideration for a public service used. The amount is set unilaterally by a public body and can be determined in advance. Other charges too, especially taxes, are fixed unilaterally by a public body and laid down according to certain predetermined criteria, such as the tax rate and basis of assessment.

It would be unusual, to put it mildly, to describe as a charge or tax the purchase price paid for an emission allowance, which is based on supply and demand according to free market forces, notwithstanding the fact that the Member States do have a certain discretion regarding the use to be made of revenues generated.[57]

Advocate General Kokott also considered whether the EU's scheme constituted a 'duty, tax, fee, or charge on fuel consumption', in violation of Article 24 of the Chicago Convention, and also Article 11 of the US–EU Open Skies Agreement. She dismissed the possibility, *inter alia*, referring back to her earlier reasoning.[58]

For its part, the CJEU did not deal with the first question, but it made similar comments when dealing with the second. It said:

[U]nlike a duty, tax, fee or charge on fuel consumption, the scheme … apart from the fact that it is not intended to generate revenue for the public authorities, does not in any way enable the establishment, applying a basis of assessment and a rate defined in advance, of an amount that must be payable per tonne of fuel consumed for all the flights carried out in a calendar year.[59]

While there are some differences of opinion concerning the importance of the fact that auctioned allowances generate revenue accruing to the state,[60] the central point made by both the Advocate General and the Court is that the EU's scheme does not constitute a duty, charge, or tax because the 'price' paid for an allowance is not fixed by the state in advance, but depends on free market forces.[61] This argument has direct application to the present case. If a measure cannot be a duty, charge, or

---

Federation of Tour Operators v. *HM Treasury* [2007] EWHC 2062 (Admin.), which was appealed to the Court of Appeal on another issue.

[57] Case C-366/10, *ATAA* (AG's Opinion), paras. 214 and 216.

[58] *Ibid.*, para. 227. Meltzer, 'Climate Change and Trade', 130, points out that AG Kokott should not at this stage have addressed the question whether the scheme constituted a 'tax', in applying art. 15 of the Convention, although he does not mention the ruling of AG Kokott on art. 24, where the term is relevant.

[59] Case C-366/10, *ATAA*, para. 143.

[60] For Meltzer, 'Climate Change and Trade', 130, this is conclusive; see also Maruyama, 'Climate Change and the WTO', 695.

[61] Meltzer, 'Climate Change and Trade', does not address this point.

tax for this reason, then it makes no difference whether the measure is applied to fuel consumption, products, or to some other activity or subject matter.[62] It would follow, therefore, that the measure should not be considered a fiscal measure for the purposes of the GATT.

Beyond this, there is also another reason for thinking that the EU's aviation scheme does not constitute a tax or a charge, which is that the scheme requires airlines to purchase carbon emission allowances. This is quite different from imposing a fiscal charge on an activity, as the airlines gain a tradable property right in exchange.[63] The fact that some of the revenue earned as a result of such a measure flows back to the state is unimportant. The EU's scheme is more similar to a law requiring motor-cycle riders to purchase helmets. This is obviously a regulatory measure, and it does not cease to be one just because the state sells an initial quantity of those helmets. The point is that the compulsory purchaser retains something of value – indeed, in the case of emissions allowances, this is something the value of which could increase significantly on the open market.[64] For this reason, too, the EU's aviation scheme (and ETS more generally) should not be considered a tax or a charge within the meaning of GATT, more precisely Article III:2 GATT.[65]

2. The EU's aviation scheme as a quantitative restriction (Article XI:1 GATT)

If the EU's aviation scheme is not a fiscal measure, the first question is whether it might constitute a quantitative restriction within the meaning of Article XI:1 GATT. This provision states, relevantly, as follows:

---

[62] Note also that Australia describes the first phase of its Clean Energy Act, which sets a fixed price for carbon emissions, but not its second phase, which is a 'cap and trade' scheme, as a 'carbon tax' (Clean Energy Bill 2011, Explanatory Memorandum, 29, http://parlinfo.aph.gov.au/parlInfo/search/display/display.w3p;query=Id%3A%22legislation%2Fbillhome%2Fr4653%22).

[63] Vranes, 'Climate Change and the WTO: EU Emission Trading and the WTO Disciplines on Trade in Goods, Services and Investment Protection', *J. World Trade* 43 (2009), 707, concludes that certificates may constitute both goods, 717–18, and financial instruments, 719–20. For the view that EU emissions allowances may constitute property under the European Convention on Human Rights, see A. Boute, 'The Protection of Property Rights under the European Convention on Human Rights and the Promotion of Low-Carbon Investments', *Climate L.* 1 (2010), 111.

[64] For a similar view, though expressed somewhat differently, see Quick, '"Border Tax Adjustment"', 166.

[65] For the view that it does, most likely, constitute a tax, see Meltzer, 'Climate Change and Trade'.

No prohibitions or restrictions other than duties, taxes or other charges, whether made effective through quotas, import or export licences or other measures, shall be instituted or maintained by any contracting party on the importation of any product of the territory of any other contracting party.

WTO panels have interpreted the term 'other measures' as a broad residual category covering 'any form of limitation imposed on, or in relation to importation'.[66] For example, in *Colombia – Ports of Entry*, the panel considered whether this phase covered a measure that restricted the ports that could be used by importers. The panel decided that it would if the measure affected the cost of shipping products from the port of origin to the place of sale;[67] or if it were applied in an arbitrary manner, thereby increasing the uncertainty of private actors involved in the importation of the product. In other words, what is important is the restrictive *effect* of the measure on the importation of any given product, not whether it concerns a right of importation. This has now been confirmed in *China – Raw Materials*, where the Appellate Body said that 'Article XI of the GATT 1994 covers those prohibitions and restrictions that have a limiting effect on the quantity or amount of a product being imported or exported'.[68]

In so far as it applies to products prior to importation that are being transported on international flights, the EU's scheme shares certain features with the measure in *Colombia – Ports of Entry*. For airlines complying with the scheme, the result is likely to be increased transportation costs. Furthermore, its impacts on imported products vary, unpredictably, according to the price of allowances. For airlines that do not comply the costs are far greater, at €100 per missed allowance in addition to the usual compliance costs. In all of these cases it seems reasonable to conclude that the EU's aviation scheme has restrictive effects – no matter how small – on the importation of products into the EU, within the meaning of Article XI:1 GATT.

---

[66] WTO Panel Report, *Colombia – Ports of Entry*, WT/DS366/R, adopted 20 May 2009, para. 7.227, referring to WTO Panel Report, *India – Automobiles*, WT/DS146/R, adopted as modified by the Appellate Body Report, 5 Apr. 2002, paras. 7.254–7.263 and 7.265 and WTO Panel Report, *Brazil – Retreaded Tyres*, WT/DS332/R, adopted as modified by the Appellate Body Report, 17 Dec. 2007, para. 7.371.

[67] WTO Panel Report, *Colombia – Ports of Entry*, paras. 7.258–7.275.

[68] WTO Appellate Body Report, *China – Raw Materials*, WT/DS394/AB/R, para. 320. It is significant that the defendant did not dispute that the focus should be on effects (see para. 57).

444 LORAND BARTELS

Over and above this, the EU's aviation scheme directly regulates the *means* by which products are imported into the EU. Admittedly, Advocate General Kokott, in her Opinion in the *ATAA* case, denied that the EU's scheme was '[a] concrete *rule* regarding [foreign airlines'] conduct within airspace outside the European Union'[69] and the Court by implication agreed.[70] But it is difficult to see how a measure that imposes fines of €100 for any allowance not obtained and 'surrendered' to the EU can be seen as anything but just such a 'concrete rule', regardless of whether it might be justified under international law. On this basis, too, one could argue that, in so far as it applies to international flights carrying imported products landing in the EU,[71] the EU's scheme amounts to a quantitative restriction contrary to Article XI:1 GATT.

3. The EU's aviation scheme as an internal measure (Article III:4 GATT)

Where Article XI:1 applies to restrictions on the importation of products, Article III:4 regulates measures (other than fiscal measures) affecting imported products. It states, relevantly, that:

> The products of the territory of any contracting party imported into the territory of any other contracting party shall be accorded treatment no less favourable than that accorded to like products of national origin in respect of all laws, regulations and requirements affecting their internal sale, offering for sale, purchase, transportation, distribution or use.

---

[69] Case C-366/10, *ATAA* (AG's Opinion), at para. 147.
[70] The CJEU addressed this issue with a *non sequitur*, focusing on EU internal competences. It said, '[a]s for the fact that the operator of an aircraft in such a situation is required to surrender allowances calculated in the light of the whole of the international flight that its aircraft has performed or is going to perform from or to such an aerodrome, it must be pointed out that, as European Union policy on the environment seeks to ensure a high level of protection in accordance with Article 191(2) TFEU, the European Union legislature may in principle choose to permit a commercial activity, in this instance air transport, to be carried out in the territory of the European Union only on condition that operators comply with the criteria that have been established by the European Union and are designed to fulfil the environmental protection objectives which it has set for itself, in particular where those objectives follow on from an international agreement to which the European Union is a signatory, such as the Framework Convention and the Kyoto Protocol' (see Case C-366/10, *ATAA*, para. 128).
[71] The case of intra-EU flights carrying products prior to importation is considered below.

(i)   The application of Article III:4 to measures affecting imported products

Article III:4 is not limited to measures specifically regulating the particular activities (internal sale, purchase, transportation, etc.) which it mentions. Rather, it applies to all measures affecting the conditions of competition of imported products on the domestic market.[72] However, this should not obscure the fact that Article III:4 is concerned with *internal* measures applicable to products *after* they have been imported. There are other provisions, such as Article XI:1 (quantitative restrictions) and Article V GATT (transit), that protect foreign products prior to their importation. Thus, Article III:4 should be understood as applying to all internal measures affecting products once they are imported except for measures affecting products before they are imported or on importation.

This assessment of the proper scope of Article III:4 is admittedly made against the background of somewhat inconsistent jurisprudence. In one of the few cases actually to deal with the issue, *US – Malt Beverages*, the GATT Panel said as follows:

> Having regard to the past panel decisions and the record in the instant case, the present Panel was of the view that *the listing and delisting practices here at issue do not affect importation as such* into the United States and should be examined under Article III:4. The Panel further noted that the issue is not whether the practices in the various states *affect the right of importation as such*, in that they clearly apply to both domestic (out-of-state) and imported wines.[73]

Thus, in accordance with the view expressed here, the panel considered Article III:4 to apply only to measures that did not apply to importation 'as such'. It was unnecessary for the panel to state that Article III:4 also does not apply to measures affecting products *before* they are imported, but this would seem to follow.

---

[72] GATT Panel Report, *Italy – Agricultural Machinery*, L/833, adopted 23 Oct. 1958. R. Howse and D. Regan, 'The Product/Process Distinction – An Illusory Basis for Disciplining "Unilateralism" in Trade Policy', EJIL, 11 (2000), 254–5, argue that all process-based measures fall under art. III:4 because they affect the sale of products. They dismiss a reading of art. III:4 that focuses on the acts specifically mentioned in this provision, on the ground that this would exclude regulations affecting internal acts not listed there, such as possession, storage, advertising, and so on.

[73] GATT Panel Report, *US – Malt Beverages*, DS23/R, adopted 19 June 1992, para. 5.63, emphasis added.

In contrast to this GATT Panel Report, in *EC – Bananas III* the Appellate Body dealt with a similar question in a less satisfactory manner. In this case the question arose whether a measure allocating import licences to domestic distributors was an internal measure falling under Article III:4.[74] The Appellate Body said it was, on the basis that the measure was *intended* to have an effect on the sales of competing domestic products. But 'intention' is, at most, useful in characterizing measures according to whether they fulfil a specific purpose, such as sanitary measures;[75] it has no application in the present context. And, indeed, when the Appellate Body came to determine the equivalent question in the context of fiscal measures, it held that taxes and charges are 'internal', and therefore subject to Article III:2 GATT, only when they 'accrue' on the basis of an internal condition or event.[76] Intention was ignored, and quite properly so.

Given this, it is suggested that Article III:4 applies to all internal measures affecting competitive conditions in the marketplace for imported products, except for measures which have potentially restrictive effects on the importation of products.[77] What, then, does this mean for the EU's scheme? To the extent that the EU's scheme applies to flights transporting imported products, it would seem to be regulated by Article III:4. This, most obviously, includes intra-EU flights transporting products that have been imported into the EU. But in so far as the EU's scheme covers international flights transporting products that have yet to be imported, it would be covered by Article XI:1.

---

[74] WTO Appellate Body Report, *EC – Bananas III*, para. 211.

[75] WTO Panel Report, *US – Poultry (China)*, WT/DS392/R, adopted 25 Oct. 2010, para. 7.102.

[76] See WTO Appellate Body Report, *China – Auto Parts*, WT/DS339/AB/R, adopted 12 Jan. 2009, paras. 161–2.

[77] See GATT Panel Report, *US – Tuna (Mexico)*, DS21, unadopted, circulated 3 Sept. 1991, which concerned a measure with two aspects. The first was a prohibition on the harvesting of tuna by persons and vessels subject to US jurisdiction in a manner that harmed dolphins; the second was a prohibition on the importation of commercial fish and fish products harvested in the same manner (see para. 2.4). The GATT Panel held that art. III:4 did not apply because the measure did not affect tuna 'as such' (at paras. 5.1 and 5.14). This reasoning is obviously incorrect, due to the fact that art. III:4 covers measures indirectly affecting products: Howse and Regan, 'The Product/Process Distinction', 255. However, the result was correct. While the prohibition on production by persons within US jurisdiction fell within art. III:4, the prohibition on importation fell under art. XI:1. Only if the latter aspect of the measure had been designed to enforce the former (which does not seem to have been the case) could it have been legal.

(ii) The Note Ad Article III

There is, however, a special rule applicable to measures that, due to their connection with an otherwise internal measure, are imposed at the time or point of importation. By virtue of the Note Ad Article III GATT, such measures are to be seen as aspects of internal measures applicable to imported products, and by implication not as quantitative restrictions subject to Article XI:1 GATT. The distinction makes a tremendous difference, as quantitative restrictions are prohibited, while Article III:4 only requires national treatment. The Note states as follows:

> Any internal [measure] which applies to an imported product and to the like domestic product and is collected or enforced in the case of the imported product at the time or point of importation, is nevertheless to be regarded as an internal [measure], and is accordingly subject to the provisions of Article III.

There is a certain degree of flexibility in relation to such measures; for example, they do not need to be identical in form to the relevant internal measure.[78] But they do need to be justified by some administrative rationale if they are to escape classification as quantitative restrictions. In the present case, it would seem that the application of the EU's scheme to international flights (and hence to products before they have been imported) is neither directly linked to nor justified by the system's application to intra-EU flights (and hence to products once they have been imported). It cannot be said that this represents the enforcement of an otherwise internal measure. However, the Note should apply to intra-EU flights carrying foreign products between an

---

[78] Such 'enforcement' measures need not have any formal correlation to the internal measure being enforced: WTO Panel Report, *EC – Asbestos*, WT/DS135/R, adopted as modified by the Appellate Body Report on 5 Apr. 2001, paras. 8.94–8.95. Indeed, it seems permissible for an internal charge to be enforced by an administrative requirement imposed at the border. In WTO Panel Report, *Argentina – Hides and Leather*, paras. 11.143–11.145, the Panel held that a charge enforcing an internal tax fell under the Note Ad Article III. Cf. WTO Panel, *China – Auto Parts*, WT/DS339/R, adopted 12 Jan. 2009, para. 7.249–7.258, in which the Panel considered administrative measures enforcing a tax to be internal measures because they affected the conditions of competition of the relevant products once they had been imported. For the reasons suggested here, it is suggested that the result was correct, but the reasoning flawed. It would have been more correct to consider these internal because they were enforcing an internal charge within the meaning of the Note Ad Article III. This issue was not appealed, and the Appellate Body seems to have thought that the Panel's approach was appropriate (WTO Appellate Body, *China – Auto Parts*, para. 196).

EU hub and an EU destination airport when importation takes place at the destination airport.

(iii)   Application of Article III:4 to the EU's scheme

On the assumption that Article III:4 applies to such flights, the next question is whether the EU's scheme accords 'less favourable treatment' to imported products than to 'like' domestic products.[79] It would appear that it does not. There are no differences in treatment of domestic and imported products on intra-EU flights, either formally or, as far as can be imagined, de facto. It is true that the EU's scheme is less favourable to air transport than to other forms of transport, which are not covered by the ETS, but it is difficult to see that this puts imported products at a disadvantage. It is perfectly possible, and common, for imported products to be offloaded at the airport of entry, and then transported to the final EU destination by road. The result is that the EU's scheme does not appear to violate Article III:4 GATT to the extent that it applies to foreign non-imported products carried on intra-EU flights.[80]

4.   The most-favoured nation obligation (Article I:1 GATT)

Both internal measures and measures imposed on importation are subject to the most-favoured nation obligation established in Article I:1 GATT. This states, relevantly, that:

> With respect to ... all rules and formalities in connection with importation ..., and with respect to all matters referred to in paragraphs 2 and 4 of Article III, any advantage, favour, privilege or immunity granted by any contracting party to any product originating in or destined for any other country shall be accorded immediately and unconditionally to the like product originating in ... the territories of all other contracting parties.

It is difficult to see how the internal aspects of the EU's scheme (in relation to intra-EU flights) would violate this provision. But it is possible that Article I:1 GATT might apply to the EU's scheme in so far as it

---

[79] This is independent of whether the measure discriminates against a particular airline, a question answered in the negative by AG Kokott in Case C-366/10, *ATAA* (AG's Opinion), paras. 195–201.

[80] Meltzer, 'Climate Change and Trade' 135, considers art. III:4 applicable to all flights covered by the EU's scheme, and finds a violation on this basis.

affects international aviation, with negative results.[81] The question, interestingly, is one that is fundamental to international trade, and yet rarely addressed: does the most-favoured nation obligation, the 'cornerstone' of the GATT, apply to the international transportation of products?

Article I:1 GATT describes the measures to which it applies as, relevantly, 'rules and formalities in connection with importation'. On a narrow reading, this phrase is limited to rules regulating the actual act of importation, such as customs formalities. However, it is arguable that Article I:1 GATT should be read in light of Article XI:1, so that it applies to any measure imposed on but also 'in connection with' importation. If not, a WTO member could discriminate against products arriving by sea, to the advantage of its neighbours with which it shares a land border.[82] The following assumes that Article I:1 GATT applies to international transportation.

(i)   According an 'advantage'

On the basis that Article I:1 GATT does apply to the EU's scheme, the next question is whether the EU's scheme accords an 'advantage' to 'like' products from different WTO members.[83] In the first instance, this requires one to identify the 'advantage' at issue. This, in turn, has to be assessed in terms of the conditions of competition between the affected products in the domestic market.[84] In the present case, the effect of the EU's aviation scheme is to impose costs on products from certain origins according to the distance they travel by air to the EU. These costs have the potential to be reflected in the final price of the products, and thus their competitiveness. It is suggested, therefore, that the 'advantage' be defined as the most-favourable compliance cost imposed on airlines transporting products to the EU.

If this is the advantage, is it accorded equally to products from all WTO members? It seems that it will not be so accorded, assuming that

---

[81] Art. XIII:1 GATT requires quantitative restrictions to be applied in a non-discriminatory manner. A number of panels (e.g. WTO Panel Report, *EC – Bananas III*, WT/DS27/R, adopted as modified by the Appellate Body Report, 25 Sept. 1997, para. 7.68) and academic commentators (e.g. P. Mavroidis, *Trade in Goods* (Oxford University Press, 2007), at 64, limit this to permitted quantitative restrictions.

[82] Such situations are not covered by art. V:6 GATT (discussed below), which requires non-discrimination between different routes from the *same* origin.

[83] See WTO Appellate Body Report, *Canada – Automobiles*, WT/DS139/AB/R, adopted 19 June 2000, para. 78.

[84] Sometimes, this involves a duty tax rate, or a regulatory procedure that is not available.

there is a correlation between the origin of a product and distance travelled by such a product by air to the EU, and that it would be disadvantageous for a given product to be transported in some other way (e.g., by ship). In this scenario, there is little doubt that products from one origin (e.g., Hong Kong) are not 'accorded' the same 'advantage' (the lowest possible compliance costs) that is 'accorded' to products from another origin (e.g., Dubai).

Indeed, in its reliance on geographical facts (distance from the EU), the EU's scheme is reminiscent of the 'classic' case of de facto discrimination: the 1904 German measure granting market access to all cows that grazed at Alpine altitudes.[85] Just as, in reality, the 'advantage' of market access was not accorded to Danish or Dutch cows,[86] here the 'advantage' of the lowest possible airline compliance cost is not accorded to products from Hong Kong. Likewise, in *EC – Tariff Preferences*, a panel rejected a measure according to which products were charged different duties depending on whether their country of origin had difficulties in regulating drugs.[87] And in *EC – Fasteners*, a panel rejected a measure applying different duties to products according to whether their country of origin had a 'market economy'.[88] The geographical factor underlying the discrimination also undermines any argument that the 'detrimental effect [of the measure] is explained by factors or circumstances unrelated to the foreign origin of the product'.[89]

---

[85] League of Nations, Economic and Financial Section, *Memorandum on Discriminatory Classifications* (Ser LoNP 1927.11.27), 8, quoted in *Second Report on the Most-Favoured-Nation Clause*, by Mr Endre Ustor, Special Rapporteur, A/CN.4/228 and Add.1, II Yrbk ILC (1970) 199, para. 148. Note however the comment of the Food and Agriculture Organization (FAO) that 'it would seem that the specialized tariff may have been technically justified because of the genetic improvement programme which was carried out in Southern Germany at that time. At present, this specialized tariff would presumably have been worded in a different way, but in 1904 terms like Simmental or Brown Swiss were probably not recognized as legally valid characteristics' (undated, quoted *ibid.*).

[86] Though see 'Peak of Insanity? Dutch Dream of Building Artificial Mountain', www.spiegel.de/international/zeitgeist/0,1518,784085,00.html (2 Sept. 2011), and www.cyclingthealps.com/tour/NederlandseBerg.html

[87] WTO Panel Report, *EC – Tariff Preferences*, WT/DS246/R, adopted as modified by the Appellate Body Report, 20 Apr. 2004, para. 7.60.

[88] WTO Panel Report, *EC – Fasteners*, WT/DS397/R, adopted as modified by the Appellate Body Report, 28 July 2011, paras. 7.124–7.127. This finding was declared moot by the Appellate Body on other grounds, in WTO Appellate Body Report, *EC – Fasteners*, WTO/DS397/AB/R, adopted 28 July 2011, paras. 397–8.

[89] WTO Appellate Body Report, *Dominican Republic – Cigarettes*, WT/DS302/AB/R, adopted 19 May 2005, para. 96. See also WTO Appellate Body Report, *US – Clove*

There is, of course, a difference between the EU's scheme and these other cases, in so far as the effects of the EU's scheme depend upon business decisions made by private actors. It is conceivable that some airlines will choose to absorb the cost of complying with the EU's scheme, in which case there will be no disadvantage to products carried on these airlines. In turn this would mean that any disadvantage could be attributed to decisions taken by airlines rather than the EU's measure. However, as mentioned above, it is unlikely that airlines will or can absorb these costs. Moreover, even if they did, this would make no difference in legal terms. It is sufficient under WTO law that a regulatory measure gives an incentive to a private actor to act in a manner negatively affecting conditions of competition in the marketplace. It is not necessary that the private actor be compelled to act in that manner.[90] On this basis, it appears that the EU's scheme fails to accord an 'advantage' to products from all WTO members.[91] The fact that the effects of this

---

Cigarettes, WT/DS406/AB/R, adopted 24 Apr. 2012, para. 179 n. 372, casting doubt on this test.

[90] WTO Appellate Body Report, *Korea – Beef*, para. 146 (art. III:4 GATT); WTO Appellate Body Report, *US – FSC (Article 21.5 – EC)*, WT/DS108/AB/RW, adopted 29 Jan. 2002, at paras. 219–20 (art. III:4 GATT); WTO Panel Report, *US – COOL*, WT/DS384/R, circulated 18 Nov. 2011, para. 7.391.

[91] There are other cases on art. I:1 GATT which might appear to be of relevance. However, these are of limited analytical value, as they are based on the erroneous assumption that the requirement in art. I:1 GATT to accord such advantages 'immediately and unconditionally' applies to conditions which private actors must meet in order to obtain an advantage (WTO Panel Report, *Indonesia – Automobiles*, WT/ DS54/R, adopted 23 July 1998, para. 14.145 and WTO Panel Report, *Canada – Automobiles*, adopted as modified by the Appellate Body report 19 June 2000, paras. 10.24–10.26). Following this, some panels have even analysed straightforward cases of *de jure* discrimination in light of this requirement (WTO Panel Report, *EC – Bananas (Article 21.5 – Ecuador II)*, WT/DS27/ RW2/ECU, adopted as modified by the Appellate Body Report, 11 Dec. 2008, at paras. 7.158–7.159 and WTO Panel Report, *EC – Bananas (Article 21.5 – US)*, WT/DS27/RW2/ USA, adopted as modified by the Appellate Body Report, 11 Dec. 2008, at paras. 7.565–7.566); WTO Panel Report, *Colombia – Ports of Entry*, para. 7.366; WTO Panel Report, *US – Poultry (China)*, WT/DS392/R, adopted 25 Oct. 2010, para. 7.437. In fact, the requirement of unconditional most-favoured-nation treatment, historically an alternative to *conditional* most-favoured treatment (on which see S. Schill, *The Multilateralization of International Investment Law* (Cambridge University Press, 2009), 129–39), is concerned with conditions addressed to WTO members, not to private actors. It precludes WTO members from according an advantage to products on condition that the other WTO member act in a certain way e.g. by adopting a certain regulatory system, or entering into a treaty (GATT Panel Report, *Belgian Family Allowances*, GATT Doc G/32, adopted 7 Nov. 1952, para. 3; *Report of the Working Party on the Accession of Hungary*, adopted 30 July 1973, BISD 20S/34, para. 12; WTO Panel, *EC – Trademarks and Geographical Indications (US)*, WT/DS174/R, adopted 20 Apr. 2005, para. 7.704

treatment might be minor, even trivial, does not matter. It is the potential
negative effect that is important.

This problem could be further amplified by the selective exemption of
certain airlines. The EU Directive provides that airlines from 'third
countries [that adopt] measures for reducing the climate change impact
of flights departing from that country which land in the Community'
shall be exempted from the ETS.[92] No such exemption has yet been
granted, but if it were and granted selectively, this would clearly violate
the requirement in Article I:1 GATT that an advantage be accorded
'immediately and unconditionally' to products from all WTO
members.[93] It is no answer to say that products from other countries
might be entitled to the same 'advantage' if these other countries adopted
'equivalent measures': this is precisely what the 'unconditionality'
requirement in Article I:1 is designed to prevent.

5. Freedom of transit (Article V GATT)

Further questions arise as to the transit aspects of the EU's measure. The
EU's scheme also involves goods in transit, in two ways: first in relation
to products that transit across the EU, and second in relation to products
that have been in transit before they arrive in the EU as a final destination. Article V GATT sets out obligations in relation to both scenarios.

(i)   A carve-out for air transport?

Before engaging in a discussion on Article V, it is appropriate to comment on the carve-out set out in Article V:7. This paragraph states that
'[t]he provisions of this Article shall not apply to the operation of aircraft
in transit'. However, it goes on to stipulate that it 'shall apply to air transit

---

(on art. 4 TRIPS)); and see also WTO Panel in *Canada – Automobiles*, WT/DS139/R,
para. 10.25. It does not, however, preclude WTO members from according advantages
requiring private actors to comply with certain conditions. This depends on whether the
advantage is, in reality, accorded to products from all WTO members.

[92] Art 25(a) of the Directive. The European Commission is reportedly in discussions with
Russia, China, and the USA on 'equivalent measures' ('US, China, Russia Try to Fly Free
of EU Aviation Emissions Cap', *Carbon Finance*, 14 July 2011, www.carbon-financeon-
line.com/index.cfm?section= lead and action=view and id=13817); but at this stage, it is
not known what such measures might involve (E-005387/2011). Answer given by Ms
Hedegaard on behalf of the Commission, to written question P-005387/2011 by Holger
Krahmer (ALDE), 'Aviation in the European Union Emissions Trading Scheme (ETS)',
15 July 2011.

[93] Meltzer, 'Climate Change and Trade', 138, is of the same opinion.

of goods (including baggage)'. Goods carried on air transport are there-fore fully covered.[94]

(ii) The EU as a transit territory

Article V applies in the first instance to the EU in its capacity as a transit territory.[95]

Article V:3 states, relevantly, that:

> traffic coming from or going to the territory of other contracting parties shall not be subject to any unnecessary delays or restrictions and shall be exempt from ... all transit duties or other charges imposed in respect of transit, except charges for transportation.

If the EU's scheme is considered a transportation 'charge', it is then subject to Article V:4, which specifies that '[a]ll charges and regulations imposed by contracting parties on traffic in transit ... shall be reason-able, having regard to the conditions of the traffic'. However, for the reasons given above, it is difficult to conceive of the EU's scheme as a 'charge' at all, whether on transportation or otherwise. It is better seen as a regulatory scheme which imposes compliance costs on airlines, and therefore on their customers.[96]

The question is then whether or not the scheme constitutes an 'unnecessary restriction' (Article V:3) or 'unreasonable regulation' (Article V:4). There remains some ambiguity as to the meaning of these terms, in particular because there is no benchmark against which the 'necessity' or 'reasonableness' of the measure could be tested. The argu-ment, presumably, would be that the EU's scheme is 'necessary' to implement the 'polluter pays' principle in connection with transport and a 'reasonable' regulation for the same reason.[97] Some support for this approach might be found in the second sentence of Article III:4, which permits differential charges on internal transportation corres-ponding to its real economic costs. If so, the EU's scheme would appear consistent with Article V:3 and Article V:4.

---

[94] See also WTO Secretariat, *Air Transport Services – Background Note by the Secretariat*, WTO Doc. S/C/W/59, 5 Nov. 1998, para. 6.

[95] The commercial significance of this traffic is uncertain, as the EU does not keep statistics of transited goods. It may nonetheless be assumed sufficient to warrant a discussion.

[96] For the same conclusion, for different reasons, see Meltzer, 'Climate Change and Trade', 139.

[97] *Ibid.*

(iii)   The EU as destination

The obligations just discussed are imposed on WTO members through whose territory products are in transit to (or from) other WTO members. This is complemented by Article V:6, which offers a certain degree of protection to the same products against regulation by the WTO member of final destination.[98] Article V:6 prevents WTO members from discriminating against products because they have transited via the territory of another WTO member, rather than using some other route.[99] It states:

> Each contracting party shall accord to products which have been in transit through the territory of any other contracting party treatment no less favourable than that which would have been accorded to such products had they been transported from their place of origin to their destination without going through the territory of such other contracting party.

Article V:6 only protects products that travel to the EU via the territory of another WTO member. As such, it does not cover products from neighbouring countries, or products that travel to the EU only via the high seas or a non-WTO member such as the Ukraine. It does, however, cover products that arrive in the EU having transited via the airspace of a WTO member, such as Singapore.

For these products, Article V:6 mandates that they must be accorded no less favourable treatment than if they had been transported on another route (regardless of whether that other route is via another WTO member). The EU scheme could be inconsistent with this obligation if the same products from the same origin would be subject to lower compliance costs if they transited via another country. For example, a direct flight from Hong Kong to Frankfurt would need to be covered by permits for the full 9,130km, while an indirect flight via Dubai would need permits for only approximately 4,800km. This disadvantage, one could argue, translates into a violation of Article V:6.[100]

---

[98] WTO Panel Report, *Colombia – Ports of Entry*, para. 7.475. This interpretation was foreshadowed and strongly supported by Ehring, 'Freedom of Transit under Article V of the General Agreement on Tariffs and Trade: A Sleeping Beauty of the Multilateral Trading System', draft on file with author, 16. J. H. Jackson, *World Trade and the Law of GATT* (Indianapolis, IN: Bobbs-Merrill, 1969), 510–11, calls this para. 'perplexing'.

[99] See WTO Panel Report, *Colombia – Ports of Entry*, para. 7.477, n. 783.

[100] Meltzer, 'Climate Change and Trade', disagrees.

6.   The justification of the EU's aviation scheme on the basis of its climate change objectives (Article XX GATT)

The foregoing analysis indicates that the EU's scheme may be inconsistent with at least some of its obligations under the GATT, principally Article XI:1 GATT (in so far as the EU's scheme applies outside EU airspace), Article I:1 (if the EU grants a selective exemption to certain airlines), and to some extent Article V:6 (depending on the journey). Whether it is non-discriminatory in other ways depends on the facts. But, regardless of any such violations, it is possible that the scheme might be justified under Article XX GATT. This is a general exceptions clause that permits WTO members to adopt measures for a variety of policy reasons, subject to various conditions.

There are two exceptions that need to be considered. The first is Article XX(g), which permits WTO members to take measures 'in relation to the conservation of exhaustible natural resources', provided that such measures are 'made effective in conjunction with restrictions on domestic production or consumption'. The second is Article XX(b) GATT, which permits WTO members to adopt measures necessary for the protection of human or animal or plant life or health. Generally speaking, measures that can fall under both of these provisions are defended under Article XX(g), because it is easier to defend a measure as being 'in relation to' the objective in this subparagraph than it is to defend a measure as being 'necessary' to the objective in the latter. Nonetheless, both exceptions will be analysed here.

(i)   The conservation of exhaustible natural resources (Article XX(g) GATT)

The present measure is adopted to reduce aviation emissions and thereby to mitigate climate change. The Appellate Body has thus far not been confronted with the question whether climate change mitigation measures could be justified as measures related to the conservation of natural resources. It is, however, noteworthy that in *US – Gasoline* the Appellate Body had no difficulty with the panel's finding that 'clean air' was an exhaustible natural resource.[101] The atmosphere is not synonymous with air, but it would seem consistent with this to consider the atmosphere

---

[101] WTO Appellate Body Report, *US – Gasoline*, WT/DS2/AB/R, adopted 20 May 1996, 14–15. Technically the issue was not appealed (see 9–12).

also as an exhaustible natural resource.[102] In addition, the EU's aviation scheme also seeks to protect the living and non-living resources that would be affected by climate change, and in this respect also is concerned with the conservation of exhaustible natural resources.

The other conditions of Article XX(g) are also easily satisfied. The EU's measure is clearly 'in relation to' the conservation of the respective resources, in the sense that there is 'a close and genuine relationship between ends and means'.[103] And it is also 'made effective in conjunction with similar domestic measures', in the sense that it 'work[s] together with restrictions on domestic production or consumption, which operate so as to conserve an exhaustible natural resource': *in casu*, the EU's ETS in its entirety.[104]

Nor do the extraterritorial aspects of the measure present any problem.[105] In *US – Shrimp*, the Appellate Body held that turtles, as a species, were an essentially migratory species, and therefore sufficiently within US territory to provide a 'jurisdictional nexus' for the regulation.[106] The 'atmosphere' that the EU seeks to protect has, if anything, an even closer 'jurisdictional nexus' to the EU. As Advocate General Kokott said in her Opinion in the *ATAA* case, '[i]t is well known that air pollution knows no boundaries and that greenhouse gases contribute towards climate change worldwide irrespective of where they are emitted; they can have effects on the environment and climate in every State and association of States, including the European Union.'[107]

It seems safe to conclude that the EU's aviation scheme can be provisionally justified under Article XX(g).

(ii)   Measures necessary to protect human, animal or plant life or health (Article XX(b) GATT)

It needs also to be considered whether the EU's aviation scheme is 'necessary' to the protection of human, animal, or plant life or health

---

[102] For the same opinion, see Meltzer, 'Climate Change and Trade', 141–2; Pauwelyn, *US Federal Climate Policy*, 35; Howse and Eliason, 'Domestic and International Strategies to address Climate Change: An Overview of the WTO Legal Issues', in T. Cottier, O. Nartova, and S. Bigdeli (eds.), *International Trade Regulation and the Mitigation of Climate Change* (Cambridge University Press, 2009), 61.

[103] WTO Appellate Body Report, *US – Shrimp*, WT/DS58/AB/R, adopted 6 Nov. 1998, para. 136, quoted with approval in WTO Appellate Body Report, *China – Raw Materials*, para. 355.

[104] *Ibid.*, para. 360.   [105] See above at section IV.2.

[106] WTO Appellate Body Report, *US – Shrimp*, para. 133.

[107] Case C–366/10, *ATAA* (AG's Opinion), para. 154. See also the Court's judgment, para. 129.

within the meaning of Article XX(b) GATT. The first question that arises is whether the EU's aviation scheme measure makes or is 'apt' to make a 'material contribution' to the protection of 'human, animal or plant life or health'.[108] In this regard, it is relevant to note that, on current carbon prices, and with full pass-through of costs to consumers, there appears to be very little effect at all on the aviation industry, and, correspondingly, it is not entirely certain that the scheme will have its desired effects. However, as the Appellate Body said in *Brazil – Retreaded Tyres*:

> [T]he results obtained from certain actions – for instance, measures adopted in order to attenuate global warming and climate change, or certain preventive actions to reduce the incidence of diseases that may manifest themselves only after a certain period of time – can only be evaluated with the benefit of time.[109]

Taking the long-term view, it is possible to say that the EU's aviation scheme is at least 'apt' to make a material contribution to its objectives. This hurdle would seem therefore to be passed.

Beyond this, it would also need to be shown that the EU could not achieve the same objective by an alternative measure that is both reasonably available and less trade restrictive than the measure adopted. This is notoriously difficult to assess in the abstract. Indeed, in *US – Gambling*, the Appellate Body said that:

> [A] responding party need not identify the universe of less trade-restrictive alternative measures and then show that none of those measures achieves the desired objective. The WTO agreements do not contemplate such an impracticable and, indeed, often impossible burden.[110]

Nor can such an exercise be attempted here. At most, it is possible to say that excluding international flights, or non-EU airlines, would not meet the EU's objectives, as too few emissions would be captured. As for alternative measures, some have been mooted, such as an international air passenger (or travel) adaptation levy (IAPAL, or IATAL),[111] but it is not possible to consider these alternatives within the confines of this chapter. The result is that it is difficult to know whether there is another

---

[108] WTO Appellate Body Report, *Brazil – Retreaded Tyres*, WT/DS332/AB/R, adopted 17 Dec. 2007, paras. 143–51.
[109] *Ibid.*, para. 151.
[110] WTO Appellate Body Report, *US – Gambling*, WT/DS285/AB/R, adopted 20 Apr. 2005, para. 309.
[111] e.g. C. Hepburn and B. Müller, 'International Air Travel and Greenhouse Gas Emissions: A Proposal for an Adaptation Levy', *World Economy* 33 (2010), 830.

measure reasonably available that can achieve the EU's objectives with less of an impact on trade. It does, however, seem plausible that the EU's aviation scheme will survive this hurdle as well.

(iii) The chapeau of Article XX

A somewhat more difficult question is whether the measure would also meet the additional requirements set out in the chapeau of Article XX. There are three such conditions: a measure may not be applied in a manner constituting unjustifiable discrimination or arbitrary discrimination between countries where the same conditions prevail, or be a disguised restriction on trade. The last of these is not an issue: the EU's scheme is not adopted for protectionist reasons.[112] But it may amount to arbitrary or unjustified discrimination.

Preliminary points The Appellate Body has described the chapeau as designed to prevent the abuse of the exceptions,[113] and as an expression of the principle of good faith.[114] More concretely, the practice of the WTO Appellate Body and panels – discussed shortly – shows that the point of the discrimination conditions is to spread the burden of a provisionally justified regulation, so that the products of the complainant WTO member suffer no greater burden than their competitors. Thus it is possible to understand the Appellate Body's statement that the chapeau is concerned with the application of a measure.[115]

---

[112] Quite what amounts to a 'disguised restriction' remains unclear, although it has been clarified that the measure need not be 'concealed' or 'unannounced' (WTO Appellate Body Report, US – Gasoline, 24 and WTO Panel Report, Brazil – Retreaded Tyres, paras. 7.315–7.323). It seems to be a synonym for protectionism. This is supported by the Appellate Body's reference to 'warning signals', in WTO Appellate Body Report, Australia – Salmon, WT/DS18/AB/R, adopted 6 Nov. 1998, para. 177, when considering 'disguised discrimination' under art. 5.5 of the SPS Agreement.

[113] WTO Appellate Body Report, US – Gasoline, 2.

[114] WTO Appellate Body Report, US – Shrimp, para. 158. Somewhat questionably, the Appellate Body went on to say that the chapeau marks a 'line of equilibrium' between one member's rights under the exceptions and other members' rights under the substantive obligations of the GATT, para. 159. An exception cannot logically be restricted by an obligation to which it is an exception.

[115] WTO Appellate Body Report, US – Gasoline, 22, US – Shrimp, para. 116; WTO Appellate Body Report, US – Gambling, para. 339. This does not mean that the policy underlying a measure is irrelevant to a chapeau analysis, as the Appellate Body wrongly said in US – Shrimp, para. 149. For an early and convincing criticism, see S. E. Gaines, 'The WTO's Reading of the GATT Article XX Chapeau: A Disguised Restriction on Environmental Measures', U. Pennsylvania J. Int'l Economic L. 22 (2001), 778; A. Davies,

The *chapeau* ensures that there are no unexplained gaps in the application of a measure in situations in which it should be applied. One might say that the *chapeau* is concerned with *under*-regulation, where the subparagraphs of Article XX are concerned with *over*-regulation.

Practice has, however, been less of a useful guide as to the order in which the different elements should be analysed. In *US – Shrimp*, the Appellate Body said that one should first determine discrimination, then whether it is unjustified, and then whether it is applied to countries in which the same conditions prevail.[116] But this suggestion, regularly followed, is not logical. The problem is that discrimination does not exist in the abstract; it depends on comparators between which discrimination is alleged to occur. It seems inevitable, therefore, that one must first identify the relevant comparators; then discrimination between these comparators (according to a given standard); and finally, where relevant, whether any such discrimination is justified.[117]

Accordingly, and contrary to the Appellate Body's suggestion, the following will identify these comparators – the 'countries' where the same 'conditions' prevail – before considering whether there is discrimination, and, if so, whether any such discrimination is justified.[118]

The relevant comparators: 'countries' in which the same 'conditions' prevail Textually, the *chapeau*'s reference to 'countries' is delinked from the subject matter of the agreement. But it is clear from the

---

'Interpreting the *Chapeau* of GATT Article XX in Light of the "New" Approach in *Brazil – Tyres*', *J. World Trade*, 43 (2009), 519, notes that the Appellate Body ignores its own statement in *US – Shrimp* a few paragraphs later (para. 165 of the Report). The Appellate Body now agrees: *Brazil – Retreaded Tyres*, para. 227, citing *US – Shrimp*, para. 165.

[116] WTO Appellate Body Report, *US – Shrimp*, para. 150.

[117] Davies, 'Interpreting the *Chapeau* of GATT Article XX', 514–15, also criticizes the usual three-stage approach. However, his own alternative is also not without difficulties: he would first determine discrimination, then identify the comparators, and then deal with justification.

[118] Something should be said about methodology. The reading of the *chapeau* offered here combines economic tests, in identifying the relevant pool of 'countries' to be compared, and in determining discrimination, with policy-based tests, in narrowing down the countries to be compared to those with the same 'conditions', and considering the reasons for any discrimination. This may appear to be inconsistent with the occasional statements made by the Appellate Body which give the impression that neither policy nor economics has any role in the application of the *chapeau*. However, it is submitted that this model, based on an oscillation between competitive effects and regulatory purpose, is supported by the jurisprudence on the issue, and also makes doctrinal sense.

jurisprudence on the issue that the potential 'countries' to be compared are those with products in competition with the product at issue.[119] Thus, in *US – Shrimp*, the Appellate Body identified the relevant set of 'countries' in the *chapeau* as 'exporting countries desiring certification in order to gain access to the United States shrimp market',[120] and in *US – Gasoline* the Appellate Body defined the relevant 'countries' to include the regulating importing member, where the competing products were to be found.[121] The panels in *EC – Asbestos* and *Argentina – Hides and Leather* did the same.[122] This appears consistent with the purpose of the *chapeau*, which is to ensure that the products of the complainant's competitors are not unfairly exempted from the application of a given measure.

Importantly, it is not competitor products from *all* countries that are compared, but only those from countries in which the same 'conditions' prevail. As practice has demonstrated, these 'conditions' are to be assessed in terms of the policy underlying the measure.[123] In *US – Shrimp*, the relevant 'conditions' concerned the overall risks posed to turtles resulting from shrimp fishing in different locations, taking into account the relevant regulatory frameworks governing these activities. In this respect, 'conditions' in the complainant countries and in the United States were the 'same'.[124] As the Appellate Body said, 'shrimp caught using methods identical to those employed in the United States have been excluded from the United States market solely because they have been caught in waters of countries that have not been certified by the United States'.[125] As between the complainants and other competitor

---

[119] Davies, 'Interpreting the *Chapeau* of GATT Article XX', 513, recognizes that competition is the core issue in determining the comparators, but asks the question of the 'conditions' prevailing, not the 'countries' where these conditions prevail. As argued here, the 'conditions' are determined by reference to the policy of the measure.

[120] WTO Appellate Body Report, *US – Shrimp*, para. 176.

[121] WTO Appellate Body Report, *US – Gasoline*, para. 23.

[122] WTO Panel Report, *EC – Asbestos*, para. 8.227; WTO Report, *Argentina – Hides and Leather*, para. 11.314. In WTO Panel Report, *EC – Tariff Preferences*, para. 7.235, the Panel considered Iran to be a relevant 'country' and a failure to grant Iranian products the same treatment as Indian products as discriminatory. This is a somewhat peculiar finding, given that Iran, a non-WTO member, was not entitled to any treatment whatsoever.

[123] Gaines, 'The WTO's Reading of the GATT Article XX *Chapeau*', 779.

[124] WTO Appellate Body Report, *US – Shrimp*, para. 149.

[125] *Ibid.*, para. 165. There is admittedly a way of understanding *US – Shrimp* as prohibiting the *same* treatment of countries where *different* conditions prevail. Some of the language of the Report supports this e.g. para. 164. Gaines, 'The WTO's Reading of the GATT

countries, the 'conditions' were also the same, and this led to a second discrimination finding (discussed below). In *US – Gasoline*, the objective of the US measure was to protect domestic air quality, but this, in turn, depended on enforcement conditions in the place of production. The United States argued that in this respect 'conditions' in Venezuela were not the 'same' as in the United States.[126] The Appellate Body disagreed.[127]

These cases are atypical. Normally it is assumed that the same conditions prevail between the countries concerned, and this is for the simple reason that the disputes do not involve any factors outside the jurisdiction of the regulating state. So, in *US – Gambling*, it was not suggested that there was any difference in relevant 'conditions' in Antigua and the United States: Antiguan online gambling services were not more dangerous to US public morals than domestic online gambling services. And in *Brazil – Retreaded Tyres*, there was no difference in any relevant 'conditions' between Brazil and other WTO members, or between these members: each country's retreaded tyres presented the same dangers to public health in Brazil.[128]

Discrimination   For different reasons, there is a paucity of jurisprudence on the meaning of discrimination under the *chapeau*. Sometimes this is because discrimination is assumed: thus, in *US – Gasoline*, once it was determined that the relevant conditions in the United States and Venezuela were the same, the Appellate Body considered it obvious that there was discrimination, and the same can be said of *Brazil – Retreaded Tyres* and *US – Gambling*. At other times the question of discrimination has been bundled with an assessment of 'arbitrary or unjustifiable' discrimination.[129]

However, based on the overall practice of the Appellate Body, it is suggested that there is discrimination under the *chapeau* when a measure detrimentally affects conditions of competition between products from

Article XX *Chapeau*', 784–6, analyses the case on this basis. However, one can also say that the imposition of a certification requirement was simply an unnecessary burden on products in similar situations.
[126] WTO Appellate Body Report, *US – Gasoline*, 25–6.
[127] *Ibid.*, 26.
[128] WTO Panel Report, *Brazil – Retreaded Tyres*, para. 7.307.
[129] See e.g. WTO Panel Report, *Argentina – Hides and Leather*, para. 11.315 fn. 570. This did not prevent the Panel from dealing with the question of justification later, after all.

countries where the same conditions prevail.[130] This was implicit in those
Appellate Body reports in which discrimination was assumed, without
being discussed. But it is also implicit in *US – Shrimp*, where the issue
was considered at some length. In this case, the measure was discriminatory for essentially two reasons: first, it banned imports of the complainants' products;[131] second, it imposed burdens on the complainants'
products, such as short phase-in periods and an absence of technical
assistance, that were not imposed on competitive products from countries where the same 'conditions' prevailed.[132] The effect, in both cases,
was that conditions of competition for the complainants' products were
detrimentally affected, and there was discrimination – the *reasons* for
discrimination, an issue now to be discussed, is a separate issue.

Justification   The jurisprudence is also rather meagre, and inconsistent,
when it comes to assessing whether any discrimination is arbitrary or
unjustified. One thing, however, is clear: the key question concerns the
reason for the discrimination, not the *process* by which a discriminatory
measure is implemented. In *Brazil – Retreaded Tyres*, the Appellate Body
said:

> [D]iscrimination can result from a rational decision or behaviour, and still
> be 'arbitrary or unjustifiable', because it is explained by a rationale that
> bears no relationship to the objective of a measure provisionally justified
> under one of the paragraphs of Article XX, or goes against that
> objective.[133]

This may be glossed as follows. First, if there is no reason for the
discriminatory aspects of a measure, it will be arbitrary and therefore
also unjustifiable. Second, if there *is* a reason for the discriminatory
aspects of a measure, but it bears *no* relationship to the objective of the
measure, it will also be arbitrary and therefore unjustifiable. Third, if
there is a reason for the discriminatory aspects of a measure, and it bears
some relationship to the objective of the measure, it is perhaps not
arbitrary, but it may still be unjustifiable. In other words, it seems, it is
only when there is a reason for the discriminatory aspects of a measure
that bears a rational relationship to the objective of the measure that it
will not be arbitrary and unjustifiable. By way of comment, it may be said

---

[130] *Ibid.*, para. 11.314; see also art. 5.5 of the SPS Agreement.
[131] WTO Appellate Body Report, *US – Shrimp*, para. 165.   [132] *Ibid.*, paras. 174–5.
[133] WTO Appellate Body Report, *Brazil – Retreaded Tyres*, para. 232.

that, up to a point, this is consistent with the Appellate Body's previous jurisprudence. However, for reasons to be explained, there is one point on which some refinement is desirable.

A number of disputes have involved the first scenario, involving a failure to give reasons for the discriminatory aspects of a measure. This was perhaps most obvious in *US – Gambling*, but it was also the case in *US – Shrimp*, where the discrimination (lack of equal market access) was the result of the USA applying its measure in a 'rigid' manner[134] and failing to negotiate with the complainants.[135] The USA offered no reason for having conducted itself in this way, or for the resulting discrimination. An example of the second scenario is *Brazil – Retreaded Tyres*, where there was a reason for the discriminatory aspects of the measure, but it was unrelated to its objective. This was also seen in *US – Gasoline*, where the USA offered, as a reason for not imposing a standard baseline on all gasoline the physical and financial costs to domestic producers. The Appellate Body rejected this out of hand.[136] There have not apparently been any cases involving the third scenario, where there is a reason for the discrimination, and it is somewhat but insufficiently related to the objective of the measure. This explains why there has not yet been a determination that a measure resulted in non-arbitrary but still unjustifiable discrimination.

But, as mentioned, there is a difficulty with the formulation in *Brazil – Retreaded Tyres*, and this has to do with its insistence that the discriminatory aspects of a measure can only be justified in terms of the rationale of the measure. The difficulty is that this fails to account for those cases in which discrimination is explained by administrative constraints. Thus, in *US – Gasoline*, the USA argued that it was not possible to give all producers the option of individual baselines because of a lack of data and control (i.e., administrative constraints). The Appellate Body rejected this

---

[134] WTO Appellate Body Report, *US – Shrimp*, t para. 184. This aspect of the measure was subsequently amended by providing for an investigation of the 'conditions', in other countries. While no such investigation was commenced, the mechanism alone was held to be sufficient in the WTO Appellate Body Report, *US – Shrimp (Article 21.5 – Malaysia)*, WT/DS58/AB/RW, adopted 21 Nov. 2001, paras. 148–50.

[135] WTO Appellate Body Report, *US – Shrimp*, para. 176. In WTO Appellate Body Report, *US – Shrimp (Article 21.5 – Malaysia)*, para. 134, the Appellate Body determined that, due to subsequent negotiations, the measure was no longer being applied in a manner constituting unjustified or arbitrary discrimination.

[136] WTO Appellate Body Report, *US – Gasoline*, 28. The Appellate Body also said that this solution would have avoided any discrimination at all (*ibid.*, 25).

contention, on the basis that in some cases data were available, and in any event data could be obtained by agreement with the complainants.[137] But in considering the argument, the Appellate Body also left the door open to the possibility that the discriminatory aspects of a measure could be justified on the basis of valid administrative constraints. Indeed, in a footnote, the Appellate Body said that 'it is not for the Appellate Body to speculate where the limits of effective international cooperation are to be found'.[138] Later, in *US – Shrimp (Article 21.5 – Malaysia)*, the Appellate Body picked up this theme when it denied that a failure to conclude an agreement would amount to discrimination under the *chapeau*.[139] Again, this indicates that there is room for justifying discrimination under the *chapeau* on the basis of genuine administrative constraints.

It is therefore suggested that *Brazil – Retreaded Tyres* should not exclude the possibility that the discriminatory aspects of a measure may be not arbitrary or unjustifiable if these are explained by reference to valid administrative constraints. At the same time, the jurisprudence on the issue gives certain indications as to invalid administrative constraints: these include domestic and international legal obligations, failures to obtain domestic funding, and failures to attempt to negotiate a solution. Beyond this, however, the question remains open.

(iv)   Application to the EU's scheme

How, then, does this reading of the *chapeau* apply to the EU's scheme? Applying the order of analysis identified above, it may be said, first, that the 'countries' at issue are those whose imports are affected by the EU's scheme. This is, to all intents and purposes, all WTO members. For purposes of determining discrimination, it is necessary to draw from this pool of 'countries' those in which the same 'conditions' prevail. In line with the considerations expressed above, these 'conditions' are to be identified by reference to the policy underlying the measure. In the present case, the policy underlying the measure can be understood as the reduction of carbon emissions produced by flights or, more narrowly, carbon emissions on flights to, from, and within the EU. Accordingly, the relevant 'conditions' would seem to be of two types: the emissions

---

[137] *Ibid.*, 27.   [138] *Ibid.*

[139] WTO Appellate Body Report, *US – Shrimp (Article 21.5 – Malaysia)*, paras. 123–4. In fact, this was an *obiter dictum*, as the Appellate Body had already found that there was no discrimination in the first place.

produced by the relevant flights and the existence of any regulatory 'equivalent measures' targeting these emissions.

The first of these conditions may be considered to be equal for all affected countries. The fact that the affected countries all have flights producing emissions makes them relevantly the 'same' for these purposes, even if some produce greater emissions than others. Likewise, in US – Shrimp, the Appellate Body did not quantify the number of turtles that might be protected by the US measure; it was sufficient that they existed in relevantly affected countries.[140] Beyond this, however, one can draw a distinction between countries with regulatory measures targeting these emissions (at present only the EU), and countries without such measures (at present all other affected countries). Accordingly, if the key difference is the existence of regulatory measures targeting climate change, then the result is that countries with regulatory measures are, relevantly, countries in which the 'same' conditions prevail. Likewise, countries without any regulatory measures are, relevantly, countries in which the 'same' conditions prevail. However, countries with regulatory measures are not, relevantly, the same as countries without regulatory measures.

Discrimination between countries with regulatory measures For countries with regulatory measures (including the EU), it follows that, if the EU were to impose regulatory costs on products that are already bearing regulatory costs, the effect would be 'double counting' (contrary to express ICAO Guidelines) and therefore discriminatory.[141] This has the following consequence. Not only is the EU's exemption for flights from countries that adopt 'equivalent measures' not discriminatory, but the absence of any such exemption would be discriminatory.

But there is more to be said on this point: the EU's exemption applies only to states of departure. Seen in the light of the above discussion, this appears to be only a partial solution, because states may also choose to regulate aircraft on the grounds of nationality, or possibly even on the

---

[140] Arguably, one could treat the different degrees of risk in affected countries as rendering them not the 'same' for these purposes. Such an analysis would achieve a similar outcome to that proposed here.

[141] Guideline (f) of the Guidelines on market-based measures (MBMs) in the Annex to ICAO Resolution A37- 19, Consolidated Statement of Continuing ICAO Policies and Practices Related to Environmental Protection states that 'MBMs [market-based measures] should not be duplicative and international aviation CO_2 emissions should be accounted for only once'.

grounds of overflight.[142] In these instances, it might be necessary for the EU also to exempt flights regulated on these jurisdictional bases.

Discrimination between countries without regulatory measures By contrast, it seems that the EU's scheme produces discrimination between exporting countries without regulatory measures. The reason is simple: products from these countries are burdened with regulatory costs according to the distance they must travel to the EU.

This does not mean that there is always discrimination between these countries. For example, it is difficult to see that there is any discrimination between products from the same origin, even if they travel by different routes to the EU.[143] Nor is there discrimination in scenarios in which competing products are subject to the same regulatory costs: this would include products travelling on direct flights to the EU from roughly equidistant origins (e.g., Hong Kong and Guangzhou), as well as products travelling directly to the EU from a certain origin (e.g., Hong Kong) and products travelling indirectly to the EU from a more distant origin (e.g., Sydney) but stopping on the way in the first location (Hong Kong).

But this leaves two cases in which there may still be discrimination. There may be discrimination between products from two countries that are not equidistant from the EU (e.g., Hong Kong and Dubai). And there may be discrimination between products from equidistant origins (e.g., Hong Kong and Guangzhou) if it is relatively easier for the products of one of these countries (Hong Kong) to fly to the EU on an indirect flight (or via a hub closer to the EU), thereby incurring lower compliance costs. Depending on air services and air service agreements, this is not an unforeseeable scenario, although it would be unwise to overstate its likelihood.

(v) Justification

Even if there is discrimination, it is not necessarily arbitrary or unjustified. Indeed, the first instance of discrimination identified here is easily

---

[142] Activities occurring on aircraft are subject to the jurisdiction of the flag state over the high seas, and a concurrent jurisdiction between the flag state and any state over whose territory the aircraft is flying at the time of the activity, with priority granted to the flag state. This applies e.g. to questions of the nationality of children born while on an aircraft (S. Rosenne, 'The Perplexities of Modern International Law: General Course on Public International Law', *Recueil des Cours*, 291 (2001), 336–7).

[143] *Ibid.*

justified in terms of the policy underlying the measure. There is a rational justification, based on the policy of reducing carbon emissions, for the fact that products from Hong Kong are subject to higher compliance costs than products from Dubai, and the fact that both are subject to higher compliance costs than EU products.

The same cannot be said, however, of the second type of discrimination – between direct and indirect (or between different indirect) travel for products of roughly equidistant origins, in which it is relatively easier for a product to travel on an indirect than a direct flight to the EU. This discrimination results from the fact that the EU's aviation scheme does not apply to any 'leg' of a flight that does not terminate in the EU. So a product from Hong Kong transiting in Dubai is subject to lower compliance costs than a product from (equidistant) Guangzhou that flies directly to the EU. As mentioned above, this is the result of a Commission decision defining the term 'flight', in the EU's Directive, in these narrow terms.[144] So what are the possible rationales?

One rationale is that the EU is unable, by reason of its international obligations, to regulate such flights. This may seem reasonable, but on the current state of the law it is, perhaps surprisingly, no defence. As mentioned, the Appellate Body has made it clear that adopting a measure to comply with international obligations without any reference to the purposes of the measure amounts to arbitrary discrimination.[145] Nor does it help the EU's case that the CJEU itself took the view that its scheme was entirely unconstrained by any such obligations. As the Court said:

> [T]he fact that, in the context of applying European Union environmental legislation, certain matters contributing to the pollution of the air, sea or land territory of the Member States originate in an event which occurs partly outside that territory is not such as to call into question, in the light of the principles of customary international law capable of being relied upon in the main proceedings, the full applicability of European Union law in that territory.[146]

If this is correct (and this is not entirely certain), the EU should be able to extend its scheme to all flights – and indeed all emissions producing activities – in the world, on the basis that they have 'effects' in the EU.

---

[144] Annex I to the Directive.
[145] WTO Appellate Body Report, *Brazil – Retreaded Tyres*, para. 227. The same point was argued by the EU in the case (*ibid.*, para. 31).
[146] Case C–366/10, *ATAA*, para. 129; see also the AG's Opinion, para. 154.

It barely needs to be said that this ruling has implications well beyond the narrow confines of this chapter.

But this is not the only justification for the discriminatory aspects of the measure: it is also possible that these aspects could also be justified on the grounds that the EU cannot obtain data relevant to flights without a terminal point in the EU. In the abstract, it is difficult to assess such a claim, but the omens of *US – Gasoline* are not positive. But even if this were a valid reason for the discrimination, the EU's aviation scheme faces another hurdle. In *Brazil – Retreaded Tyres*, the Appellate Body criticized the discriminatory aspects of Brazil's measure not only because these were not related to the objective of the measure, but also because these aspects of the measure had the effect of *worsening* the risk to public health, due to potential increases in imports of retreaded tyres from Uruguay (even if only to a 'small degree').[147] The present case is similar. There is a risk that the EU's aviation scheme will, at least in individual cases, have a negative effect on aviation emissions. As Lufthansa has pointed out, an indirect flight, which requires fewer carbon emissions, may actually emit more carbon than the equivalent direct flight.[148] In such cases, the EU's aviation scheme establishes an incentive to create carbon emissions.

The result of this analysis is somewhat negative for certain aspects of the EU's scheme. However, it must be borne in mind that the facts underlying these aspects of the scheme may be largely hypothetical, and therefore of little real consequence. The important point is that the core of the EU's aviation scheme appears to be justified under Article XX GATT.

V. The legality of the EU's aviation scheme under the GATS

A second issue raised by the EU's scheme, and one of more economic importance, concerns its effect on trade in services, especially services delivered outside the EU. The question arises whether the EU's scheme

---

[147] WTO Appellate Body Report, *Brazil – Retreaded Tyres*, para. 228; WTO Panel Report, *Brazil – Retreaded Tyres*, para. 7.288, quoted in WTO Appellate Body Report, *Brazil – Retreaded Tyres*, para. 219 and n. 417.

[148] Lufthansa calculates that a Hong Kong–Dubai–Frankfurt flight would result in emissions of 296t of carbon, 18 per cent more than a direct Hong Kong–Frankfurt flight: Lufthansa, 'EU Emissions Trading: Europe Headed Down a Dead End', Policy Brief, Dec. 2009, http://presse.lufthansa.com/fileadmin/downloads/en/policy-brief/12_2009/LH-Policy-Brief-December-Emissions-trading.pdf

raises any issues under the GATS, which applies, in principle, to all measures affecting trade in services.[149]

1.   The Annex on Air Transport Services

The first, and most obvious, question concerns the application of the GATS Annex on Air Transport Services, which purports to exempt air transport services from regulation under the GATS. The following will consider the extent to which this means that the GATS does not protect services dependent on air transport, such as tourism.

(i)   Scope of the Annex

Paragraph 1 of the Annex states that it applies to 'all measures affecting trade in air transport services, whether scheduled or non-scheduled, and ancillary services'. The language used is reminiscent of the phrase 'measures affecting trade in services' in Article I:1 GATS, which the Appellate Body has described as a broad term covering any measures which have an effect on trade in services.[150] It seems appropriate to interpret both in a similar way.[151]

But does this phrase also cover all measures affecting trade[152] or, more narrowly, only those measures affecting conditions of competition for foreign services and service suppliers? In relation to Article I:1 GATS, the narrower view is common, even among complainants in litigation.[153] But this cannot be correct. This would lead to the duplication of an inquiry properly conducted in the context of relevant non-discrimination obligations.[154] In addition, the GATS contains provisions, such as those on domestic regulation in Article VI, which are not related to discrimination. The answer must therefore be that Article I:1 GATS applies also to

---

[149] Art. I:1 GATS.

[150] WTO Appellate Body Report, *EC – Bananas III*, para. 220; WTO Appellate Body Report, *Canada – Automobiles*, paras. 160–7.

[151] Koebele, 'Commentary on the Air Transport Services Annex', in R. Wolfrum *et al.* (eds.), *WTO – Trade in Services* (Leiden: Nijhoff, 2008), 611 n. 67.

[152] This would be equivalent to what has been termed the 'market access' test in EU law (C. Barnard, *The Substantive Law of the EU: The Four Freedoms* (2010), 19–20).

[153] See e.g. the EU argument as reported in WTO Panel Report, *US – Gambling*, WT/DS285/R, adopted as modified by the Appellate Body Report, 20 Apr. 2005, para. 4.16.

[154] See also Zdouc, 'WTO Dispute Settlement Practice Relating to the General Agreement on Trade in Services', in F. Ortino and E.-U. Petersmann (eds.), *The WTO Dispute Settlement System, 1995–2003* (The Hague: Kluwer, 2004), 394.

measures that have no effect on conditions of competition, or – to put it another way – non-discriminatory measures. This has a direct bearing on paragraph 1 of the Annex, where similar considerations also apply. As will be seen, the Annex contains provisions that apply also to non-discriminatory measures. The phrase 'measures affecting trade in air transport services' must therefore also be understood to mean measures affecting the quantity and type of services provided by foreign service suppliers, not just measures affecting their conditions of competition, which might exclude non-discriminatory measures.

(ii)   Paragraph 2 ATS

The main substantive carve-out for measures affecting trade in air transport services is set out in paragraph 2 ATS. This paragraph states as follows:

> 2. The Agreement [GATS], including its dispute settlement procedures, shall not apply to measures affecting:
> (a) traffic rights, however granted, or
> (b) services directly related to the exercise of traffic rights, except as provided in paragraph 3 of this Annex.

Both of these subparagraphs are relevant to the EU's scheme.

Paragraph 2(a) ATS   Paragraph 2(a) exempts 'measures affecting traffic rights' from GATS obligations. 'Traffic rights' are defined in paragraph 6(d) as follows:

> 'Traffic rights' mean the right for scheduled and non-scheduled services to operate and/or to carry passengers, cargo and mail for remuneration or hire from, to, within, or over the territory of a Member, including points to be served, routes to be operated, types of traffic to be carried, capacity to be provided, tariffs to be charged and their conditions, and criteria for designation of airlines, including such criteria as number, ownership, and control.[155]

The most likely way in which the EU scheme might be deemed a 'measure affecting traffic rights', as per the definition of such measures

---

[155] In the 'Dunkel Draft' of GATS, GATT Doc. MTN.TNC/W/FA, 20 Dec. 1991, this paragraph referred expressly to the ICAO agreements: '[e]xcept as set out in paragraph 3, no provision of the Agreement shall apply to measures affecting: (a) traffic rights covered by the Chicago Convention, including the five freedoms of the air, and by bilateral air services agreements'.

in paragraph 6(d), is if the scheme affects 'tariffs to be charged and their conditions'.

The phrase 'tariffs and their conditions' refers to negotiated tariffs, not to all forms of air service pricing. The negotiations to which the phrase refers are those undertaken by states (usually within the International Air Transport Association (IATA)) on tariffs to be charged on given international flights. In practice, however, tariff negotiations have, in almost all cases, been superseded by fares set unilaterally by the airlines themselves.[156] Indeed, the UK Civil Aviation Authority no longer even requires airlines to notify their tariffs.[157] While it is, therefore, theoretically possible that the EU's scheme could affect a negotiated tariff that is still in effect between an EU member state and a third country, in practice this is highly unlikely. It is therefore also no surprise that this issue has not arisen in any of the many ICAO based challenges to the EU's scheme to date. Indeed, the claimants in the *ATAA* case did not even claim that the EU's scheme affected their ability to set prices under Article 11 of the US–EU Open Skies Agreement.[158]

The conclusion must be that the EU's scheme does not affect 'tariffs to be charged or their conditions' within the meaning of paragraph 6(b), and consequently that it is not a measure covered by the exemption in paragraph 2(a).[159]

---

[156] IATA still sets a base rate, but it is of minor importance. For example, in 2002 it was estimated that as little as 5 per cent of British Airways freight was carried at published IATA rates (R. Doganis, *Flying off Course: The Economics of International Airlines* (3rd edn, London: Routledge, 2002), 325).

[157] The UK Civil Aviation Authority (CAA) no longer even requires airlines to file their fares. In its view, 'the interests of users will be best served if airlines are free to set their own prices without regulatory intervention, subject only to the application of normal competition policy' (CAA, *CAA Statement of Policies on Route and Air Transport Licensing*, www.caa.co.uk/default.aspx?catid=589 and pagetype=90 and pageid=7228).

[158] See complainants' arguments, Case C-366/10, art. 11 of the Open Skies Agreement guarantees, *inter alia*, that '[p]rices for air transportation services operated pursuant to this Agreement shall be established freely'.

[159] Meltzer, 'Climate Change and Trade', 125–7, comes to the same conclusion, though via a different route. Meltzer's argument is that a measure comes within the scope of para. 2(a) of the Annex if it does not violate the Chicago Convention. Historically, there is much to be said for this view, particularly in light of the drafting history of para. 2(a), as per WTO Appellate Body Report, *Brazil – Retreaded Tyres*, para. 228; see also WTO Panel Report, *Brazil – Retreaded Tyres*, para. 7.288, but it is probably overstating the connection to imply that there is mutual exclusivity between the Chicago Convention and the GATS. Among other things, it renders para. 4 of the Annex redundant.

Paragraph 2(b) ATS   Paragraph 2(b) ATS establishes another substantive carve-out for 'measures affecting services directly related to the exercise of traffic rights'. These services are undefined, but correlate broadly to the so-called 'soft rights' involving currency exchanges, ground and baggage handling, catering, marketing, and airport usage.[160] It is possible that the EU's scheme might affect these services, as a result of airlines changing routes to minimize their compliance costs under the EU's scheme. To the extent that it does, paragraph 2(b) would be applicable and the EU's scheme would be exempt from scrutiny under the GATS. However, this is by no means certain, and it is therefore still appropriate to pursue an analysis under the GATS.

(iii)   Paragraph 4 ATS

Paragraph 4 of the Annex establishes a procedural carve-out for measures affecting trade in air transport services. It states that, in relation to the measures defined in paragraph 1, WTO dispute settlement is available only 'where . . . dispute settlement procedures in bilateral and other multilateral agreements or arrangements have been exhausted'.

When, then, are the conditions in paragraph 4 satisfied? The point of this paragraph, and the point of the Annex more generally, is to ensure the primacy of the ICAO system over the WTO system in cases of regulatory overlap,[161] and perhaps also to prevent true conditions of competition in the market for air transport services. But primacy can be applied in different ways. On a narrow view, primacy would apply in relation to matters prohibited by an ICAO agreement. More generally, it might be thought that paragraph 4 applies also to matters governed by the ICAO, including by positive authorization. But at least the matter would have to fall within ICAO competence to some degree.

In the case at hand, there is good reason to believe that the EU's scheme does not violate any ICAO obligations. There is no definitive ICAO ruling on the matter, but the CJEU has decided that the EU's scheme does not violate any relevant ICAO obligations,[162] and this

---

[160] Koebele, 'Commentary on the Air Transport Services Annex', 613–14.
[161] *Ibid.*, at 610. Air services agreements are concluded as a result of the principle of national sovereignty over airspace (art. 1 Chicago Convention) and the requirement for special permission or other authorization to operate a scheduled international air service into or over another contracting state and in accordance with the terms of that permission or authorization (art. 6 Chicago Convention): see e.g. GATT Doc. MTN.GNS/W/36, 16 May 1988, 5.
[162] Case C-366/10, *ATAA*.

echoes decisions to similar effect by the UK High Court[163] and the Dutch Supreme Court[164] with respect to 'ticket taxes'. In practical terms, it is also unlikely that the EU, the UK, the Netherlands, and perhaps other governments would argue in WTO dispute settlement proceedings that the EU's scheme does (or even *might*) violate their ICAO obligations. This is particularly true for the UK, which has argued (successfully) that the Chicago Convention does not even have any 'application' to its air passenger duty.[165] If the narrow view is taken, the result would be that the conditions in paragraph 4 are not satisfied, and the EU's scheme can be challenged in WTO dispute settlement proceedings.

However, the answer is likely to be different if the broader view is taken that paragraph 4 applies if a matter is governed by the ICAO. In Resolution A37/19, in a paragraph not subject to reservations,[166] the ICAO Assembly 'request[ed] the Council to ensure that ICAO exercise continuous leadership on environmental issues relating to international civil aviation, including GHG emissions'.[167] It is true that some countries have claimed that the ICAO should cede this primary role to the UN Framework Convention on Climate Change (UNFCCC).[168] However, on the present state of affairs, this should not change the conclusion that the ICAO has competence over the issue. The result is that, on the broad view, for purposes of paragraph 4, the ICAO continues to govern the matter, and the issue would not be justiciable in the WTO.

There is no way of knowing whether a broad or narrow approach to paragraph 4 is correct. The matter is essentially one of comity between international tribunals, on which there is very little by way of a common approach. At a minimum, though, it is to be expected that a WTO panel would have to be established to examine the issue whether it has

---

[163] *Federation of Tour Operators* v. *HM Treasury* [2007] EWHC 2062 (Admin.), para. 84.

[164] *Board of Airline Representatives in the Netherlands (BARIN)* v. *The Netherlands, Ministry of Finance*, LJN: BI3450, Hoge Raad, 08/04121, 10 July 2009 (applying the relevant test of 'manifest incompatibility'). For an English translation, see Barnhoorn, 'Netherlands Judicial Decisions Involving Questions of Public International Law, 2008–2009', *Netherlands Yearbook Int'l L.* 40 (2010), 432. The case is discussed by Havel and van Antwerpen, 'The Dutch Ticket Tax and Article 15 of the Chicago Convention', *Air and Space L.* 34 (2009), 141 and Havel and van Antwerpen, 'The Dutch Ticket Tax and Article 15 of the Chicago Convention (continued)', *Air and Space L.* 34 (2009), 449.

[165] See *Federation of Tour Operators* v. *HM Treasury*, para. 3.

[166] 'ICAO Assembly Res. A37-19', Consolidated Statement of Continuing ICAO Policies and Practices, and 'Reservations', Commission Dec. 2011/638/EU, OJ (2011) L252/20.

[167] *Ibid.*, para. 2(a).

[168] This is discussed in Truxal, 'The ICAO Assembly Resolutions', 219–22.

jurisdiction over the matter, and it is at this point that this question would be addressed.[169]

(iv) Summary

If this analysis is correct, then even if one of the substantive carve-outs in paragraph 2 does not apply, it is possible that a WTO panel would lack jurisdiction to determine whether there is a GATS violation until ICAO remedies have been exhausted. However, this does not mean that the WTO member would be complying with its WTO obligations. It just means that dispute settlement is not available. For this reason, and also in the event that the preceding analysis is incorrect, the following considers the applicable GATS obligations and exceptions.

2. The most-favoured nation obligation (Article II:1 GATS)

Article II:1 GATS, inspired by Article I:1 GATT, requires that any 'advantage' accorded by the EU to any service or service provider must be accorded immediately and unconditionally to the like service or service provider of any other WTO member.[170]

Unlike Article I:1 GATT, there is no doubt that Article II:1 GATS applies to the EU's scheme. By virtue of Article I:1 GATS, Article II:1 applies to all measures with an effect on services. Clearly this measure has such an effect, most notably on services supplied to EU consumers travelling outside the EU, such as tourism. It seems also relatively clear that the EU's scheme has a disproportionate effect on services and service suppliers in certain countries; tourism in Barbados will be proportionately more affected than tourism in Israel. Nor is there any possibility of arguing that the reasons for this situation are unconnected with the origin of the service: clearly, it is linked directly to geographical factors. For the reasons mentioned in the context of Article I:1 GATT, this would seem to be sufficient for there to be a failure to accord an 'advantage' to all 'like services' and 'service suppliers'. Furthermore, as in that context, if

---

[169] The Appellate Body has said that Panels have *Kompetenz–Kompetenz*, and this is a perfect example of when that power would need to be exercised (WTO Appellate Body Report, *Mexico – Corn Syrup (Art 21.5 – US)*, WT/DS132/AB/RW, adopted 21 Nov. 2001, para. 36). For the same conclusion, and an interesting discussion, see Meltzer, 'Climate Change and Trade', 127.

[170] It is possible for WTO members to schedule exemptions from art. II:1 GATS, but the EU has not listed any relevant exemptions (*European Communities and their Member States – Final List of Article II (MFN) Exemptions*, GATS/EL/31, 15 Apr. 1994).

the EU granted an 'equivalent measures' exception to some countries only, there would also be a violation of the requirement to grant such an advantage 'immediately' and 'unconditionally' to all WTO members.

2. *Obligations applicable to commitments on service sectors*

Unlike Article II:1, most of the other obligations under the GATS apply only to the extent that a WTO member has made specific commitments in relation to those services. The EU has made full commitments in Mode 2 (consumption abroad) in relevant tourism and recreational services.[171] The question arises whether the EU's scheme violates any obligations with respect to these service sectors.[172]

(i) Market access (Article XVI GATS)

In the first place, one might consider whether the scheme violates Article XVI GATS. In respect of scheduled services, this forbids the measures described in Article XVI:2 GATS.[173] Relevantly, this applies to measures setting a maximum number of suppliers or various elements of services, whether in their form or in their effect.[174] The EU's scheme does not, however, set any maximum limits, even if it has a restrictive effect on the supply of services. Article XVI GATS does not therefore apply.

(ii) National treatment (Article XVII GATS)

The remaining question, then, is whether the EU's scheme discriminates in favour of domestic services and service suppliers in these (and other) sectors, contrary with Article XVII:1 of GATS.[175] This provision reads as follows:[176]

---

[171] *European Communities and their Member States, Schedule of Specific Commitments*, GATS/SC/31, 15 Apr. 1994.

[172] Meltzer, 'Climate Change and Trade', 147–50, mentions tourism but focuses on the impacts of the EU's aviation scheme on the aviation transport sector. This, however, is excluded by para. 2(a) of the Annex, which excludes measure affecting 'traffic rights', defined to include 'the right for scheduled and non-scheduled services to operate and/or to carry passengers.'

[173] WTO Panel Report, *US – Gambling*, WT/DS285/R, para. 6.298.

[174] WTO Appellate Body Report, *US – Gambling*, para. 232.

[175] It is not necessary to consider the application of art. VI GATS, on domestic regulation of services.

[176] Art. XVII:2 and 3 add some interpretive gloss.

> In the sectors inscribed in its Schedule, and subject to any conditions and qualifications set out therein, each member shall accord to services and service suppliers of any other Member, in respect of all measures affecting the supply of services, treatment no less favourable than that it accords to its own like services and service suppliers.

It seems clear that the EU's scheme could have the effect of modifying the conditions of competition in favour of EU services and service suppliers, compared with those of other WTO members. As tickets become more expensive, it is foreseeable that EU residents will prefer to holiday at home. But does the disproportionate impact of the EU's scheme amount to 'no less favourable treatment' for those services and service suppliers? Arguably, it does, for the same reasons mentioned in the context of Article II:1 GATS and Article I:1 GATT. Among other things, the reasons for discrimination are not independent of the origin of the service or service provider.[177] They could hardly be more connected.

Footnote 10 This is not quite the end of the analysis. Article XVII is subject to a footnote 10, which states that:

> Specific commitments assumed under this Article shall not be construed to require any Member to compensate for any inherent competitive disadvantages which result from the foreign character of the relevant services or service suppliers.

It might appear that footnote 10 protects the EU's scheme. However, as the Panel in *Canada – Automobiles* said, footnote 10 'does not provide cover for actions which might modify the conditions of competition against services and service suppliers which are already disadvantaged due to their foreign character'.[178] In the context of Mode 2 services, footnote 10 protects the EU from having to subsidize the costs of international transportation of consumers. However, it does not, of itself, permit the EU to add to these costs.

4. Exceptions for environmental reasons (Article XIV(b) GATS)

Even if the EU's scheme encounters the legal difficulties described, its GATS-illegal aspects may be justified under Article XIV GATS. While

---

[177] See WTO Appellate Body Report, *Dominican Republic – Cigarettes*, WT/DS302/AB/R, adopted 19 May 2005, para. 96. See also WTO Appellate Body Report, *US – Clove Cigarettes*, WT/DS406/AB/R, adopted 24 Apr. 2012, para.179 n. 372, casting doubt on this test.

[178] WTO Panel Report, *Canada – Automobiles*, para. 10.300.

this provision does not include an equivalent to Article XX(g) GATT, Article XIV(b) GATS is exactly the same as Article XX(b) GATT. Correspondingly, the analysis of the legality of the EU's aviation scheme under Article XIV GATS follows that already undertaken in the context of Article XX(b) GATT, with the result that (alternative measures aside) the EU's aviation scheme should be justifiable, except perhaps for the scenario in which services and service providers are located in a country which, compared with a country equidistant from the EU, is more easily accessible by direct flights than indirect flights. Concretely, this would mean that there might be arbitrary or unjustified discrimination if, for example, Barbados were serviced mainly by direct flights to the EU, while a neighbouring equidistant island were serviced mainly by indirect flights to the EU, and as a result services and service providers in Barbados would be burdened by higher regulatory costs than their competitors. However, this is probably a hypothetical scenario. In short, even if the EU's aviation scheme is covered by the GATS, and even if it is justiciable, in all of its essential aspects it would most likely be justified under Article XIV(b) GATS – so long as there is no reasonably available alternative measure that meets the EU's objectives in a less trade restrictive manner.

VI. Final remarks

The foregoing analysis has illustrated the complexities of the WTO aspects of the EU's aviation scheme, with the result that, except in certain limited cases, any discriminatory effects of the measure are likely to be justified on environmental grounds. However, this analysis has also shown up some more long-term structural issues for the WTO, which are of particular relevance to climate change issues, but not limited to these. One of the more surprising points to emerge from this case study is the fact that a WTO member cannot justify discrimination under the *chapeau* to Article XX GATT and Article XIV GATT on the basis that it needs to comply with its international obligations. This rule, which was stated in *Brazil – Retreaded Tyres*, has one obvious merit, which is to prevent WTO members from seeking to circumvent their WTO obligations by entering into contradictory international agreements. However, it also has less than salutary effects on the coherence of WTO law with the remainder of the international legal system. One wonders whether perhaps another solution might not be found such that WTO members are able to avail themselves fully of the general exceptions in the WTO Agreements while still remaining in compliance with their international obligations.

But even if the WTO dispute settlement system manages to open up more effectively to other international regimes, this will only solve a subset of the broader issues raised by the EU's aviation scheme. The attempt to allocate competences between the WTO and the ICAO in the GATS Annex on Air Transport Services is only a partial solution, and, as this chapter has shown, not a very satisfactory one at that. Nor is this the only area in which these problems of regulatory competence have arisen. The EU has proposed extending its ETS to shipping, which has been controversial within the International Maritime Organization (IMO), in part due to the possibility that these measures violate WTO law.[179] These disputes therefore show the need for a broader regulation of transportation, taking into account the ICAO, the IMO, and also the WTO. It is impractical, in the long term, to leave such matters to be solved by the judicial body of one of these organizations – no matter how open that judicial body proves itself to be.

Postscript

Since this chapter was written there have been significant changes to the EU's approach to including aviation emissions in its Emissions Trading System. Aviation emissions were to be included from 1 January 2012, with permits covering this period to have been purchased and surrendered by 30 April 2013. On 12 November 2012 the European Commission announced that it would defer that requirement for non-EEA flights for one year, pending the outcome of ICAO negotiations.[180] On 4 October 2013 these negotiations produced ICAO Resolution 38/18, in which the ICAO Assembly decided to develop a global market based mechanism (MBM) for international aviation by 2020.[181] In addition,

---

[179] IMO MEPC 64/5/3, 64th Session, Agenda item 5, Reduction of GHG Emissions from Ships: Possible incompatibility between the WTO rules and MBMs for International Shipping, submitted by India and Saudi Arabia, 29 June 2012. I owe this reference to Mihalis Loizou.

[180] 'Stopping the clock of ETS and aviation emissions following last week's International Civil Aviation Organisation (ICAO) Council', European Commission PR, Memo/12/854, 12 November 2012.

[181] ICAO Resolution A38/18 – Consolidated statement of continuing ICAO policies and practices related to environmental protection – Climate change, adopted 4 October 2013, para. 18 (www.icao.int/Meetings/a38/Pages/resolutions.aspx).

Resolution 17/2 resolved that states 'should grant exemptions for application of MBMs on routes to and from developing States whose share of
international civil aviation activities is below the threshold of 1% of total
revenue ton kilometres of international civil aviation activities'.[182] However, this paragraph was subject to a reservation by the 28 EU member
states, the 14 other members of the European Civil Aviation Conference,
and 8 other countries.[183]

Following this resolution, on October 16, 2013 the European Commission has proposed an amendment to the EU ETS Directive. According to
its proposal, all EEA flights would continue to be covered. Non-EEA
flights would be exempted for the full year.[184] From 2014, there would be
an exemption for the flights to and from developing countries accounting
for less than 1 per cent of total revenue ton kilometres, as specified in the
ICAO Resolution, but only if they are also beneficiaries of the EU's
Generalized System of Preferences (GSP). There would also be exemptions for overflights and flights to and from EEA dependent territories.
For all other flights, emissions permits would be required in respect of
the proportion of the flight taking place over EEA territory. This proposed amendment to the EU's ETS scheme would significantly diminish
the economic effects on imported goods and services. Nonetheless, it still
presents some of the former legal problems, and adds some of its own.

First, the proposal would still result in a charge for airline operators,
and hence imported products and services dependent on these operators.
In so far as this charge constitutes a 'restriction' on the importation of
products prior to their actual importation, the amended scheme would
continue to violate Article XI:1 GATT. Added to this are potential
violations of various non-discrimination rules (Article I:1 and Article
V:6 GATT and Article II:1 GATS), insofar as the economic effect of the
amended system still depends upon the distance between the EU airport

---

[182] *Ibid.*, para. 16(b).

[183] Reservations were lodged by the EU as well as Albania, Armenia, Azerbaijan, Bosnia and
Herzegovina, Georgia, Iceland, the Republic of Moldova, Monaco, Montenegro, Norway,
San Marino, Serbia, Switzerland, and the former Yugoslav Republic of Macedonia
(ECAC) as well as Afghanistan, Australia, Canada, Japan, New Zealand, Qatar, Singa-
pore, the United Arab Emirates and the United States. See www.icao.int/Meetings/a38/
Pages/resolutions.aspx

[184] Proposal for a Directive of the European Parliament and of the Council amending
Directive 2003/87/EC establishing a scheme for greenhouse gas emission allowance
trading within the Community, in view of the implementation by 2020 of an international agreement applying a single global market-based measure to international
aviation emissions, COM(2013) 722, 16 October 2013.

and the origin of the affected imported goods and services. This, however, is more complicated to analyse. These distances are now calculated in a different way. Second, it is more difficult to link the geographical origins of imported product or service and the economic costs to which they would be subjected. For example, if one were to compare US and Turkish products and services, one could say that a Bucharest–New York flight would be subject to a higher charge than a Bucharest–Ankara flight. But a London–New York flight would cost less than a London–Ankara flight. For any given products or services, it is possible that discrimination could be found against both US and Turkish 'like' products and services. However, the matter is complicated by the fact that one needs to find an overall negative impact on US or Turkish products. This is much more difficult to ascertain, and finding violations of Article I:1 GATT and Article II:1 GATS is also now correspondingly more difficult to establish. On the other hand, Article V:6 compares journeys, not overall impacts on all like products, meaning that finding this form of discrimination will presumably be more straightforward.

Another difference in the proposed amendment to the EU's scheme goes to the other side of the ledger. The exemptions are now almost entirely arbitrary from an environmental perspective. While there is some justification for the exemption for developing countries accounting for only a very small share of emissions, particularly in light of the ICAO resolution to this effect, there is no justification for limiting this to EU GSP beneficiaries. This has nothing at all to do with an environmental rationale. Nor does the exemption for EU dependencies make much sense from an environmental perspective. This means that even if the proposed amendment can be justified as a measure adopted for environmental reasons, it will fail to meet the conditions in the *chapeaux* of Articles XX GATT and Article XVI GATS which, as explained in the article, govern under-regulation – in other words, illegitimate exclusions from a regulatory scheme.

In short, the proposed amendment to the EU scheme seems less likely to pass WTO muster than the previous version. But it also has to overcome other hurdles. First, the amendment must be adopted by the European Parliament and the EU Council, and it is uncertain whether the Parliament will be minded to agree. On 23 October 2013, only one week after the Commission's proposal, the Parliament adopted a resolution in which it emphasized that 'even though the EU recently agreed to "stop the clock" in relation to the inclusion of international aviation flights in its ETS, this derogation is limited to one year only and is

conditional on the international negotiations producing tangible decisions on a global market-based measure on emissions from international
aviation'.[185] On the other side of the Atlantic, on 20 November 2013
senior members of the US House of Representatives Committee on
Transportation and Infrastructure wrote to the US Transportation Secretary claiming that the European Commission's proposed amendment
'violates the spirit and the letter of the ICAO agreement' and represents
an approach that was rejected by ICAO in October, and requesting the
Secretary to ensure that US operators are 'held harmless' from the EU's
unilateral approach.[186] The drama looks set to continue for some time,
both within and beyond the EU.

[185] European Parliament resolution of 23 October 2013 on the climate change conference in
Warsaw, Poland (COP 19), para. 42.
[186] Letter from Bill Shuster *et al.* to Anthony Foxx dated 20 November 2013 (http://
transportation.house.gov/uploadedfiles/2013-11-22-foxx_ets_letter.pdf).

19

Certain legal aspects of the multilateral trade system and the promotion of renewable energy

RAFAEL LEAL-ARCAS AND ANDREW FILIS

I. Introduction

Environmental degradation occurs due to a variety of reasons, including processes that are entirely inherent to nature.[1] However, in recent history, the rate of environmental degradation has been ostensibly more rapid than during the previous millennia of organized human society.[2] What is more, we are fast approaching the tipping point after which environmental degradation may become irreversible.[3] This excessiveness in 'climate change' has largely been anthropogenic in that it flows from

---

[1] For further explanation, see R. Leal-Arcas, *Climate Change and International Trade* (Cheltenham: Edward Elgar, 2013), ch. 2.

[2] See the executive summary to the IEA 2013 'Redrawing the Energy-Climate Map' World Energy Outlook Special Report, where it is stated that: *"The world is not on track to meet the target agreed by governments to limit the long- term rise in the average global temperature to 2 degrees Celsius (°C).* Global greenhouse-gas emissions are increasing rapidly and, in May 2013, carbon-dioxide (CO_2) levels in the atmosphere exceeded 400 parts per million for the first time in several hundred millennia. The weight of scientific analysis tells us that our climate is already changing and that we should expect extreme weather events (such as storms, floods and heat waves) to become more frequent and intense, as well as increasing global temperatures and rising sea levels. Policies that have been implemented, or are now being pursued, suggest that the long-term average temperature increase is more likely to be between 3.6 °C and 5.3 °C (compared with pre-industrial levels), with most of the increase occurring this century. While global action is not yet sufficient to limit the global temperature rise to 2 °C, this target still remains technically feasible, though extremely challenging. To keep open a realistic chance of meeting the 2 °C target, intensive action is required before 2020, the date by which a new international climate agreement is due to come into force. Energy is at the heart of this challenge: the energy sector accounts for around two-thirds of greenhouse-gas emissions, as more than 80% of global energy consumption is based on fossil fuels" (1, emphases in the original).

[3] See the Intergovernmental Panel on Climate Change 'Climate Change 2007: Synthesis Report,' 2007, where it is stated that: "Anthropogenic warming could lead to some impacts that are abrupt or irreversible, depending upon the rate and magnitude of the climate change" (53).

the effects of human habitation. Moreover, environmental degradation operates dynamically in that the anthropogenic effects on the environment may themselves cause or contribute to further environmental degradation.

To illustrate this point, let us take the example of greenhouse gases (GHGs),[4] which are almost entirely human caused.[5] The concentration of GHGs in the atmosphere not only degrades the content of the atmosphere, but also reproduces the 'greenhouse effect,' thus trapping a significant part of energy and heat that the earth, having previously absorbed these from the sun, subsequently reflects back into space. The effect of this phenomenon is the rise of the temperature of the earth that, in turn, has far-reaching consequences – including desertification and the melting of frozen parts of polar water-bodies and territories – for the natural landscape and the human, animal, and plant populations sustained by the ecosystem.

In light of the above, it is unsurprising that climate change is a concern to many a state and an inter-state actor. What may to some be more surprising, though not entirely bemusing, are the underwhelming efforts on the part of the international 'community' to meaningfully address climate change.[6] While a *gathering* – for lack of a better word – of state

---

[4] Art. 1 UN Framework Convention on Climate Change (UNFCCC) defines greenhouse gases as "those gaseous constituents of the atmosphere, both natural and anthropogenic, that absorb and re-emit infrared radiation."

[5] During 2004, the breakdown of global GHG emissions was the following: 26 percent regarding the energy supply, 19 percent regarding industry, 17 percent regarding gases released from land-use change and forestry, 14 percent from agriculture, 13 percent regarding transport, 8 percent regarding residential, commercial, and service sectors, and 3 percent regarding waste. See IPCC, 2007: 'Contribution of Working Group III to the Fourth Assessment Report of the Inter- governmental Panel on Climate Change,' in B. Metz, O. R. Davidson, P. R. Bosch, R. Dave, L. A. Meyer (eds.), *Climate Change 2007: Mitigation* (Cambridge University Press, 2007), 27 and 104. It is worth noting that the breakdown of GHG indicates that the overwhelming majority of GHG emissions relates to CO_2. The breakdown is: 57 percent from CO_2 (produced due to fossil-fuel use), 17 percent from CO2 (related to biomass and deforestation), 14 percent from methane, 8 percent from nitrous oxide, and 8 percent from various fluorinated gases. These figures have been calculated by the US Environmental Protection Agency (EPA) based on data in the IPCC, 2007: 'Contribution of Working Group III to the Fourth Assessment Report' (see www. epa.gov/climatechange/ghgemissions/global.html for EPA's calculations).

[6] The 1992 UNFCCC and its 1997 Kyoto Protocol may have laid the foundations for a nigh-universal climate change mitigation regime that is predicated, among others, on the principle of *equity* (see art. 3.1 UNFCCC) that differentiates the climate change mitigation duties owed by the industrialized states from those owed by less- and least-developed states, according to their emitting history and their current capabilities. The UNFCCC and

actors indeed exists, in our view, this does not possess the characteristics of a community with paritous interests. References to an *international community* often disguise the fact that what we are dealing with is, essentially, a collection of sovereign entities that, while formally enjoying the legal equality flowing from their sovereign status, in reality, are as highly disparate among themselves as their interests. How this may translate at the inter-state cooperation level is that meaningful efforts to address climate change might founder on the fact that certain states – including those with significant hydrocarbon/fossil fuel[7] endowments and those whose privately and/or state-owned enterprises have considerable interests in the conventional energy sector, along with highly polluting states with heavy industries – do not share the same sense of urgency as those states who seek to spearhead collective inter-state efforts aimed at climate change mitigation (e.g., such as the group of small island developing states[8] that face existential threats by rising sea levels).[9] In this respect, we shall be avoiding the term *international community* and shall be utilizing references to *inter-state cooperation*. We see some instances of unilateralism in respect to measures taken on the basis of the need to address climate change; however, these are not enough. The European Union's (EU) emissions trading system (ETS) is a case in point, where an economic area – namely the EU – that is also a WTO member in its own right had unilaterally, and much to the ire of several other states and WTO peers,[10] sought to include within its ETS all commercial aviation industry actors whose flight operations engaged

---

its Kyoto Protocol are significant multilateral steps for the cause of environmental protection; however, in the grander scheme of things, they may have been of little consequence. We say this as we are astonished to note that, while the strength of the Kyoto Protocol lies in the fact that 191 out of 192 of its parties have ratified it (with the notable exception of the US), its Clean Development Mechanism (CDM) (pursuant to art. 12 Kyoto Protocol) has only resulted in a 1 percent containment of global CO_2 levels (see A. Goldthau and J. M. Witte, *Global Energy Governance: The New Rules of the Game* (Washington, DC: Brookings Institution Press, 2010) 146.

[7] We refer to fossil fuel/hydrocarbon-based fuel as 'conventional' energy sources throughout the present chapter.

[8] See www.un.org/special-rep/ohrlls/sid/list.htm

[9] For a call to change the current approach to climate change mitigation and to suggest that major economies be more active in the fight against climate change, see R. Leal-Arcas, 'Top-down versus Bottom-up Approaches for Climate Change Negotiations: An Analysis,' *IUP Journal of Governance and Public Policy* 6 (2011), 7–52; R. Leal-Arcas, 'The BRICS and Climate Change,' *International Affairs Forum*, 2013, 1–5,

[10] See 'India Joins China in EU Aviation Emissions Scheme Boycott,' *Bridges Trade BioRes* 12 (2012), International Center for Trade and Sustainable Development, where it is stated

EU territory, before the EU finally suspended this policy under the pressure of the reaction that ensued – this could be seen as EU deference towards multilateralism.[11] Unsurprisingly, the EU had argued that such instances of unilateralism were necessary, if not justified, given the urgency that climate change caused and given the rather inadequate efforts of the international 'community' through its various relevant organizations, including the International Civil Aviation Organization.[12]

Having accepted that the threat of irreversible environmental degradation is real rather than imagined, and having understood that the political realities of inter-state cooperation – namely, the disparity of interests at play – are, to say the least, partly to blame that meaningful inter-state action has not been forthcoming, it seems reasonable to expect that measures – be they unilateral or collective –aimed at climate change mitigation and adaptation ought to be systemically encouraged and supported. Such measures may be schemes at the domestic, regional, and/or inter-state levels aimed at promoting the development and use of energy sources that are less polluting.[13] We have seen how the lion's

that 20 countries met in Moscow, Russia, in February 2012 to discuss the possible adoption of counter-measures (http://ictsd.org/i/news/biores/129175).

[11] The inclusion of the aviation industry into the EU's ETS was suspended on April 30, 2013 on the basis that multilateral negotiations on aviation industry emission containment are currently taking place in other organizations (see: http://ictsd.org/i/news/bridgesweekly/158472). For information regarding this temporary suspension, see European Parliament, 'CO$_2$: MEPs want ETS exception for intercontinental flights and progress in ICAO,' PR, February 26, 2013, www.europarl.europa.eu/sides/getDoc.do?pubRef=-%2f%2fEP%2f%2fTEXT%2bIM-PRESS%2b20130225IPR06039%2b0%2bDOC%2bXML%2bV0%2f%2fEN and language=EN. For an analysis of the inclusion of aviation in the EU's ETS, see R. Leal-Arcas, 'Unilateral Trade-related Climate Change Measures,' *Journal of World Investment and Trade* 13 (2012), 875–927.

[12] See http://ec.europa.eu/clima/policies/transport/aviation/index_en.htm on this issue, where it is stated that the EU had been pressing ICAO for more than fifteen years to take meaningful action in relation to GHG emissions. Also at the same link, read the official EU narrative on this issue. The EU holds to the view, further to a December 2011 CJEU case brought by some US airlines, that the inclusion of aviation in the EU ETS is compatible with the EU's international obligations (see Case C-366/10).

[13] We refer throughout this chapter to such sources as: renewable energy/renewables/renewable energy sources. In terms of what this term includes, we draw from how this concept is handled by the International Energy Agency (IEA) in its publications and periodical reports. See the FAQ page of the IEA, where it is stated that renewable energy is "Energy derived from natural processes (e.g. sunlight and wind) that are replenished at a faster rate than they are consumed. Solar, wind, geothermal, hydro, and some forms of biomass are common sources of renewable energy" (available at www.iea.org/aboutus/faqs/renewableenergy); see also the 2012 IEA report, where the sort of energy sources that, for the purposes of this chapter, we could aggregate together as 'renewable energy'

share of GHG emissions derives from CO_2 emissions that, in turn, are caused by, or linked to, the energy supply through the combustion of fossil fuels. Energy-related CO_2 emissions reached 31.6 gigatons (Gts) in 2012 – that is 31.6 billion tons of CO_2.[14]

Diversifying the global energy supply mix in a manner that increasingly draws from renewable sources could have far-reaching geo-economic and geo-strategic implications,[15] including: the containment of GHG emissions to levels that would avert more costly future redress; the conservation of the ecosystem and the safeguarding of the welfare of the human, animal, and plant populations it sustains; a more enhanced energy security for those states and group of states that are net energy importers; and foreign relations that are less skewed by energy considerations. The scope of this chapter relates to the implications of renewable energy for the environment, and how, therefore, measures taken to promote the development and take-up of renewable energy may engage the rules of the multilateral trade system.[16]

---

are those that yield energy through the processing of: 'biofuels & waste,' 'hydro,' 'geothermal,' 'solar,' 'wind,' and 'heat,' etc. See International Energy Agency, 2012 Key World Energy Statistics, OECD/IEA, 2012 (at 6, at the legend to the 2010 pie chart). Moreover, Article III of the International Renewable Energy Agency (IRENA) statute defines renewables to be: "all forms of energy produced from renewable sources in a sustainable manner, which include, inter alia: bioenergy; geothermal energy; hydropower; ocean energy, including inter alia tidal, wave and ocean thermal energy; solar energy; and wind energy." In our view, certain energy sources that are more environmentally friendly due to their lower CO_2 emissions when compared with fossil fuels – namely, biomass/biofuels – are rightly considered non-conventional energy sources. That said, given that they are produced by processing mainly plants that need to be replanted, strictly speaking, these sources are not *renewable* in the way that wind, solar, hydro, and geothermal are renewable. Despite this, we have also followed the practice of the IEA and IRENA to aggregate these too as *renewables*.

[14] See the executive summary to the IEA 2013 'Redrawing the Energy-Climate Map' World Energy Outlook Special Report, 1.

[15] See IPCC, 'Summary for Policymakers,' in O. Edenhofer, R. Pichs-Madruga, Y. Sokona, K. Seyboth, P. Matschoss, S. Kadner, T. Zwickel, P. Eickemeier, G. Hansen, S. Schlömer, C. von Stechow (eds.), *IPCC Special Report on Renewable Energy Sources and Climate Change Mitigation* [(Cambridge University Press, 2011), 4–26, for an exposition of the potential benefits of increasing the proportion of renewables in the global supply energy mix. See also A. Ghosh and H. Gangania, 'Governing Clean Energy Subsidies: What, Why and How Legal?,' International Centre for Trade and Sustainable Development (2012), 11–18, for an exposition of the various arguments for the promotion of renewable energy.

[16] A similar line of thought is to be found in R. Leal-Arcas, 'Climate Change Mitigation from the Bottom up: Using Preferential Trade Agreements to Promote Climate Change Mitigation,' *Carbon and Climate Law Review* 7 (2013), 34–42 (discussing how to promote climate change mitigation by using preferential trade agreements).

This chapter is principally concerned with how the existing multilateral trade system, based on the World Trade Organization (WTO), countenances the promotion of renewables. We carry out this examination by discussing certain WTO norms that have, or may, come to bear on measures that WTO members take which have a distortive or restrictive effect on cross-border intra-WTO trade and which have been argued in connection with environmental protection and/or with renewable energy,[17] and by reviewing the relevant WTO jurisprudence.

This contribution is therefore part of the so-called 'trade and ...' debate, which relates to concerns surrounding the fragmentation of the international legal system, and of international law, along thematic or other lines that lead to artifacts such as 'international' 'economic' law and international 'energy' law. The International Law Commission set up a Study Group on fragmentation which issued its report to the United Nations General Assembly in 2006. In that report, the Study Group referred to the reasons that fragmentation of the international legal system has arisen, identified the advent of special regimes – including not only legal orders, but also fields of law such as 'international' 'trade' law – that reinforced perceptions that these were 'self-contained,' itself a fallacy when, among other things, any special legal regime set up further to inter-state contracting is predicated upon general international law to function.[18] Starting from the premise that the ecosystem, its preservation,

---

[17] While the WTO and its norms apply to intra-WTO trade, they may also have implications for trade flows involving a nexus between states where at least one party is a WTO member. For instance, the requirement under art. I GATT (regarding the principle that WTO members ought to treat all their WTO peers as they would their 'most-favored nation') makes clear that any trade privilege that a WTO member affords to any other state must, in effect, be unconditionally extended to all of its WTO peers. Naturally, this does not create obligations for non-WTO members.

[18] See ILC, Report of the Study Group, Fragmentation of International Law: Difficulties Arising from the Diversification and Expansion of International Law (A/CN.4/L.682) (April 13, 2006) (14, para. 15) where it is stated that: "The rationale for the Commission's treatment of fragmentation is that the emergence of new and special types of law, 'self-contained regimes' and geographically or functionally limited treaty-systems creates problems of coherence in international law. New types of specialized law do not emerge accidentally but seek to respond to new technical and functional requirements. The emergence of 'environmental law' is a response to growing concern over the state of the international environment. 'Trade law' develops as an instrument to regulate international economic relations. 'Human rights law' aims to protect the interests of individuals and 'international criminal law' gives legal expression to the 'fight against impunity.' Each rule-complex or 'regime' comes with its own principles, its own form of expertise and its own 'ethos,' not necessarily identical to the ethos of neighbouring specialization. 'Trade law' and 'environmental law,' for example, have highly specific objectives and rely

and climate change mitigation are global public goods, there is a nexus between energy and climate change, which encompasses a range of issues such as clean energy subsidies, and emission-related levies (e.g., carbon taxes, and border adjustment taxes for carbon emissions). International law is threatened by incoherence due to its fragmentation, and there is a need to bring greater coherence not least for the promotion of environmental protection through the entire normative context that is international law.[19] One would need to look at various special regimes (such as the WTO, the EU, the North American Free Trade Agreement (NAFTA)) and institutions (such as civil society and markets) for resolving disputes that pitch environmental against other (say, investment protection, market liberalization) objectives in a manner that sufficiently promote environmental objectives, or that induct environmental protection norms in the normative context that is to be taken into account for resolving such disputes so that, ultimately, we may come closer to achieving more coherent global environmental governance.

After the introduction, for context purposes, we shall briefly refer to some general global energy data and to some data that are more specific to renewable energy in section II. In section III, we shall sum up arguments in relation to the suitability of the existing multilateral system to sufficiently balance the inter-state environmental objectives with those relating to inter-state trade liberalization objectives. Section IV concludes the chapter.

II.   Facts and figures on renewable energy and its governance

The latest readily available global data compiled by the International Energy Agency (IEA) indicate that renewable energy sources made up 13.2 per cent of the global energy supply mix in 2010, while conventional energy sources (oil, natural gas, and coal) made up 81.1 per cent of the

on principles that may often point in different directions. In order for the new law to be efficient, it often includes new types of treaty clauses or practices that may not be compatible with old general law or the law of some other specialized branch. Very often new rules or regimes develop precisely in order to deviate from what was earlier provided by the general law. When such deviations or become general and frequent, the unity of the law suffers."

[19] On the fragmentation of international law, see the work of the ILC, 58th session, Final Report of the study group on fragmentation, UN Doc. A/CN.4/L.682, and the conclusions of the study group on fragmentation, UN Doc. A/CN.4/L.702, http://untreaty.un.org/ilc/guide/1_9.htm. On the specific case of international trade law, see also R. Leal-Arcas, 'The Fragmentation of International Trade Law: Is Now the Time for Variable Geometry?,' *Journal of World Investment and Trade* 12 (2011), 145–195.

mix.[20] The figures for 1973 – the year used in successive IEA reports as a comparator – were 12.4 per cent and 86.7 per cent, respectively.[21] In almost forty years, the composition of the global primary energy supply has changed very little. Any reduction in the proportion of conventional energy sources has largely been replaced by the rise in the proportion of nuclear energy from 0.9 in 1973 to 5.7 per cent by 2010.[22] While nuclear energy is an alternative energy source, it is far from environmentally friendly. As the disasters at the nuclear power plants of Chernobyl (Ukraine) in 1986 and Fukushima Daiichi (Japan) in 2011 tragically testify, nuclear energy poses nigh-apocalyptic consequences for the environment.

We fleetingly alluded to political realities (i.e., briefly, the disparate interests of states in preserving the *status quo* in relation to the primacy of convention energy sources) that, generally, seem to undermine meaningful concerted action to protect the environment. In relation to the global energy mix, there are other practices that stack the odds against the proliferation of renewables – namely, pervasive fuel subsidies[23] that have implications for conventional energy demand and, consequently, that retard the move towards a more environmentally friendly composition of the global energy supply mix.[24] It should be noted that such conventional energy subsidies have been tolerated within the WTO system.[25]

---

[20] Figures calculated based on data as these appear in International Energy Agency, 2012 Key World Energy Statistics, OECD/IEA, 2012, 6. During 2010, the global primary energy supply was 12,717 million tons of oil equivalent (Mtoe). During 1973, it stood at 6,107 Mtoe.

[21] *Ibid.*   [22] *Ibid.*

[23] According to the IEA 2012 World Energy Outlook factsheet, "[e]nergy subsidies – government measures that artificially lower the price of energy paid by consumers, raise the price received by producers or lower the cost of production – are large and pervasive. When they are well-designed, subsidies to renewables and low-carbon energy technologies can bring long-term economic and environmental benefits. However, when they are directed at fossil fuels, the costs generally outweigh the benefits" (6) (www.worldenergyoutlook.org/media/weowebsite/2012/factsheets.pdf).

[24] UNCTAD, World Trade Law and Renewable Energy: The Case of Non-Tariff Barriers, 2009, 17, and J. Pershing and J. Mackenzie, 'Removing Subsidies: Leveling the Playing Field for Renewable Energy Technologies,' 2004, www.ren21.net/Portals/0/documents/irecs/renew2004/Removing%20subsidies.pdf

[25] See Thomas Cottier's comments at the 2011 WTO public forum discussions on International Governance of Energy Trade: WTO and Energy Charter Treaty (www.wto.org/english/forums_e/public_forum11_e/programme_e.htm#session40).

In recent years, there has been an increase in subsidies directed at the promotion of renewable energy. The global figures for subsidies in the renewable energy sector increased from US$39 billion in 2007 to US$66 billion by 2010.[26] While this increase is laudable, the figures are eclipsed by the enormity of fossil-fuel-related subsidies that in 2010 stood at US $409 billion.[27] The IEA projects that by 2035, under its various policy scenarios, should renewables subsidies rise to US$250 billion, a variety of positive developments could take place, such as onshore wind becoming competitive by 2020 in the EU and by 2030 in China,[28] and the containment of up to 3.4 gigatons – that is, 3.4 billion tons – of energy-related CO_2 when compared with the current total energy supply fuel mix.[29]

At the inter-state level, there are various initiatives that concern renewable energy. There are several intergovernmental organizations (IGOs) and/or supranational organizations – including the IEA, the EU, and the United Nations (UN) – whose remits to varying degrees concern renewable energy. What is more, there are numerous instances of inter-state cooperation along the lines of transnational policy networks and discussions at summit meetings.[30]

The most ostensibly renewables-related IGO is the International Renewable Energy Agency (IRENA),[31] which counts 116 member states (plus the EU in its own right) and another forty-four in accession talks.[32] The declared purpose of IRENA is to promote the adoption and sustainable use of all forms of renewables in a manner that takes into account

---

[26] IEA 2012 World Energy Outlook factsheet, 6.

[27] *Ibid.*   [28] *Ibid.*   [29] *Ibid.*

[30] See B. Sovacool and A. Florini, 'Examining the Complications of Global Energy Governance,' *Journal of Energy and Natural Resources Law* 30 (2012); A. Steiner, T. Wälde, A. Bradbrook and F. Schutyser, 'International Institutional Arrangements in Support of Renewable Energy,' in D. Abmann, U. Laumanns, and D. Uh (eds.), *Renewable Energy: A Global Review of Technologies, Policies, and Markets* (London: Earthscan, 2006), 152–165, for a rundown of such organizations and instances concerning renewable energy at the inter-state governance/co-operation level. Some relevant examples are the Organización Latinoamericana de Energía, the World Council for Renewable Energies (the precursor to IRENA), the Inter-American Development Bank, the Organization of the Black Sea Economic Cooperation, the South Asian Association for Regional Cooperation, the Renewable Energy and Energy Efficiency Partnership, the Global Network on Energy for Sustainable Development, the Renewable Energy and Energy Efficiency Partnership, the International Institute for Energy Conservation, and the Global Energy Efficiency and Renewable Energy Fund (an EU associated scheme).

[31] See www.irena.org/menu/index.aspx?mnu=cat&PriMenuID=13&CatID=30.

[32] See www.irena.org/Menu/Index.aspx?mnu=Cat&PriMenuID=46&CatID=67.

"national priorities."[33] IRENA lacks the power to make binding recommendations on its members and its members are under no obligation[34] to implement the advice they periodically receive from IRENA.

Having briefly referred the instances of inter-state cooperation concerned with renewables, we turn to another instance of inter-state cooperation, albeit one with a very different mandate from those mentioned above, and with a much stronger normative effect – namely, the WTO. The WTO has been the main component of the multilateral trade system since 1995. It evolved from the 1947 General Agreement on Tariffs and Trade (GATT), which it entirely incorporated. The WTO provides degrees of governance over the trade flows between its members to the extent that their policies and practices may engage WTO norms. We should also like to add that the WTO system is neither *expressly* concerned with energy trade in general, nor with renewables trade in particular. Unless expressly stated (for instance, there is a degree of divergence from standard WTO rules in the field of agricultural trade,[35] trade in services[36] and, as had been the case, for clothing and textiles up to 2005),[37] WTO norms could potentially apply, and habitually apply, evenhandedly to all cross-border trade involving WTO members,

---

[33] See Article II of the IRENA Statute, where the objectives are stated to be as follows: "The Agency shall promote the widespread and increased adoption and the sustainable use of all forms of renewable energy, taking into account: a.) national and domestic priorities and benefits derived from a combined approach of renewable energy and energy efficiency measures, and b.) the contribution of renewable energy to environmental preservation, through limiting pressure on natural resources and reducing deforestation, particularly tropical deforestation, desertification and biodiversity loss; to climate protection; to economic growth and social cohesion including poverty alleviation and sustainable development; to access to and security of energy supply; to regional development and to inter-generational responsibility."

[34] See art. IV(1)(a) IRENA Statute.

[35] See www.wto.org/english/thewto_e/whatis_e/tif_e/agrm3_e.htm for a rundown of the issues.

[36] WTO members are under no obligation to liberalize their services sectors. However, they are obligated to provide the same treatment to all WTO peers indiscriminately in relation to those sectors which they have previously liberalized in their respective Schedules of Commitments (see arts. II and XVI of the General Agreement on Trade in Services (GATS). What is more, WTO members are obligated, in relation to those sectors previously liberalized, to not discriminate between domestic service providers and those of their WTO peers (see art. XVII of the GATS).

[37] The Agreement on Textiles and Clothing (ATC), which permitted departures from the general WTO rules, terminated on January 1, 2005. Its expiry means that trade in textile and clothing products is no longer subject to quotas under a special regime outside normal WTO rules, but is now governed by the general WTO rules and disciplines.

including energy-related trade.[38] Consequently, cross-border trade in renewable energy goods and services that involve at least one WTO member is potentially within the WTO ambit.

The following section provides a *tour d'horizon* of the sort of WTO norms that have been, and might be, engaged by measures linked to the promotion of renewables, and a commentary on how the WTO system may generally countenance the promotion of renewables.

III.   The WTO and renewables

1.   Initial remarks

The WTO system does not handle general energy trade, or particular renewables trade, any differently from any other trade sector that is within the WTO's scope. While there have been calls for an energy-specific multilateral agreement to be adopted under the WTO auspices,[39] these have yet to result in a WTO agreement that is energy specific. Arguably, the Energy Charter Treaty (ECT) – an international

---

[38] See R. Leal-Arcas and A. Filis, 'The Fragmented Governance of the Global Energy Economy: A Legal–Institutional Analysis,' *Journal of World Energy Law and Business* 6 (2013), 1–58 (at 21–22); WTO, 'World Trade Report 2010: Trade in Natural Resources' (2010), for a more thorough exposition of the relationship between WTO and energy trade.

[39] See T. Cottier *et al.*, 'Energy in WTO Law and Policy,' in T. Cottier and P. Delimatsis (eds.), *The Prospects of International Trade Regulation: From Fragmentation to Coherence* (Cambridge University Press, 2011), 211–244; in relation to a speculative proposal for a Sustainable Energy Trade Agreement (SETA), see M. Kennedy (2012), 'Legal Options for a Sustainable Energy Trade Agreement,' International Centre for Trade and Sustainable Development; see the May 2013 ICTSD news item (http://ictsd.org/i/news/bridge-sweekly/162166) reporting proceedings from a workshop held at the WTO headquarters in Geneva, where several attendees commented on the need for the WTO system to better accommodate the promotion of renewables and energy particularities. We would add that such statements generally support the misperception that the current normative framework may be woefully inadequate. While we believe that guidelines based on the WTO rules and jurisprudence would be helpful to WTO members – imaginably, these could be drafted by the WTO legal division in cooperation with the WTO's Committee on Trade and the Environment, and any other relevant WTO organ – the rules and jurisprudence, as they currently stand, do not obstruct measures taken to promote renewable, so long as such measures are, generally, bona fide, not unduly discriminatory, and not unduly restrictive. It is therefore one thing to call for far-reaching – through e.g. guidelines, clarifications, and other means – systemic encouragement of the scaling-up and taking-up of renewables, and quite another to attempt to do away with the existing safeguards in WTO rules and jurisprudence that seek to prevent abuse (e.g. discriminatory treatment and/or protectionism).

treaty relating to various aspects, including trade, investment, and environmental protection, of its parties' respective energy sectors – may fit that bill. The ECT could appropriately be regarded as an inter-state arrangement that arose out of the GATT/WTO system, given that the ECT was concluded as an alternative to previously unsuccessful efforts on the part of several developed net energy-importing WTO members to have an energy-specific agreement adopted within the WTO.[40]

In the absence of a specific energy–trade agreement, the WTO system and its multilaterally covered agreements are the principal structures that provide governance in cross-border energy trade, including cross-border renewable energy trade, to the extent that such trade flows involve a WTO member.[41] In addition, the multilateral trade rules that come to bear on such trade flows may further be enhanced by the rules contained in the WTO's *plurilateral* agreements so long as the WTO member(s) concerned have acceded to these and have, therefore, assumed that further layer of WTO obligation. An example of one such plurilateral agreement would be the Agreement on Government Procurement (GPA), to which a minority of WTO members are parties,[42] and which may be relevant to instances, say, where a WTO member which is a party to the GPA takes some trade-distortive measure connected to government procurement.

---

[40] See T. Wälde, *The Energy Charter Treaty: An East–West Gateway for Investment and Trade* (The Hague: Kluwer Law International, 1996).

[41] The Agreement Establishing the WTO, signed in Marrakesh on April 15, 1994, sets the WTO's terms of reference. Annexes to this Agreement specify which the covered agreements are. The GATT is the principal multilateral trade agreement under the WTO concerning tradable goods. See the Agreement Establishing the WTO's Annex 1A. Note that Annexes 1 and 4 to the Agreement Establishing the WTO distinguish between 'multilateral' and 'plurilateral' WTO agreements, with the former being binding to the entire WTO membership, while the normative effect of the latter set relies on WTO members having specifically acceded to this class of international agreements. The entire WTO system is predicated on the core principle of non-discrimination by prohibiting discrimination along the following two axes: namely, among WTO peers (art. I GATT) and among domestic and imported tradables (art. III GATT). Certain trade-distortive measures argued to have been taken to promote renewables may, and often do, engage any, or both, of these twin aspects of the non-discrimination principle.

[42] Currently there are 41 parties to the GPA, including all 28 EU members (with the Netherlands in its own right and on account of Aruba). Note that the EU is not a party in its own right to the GPA (see www.wto.org/english/tratop_e/gproc_e/memobs_e.htm#pArties).

494 RAFAEL LEAL-ARCAS AND ANDREW FILIS

For their part, measures aimed at the promotion of renewable energy can be highly varied,[43] and, consequently, might each engage a variety of WTO norms; norms, however, that are not necessarily all applicable in every single case that involves a measure argued to be taken to promote renewables. In that respect, any assessment of a measure's WTO compatibility would have to be performed on a case-by-case basis and in relation to the facts of each case.

For instance, certain measures may rely on the subsidization of the renewables generation industry by financial incentives for market actors, and, say, by subsidizing partly or entirely the cost of technologies for households to generate renewable electricity. Those examples alone could illustrate how different WTO norms might be engaged; while there is little in the WTO rules to obstruct a government from assuming or otherwise supporting, say, the cost of renewable technologies for *households* to generate their own electricity, this is, generally, not the case, were a government to subsidize a specific sector in a manner that, by conferring a benefit to that sector, consequently, injures the domestic industry of another WTO member. Again, it would be necessary to examine all relevant aspects of a measure and its effect to establish whether imports are indeed injured and whether this may be justified under WTO rules. The Agreement on Subsidies and Countervailing Measures (SCM Agreement) defines what may be a subsidy, provides a typology of subsidies to list those that are *prohibited*, *actionable*, and *non-actionable*, along with listing the available remedies.[44]

Building on the previous example involving households, another brief example of WTO incompatibility would be where a government financially supports only such households that install, say, domestically manufactured and/or assembled renewable energy technologies, given that, among other things, such a measure would clearly favor domestic producers/market actors, and thus disadvantage identical or substitutable imported goods vis-à-vis domestically produced goods. Such a measure

---

[43] In terms of the diverse typology of policy tools to promote renewables, see Ghosh and Gangania, 'Governing Clean Energy Subsidies: What, Why and How Legal? ,' 20–26.

[44] The SCM Agreement is also a covered agreement listed in Annex 1A of the Agreement Establishing the WTO. Art. 1 defines subsidies; art. 3 defines which subsidies are prohibited; art. 4 relates to remedies for prohibited subsidies; art. 5 relates to actionable subsidies; art. 7 to remedies for actionable subsidies; and art. 8 defines what type of subsidies may be non-actionable. For further details on how WTO subsidies provisions apply to renewable energy, see R. Leal-Arcas, *Climate Change and International Trade*, 136–150.

would, on its face, be offending a principal tenet of the WTO system that *like* products, once over the border, be treated in a non-discriminatory manner, irrespective of whether they are imports or domestically produced.[45] Such measures are unlikely to be permitted under the general exceptions (see Article XX of the GATT), given that, should imported goods also do as good a job as those domestically sourced, the consequent discrimination may actually be mercantilist protectionism veiled by environmental protection pretexts.[46]

What is more, what often defines the outcome of a dispute before the WTO Dispute Settlement Body's (DSB) adjudicative organs – namely, at first instance, the Panel, and, on final appeal, the Appellate Body – are the issues that parties choose to raise along with how they choose to argue these, thus somewhat restricting the ability of the adjudicative bodies concerned to approaching the dispute in a more autonomously coherent manner.[47]

---

[45] See art. III GATT, which states that: "The contracting parties recognize that internal taxes and other internal charges, and laws, regulations and requirements affecting the internal sale, offering for sale, purchase, transportation, distribution or use of products, and internal quantitative regulations requiring the mixture, processing or use of products in specified amounts or proportions, should not be applied to imported or domestic products so as to afford protection to domestic production."

[46] The art. XX general exceptions, if applicable, could allow WTO members to derogate from their core obligations under the GATT and potentially other covered agreements. Art. XX(b) and (g) are the exceptions evidently related to the ecosystem. Art. XX(b) contemplates that trade-restrictive measures necessary to protect human, animal, and plant health of life could potentially be justified, and art. XX(g) contemplates that trade-restrictive measures taken to conserve exhaustible natural resources could potentially be justified. There is a wealth of WTO jurisprudence that articulates the application of these two grounds further. We shall refer to the relevant cases elsewhere in this chapter. What is more, it is worth noting that the *chapeau* to art. XX conditions the application of the general exceptions to ensure that it is not used to offer protection to domestic industry or to discriminate between trade partners. Thus, the *chapeau* reiterates the non-discriminatory dual principle upon which the WTO system is predicated, namely art. I (most-favored nation treatment) and art. III (national treatment) of the GATT.

[47] See the Understanding on Rules and Procedures Governing the Settlement of Disputes (being Annex 2 of the Agreement Establishing the WTO), where arts. 7 and 17 suggest that the Panel and Appellate Body terms of reference, unless otherwise agreed by the parties in dispute, ought to follow the issues and pleadings of the parties. Article 7 (regarding Panels terms of reference): "1... To examine, in the light of the relevant provisions in (name of the covered agreement(s) cited by the parties to the dispute), the matter referred to the DSB by (name of party) in document . . . and to make such findings as will assist the DSB in making the recommendations or in giving the rulings provided for in that/those agreement(s)." "2. Panels shall address the relevant provisions in any covered agreement or agreements cited by the parties to the dispute," and art. 17(6), in

2. Environmental Protection Objectives and the WTO

Throughout section III, we shall be looking at the specific WTO norms that have been, and are likely to be, engaged by trade-distortive measures that WTO members may seek to argue have been taken to promote renewables. Before doing so, it may be helpful to briefly consider how environmental concerns have been handled within the GATT/WTO system since the beginning. Essentially, the GATT/WTO system is concerned with trade liberalization. Its advent was shortly after the end of World War II as part of broader efforts to formalize inter-state cooperation along pro-market development lines during the Cold War. The GATT was agreed within the context of the 1944 United Nations' Monetary and Financial Conference, at Bretton Woods, New Hampshire (UAS), along with the other 'Bretton Woods' institutions – namely, the International Monetary Fund and the International Bank of Reconstruction and Development (commonly known as the World Bank). In that sense, its pro-market/pro-trade liberalization bias is inherent and systemic.[48] For the purposes of the GATT, all other policy objectives, while not unimportant, were relegated as systemically *external* considerations.

Within the GATT regime, the principal vehicle to accommodate other policy objectives – including environmental protection – has been Article XX of the GATT. This provision contains *general exceptions* to GATT/WTO obligations, which, if applicable, may justify derogation on the part of WTO members. The grounds of derogation pertinent to the ecosystem are: Article XX (b), concerning measures *necessary* for the protection of human, animal and plant life or health; and Article XX (g), regarding measures *in relation* to the conservation of exhaustible natural resources.[49]

relation to the Appellate Body: 'An appeal shall be limited to issues of law covered in the panel report and legal interpretations developed by the panel.'

[48] See preamble to the GATT 1947, which states that: "Recognizing that [parties'] relations in the field of trade and economic endeavour should be conducted with a view to raising standards of living, ensuring full employment and a large and steadily growing volume of real income and effective demand, developing the full use of the resources of the world and expanding the production and exchange of goods, Being desirous of contributing to these objectives by entering into reciprocal and mutually advantageous arrangements directed to the substantial reduction of tariffs and other barriers to trade and to the elimination of discriminatory treatment in international commerce."

[49] For an analysis, see E. Abu-Gosh, and R. Leal-Arcas, 'The Conservation of Exhaustible Natural Resources in the GATT and WTO: Implications for the Conservation of Oil Resources,' *Journal of World Investment and Trade* 14 (2013), 480–531.

During the GATT era (i.e., in the pre-WTO era, before the conclusion of the Uruguay Round of trade negotiations, which resulted in the Agreement on the Establishment of the WTO in 1994), interpretations of Article XX had been very scarce.[50] This, however, changed with the advent of the WTO system. The advent of the WTO system in 1995, however, also saw the inclusion of the notion of "sustainable development" in the preamble of the Agreement Establishing the WTO (to which the GATT 1994 and all other covered agreements are annexed).[51] Furthermore, in 2001 WTO members issued the Doha Ministerial statement, in which they affirmed the importance of "sustainable development"[52] to the multilateral trade system. This is not an inconsiderable addition for the purposes of interpreting treaty obligations; the principle of effective treaty interpretation presumes that all relevant textual elements ought to be afforded what may be their appropriate weight in the circumstances.

---

[50] See G. Marceau, 'The WTO's Efforts to Balance Economic Development and Environmental Protection: A Short Review of Appellate Body Jurisprudence,' *Latin American Journal of International Trade Law* 1(2013), 293.

[51] "Recognizing that their relations in the field of trade and economic endeavour should be conducted with a view to raising standards of living, ensuring full employment and a large and steadily growing volume of real income and effective demand, and expanding the production of and trade in goods and services, while allowing for the optimal use of the world's *resources in accordance with the objective of sustainable development, seeking both to protect and preserve the environment and* to enhance the means for doing so in a manner consistent with their respective needs and concerns at different levels of economic development" (emphasis added).

[52] WT/MIN(01)/DEC/1 (November 20, 2001). At point 6 of the Declaration, it is stated that: "*We strongly reaffirm our commitment to the objective of sustainable development,* as stated in the Preamble to the Marrakesh Agreement. We are convinced that the aims of upholding and safeguarding an open and non-discriminatory multilateral trading system, and acting for the protection of the environment and the promotion of sustainable development can and must be mutually supportive. We take note of the efforts by members to conduct national environmental assessments of trade policies on a voluntary basis. We recognize that under WTO rules no country should be prevented from taking measures for the protection of human, animal or plant life or health, or of the environment at the levels it considers appropriate, subject to the requirement that they are not applied in a manner which would constitute a means of arbitrary or unjustifiable discrimination between countries where the same conditions prevail, or a disguised restriction on international trade, and are otherwise in accordance with the provisions of the WTO Agreements" (emphasis added). See www.wto.org/english/thewto_e/minist_e/min01_e/mindecl_e.htm

(i)   US – Shrimp

The WTO's Appellate Body has certainly thought as much; in its determination of the US – Shrimp case,[53] the Appellate Body expressly referred to the need to utilize the addition of "sustainable development" in its determinations.[54] Gabrielle Marceau goes further to refer to this interpretative development, which has paid heed to the "sustainable development" objective, as the: 'consecration of WTO Members' fundamental right to take measures to protect the environment . . . at a level *they* consider appropriate' (emphasis added).[55]

A further development during the WTO years has been the establishment of the Committee on Trade and Environment (CTE)[56] – a deliberative and advisory body set up to examine the interplay between trade and the environment – created under the 1994 Ministerial Decision on Trade and Environment.[57]

In fact, in the WTO era, there have also been disputes resolved by the WTO's DSB adjudicative bodies that, in effect, have extended the level of environmental protection acceptable within the WTO. In the US – Shrimp case, it was confirmed that the meaning of GATT Article XX(g) notion of *exhaustible natural resources* had evolved to contain living beings (in that specific case, these being sea turtle populations). The Appellate Body did this by applying an evolutionary–teleological take on interpreting that notion. What is more, the interpretation of this notion was, to an extent, colored by extraneous considerations, given that the Appellate Body had regard to other international agreements to which not all WTO members had been parties. This allowed the Appellate Body, in interpreting the obligations of WTO members, to take into account contemporary concerns expressed at the level of inter-state cooperation.[58]

---

[53] *United States – Import Prohibition of Certain Shrimp and Shrimp Products* (October 12, 1998) (WT/DS58/AB/R).

[54] See the Appellate Body report, where it is stated that: "It is proper for us to take into account, as part of the context of the *chapeau*, the specific language of the preamble to the WTO Agreement, which, we have said, gives colour, texture and shading to the rights and obligations of Members under the WTO Agreement, generally, and under the GATT 1994, in particular" (paras. 153–155).

[55] Marceau, 'The WTO's Efforts to Balance Economic Development,' 294.

[56] See www.wto.org/english/tratop_e/envir_e/wrk_committee_e.htm for background information on the CTE.

[57] Accessible at www.wto.org/english/docs_e/legal_e/56-dtenv.pdf

[58] See the Appellate Body report in the US – Shrimp dispute, where it is stated that: 'contemporary concerns of the community of nations about the protection and conservation of the environment' (para. 129). This is a fine example of *systemic integration*,

It is worth stating that the WTO adjudicative agencies have, on balance, adhered to the general international law rules on interpretation in a manner that has been consistent with general international law so as to give appropriate weigh to agreements that are outside the WTO scope. The Appellate Body has corrected interpretative errors at the lower adjudicative level,[59] thus not ceasing to regard treaty-based systems – such as the WTO – as being operative against the backdrop of general international law, and, might we add, thus not ceasing to regard the treaties themselves as anything other than *creatures*[60] of public international law.

(ii)   *US – Gasoline*

The *US – Gasoline* case[61] is another seminal case illustrating the extent to which the WTO system may be amenable to environmental protection. While the case was resolved against the party who sought to rely on an Article XX(g) ground to derogate – namely, the USA[62] – the case has important implications for environmental protection, given that the panel in that case held that "clean air," may, for the purposes of Article XX(g) be considered an *exhaustible natural resource*;[63] a finding subsequently upheld by the Appellate Body on appeal. It is an important development for environmental protection within the WTO system and jurisprudence. In fact, the panel had drawn from previous (GATT-era) jurisprudence, where resources capable of renewal – such as air and living organisms – had been considered *exhaustible natural resources* within the meaning of Article XX(g) of the GATT and, thus, that trade-

where the entire international law edifice is approached cohesively and its elements sympathetically to one another. This systemically integrative approach had previously been confirmed by the Appellate Body in *United States – Standards for Reformulated and Conventional Gasoline*, April 29, 1996 (WTO/DS2/AB/R), where the Appellate Body had stated that the GATT ought not be considered 'in clinical isolation of public international law' (*US – Gasoline* Appellate Body report, 17).

[59]   See M. Fitzmaurice and P. Merkouris, 'Canons of Treaty Interpretation: Selected Case Studies from the World Trade Organization and the North American Free Trade Agreement,' in M. Fitzmaurice *et al.* (eds.), *Treaty Interpretation and the Vienna Convention on the Law of Treaties: 30 Years On* (Leiden: Nijhoff, 2010), 234–237.

[60]   See C. McLachlan 'The Principle of Systemic Integration and Article 31(3)(C) of the Vienna Convention,' ICLQ 54 (2005), 280.

[61]   *United States – Standards for Reformulated and Conventional Gasoline* (WTO/DS2/AB/R).

[62]   The Appellate Body found that the measure in question unjustifiably discriminated against imports and therefore did not satisfy the non-discrimination requirements of the *chapeau* of art. XX and of the remaining part of art. XX(g).

[63]   See Panel Report, para. 6.37.

restrictive measures in relation to their conservation or in order to protect the life or health of human, animal, or plant populations may be justified under Article XX(g).[64]

What is more, in the *US – Gasoline* case, in finding against the US measure and thus disallowing its justification under Article XX(g), the Appellate Body clearly felt the need to reiterate that the specific finding does not compromise in any way the *autonomy* of WTO members to take environmental protection measures that may be trade restrictive/distortive so long as they are WTO consistent, which largely means they are bona fide and non-discriminatory.[65]

It is worth noting at this point that, while, undoubtedly, there is a preference within the WTO system for multilateralism[66] in trade-restrictive

---

[64] In *US – Gasoline*, the Panel stated that: "the fact that a resource was renewable could not be an objection. A past panel had accepted that renewable stocks of salmon could constitute an exhaustible natural resource" (44, para. 6.37 of the Panel report). The case cited by the Panel had been a GATT-era dispute, namely, the *Canada – Measures Affecting Exports of Unprocessed Herring and Salmon* (BISD 35S/98) (adopted on March 22, 1988), dispute in which herring and salmon were considered exhaustible natural resources for the purposes of art. XX(g). In that case, however, Canada could not cite art. XX given that it applied the measure in question discriminatorily in favor of the domestic fisheries processing industry. Also note that dolphins were considered exhaustible natural resources for the purposes of art. XX(g) as per the Panel report (not adopted) in the *United States – Restrictions on Imports of Tuna* dispute (DS29/R) (see para. 5.13).

[65] "It is of some importance that the Appellate Body point out what this does not mean. *It does not mean, or imply, that the ability of any WTO Member to take measures to control air pollution or, more generally, to protect the environment, is at issue. That would be to ignore the fact that Article XX of the General Agreement contains provisions designed to permit important state interests – including the protection of human health, as well as the conservation of exhaustible natural resources – to find expression.* The provisions of Article XX were not changed as a result of the Uruguay Round of Multilateral Trade Negotiations. Indeed, in the preamble to the WTO Agreement and in the [1994 Ministerial] Decision on Trade and Environment *there is specific acknowledgement to be found about the importance of coordinating policies on trade and the environment. WTO Members have a large measure of autonomy to determine their own policies on the environment (including its relationship with trade), their environmental objectives and the environmental legislation they enact and implement.* So far as concerns the WTO, that autonomy is circumscribed only by the need to respect the requirements of the General Agreement and the other covered agreements" (emphases added, 29–30).

[66] See arts. 1.1 and 2.4 Agreement on Technical Barriers to Trade (TBT Agreement). The TBT Agreement is also in the Annex 1A to the Agreement Establishing the WTO and, therefore, binding on all WTO members. Article 1.1 states that: "*General terms for standardization and procedures for assessment of conformity shall normally have the meaning given to them by definitions adopted within the United Nations system and by international standardizing bodies* taking into account their context and in the light of the object and purpose of this Agreement" and Article 2.4 TBT Agreement states that:

measures taken in pursuit of legitimate objectives – including environmental protection – as the Appellate Body's comments in *US – Gasoline* suggest, this does not negate WTO members' right to autonomously – i.e., unilaterally – take such measures.[67]

(iii)   The SPS Agreement

The Agreement on the Application of Sanitary and Phytosanitary Measures (SPS Agreement)[68] further contemplates the relationship between WTO trade obligations and environmental protection. It acknowledges that it may be appropriate for WTO members to take such trade-restrictive measures that seek to protect the life or health of human, animal, and plant populations within their territory (Article 2.1). The SPS Agreement tightly conditions recourse to justificatory grounds in order to prohibit its discriminatory application (Article 2.3), and to ensure that there is *some* scientific basis to such trade-restrictive measures (Articles 3.2 and 3.3). That said, it affords discretion to members to take measures that seek to offer a higher degree of protection than what may be possible, say, under international standards.[69] In other words, it is for members to determine the level of risk they are willing to assume. In the

---

[67] "*Where technical regulations are required and relevant international standards exist or their completion is imminent, Members shall use them, or the relevant parts of them, as a basis for their technical regulations* except when such international standards or relevant parts would be an ineffective or inappropriate means for the fulfilment of the legitimate objectives pursued, for instance because of fundamental climatic or geographical factors or fundamental technological problems" (emphases added). See also the 1994 Ministerial Decision on Trade and Environment, where it is stated that there should be: "adherence to effective multilateral disciplines to ensure responsiveness of the multilateral trading system to environmental objectives set forth in Agenda 21 and the Rio Declaration, in particular Principle 12." In relation to Principle 12 of the Rio Declaration, it relates to the 1992 UN Conference on Environment and Development, where participants declared their commitment: "Unilateral actions to deal with environmental challenges outside the jurisdiction of the importing country should be avoided. Environmental measures addressing transboundary or global problems should, as far as possible, be based on an international consensus."

[67] Comments as appear in the above note. What is more, in the *US – Shrimp* case, the Appellate Body, while citing a list of WTO documents and other agreements in which a preference for multilateralism is articulated, stated that: "WTO Members are free to adopt their own policies aimed at protecting the environment as long as, in so doing, they fulfill their obligations and respect the rights of other Members under the WTO Agreement" (71, Appellate Body report).

[68] The SPS Agreement is an Annex 1A (to the Agreement Establishing the WTO) multilateral WTO covered agreement, binding on the entire WTO membership.

[69] See Article 3.3 SPS Agreement.

European Communities – Measures Affecting Asbestos and Asbestos-containing Products case,[70] the Appellate Body reiterated the prerogative of WTO members to determine the level of risk[71] so long as this exercise, predictably, is bona fide and not unjustifiably discriminatory in relation to the treatment of trade partners and of imports vis-à-vis domestic products.

(iv)   The TBT Agreement

Another relevant aspect of the WTO system and measures taken in relation to a wide range of policy objectives is the Agreement on Technical Barriers to Trade (TBT Agreement). The general obligation under the TBT Agreement is that technical regulations taken on the part of members in pursuit of certain legitimate policy objectives not be unduly restrictive, discriminatorily applied, or otherwise improperly used. The TBT Agreement does not provide derogation grounds per se in the sense that Article XX of the GATT does. What it does is allude to a non-exhaustive list of legitimate objectives that may be behind a WTO member's technical regulation.[72] That said, in one recital in the preamble, it is made clear that WTO members preserve their rights in relation to, among other things, environmental protection.[73] What is more, the TBT Agreement systemically defers to the SPS Agreement for measures that may more appropriately fall within the scope of the

---

[70] WT/DS135/AB/R.

[71] The Appellate Body stated: "we note that it is undisputed that WTO Members have the right to determine the level of protection of health that they consider appropriate in a given situation" (para.168).

[72] Article 2.2 TBT Agreement reads: "Members shall ensure that technical regulations are not prepared, adopted or applied with a view to or with the effect of creating unnecessary obstacles to international trade. For this purpose, *technical regulations shall not be more trade-restrictive than necessary to fulfil a legitimate objective, taking account of the risks non-fulfilment would create. Such legitimate objectives are, inter alia: national security requirements; the prevention of deceptive practices; protection of human health or safety, animal or plant life or health, or the environment.* In assessing such risks, relevant elements of consideration are, inter alia: available scientific and technical information, related processing technology or intended end-uses of products" (emphasis added).

[73] "Recognizing that *no country should be prevented from taking measures necessary to ensure the quality of its exports, or for the protection of human, animal or plant life or health, of the environment, or for the prevention of deceptive practices, at the levels it considers appropriate,* subject to the requirement that they are not applied in a manner which would constitute a means of arbitrary or unjustifiable discrimination between countries where the same conditions prevail or a disguised restriction on international trade, and are otherwise in accordance with the provisions of this Agreement" (emphasis added).

latter.[74] Gabrielle Marceau considers that the TBT Agreement could potentially be more accommodative than Article XX of the GATT.[75]

(v)   The SCM Agreement

A further pro-environment aspect of the WTO system is contained in the SCM Agreement, which permits, as non-actionable, such subsidies that are directly related to making existing industrial facilities more environmentally friendly.[76] Furthermore, under Article 8 of the SCM Agreement, government subsidies for, say, renewables research could potentially be acceptable so long as certain conditions are met to ensure it is not protectionism under the veneer of environmentalism.[77] Article 8, however, expired in 1999[78] and no new list of non-actionable subsidies appears to have been agreed upon.[79]

(vi)   Discussion

All the above developments point toward a multilateral trade system that has evolved to its current WTO form to better and more meaningfully integrate non-core objectives – e.g., environmental protection – with its core trade liberalization objectives. And toward a system that affords, if

---

[74] See art. 1.5 TBT Agreement.

[75] Marceau persuasively argues that: "TBT Article 2.2 'provides a non-exhaustive, open list of legitimate objectives' and the complaining Member bears the burden of proving that the responding Member's objective is not legitimate. The practical effect of this difference is that some policy objectives that would not be permissible to justify a prima facie GATT breach through GATT Article XX will be admitted under TBT Article 2.2 as legitimate objectives capable of justifying technical regulations that create obstacles to trade. Already in the *US – COOL* dispute [*United States – Certain Country of Origin Labelling (COOL) Requirements* (WT/DS384/DS386)], an objective that would most probably not have come within any of the sub-paragraphs of GATT Article XX the US objective of providing consumers with information on the countries in which the livestock from which the meat they purchase is produced were born, raised, and slaughtered, was considered legitimate for the purposes of TBT Article 2.2" ('The WTO's Efforts to Balance Economic Development,' 311).

[76] See Article 8.2(c) of the SCM Agreement, which lays down the conditions for non-actionable subsidies, including that the environmental protection levels an existing facility seeks to meet be prescribed by law and that the subsidy not exceed 20 percent of the total cost of adaptation.

[77] *Ibid.,* art. 8.2(a) in relation to the conditions that emphasize the need for the benefit of any such subsidy to accrue to the beneficiary during the pre-competitive stage.

[78] *Ibid.,* art. 31 which states that the provisions of art. 8 of the SCM Agreement, among others, shall apply not more than five years after the date that the Agreement on the Establishment of the WTO comes into force.

[79] See Ghosh and Gangania, 'Governing Clean Energy Subsidies,' 39.

not preserves, the necessary policy space for WTO members to continue to pursue a wider range of policy objectives, including linked to environmental protection.

While it is evident from the above that the multilateral trade system has evolved to better accommodate environmental protection objectives, we have also witnessed a significant development in WTO jurisprudence to strengthen the safeguards against abuse.[80] This has happened to ensure that trade-restrictive measures remain bona fide and that the multilateral trade system remains credible. There is a raft of cases relating to Article XX of the GATT derogatory grounds, where recourse to it has been disciplined to ensure that it is not abused. The adjudicative bodies of the WTO have sought to articulate what ought to be the relationship between a trade restrictive measure at issue and the GATT Article XX derogatory grounds cited. While such an exercise would depend on the actual Article XX paragraph(s) that a WTO member chooses to cite,[81] the *chapeau* to Article XX makes clear that such measures that are arbitrary and unjustifiable discrimination between WTO peers and/or disguised restriction on international trade may not be justified under Article XX.

While the purpose of the present chapter is to discuss pro-renewable energy measures and their relationship to WTO rules, we have provided

---

[80] There is a wealth of cases that contain findings that, in effect, regulate reliance on art. XX. For the purposes of this chapter, however, we are not drilling down to such level, as we are mainly concerned with presenting aspects of the WTO system that are amenable to environmental protection objectives. Such cases are aspects of the *US – Gasoline*, which articulates the relationship between the measure and the policy objective it seeks to advance (the *means–ends* relationship); *Brazil – Measures Affecting Imports of Retreaded Tyres* (WT/DS332) and *Korea – Measures Affecting Imports of Fresh, Chilled and Frozen Beef* (WT/DS161/WT/DS169), which are concerned, among other things, with the necessary degree of proximity between the means and ends; and *China – Measures Related to the Exportation of Various Raw Materials* (WT/DS394/WT/DS 395/WT/DS398) in relation to analyzing the relationship between the means and ends to also examine when the measure in question was likely to have any positive impact for the objective cited by a state defending its trade-restrictive measure. See Marceau, 'The WTO's Efforts to Balance Economic Development,' 297–300, for a recent rundown of the relevant cases.

[81] Note that the wording between groups of Article XX grounds (namely, the use of 'necessary,' in paragraphs (a) (b) and (d); 'relating to,' in paragraphs (c) (e) and (g); 'in pursuance of,' in paragraph (h); 'essential,' in paragraph (j); 'for the protection of,' in paragraph (f); and 'involving,' in paragraph (i)) varies, which suggests that its effect on the required degree of relationship between the objective behind the trade-restrictive measure and the measure taken may vary. See the Appellate Body's comments in the *US – Gasoline* dispute, where it refers to the significance of textual nuances (17–19).

section III about environmental protection in relation to WTO rules,[82] as these are issues that we see frequently arising in disputes involving such measures.

3.   The promotion of renewables and the WTO

This section makes reference to disputes at the WTO over subsidies for renewable energy.[83]

(i)   The *Canada Renewables* cases

As we have briefly alluded to earlier, government measures connected to the promotion of renewables may be highly divergent. In the recent WTO disputes in which Canada responded to complaints raised by the EU[84] and Japan[85], the pro-renewables measures that could be teased out of the facts of these cases were: the offer on the part of the provincial government of Ontario of financial support for those who fed into the electricity grid energy that was derived from renewable sources, and the favoring of the local renewables technology manufacturing and/or assembling industries. In relation to the latter, we say this because the offer of financial support[86] to those generating electricity through renewable sources (wind and solar means, in these particular cases) was

---

[82] See www.wto.org/english/tratop_e/envir_e/climate_change_e.pdf for a WTO take on the intersection between the WTO system and climate change. For a more general discussion on the link between trade and climate change, see R. Leal-Arcas, *Climate Change and International Trade*.

[83] On renewable energy, see L. Rubini, 'Ain't Wastin' Time no More: Subsidies for Renewable Energy, the SCM Agreement, Policy Space, and Law Reform,' *Journal of International Economic Law* 15 (2012); R. Howse (2009), 'World Trade Law and Renewable Energy: The Case of Non-Tariff Barriers,' UNCTAD/DITC/TED/2008/5; R. Howse and A. Eliason, 'Domestic and International Strategies to Address Climate Change: An Overview of the WTO Legal Issues,' in Cottier, T. *et al.* (eds.), *International Trade Regulation and the Mitigation of Climate Change* (Cambridge University Press, 2009), 48–93.

[84] *Canada – Measures Relating to the Feed-in Tariff Program* (WT/DS426/AB/R). The Appellate Body report published in tandem with *Canada – Certain Measures Affecting the Renewable Energy Generation Sector* (*Canada – Renewable Energy*) (WT/DS412/AB/R).

[85] *Canada – Certain Measures Affecting the Renewable Energy Generation Sector* (WT/DS412/AB/R). Appellate Body report published in tandem with *Canada – Measures Relating to the Feed-in Tariff Program* (WT/DS426/AB/R).

[86] Let us refer to this as the feed-in tariff and micro feed-in tariff contracts, as well as by the shorter 'FITs and micro-FITs contracts.'

contingent to their drawing a substantial part (50–60 per cent)[87] of the technological components from domestic manufacturers or assemblers. In that sense, these two distinct, yet linked, measures engage different aspects of the WTO. While the former measure may immediately call into question the consistency of a subsidy-like measure with WTO rules and, more broadly, of appropriate levels of government support and market intervention, the latter, most crucially, engages several WTO rules that relate to local content requirements (LCR).

The pleadings and findings in the *Canada – Renewable Energy* and *Canada – Feed-In Tariff Program* disputes brought to the fore a catalogue of matters engaged, including the WTO's core non-discrimination provisions (Articles I and III of the GATT), as well as provisions in the SCM Agreement, the GPA[88], and in the Agreement on Trade-Related Investment Measures (TRIMs Agreement).[89]

The production of electricity through renewable means is less regular than through the combustion of hydrocarbons or through nuclear fission. Energy production through the harnessing of, say, solar and power is contingent upon weather conditions. There can be no steady production outside the vagaries of the weather. What is more, the cost of the necessary infrastructure makes this field of the renewables industry uncompetitive when compared with conventional energy production.[90] The short of it in relation to these cases is that the Appellate Body – having upheld some and having nullified other earlier findings by the Panel – ended up recommending that Canada abandon the LCR component of its measure as it found, among other

---

[87] There are various figures ranging from 25–60 percent. However, from 2012, the range has been 50–60 percent. See joint Appellate Report, 18.

[88] As stated earlier, the GPA is a plurilateral agreement annexed to the Agreement Establishing the WTO. Canada and Japan are parties to the GPA. The EU is listed as a party "with respect to its 28 member states," which suggests it is not a party in its own right. See www.wto.org/english/tratop_e/gproc_e/memobs_e.htm. In any event, the GPA has been cited in the Appellate Body report in side comments 50 and 58.

[89] The TRIMs Agreement is also an Annex 1A (to the Agreement Establishing the WTO) covered multilateral agreement and, therefore, binding on all WTO members.

[90] See para. 5.174 (p. 124) of the Appellate Body joint report, where it is stated that: "In the present disputes, supply-side factors suggest that wind power and solar PV producers of electricity cannot compete with other electricity producers because of differences in cost structures and operating costs and characteristics. Windpower and solar PV technologies have very high capital costs (as compared to other generation technologies), very low operating costs, and fewer, if any, economies of scale. Windpower and solar PV technologies produce electricity intermittently (depending on the availability of wind and sun) and cannot be relied on for base-load and peak-load electricity."

things, this to be an unjustifiable breach of Article III of the GATT in relation to the non-discrimination principle that imported products be treated similarly to *like* domestic products (i.e., the 'national treatment' aspect of the non-discrimination principle that underpins the multilateral trade system).

The complainants had sought to have the measure examined primarily under the specific provisions in the SCM and TRIMs Agreements as they considered these to be the *lex specialis* applicable to the measure in question. Article 3.1(b) of the SCM Agreement expressly places subsidies contingent on LCRs in the prohibited category[91] and paragraph 1(a) in the Annex to the TRIMs Agreement makes clear that trade-related investment measures requiring the use or purchase of domestic products are inconsistent with Article III of the GATT. In that sense, both Agreements condemn LCRs. While no loophole exists in the SCM Agreement for measures containing LCRs, the TRIMs Agreement admits some departure by its reference to Article III of the GATT. We say this because, while Article III of the GATT prohibits discriminatory treatment of imports vis-à-vis domestic products[92] and prohibits the use of LCRs,[93] it permits derogation in relation to government procurement[94] so long as there is no subsequent commercial dimension to this procurement.[95] The Appellate Body rejected the argument that both of these instruments were somehow more specific to the measure and considered that the measure could appropriately be examined under Article III of the GATT. Also, the Appellate Body rejected the view that, when confronted with claims engaging all three instruments (namely, the GATT, the SCM, and

---

[91] Readily we see the prohibition of any subsidy that seeks to boost exports or substitute imports.

[92] Article III:4 GATT.

[93] Article III:1 GATT states that: "contracting parties recognize that internal taxes and other internal charges, and laws, regulations and requirements affecting the internal sale, offering for sale, purchase, transportation, distribution or use of products, and internal quantitative regulations *requiring the mixture, processing or use of products in specified amounts or proportions, should not be applied to imported or domestic products so as to afford protection to domestic production*" (emphasis added).

[94] Article III:8 GATT.

[95] The precise wording in Article III:8 GATT: "(a) The provisions of this Article shall not apply to laws, regulations or requirements governing the procurement by governmental agencies of products purchased for governmental purposes *and not with a view to commercial resale or with a view to use in the production of goods for commercial sale*" (emphasis added).

TRIMs Agreements), it ought take into consideration and examine these in a sequence that promoted the last two.[96]

As one may expect, the Appellate Body report contains several nuanced interpretations over various matters, including over terms from the GATT, the SCM, and TRIMs Agreements and their respective jurisprudence.[97] It is outside the immediate scope of this chapter to review these here. However, what we want to emphasize is that this report *does not* condemn pro-renewables policies or measures per se. What it does condemn are unnecessarily discriminatory practices that favor domestic commercial production. The measure was, ultimately, found to be inconsistent because it unjustifiably discriminated between domestic and imported products (under Article III of the GATT and, as a trade-related investment measure, also under Article 2.1 of the TRIMs Agreement); and not because preferential rates were paid to Ontario's renewable energy producers under their FIT and micro-FIT contacts.[98]

The Panel and the Appellate Body attempted to carry out an analysis under the SCM Agreement. The Appellate Body upheld the Panel's earlier finding that the payment of higher rates for renewables-derived electricity under the FIT and micro-FIT contracts had been a 'purchase of goods' for the purposes of Article 1.1(a)(1)(iii) of the SCM Agreement. However, in relation to satisfying the other aspect that a subsidy exists – namely, that there is a 'benefit' that may accrue to another (as per Article 1.1(b) of the SCM Agreement) – the Appellate Body was unable to carry out an assessment of 'benefit,' given, in this case, the complexities of establishing what is the likely market benchmark that ought to be used to assess what the 'benefit' had been in that particular case. Also, in

---

[96] See 84, para. 5.5 of the Appellate Body joint report, where it stated that: "Both the national treatment obligations in Article III:4 of the GATT 1994 and the TRIMs Agreement, and the disciplines in Article 3.1(b) of the SCM Agreement, are cumulative obligations. Article III:4 of the GATT 1994 and the TRIMs Agreement, as well as Article 3.1(b) of the SCM Agreement, prohibit the use of local content requirements in certain circumstances. These provisions address discriminatory conduct. We see nothing in these provisions to indicate that there is an obligatory sequence of analysis to be followed when claims are made under Article III:4 of the GATT 1994 and the TRIMs Agreement, on the one hand, and Article 3.1(b) of the SCM Agreement, on the other hand."

[97] Issues examined were, among other things, the extent to which the measure amounted to government purchases, whether it had been government purposes, and what the conditions were which governed the government procurement. Note: there was recourse to the French and Spanish version of the text of GATT 1994 to establish the meaning of 'purposes.'

[98] See 103, para. 5.84 of the Appellate Body joint report.

assessing what may have been the 'subsidy' and its 'benefit,' the parties where concerned with those who benefited from the higher tariffs under the FIT and micro-FIT contracts – that is to say, the renewable energy producers – rather than the domestic producers and/or assemblers of the renewables technology who, despite their being third parties, clearly benefited under the LCRs of the FIT and micro-FIT contracts vis-à-vis foreign producers and/or assemblers of such technologies. Eventually, there were sufficient grounds to find against Canada under Article III of the GATT.

Finally, the political reasons behind Canada's insistence to defend the LCR aspect of its measure – namely, regional job creation – is a trade-restrictive 'externality' for the purposes of WTO rules that cannot be accommodated when it exceeds the limits afforded to WTO members under, among others, Article XX of the GATT, Article III:8 of the GATT, and Article 8 of the SCM Agreement. However, the objectives of job creation and of environmental protection are inherently different and, while the multilateral trade system has evolved to better accommodate environmental protection, this is not so in relation to job creation.

(ii)   Other WTO cases connected to renewable energy[99]

China – Wind Power[100]   In December 2010, the USA requested consultations with China concerning certain measures it alleged benefited wind-power technology manufacturers in China. The USA contended, among other things, that such measures appeared to be contingent on the use of domestically produced goods and, therefore, inconsistent with Article 3 of the SCM Agreement. The USA argued that, as these measures appear to be subsidies that had not been notified to the WTO, they also breached, among others, Article XVI of the GATT regarding subsidies and Article 25 of the SCM Agreement regarding the duty to notify. There has been no further progress published so far.[101]

US – Countervailing Measures (China)[102]   In May 2012, China requested consultations with the USA concerning countervailing duties that the USA was levying on certain Chinese products, including

---

[99] This section refers to other renewable energy-related complaints that have engaged the WTO dispute settlement processes; however, not all cases necessarily resulted in determinations.

[100] WT/DS419.

[101] See www.wto.org/english/tratop_e/dispu_e/cases_e/ds419_e.htm.   [102] WT/DS437.

renewable energy technologies, on the basis that they are state-owned enterprise products with subsidized inputs on the part of the Chinese government. China also challenged the US Department of Commerce's presumption that enterprises with majority government ownership ought to be treated as *public bodies* for the purposes of WTO rules.[103] China claimed that the measures in question infringed the following provisions: Article VI of the GATT; Articles 1, 2, 11, 12, and 14 of the SCM Agreement; and Article 15 of the Protocol of Accession of China to the WTO. A panel was established in September 2012 and its composition was determined in November 2012. At the time of writing this chapter, the panel was expected to issue its report by January 2014.[104]

EU and a Member State – Importation of Biodiesels[105]   In August 2012, Argentina requested consultations with the EU and Spain concerning certain measures affecting biofuel imports into the EU and how related data collection practices discriminated against certain biofuels imports. Argentina claimed the measure was inconsistent with, among others, Articles III and XI of the GATT as well as Article 2 of the TRIMs Agreement. In December 2012, Argentina requested a panel be established, which was then deferred by the DSB. No further progress has been published so far.[106]

US – Countervailing and Anti-Dumping Measures (China)[107]   In September 2012, China requested consultations with the USA in relation to US measures that affected, among other Chinese exports, wind-power technologies. These measures related to the following: US legislation that permitted the application of countervailing measures (i.e., a type of trade-balancing remedy permissible, subject to conditions, under WTO law) to tradables from 'non-market' economies; the countervailing duties pursuant to that legislation; and to countermeasures taken by the USA in

---

[103] This is despite an earlier Appellate Body determination in a case brought by China against the USA, where the Appellate Body reversed the Panel's interpretation of the term 'public body,' in art. 1.1(a)(1) SCM Agreement and found that a public body is an entity that possesses, exercises, or is vested with, governmental authority, and where it found that the USA had acted inconsistently with arts. 1.1(a)(1), 10, and 32.1 of the SCM Agreement, in finding that certain state-owned enterprises constituted public bodies. See *United States – Definitive Anti-Dumping and Countervailing Duties on Certain Products from China* (WT/DS379).

[104] See www.wto.org/english/tratop_e/dispu_e/cases_e/ds437_e.htm   [105] WT/DS443.
[106] See www.wto.org/english/tratop_e/dispu_e/cases_e/ds443_e.htm   [107] WT/DS449.

relation to its subjective findings of dumping practices on the part of China. China claimed that the measures in question are inconsistent with the following provisions: Articles 10, 15, 19, 21, and 32 of the SCM Agreement; Articles VI and X of the GATT; and Article 9 of the Anti-Dumping Agreement (ADA).[108] The DSB established a panel in December 2012, which the WTO Director-General composed in March 2013. No further progress has been publicized.[109]

EU and Certain Member States – Renewable Energy Measures[110]   In November 2012, China requested consultations with the EU, Greece, and Italy in relation to certain measures, including domestic content restrictions that affect the renewable energy generation sector relating to the feed-in tariff (FIT) programs of EU member states, including Italy and Greece. China cited ten separate pieces of EU and member state legislation that it considered affected its trade interests. Among the WTO rules cited by China are the following: Articles I and III of the GATT; Article 3 of the SCM Agreement; and Article 2 of the TRIMs Agreement. There has been no reported progress since November 2012.[111]

India – Solar Cells Measures[112]   In February 2013, the USA requested consultations with India in relation to certain measures linked to renewable energy generation in India that contained a local content requirement for solar energy technologies. On the face of it, this measure would injure *like* imports as it encouraged use of domestic components. The USA claims that this is inconsistent with: Article III of the GATT; Article 2 of the TRIMs Agreement; Articles 3, 6, and 25 of the SCM Agreement, and that it directly or indirectly nullifies or impairs the benefits that accrue to the USA due to its and to India's WTO membership. There has been no publicized progress to date.

EU and Certain Member States – Importation and Marketing of Biodiesel and Supporting the Biodiesel Industry Measures[113]   In May 2013, Argentina requested consultations with the EU and its member states

---

[108] The ADA is officially listed as the Agreement on Implementation of Article VI of the GATT 1994 and is an Annex 1A (to the Agreement Establishing the WTO) multilateral agreement binding on all WTO members.
[109] See www.wto.org/english/tratop_e/dispu_e/cases_e/ds449_e.htm   [110] WT/DS452.
[111] See www.wto.org/english/tratop_e/dispu_e/cases_e/ds452_e.htm
[112] WT/DS456.   [113] WT/459.

regarding certain measures that it deemed to affect Argentinian biofuels imports and their marketing within the EU. Argentina's request relates to two types of EU and member state measures: (a) measures to promote the use of renewable energy and to introduce a mechanism to control and reduce GHG emissions; and (b) measures to establish support schemes for the biodiesel sector. Argentina considers that the measures in question are inconsistent with, among others: Articles I and III of the GATT; Articles 1, 2, 3, 5, and 6 of the SCM Agreement; Article 2 of the TRIMs Agreement; and Articles 2 and 5 of the TBT Agreement. Argentina referred to the TBT Agreement, which clearly expresses a preference for multilateralism[114] in that any technical barriers to trade – in this case, arguably, the EU's definition of 'sustainable'– be based on international standards and not be more restrictive than necessary in addressing some legitimate objective(s) contemplated by the TBT Agreement.[115]

Argentina contests EU measures, and member state implementation legislation pertinent to these, that define as 'sustainable' such energy sources that reduce GHG emissions by at least 35 per cent when compared to fossil fuels. Its soya-related biofuels products reduce emissions by no more than 31 per cent, thus disqualifying for the EU definition. What is more, Argentina further challenges an EU measure requiring that certain fossil-fuel distributors also make available *sustainable* fuel through their distribution operations, given that its biofuels would be excluded. Argentina contends that this results in treatment less favorable for its own products. No further progress has been published.[116]

Recurring issues in renewables-related complaints   An overview of the above complaints suggests that the commonest issue complainants raise is that some LCR aspect of a measure has been harmful to their industries and is unjustified under WTO rules. Other issues appear to be whether countermeasures taken to address dumping concerns have been justified in the circumstances, and whether some technical barrier exits – such as a definition employed by a WTO member – that leads to less favorable treatment for imports. As we have stated, the above listed disputes, for the most part, are at the early stages of the dispute resolution process. However, there is WTO jurisprudence that, although

---

[114] See the interplay of arts. 1.1 and 2.4 TBT Agreement, discussed earlier in this chapter.
[115] Art. 2.2 TBT Agreement, discussed earlier in this chapter.
[116] www.wto.org/english/tratop_e/dispu_e/cases_e/ds459_e.htm

not directly concerned with renewables, has implications for renewables within the WTO.

The issues that arise in the list of complaints above often hinge on whether *like* products are treated even-handedly. Articles III:2 and III:4 of the GATT refer to the obligation to treat *like* products in a non-discriminatory manner. Therefore, the first step in assessing whether less favorable treatment indeed exists is itself complicated by the need to establish that there is sufficient *likeness* between the products for an allegation to be legally relevant. What establishes *likeness* is determined on a case-by-case basis. While the competitive relationship between the products in question is clearly material to a determination of *likeness*, it is not the sole determinant, nor are all products in a strong competitive relationship with one another necessarily *like* products under the WTO rules.[117]

Likeness could potentially depend on a wide range of issues, including the physical characteristics of the products, end uses, consumer habits, and sensibilities,[118] with the possibility that other factors may, in certain cases, also be relevant for establishing whether there is *likeness*. Once likeness has been established, the question is to then establish whether imports have been treated less favorably than domestic products.[119] In that sense, Article III of the GATT is aimed at curing against protectionism[120] and, therefore, determinations of *likeness* cannot be restricted to an inflexible array of issues to be taken into consideration. *Likeness* considerations could be relevant to, say, complaints alleging that electricity produced through renewable means is treated more favorably than other products that exist in a competitive relationship and, on a number of parameters – including substitutability, physical likeness, and others – are sufficiently *alike*.

Potentially, an importer of electricity may argue that the higher tariffs paid to, or preferential price levels set by government for, renewable-

[117] See 37, para. 99 of the Appellate Body Report, *European Communities – Measures Affecting Asbestos and Asbestos-Containing Products*, WT/DS135/AB/R, adopted 5 April 2001.

[118] For instance, consumer sensibilities around the use of asbestos were held to be sufficiently material in establishing likeness in *EC – Asbestos* (WT/DS135/AB/R).

[119] See the report by the United Nations Conference on Trade and Development, World Trade Law and Renewable Energy: The Case of Non-Tariff Barriers, New York and Geneva, 2009, for a fuller analysis on this two-step test in the relevant WTO jurisprudence (at 5–7).

[120] See Appellate Body report, *Japan – Taxation on Alcoholic Beverages* (WT/DS8/AB/R), 16.

energy domestic producers breach Article III, GATT. Here there is a series of questions that would have to be addressed. For instance, are the electricity imports, which are alleged to be treated less favorably, *like* products for the purposes of Article III of the GATT? A determination of *likeness* could foreseeably focus on how this electricity has been produced. While a single unit of electricity is identical to any other unit of electricity – and, therefore, while the physical aspects of electricity may make electricity derived from different energy sources (e.g., conventional (fossil fuel), nuclear, or renewables) a *like* product – their production method may well make these sufficiently *unlike*.[121]

It is worth noting that, in the Canada cases, the Appellate Body – albeit for the purposes of assessing what might be the appropriate market benchmark for an assessment of 'benefit' under Article 1.1(b) of the SCM Agreement – contemplated the differences between the electricity generation industries drawing from conventional sources and those drawing from renewables as being rather distinct.[122] In that respect, less favorable treatment towards electricity produced by conventional or nuclear means and that of electricity produced by renewables may be entirely justified under WTO rules if they are determined to be *unlike, so long as* domestically produced electricity derived by conventional or nuclear means is also treated in an even-handed manner. Otherwise, the complaint by foreign electricity producers could be structured on the less favorable treatment accorded to those *like* products – namely,

---

[121] UNCTAD, World Trade Law and Renewable Energy: The Case of Non-Tariff Barriers, 2009, where it is stated that: "Much of the debate as about how this analysis might be done revolves around the controversy over the so-called 'product/process distinction,' the notion that the GATT does not permit differential treatment of products based on their method of production as opposed to their properties as products for consumption. Without rehashing this controversy here, we note to begin with that the approach to 'likeness' and 'directly competitive and substitutable' articulated by the Appellate Body does not predetermine a conclusion one way or another concerning methods of production. The AB has emphasized (Japan – Alcohol and EC – Asbestos) that factors other than those in the Border Tax Adjustment working party may, in an appropriate case, be dispositive of whether two products are 'like' or 'unlike.' *The Appellate Body has also emphasized the need for the adjudicator to examine all relevant factors in a given case and context, and to consider all the evidence pointing either in the direction of a finding of 'likeness' or otherwise. There is simply nothing in the jurisprudence that would justify a per se exclusion of production methods from the analysis of 'likeness' or 'directly competitive or substitutable' nor, on the other hand, is there anything to suggest that productions methods could be, on their own, dispositive of a finding of 'unlikeness' or a lack of direct competitiveness or substitutability*" (3, emphasis added).

[122] See Appellate Body joint report, 124, para. 5.174.

imported electricity produced by conventional or nuclear means vis-à-vis domestically produced electricity produced by conventional or nuclear means, given that discriminatory treatment could then be said to exist between *like* products.

Other issues that appear repeatedly in the renewables-related complaints we have listed earlier relate to whether a particular measure actually amounts to a prohibited or otherwise actionable subsidy within the context of the SCM Agreement. Again, making such a determination relies on a thorough review of all relevant aspects of a measure. Does the measure involve some sort of material support on the part of a government to its domestic industry in a manner that is trade distortive? In that sense, "government," or "public body" (or even a "private body" where it is clear or imputed that it exercises some government-like functions)[123] and "subsidy" have a specific meaning within the SCM Agreement; there must be some sort of "financial contribution"[124] *or* price or income support;[125] it must confer a "benefit" on the recipient;[126] and, unless it involves a subsidy that on its face is prohibited,[127] in order for it to be actionable, it would be necessary to establish that the subsidy is "specific,"[128] that it has "adverse effects"[129] to the trade interests of another WTO member, and that the level of support is above the permissible limits of Article 8 of the SCM Agreement.

Findings as to whether the above elements are present in a measure that is the subject of a complaint are not without their complexities. There would be little doubt that a measure aimed at the development of the renewables industries – e.g., by providing interest-free or low-interest loans to the domestic renewable energy technology industry – would be a clear case of a financial contribution that confers a benefit and that is specific to a particular industry. It is less clear on first inspection whether

---

[123] See art. 1.1(a)(1)(i) and (iii) of the SCM Agreement.   [124] *Ibid.*, art. 1.1(a)(1).
[125] *Ibid.*, art. 1.1(a)(2). In relation to findings as to whether a financial contribution exists, it is not necessary for a state to be financially burdened or forego, say, tax income, given that the material support it gives may be indirect and, at the same time, fulfill the requirement of Article 1 of the SCM Agreement. See A. Jerjian, 'The Feed-in Tariff Controversy: Renewable Energy Challenges in WTO Law,' for a review of the relevant WTO jurisprudence relating to art. 1 SCM Agreement (5–8), www.sielnet.org/Resources/Documents/SIEL%20CUP%202012%20highly%20comended%20%20-%20article%20by%20Jerjian.doc
[126] Art. 1.1(b) of the SCM Agreement.
[127] e.g. such subsidies designed to boost export performance or import substitution as per Article 3 of the SCM Agreement.
[128] *Ibid.*, art. 2.   [129] *Ibid.*, art. 5.

it would be inconsistent with WTO rules. While such a measure would appear less likely, on the face of it, to amount to a prohibited subsidy aimed at export stimulation or import substitution per se, it is likely to be actionable under Article 5 of the SCM Agreement, should it have adverse effects for the trade interests of other WTO members; and should the level of support conferred by it be outside the permissible limits stipulated in Article 8 of the SCM Agreement.

We acknowledge that there may be various measures connected to the promotion of renewables that may infringe WTO rules; not only such measures that are linked to feed-in tariff renewables schemes. However, the relationship between FIT schemes and WTO rules seems to have attracted a fair amount of scholarly attention and scrutiny.[130] The purpose of this chapter has been to present sufficient high-level background in relation to environmental protection and the WTO system in which to then situate the relationship between renewables promotion and the WTO system. The rules and jurisprudence appear to suggest that bona fide non-discriminatory measures linked to environmental protection objectives – including the promotion of renewable energy – are not actually blocked or otherwise discouraged within the multilateral trade system, particularly since the advent of the WTO.

IV. Conclusion

The main barriers to the scaling-up and proliferation of renewables relate to the infrastructural costs that make energy production uncompetitive when compared with energy production based on conventional energy sources. This is a barrier that is certainly compounded by the long-standing subsidization of conventional energy sources. What is more, conventional energy source-related subsidies – amounting to up to 90 per cent of energy subsidies – which, incidentally, negatively impact the ecosystem, are actually tolerated within the WTO system. Predictably, these are unlikely to be addressed in WTO litigation, given that these are popular measures among states, but also because demand for

---

[130] See among others, A. Jerjian, 'The Feed-in Tariff Controversy: Renewable Energy Challenges in WTO Law.' Jerjian carries out an extensive analysis of how FIT schemes for renewables engage WTO rules. See also M. Wilke, 'Feed-in Tariffs for Renewable Energy and WTO Subsidy Rules: An Initial Legal Review,' Trade and Sustainable Energy Series, Issue Paper No. 4, International Centre for Trade and Sustainable Development (2011).

conventional energy sources exists to a large extent due to the distortive effects of such subsidization. For instance, if there were fewer conventional energy subsidies, at best, renewable energy may have been more competitive and therefore more viable; however, at worst, perhaps a larger part of the human population would have been denied access to affordable energy and would have been condemned to pre-modern standards of life.[131]

Our conclusion is that the main obstacles to the scale-up and take-up of renewable energy are not normative/institutional per se. Rather, they are economic. The only systemic 'obstacle' that the WTO presents is its requirements that measures not be disguised mercantilism and that they be applied even-handedly. The WTO system, as it stands, could, and does, accommodate bona fide non-discriminatory measures that promote the scale-up and take-up of renewable energy. After all, we see that it tolerates conventional energy subsidies, which certainly are not predicated on the general exceptions to WTO rules or other dispensations, as these appear in the covered agreements.

Having said that, we acknowledge that confusion about how the WTO system may accommodate measures aimed at the promotion of renewable energy could strengthen the case for a separate specific agreement. However, such an agreement is likely to contain clarifications of, or even replicate the policy space that we believe currently exists within, the existing normative framework. As such, we believe it may be an unnecessary legislative step when its objectives (e.g., legal certainty) could be addressed by the adoption of an explanatory note containing clarificatory guidelines issued by the WTO Ministerial Conference[132] under its existing mandate and powers.[133] Such a note could contain an illustrative

---

[131] Almost 2 billion people currently go without modern forms of energy such as electricity. That is nearly more than 1 in 4 people globally. See the World Bank Report, *Meeting the Challenge for Rural Energy and Development for Two Billion People*, 3, http://siteresources.worldbank.org/INTENERGY/Resources/Rural_Energy_Development_Paper_Improving_Energy_Supplies.pdf. Note that this report draws from a previous World Bank report (No. 16002, published September 30, 1996) entitled *Rural Energy and Development: Improving Energy Supplies for Two Billion People*, vol. I, http://go.worldbank.org/G6ZXYV3ER0

[132] Art. IV.1 Agreement Establishing the WTO.

[133] *Ibid.*, arts. III, IV, IX, and X, which relate to the competences of the Ministerial Conference. The Ministerial Conference may either consensually or on the basis of a three-fourths majority – whichever may be required under the specific requirements of these provisions – adopt amendments to the agreements or interpretations of terms within the agreements.

index/table with a series of examples of pro-renewables measures and their classification as *WTO consistent* or *inconsistent*, according to the policy motivation behind these (given that there may be a variety of policy objectives hidden behind these), their adverse effects, and the specific WTO rules that are engaged.[134]

As we have attempted to outline in this chapter, the policy space appears to be preserved for WTO members to take measures to support environmental goals, including the promotion of renewables. This is particularly the case in the WTO era. Rather than finding fault with the existing normative framework of the multilateral trade system in relation to the further development and proliferation of renewables, we believe the obstacles to the promotion of renewables do not flow from some normative failure, but from the economics that underlie energy.

---

[134] In fact, an excellent example, albeit one that considers these from a subsidies point of view, appears in Ghosh and Gangania 'Governing Clean Energy Subsidies: What, Why and How Legal?,' 41.

PART V

Concluding observations

20

Conclusion: beyond fragmentation?

C. L. LIM AND BRYAN MERCURIO

In this volume, we have surveyed many of the diverse aspects of the evolution of the Bretton Woods system in the aftermath of two crises. We undertook this survey in order to gain greater insight and understanding into the constitutional, legislative, and regulatory aspects of the contemporary international economic order. Despite discussion of specific incidents, disputes, and the contribution of a number of different international economic dispute resolution mechanisms to the jurisprudence and body of case law of international economic law, our theoretical focus has been on fragmentation. Specifically, the fragmentation of norms, authority, and modalities of rule creation in the contemporary globalized economy.

I. Fragmentation of norms, authority, and modalities of rule and regime creation

1. The first sense of 'fragmentation': norm fragmentation

(i) Variable geometry, norm fragmentation, and varying treaty obligations

Sometimes different laws apply. One of the recurring themes underlying the focus of the book has been the fragmentation of norms and variable geometry between and among the differing treaty obligations. This has been highlighted most obviously in the chapters on investment law. There, we have seen how different norms – that is, substantive rules – apply to investment-related activities and bilateral relationships due to the absence of a unifying, global treaty in the field of investment regulation. Instead, a *mélange* of over 3,000 treaties regulate the investment field and while the guiding principles of most of these agreements are harmonized, the text and therefore the substantive obligations and operation of the agreements differ widely. International investment law is thus very much a fragmented regime. Another example of norm fragmentation is the field of intellectual property protection. As illustrated by Bryan Mercurio's chapter, FTAs including substantive intellectual property protection contain variable intellectual property commitments. While some agreements go far beyond the minimum standards of the TRIPS Agreement, both in terms of substance and procedure, others do little more than to restate the commitments and obligations of the TRIPS Agreement. The controversy surrounding the ACTA, a treaty negotiated outside the confines of the WTO or any other existing international organization, further underscores the fragmented norms of international intellectual property.

These examples illustrate the first, simple sense in which fragmentation features in international economic law – the variable geometry provided by varying treaty regulation of common activities due to the diversity of treaty commitments entered into by different states and economies. Broken down into a simple example – because the treaty commitments of Singapore and Switzerland in these and other fields vary, their rights and obligations are different from one treaty to the next.

(ii)   Janus-faced issues and concepts, and norm fragmentation

A second variant of this sense of fragmentation – i.e. norm fragmentation – looks not to the different treaties entered into by sovereigns within a particular area of economic activity, but to the Janus-faced nature of some disputes where the dispute transcends and crosses from one regulatory area characterized by its own distinct body of rules to another. In this regard, the issues surveyed in this book with this feature include allegations of Chinese currency manipulation, which is addressed by C. L. Lim (Chapter 6), the dispute over plain cigarette packaging of tobacco products which is the subject of the chapter by Andrew Mitchell, Tania Voon, and James Munro (Chapter 16), and Greek debt restructuring in Julien Chaisse's chapter (Chapter 13). This is a species of norm fragmentation, since different bodies of rules apply to the same issue because the issue in question is multifaceted. The currency issue involves both the application of global trade and currency rules; the plain packaging issue involves investment, intellectual property, and trade treaty rules; while the Greek debt issue involves the concurrent application of investment and debt workout norms (specifically the use of collective action clauses – CACs) in the absence of a global insolvency regime. This is not to say that the phenomenon is entirely novel – Dr F. A. Mann observed in a seminal article that intellectual property loans and sales could fall within an expansive treaty definition of investment.[1] In recent times, it is this form of fragmentation which has exercised the imagination of public international lawyers.[2] The examples provided in this book indicate that indeed such thinking in recent years has been well worth the time and effort.

A more subtle example of this variant of norm fragmentation is the current absence of a safeguard mechanism in the regulation of services trade, compared to global and indeed regional rules governing the international trade in goods. Shin-yi Peng's chapter contains, in this regard, a proposal which – not unlike the issues of Chinese currency or cigarette plain packaging – involves the application, or proposed application of a trans-substantive, or at least cross-sectoral norm (Chapter 10). The regulation of international trade in goods and services are correctly treated as the regulation of different 'sectors'. This makes good sense, as the attributes of goods and services trade cannot be assumed to be similar. Take for instance the investment dimension to the provision of services through commercial presence. We would certainly think twice before halting the trading permission granted to a foreign bank which has already established a commercial presence.

(iii)   Regionalism and norm fragmentation

A third variant of norm fragmentation demonstrates a concurrence of global and regional regulation – i.e. the phenomenon of regionalism in international politics.[3] What is clear, for example from Emilios Avgouleas and Douglas Arner's joint chapter, is that the present European debt crisis has stimulated regime innovation at the European (regional) level which competes with and simultaneously complements the IMF's long-standing function as a lender of last resort (Chapter 4). The more well-known example which has been the subject of a tremendous volume of literature, and is therefore not subjected to further treatment in this volume, has to do with the proliferation of preferential trade agreements

---

[1] F. A. Mann, 'British Treaties for the Promotion and Protection of Investments,' BYIL 50 (1982), 241.

[2] See J. Pauwelyn, *Conflict of Norms in Public International Law: How WTO Law Relates to Other Rules of International Law* (Cambridge University Press, 2003); UN Doc. A/CN.4/ L.682, 13 April 2006, 19.

[3] S. Breslin and R. Higgott, 'Studying Regions: Learning from the Old, Constructing the New,' *New Political Economy* 5 (2000), 333.

at the regional level which compete with the functions of global trade regulation by the WTO, with attendant uncertain effects.[4]

(iv)   Parallel treaty and customary rules

A final variant of norm fragmentation surveyed here deals with one of the longest-standing problems of norm fragmentation known to public international law – parallel treaty and customary rules.[5] In the international economic law context, the problem is best known in the field of international investment law. It concerns the concurrent application of customary international law and treaty law in imposing, for example, the minimum standard of treatment. Many tribunals have grappled with the interrelationship of such concurrent application, with the tribunal in *Sempra* v. *Argentina* even famously pronouncing that 'international law is not fragmented'.[6] However, the study of countermeasures in the chapter by Martins Paparinskis shows that such fragmentation occurs

---

[4] J. Bhagwati, *Termites in the Trading System: How Preferential Agreements Undermine Free Trade* (New York: Oxford University Press, 2008); S. Lester and B. Mercurio, *Bilateral and Regional Trade Agreements: Commentary and Analysis* (Cambridge University Press, 2009); F. M. Abbott, 'A New Dominant Species Emerges: Is Bilateralism a Threat?,' *J. Int'l Econ L.* 10 (2007), 571; L. Trakman, 'The Proliferation of FTAs: Bane or Beauty?,' *J. World Trade* 42 (2008), 367. See also, criticism of preferential trade agreements in the Sutherland Commission Report and the Warwick Commission Report; P. D. Sutherland, 'Leadership and Vision: Some Lessons From the Uruguay Round', in M. E. Janow, V. Donaldson and A. Yanovich (eds.), *The WTO: Governance, Dispute Settlement, and Developing Countries* (New York: Juris Publishing, 2008), 54–5; Report of the First Warwick Commission, 'The Multilateral Trade Regime: Which Way Forward' (University of Warwick, 2007).

[5] Parallel custom may emerge alongside a treaty provision, either because the treaty (a) codifies a pre-existing customary rule, or (b) the treaty negotiations supply state practice proving the emergence of a new customary rule, or (c) subsequent practice of non-treaty parties nonetheless 'look to' a treaty rule as the basis for guiding their subsequent practice. The issue was dealt with by the ICJ in the *North Sea Continental Shelf Cases* (*FRG* v. *Denmark*; *FRG* v. *Netherlands*), Merits (1969) ICJ Rep. 3, paras. 70–4; *Nicaragua Case* (*Nicaragua* v. *USA*), Merits (1986) ICJ Rep. 14, paras. 175–86.

[6] ICSID Case No. ARB/02/16, 28 September 2007, para. 378. Like the Tribunal in *Enron*, the tribunal in *Sempra* considered – at para. 302 – that the treaty fair and equitable treatment rule under the relevant bilateral investment treaty could be more precise, specific, less generic and spelled out compared to its customary international law equivalent; see also *Enron* v. *Argentina*, ICSID Case No. ARB/01/3, 22 May 2007, para. 258. Other tribunals have found that the customary international law rule could however set a 'floor' to the treaty standard of protection; see *Azurix* v. *Argentina*, ICSID Case No. ARB/01/12, 14 July 2006, para. 361 (but is substantially similar to the treaty rule); *Vivendi* v. *Argentina* ('*Vivendi II*'), ICSID Case No. ARB 97/3, 20 August 2007. Other tribunals have similarly echoed the tribunal in *Azurix*, stating that in many cases the relevant treaty and customary rules were substantially similar.

by examining a combination of the third and fourth senses of norm fragmentation – i.e. regionalism and the phenomenon of parallel customary and treaty rules (Chapter 11).

II. Authority fragmentation: the growth of 'trans-substantive' authority fragmentation in international economic law

Closely allied to norm fragmentation is the idea of fragmented authority.[7] Different international institutions coexist on the global plane.

Where each body of norms operates within its own institutionalized setting or through discrete regimes which constitute sites of formal treaty authority, questions of competing jurisdictional competence can arise. With a dearth of rules which properly allocate jurisdictional competence between diverse institutions and regimes, difficulties emerge: for example, where tribunals operating under one institution or treaty regime compete jurisdictionally with other tribunals outside that institution or formal treaty regime.

This volume did not address one of the most common examples of such phenomena, that being the conflict of jurisdiction between regional dispute settlement regimes under preferential trade agreements and the WTO.[8] This involves a conflict of jurisdiction between treaty authorities typically handling the same subject matter; namely, 'overlapping' WTO and preferential agreement obligations. Again, with a substantial body of literature already having been generated on this topic we focused attention on less obvious examples of authority fragmentation between different institutions handling the sort of legal subject matter which transcends one regulatory area, and crosses into another.[9]

---

[7] T. Broude and Y. Shany, *The Shifting Allocation of Authority in International Law* (Oxford: Hart, 2008).

[8] See e.g. H. Gao and C. L. Lim, 'Saving the WTO from the Risk of Irrelevance', *Journal of International Economic Law* 11 (2008), 899; G. Marceau and J. Wyatt, 'Dispute Settlement Regimes Intermingled: Regional Trade Agreements and the WTO', *Journal of Dispute Settlement* 1 (2010), 67; C. L. Lim and H. Gao, 'Competing WTO and RTA Jurisdictional Claims', in T. Broude, M. Busch, and A. Porges (eds.), *The Politics of International Economic Law* (Cambridge University Press, 2011).

[9] In a sense, this is even more well known than WTO–PTA jurisdictional disputes, at least among international lawyers. See e.g. C. L. Lim, 'Free Trade Agreements in Asia and Some Common Legal Problems', in Y. Taniguchi, A. Yanovich, and J. Bohanes (eds.), *The WTO in the Twenty-First Century: Dispute Settlement, Negotiations, and Regionalism in Asia* (Cambridge University Press, 2007), 434, at 452ff.

We see this 'trans-substantive' version of authority fragmentation as a potent issue in international economic law. Again, the currency problem is illustrative of the potentially competing authority of the WTO and IMF. Where two or more institutions or treaty regimes exist – such as between the WTO and IMF, or the WTO Dispute Settlement System (WTO DSS) and a PTA dispute settlement system – jurisdictional competition and conflict may be easily discernible.

We are also seeing this situation play out in the case involving cigarette plain packaging, with bilateral investment treaties granting authority to ICSID or to ad hoc tribunals to deal with investor-state disputes which will likely compete (or, more generously, complement) the ongoing trade dispute settlement cases filed under the WTO DSS. Andrew Mitchell, Tania Voon, and James Munro discuss this issue in some detail in Chapter 16.

Moreover, the phenomenon also exists in the interrelationship between climate change initiatives, for example in the case of the EU's attempt to reduce the carbon footprint of private air carriers, and the existing international civil aviation regime. This issue is explored in Chapter 18 by Lorand Bartels. Likewise, the scenario may play out in relation to specific investments in agricultural lands in developing countries, as explored by Antoine Martin in Chapter 15.

Beyond these, perhaps the most basic example of jurisdictional fragmentation is that between sovereign competing authorities where international regulation is thin or absent. An example in this regard is provided by Elisabetta Cervone (Chapter 3) – differential regulation of credit rating agencies in the USA and the EU. At its most basic level, when international economic law ceases to regulate all that exists is divergent, sovereign regulation. The example is imperfect (banking regulation may have been a better example) to the extent that the EU is not a sovereign state but a supranational organization, but it is an especially apt example in demonstrating the continued influence of the USA and Europe in producing regulatory models for potential adaptation on an international plane.

A more complex subject is the Greek sovereign debt dispute, discussed by Chaisse (Chapter 13). In this case, there is no competing authority to the regulation of investment under bilateral investment treaties (the mechanics and terms of a European bailout not being directly connected to the main features of the dispute itself). The real dispute has to do with the introduction of CACs – being a private contractual term to facilitate a debt workout[10] – by way of Greek legislation. It is at one level, a simple case of legislation which allegedly violates Greek investment treaty commitments. But the case also has to do with the different modes for creating rules of investment law, and the rules which would apply to sovereign debt restructurings. The former uses treaties, while the latter uses a contractual term which in the Greek case could be introduced by Greek legislation because the bonds in question are governed by the choice of Greek law. Here is a different sense of fragmentation altogether – involving fragmented modes of rule creation. At its core, however, it is related to a well-known type of problem, albeit in a new guise – the 'internationalization' of bond contracts expressly governed by Greek law.[11]

As we shall see, below, authority fragmentation is an essential component in understanding fragmentation. Norm fragmentation alone hardly explains how international actors behave, and are behaving, including their behaviour in making and organizing the contemporary norms of the international economic order.

III.   Fragmented modalities of rule/law creation

We also need to keep in mind fragmented modalities of international lawmaking, and the diverse sources of both 'hard' and 'soft' international law. Fragmented modalities of law creation have to do with different regimes electing different sources and methods of formal lawmaking. Rolf Weber and Ross Buckley address this aspect (in Chapter 2 and

---

[10] Otherwise known as majority amendment clauses, which have been in common use for bonds governed by New York law since 2003; P. Bedford, A. Penalver, and C. Salmon, 'Resolving Sovereign Debt Crises: The Market Based Approach and the Role of the IMF', *Financial Stability Review* (June 2005), 102.

[11] The difficulty of classifying the Greek issue lies in the fact that true 'internationalization' does not even require the choice of international law, or some more nebulous definition (e.g. 'general principles of law') in contracts in order to resist governance by host state law (*Revere Copper* v. *OPIC* (1978) 17 ILM 1321, criticized in M. Sornarajah, 'The Myth of International Contract Law', *Journal of World Trade Law* 15 (1981), 187, although choice of international law to govern the contract will be a more direct method. The growth of 'umbrella clauses' was a separate development altogether (see T. W. Wälde, 'The 'Umbrella' (or Sanctity of Contract/Pacta Sunt Servanda) Clause in Investment Arbitration: A Comment on Original Intentions and Recent Cases', *Transnational Dispute Management* 1 (2004), 1). Although it is not entirely clear yet what the precise strategy for bringing a BIT claim will be, the more direct approach would be an extension of the concept of investment to cover bonds as loans, a view expressed early on by Mann, 'British Treaties for the Promotion and Protection of Investments', 243.

Chapter 5, respectively) partly because 'soft laws' feature in international financial law.[12] In this regard, the 'trade law model' of international economic regulation has often stood in contrast to lawmaking in the international financial law field. 'Hard' (i.e. legally binding) treaty laws have long been a characteristic of trade law, and also in the fields of investment and intellectual property protection. This is also true of the international treaty regime of international monetary cooperation although the treaty rules in the IMF Articles are by and large framed in the language of 'soft' obligations (which is different from the binding quality of treaty law under-pinning the IMF Articles). The same however is not true of banking regulation, for example, which avoids formal international law sources and methods of lawmaking, depending instead upon non-legal agreements towards having coordinated national regulatory convergence. Capable international adjudication is a further feature of trade regulation, and investment protection but occurs hardly anywhere else.

In short, treaty-making is not evenly employed across the field of international economic law. Other areas of treaty-based international economic law exist in private international law, where international pri-vate treaties – common examples being the 1979 Vienna Sales Convention (United Nations Convention on Contracts for the International Sale of Goods, or CISG), and the 1958 Convention on the Recognition and Enforcement of Foreign Arbitral Awards ('New York Convention') – govern. Yet even in this sphere, non-legal sources of 'law' such as the UNIDROIT Principles of International Commercial Contracts or the Uniform Customs and Practice for Documentary Credits (UCP) are translated into private obligations through their incorporation in inter-national contracts. It is in this last respect, that the novel attempt by Greece to introduce further contractual provisions into Greek bonds has caused controversy and allegations of violation of investment treaty obligations.

IV.   Developments post-crises, persistent fragmentation, a range of concerns and coherence lost

Some of the examples given are of events which have been the direct result of the global financial or European debt crises – such as the Greek introduction of CACs explored in the chapter by Chaisse. Others have

---

[12] See especially, G. J. H. van Hoof, *Rethinking the Sources of International Law* (Boston, MA: Kluwer, 1983); O. A. Elias and C. L. Lim, '"General Principles of Law", "Soft Law" and the Identification of International Law', *Netherlands YBIL* 28 (1997), 3.

been raised as potentially related to the causes of or as solutions to the global financial crisis – soft international financial regulation, better regulation of credit rating agencies. The chapters by Weber and Cervone in this volume discuss such issues at length (Chapters 2 and 3, respectively). In all these examples there is also the popular expectation that lessons will have been learned which might in turn suggest new or innovative forms of international economic regulation.

The editors of this volume have not presumed that the 2008 global financial and economic crisis or the subsequent European debt crisis were necessarily significant turning points in the continuing evolution away from the original Bretton Woods design of the post-war international economic order. But by juxtaposing our study of fragmentation against the backdrop of a broad range of contemporary scholarly and regulatory concerns, two noteworthy features emerge. The first has been the persistence of fragmented regulation. The second feature is the broad and varied range of concerns which have been taken by the collaborators in this volume to be equally, if not more, pressing than the need to address the perceived causes and lessons from the two crises through regulatory reform and innovation.

Put together, however, the picture of a fragmented international economic regime amidst a range of concerns about the development of the global economic order dovetails with at least one overriding concern in the aftermath of the two crises – the legitimacy of current global economic arrangements which had once begun with but has since lost their original coherence and overall design as new areas of regulatory need and concern continue to emerge. An international economic order which has undergone severe scrutiny due to the external shocks created by events since 2008 ought to be attentive towards popular perceptions about its legitimacy.

It cannot be disputed that we have lost the coherence and overarching design of a now bygone era of global economic management. Where, in the aftermath of the Second World War there had been an urgent need to restart trade and payments on a secure footing, and to reconstruct nations, the aims of the contemporary order are more diverse. Today's concerns range beyond sovereign agreement over the rules governing trade and monetary stability. After the Second World War they evolved from concerns with reconstruction to development, which in turn focused greater concern on facilitating investment and not simply the protection of foreign-owned property. With the global movement of capital following the emergence of a Eurodollar market, there was first the emergence of regulation of cross-border banking activities and effects, and now the stability of the global financial order. From oil, we now see contemporary concern over renewable energy. Elsewhere climate change, food price stability, and the related issues of foreign direct investment in the agricultural sector and biofuels have come to the fore.

The definition of international economic law has always been uncertain, but, by and large, trade, investment, development, currency policy cooperation, and international financial regulation have occupied the core of that definition. At the present time, a shift away from the Washington Consensus is occurring in an uncertain manner, and social and environmental concerns and initiatives have gone on to occupy that core of the contemporary global economic agenda.

V.   Regionalism, asymmetry, and pluralism in decision-making

Today the management of the global economic order is not just multi-tiered, and multi-speed – as the proliferation of PTAs has demonstrated, challenging the global trading system managed in Geneva by the WTO. There is an asymmetry between the range of issues handled regionally and globally, and the example from trade regulation shows this where PTAs are handling competition regulation, investment protection issues, intellectual property protection, and regulatory coherence in a more comprehensive manner and deeper way than the WTO can at present,[13] assuming that to be even desirable. A more mature and far-reaching example shows this asymmetry between what PTAs and the WTO do in the way the EU is handling issues of financial stability and sovereign debt bailouts. In that sense, trade regionalism represents more than having two tiers of lawmaking, legal surveillance and adjudication, and a multi-speed global trading system. Regionalism is a phenomenon in its own right, which has been explored in a resurgence of writing beginning in the 1990s in the political science field, and with potentially very far-reaching consequences for the overall architecture of the international economic order.[14]

In addition to regionalism, global economic decision-making is evolving, the most noticeable feature being what Buckley (in Chapter 5)

---

[13] See e.g. C. L. Lim, Deborah K. Elms, and Patrick Low, *The Trans-Pacific Partnership: A Quest for a Twenty-first-Century Trade Agreement* (Cambridge University Press, 2012).

[14] Breslin and Higgott, 'Studying Regions', generally; Richard Baldwin and Patrick Low (eds.), *Multilateralizing Regionalism* (Cambridge, 2009).

identifies as the emergence of the G20 since the 2008 Washington Summit as the 'high table' of global economic governance. Scholarly research on this issue is still at a relatively early, reactive stage, but the issue underscores a larger point about the plurality of the forms in which global systemic and legal reform could take place. In terms of the forms of decision-making, the cumbersome process of convening formal treaty-making conferences is simply too slow both in generating practical agreements and in accommodating the geopolitical changes which the 2008 crisis may in part have contributed to. Time will tell.

VI.   Through a glass, darkly: the search for deeper analytical tools

In the aftermath of the two crises, this plurality in rules, sites, decision-making, and methods of regulation has continued in an asymmetrical, overlapping, multi-tiered, and multi-speed manner. The growth in new subject matter and issue areas promises to continue while lawyers grapple against the backdrop of fragmentation to make sense of recent disputes over dolphin-safe labelling,[15] Ontario's feed-in tariff programme,[16] the importation of Chinese solar panels into Europe,[17] and the US country-of-origin labelling laws;[18] while the legal consequences of the plain packaging of tobacco products and EU emissions policy for international civil aviation continue to be debated.[19]

For now we see through a glass, darkly. One reason for this may be that there is no overall design to guide us in organizing the fragments of the international economic order. Our survey of fragmentation across the field takes place only against an imaginary backdrop provided by the now lost original institutional design of the Bretton Woods system. The importance of taking institutional design into account has been made, in more or less express terms, in the investment context, in Ratner's 2008 study of regulatory takings in the *American Journal of International Law*. In that study, Ratner cautioned against applying scattered

---

[15] *US – Tuna II*, WT/DS381/AB/R, 16 May 2012.
[16] *Canada – Feed-In Tariff Programme*, WT/DS426/AB/R, 6 May 2013.
[17] J. Steams, 'European Commission Approves Chinese Solar-Panel Pact', *Bloomberg*, 3 August 2013.
[18] *US – COOL*, WT/DS386, 384/AB/R, 29 June 2012.
[19] At time of writing – see D. Keating, 'ICAO Rebukes EU ETS', *European Voice*, 4 October 2013.

investment law doctrines to the facts of disputes without also taking the institutional design of diverse investment regimes into account.[20]

Ratner's application of regime theory to this branch or sub-discipline of international economic law invokes the insights of Stephen Krasner and Robert Keohane.[21] For Krasner, regimes are in the words of his often-quoted definition 'institutions possessing norms, decisions, rules, and procedures which facilitate a convergence of expectations'.[22] This emphasizes the institutional nature of regimes. On the behavioural side, Keohane's work has stressed the influence which institutional membership itself exerts upon sovereign behaviour, particularly compliance behaviour. He quotes the late Thomas Franck at the very outset of his best-known piece of writing: 'The surprising thing about international law is that nations ever obey its strictures or carry out its mandates.'[23] This recalls regime theory's roots in that school of thought in international politics – liberalism – which has as a central tenet a belief in sovereign cooperation and legal compliance. Many of the chapters in this volume have sought to identify, explore, and map out the doctrinal and jurisdictional aspects of specific areas of international economic law against this backdrop of fragmentation, but in some important respects the sort of fragmentation identified cannot also ignore what regime theory has to say. In this regard, we as editors of this volume would advocate regime theory as a fruitful avenue for further research work on the full spectrum of forms of fragmentation in international economic law.

At first glance there may be a need to distinguish 'pure' norm fragmentation, from fragmentation which clearly implicates jurisdictional, institutional, and regime fragmentation. For example, Stampalija's treatment of fragmentation is purely of the first variety of norm fragmentation discussed earlier, above – i.e. the variable investment obligations of

---

[20] S. Ratner, 'Regulatory Takings in Institutional Context: Beyond the Fear of Fragmented International Law', AJIL 102 (2008), 475.

[21] S. D. Krasner, 'Structural Causes and Regime Consequences: Regimes as Intervening Variables', *International Organization* 36 (1982), 185; R. Keohane, 'International Relations and International Law: Two Optics', *Harvard International Law Journal* 38 (1997), 487.

[22] See Krasner, 'Structural Causes and Regime Consequences', 186 for this and other definitions.

[23] See Keohane, 'International Relations and International Law', 487 and generally; Thomas M. Franck, 'Legitimacy in the International System', AJIL 82 (1988), 705. See also, A. Chayes and A. H. Chayes, 'On Compliance', *International Organization* 47(1993), 175.

sovereigns due to their varying investment treaty commitments ('variable geometry norm fragmentation'). Ratner's point, however, is that insights from regime theory are equally applicable here, even though fragmentation has been viewed primarily in terms of norm fragmentation thus far. As Ratner has shown, sometimes norm fragmentation cannot be properly understood without accounting for the contexts – the different regimes – in which even apparently similar norms operate, in order to understand their precise operation and subtle differences in the ultimate shape of those norms from one context to another, shaped that is by the individual aims of each regime. Thus, the investment norm on regulatory takings may differ from the NAFTA context to the China–ASEAN investment treaty context.[24]

In other cases, the potential for regime theory to yield insights may be more obvious. One example of such an instance is the Chinese currency issue (i.e. norm fragmentation in a second sense, discussed earlier above – or 'Janus-faced norm fragmentation'). Since the IMF does not possess any meaningful dispute settlement arrangement, the issue has been reframed as a trade-related dispute in order to come within the mandate of the WTO DSS. Even more nuanced is the example of norm fragmentation given by Peng's application of the safeguards concept in the regulation of services trade. It raises the question of whether regulation of trade in goods and services at the WTO may be treated as different 'sub-regimes' within the institutional framework of the WTO. Do rule-makers and the industries which lobby for rule change, who spend their time thinking about services, and those who spend their time thinking about goods, think differently within different, even different institutional, settings?

The third and fourth senses of norm fragmentation are more obvious candidates for regime theory – being, respectively, norm fragmentation caused by regionalism and parallel treaty and customary rules. Likewise jurisdictional fragmentation and divergent modes of lawmaking are characteristic of the existence of multiple regimes.

Assuming therefore that regime theory could yield insights in most if not all of the forms of fragmentation surveyed or touched upon in this

---

[24] Ratner, 'Regulatory Takings in Institutional Context', uses other examples. For the China–ASEAN treaty as a key point in the evolution of China's BITs, see W. Shen, 'Leaning towards a More Liberal Stance? An Evaluation of Substantive Protection Provisions under the New ASEAN–China Investment Agreement in Light of Chinese BIT Jurisprudence', *Arb. Int'l* 26 (2010), 549.

collection, and indeed in other areas which have not, it would be useful to ask, first, what regime theory could teach us about the prospects of a more unified international economic system. Here too, regime theory may contain some answers. The different regimes advance their own goals and purposes, even to the exclusion of other regimes. Conditioned by their aims, they could produce outcomes which conflict with other regimes in the forms of norms, decisions, and rulings. For example, ICAO may yet produce an answer towards reducing the carbon footprint of international civil aviation where the EU's proposals have since run into deep resistance.[25] Second, regime theory is closely allied to another strand of social science scholarship – regionalism – where the latter has yielded important insights into responses by regional regimes to crises, and in particular how APEC and ASEAN responded to the 1997 Asian financial crisis.[26] This may contain lessons for the study by Avgouleas and Arner in this volume, for example. Third, regime theory emphasizes the way regimes channel and regulate access, participation, and information as well as coordination and reputation (i.e. based on compliance).[27] The coordination role is explored by Lim (Chapter 6), for example, in terms of the coordination rules that exist, however imperfectly, between the WTO and the IMF in relation to something like the Chinese currency issue. As Keohane puts it:[28]

> Two of the most important functions of institutions are to provide information to participants and to link issues to one another in the context of a larger set of valued activities.

More importantly:[29]

> Institutions that states strongly value can promote cooperation by linking normatively prescribed behavior, such as fulfilling commitments, to the continued receipt of material or normative beliefs from the institutions.

This prompts two lines of thought. First, that states may value regimes differently at different times, and between one regime and another. For example, Nakagawa's chapter – where he seems to dismiss the constraint imposed by WTO rules upon the policy directions of nations – almost assumes the enduring value of the WTO regime to developing nations

---

[25] D. Michaels, 'Global air emissions deal approved: UN's International Civil Aviation Organization votes to back plan', *Wall Street Journal*, 4 October 2013; cf. 'China bans airlines from joining EU emissions scheme', Reuters, 6 February 2012.

[26] Breslin and Higgott, 'Studying Regions', 336ff.

[27] Keohane, 'International Relations and International Law', 499–500.

[28] *Ibid.*, 499.   [29] *Ibid.*, 500.

without any need to accord attention to such developing country perspectives (Chapter 8). This may not reflect the way such nations attribute value to the WTO across time or between trade law and international developmental norms.[30] Second, that future attempts at overcoming or alleviating the effects of excessive fragmentation and the calculation of the costs of such fragmentation ought to take into account existing regimes and the prestige they enjoy in the eyes of sovereigns.[31] This may also explain why international investment, and supranationalization of competition regulation are issues which the EU has sought to promote within the WTO framework, in order to increase the functional value of the WTO regime, or why detractors of the extension of the EU's Emissions Trading Scheme to international civil aviation have chosen to discuss the matter in the ICAO. Should Greece prize its reputation under investment treaty rules in the way it has chosen to restructure Greek debt?

To be sure, because the definition of fragmentation has been so broadly applied in this collection, we may need to distinguish between the prosaic and the sublime. Doctrinally orientated legal scholars may be surprised to find that the idea that treaties bind only those party to them – the doctrine of *pacta sunt servanda* – to be an instrument of 'fragmentation', and might respond by saying 'So what if it is?' The

---

[30] See C. Picker, 'International Trade and Development Law: A Legal Cultural Critique', 4 (2011) *Law and Development Review* 49, 54 for the argument that legal cultural differences also matter, and that one difference between international (trade) law and international developmental law – i.e. as fragmented bodies of international economic regulation – is that the latter field is particularly tuned towards the handling of asymmetric relations, whereas the former is not. For another perspective about the interrelationship between developing nations' concern about policy space and the GATT–WTO regime, see C. L. Lim, 'The Turn to Trade', *Proceedings of the American Society of International Law* 103 (2008), 231. For China's views as a developing country member, see C. L. Lim and J. Wang, 'China and the Doha Development Agenda', *Journal of World Trade* 44 (2010), 1309. For the history of developing country claims in the GATT/WTO, see C. L. Lim, 'The Conventional Morality of Trade', in C. Carmody, F. J. Garcia and J. Linarelli (eds.), *Global Justice and International Economic Law: Opportunities and Prospects* (Cambridge University Press, 2012), 129.

[31] Regime theorists have, by employing the metaphor of 'chessboard politics', sought to explain how moves made in a single institution, in case of overlapping institutions, may be decisive in 'repositioning pawns, knights and queens within other institutions'. Karen J. Alter and Sophie Meunier, "The Politics of International Regime Complexity," (2009) 7 *Perspectives on Politics* 13, 16. Likewise, the prestige and influence of an individual sovereign within a particular regime may shift over time and this may contain consequences for how that sovereign in turn views the regime; see further, C. L. Lim 'On Free Trade and the Post-American World', in Sabrina Hoque and Sean Clark (eds.), *What Lies Ahead? Debating the Prospects for a 'Post-American World'* (Abingdon, Oxon.: Routledge, 2011), 230.

international lawyer who is told that parallel treaty and customary rules contribute to fragmentation may respond in like manner. These, if any, are problems which routine doctrinal legal analysis is already adept at handling. Investment lawyers scour the terms of applicable bilateral treaties in the absence of a multilateral agreement on investment, while public international lawyers know how to account for the object and purpose of a regime's constitutive treaty under the principles of treaty interpretation, and are versed in the subtleties of untangling customary international law formation and proof of custom from treaty rules. International economic lawyers in particular have experience of needing to do so in both trade law and investment law contexts.[32] Others like Ratner argue that regime theory may yet yield further insights. In any event, other forms of norm and authority fragmentation, as well as forms of fragmented lawmaking modalities are natural areas of application for regime theory and regionalism and cannot be adequately satisfied by responses based purely on accepted legal doctrine.

For some lawyers the importance of systematic study of fragmentation is the prospect of the systematization of the law itself and its allocations of institutional competence. The search is for an international economic *system*. Others seek merely to relieve the tensions caused by the conflict of norms and competences.[33] But, at its most basic level, understanding fragmentation is about understanding how the global economy is presently regulated.

The global crisis has not led to a grand redesigning of the international economic system. The reality is that it could not have. Understanding how the design at Bretton Woods never worked as originally contemplated, and the range of pressing issues today, shows instead an international economic system which operates not by design but by accommodating new issues and events without the luxury (or ability) of providing systemic responses.

---

[32] For parallel arguments in the trade law and investment law literature on how customary international law features in the application of trade and investment treaties, see e.g. J. Pauwelyn, 'The Role of Public International Law in the WTO: How Far Can We Go?', AJIL 95 (2001), 560; J. Pauwelyn, *Conflict of Norms in Public International Law: How WTO Law Relates to other Rules of International Law* (Cambridge University Press, 2003), 460ff.; M. Paparinskis, 'Investment Treaty Interpretation and Customary International Law: Preliminary Remarks', in Chester Brown and Kate Miles (eds.), *Evolution in Investment Treaty Law and Arbitration* (Cambridge University Press 2011), 70ff.

[33] See e.g. Lim and Gao, 'Competing WTO and RTA Jurisdictional Claims'.

INDEX

Lightning Source UK Ltd.
Milton Keynes UK
UKOW06n2141060815

256529UK00003B/69/P

9 781107 0756